BARRON'S

AP

WORLD HISTORY

4TH EDITION

John McCannon, Ph.D.
Department of History
University of Saskatchewan
Saskatoon, Saskatchewan, Canada

BARRON'S

ABOUT THE AUTHOR

John McCannon earned a Ph.D. in history from the University of Chicago in 1994. He has taught Russian history, modern European history, and world history at several universities in the United States and Canada, and he has worked as an Advanced Placement faculty consultant for the College Board. He is the author of *Red Arctic: Polar Exploration and the Myth of the North in the Soviet Union, 1932–1939.* Professor McCannon is a faculty member in the Department of History at the University of Saskatchewan; he also serves as editor-in-chief of the *Canadian Journal of History.*

ABOUT THE CONTRIBUTOR

Pamela Jordan received a Ph.D. in political science from the University of Toronto in 1997. In addition to her academic background, she has worked as a news writer for Facts on File News Services, Inc., and as executive director of a nongovernmental organization affiliated with the United Nations. Dr. Jordan is a faculty member in the Department of History at the University of Saskatchewan, as well as author of *Defending Rights in Russia: Lawyers, the State and Legal Reform in the Post-Soviet Era.*

ACKNOWLEDGMENTS

This book is dedicated to Pamela Jordan, a co-author in every sense of the word. Without her formidable research skills, her invaluable written contributions to the manuscript, and her sharp editorial eye, this book could never have come into being.

Both the author and contributor would like to thank David Rodman and Anna Damaskos, whose editorial supervision made the preparation of this manuscript a smooth and easy process. We are also grateful to Bill Kuchler for art direction, to Debby Becak and Frank Pasquale for production assistance, and to the anonymous reviewers of this manuscript for their insightful and encouraging comments.

All inquiries should be addressed to:
Barron's Educational Series, Inc.
250 Wireless Boulevard
Hauppauge, New York 11788
www.barronseduc.com

ISBN-13: 978-0-7641-4367-0 (Book)
ISBN-10: 0-7641-4367-0 (Book)

ISBN-13: 978-0-7641-9697-3 (Book/CD Package)
ISBN-10: 0-7641-9697-9 (Book/CD Package)

ISSN: 1937–8874

PRINTED IN THE UNITED STATES OF AMERICA

9 8 7 6 5 4

FSC
Mixed Sources
Product group from well-managed
forests and other controlled sources

Cert no. SW-COC-002507
www.fsc.org
© 1996 Forest Stewardship Council

Contents

UNIT ONE

INTRODUCTION

How to Use This Book

TO TEACHERS AND STUDENTS

This book can be a useful supplement to classwork and study materials. For readers who are not taking—or have never taken—a course in world history, it can serve as an independent study aid. Ideally, however, it will be used in conjunction with an actual academic course in world history, or by students who have taken such a course and are attempting to review.

Unit One offers strategies for approaching the various types of questions encountered on the Advanced Placement Examination in World History. These include multiple-choice questions, the document-based essay question, the continuity and change over time essay question, and the comparative essay question.

Units Two through Six contain review chapters. Each unit is dedicated to one of the major historical periods covered by the exam and contains five to eight chapters dealing with major geographical areas or historical topics. Each unit is preceded by a historical overview. A review section, consisting of 20 multiple-choice questions and four essay questions, follows each of these five units.

TO THE TEACHER

This book's review chapters can be used as supplements to summarize or reinforce particular teaching units and classroom or homework assignments. Unit overviews and chapter introductions assist students in looking at historical events from a broad perspective. The unit overviews also strive to place historical events and developments in the comparative context that the World History exam emphasizes.

The sample examinations in Unit Seven can be used near the end of the academic year as a culmination of a world history course. The sample exams also serve as good practice for the actual Advanced Placement exam.

Unit One should be covered with students at the beginning of a world history course and then at several points afterward. The sooner students are familiar with the structure and procedures of the Advanced Placement Examination in World History, the more comfortable they will be with the exam process itself.

TO THE STUDENT

This book can be used as an independent review device, whether or not you are taking an Advanced Placement course in world history. Even for those who have never taken an academic or Advanced Placement course in world history, this book can prove helpful. It is optimal, however, if you are using this book while taking a course in world history, or if you have taken a world history course in the past and are using this book as a refresher.

It is best to use this book over a long period of time, rather than trying to cram at the last minute. You will want to absorb information and ideas thoroughly.

At the beginning, read Unit One, on the structure of the Advanced Placement exam and the types of questions asked by it. To do well on the exam, it is crucial to know the procedure and follow directions closely. The sooner you acquaint yourself with the rules and procedures, the more natural they will feel when you take the actual test.

Pay special attention to unit overviews and chapter introductions. These will help you to see world history from a "big picture" perspective. They place trends and facts in a comparative context. Your ability to compare and contrast different eras and parts of the world will be tested extensively by the Advanced Placement exam.

SUGGESTED TIMELINES

How you use this book will largely depend on how much time you have to prepare. The more time, the better. Three possible timelines are provided; adapt as necessary to your own situation and abilities.

7-DAY TIMELINE

With such limited time, it is best to concentrate on test-taking methods and big-picture issues.

Day 1: Read Sections B through G of Unit One carefully. Take one of the model exams in Unit Seven to get a sense of how ready you are.

Day 2: Read Unit Two. Read ALL the overviews for Units Two through Six.

Day 3: Read Unit Three. Again, read all the unit overviews.

Day 4: Read Unit Four. Read all unit overviews.

Day 5: Read Unit Five. Read all unit overviews.

Day 6: Read Unit Six. Read all unit overviews.

Day 7: Review Unit One. Take the second model exam in Unit Seven.

4-WEEK TIMELINE

Having roughly a month to prepare will allow you some time to examine topics in depth, in addition to focusing on essentials.

Week 1: Read Sections B through G of Unit One to get a sense of how the AP exam works. Move on to study Unit Two.

Week 2: Study Units Three and Four.

Week 3: Study Units Five and Six.

Week 4: Take the model exams in Unit Seven. Review Unit One about the exam itself, as well as the overviews for Units Two through Six.

SCHOOL-YEAR (9-MONTH) TIMELINE

This is the ideal scenario. Here, you are likely using this book as a supplement to a world history course. If so, you should proceed at the same pace and in the same order as your teacher and classmates. Otherwise, the following will give you a good grounding.

Month 1: Read Unit One. Study Unit Two.

Month 2: Review Unit Two. Study Unit Three.

Month 3: Review Unit Three. Study Unit Four.

Month 4: Review Unit Four. Study Unit Five.

Month 5: Review Unit Five. Study Unit Six.

Month 6: Review Unit Six. Take the model exams in Unit Seven. Assess your strengths and weaknesses.

Month 7: Skim Units Two through Six, focusing on weak points. Use the unit overviews to help you think about comparisons.

Month 8: Continue reviewing the unit overviews. Reread Unit One carefully.

Month 9: Review as needed. Skim unit overviews and Unit One a final time.

GENERAL NOTES

Dates are given according to the standard Western calendar, with one exception. The abbreviations B.C.E. ("before common era") and C.E. ("common era") are used, rather than the traditional B.C. ("before Christ") and A.D. (*anno domini,* or "year of our Lord"). This usage shows more respect to those world cultures whose traditions are not based on Christianity. The Western calendar is only one of many systems used for measuring time. According to the Hebrew calendar, for example, year 1 is the equivalent of 3760 B.C.E. Year 1 of the Muslim calendar, by contrast, is 622 C.E.

Dates with no designation—those that appear simply as numerals—are assumed to be C.E.

Names and terms from a variety of languages are used throughout this book. Many, such as Russian, Chinese, Arabic, Japanese, and Hebrew, use different alphabets, rather than the Latin script used by English speakers. There is no single way of transliterating, or converting, one alphabet to another.

When referring to people or terms transliterated from non-Latin scripts, this book will try to use versions that are both linguistically accurate and easily recognizable. Be aware that there are several variants of certain well-known names and terms. For example, Genghis Khan versus Chinggis Khan (or Jenghiz Khan), Mao Tse-tung versus Mao Zedong, Mohammed versus Muhammad, or Sundiata versus Son-Jara. Students may encounter some or all of these different versions in different textbooks and readings.

The Advanced Placement Examination in World History: An Overview

FORMAT

The Advanced Placement exam lasts a total of 3 hours and 5 minutes.

Students are allowed 55 minutes to complete 70 multiple-choice questions.

For the completion of the free-response, or essay, section of the examination, 130 minutes are allotted. This section of the test consists of the following types of questions:

- *Document-based question (DBQ):* Roughly 50 minutes, including a mandatory period of 10 minutes to read documents.
- *Continuity and change over time essay question (CCOT):* Roughly 40 minutes, devoted to a thematic essay touching on at least one of the time periods covered in the exam.
- *Comparative essay question:* Roughly 40 minutes given to a question focusing on broad issues and dealing with at least two societies.

The free-response portion of the exam begins with a 10-minute document-reading period. During this time, students may make notes on the document sheets, but they are not allowed to work on actual essays. Once the document-reading period is over, it is recommended that students spend 5 or so minutes planning answers for each essay question.

GRADING

Grades for the exam are calculated as follows:

- The 70 multiple-choice questions: one half of the total raw score (60 out of 120 possible points).
- The 3 free-response questions: one half of the total raw score. Each essay receives a grade of 0 (the worst) to 9 (the best). A complex formula converts

the total of 0 to 27 to a raw score of 0 to 60. This is added to the raw multiple-choice score, for a total of 0 to 120.

Another calculation converts the 0–120 raw score to a standard score of 1 through 5. This is the number students will see at the end. Scores can be interpreted as follows:

5: Extremely well qualified. Accepted by the majority of colleges and universities for some kind of academic credit or benefit. Earned by roughly 10 percent of students.

4: Well qualified. Accepted by many colleges and universities for some kind of academic credit or benefit. Earned by roughly 15 percent of students.

3: Qualified. Accepted by many colleges and universities for some kind of academic credit or benefit, but often of a limited nature. Earned by roughly 25 percent of students.

2: Possibly qualified. Accepted by a few colleges and universities for credit or benefit, generally quite limited. Earned by roughly 25 percent of students.

1: No recommendation. Not accepted anywhere. Earned by roughly 25 percent of students.

Universities and colleges have different policies regarding Advanced Placement exams. Students should contact the school of their choice to determine what benefit, if any, a particular score will give them.

TIME FRAME

The Advanced Placement Examination in World History focuses on global developments between 8000 B.C.E. and the present. The percentage of multiple-choice questions pertaining to each era is approximately as follows:

- Foundations period (prehistory to 600 C.E.): 19–20 percent of questions
- 600 to 1450: 22 percent of questions
- 1450 to 1750: 19–20 percent of questions
- 1750 to 1914: 19–20 percent of questions
- 1914 to the present: 19–20 percent of questions

THEMES

The Advanced Placement World History exam is broad in scope and seeks to test students on critical and interpretive skills, as well as the ability to examine and analyze historical issues from a "big-picture" perspective. Questions will emphasize social, economic, and cultural trends; issues of gender and ethnic identity; interrelationships and exchanges among various civilizations; and the ability to compare different historical eras and societies.

Topics such as battles, the lives of monarchs and political leaders, and the careers of individual "great figures" will receive some coverage, but less than on traditional history exams. It will be necessary to place such events, lives, and careers in their broader political, economic, cultural, and social contexts.

No more than 30 percent of the questions (multiple-choice or free-response) will cover topics in European history. The United States will be included only as part of global or comparative topics, such as colonization, foreign affairs, and the globalization of trade and culture. There will be no coverage of the internal politics of the United States.

Six overarching themes are outlined by the Advanced Placement World History course to assist students in analyzing broad trends and making insightful comparisons across time and place.

- The impact of interaction among major societies. Interaction can take many forms, including trade, war, and diplomacy.
- The relationship of change and continuity within periods of world history, as well as between different historical periods.
- The impact of technology and demography on people and the environment. Such issues might touch on population growth and decline, disease, manufacturing, migrations, agriculture, and weaponry.
- Systems of social organization and gender structure. Who has power and status? What is the place of minority populations? How are women and men treated by various societies and at different times?
- Intellectual and cultural developments and interactions among or within societies. How do art, literature, ideas, and religions affect societies and individuals?
- Changes over time in the functions and structures of states. This includes discussion of various types of political organization, principally the nation-state.

HABITS OF MIND

One purpose of the Advanced Placement World History course is to develop certain "habits of mind." The exam will test students on these skills:

- The construction and evaluation of arguments.
- The analysis of documents, data, and primary material.
- The assessment of continuity and change over time.
- The analysis of differing interpretations, biases, and perspectives.
- The perception and understanding of global patterns across geographic space and over time.
- The ability to compare different societies and their reactions to global processes.
- A sensitivity to the common denominators and differences that unite and divide human communities, and awareness of the historical context of ideas, beliefs, and values.

Multiple-Choice Question Strategies

The Advanced Placement Examination in World History will require you to answer 70 multiple-choice questions. Each question will have five answer choices. Your goal is to pick the one answer that BEST responds to the question.

You will be given 55 minutes to complete this section of the test.

The percentage of questions devoted to each historical period will be the same as described earlier (foundations, 19–20 percent; 600–1450, 22 percent; 1450–1750, 19–20 percent; 1750–1914, 19–20 percent; 1914–present, 19–20 percent). The questions will NOT appear in chronological order.

Assuming that you complete the free-response (essay) parts of the exam acceptably, you must answer 50 percent of the multiple-choice questions correctly in order to qualify for an overall score of 3. For a 4 or 5, you should aim for at least 70 percent. You receive a point for each correct answer and nothing for a question left blank. Incorrect responses will not be penalized, so it is in your interest to answer EVERY question.

TIPS FOR THE MULTIPLE-CHOICE QUESTIONS

Here are some guidelines to keep in mind when taking the multiple-choice section of the Advanced Placement exam:

- *Look for the BEST answer.* Read the question's key words carefully. Is it calling for the "most important"? The "most influential"? Does it qualify the issue some other way? A question asking you to identify the IMMEDIATE cause of World War I might give you a choice among "the assassination of Archduke Francis Ferdinand," "the Anglo-German naval race," and "competition over colonies in Africa." All three helped cause World War I. But because the question asks for the most immediate cause, the BEST answer is "the assassination of Archduke Francis Ferdinand." The other responses deal with long-term causes.

> **SCORING CHANGE**
>
> As of 2011, the College Board eliminated the $1/4$ point penalty for incorrect answers on the AP World History exam. So it pays to guess—but guess wisely.

- *Watch out for "except" and "which of these is not true" questions.* These reverse the normal logic by asking what is NOT true. If you are told that "the Columbian Exchange brought all of the following to the Americas EXCEPT…," the list might include "smallpox," "horses," "the potato," "gunpowder weapons," and "coffee." Here, you must avoid the four "correct" choices in favor of the "incorrect" one (in this case, "the potato"), which is actually the right response.

- *Answer every question.* With no penalty for incorrect responses, there is no reason to leave any question blank. Answering 70 questions in 55 minutes requires a pace of 45 seconds per question. If you cannot work that quickly, skip the questions that seem like they will take too long for you to think through, aiming instead to answer 70 to 75 questions quickly and confidently—in other words, without guessing. (Topping 50 percent correct is generally enough to earn an overall score of 3; 70 to 75 percent will typically put you in a position to earn a 4, perhaps even a 5, depending on the quality of your essays.) In the last 5 or so minutes, return to the questions you've skipped. Guess carefully where possible, but make sure that, by the time runs out, you've left nothing blank, even if that calls for some random choices in the end.

- *Save time by eliminating obviously incorrect answers.* This is the first and most effective part of the narrowing process. As you read through the question and the answers, strike out any answer that is obviously false. Answers containing absolute statements (such as "never," "always," "none of," or "all of") are almost always incorrect. Ideally your first read-through will eliminate at least one or two answers, leaving you with three or so to think about more carefully.

- *Trust your intuition—to a point.* Most teachers and exam-preparation specialists say that your first choice is generally the correct one, *if* you have read the question and the answers carefully. Unless you have a concrete reason for changing your mind (for example, you remember a crucial piece of information or notice something in the question that you missed when you skimmed through it), you should probably stick with your first choice. On the other hand, this should not be used as an excuse for lazy reading or sloppy thinking. Don't make that first choice until you have closely read and thought about the question.

SAMPLE MULTIPLE-CHOICE QUESTIONS

Advanced Placement multiple-choice questions test the "habits of mind" referred to earlier. The simplest questions will ask you to **identify** correct facts. The majority are more **analytical** and require you to think about historical relationships, to understand cause and effect, to compare and contrast effectively, and to ponder more abstract issues.

A portion of the multiple-choice questions—generally no more than 20 percent—will call upon you to interpret **maps**, **images** (artwork, cartoons, photographs of architecture or artifacts), **quotations**, and **graphs** and **charts**.

Below are examples of possible multiple-choice questions, along with answers and explanations.

1. Which of the following religions or philosophies did Qing emperors such as Kangxi encourage in their attempt to increase public respect for political authority in China?

   (A) Stoicism
   (B) Taoism
   (C) Christianity
   (D) Confucianism
   (E) Shinto

ANSWER: **D**

Because they are principally Western, A and C can be readily eliminated. Knowing that Shinto is Japanese, not Chinese, allows you to strike E as well. You might decide between B and D based on knowledge of the Qing emperors, but you might also recall that Taoism is more about living in the moment, whereas Confucianism places stress on proper social relations and hierarchy, making it more suitable for a ruler hoping to encourage political obedience.

2. This city became one of West Africa's greatest centers of trade and Islamic scholarship from the thirteenth to the fifteenth centuries.

(A) Timbuktu
(B) Zimbabwe
(C) Mogadishu
(D) Zanzibar
(E) Alexandria

ANSWER: **A**

This may seem to be a straightforward identification question: You either know the answer or you don't. Still, basic geographic knowledge can assist your process of elimination. Zanzibar and Mogadishu are on Africa's east coast. Alexandria is in Egypt, to the north, and flourished most as a cultural center before the emergence of Islam. Zimbabwe is far to the south and experienced its peak as a civilization in the pre-Islamic period.

3. Which of the following is NOT true of most human societies during the Stone Age?

(A) Despite technological limitations, Stone Age humans designed many innovative tools.
(B) Biological differences between men and women often gave rise to a gendered division of labor.
(C) Human beings tended to be more aggressive during the Stone Age than during later periods.
(D) Human beings settled the Americas later than they did Africa, Asia, and Europe.
(E) Stone Age societies were capable of developing complex forms of tribal organization.

ANSWER: **C**

This question requires you to choose the one INCORRECT answer. Answers A and E remind us that societies are not necessarily "primitive" just because they lack metal-based technology. Although labor was not as specialized during the Stone Age as it would be in more advanced societies, specific gender roles were common from the start, making B correct as well. Academic consensus has it that human beings appeared first in Africa, then spread throughout Eurasia, so D is also correct. Given the catastrophic nature of wars in recent history, C is clearly incorrect, making it the "right" choice in this case.

4. How did the storming of the Bastille affect the course of the French Revolution?

   (A) It led directly to the imprisonment and execution of Louis XVI.
   (B) Robespierre seized it as an opportunity to begin the Reign of Terror.
   (C) It ended the Third Estate's attempt to negotiate a reformist solution to France's financial crisis.
   (D) Louis XVI agreed soon afterward to call the Estates General to Versailles.
   (E) Women were granted the vote as a reward for their role in the uprising.

ANSWER: **C**

Proper understanding of the revolution's chronology allows you to ignore A, B, and D, because the first two took place many months after the Bastille uprising, whereas the last took place beforehand. Despite their grand ideals, the Revolution's leaders did not extend suffrage to women, making E incorrect. Answer C correctly identifies how Bastille Day marked the shift from negotiation to revolution.

5. Which of the following best summarizes the beliefs of a practicing Buddhist?

   (A) Conversion of nonbelievers by force is justified by God's will.
   (B) Each individual should place trust in a personal savior to ensure a place in heaven.
   (C) At the end of the world, God will judge all sinners and condemn them to eternal torment.
   (D) Justice should be based on the principle of an eye for an eye, a tooth for a tooth.
   (E) People are born and reborn into lives of suffering but can escape this cycle by attaining enlightenment.

ANSWER: **E**

Basic knowledge of religious tenets is necessary here. Answer D is associated with the retributive justice of Hammurabi's law code and Judaic scripture. Answers A, B, and C are more characteristic of monotheistic religions like Islam, Judaism, and Christianity (even though the history of Buddhism has not been without violence). Although there are many forms of Buddhism that differ on key questions, answer E captures the core belief that one transcends the karmic cycle of birth, death, and rebirth by gaining enlightenment.

6. Which of the following did World War II help to bring about?

(A) Women in Great Britain and the United States received the vote partly as recognition for their homefront labor efforts.
(B) The war concentrated strategic might and economic power in the hands of the United States and the Soviet Union.
(C) Nurses like Florence Nightingale improved military medicine by introducing modern methods and hygenic practices.
(D) The Ottoman Empire collapsed, paving the way for Mustafa Kemal's modernization of Turkey.
(E) Spain's Latin American colonies took advantage of the monarchy's weakness and declared independence.

ANSWER: **B**

All these changes resulted from various wars, but only B, the creation of the Cold War superpowers, has to do with World War II. Answers A and D are the products of World War I, and Florence Nightingale rose to fame during the Crimean War, making C false. The Latin American wars of independence alluded to in E followed the wars of Napoleon.

7. "Although the empire was conquered on horseback, it could not be governed from there."

The quotation above, adapted from Sun Tzu's *Art of War* by the thirteenth-century Chinese official Yeh-lü Ch'u-ts'ai, most likely refers to which conquering force?

(A) the Hun armies led by Attila
(B) the Mongol Empire created by Genghis Khan
(C) the Aryan forces thought to have invaded India around 1500 B.C.E.
(D) the infantry of the Roman Republic
(E) the army of Alexander the Great

ANSWER: **B**

Although this proverb dates back to centuries before Genghis Khan's invasions, it is most commonly cited to describe the Mongols' dilemma: that although they conquered vast stretches of territory, they did not have the capability to control them for very long. A Chinese speaker during the 1200s would most likely be referring to the army most relevant to him in terms of time and geography, making it safe to eliminate A, C, D, and E.

8. The sculpture pictured below is most likely

(A) a personal likeness commissioned by a wealthy patron.
(B) an example of Asian influence on Western art.
(C) an experiment in modernist abstraction.
(D) a ritual object with religious significance crafted in Africa.
(E) an artistic protest against wage inequality suffered by women in the workplace.

ANSWER: **D**

Image-based questions may ask you to interpret the image—especially if there is accompanying text, as in a poster or cartoon—or simply identify it. As in this case, you will often have to be familiar with the basic characteristics of different artistic and architectural traditions. Based on logic, you can feel fairly safe in discarding A and E; only in a nontraditional sense can this be considered a portrait, and it would need more context to make the sort of comment referred to in E. Although many modern artists were inspired by non-Western "primitive" art in the late 1800s and early 1900s, this does not look like a truly abstract piece, as in C. Left to decide between B and D, you will ideally have a sense of how Asian and African art differ—but even if you don't, it would be worth guessing, with the number of possible answers whittled down to two.

9. What historical development does this map depict?

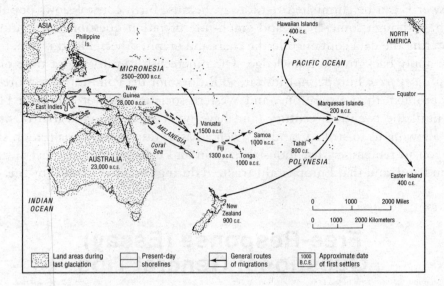

(A) the expansion of Chinese trade routes
(B) James Cook's voyages of discovery
(C) Japan's military assault on the South Pacific
(D) Thor Heyerdahl's *Kon-Tiki* expedition
(E) the migration of Polynesian peoples

ANSWER: **E**

A close look at the dates referred to on the map is all it takes to reject B, C, and D, which took place in the 1700s or the 1900s. Premodern China did not trade so far to the east (and the lines do not go back and forth to China, as one would expect with trade routes), making A incorrect.

10. What is the most likely explanation for the population rise experienced by the cities included on the chart below?

Year	Cities (Pop. in thousands)				
	London	Paris	Antwerp	Berlin	Moscow
1800	960	600	60	170	250
1850	2,700	1,400	90	500	360
1900	6,500	3,700	280	2,700	1,000

(A) industrialization
(B) foreign immigration
(C) increased levels of pollution in the countryside
(D) the elimination of diseases such as tuberculosis and polio
(E) more advanced forms of birth control

ANSWER: **A**

Answer E can be eliminated right away, because birth control slows population growth. Although some chart- and graph-interpretation questions focus more on interpreting the data contained in the chart and graph, others, like this one, require you to apply background knowledge. The nineteenth century was a time of emigration *away from* Europe, not into it, so B does not fit. Pollution was more of an urban problem than a rural one, and Western societies did not eliminate TB and polio until the twentieth century (and have not *completely* eradicated them even now), allowing us to strike C and D. Even a basic grasp of industrialization should allow you to remember that industrialization and urban growth almost always go hand in hand, and that Europe industrialized during the years covered by this chart.

Free-Response (Essay) Questions: General Tips

The free-response section of the Advanced Placement Examination in World History lasts 130 minutes. During this time, you will be required to write three essays: a document-based question (DBQ), a continuity and change over time question (CCOT), and a comparative essay.

Once the 10-minute document-reading period is over, you can write the essays in whichever order you like, and you can use the 120 minutes however you please—no one will tell you when to finish one essay or start another. You SHOULD spend roughly 40 minutes on each essay, and the one you SHOULD write first is the DBQ. The documents will be fresh in your mind, and the DBQ is the most complicated essay you will write, so it will be good to have it out of the way. This section outlines general tips for successful essay writing.

APPROACHING THE ESSAYS

Unlike the multiple-choice questions, which are graded by machine, the written portions of AP examinations are evaluated by high-school teachers, university professors, and other specialists. For each subject area, several hundred of these evaluators gather together for about a week.

In that time, an AP reader is likely to mark several hundred essays. He or she is careful and well-trained. Still, because your reader will be looking over so many essays in such a short time, it is up to you to make the quality of your work stand out.

Each of your essays will receive a score of 1 through 9 (later, these numbers are plugged into a complicated formula to determine your overall free-response score). In each case, the AP grader will check to see if your essay meets five or-six elementary requirements (the *basic core*); you can earn up to 7 points this way. If you fulfill ALL the requirements of the basic core, the grader will check your essay against a list of advanced criteria (the *expanded core*). Here, you can earn an additional 1 or 2 points.

The requirements for fulfilling the basic core and moving on to the expanded core are different for each essay. However, one thing is the same for all three: you CANNOT earn ANY of the expanded-core points unless you earn ALL the basic-core points. Think of this as opening a gate with five or six locks. Until you open them all, you cannot go any farther. The happy news is that, if you do a good job on each part of the basic core, you will already be doing some of the things necessary to score well on the expanded core.

Here are some ways to impress your readers:

- *Develop a thesis and state it clearly.* You must make an argument or draw a concrete conclusion, and you must let your reader know you are doing it. No matter how good the rest of your essay is, you will lose many points if you fail to do so. See the section below for more details.
- *Read the directions and follow them closely.* You are writing three different essays, each with its own set of rules. Advanced Placement readers are trained to judge your work based on how well you follow those rules. Even if your essay is beautifully written, it will lose points if you do not follow the directions.
- *Look at the question's key verb.* Answer the question on that basis. Questions will ask you to *defend* or *refute* (argue for or against); *assess the validity of* (judge the truth of); *evaluate* (determine the worth of, discuss advantages and disadvantages); *describe, discuss,* or *detail* (tell about, consider points of view); *outline* (list); *explain* (offer reasons for, make clear); *analyze* or *examine* (look at in detail, consider relationships, take into account cause and effect); and *compare* and *contrast* (show differences and similarities).
- *Write neatly and clearly.* Your reader will be marking hundreds of essays, and he or she will not grade generously if he or she has to struggle to understand what you are saying. Guidelines state that "substance takes precedence over neatness," but neatness helps the reader appreciate the substance more fully.
- *Divide your essay into paragraphs.* Paragraphs should be clearly indented. Correct and effective use of paragraphs shows the reader that you know how to think and write in an organized fashion.
- *Give an answer of appropriate length.* There is no hard-and-fast rule as to how long your essay should be. Length may depend on how large your handwriting is or whether you skip lines. Also, quantity does not always mean quality. A good argument can be made concisely, and a bad essay can ramble on for pages. However, an essay less than two pages long will be regarded with suspicion. Assuming your handwriting is of average size, a MINIMUM length to aim for is two FULL pages (not skipping lines, except maybe between paragraphs). Three or four pages is optimal.
- *If you have time, reread your essay.* If necessary, revise it. Cross out mistakes or awkward phrasings. If new information or a good idea occurs to you, add it. Make corrections neatly.

Organization is as important as the points discussed above. Your essay should have an introduction, and it should include an explicitly stated thesis. Your essay should be divided into paragraphs. Make sure your reader can tell where your paragraphs begin and end (indent clearly and/or skip a line between paragraphs).

Paragraphs should correspond with specific points or arguments you wish to make. These should serve to back up or prove your thesis. You should have at least three main points, although there can be more. If you have time, write a conclusion to sum up your arguments or make some general remarks about the topic.

GENERAL TIPS FOR WRITING THESIS PARAGRAPHS

To get a high score—a 7 or above—on your essays, begin each of your answers with an effective thesis paragraph, containing a clear thesis statement.

A good thesis is the first thing your grader will look for. According to AP guidelines, your essay must have "an acceptable thesis" to meet the standards of the *basic core*. To get through the gateway to the *expanded core*, your essay has to start off with "a clear, analytical, and comprehensive thesis." In other words, without an effective thesis, your maximum possible score will be 6 or 7 out of 9.

In addition, a well-written thesis paragraph strengthens the whole essay. It creates a good first impression and shows the reader that you understand the question. It demonstrates your ability to analyze a complex issue and construct an argument (meaning a logical assertion, NOT a quarrelsome or aggressive rant) about it. It allows you to display some general historical knowledge. You can get a lot done—and earn some key points—with just this one paragraph.

Each type of question calls for a slightly different approach to the thesis paragraph. No matter what, though, you want to do the following things, all of which are interrelated:

- Begin with a restatement of the question. This step gets you started, and it keeps you focused on the subject at hand.
- Refer to the principal elements contained in the question. Who or what is this question about? What regions and/or time periods are you being asked about? What sort of relationships (between cultures, events, social classes, etc.) are being stressed?
- Pay attention to the question's key verb. This is how you determine what the question is asking you to do. Your thesis paragraph should tell the reader right away that you have figured this out.
- Show up front that you are aware of the bigger picture. Most questions are designed to get you to talk about a larger historical issue: sometimes a standard debate or interpretive point, sometimes an important phenomenon or historical pattern.
- Be balanced. Stories and debates have more than one side. More than one reasonable argument can be made about an issue. Events and phenomena generally have more than one cause. Acknowledge this fact, even if you favor a particular argument or explanation.
- Give some hint about what the rest of the essay will cover. Preview what your main points will be—but do it briefly.
- Provide a clear transition to the next paragraph. Your reader should know when it is time to move on. (Even something as simple as clearly indenting will make your essay appear better organized.)

Here's one example of how a thesis paragraph might be constructed. The following question combines the characteristics of the CCOT and comparative essays; with some adjustment, it could appear as either:

3. Choose one of the following regions. Compare and contrast Europe's colonial and imperial relationship with it, first during the fifteenth and sixteenth centuries and then during the nineteenth century.

Central and South America
South and East Asia
Africa

POSSIBLE THESIS PARAGRAPH

Although certain things remained constant over the centuries, the character of Europe's relationship with South and East Asia changed considerably between the 1400s–1500s and the 1800s.

[In one sentence, the question has been restated. Most of the question's principal elements—Europe, South and East Asia, and the time periods—have been mentioned. The key verbs ("compare and contrast") are not mentioned explicitly, but they are implied by the phrases "remained constant" and "changed considerably." This is already an "acceptable" thesis (although, by itself, not a very sophisticated one), because it makes a clear assertion and shows some scholarly judgment.]

During both eras, Europeans traveled to Asia to seek profit, spread Christianity, and expand their global power. In the nineteenth century, however, a newer group of nations—England and France, for example, as opposed to Spain and Portugal—held sway. Religious activity was carried out by Protestants as well as Catholics, and it was reinforced by a clearer sense of racial superiority, reflected in the doctrine of "social Darwinism."

[These sentences (1) continue what the key verbs ("compare and contrast") say to do; (2) preview some of the things the essay is likely to talk about in more depth; and (3) show that the author has a big-picture grasp of the historical context. The concept of social Darwinism could have been introduced later, but it does not hurt to get credit now for mentioning it—and it can be brought up again.]

Perhaps most important, European colonial efforts in nineteenth-century Asia met with greater success than before. Many historians refer to the "new imperialism" of the late 1800s, recognizing how military, economic, and technological superiority gave European empire builders advantages that had not existed earlier. When one compares and contrasts the European imperial experience in Asia during the 1400s–1500s with that of the 1800s, it appears that the differences outweigh the similarities.

[Here, the essay highlights an important difference (the greater degree of European power in the 1800s). It strengthens the thesis by suggesting that change is greater than continuity. It introduces a major historiographical concept—the "new imperialism"—and, while this concept could have been mentioned later, it is a good way of demonstrating historical knowledge and an appreciation of the big picture. As with social Darwinism, it can be discussed again later. The last sentence does three important things. It tells the reader what to expect in the rest of the essay. It formally mentions that the essay will be about comparing and contrasting. Finally, it restates the thesis and adds extra punch to it by taking a definite position.]

Ideally, this paragraph would be followed by at least three main points and then a conclusion, for a MINIMUM of two full pages. As you study the answers to sample essay questions in the rest of this book, take some time to look at how the thesis paragraphs are written. They are constructed according to the same principles as this one.

Document-Based Question Strategies

You should spend 50 minutes on the DBQ. This includes the 10 minutes you will be given to read the documents (during which time you will not be allowed to write).

As noted earlier, the DBQ should be the first essay you write (although you can choose differently). The DBQ is the essay with the most elaborate rules, and it is extremely important to be familiar with the procedure.

APPROACHING THE DOCUMENT-BASED QUESTION (DBQ)

You will be provided with four to ten documents. Most will be traditional written texts: excerpts from books, memoirs, and essays; transcriptions of speeches or radio and television addresses; government papers; and so on. Sometimes song lyrics, poetry, or images will be included. The authors cited may or may not be famous.

The DBQ's purpose is to assess your ability to evaluate and comment on primary documents. Therefore, you must not only write a good essay with a clear thesis but actively incorporate all, or all but one, of the documents. You must also comment on at least one OTHER type of document, NOT included, that might shed light on the question.

Following is the official AP scoring guide for the DBQ.

Generic Scoring Guide for AP World History Document-Based Question

Basic Core	Points	Expanded Core	Points
1. Has an acceptable thesis.	1	Expands beyond the basic core of 1–7 points. A student must earn **7** points in this core area before earning points in the expanded-core area.	**0–2**
2. Addresses and shows understanding of all (or all but one) of the documents.	1	Examples:	
3. Thesis is supported by evidence from all documents or all but one. (Supported by all but two documents.)	2 (1)	• Has an analytical, clear, comprehensive thesis.	
		• Demonstrates careful and insightful analysis.	
4. Analyzes point of view in two or more documents.	1	• Makes convincing use of documents as evidence.	
5. Analyzes documents by clustering them in two or three ways.	1	• Discusses point of view in most or all documents.	
		• Compares, groups, and synthesizes the documents in additional ways.	
6. Identifies one type of additional document and explains why it is needed.	1	• Employs useful external historical content.	
		• Identifies and explains the need for two or more additional document types.	
Subtotal	**7**	**Subtotal**	**2**
TOTAL 9			

A few of these items deserve additional attention because they must be done in specific ways to avoid losing points.

Using and analyzing documents, and adding "outside" content. As the directions state, use all the documents or all but one (better to use them all if possible). "Careful and insightful analysis" will follow if you group the documents effectively, discuss point of view well, and present interesting comparisons and contrasts. Demonstrating external knowledge—by providing information about the author of a document or a document's historical context—is a good way to earn expanded-core points, and it can be done in combination with attribution.

Attribution. You are allowed to refer to documents simply by number (e.g., "Document 1," "# 5," or "doc. 3"). However, it is better to identify the author and title. This leads more naturally to providing information about the author and/or text—a good way of bringing in "outside" historical knowledge.

Point of view. Simply attributing the documents is not sufficient. You must also comment on point of view. What is the bias or perspective of the author, speaker, or artist? The point of view may be clear from nationality, ethnicity, gender, social class, religion, or political affiliation. If the speaker/writer is famous, his or her point of view may be easy to describe. If he or she is not well known, you will have to read the document closely to determine its point of view. For partial credit, you must analyze the point of view of two or three documents. For full credit, especially if there are fewer than five or six documents, you must do this for all or most of the documents.

Grouping documents. One of the skills you MUST demonstrate is an ability to group documents into useful and meaningful categories. Can the documents be grouped by national origin (generally a weak approach)? By chronology? From a class perspective? According to a political philosophy or outlook? By purpose? By gender? According to cultural attitudes? There is no single right way to group. However, your groupings must make sense, and the DBQ will be designed in such a way that some methods of grouping will be more appropriate than others. Also, the NUMBER of groups is typically two or (generally more preferable) three. More may be too complicated or, with a small set of documents, not feasible.

Identifying additional documents. The DBQ asks you to demonstrate your historical judgment by commenting on what is missing from the picture presented to you. If OTHER documents could be provided to you, what types would you find useful? And why would you choose them? This must be done at least once. Doing it more than once is a way to earn expanded-core points.

Thesis. Don't forget your thesis. Most often, your thesis will determine how you group your documents. Conveniently, each category—especially if you have three or four—can be used as a main point in the body of your essay.

SAMPLE QUESTION

1. In the modern world, major political and social changes have been brought about by different means. Using the documents presented below, discuss the various methods of political and social transformation that they call for or advocate. Be sure to explain the need for at least one additional type of document.

DOCUMENT 1

Source: Vladimir Lenin, Russian revolutionary leader and head of the Soviet state, *What Is to Be Done?* (1902).

A small, compact core of the most reliable, experienced, and hardened workers, with responsible representatives in the principal districts and connected by all the rules of strict secrecy with the organization of revolutionaries, can . . . perform all the functions of a trade union organization.

I assert: 1) that no revolutionary movement can endure without a stable organization of leaders that maintains continuity . . . 3) that such an organization must consist chiefly of people professionally engaged in revolutionary activity; 4) that in an autocratic state, the more we confine the membership of such an organization to people who are professionally engaged in revolutionary activity and have been professionally trained in the art of combatting the political police, the more difficult it will be to wipe out such an organization. . . .

Only a gross failure to understand Marxism . . . could prompt the opinion that the rise of a mass, spontaneous working-class movement relieves us of the duty of creating a good organization of revolutionaries. On the contrary, this movement imposes this duty upon us, because the spontaneous struggle of the proletariat will not become its genuine "class struggle" until this struggle is led by a strong organization of revolutionaries.

DOCUMENT 2

Source: Gamal Abdel Nasser, Arab nationalist and president of Egypt, "The Philosophy of the Revolution" (1959).

As I often sit in my study and think quietly of this subject, I ask myself: "What is our positive role in this troubled world, and where is the scene in which we can play that role?"

Can we ignore that there is a Muslim world to which we are tied by bonds which are not only forged by religious faith, but also tightened by the facts of history? . . . It is not in vain that our country lies to the southwest of Asia, close to the Arab world, whose life is intermingled with ours. . . . It is not in vain that Islamic civilization and Islamic heritage, which the Mongols ravaged in their conquest of the old Islamic capitals, retreated and found refuge in Egypt, where they found shelter and safety as a result of the counterattack with which Egypt repelled the invasion of these Tartars at Ein Galout.

All these are fundamental facts, whose roots lie deeply in our life. Whatever we do, we cannot forget them or run away from them.

DOCUMENT 3

Source: Mikhail Bakunin, nineteenth-century anarchist, "Principles of Revolution" (1869).

We recognize no other activity but the work of extermination, but we admit that the forms in which this activity will show itself will be extremely varied— poison, the knife, the rope, etc. In this struggle, revolution sanctifies everything alike.

DOCUMENT 4

Source: Kwame Nkrumah, leader of Ghana's independence movement, "The African Personality," speech delivered to a conference of independent African states (April 13, 1958).

Africa is the last remaining stronghold of colonialism. Unlike Asia, there are on the continent of Africa more dependent territories than independent sovereign nations. Therefore we, the free independent states of Africa, have a responsibility to hasten the total liberation of Africa . . .

We, the delegates of this conference, in promoting our foreign relations, must endeavor to seek the friendship of all and the enmity of none. We must stand for international peace and security, in conformity with the United Nations charter.

This will enable us to assert our own African personality and to develop our own ways of life, our own customs, traditions, and cultures. . . .

If we can as independent African states show by our own efforts that we can settle our own problems in Africa, then we shall be setting an example to others. . . . For this reason it may be necessary for this conference to examine the possibility of setting up some sort of machinery to maintain the links we shall forge here and to implement the decisions we shall reach. . . .

Today we are one. . . . An injury to one is an injury to all of us. From this conference must go out a new message: "Hands off Africa! Africa must be free!"

DOCUMENT 5

Source: Gloria Steinem, American feminist, "Far from the Opposite Shore" (1978).

Even the late suffragists, the ones who are most often labeled reformers because of their concentration on the vote, used radical tactics. Yes, they lobbied politely, sometimes, and took tea with their friends in Congress, but they also picketed the White House and engaged in the civil disobedience that those same congressmen abhorred. . . .

Chaining themselves to the White House fence, going to jail, declaring a hunger strike, being cruelly force-fed: those events are now famous. But the range of tactics [also] included humor, theatrics, passive resistance, [and] persuasion.

DOCUMENT 6

Source: Mao Tse-tung, leader of the Chinese Communist Party, "The Peasant Movement in Hunan" (1926).

In a very short time, . . . several hundred million peasants will rise like a mighty storm. . . . There are three alternatives. To march at their head and lead them? To trail behind them, gesticulating and criticizing? Or to stand in their way and oppose them?

Every revolutionary comrade should know that the national revolution requires a great change in the countryside. The Revolution of 1911 did not bring about this change, hence its failure. This change is now taking place, and it is an important factor for the completion of the revolution. Every revolutionary comrade must support it, or he will be taking the stand of counterrevolution.

DOCUMENT 7

Source: Henry David Thoreau, American philosopher and activist, *On the Duty of Civil Disobedience* (1848).

How does it become a man to behave toward this American government today? I answer that he cannot without disgrace be associated with it. I cannot for an instant recognize that political organization as *my* government which is the *slave's* government also.

All men recognize the right of revolution; that is, the right to refuse allegiance to and to resist the government, when its tyranny or its inefficiency are great and unendurable . . . those who call themselves abolitionists should at once effectually withdraw their support, both in person and property, from the government of Massachusetts. . . . Under a government which imprisons any unjustly, the true place for a just man is also a prison. . . . A minority is powerless while it conforms to the majority . . . but it is irresistible when it clogs by its whole weight.

DOCUMENT 8

Source: Mohandas K. Gandhi, member of the Indian National Congress and leader of the Indian independence movement, letter to Russian novelist Leo Tolstoy (1909).

These Indians [living in South Africa] have for several years labored under various legal disabilities. The prejudice against color and in some respect against Asiatics is intense in that colony. . . . The climax was reached three years ago, with a law which I and many others considered to be degrading and calculated to unman those to whom it was applicable. I felt that submission to a law of this nature was inconsistent with the spirit of true religion. I and some of my friends were and still are firm believers in the doctrine of non-resistance to evil. The result has been that nearly one-half of the Indian population [of Transvaal], that was unable to stand the heat of the struggle, to suffer the hardships of imprisonment, have withdrawn from the Transvaal rather than submit to a law which they have considered degrading. Of the other half, nearly 2,500 have for conscience's sake allowed themselves to be imprisoned, some as many as five times. . . . The struggle still continues, and one does not know when the end will come. This, however, some of us at least have seen most clearly, that passive resistance will and can succeed where brute force must fail.

Sample Answer

Many times throughout history, legal means of political and social change have failed to bring about desired results. On such occasions, there are frequently calls for radical or drastic forms of transformation. As the documents discussed in this essay demonstrate, these include national liberation, revolution, and civil disobedience. As a rule, when any of these options—as opposed to reform or gradual change—is seen as necessary, it is a sign that the existing system has failed in some fundamental way.

[The thesis paragraph correctly identifies the nature of the documents and tells the reader how they will be categorized. A simple but acceptable thesis results from the grouping of the documents into three categories of political and social change. The last sentence adds an insightful observation—even a secondary thesis—about how radical forms of change tend to be caused by general social or political failure.]

Documents 2 (Nasser's "The Philosophy of the Revolution") and 4 (Nkrumah's "The African Personality") have to do with decolonization in Africa and Asia after World War II. Like Sukarno in Indonesia, Nasser, president of Egypt, was one of several modernizing strongmen who led successful national liberation movements, then encouraged the so-called Third World to assert its global power and defy the West. Nkrumah came to power in Ghana, the first British colony in sub-Saharan Africa to gain freedom. Both appeal not just to their own people but to larger cultural units: the Muslim world in Nasser's case, all of Africa in Nkrumah's. Both are politicians, and this is a way to boost their international influence (but it also reflects the fact that boundaries in Africa and the Mideast had been artificially imposed by Western colonizers). Such appeals stirred up pride, but had limits. Nasser's pan-Arab nationalism did not catch on, and his patriotic appeal at home has to be balanced against his authoritarianism. Nkrumah's pan-Africanism was too unrealistic to succeed in a region of such extreme ethnic and linguistic diversity.

[Two documents are grouped here. They are attributed by number, title, and author. There is historical context about postwar decolonization, including an outside reference to a similar political leader. The documents are not just listed; their political purpose is discussed, as is the question of whether the ideals they express were met. Point of view—that of politicians trying to increase their stature—is touched on. So far, there has been no discussion of what other documents might be helpful. (One possibility would have been to suggest diaries, newspaper editorials, or other materials to indicate whether ordinary people found pan-Arabism or pan-Africanism appealing.) Another option to be aware of: Document 8 (Gandhi) could have been included here, but this essay uses it differently. There will generally be more than one "right" way to group documents.]

Revolutionary ideologies are a hallmark of modern history, as shown by Documents 3 (Bakunin's "Principles of Revolution"), 1 (Lenin's *What Is to Be Done?*), and 6 (Mao's "The Peasant Movement in Hunan"). Bakunin, founder of the anarchist movement, is the most extreme: in declaring that "revolution sanctifies everything alike," he restates the age-old argument that the ends justify the means. Lenin, leader of the Soviet Union, subscribes to the same idea in *What Is to Be Done?*, written while he was still a young Marxist, plotting to overthrow the tsar. Lenin discourages working-class democracy on the grounds that absolute secrecy is necessary for revolution to succeed. This stance can be explained partly by Lenin's point of view: he was leader of an illegal party in a repressive country with a powerful secret police. Unfortunately, Lenin's antidemocratic approach was one of many things that later turned the USSR, a state founded on utopian ideals, into a dictatorship. In #6, Mao, years before communist victory in China, appears more committed to open mass movements as he describes the revolutionary power of the peasantry (an unusual position for a Marxist, because Marxism puts more stress on the industrial working class). After coming to power, however, Mao proved just as much a dictator as Lenin did in the USSR. All three documents propose that the potential benefits of revolution are worth any price, but they say nothing about actual costs. For the sake of balance, it would be useful to have statistics or first-hand accounts related to the mass arrests, persecutions, and famines that resulted from revolution in Soviet Russia and Maoist China.

[This paragraph provides a second effective grouping, dealing with revolution. Transition from the previous paragraph is clear, and the attribution of documents remains explicit. Historical information is included for the sake of context. Detailed point of view is provided in Lenin's case. (Also, a reader might give point-of-view credit for mentioning the unorthodoxy of Mao's Marxist views.) This paragraph fulfills the basic core by making a suggestion about possibly useful additional documents.]

Another way to bring about change is nonviolent resistance. The American thinker Henry David Thoreau argues in *On the Duty of Civil Disobedience* (#7) that even democratic governments can do wrong. An idealist philosopher angry about the Mexican-American War and slavery, Thoreau asks whether a good person acting in a good cause is justified in violating his or her country's laws. His answer is "yes." In her essay "Far from the Opposite Shore" (#5), American feminist Gloria Steinem describes how nineteenth-century suffragettes used civil disobedience, not just lawful reform, to fight for the vote. (She seems to be encouraging similar action in her own day, and the fact that she is writing about history to a modern audience for political purposes should be noted.) Perhaps the most admired advocate of civil disobedience is Gandhi, spiritual father of India's freedom movement. In a 1909 letter (#8) to Russian author Leo Tolstoy—also known for his activism and pacifism—Gandhi explains his strategy of passive resistance in South Africa, where Indians, like blacks, were racially discriminated against. Later, Gandhi's method of *satyagraha*, which combined Hindu faith with nonviolent political action, was an effective tool in persuading the British to grant India its independence. As effective as civil disobedience has been, however, it works only under certain circumstances. Gandhi's confident assertion that "passive resistance will and can succeed where brute force must fail" applies only in liberal or democratic societies, where the use of brute force is seen as embarrassing or shameful. It is hard to imagine civil disobedience bringing about change in a truly dictatorial regime such as Hitler's, Stalin's, or Mao's.

[A third and final grouping appears in this paragraph. Attribution is complete, and Steinem's point of view is noted. So are Thoreau's and Gandhi's, to a lesser extent. (Many readers would assign an expanded-core point to this essay for analyzing the point of view of "all or most" of the documents.) Much historical information is provided, as well as an evaluation of civil disobedience as a political strategy.]

None of the documents discuss what is perhaps the fairest and most desirable means of social and political change: the proper functioning of democratic government. Also, while the documents provide examples of one extremist form of change, communist revolution, they do not mention fascism, another common form of extremism. Memoirs or newspaper reports demonstrating fascist excess and the effective operation of democracy would have been useful.

[This brief conclusion caps off the essay, even though time is running out. It also raises a general analytical point about democratic change. Most important, it earns an expanded-core point by making a second suggestion about potentially useful documents.]

Continuity and Change Over Time Essay Question Strategies

Another type of essay the World History exam will ask you to write is the continuity and change over time (CCOT) question. This exercise tests your ability to trace a broad trend or development over a long period of time. Topics may include cultural interchange, global trade, the movement and migration of peoples, the role of minorities in a given society, the status of women, environmental issues, biological developments, changes in technology, artistic and cultural attitudes, and scientific innovations.

The CCOT lends itself to a topical approach. In order to follow how a particular issue changed or stayed the same through long periods of time, consult the overviews at the beginning of Units Two through Six. These track "big-picture" issues as they played out over different eras.

Moreover, as you read through the material covered in Units Two through Six, keep in mind how long-term trends develop, not just within geographical areas but across borders.

APPROACHING THE CONTINUITY AND CHANGE OVER TIME ESSAY

As with all essays, follow the General Tips provided earlier in this unit.

It is recommended that you take 40 minutes to complete the CCOT. Spend 5 or so minutes (no more than 10) looking over the question, thinking about it, then organizing and outlining your thoughts.

The CCOT will request that you analyze the evolution of a trend or phenomenon over a long period of time. You will be asked to focus on a particular nation or geographical region, although you may be given a choice. On the next page is the official AP scoring guide for the CCOT.

The CCOT's requirements are more straightforward than those for the DBQ. Aside from following the general essay-writing tips, concentrate on showing that you understand what changed, and how. Start by establishing a baseline: what were things like at the beginning of the period you have been assigned? What changed? How and why did it change? What were things like at the end of the period in question? What differences did those changes make? What remained the same?

One easy way to create a thesis is to focus on the cause(s) and/or effect(s) of the change(s) you are writing about. Another is to discuss whether change outweighed continuity or vice versa. Either way, discuss both for the sake of balance.

Generic Scoring Guide for AP World History Continuity and Change Over Time Essay

Basic Core	Points
1. Thesis deals acceptably with the global issues and time period(s) in question.	1
2. Deals with all parts of the question, though not necessarily evenly or completely.	2
(Deals with most parts of the question; for instance, change but not continuity.)	(1)
3. Backs up the thesis with appropriate historical evidence.	2
(Partially backs up thesis with appropriate historical evidence.)	(1)
4. Uses historical context to illustrate continuity and change over time.	1
5. Analyzes the process of change and continuity.	1
Subtotal	**7**

Expanded Core	Points
Goes beyond the basic core of 1–7 points. A score of **7** must be earned before a student can gain expanded-core points.	0–2

Examples:

- Begins with an explicit, analytical, and comprehensive thesis.
- Deals with all aspects of the question: global issues, chronology, causation, change, continuity, content.
- Gives ample historical evidence to back up thesis.
- Creatively links topic to relevant ideas, trends, and events.

Subtotal	**2**

TOTAL	**9**

SAMPLE QUESTION

2. Choose one of the following regions. Discuss the changes and continuities in how women were treated—socially, economically, and politically—between 1000 C.E. and 1750 C.E. If a woman's social class factored into the way she was treated, discuss that in your answer.

the Middle East
India
China and Japan
sub-Saharan Africa

Sample Answer

In most times and places, women have occupied a secondary status in society, whether because of gender division of labor, cultural and religious bias, or simple sexism. However, the type of discrimination a woman experienced and how bad it was varied greatly, depending on where and when she lived, as well as her social class. Neither China nor Japan between 1000 and 1750 is an exception. In both places, women remained subservient to men. There were also changes, and, in both cases, they tended to go from bad to worse.

[This introduction refers to all key elements in the question. It tells the reader what region the essay will focus on. It recognizes that change and continuity are both relevant. Most important, it clearly states a complex thesis by discussing the secondary status of women generally and asserting that, both in China and Japan, the situation of women worsened over time.]

Around 1000 C.E., women in Song China and Heian Japan enjoyed some rights and privileges, although their situation was still secondary. As in many societies, they could own and inherit property, and they had informal influence over the management of households. Women of the upper classes could exercise indirect power through their husbands or personal connections at the imperial court. Japanese women were luckier: the Heian aristocracy placed a great emphasis on cultural brilliance, and the literary achievements of women like Lady Murasaki, author of *The Tale of Genji*, gained them some prestige. Also, Confucianism, which did nothing to improve the status of women, was not yet as prevalent as it was in China, where it had been part of tradition for centuries. One woman, Wu Zhao, actually ruled China as empress, but hers was an extremely rare case that says little about the lives of most women there.

[This paragraph establishes a baseline by describing the situation as it was at the beginning of the time period in question. It provides much outside historical knowledge. It shows analytical awareness by noting that generalizing from one unusual case (Wu Zhao's) is risky.]

In China, conditions worsened for women mainly because of religious and cultural reasons. Since the 400s B.C.E., Confucianism, with its strict sense of hierarchy, had done much to lower the status of Chinese women, but its influence had waxed and waned over time. Starting in the 600s C.E., though, Confucianism revived more permanently in the form of Neo-Confucianism. The Song, Yuan, and Ming dynasties were increasingly drawn to Neo-Confucianism, and the place of women lessened as a result. Brides' families now paid dowries to the groom; earlier, it had been the other way around. This change in custom made it expensive to marry off daughters, and families came to want girl children less. The most infamous means of subjugating women was foot binding. Tiny feet were considered to be more attractive, but observing this fashion had the effect of crippling women and turning them into little more than beautiful objects. Foot binding gradually gained in popularity, spreading from the upper classes downward. It was widely practiced by 1200 and continued till the 1900s.

[This paragraph discusses change in China. It identifies a primary agent of change and provides concrete historical information.]

Political events were more important in changing the role of women in Japan. The transition from the culturally refined Heian regime to the feudal shogunates in the late 1100s led to a steep decline in the status of women. During the first shogunates and the disunity of the 1400s and 1500s, prestige belonged to the samurai class, and their warrior ethic left little room for the accomplishments or abilities of women. Also, unlike European chivalry, which at least required knights to respect and cherish women (however condescending this was), the Japanese code of Bushido did nothing to encourage samurai to treat women well. Things got even worse as Japan reunited in the late 1500s and early 1600s. Society became tremendously stratified, and under the Tokugawa shoguns, women were required to obey their husbands without question—if they did not, they could be put to death.

[Like the previous paragraph, this one discusses change, this time in Japan. It identifies the principal reason for change and provides specific details and information.]

It should be noted that all these changes were less pronounced among the lower classes, as was often the case in most societies. In China, lower-class families were less likely than upper-class families to follow Confucian rules closely. Foot binding was for the aristocracy: A peasant woman with bound feet would be useless for farm or household work. In Japan, samurai ideals were irrelevant to the lives of people farther down in society. Even among the lower classes, though, the question of who paid dowries for marriage was important, and in both countries, regardless of class, the overall desirability of girl children decreased. (This is still a cultural problem today in much of Asia, especially in China.) During the premodern era, female infanticide was not uncommon.

[This supplemental paragraph addresses the question of social class, talking about likenesses AND differences. Links with the present ("still a cultural problem today") are a way of earning expanded-core points.]

To sum up, the condition of women tended to worsen, both in China and Japan, between 1000 and 1750. The increased role of Neo-Confucian beliefs was mainly responsible for change in China, while the rise of warrior government was the primary cause in Japan. Feminism and equal rights took a long time to come to both countries—not until late in the twentieth century—and one could argue that the influence of this traditional sexism is still felt today.

[This short conclusion recaps the thesis and its main points. It gives a sense of what followed the historical period in question and also comments on the present (one way to get an expanded-core point).]

Comparative Essay Question Strategies

Yet another exercise you will complete on the World History exam is the comparative essay, which will ask you to compare and contrast the ways different societies deal with major issues and phenomena. These may include technological innovation; the social and economic impact of warfare; the treatment of minorities and women; the evolution of political systems; international trade and economic exchange; and systems of labor organization.

The organizers of the AP World History course consider the comparative approach especially important. The overviews preceding Units Two through Six provide lists of issues that lend themselves well to comparative questions. Read them carefully. In addition, as you study the material covered in Units Two through Six, think about broad patterns and see if you can come up with examples of major developments that most, if not all, societies undergo as they evolve historically.

APPROACHING THE COMPARATIVE ESSAY

As with all essays, follow the General Tips provided.

You should devote 40 minutes to complete the comparative essay. Spend 5 or so minutes (no more than 10) looking over the question, thinking about it, then organizing and outlining your thoughts.

The comparative essay will require you to compare and contrast how at least two (perhaps more) civilizations or nations have undergone or responded to a historical event or experience. Give equal weight to both (or all) civilizations or nations specified in the question. Also be sure to balance similarities and differences, although you may decide that one is more important than the other.

The official AP scoring guide for the comparative essay is on the next page.

Because the central task of this essay is so heavily focused on comparison, rather than a specific theme, developing a strong thesis for it may appear difficult. The question, or the way you want to answer it, may not lend itself to a clear-cut theme or argument. In that event, you can still create a thesis by stating that, in the case you are discussing, the likenesses outweigh the differences, or vice versa. You may argue that likenesses and differences are equally balanced. This is not the most sophisticated approach, but it will fulfill the requirement.

SAMPLE QUESTION

3. Compare and contrast the degree to which TWO of the following regions modernized between the end of the First World War and the beginning of the Second World War.

   South Asia
   Latin America
   the Middle East
   Russia

Generic Scoring Guide for AP World History Comparative Essay

Basic Core (Competence)	Points
1. Opens with acceptable thesis. (Compares the issues or themes specified.)	1
2. Deals with all parts of the question, perhaps not evenly or thoroughly.	2
(Deals with most parts of question.)	(1)
3. Backs up thesis with appropriate historical evidence.	2
(Partly backs up thesis with appropriate historical evidence.)	(1)
4. Provides one or two relevant, direct comparisons between or among societies.	1
5. Analyzes one or more reasons for a difference or similarity discussed in a direct comparison.	1
Subtotal	**7**

Expanded Core (Excellence)	Points
Goes beyond the basic core of 1–6 points. The basic core score of **7** must be earned before a student can gain expanded core points.	0–2

Examples:

- Opens with an analytical, clear, comprehensive thesis.

- Deals with all relevant parts of the question: comparisons, chronology, causation, connections, themes, interactions, content.

- Gives ample historical evidence to back up thesis.

- Links comparisons to larger global context.

- Draws several direct comparisons between or among societies.

- Regularly examines the reasons for and the resullts of key similarities and differences.

Subtotal	**2**

TOTAL 9

Sample Answer

The two decades that followed World War I brought immense changes to most parts of the globe. Among the regions affected were the Middle East and Latin America, each of which modernized during the 1920s and 1930s. Both had several things in common, such as relative backwardness, heavy influence from outside powers, and not much success with representative government. However, there were also key differences that, arguably, outweigh the similarities: Latin American states were already more modern and more independent, traditional Islam was more an obstacle to change than Catholicism, and events like WWI and the Depression affected both areas differently.

[This introductory paragraph addresses the question's key elements and identifies the regions to be compared. It acknowledges that there are similarities and differences, and it tackles the basic core by starting the process of comparison right away. It lays out a thesis about modernization in both regions, then strengthens the thesis by proposing that differences may outweigh similarities.]

Prior to WWI, the Middle East was backward in comparison to the West, and it was dominated by outside powers. Egypt was under British control, and Persia, while technically free, was divided into British and Russian spheres of influence. The one major independent state, the Ottoman Empire, was in decline and widely known as the "sick man of Europe." The Ottomans attempted some changes, the Tanzimat reforms, in the nineteenth century, and there was some social modernization and industrialization—but not enough to prevent the Young Turks from taking over in 1908 and attempting even faster change. Unfortunately for the Ottomans, the Young Turks sided with the Germans in WWI. Therefore, more so than Latin America, the Middle East was directly involved in the war. The Ottomans were among the losers, and their empire was broken up.

[This paragraph sets the stage by describing the existing state of modernization in the Middle East before and during World War I. This essay is about comparing two processes of change, so a starting point has to be established in both cases. One comparative note—the Middle East's greater involvement in World War I—has already been included.]

At first, the end of WWI brought greater foreign domination to the Middle East. Egypt and Persia remained under British influence. Arabs, who had rebelled against Ottoman rule and sided with the Allies, hoping to gain a united, independent Arab state, were disappointed. The English and French imposed a mandate system over Arab regions such as Iraq, Syria, Lebanon, Jordan, and Palestine. These were not technically colonies, but were dominated by the French and British. (Britain's Balfour Declaration, which guaranteed a Jewish homeland in Palestine, also alienated the Arabs.) In 1932, Ibn Said created the state of Saudi Arabia, but it remained very traditionalist. Economic modernization came only after the discovery of oil in 1938, and even then, it benefitted only the Saudi elite and foreign investors.

Real modernization in the Middle East occurred in Turkey and Persia, in both cases as a result of bold action by strong-willed and authoritarian leaders. In 1923, Mustafa Kemal took over the Turkish government and renamed himself Ataturk ("father of all Turks"). In 1925, Reza Khan Pahlavi rose to power in Persia, threw out the British, and crowned himself shah. Both were Westernizers who industrialized their economies and encouraged Western ideas and education (Ataturk even gave women the vote). Both saw Islam as a backward force standing in the way of change, and both sought to reduce, even eliminate, Islam's role in law and politics. Middle Eastern modernization took place only in a handful of countries, and it was imposed from above.

[These two paragraphs describe where and how modernization in the Middle East occurred. Good historical detail is provided, and several examples are analyzed in order to demonstrate a general pattern.]

Like the Middle East, Latin America before and during WWI was relatively backward and heavily influenced by outside powers, especially the United States. On the other hand, most nations in Latin America had been free since the early 1800s, thanks to the Latin American wars of independence, and foreign domination was economic, not directly colonial. There was also more industrialization in Latin America—although most Latin American economies were based on the exploitation of one or two commodities, such as an agricultural crop (coffee or bananas) or a natural resource (copper, fertilizer, or steel), and foreign investors had great control over those economies. One more difference is that Latin American nations had almost no direct involvement with WWI.

[Just as the second paragraph did for the Middle East, this paragraph establishes a starting point for Latin America. It also continues the process of comparing the Middle East with Latin America directly.]

After WWI, American economic influence over Latin America increased, because countries like Britain and France were in such bad economic shape that they pulled out many of their investments. During the 1920s, the U.S. backed up its business interests with political pressure and military force. This lessened only when President Franklin Roosevelt started his Good Neighbor Policy. By that point, though, the Great Depression had begun, and because Latin American economies were so dependent on U.S. investment, the Depression hurt Latin America badly and slowed down modernization. (The Middle East was less affected by the Depression, another important difference.)

Industrialization and modernization took place in Latin America during the 1920s and 1930s but not, as in the Middle East, because of one ruler's will. Instead, the economic interests of a larger elite—and foreign investors—stimulated growth. Dictatorial governments, some mild (like Mexico's PRI party), some severe, were common. This authoritarianism grew worse in the 1930s, largely because of economic stress caused by the Depression, partly because of the influence of European fascism. A military government seized control of Argentina in 1930, and that same year, the right-wing dictator Vargas took power in Brazil and created one of the continent's most brutal regimes.

[These two paragraphs describe change in Latin America during the 1920s and 1930s. They provide concrete details but also discuss general trends. There are direct comparisons to the Middle East.]

During the interwar period, both Latin America and the Middle East modernized and industrialized despite lingering backwardness from the 1800s, outside interference, and, on the whole, undemocratic government. Latin America started from a more advanced position, however, with politically independent countries and partially industrialized economies and societies. In the Middle East, modernization was rarer and, when it happened, was pushed through by westernizing politicians opposed to Muslim traditionalism.

[This conclusion restates key similarities and differences. It is somewhat rough and rushed, but when time is running out, it is more important to get points across than to worry about style.]

UNIT TWO

FOUNDATIONS OF WORLD CIVILIZATION
(ca. 8000 B.C.E.–600 C.E.)

Unit Overview

GENERAL REMARKS

This "foundations" unit is so wide-ranging in terms of time and geography that it is difficult to encapsulate in a brief overview.

Humanlike, or hominid, creatures emerged on earth approximately 3 to 4 million years ago. Modern humans (*Homo sapiens sapiens*) developed sometime between 100,000 and 250,000 years ago. According to most scholars, humanity's birthplace was Africa. From there, humans spread to the rest of the globe, starting around 100,000 years ago.

The period from approximately 2.5 million years ago to 5,000 or 6,000 years ago is referred to as the Stone Age. During this time, human communities took shape, but remained at a relatively primitive state of development, socially and technologically. After around 10,000 years ago, thanks to the phenomenon generally known as the Neolithic revolution, human societies gradually became more advanced. Various peoples learned how to domesticate plants and animals. They developed what are generally considered to be the basic attributes of civilized society. They practiced agriculture, invented systems of recordkeeping (especially writing), and made metal (rather than stone) tools. They developed complex forms of social and political organization, and sophisticated modes of economic exchange.

The earliest "civilized" societies appeared between 3500 and 2000 B.C.E. All four were born along the banks of major river systems. They were

- The Sumerian-Babylonian civilization of Mesopotamia (the Tigris and Euphrates rivers)
- Egypt (the Nile River)
- The Indus valley civilization (the Indus River)
- Early China (the Yellow River, or Huang Ho)

Also among the world's oldest civilizations were the Olmec, who arose in Central America around 1200 B.C.E., and the Chavin, who appeared in the Andes Mountains after 900 B.C.E.

Quickly, other developed societies appeared throughout the world. By 600 C.E., civilizations had emerged in Asia, Europe, North Africa, sub-Saharan Africa, North America, and Central and South America. Many were connected by trade, warfare, and other forms of interaction. Most of the major religions of the world had been born by 600 C.E. (Islam is the key exception).

BROAD TRENDS

Global Power and International Relations

- Early on, the most advanced civilizations were to be found in the Middle East (especially the river valleys of Egypt and Mesopotamia) and China.
- As time passed, other developed societies emerged. Especially powerful and sophisticated was the Mediterranean world (particularly Greece and Rome).
- Cultures in North and South America were physically and culturally isolated from the rest of the continents.
- The peoples of Europe, North Africa, the Middle East, South Asia, and East Asia were linked, directly or indirectly, by war, conquest, trade, travel, and cultural and religious exchange.
- By 600 C.E., several civilizations were among the world's most powerful and advanced, especially China, Persia, and Byzantium. Europe was slowly recovering from the collapse of Rome in the late 400s.

Political Developments

- With the development of agriculture during the Neolithic revolution, advanced forms of political organization began to appear.
- Most governments were monarchies (rule by a single leader) or oligarchies (rule by a small elite). Representative forms of government, such as republics and democracies, were very rare.
- Decentralized civilizations were often governed by confederations of independent city-states (such as Greece) or feudal systems (such as Europe after the fall of Rome).
- Many civilizations built empires by means of military conquest. Among the largest and longest lasting were Assyria's, Persia's, Rome's, and China's.

Economic and Environmental Developments

- Until the development of agriculture during the Neolithic revolution, systems of economic exchange remained primitive. Most prehistoric cultures, mainly hunting and gathering societies, lived at subsistence (they gathered or grew only enough food to feed themselves) and possessed few goods. There was little specialization of labor. Trade tended to be limited, and based on simple barter.
- The development of agriculture allowed the accumulation of food surpluses, which enabled some members of society to make a living by means other than growing food. The result was specialization of labor.
- Specialization of labor led to social stratification and the emergence of socioeconomic classes (upper-class aristocracies, middle-class merchants and artisans, lower-class urban dwellers and peasants).
- The switch from nomadic life to sedentary, or settled, life led to the concept of private property.
- Resource consumption and resource extraction increased, causing human societies to have a greater (and often negative) impact on the environment.

- As settled civilizations encountered each other, they traded. Trade became one of the most important forms of interaction between civilizations. Trade networks tended to follow waterways, for ease of transport. Trade routes were especially wide-ranging in Eurasia, connecting civilizations in Europe with those as far away as East Asia.
- Systems of currency (particularly coinage) were devised.

Cultural Developments

- Even during the Stone Age, human beings expressed themselves artistically, by means of painting and music.
- Prehistoric societies buried their dead, worshipped gods, and practiced religious rituals.
- Writing and other forms of recordkeeping emerged in most civilized societies, starting around 3000 B.C.E.
- Systematic scientific observation, experimentation, and thought emerged, especially in China, the Middle East, and the Mediterranean world.
- The world's major religions were born (except for Islam).

Gender Issues

- The ability of humans to mate when and with whom they chose gave rise to family units during the prehistoric era.
- Basic physical differences between the sexes led to a gender division of labor in most Stone Age societies.
- The emergence of agriculture deepened the gender division of labor. In most agricultural and settled societies, gender division gave rise to gender inequality.
- Organized religions often reinforced this sense of inequality.
- In most societies up to 600 C.E., women were relegated to a secondary, subservient role. The degree of subservience depended on the society. In some cultures, women had at least some rights (divorce, inheritance, and ownership of property, for example). They might also exercise certain forms of influence within their societies or over their families. In other cultures, women had almost no rights or influence. Whatever the case, in almost no society were women granted a status equal to that of men.

QUESTIONS AND COMPARISONS TO CONSIDER

- What roles do geography, climate, and environment play in shaping human societies? How have different societies affected their environments?
- How do human societies develop into civilizations? What does it mean to be "civilized"?
- How do agricultural and urban societies compare with pastoral and nomadic ones?
- What is the importance of cultural interaction and diffusion versus that of independent innovation in changing societies technologically, scientifically, or culturally?

- Compare how different religious and philosophical traditions have determined how societies organize themselves, justify class systems and hierarchies, and treat women.
- Examine and compare various forms of social inequality (slavery, caste systems, patriarchy, gender inequality) in different cultures.
- How have different societies organized themselves economically? What role did trade play? Be able to describe the features of at least one interregional trading system (for example, the Indian Ocean trade network or the overland route linking the Mediterranean and Middle East with East Asia).
- What are "classical" civilizations? What does that concept mean? Be able to compare major civilizations—such as India, China, Greece, or Rome—during their classical phases.
- How and why do empires and major civilizations decline or collapse? Good comparisons might include Egypt versus Mesopotamia or the Roman Empire versus Han China. More generally, why did imperial collapse prove more devastating in western Europe than it did farther to the east?
- What roles did large-scale migrations play in various parts of the world during this period? Consider the passage of Asiatic peoples to the Americans over the Bering land bridge, the Pacific-wide migration of the Polynesians, the Bantu migrations throughout Africa, and the movement of Eurasian nomads into Roman and Chinese territory.

Geography, Environment, and Humanity

- Major continents and regions
- Major oceans, seas, and rivers
- Water transport versus overland travel

- Environmental impact ("ecological footprint")
- Resource extraction and consumption
- Agriculture

A key force shaping human societies is physical environment. Knowledge of the earth's major geographical features is indispensable for any understanding of world history. There are also certain patterns where human interaction with the environment is concerned.

GEOGRAPHIC ORIENTATION

While the earth is approximately 5 to 6 billion years old, the present configuration of the continents dates back to less than 60 million years ago. Scientists speculate that all the earth's landmasses were originally clustered into a single supercontinent called **Pangaea**. Over time, geological forces separated Pangaea into smaller bodies of land, which eventually became today's continents and major islands.

Antarctica, covering the south polar region, has no native human population. Australia, the smallest continent, is home to the earth's oldest surviving ethnic group (the Aborigines) but remained largely isolated for most of its history. The thousands of islands sprinkled throughout the Pacific form no continent but are often referred to, along with Australia, as **Oceania**.

Africa is considered by most scholars to be the birthplace of humanity. Its northern third is home to the world's largest desert, the **Sahara**. (The AP World History course prefers the following terms to describe African subregions: North Africa, West Africa, East Africa, Central Africa, and Southern Africa.) **Asia** is the largest and most populous continent on earth, ranging from the Middle East (also called the Near East) to the Indian subcontinent and, farther east, China and Japan. The island chains that make up Indonesia, Malaysia, and the Philippines are also considered part of Asia. Thanks to its size, Asia contains the world's most diverse mix of climates, geographical features, ethnicities, languages, and cultures. (In addition to the Middle East and Siberia, the continent contains three distinct regions: South Asia, Southeast Asia, and East Asia.) **Europe**, a rela-

> **NOTE**
>
> There are seven continents (Africa, Antarctica, Asia, Australia, Europe, North America, and South America) and four oceans (Arctic, Atlantic, Indian, and Pacific). Several seas—including the **Caribbean** Sea, the **Mediterranean** Sea, the Red Sea, the Arabian Sea, and the seas of Japan, East China, and South China—are important as well.

tively small continent with a large population, is resource-rich and, on the whole, mild and temperate in climate. Europe is physically joined to Asia, and the two continents together are referred to as **Eurasia**. From humanity's earliest days, there was constant interaction among the populations of Africa and Eurasia.

North and **South America** were originally settled by nomadic peoples from Asia, crossing a land bridge that existed only temporarily. Until the late 1400s C.E., the Americas developed in isolation from the other three major continents. Abundant in resources and, in most parts, agriculturally fertile, the Americas became home to many advanced cultures. Contact with European societies changed the Americas dramatically. From 1492 C.E. onward, cross-oceanic transportation, trade, and communication turned the Atlantic basin into a gigantic cauldron of economic, cultural, religious, ethnic, political, and military interaction.

HUMANITY AND THE ENVIRONMENT

Human societies and their physical environments mutually influence each other. Geography is not the only, or even the most important factor, shaping a society, but it can play a crucial role.

Human beings have lived and created societies in all but the most inhospitable environments on earth. As a general rule, though, preindustrial societies—the only type in existence until the 1700s C.E.—tended to develop into advanced civilizations if one or more of the following preconditions existed:

- the climate was not extremely hot, cold, dry, or wet
- a suitable amount of arable, fertile land, preferably flat, was available
- a reliable source of water was present
- topography (the shape of the land) permitted reasonably easy movement
- access to a river or a seacoast or both, for the sake of transport (and food supply), was helpful
- the presence of one or more desirable natural resources was a bonus, as was proximity to one or more trade routes, whether overland or by water

> **NOTE**
>
> An older school of historical thought, **geographic determinism**, used to argue that geography was the paramount force behind a society's development, but few subscribe to that view now.

Not all these conditions have to prevail; think of the monsoons of India (extreme weather) or the terraced fields of the Andean civilizations (little or no flat land for agriculture). However, a society is unlikely to develop without at least some of these advantages. To some degree or another, human societies are compelled to adapt to their geographical setting; in many ways, environment does shape society.

One especially important geographic reality during the long preindustrial era has to do with oceans, seas, and rivers. For centuries, **water transport** remained much easier, cheaper, and more efficient than overland travel. Lakes and river systems were vital to the birth, growth, and continued viability of human societies. Rivers served as sources of food (fish) and drinkable water. They stimulated the invention of agriculture and the emergence of cities. They made possible the large-scale movement of passengers and freight, encouraged trade and travel, and linked communities.

Likewise, oceans and seas not only provided food and other resources, but enabled the transfer of people, goods, ideas, technology, religious beliefs, and cultural practices. For civilizations without the scientific knowledge and technological ability to cross them, large bodies of water were formidable barriers. (The first known transatlantic voyage, that of Leif Eriksson, did not take place until the eleventh century C.E., and the Pacific is thought not to have been crossed until Ferdinand Magellan's circumnavigation of the globe in 1519–1522.) However, early societies were generally capable of coastline navigation. Once oceans and seas became fully navigable, they offered coastal societies an effective means by which to communicate, trade, fight, and otherwise interact. The **Atlantic**, **Indian**, and **Pacific** oceans, as well as the seas listed above, have been particularly important in this respect. Major river systems include the **Nile**, the Congo, the **Tigris** and **Euphrates**, the **Indus**, the Ganges, the **Huang Ho** (**Yellow**), the **Yangzi** (Yangtze), the Volga, the **Danube**, the Rhine, the **Mississippi-Missouri**, and the **Amazon**.

The larger and more advanced the society, the greater its level of **resource consumption** and **resource extraction**. Even less advanced modes of economic production influence the environment: the gathering of nuts, berries, and other foodstuffs; the grazing of herds; and the creation of simple tools all involve resource consumption. Also, although it is common to think of these as modern problems, all societies, even early and less-advanced ones, produced waste and **pollution**.

As societies developed, they became more able to shape their environment. Practices such as **forest clearing**, **irrigation**, and **agriculture** increased humanity's impact, or "ecological footprint," on the land. The same is true for **mining**, as well as engineering projects such as swamp dredging, dam building, and canal digging. Even in the preindustrial era and surprisingly early in the historical record, advanced societies were capable of such accomplishments—and thus capable of affecting their environments, just as their environments affected them. (From the late 1700s onward, industrialization vastly heightened humanity's ability to affect and control the environment, though not always for the better.)

> **NOTE**
>
> If the environment helps to influence the development of human societies, the development of human societies, in return, has a profound environmental impact.

CHAPTER 2

Building Blocks of Civilization

- Prehistory
- Civilization
- Hominid development and the "Out of Africa" thesis
- The Stone Age (Paleolithic and Neolithic)
- Hunter-gatherer societies
- Gender division of labor and gender inequality
- The Neolithic revolution
- Pastoralism and herding societies
- Agriculture
- Urbanization and the role of cities
- Specialization of labor
- Metallurgy
- The Bronze Age
- Writing and systems of recordkeeping

Hominid, or humanlike, life has existed on earth for 3 million to 4 million years. Humans and their immediate ancestors appeared 100,000 to 200,000 years ago and have gathered themselves into social groups for almost as long. The history of human civilization, however, stretches back only a little more than 5,000 years. The vast expanse of time preceding the birth of civilized societies is called **prehistory**. During this long prehistoric period, human beings evolved into their present biological form.

Much of the knowledge historians have of the prehistoric period comes from the work of other scholars, including paleontologists (who study the physical remains and fossils of animals and plants), anthropologists (who study the physical, social, and cultural characteristics of human beings), and archaeologists (who study the objects and buildings left behind by humans). These scientists constantly make new discoveries and form new theories, and so the ways historians understand the prehistoric age frequently change.

What distinguishes a civilization from less advanced forms of society (often referred to as "primitive" or "barbaric")? Webster's Dictionary defines **civilization** as "social organization of a high order, marked by advancements in the arts and sciences." Four features are commonly associated with the development of civilization:

- An economic system able to provide basic goods and services
- A form of political organization to govern, create social institutions, enforce laws, and protect people from outside threats
- A moral code, generally in the form of a shared religion
- An intellectual tradition that typically includes a written language and encourages the pursuit of knowledge, science, and the arts

EARLY HUMANS AND THE STONE AGE

The earliest hominids, or humanlike creatures, emerged in southern and east Africa around 3 to 4 million years ago. They were part of the zoological order called primates, which includes apes and monkeys. Between 2 and 3 million years ago, humanity's immediate ancestors, the early members of the genus *Homo*, appeared, also in Africa. Later versions of genus *Homo* made basic stone and wooden tools and clothed themselves in skins and furs.

At some point between 100,000 and 200,000 years ago, true humans (*Homo sapiens*, meaning "wise human") appeared. The best-known of *Homo sapiens*'s early variants are the Neanderthal and Cro-Magnon. Modern humans, known as *Homo sapiens sapiens,* may have lived as early as 200,000 years ago. How or whether *Homo sapiens sapiens* interacted with Neanderthals or Cro-Magnons is unknown. What seems more certain is that *Homo sapiens sapiens* emerged in Africa and then migrated outward. This theory is informally referred to as the **"Out of Africa" thesis.** (An opposing model held by a minority of scholars, the multiregional thesis, proposes that modern humans, descending from earlier hominid groups that had already left Africa, appeared simultaneously throughout the world.) *Homo sapiens sapiens* continued the pattern of worldwide hominid movement, spreading first to Asia and Europe and then to Australia, the Arctic, and the Americas.

Early humans made tools out of many materials, such as wood, bone, and animal skins. The most important (and the most numerous today, because they have survived best over time) were made of stone. Consequently, the first period of hominid prehistory is known as the **Stone Age,** which lasted roughly from 2.5 million years ago to 5,000 or 6,000 years ago. The Stone Age is typically subdivided into the Paleolithic ("Old Stone Age," ending approximately 12,000 years ago, and overlapping with the Great, or Pleistocene, Ice Age), the Mesolithic ("Middle Stone Age," a transitional period lasting from about 12,000 years ago to 10,000 years ago), and the **Neolithic** ("New Stone Age," beginning around 8000 B.C.E.).

Humans moved out of natural dwellings (such as caves and canyons) and learned to build tents, huts, and wooden and stone structures that demanded advanced carpentry and construction skills. They used fire for light and heat. At what point organized warfare began to be practiced is unknown, but Stone Age humans had to protect themselves against dangers of many sorts. The first weapons included rocks and clubs.

The greatest concern of Stone Age humans was ensuring a steady and plentiful food supply. Clothing was important as well. Most tools were designed to serve these needs.

Multipurpose devices such as knives and axes were especially useful. Spears, bows and arrows, fishhooks, and harpoons were used for hunting and fishing. There were wooden implements to dig roots from the ground, as well as mats and baskets to carry nuts, berries, and other foodstuffs. Clay pots were used for cooking as early as 12,500 years ago. The earliest clothes were made from furs or animal hides. As time passed, humans also began to use plant fibers. By 26,000 years ago, at least some Stone Age peoples were weaving cloth and even dyeing it to add color.

> **NOTE**
>
> Certain tools meant for hunting and food preparation, such as the knife, spear, ax, and bow and arrow, could also be used in combat.

Almost universally, early Stone Age social groups sustained themselves by **hunting and gathering**. Rather than produce food themselves, these societies lived off the resources they could take directly from the land, including birds and animals. They fished lakes, rivers, and seashores. They gathered nuts, berries, and roots. If resources grew scarce, hunter-gatherers practiced **nomadism**, moving on to another area.

Primitive by later standards, the hunter-gatherers of the Stone Age had their own social and cultural complexities. The organization of clans and tribes could be quite sophisticated. Some historians speculate that the coordination and teamwork necessary to hunt large creatures helped to develop effective means of waging war.

Stone Age humans worshipped deities and practiced a variety of religious rituals. They buried their dead, made sacrifices to gods and spirits, and performed ceremonies. Prehistoric humans also expressed themselves by means of art and music.

A final social feature to note is the **gender division of labor**. Because of basic physical differences, various food-gathering tasks and everyday activities tended to be assigned by sex. Men, who were on average stronger and larger, hunted, made war, and performed heavy labor. Women, for the most part smaller and weaker, gathered nuts, berries, and plants; prepared food; maintained the home; and tended children. Some historians theorize that, during the Stone Age, division of labor did not necessarily mean that men's roles were seen as superior to women's, although this assumption remains open to debate. The division of labor by gender continued long after the Stone Age and gave rise to a long-standing **gender inequality** that most commonly favored men and greatly disadvantaged women. Regrettably, traces of this inequality are still found today, in even the most advanced societies, despite technological advances that have made the genders' differences in physical strength less important.

> **NOTE**
>
> Social organization during the Stone Age was based on the family unit, which took shape during this time. Extended families tended to cluster together, forming clans bound by ties of kinship as well as larger groups such as bands and tribes.

> **NOTE**
>
> The oldest cave paintings discovered to this date are 32,000 years old. The first known musical instruments are flutes from 30,000 years ago.

NEOLITHIC REVOLUTION: PASTORALISM AND AGRICULTURE

The Neolithic Revolution

The end of the Great (Pleistocene) Ice Age around 10,000 to 12,000 years ago brought about milder conditions, warmer temperatures, and higher ocean levels. These and other climate changes profoundly altered the lives of Stone Age people. Human population increased rapidly. It is estimated that fewer than 2 million humans were alive during the ice age. There were at least 10 million by 5000 B.C.E. By 1000 B.C.E., the human population had reached somewhere between 50 million and 100 million.

Just as important as population growth (and a major cause of it) was a key transformation in how human societies provided themselves with food. Although activities such as hunting and gathering did not cease, different groups in various parts of the world, starting around 12,000 years ago, began to produce their own food. This lifestyle depended on a new skill: the domestication of animals and plants.

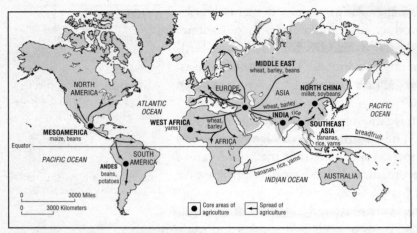

The Practice of Agriculture, ca. 8000 B.C.E.
During the transition from the Paleolithic Era to the Neolithic, communities in the Middle East and northern China began to practice agriculture systematically.

This skill gave birth to the practices of pastoralism and agriculture, which allowed humans to manipulate their environment to a greater degree than ever before.

The tremendous importance of pastoralism and agriculture has made it traditional to refer to a **Neolithic revolution**. Some scholars have questioned the validity of this label on the grounds that the "revolution" took place over a long period of time and that, in some parts of the world, the changes began in the Mesolithic. Whether one considers them revolutionary or gradual, the changes were immense.

NOTE

Because it required great effort and organization, agriculture encouraged closer social ties and the formation of long-lasting settlements. The permanence and stability associated with agriculture proved crucial in civilizing early societies.

Pastoralism and Herding Societies

Pastoralism resulted from humankind's **domestication of animals**. The first to be tamed was the dog, which, early in the Stone Age, provided many societies with companionship, security, and help in hunting. The goat was also domesticated for meat and milk.

The Neolithic era saw the full-scale domestication of many more animals. Horses, water buffalo, oxen, and (in the Americas) llamas provided transport and labor. For groups involved in agriculture, animal droppings were useful as fertilizer. Many animals, particularly sheep, were raised for wool or hides, in order to make clothing. Most important, animals provided a steady source of food. Sheep, goats, cattle, pigs, and poultry yielded meat, milk, eggs, and other edible products.

Pastoralism affected early social development primarily in two ways. Groups that domesticated animals, but not plants, became **herding societies**. Because livestock consumed great quantities of grass or fodder, herders had to migrate constantly, generally according to the pattern of the seasons. This nomadic wandering made it harder for herding groups to develop into civilized societies. Other pastoral societies began to mix pastoralism with the domestication of plants. This combination became a powerful engine driving the emergence of the first civilizations.

Agriculture

The cultivation of plants, or **agriculture**, began in many parts of the world about 10,000 years ago. In the Middle East, wheat and barley cultivation began around 8000 B.C.E. From there, it spread to the Balkans (6500 B.C.E.), the Nile valley (6000 B.C.E.), other parts of northeast Africa (5500 B.C.E.), and continental Europe (4000 B.C.E.). Central Africa developed its own agricultural tradition, growing plantains, bananas, and yams. The peoples of North and South America, isolated from the other continents, learned agriculture on their own. Their early crops were maize (corn), beans, and squash. Millet and barley were grown in India as early as 7000 B.C.E. Probably independently, the people of northern China were growing millet by 6000 B.C.E. Rice cultivation began in Southeast Asia around 5000 B.C.E. and seems to have spread from there to southern China.

After the initial emergence of agriculture in separate parts of the world, cultural diffusion played a greater role. As more societies began to domesticate plants, certain techniques were borrowed and handed on. Seeds and crops were exchanged as well.

The most primitive forms of agriculture included migratory farming and slash-and-burn farming. The former involved farming in a single area for a brief time and then moving on when the soil was exhausted. The latter involved burning down forest land to clear a space for cultivation. For a time, ashes from the trees kept the soil fertile. When the soil wore out, the people moved on and started the cycle elsewhere. Later, a more sophisticated technique, shifting (swidden) agriculture, avoided using up all the soil's nutrients. Rather than cultivating all the fields in a given region, farmers planted some fields, left others fallow (that is, unfarmed), then switched on a regular basis. Other innovations, such as fertilizing, irrigation, and mixing crop types, were also helpful.

As the Neolithic era continued, more societies combined agriculture with the domestication of animals. They also raised a wider variety of crops, including grains (such as wheat and barley), rice (especially in Asia), peas, beans, corn (particularly, if not only, in the Americas), and roots (such as potatoes and yams). Near the end of the Neolithic, the fermentation of alcoholic beverages, beginning with beer, had been discovered in the Middle East.

> **NOTE**
>
> Whether the concept of agriculture arose in one place and then spread through a process of cultural diffusion or originated independently among many peoples at the same time is a matter of debate. The prevailing theory combines both views.

> **NOTE**
>
> The majority of scholars agree that women, already responsible for food collection in most Stone Age cultures, played a key part in stimulating the transition from hunting and gathering to agriculture.

FROM STONE AGE TO CIVILIZATION: EARLY CITIES, METALLURGY, AND WRITING

Transition to Civilized Societies

More elaborate types of social organization took root throughout the Neolithic era. Agriculture required an increased commitment to a single region and caused social groups to give up nomadic life.

There was a corresponding increase in the complexity of religious practices. Rituals became more complicated. Stone Age peoples worshipped a greater variety of deities, in addition to forces of nature and the spirits of departed ancestors. They built permanent sites of worship, including shrines, temples, and megaliths (large standing stones, such as those used at Stonehenge).

Cities and the Specialization of Labor

In some places, the increased social sophistication of the Neolithic era led to the emergence of the **city**. Cities offer protection and defense for large numbers of people. They serve as points of trade and economic activity. They enable the exchange of ideas, information, religious beliefs, and cultural values. They also permit people with different skills and talents to gather in a single area, allowing **specialization of labor**, an important feature of civilized societies. Artisans and craftspeople joined agricultural laborers in increasingly diverse social groups. The first cities date to 8000 to 7000 B.C.E. They include Jericho, on the west bank of the Jordan River, and Çatal Hüyük, in what is today Turkey. An urban center, Danpo, also appeared in China, between 5000 and 4000 B.C.E.

New Tools and the Bronze Age

All during the Neolithic, technological aptitude improved. Tools invented during the Paleolithic became more refined. Newer devices, such as plows, needles, baskets, hoes, shovels, chisels, and saws, appeared. Peoples in the Middle East invented the **wheel**. Many groups taught themselves the multipurpose craft of **pottery**. The **plow** extended the areas of land under cultivation and increased labor productivity. The result was **surplus production**, and such surpluses gave rise to the specialization of labor and the stratification of society.

By the middle of the Neolithic, many societies were on the brink of discovering how to use metals. As a tool-making material, metal is stronger and more versatile than stone. However, **metallurgy** (the science of extracting and refining metal from raw ore) and **metalworking** (the craft of shaping refined metal into tools) are highly advanced skills that took thousands of years to discover and perfect.

Large-scale metallurgy first began in the Middle East and China, sometime between 4000 and 3000 B.C.E. In both areas, toolmakers hit upon the idea of mixing copper and tin to create a harder alloy, bronze. The Neolithic era ended, and the **Bronze Age** (ca. 3500–1200 B.C.E.) began. With the development of **iron**, a metal of even greater strength and usefulness, the Bronze Age came to a close.

One innovation almost always accompanying the emergence of civilization is **writing**. Ancient societies developed rich oral traditions, but the written word enabled them to keep records, pass on learning, and transfer information more effectively than before. Perhaps the earliest form of writing was developed in the ancient Middle East, by the Sumerians, between 3500 and 3000 B.C.E., followed by the Egyptians in 3000 B.C.E. and the Indus River people around 2200 B.C.E. A handful of cultures, including the Incas, reached a civilized state without the benefit of writing, but this happened rarely.

Major Societies, Kingdoms, and Empires to 600 C.E.

CHAPTER 3

- The river valley civilizations
- Hammurabi's law code
- Alphabets (including cuneiform and hieroglyphics)
- The *Gilgamesh Epic* and the Egyptian *Book of the Dead*
- The role of cities
- Classical Greece and Hellenic culture
- The Roman Republic and Empire
- Qin and Han China
- The mandate of heaven
- Mauryan and Gupta India
- The Indian caste system
- Migrations
- Europe's medieval period
- The Bantu
- Nubia and Ghana
- The Olmec
- The Anasazi

This chapter provides an overview of the principal states, kingdoms, and empires of the world before 600 C.E. It begins with the four earliest civilizations, then focuses on various regions of the globe, highlighting key societies. Of particular interest are the political, ecomomic, and cultural–intellectual legacies left behind by these older societies (often referred to as "classical").

THE RIVER VALLEY CIVILIZATIONS

Mesopotamian Societies

From around 3500 to 2000 B.C.E., river systems in the Middle East, India, and China gave birth to the world's first four civilizations. One of the two oldest—if not the oldest—was the Sumerian-Babylonian civilization that arose in the region of **Mesopotamia** (a Greek term meaning "land between the waters"). The rivers that gave life to this so-called Fertile Crescent were the Tigris and Euphrates. Settlement began in this area as early as 8000 B.C.E., and large-scale agriculture was practiced by 5000 B.C.E. Between 3500 and 2350 B.C.E., the first true civilization in Mesopotamia was begun by the **Sumerians**. As time passed, a variety of other local groups, especially the Babylonians (1900–1600 B.C.E.), achieved political dominance. Still, the language, culture, and religious traditions of the Sumerians influenced the peoples of Mesopotamia for centuries to come.

The Mesopotamians built many cities (including **Babylon**) and were governed by a small ruling class of priests and a kinglike figure known as the *lugal* (literally, "big man"). Mesopotamia was not always politically centralized; at times, individual city-states enjoyed much autonomy.

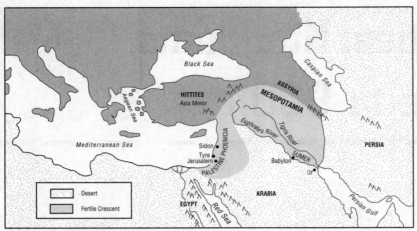

The Ancient Middle East, ca. 1200 B.C.E.

Note the importance of bodies of water in giving birth to ancient civilizations. The Fertile Crescent, between the Tigris and Euphrates rivers, encouraged the formation of advanced societies in Mesopotamia. The Nile did the same in Egypt. The Mediterranean Sea was crucial for the movement of people and trade goods.

In the Western tradition, if not worldwide, the Sumerians were the first to develop a written language. Around 3300 B.C.E., they created a script called **cuneiform**, in which wedge-shaped characters were pressed into clay tablets with a small stick. Sometime before 2000 B.C.E., one of the world's oldest literary works, the *Gilgamesh* epic—which tells the story of a king's quest to achieve immortality—appeared in Sumeria. One of the world's first law codes was designed in Mesopotamia, by the Babylonian king Hammurabi (1792–1750 B.C.E.). Although **Hammurabi's law code** was very harsh (death and mutilation were common punishments) and favored the upper classes, the idea that a consistent set of regulations, rather than the arbitrary will of a ruler, should govern society was an important innovation.

The peoples of Mesopotamia were skilled builders and craftspeople. Using clay, they erected dozens of large cities and, to honor their gods and goddesses, pyramid-like temples called **ziggurats**. They built canals and dams. They were accomplished at pottery and metalworking (bronze working began here around 3000 B.C.E.). Skilled astronomers, the Sumerians and Babylonians developed a high level of mathematical knowledge, originating the **base-60 number system** still used today to measure time and navigational calculations. The peoples of Mesopotamia were great traders, and their economic network extended throughout the Middle East, as well as North Africa and the Indian Ocean.

Egypt

The other early civilization of the Middle East appeared in Egypt, on the banks of **the Nile**. Surrounded by desert, Egypt depended for survival on the Nile's waters. Agricultural settlements began to emerge there as early as 5500 B.C.E.

Egypt's history as a civilization is considered to have begun in 3100 B.C.E., when the king Menes united Upper (southern) and Lower (northern) Egypt. Its ancient history is traditionally divided into several long periods. During the Early Dynastic (ca. 3100–2575 B.C.E.) and Old Kingdom (2575–2134 B.C.E.) periods, basic social and political features took shape. Civil war tore Egypt apart during the First Intermediate Period (ca. 2134–2040 B.C.E.), but a more powerful and culturally dynamic Middle Kingdom arose around 2040 B.C.E. The Middle Kingdom lasted until approximately 1640 B.C.E., when outside invaders called the Hyksos ushered in a Second Intermediate Period (ca. 1640–1532 B.C.E.). Rebelling against Hyksos rule around 1532 B.C.E., the Egyptians formed a New Kingdom that lasted until

1070 B.C.E. Under vigorous leaders, especially Rameses II (ca. 1304–1237 B.C.E.), New Kingdom Egypt conquered a great deal of territory in northern Africa and the Middle East. Eventually, the New Kingdom collapsed, due to internal disorder and foreign invasions. By the 900s B.C.E., most of Egypt had lost its independence.

Although Egyptian women were secondary to men in terms of power and status, they enjoyed certain privileges. They managed household finances and the education of children. They had the right to divorce their husbands and could receive alimony. They could own property. Some women managed businesses, and upper-class women could serve as priestesses. One queen, Hatshepsut, became pharaoh of Egypt in her own right.

The Egyptians had an elaborate religion. Their chief deity was Ra, the sun god. What happened to the soul after death and how to earn a happy afterlife were the subjects of the Egyptians' most important religious text, the **Egyptian Book of the Dead**. Concern about life after death gave rise to mummification (the art of preserving bodies after death) and the building of gigantic tombs (including the famous **pyramids**, which provided resting places for pharaohs after they died).

The cultural and scientific attainments of the Egyptians were many. Around 3100 B.C.E., they developed a written script made up of characters called **hieroglyphics**. Using the fiber of reeds called **papyrus**, they invented the craft of papermaking. The Egyptians were skilled engineers and architects. From the beginning, they knew how to irrigate their fields, extending the reach of the Nile's waters far from the river valley itself. They began to construct pyramids around 2630 B.C.E., and their other buildings and monuments were impressive. They were talented makers of bronze tools and weapons, and possessed a great knowledge of medicine, mathematics, and astronomy.

> **NOTE**
>
> Even more so than the Mesopotamians, the Egyptians developed a centralized society presided over by a monarch and a small caste of priests. The monarch, or pharaoh, was considered the living incarnation of the sun god. Although their society was less urban than that of the Mesopotamians and although they did not trade as widely, the Egyptians still erected many cities and built up a sizable economic network.

> **NOTE**
>
> The Egyptians devised the **365-day calendar** that, with only minor modifications, is still in use today.

The Indus Valley Civilization

Farther to the east was a third civilization, which grew up on the coast of the Arabian Sea and farther inland, in what is today Pakistan and northwestern India. This was the Indus River civilization, and it arose around 2600 B.C.E. Although the people of the Indus River had a written language, it has not been deciphered by modern scholars. As a result, much about their civilization remains unclear, especially their origins, their culture, and the reasons for their decline and disappearance.

What is known is that the Indus River civilization was quite large, about the size of present-day France and heavily urbanized. The Indus River people built several hundred cities, the largest of which, **Harappa** and **Mohenjo-Daro**, had populations of perhaps 100,000 apiece (these are the modern names, since the original names are unknown). Because the design of most of these cities is virtually identical, it is thought that their society was unified and highly centralized. The Indus River civilization produced metal tools and objects of high quality, as well as precious stones. It traded not only with its neighbors, but far beyond its borders, perhaps even with Mesopotamia.

The Indus River civilization lasted until approximately 1900 B.C.E. How it met its end is a matter of debate. It used to be thought that invasion by outside enemies, the

Aryans, destroyed the Indus River society. However, a majority of scientists now believe that environmental factors—most likely the drying up of local rivers or the erosion of soil—led to the downfall.

Early China and the Yellow River

The fourth river valley civilization emerged in China, along the Yellow River (or Huang Ho). The western reaches of China border on desert, and much of China's center is hilly or mountainous. This makes the two east–west rivers, the Yellow and the Yangtze, exceptionally important in supporting agriculture, allowing movement between communities, and fostering social and political unity. Around 8000 B.C.E., small agricultural societies formed along the Yellow River. The Chinese grew wheat, millet, and, later, rice, a high-yield crop that required an immense amount of cooperative labor. By 2000 B.C.E., the Chinese had discovered the science of bronze working.

Most of China's long history as a civilization, from the 1700s B.C.E. to 1911 C.E., is measured in dynasties, or successions of emperors. Myth and tradition speak of a dynasty called the Xia arising around 2000 B.C.E., but most scholars consider it not to have existed. Therefore, the first historically verifiable dynasty—and the bedrock of Chinese civilization—is the **Shang Dynasty**, which emerged on the banks of the Yellow River around 1750 B.C.E. and ruled a gradually growing state until 1027 B.C.E. Led by a warrior aristocracy, the Shang fought its northern and western neighbors (whom it considered to be barbarians) and expanded its boundaries by conquest.

The Shang traded extensively, its economic network stretching perhaps as far as the Middle East. Principal commodities included jade, ivory, and silk (on which the Chinese enjoyed an unbroken monopoly for over a thousand years). The Chinese system of writing, pictograms, originated with the Shang. So did two of the most important aspects of Chinese religion: fortune-telling and ancestor worship (a tradition that reinforced a strong sense of patriarchalism). The Shang also considered themselves to be at the center of the world. This idea gave rise to a sense of superiority and the long-standing tradition of viewing China as the "Middle Kingdom."

China's second and longest-lasting, dynasty was the **Zhou (Chou)**, founded when King Wu rebelled against the Shang and overthrew it in 1027 B.C.E. The Zhou lasted till 221 B.C.E., though it was in serious decline long before that, from around 800 B.C.E. The internal collapse and civil wars that plagued the Zhou are reflected in the name given to the last phase of its history: the "Warring States" period (480–221 B.C.E.).

The Zhou preserved the knowledge of the Shang but added innovations of its own. Around 600 B.C.E., the Chinese learned to make iron tools and weapons. Political sophistication increased: a central principle of the Zhou was the **Mandate of Heaven**, the idea that, as long as a leader governed wisely and fairly, he could claim a divine right to rule. Key religious and philosophical traditions, such as Confucianism and Daoism, emerged during these years (see Chapter 5).

THE CELTS

Their lack of a written tradition, as well as the fact that they never united politically, has led most scholars to consider the **Celts** noncivilized. However, the Celts are widely regarded as the first ethnic group to establish a widespread presence in Europe. They are believed to have emerged somewhere in central Europe, north of the Danube, thousands of years ago. After 500 B.C.E., they began to migrate west, spreading throughout Europe. Their legacy is strongest in northwestern France, parts of Spain, and the British Isles (particularly Ireland, Scotland, and Wales).

Although they had no written language until the 300s C.E., when they developed the ogham script, the Celts had a rich oral tradition, in the form of myths, songs, and folktales. They were highly skilled at crafts, especially metalworking. They worshipped a variety of gods and goddesses, whose priests were known as druids.

THE ANCIENT MIDDLE EAST

From 1500 B.C.E. onward, the ancient Middle East witnessed the rise and fall of a number of important civilizations besides the Egyptians and Mesopotamian peoples. Many of them made noteworthy contributions. Although they did not invent the science of ironworking, the **Hittites**, who appeared in Mesopotamia around 1700 B.C.E. and dominated the region in the 1200s B.C.E., were likely the first group to make systematic use of iron weapons.

Even more powerful were the **Assyrians**, who formed one of the world's first true empires—large states created by the conquest of one's neighbors—from 911 to 612 B.C.E. Armed with iron weapons and making use of the new skill of cavalry (horseback) warfare, the Assyrians took over most of the Middle East, including Mesopotamia and Egypt, and held their empire together by means of a deliberate policy of cruelty. Assyrian rule over the Middle East was ended by a new conqueror, the Chaldeans, or Neo-Babylonians, who controlled the region from 626 to 539 B.C.E. Their most famous ruler was **Nebuchadnezzar** (ca. 605–562 B.C.E.), renowned for building the Hanging Gardens of Babylon.

The last to dominate the Middle East politically before Alexander the Great (discussed below) were the **Persians** (550–331 B.C.E.), who, in a short time, created one of the largest empires in world history. The Persians' first ruler, Cyrus the Great, conquered present-day Iran in 550 B.C.E. By the end of the reign of the third emperor, Darius the Great (522–486 B.C.E.), the empire stretched from Turkey and Libya to India, measuring more than 2 million square miles, the largest state seen in the world to that date. The Persians governed with the help of an advanced postal system, an excellent network of roads, a single currency, and a flexible form of government, in which local officials called satraps ruled in the name of the emperor. Its 1,600-mile Great Royal Road could be traveled in less than a week. The official religion of the Persians was Zoroastrianism (see Chapter 5), but they remained relatively tolerant of other faiths. The Persians fought several wars with their Greek neighbors to the west during the 500s and 400s B.C.E. In 331 B.C.E., they fell to the Macedonian conqueror Alexander the Great.

Other notable peoples of the ancient Middle East include the **Hebrews** (later known as Israelites and Jews). Sometime after 2000 B.C.E., under the leadership of Abraham, the Hebrews became the first in the world to practice **monotheism** (worship of only one god). They were politically weak during most of their history: enslaved by the Egyptians (ca. 1400–1200 B.C.E.), conquered by the Assyrians (in

721 B.C.E.), and taken over by the Neo-Babylonians (ca. 587–539 B.C.E.). Nevertheless, their religious and cultural legacy, in the form of the Judeo-Christian tradition, has shaped world history in countless ways.

By about 1100 B.C.E., the **Phoenicians** settled on the eastern coast of the Mediterranean, in what is today Syria and Lebanon. From their great cities of Tyre and Sidon, they developed an advanced economy based on the export of timber (particularly cedar) and purple dye made from shellfish. The Phoenicians were skilled traders and sailors, and established many colonies along the coast of North Africa. One of these, Carthage, became one of the ancient world's great cities and a serious rival to Rome (discussed subsequently). Around 1400 B.C.E., the Phoenicians devised the world's first true **alphabet**: a system of writing in which the signs represent sounds, rather than pictures. These twenty-two letters made writing and reading much easier. They were adapted by the Greeks, then (in modified form) by the Romans. The Latin script devised by the Romans now serves as the alphabet for most modern Western languages, including English. A last Middle Eastern people, the **Lydians** (ca. 600–500 B.C.E.) are said to have invented metal **coinage**.

GREECE AND ROME

The ancient Greeks and Romans lay the political and intellectual foundations of Western culture. Both of these Mediterranean civilizations played a central role in shaping the history of Europe, the Middle East, and North Africa.

Early Greek History

The earliest civilizations in the Greek world were the Aegean civilizations (ca. 2000–1150 B.C.E.), centered on the island of Crete (the Minoan culture) and the Greek mainland (the Mycenaean civilization). Both were trading societies, and the Mycenaeans also grew wealthy through conquest (they are best known for fighting the **Trojan War**, ca. 1250 B.C.E.). Around 1200 B.C.E., Greek-speaking tribes invaded the southeastern tip of Europe, as well as the nearby islands. Over time, these tribes joined together into a single culture, the **Greeks** (or, as they called themselves, **Hellenes**). These years of gradual cultural union are known as the Greek Dark Ages (1150–800 B.C.E.). Although a common language and religion emerged during this period, political and social development remained at a relatively low level.

Greek City-States

More advancement characterized the archaic period (ca. 800–500 B.C.E.). Rugged, mountainous terrain and the fact that so many of the Greeks lived on islands prevented them from creating a single nation. Instead they formed dozens of independent **city-states** (urban centers that controlled the immediate regions surrounding them).

Key city-states included Corinth and Thebes, but most important were Sparta and Athens. **Sparta** was a rigid, slave-holding dictatorship that created the Greek world's most effective and most feared army. **Athens** became a culturally and politically advanced city that gained wealth through trade and power thanks to its naval strength.

The Greek city-states governed themselves in a variety of ways, but most were oligarchies, in which a narrow elite made up of rich, powerful families ruled. Slavery was common in all city-states, but most prevalent in Sparta. Greek women were treated as social and political inferiors. Ancient Greece's most significant political innovation came from the city of Athens. This was **democracy**, or rule by the people. Democratic government began in Athens in 508 B.C.E. and reached its peak under the leadership of the statesman **Pericles** (ca. 461–429 B.C.E.). As in other Greek city-states, women and slaves were excluded from Athenian political life and did not have the right to vote. Even with these restrictions, however, Athens had the most representative government in the ancient world.

> **NOTE**
>
> It is from the Greek word for city-state, *polis*, that the word "politics" comes.

The Classical Period and the Age of Alexander the Great

During the classical period (ca. 500–338 B.C.E.), the Greeks fought two major wars with the Persians, in 492–490 B.C.E. and 480–479 B.C.E. In both cases, the Persians attempted to invade Greece only to be driven back, thanks to Spartan and Athenian leadership. Afterward, competition between Sparta and Athens led to a devastating civil conflict known as the **Peloponnesian War** (431–404 B.C.E.). Although Sparta and its allies won the war, the conflict left all of Greece's city-states weakened. That weakness opened Greece first to Persian influence, then, in 338 B.C.E., to conquest by its neighbor to the north, Macedonia (whose people were related to the Greeks but not as politically or socially advanced).

It was from this Greek-Macedonian kingdom that the ancient world's most skilled general, **Alexander the Great** (356–323 B.C.E.), launched one of the most successful military campaigns of all time. Alexander crossed into Asia, took over the Persian Empire, and conquered territory all the way to the borderlands of India. Before dying at the age of thirty-three—of exhaustion, alcoholism, and fever—he had led a large army on a journey of more than 20,000 miles, lasting almost 3,600 days. Alexander preserved Greek culture and spread it throughout a vast portion of Eurasia and northern Africa. Under him, the Egyptian city of Alexandria, with its Great Library, became one of the Mediterranean world's great centers of trade, learning, and culture.

Hellenic (Greek) Culture

The Greeks' cultural outlook is known as Hellenism (after the Greeks' name for Greece, Hellas). Although the polytheistic Greeks worshipped a number of gods, Hellenism tended to be more worldly and rational than other ancient cultural traditions. Science was extremely important. From the 600s to the 300s B.C.E., Greek thinkers (influenced by learning from Egypt) outlined many of the basic laws of geometry, physics, mathematics, and astronomy.

The celebration of life and the experience of being human (as opposed to fear of the gods and fixation on the afterlife) was a hallmark of Hellenic culture. Starting with the poet Homer (ca. 850–800 B.C.E.), who composed the *Iliad* and the *Odyssey*, and ending with the classical playwrights Aeschylus, Sophocles, and Euripides (all during the 500s and 400s B.C.E.), Greek writers created the Western world's first literary masterpieces. Western thought rests on the intellectual foundation established by the philosophers **Socrates** (470–399 B.C.E.), **Plato** (428–347 B.C.E.), and **Aristotle** (384–322 B.C.E.). Aristotle's writings on logic, observation, and experimentation set into place a mode of scientific inquiry that influenced the Middle East and the Western world for centuries, and remains at the heart of the modern **scientific method**. Greek sculpture and architecture are still considered to be among the world's finest. In countless ways, ancient Greece can be considered the wellspring of much of Western culture.

Early Roman History

As the Greeks faded politically, a new power emerged in Mediterranean Europe, the city of Rome, traditionally considered to have been founded in 753 B.C.E. From their homeland on the Italian peninsula, the **Romans** spread outward to dominate the Mediterranean world and the regions bordering it, creating one of the largest and longest-lasting empires in history. For several centuries, Rome was governed by a monarchy. It was also controlled for some time by foreign overlords, the Etruscans. In 509 B.C.E., the Romans rebelled against the monarchy (and the Etruscans), forming a new government called the **Roman Republic** (509–31 B.C.E.).

The Roman Republic

During the republican period, Roman society experienced tensions between the lower (**plebeian**) and upper (**patrician**) classes. Through a long process of compromise and negotiation, the plebeians gained greater, but never complete, social and political equality. The most important governing body was the Senate, dominated by the patrician class. Executive power rested with two consuls, elected every year (but not in a completely democratic fashion). It was during the republican period that Rome expanded into a Mediterranean power. By 270 B.C.E., the Romans had conquered almost the entire Italian peninsula. From 264 to 146 B.C.E., Rome fought three bitter campaigns, collectively called the **Punic Wars**, against the powerful city of **Carthage**, a Phoenician colony on the North African coast. Rome's victory made it the strongest state in the western Mediterranean, with a large amount of new territory in Europe, the Mediterranean islands, and North Africa. From 214 to 169 B.C.E., the Romans turned east, absorbing Greece, the Balkans, and parts of what is today Turkey. The Romans later took over more territory, moving steadily to the east (into Asia and Egypt) and north (into Europe).

The Collapse of the Roman Republic

Such rapid expansion caused a number of political, economic, and social crises throughout the first century B.C.E. In particular, small farmers (the closest Rome had to a middle class) went bankrupt, thanks to falling grain prices and the increased use of slave labor by larger landowners. Poverty worsened, and many of the urban poor joined violent mobs (often manipulated by unscrupulous politicians) or sold their votes to the highest bidder.

Rome was shaken by a series of civil wars from 91 to 30 B.C.E. During this period, the republican form of government faltered, and political power began to fall into the hands of a single ruler. The most famous of the late republican politicians was **Julius Caesar**, who assumed dictatorial powers during Rome's second civil war (49–45 B.C.E.). Although Caesar seems to have wanted to use his powers to benefit Rome, he was assassinated in 44 B.C.E. by those opposed to his growing strength. More war followed, until the republic ended in 31 B.C.E.

The Roman Empire

A new regime, the **Roman Empire**, remained in place for approximately five centuries, from 31 B.C.E. to Rome's downfall in 476 C.E. The first emperor was Julius Caesar's adopted son, Octavian, who renamed himself **Caesar Augustus** (30 B.C.E.–14 C.E.). Augustus restored order, revived Roman strength and wealth, and, despite the fact that he gave himself even more power than Julius Caesar, enjoyed a long reign as a respected ruler. Over time, Rome's emperors became more despotic. During the first two and a half centuries C.E., Rome's economic and military might increased. Its huge territory extended from Spain in the west to Asia Minor in the east, from northern Africa in the south to the British Isles in the north.

From the early 200s C.E. onward, Rome found itself in crisis. During the 300s C.E., the eastern half of the empire broke away, evolving into the Byzantine Empire. Overextension of military and political strength made it difficult to govern what remained of the western empire. The army gained a large degree of control over the imperial government. The economy experienced severe downturns. Migrating waves of Asiatic and Germanic barbarians attacked Roman lands from the east and the north for more than four centuries. By the 400s C.E., the heartland of the empire lay open to barbarian invasion. The city of Rome was sacked by Gothic tribes in 410 C.E. Another wave of Goths took over the city completely in 476 C.E., the year when Rome and the western empire are considered to have fallen.

> **NOTE**
>
> Despite occasional episodes of political violence, Rome experienced a period of power and prosperity from the reign of Augustus to the 200s C.E. known as the *pax Romana* ("Roman peace"). This proved to be Rome's golden age.

Roman Society

Roman society was sharply divided into citizens and noncitizens, who were subject peoples with no civil rights. Among Rome's citizens, the primary social distinction was between upper-class patricians and lower-class plebeians. As time passed, however, Roman social divisions became less rigid. Wealth, as much as one's ancestry or birth, determined one's place.

As in ancient Greece (and most ancient societies), slavery was widely practiced. Rome's social and economic functions depended heavily on slave labor, although occasional slave revolts (such as that of Spartacus in the 70s B.C.E.) periodically disturbed the order of things.

> **NOTE**
>
> Roman imperial policy was to respect the cultural and religious practices of subject peoples, as long as they obeyed Roman law and authority.

The role of women in Roman society changed over time. During the republican period, Roman society was strictly patriarchal. The family head (**paterfamilias**), always male, had absolute power over his wife and children. By the late republican period and early empire, this tradition broke down somewhat. Although males remained dominant and women could not vote, women gained more freedom to divorce, more economic rights, and greater influence over family financial affairs.

Rome's Cultural Legacy

For the Western world, the cultural heritage of Rome is incalculable. To begin with, the Romans, who greatly admired Greek culture (to the point of adapting most of the Greeks' gods), preserved the Hellenic philosophy, literature, and scientific learning of ancient Greece.

The Romans were master builders and engineers. Many of the roads, **aqueducts**, fortifications, cities, and buildings they constructed were of use to the people who came after them for many centuries (in cases, up to the present).

The ideal of Roman imperial unity was a political concept that kings and emperors in a disunified Europe would attempt to live up to during the medieval period. Roman political thinking guided the formation of many of Europe's nations. Roman law remains one of the keystones of Western legal thought. Finally, it was at the eastern edge of the Roman Empire that the religion of Christianity was born, during the first century C.E. By making Christianity legal (313 C.E.), and then adopting it as their official faith (380 C.E.), the Romans ensured that the new religion would remain a major intellectual, cultural, and political force after the empire itself had faded away.

CHINA THROUGH THE HAN AND SUI DYNASTIES

From the 200s B.C.E. to 600 C.E., a united and steadily growing China was ruled by three major dynasties. These were the Qin, or Ch'in (221–206 B.C.E.); the Han (206 B.C.E.–220 C.E.); and the Sui (589–618 C.E.).

The Qin Dynasty

Although short-lived, the Qin dynasty was important because of its principal ruler, **Shi Huangdi**, whose name means "first emperor." Shi Huangdi turned the Qin state—which many historians believe gave the country its name, China—into a dictatorial, centralized nation. He standardized weights and measures and modernized the Chinese army by introducing iron weapons, crossbows, and cavalry warfare. He used forced labor to build thousands of miles of roads, as well as the first of the structures that collectively came to be known as the **Great Wall of China**. Many of the political institutions that the Qin handed down to later dynasties—among them the concept of a strong emperor, the emphasis on legalism, and the importance of a large **bureaucracy**—became basic features of the Chinese state.

The Han Dynasty

The Qin state survived the death of Shi Huangdi by only four years. Then, in 206 B.C.E., rebellion brought to power a new dynasty, one of China's strongest and longest lasting. This **Han Dynasty**, building on the foundations of Shi Huangdi's Qin state, created a mighty, efficiently governed empire. Especially under the emperor **Wu Ti** (140–87 B.C.E.), Han armies expanded hundreds of miles to the west, north, and south, absorbing all of Inner China, much of Outer China, parts of Southeast Asia (including northern Vietnam), portions of Korea and Manchuria, and inner Mongolia. Where they did not take over directly, they established a **tributary system**, exacting payment from neighboring states.

The Great Wall of China.
The so-called Great Wall was actually a network of many walls. Construction began as early as the 200s B.C.E., under the emperor Shi Huangdi, and took centuries. Thousands of the workers, many of them prisoners, died. As impressive a feat of engineering as the Great Wall is, it failed to defend China from attack. Note the state of disrepair depicted in this engraving.

Like the Qin before them, Han rulers put into place an effective administration, postal service, and tax-collecting system. They built roads, defensive fortifications (enlarging the Great Wall), and canals to link the country's major rivers. During most of the Han dynasty, the economy was strong, spurred by improved agricultural techniques and China's monopoly on **silk production**. By 200 C.E., however, the Han state was in decline. A downturn in agricultural production and an overall economic slump sapped its strength, as did governmental corruption and weak leadership. Outside invaders, bandits, and rebels on the frontiers made it difficult for the Han to protect their borders. In 220 C.E., the Han dynasty collapsed. It has become increasingly common for historians to draw parallels between the Han and Roman empires, which existed at roughly the same time and became large and powerful by similar combinations of conquest and effective administration. Over the next three and a half centuries, several minor dynasties rose and fell, while China itself was mired in a state of chaos and anarchy. Not until 589 C.E. did a strong dynasty, the Sui (589–618), reestablish order.

CENTRAL ASIA

Although it was not home to settled civilizations until comparatively late, Central Asia gave birth to enough important nomadic groups that it deserves mention. Living in the grasslands and deserts of Central Asia and Mongolia were many herding societies, with highly mobile lifestyles and an aptitude for horsemanship and cavalry warfare.

Many cultures originating here migrated thousands of miles to other parts of Eurasia and had a great impact on the development of civilizations and movement of peoples in Europe and Asia. Central Asia may be the birthplace of the **Indo-**

European linguistic and cultural group, although this has not been proven conclusively. Certainly many of the ethnic groups belonging to the Indo-European tradition came from Central Asia, including the Aryas (or Aryans), who invaded India in approximately 1500 B.C.E., and perhaps the Persians. Many Turkic peoples, among them the Scythians, Tatars (Tartars), Seljuks, and Ottomans, trace their origins to Central Asia. Others from Central Asia who affected the course of early history were the Huns (who helped destroy China's Han dynasty, India's Gupta Empire, and the Roman Empire), the Magyars (ancestors of the modern Hungarians), and the Mongols (see Chapter 10), who, during the 1200s and 1300s, carved out one of the world's largest empires.

EARLY JAPAN

Origins of the Japanese State

The origins of civilization on the Japanese islands remain cloudy. Communities gathered together during the Stone Age. As early as the 300s and 200s B.C.E., larger settlements appeared, but the mountainous terrain of the home islands kept them relatively isolated. Although Shinto tradition traces the ancestry of the Japanese imperial family back to the 600s B.C.E., there is no evidence of an organized Japanese government before the 300s or 400s C.E.

> **NOTE**
>
> It was from China (and through Korea) that, in 522, Buddhism arrived in Japan. Nara became famous throughout Asia as a center of Buddhist scholarship.

The Nara State

The first imperial state was ruled by the Yamato family, starting in the 300s or 400s C.E. The **Shinto** religion—which remained important even after the arrival of new faiths like **Buddhism**—legitimated the emperors, declaring them descendants of the sun goddess. The Yamato initially ruled from Nara, which, until the late 700s, served as Japan's capital. During the Nara period (ca. 300–794 C.E.), the Japanese nation's foundations were laid. Japan also came into contact with Korea and China. The Chinese had a tremendous influence on the development of Japanese art, architecture, literature, and religion.

CLASSICAL INDIA

The Aryan Invasion

To what degree the Indus River valley civilization can be considered "Indian" is unclear, and the true foundations of Indian culture remain unknown. Conventionally, Indian history is said to have begun around 1500 B.C.E., when northern India was invaded by a nomadic group known as the **Aryans** (also called the Aryas). Originally from Persia and Central Asia, the Aryans are considered to be among the earliest Indo-Europeans. (Famously and tragically, Adolf Hitler and the Nazis misinterpreted the concept of the "Aryan" race to justify their genocidal racial policies.) The light-skinned Aryans conquered the darker-skinned natives of India (collectively known as the **Dravidians**), expanding from north to south. The Aryans established a warrior aristocracy and enslaved the Dravidians, but both blended to form a truly Indian culture. However, even today, India is home to dozens of ethnicities, languages, and traditions.

The Aryan-Dravidian fusion gave India several of its characteristic features. One was an elite language, **Sanskrit**, for religious, literary, and intellectual purposes. Another was a religious tradition, the Vedic and early Hindu faiths, that shaped India for centuries to come. In addition, a **caste system** emerged, dividing society into specific social classes. Over time, the Indian caste system grew increasingly complex, with new groups and subgroups. People were born into their castes, and their descendants remained in the same caste permanently. This persisted into modern times.

> **NOTE**
>
> The original castes included, from top to bottom, priests (brahmins), warriors and political rulers (kshatriyas), commoners (vaishyas), servants and peasants (shudras), and "untouchables."

The Mauryan Empire

India is large and diverse enough that, during its ancient and classical periods, it was rarely unified as a single state. The first rulers to bring most of India together were the Mauryas, who created an empire lasting from 324 to 184 B.C.E. Mauryan India was characterized by a strong military and an extensive trade network, which stretched all the way to Mesopotamia and the eastern parts of the Roman Empire. A key good was cotton.

The best known of the Mauryan emperors was **Ashoka** (269–232 B.C.E.). A great warrior as a youth, Ashoka became sickened by war after one of his greatest victories. He converted to Buddhism and advocated peace and tolerance, spreading those ideals throughout India by means of his Rock and Pillar Acts. He encouraged trade with China, especially for its silk, and opened trade routes to the north. Ashoka was admired for his justice and wisdom, and he remains famous for his efforts to create harmony between Buddhists, Hindus, and the followers of India's other religions.

The Gupta Empire

In 184 B.C.E., the Mauryan Empire collapsed because of attacks by outside enemies. For the next five hundred years, India reverted to a state of political disunity. Not until 320 C.E. did another large empire rise up: the **Gupta Empire**, which lasted until 550 C.E. and controlled most of northern and central India. The Gupta Empire was smaller and less centralized than the Mauryan, but it thrived culturally and economically. Although the Gupta rulers were Hindu, they practiced religious toleration. Gupta India traded with China, Southeast Asia, and even the eastern Mediterranean. Gupta scholars created the **decimal system** used today (the misnamed "Arabic numerals"), along with the concepts of *pi* and **zero**.

Like the Mauryans before them, the Gupta emperors fell as a result of outside pressure, especially from Hun attacks on the northwestern frontier. From then until after 1000 C.E., India would remain decentralized. Muslim invaders then moved into the subcontinent, doing much to shape Indian politics and culture after 1000 C.E.

BYZANTIUM

When the Roman Empire split in two in 395 C.E., the eastern half flourished, even after the western empire fell. It was known as Byzantium, after the original name of its capital, better known as **Constantinople**. The city's unique position between the Black and Mediterranean seas, the crossroads of Europe and Asia, made it economically and militarily important for a millennium and a half. The **Byzantine Empire** played a crucial role in providing commercial and cultural connections among the Europeans, the peoples of the Middle East, and Asia. It also preserved Christianity in eastern Europe and the Middle East.

Under **Justinian**, who reigned during the 500s C.E., Constantinople underwent a breathtaking architectural renovation, during which the Church of Hagia Sophia was built. Now an Islamic mosque, Hagia Sophia remains one of the ancient world's finest monuments. The form of religious art known as the icon originated in Byzantium and spread throughout medieval Europe, the Middle East, and eastern Europe (especially Russia). Justinian was also responsible for the **Corpus Juris Civilis** (*Body of Civil Law*), a codification of all existing Roman laws. It became (and remains) a key foundation of most European and western legal systems.

Byzantium's territorial might reached its peak in the 500s C.E., under Justinian, who succeeded in recapturing many of the lands controlled by the western Roman Empire. From the 600s onward, the Byzantine Empire gradually lost territory in northern Africa and the Middle East, because of the rapid expansion of Islam (discussed in the next unit). Still, until the 1400s C.E., Byzantium remained a strong regional power, both in Europe and Asia.

EARLY MEDIEVAL EUROPE

The Concept of "Middle Ages"

After the fall of the western Roman Empire, Europe entered a state of relative backwardness. In the west, the centralizing institutions of Roman rule had been rotted out by economic decay and political corruption, then shattered by the incursion of Germanic and Asiatic barbarians. This collapse began Europe's long **medieval period**, also known as the **Middle Ages**, which lasted approximately from 500 to 1500 C.E.

Barbarian Invasions

During the early medieval period, Europe continued to undergo numerous invasions by **barbarian tribes** from the north and east. This **great age of migrations** was one of the principal forces shaping European culture. Most of these people were Germanic (Saxons, Angles, Goths) or Asiatic (Huns, Magyars) in origin. A number of them, especially the former, settled permanently in European lands. The kingdoms they formed tended to be unsophisticated and short-lived. Nonetheless, as the barbarian tribes of the medieval era became less nomadic and more settled, they helped form Europe's emerging (but still decentralized) nations.

BANTU AFRICA, NUBIA, AND GHANA

Africa, especially its sub-Saharan portions, is incredibly diverse ethnically and linguistically, making it difficult to generalize about early societies and civilizations there.

The Bantu

The one language-based group that most resembles a common cultural source in sub-Saharan Africa is the **Bantu**. Bantu-speaking peoples emerged in the Niger River basin of west central Africa and, between 1500 and 100 B.C.E., began to migrate throughout the continent. By 1000 C.E., their descendants had spread to the southern and eastern ends of Africa. Environmental pressures in the form of greater aridity in the Sahara may have caused the migration, by driving Saharan tribes into the Bantus' lands and displacing them.

> **TIP**
>
> It is believed that Bantu-speaking tribes spread the knowledge of agriculture and ironworking to many parts of eastern and southern Africa.

It is inaccurate to say that the Bantu provided Africa with a single cultural heritage, but they played the greatest role in shaping the region's cultural, ethnic, and linguistic character. They transformed an area that had earlier been sparsely populated by groups of hunter-gatherers to one more densely populated and dominated by farming communities. All Bantu-speaking groups of southern and eastern Africa—including the Swazi, Sotho, Tswana, Shona, Ndebele, Venda, Xhosa, and Zulu—came to depend on the ownership of cattle as the foundation of their economic and political systems.

Nubia and Ghana

Not counting Egypt, the first major civilizations in Africa appeared in Nubia and Ghana. The former is a thousand-mile region south of Egypt that links sub-Saharan Africa with the Mediterranean coast. With the Nile running through it, **Nubia** became an important corridor for trade between north and south. A particularly valuable commodity was gold. Nubia was settled around 3000 B.C.E. More advanced societies appeared about 2300 B.C.E., and a powerful kingdom known as Kush emerged in approximately 1750 B.C.E. For 500 years, the Egyptian New Kingdom dominated Nubia, but its control gradually faded.

A new Nubian kingdom rose during the 700s B.C.E. From the fourth century B.C.E. to the fourth century C.E., that kingdom was centered at the prosperous city of **Meroë**, south of Egypt. Meroë, surrounded by grasslands and rivers, could support agriculture and livestock grazing. It also contained large deposits of iron ore, and the scale of iron production in Nubia was once large. Meroë collapsed in the second century C.E., as a result of changing trade patterns in the Red Sea and environmental factors, especially the erosion of topsoil, caused by heavy deforestation.

Far to the west, on the Atlantic coast, was **Ghana**. The first major sub-Saharan kingdom, this "land of gold" dates back to the 500s C.E. Part of the **trans-Saharan trade network** that extended throughout the Sahara, Ghana grew during the next 500 years, expanding throughout northwestern Africa.

EARLY CULTURES IN THE AMERICAS

Mexico and Central America

Advanced civilizations appeared in the Americas after 1200 B.C.E. The oldest and most sophisticated were in Mexico and Central America (also known as Mesoamerica), where a succession of cultures, each influencing the ones that followed it, emerged. The first major society in the Americas was that of the **Olmecs** (ca.

1200–400 B.C.E.). Located on the east-central coast of the Gulf of Mexico, the Olmecs created what is considered to be the "mother civilization" of Central America. Although their written language remains a mystery to modern scholars, it is clear that the art (consisting mainly of large heads carved from stone), monumental architecture, and religion of the Olmecs had an impact on the peoples that came after them. One interesting comparative point is that, unlike other early civilizations—such as Mesopotamia, Egypt, Shang China, and the Indus culture—the Olmec arose without the benefit of a major river system.

The next major society in the region was centered on the vast city of Teotihuacán, founded approximately 150 to 100 B.C.E., near modern-day Mexico City. With a population greater than 200,000, Teotihuacán was one of the world's largest cities at the time. It existed until 750 C.E. By that point, it had been eclipsed, perhaps taken over, by one of the most complex societies of the ancient Americas, the **Maya**, who flourished from 250 to 900 C.E. (On the Maya, see Chapter 12.)

Mayan Pyramid of Chichén Itzá.
The Maya founded the city of Chichén Itzá around 250 C.E. It remains a treasure trove of archaeological evidence about how the Maya lived. The pyramid was constructed in approximately 1100 C.E. For more, see Chapter 12.

Andean Societies In South America

In the northwestern portion of South America, several civilizations rose up in the peaks and valleys of the Andes. Recent archaeological discoveries indicate that the first city in the Americas, Caral, was probably founded along the Supe River, in central

Peru, around 2600 B.C.E. Most Andean cultures were skilled at weaving, pottery, and metalworking. It is thought that in the Americas, metallurgy originated here, then spread northward. Andean cultures formed heavily urban, class-stratified societies. Their most important domesticated animal was the llama. The oldest of these societies was the **Chavin** (ca. 850–250 B.C.E.). Like the Olmec civilization, Andean societies created advanced cultures without growing up on the banks of a major river.

The South American plains gave rise to nomadic herders. The rain forests of the Amazon basin were home to innumerable tribes. However, in neither place did settled civilizations of the complexity found in the Andes appear before 1000 C.E.

North American Cultures

To North America, advanced social structures came comparatively late. A number of tribes formed in the forests of the eastern part of the continent. The first was the Adena (ca. 500 B.C.E.–100 C.E.), followed by the Hopewell (100–400 C.E.) and Mississippian (700–1500 C.E.) cultures. All three spread out along the Ohio and Mississippi river valleys. Their most famous legacy is a variety of giant **earth mounds**, built for ceremonial and religious purposes.

Sometime in the first millennium C.E., a civilization in North America's desert Southwest reached its peak. This was the **Anasazi** (a Navajo word meaning "ancient ones," because the original name is lost). Small settlements date to 400 C.E., but the Anasazi may have appeared years before that, and the date of their origins remains unknown. The Anasazi—and the Native Americans of the Southwest who followed them—are famous for their elaborate **cliff dwellings**, made of clay and rock, perched hundreds of feet above the floors of the canyons and desert below.

MONUMENTAL ARCHITECTURE

The modern world takes large-scale architectural projects for granted. Ancient peoples were capable of equally grand feats of construction, such as the ziggurats, Stonehenge, the Great Wall of China, the Parthenon, the Colosseum, and the pyramids of Egypt and Mesoamerica. Monumental architecture required an enormous expenditure of resources and labor, often provided by slaves or prisoners. Why did societies make such mammoth investments? Motivations include religion (burial or the performance of rituals), defense, entertainment, and the public display of political power. Over time, commerce became important as well.

Social Structure and Cross-Cultural Connections

CHAPTER 4

- Cultural diffusion versus independent innovation
- Class structures
- Specialization of labor
- Social stratification and hierarchy versus social mobility
- Monarchies, oligarchies, and feudalism
- Noble/aristocratic classes

- Republics and democracies
- The nation-state
- Slavery and serfdom
- Warfare
- Trade (water transport versus overland caravan routes)
- Religious interchange and missionaries
- Migrations

Human communities are diverse, and each possesses unique characteristics. Nonetheless, most have certain features in common, which will be discussed in this chapter.

This chapter will also show how societies interacted, especially in the early eras of world history. Cross-cultural interaction can take place in a number of ways, all of which bring civilizations into closer contact with each other, with both positive and negative consequences. By 600 C.E., many civilizations had begun to interact with others, in some cases over considerable distances. Sometimes encounters were peaceful, often they were not.

Many things about individual societies—what they knew, how they lived, the material possessions they had available to them, whether or not they survived—were deeply affected by how they met and dealt with other civilizations. One of the most common forms of social, cultural, technological, and economic change is diffusion: the spread of inventions, foods, trade goods, concepts, and practices from one people to another. Determining to what degree a given society's basic features are shaped by **cultural diffusion** or **independent innovation** is one of the most challenging and interesting questions in the study of ancient cultures. Both have played important roles in the evolution of civilizations.

CLASS STRUCTURES

Almost all societies have some form of **class distinction**, according to which people are defined by wealth, ancestry, or occupational function. Differentiation by class is limited in preagricultural societies. Typically, among hunters, gatherers, and herders, all members of the group perform similar functions and have similar skills (although in most cases, labor is divided by gender). Most possessions are shared or owned commonly. Thus, members of these societies remain more or less equal. Exceptions include chieftains and elders (who provide leadership) and priests or shamans (who provide religious guidance and, often, medical care).

True class distinction generally coincides with the adoption of agriculture. Agriculture encourages permanent settlement and technological advancement. Because land and the tools and livestock needed to work it are so important, agriculture makes the concept of **private property** meaningful. Agriculture also leads to the creation of **food surpluses**, meaning that, unlike in preagricultural societies, substantial numbers of people not directly involved in food production can be fed. These people are free to develop other skills for the benefit of their society and themselves. This gives rise to the **specialization of labor**.

Certain social roles—such as political or military leadership—are inherently more powerful than others. Also, some occupations come to be more valued than others, causing the phenomenon of **social stratification**, in which upper and lower classes emerge. A culture's system of ranking social classes is known as a **hierarchy**. Each society judges for itself which classes are more important and which are less so. Each society also has its own way of determining how classes interact with each other, how difficult it is for an individual to move from one class to another (the concept of **social mobility**), and what benefits or disadvantages each class possesses. Religion often plays a role in justifying social hierarchies. In most societies up to 600 C.E. (and even later), the privileged, or elite, classes were quite small. Social stratification tended to be rigid, meaning that upward social mobility was difficult. Certain civilizations, such as India, had extremely strict arrangements, called **caste systems**, in which movement from one class to another was impossible. In most early civilizations, lines between classes were very sharply drawn. Upper classes typically enjoyed many legal and financial advantages, such as more lenient treatment before the law and immunity from taxation.

> **NOTE**
>
> Up to 600 C.E., the vast majority of people in most societies were peasants and farmers. Still, an increasing percentage performed other functions. Ruling classes, generally in the form of royal families, emerged to run governments that became more complicated as time passed. Other examples of specialized occupations in early societies include soldiers, priests, craftspeople, artisans, scribes, and accountants.

At most times and in most parts of the world, political power, religious leadership, and important social functions have been in the hands of males, especially since the rise of settled agricultural and urban cultures. Societies in which male domination prevails are called **patriarchies**. A small minority of early societies gave more political, religious, and social power to women. These matriarchies, however, were rare. A few archaeologists and anthropologists have tried to prove that most preagricultural societies were originally matriarchal, but their theories are not accepted by most scholars. In either case, from the development of agriculture onward, the gender division of labor has remained an important (and unfortunate) way, along with class, that societies differentiate certain members from others.

FORMS OF GOVERNMENT

Few communities fail to provide themselves with a form of leadership. Even the least advanced group will have some kind of chief or war leader. As societies grow into civilizations, they develop more complex forms of government. Although details vary, most systems fall into one of a few basic categories.

Most common before the modern era was **monarchy**, or government led by a single ruler—typically a king, queen, emperor, or empress. In premodern eras, the monarch's power was often justified in religious terms: Egyptian pharaohs were said to be the sun god's incarnation, Chinese emperors ruled with the so-called Mandate of Heaven, and many European kings claimed to govern according to the principle of "divine right."

Most monarchs govern with the assistance of a small upper class, known as the **nobility** (or **aristocracy**). This political elite assists with political administration, economic development, military defense, and other matters that the monarch cannot take care of directly or alone. In cases where the monarch's powers are relatively weak, he or she often rules in tandem with a **parliament** (or some sort of lawmaking body), according to the rules of a constitution, or both. Before around 1000 C.E., such arrangements were extremely rare. In most instances, monarchical rule is hereditary (as is noble or aristocratic status). Monarchies in which the monarch possesses an unusual amount of power—or all of it—are referred to as autocratic or despotic. In highly decentralized conditions (as in medieval Europe or preunification Japan), monarchies often degenerated into **feudal** systems, in which the local authority of individual nobles outweighs the central authority of the monarch.

Also prominent was **oligarchy**, or rule by the few. In oligarchic systems, political power rests in the hands of a small elite group, generally chosen from the wealthy or the aristocracy.

Two forms of government remained uncommon before modern times: the republic and democracy. Often thought to be identical, the two are sometimes substantially different. A **republic** (from the Latin term *res publica,* meaning "public thing") is a state in which all or most adult citizens (generally, until recently, only males) play some role in government. However, the republican form does not guarantee that all citizens will play an *equal* role in government. For example, the votes of a republic's upper class may count for more than those of lower classes (as in ancient Rome). Or members of the lower classes may be allowed to vote but not to run for office. Unlike a republic, a **democracy** grants more or less equal political rights and opportunities to all adult citizens, that is, until the modern era, all adult male citizens (the word comes from the Greek phrase for "rule by the many"). It is possible for a republic to be fully democratic, but it does not have to be (the modern United States is considered a democratic republic). One of the few democracies to exist before the modern age was the Greek city-state of Athens.

A government dominated by a religious elite is known as a **theocracy**.

Nations (also **nation-states** or countries) are run by centralized governments and united by uniform legal systems and a sense of common national identity. Generally, a nation-state's population (or the majority of the population) shares a common language, ethnicity, religion, and cultural heritage. Not all societies are nation-states in the technical sense. Especially during the ancient period and even later, states tended to be less centralized, and they were thought of as a monarch's personal property. The concept of nationhood is a relatively modern phenomenon.

SLAVERY

One of history's most shameful institutions is the ownership of human beings by other human beings, or **slavery**. Until comparatively recently (the 1800s), slavery was widespread. In some parts of the world, it still exists today. Before and around

600 C.E. (and long afterward), most societies around the world practiced slavery or engaged in and benefited from economic activities reliant on it.

Slaves performed a number of functions. These were divided mainly into household tasks and hard labor (especially jobs associated with construction or agriculture). Questions such as the severity of slaves' treatment, the length of their service, and the degree to which they had legal rights or protections depended on the laws and customs of each society.

People fell into slavery in many ways. Some were prisoners of war or captives taken during raids into enemy territory. Some were debtors who were sold—or sold themselves—into slavery. Slaves were sometimes kidnapped or pressed into service by force. In some societies, slave status was hereditary, passed on from parent to child.

Trade in slave labor went on in almost every major society. Regional networks grew up around the globe for the exchange of slaves. Prior to 1000 C.E., particularly important slave markets appeared in the Mediterranean, Africa, China and the Far East, and the Arab world. From the 1400s through the 1800s, Europeans and Americans transported millions of slaves from Africa to North and South America. This infamous **Atlantic slave trade** is discussed in further detail in Units Four and Five, Chapters 18 and 26.

An institution similar to slavery existed in many times and places—**serfdom**. In serf-holding societies, the majority of a country's peasants would be unfree. Serfs were not technically slaves. They had more freedoms and protections than slaves (who were seen in most law codes simply as property). Still, serfs were bound to the land they lived on, unable to move or change profession without permission of the land's owner. Whether or not they had theoretical legal protections, serfs were, in real life, often vulnerable to many of the same abuses that slaves were. In some parts of Europe (especially Russia), serfdom persisted until the 1800s.

WAR

Regrettably, one of the most straightforward modes of human interaction is **war**. Exactly when humans began to engage in organized violence is unknown. Most scholars speculate that combat emerged among hunter-gatherer societies during the Stone Age, growing out of the cooperative efforts needed to track and kill large animals.

From the beginning, wars were fought for a variety of reasons. These included competition over resources such as hunting grounds, water sources, and livestock. Fear and hatred of other groups caused conflicts, as did the desire for captives to use as slaves or for forced labor.

During the Stone Age, few if any societies maintained any type of professional military organization. Instead of forming armies, hunter-gatherer and herding societies assigned the responsibility for fighting to all or most able-bodied males. During the Bronze Age, the character of warfare changed. The advent of agriculture, the increased permanency of farming communities, and the rise of cities made it possible and necessary to create a specialized class of soldiers for the protection of territory and property. Improved metallurgical techniques gave these new soldiers better weapons and armor.

Therefore, by the 3000s and 2000s B.C.E., sizable and well-organized armies, led by professional generals and officers, appeared in many parts of the world, especially the

Middle East and China. Military skills and equipment increased in sophistication and complexity. From the Bronze Age onward, war became a driving force in world history.

TRADE

A powerful motivator of interaction is **trade**, or the exchange of goods. From prehistory onward, humans have found it mutually beneficial to buy, sell, or barter resources with each other. Trade takes place within societies, bringing cities, villages, and rural communities into closer contact. Societies also trade with other societies, creating connections and interdependencies throughout large areas of the world.

As long as terms are relatively fair and equal, trade generally leads to increased prosperity or advantage for all parties. Economic relationships also stimulate the exchange of ideas, information, and cultural practices between civilizations. In many cases, healthy economic relationships help to preserve peace. Conversely, trade disputes have frequently led to hostility, even war. In times of conflict or disagreement, it is common for enemies to attempt to deprive each other of the ability to trade, either by means of blockade (physically interfering with a society's ability to move goods across its borders) or sanctions (refusing to trade with a society).

THE FALL OF EMPIRES

Empires like Rome, Persia, Han China, and the Abbasid Caliphate collapsed because of a complex mix of reasons—generally a combination of *internal* and *external* factors. Examples of the former include economic crisis, civil war, social tensions, and unwise political leadership (sometimes an environmental problem, such as climatic shift or the appearance of a new disease, plays a role). The most obvious external factor is military threat, whether from raiders, nomads, or an enemy state. Outside aggression is most likely to bring down an empire if it is already weakened by internal problems. Also, the larger an empire becomes, the more likely it is to suffer what many call imperial overreach: The task of holding far-flung territories together stretches the empire's authority too thin, and it falls, or at least loses outlying territories.

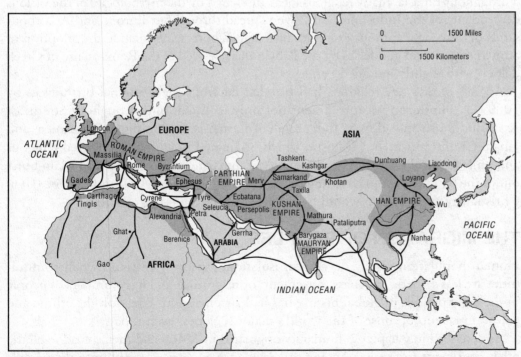

Principal African-Eurasian Trade Routes, ca. 200 B.C.E.–200 C.E.
During this time, merchants sold goods along a vast trade network that spanned from England in the northwest, to western Africa, Central Asia, and as far east as the Han Empire.

Until the invention of railroads and modern roads, the movement of goods overland was quite difficult. **Water transport** was much easier. Therefore, trade tended to flourish along rivers, lakeshores, and the coastlines of oceans and seas. In the premodern era, key international trade routes sprang up in the **Mediterranean Sea**, the North and Baltic seas, the Arabian Sea and **Indian Ocean**, the river systems of western Europe (especially the Rhine and Danube), the river basins connecting Scandinavia and Russia with the Black Sea, and East Asia's Pacific shore. Land routes included the **caravan routes** of the **Sahara desert** and the **Arabian peninsula**. The longest and most important overland trade route was the **Silk Road**. This network stretched more than 5,000 miles, linking China with the Mediterranean coast of the Middle East—and, by extension, Europe.

RELIGIOUS INTERACTION

Every society develops or adopts some kind of belief system to address questions of ethics, morality, and humanity's place in the universe. The world's major religions are described in Chapter 5. It should be noted here, however, that religious beliefs cross borders very easily, allowing different cultures and civilizations to affect each other profoundly. Sometimes, religions spread peacefully, through cultural contact or **proselytizing** and **missionary activity**. In other cases, religious faiths are brought to other societies by means of aggression and war.

As societies interact, they often absorb some of the deities and basic religious concepts of their neighbors, even if names and details change. This borrowing took place among many of the native populations of Africa, South America, and North America. Throughout Eurasia, many religious ideas are shared by the mythologies of the various descendants of the Indo-Europeans, who spread throughout Europe and Asia thousands of years ago. Famous examples of religious borrowing include the adoption of Sumerian gods and goddesses by the Babylonians, as well as the Romans' use of Greek deities, with slightly modified names.

All the world's key religions had traveled far from their original birthplaces by 1000 C.E. Hinduism was prominent not only in India, but throughout Southeast Asia. Buddhism spread from India to all of East Asia, including China, Korea, and Japan. Confucianism and Daoism, which originated in China, influenced religious and philosophical thought elsewhere in Asia. Judaism, Christianity, and Islam burst out of the Middle East to have huge effects on North Africa, Asia, and Europe (later, Christianity and Judaism would be exported to the Americas as well).

THE MIGRATION OF PEOPLES

Human populations rarely develop in isolation, especially in times when communities are less settled. The mass movement, or **migration**, of large numbers of people in the early periods of global history has had a tremendous effect on the ethnic and cultural makeup of most of the world's major societies, even today.

As described in Chapter 2, humanity originated in Africa, and then spread to all the other continents (excepting Antarctica). *Homo sapiens sapiens* moved into the Middle East and much of Asia around 100,000 years ago. Perhaps as far back as 50,000 years ago, settlers crossed from Southeast Asia to Australia. By 40,000 years ago, there were numerous human communities throughout Europe. Most scholars think that humans did not reach the Americas until comparatively late. Scientists estimate that *Homo sapiens sapiens* first came to the Americas 15,000 years ago (perhaps earlier). At that time, Asiatic peoples crossed an ice shelf or land bridge that spanned what is now the Bering Strait, the narrow waterway separating the tip of Russia from Alaska. By 8000 B.C.E., humans had settled in almost all parts of the globe.

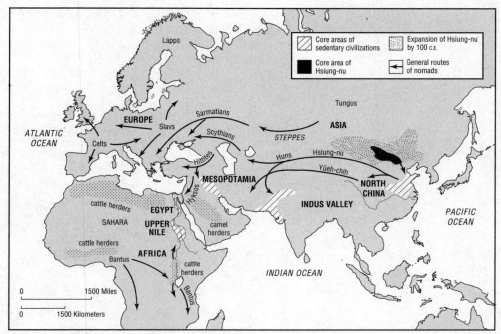

The Movement of Peoples in Eurasia and Africa after 2000 B.C.E.
Migration played a major role in the formation and development of early civilizations. Migrations often led to war and conquest, but they also facilitated cultural interaction and the spread of technology, science, languages, and religions.

After the settlement of these continents, the regions that experienced the greatest and longest-lasting waves of mass migration were Africa, the Pacific, and Eurasia. From 5,000 to 2,500 years ago, the Bantu peoples began to spread throughout sub-Saharan Africa. Starting sometime around 2500 B.C.E., the epic migration of the Polynesians from Southeast Asia throughout the vast expanse of the Pacific Ocean led to the settlement of literally thousands of islands. In Eurasia, a number of peoples, mainly from Central Asia, migrated outward, deeply affecting the ethnic and linguistic makeup of many Europeans and Asians. In particular, Europe was flooded by a tremendous influx of invaders, from approximately the 200s C.E. to 1000 C.E. During this **Great Age of Migrations**, a variety of Germanic and Asiatic peoples moved toward and into Europe. Although they were generally seen as a threat—and often perceived as barbarians—many of these peoples eventually settled throughout Europe and western Asia, playing an immensely important role in the development of many Eurasian ethnicities and cultures.

Religious Traditions and Belief Systems

CHAPTER 5

- Polytheism versus monotheism
- Judaism (the Torah and Talmud)
- Hinduism
- Buddhism
- Daoism
- Confucianism
- Christianity (the Bible)
- Islam (the Qur'an)

Integral to the growth of any civilization is the development of belief systems that address questions of ethics, morality, spirituality, and the possibility of an afterlife. Religions provide societies with a sense of unity, pride, and inspiration. Missionary activity has often led to dynamic and fruitful interactions across cultures. On the other hand, clashes between different faiths (or denominations within faiths) have resulted in bigotry, persecution, and war.

POLYTHEISM

Ancestor Worship and Other Early Forms of Religion

The earliest societies' belief systems were polytheistic, involving the worship of more than one deity. Among the oldest forms of **polytheism** are ancestor worship and the veneration of spirits. Examples of the latter are totemism (identification of the self with animal symbols), shamanism (a belief in spirit worlds, common in Central Asia, Siberia, and the Americas), "dreamtime" (a spiritual concept peculiar to the Australian aborigines), Shinto (native to Japan), and animism (a worship of life forces prevalent in Africa, the Pacific Islands, and parts of Asia).

Pantheons

Some civilizations developed elaborate pantheons of gods, each of whom had a distinct personality and function. Among the best-known are the Sumerian-Babylonian deities, shared by many peoples of the ancient Middle East; the Egyptian gods, whose worship was bound up with ritual preparation for the afterlife; the Olympian deities worshipped by the Greeks (and, in modified form, by the Romans); the Vedic gods of ancient India; the Teutonic and Norse gods worshipped in northern Europe; and the "celestial bureaucracy" of deities venerated in China.

Partial Monotheism: Zoroastrianism

Most of these polytheisms faded away, remaining as bodies of myth and legend. A few, like Hinduism and some forms of Buddhism, survive as major religions. One faith that represents a partial commitment to **monotheism** (worship of a single god or goddess) is **Zoroastrianism**, founded in ancient Persia by the priest Zoroaster (also Zarathustra), sometime in the 500s B.C.E. Basing his teachings on a collection of texts called the Avestas, Zoroaster proposed the worship of only one god, Ahura Mazda, the "wise lord." Later, Ahura Mazda's son Mithra was venerated as well. The enemy of Ahura Mazda was Ahriman, the god of darkness. Zoroastrianism flourished in Persia until the 600s C.E., when the expansion of Islam drove it out. It lingers today mainly in India, among the small religious community known as Parsis. However, basic concepts from Zoroastrianism are thought by most religious historians to have played a role in shaping later Jewish thought and early Christianity.

JUDAISM

The First Monotheistic Faith

Judaism emerged among the Middle Eastern people known as the **Hebrews** (the terms *Jews* and *Jewish* were not commonly used until the 900s B.C.E.). It is generally considered to have been the world's first monotheistic faith—that is, the first to devote itself to the worship of one deity alone. Along with Christianity, which grew out of it, **Judaism** forms a key part of the Western world's ethical, intellectual, and cultural foundation.

Abraham's Covenant

According to Judaic tradition, the patriarch **Abraham**, of the Sumerian city of Ur, entered into a covenant with the god YHWH (often rendered as Yahweh or Jehovah). YHWH swore to make the Hebrews his "chosen people" and to lead them to the "promised land" of Canaan (present-day Israel). Sometime between 2000 and 1850 B.C.E., the Hebrews left Ur and journeyed westward. Abraham's leadership was carried on by his son Isaac and grandson Jacob (who took the name **Israel** and whose sons are considered to be the founders of Israel's Twelve Tribes).

Slavery in Egypt, Exodus, and Moses's Leadership

In approximately 1700 B.C.E., during a time of famine, the Hebrews migrated to Egypt, an event narrated in the story of Jacob's son Joseph. The Hebrews became the Egyptians' slaves, but around 1300 to 1200 B.C.E., under the prophet **Moses**, escaped from Egypt. This exodus is remembered in the celebration of **Passover**, the most important holiday in the Jewish faith. Moses and the war leader Joshua took the Hebrews back to Canaan. During the journey, Moses is said to have handed down from YHWH the principles of Jewish law, including the **Ten Commandments**, revealed to him on Mount Sinai. He is also considered the author of the **Torah** ("Teaching"), the first five books in the Hebrew scriptures (the Tanakh). The Torah was later incorporated by the Christian Bible as the first five books of the Old Testament.

The Hebrew Kingdoms: Freedom and Conquest

Consolidation of the homeland followed. The Hebrews were ruled at first by judges, then by kings, starting with Saul. The Hebrew kingdom reached its zenith under its second monarch, **David** (ca. 1000–961 B.C.E.), and his son Solomon (ca. 961–922 B.C.E.). David, a talented military commander, united the kingdom of Israel and created a Hebrew capital at Jerusalem. Many of the religious songs known collectively as the Psalms are attributed to him. **Solomon** increased Israel's prosperity by taking advantage of its location at the crossroads of Middle Eastern trade routes. In Jerusalem, Solomon dedicated to YHWH the great Temple, the heart of Jewish religious life for centuries.

After Solomon's death, the Hebrew kingdom split into two lands: Israel and Judah. The Hebrews were then conquered by a number of invaders, including the Assyrians (722 B.C.E.), the Babylonian Empire of Nebuchadnezzar (587 B.C.E.), the Persians (539 B.C.E.), Alexander the Great (333–331 B.C.E.), and the Romans (66–64 B.C.E.). Under Nebuchadnezzar, the Hebrews were uprooted from their lands, and Solomon's Temple was torn down (a second temple was built during the 530s and 520s B.C.E.). In the face of their conquerors, all of whom were polytheistic, the Jews, guided by prophets and rabbis ("teachers"), remained true to their monotheistic worship. They also came to believe that a savior, or Messiah ("anointed one"), would someday appear to free them from oppression.

Roman Rule and the Jewish Diaspora

During the years of Roman rule, the Judaic tradition gave birth to the new faith of Christianity, based on the teachings of Jesus of Nazareth (see the section on Christianity). Shortly thereafter, attempts to rebel against the Romans led to the dissolution of the Hebrew state. During the Jewish Wars of 70–73 C.E., the Romans deprived the Jews of their homeland, destroyed the second Temple, and forced them into a **diaspora** that lasted until the middle of the twentieth century. While some Jews remained in the Middle East, others scattered throughout Europe, Asia, and the rest of the world.

> **NOTE**
>
> Until the establishment of the modern state of Israel in 1948, Jews were linked not by geography but by shared cultural heritage, continued dedication to the monotheistic worship of YHWH, and observation of the laws and customs laid out by scripture.

Jewish Principles

In addition to its emphasis on worshipping a single god, Hebrew scripture outlines a strict code of conduct and places a high premium on righteous behavior. The same can be said about the **Talmud** ("Instruction"), the main collection of Jewish laws. Among the ancient Hebrews, legal practices operated on a retributive principle—an eye for an eye, a tooth for a tooth—that was common throughout the ancient Middle East. Dietary restrictions were strict, as were rules governing sexual practice. Although women were respected in the home, Hebrew society as a whole was patriarchal. As did most people of the eastern Mediterranean, the Hebrews practiced slavery on a limited basis, but Jewish scripture also insisted on charity, social responsibility, and concern for the poor.

HINDUISM

Born in India, **Hinduism** is an extremely complex, polytheistic faith. Arguably, its roots extend further back in time than those of any other religion still practiced today. Rather than being a single faith in the Western sense—founded by a single individual or group, following a single god or set of gods, recognizing a single body of scripture—Hinduism is a synthesis of many traditions. Today, the vast majority of the people of India are Hindu. Sizable Hindu minorities live in Pakistan, Bangladesh, and Sri Lanka. There are Hindu populations in South and Southeast Asia, as well as in emigration throughout the world.

Vedic Roots of Hinduism and Early Hindu Scriptures

No precise date can be assigned to the birth of Hinduism. It evolved over hundreds of years from a combination of the religious practices of the Indus River people, other groups native to the subcontinent, and Aryan invaders. From this mixture emerged the tradition of **Vedism**, the foundation of Hinduism. At the core of Vedism are four Aryan scriptures called Vedas, meaning "knowledge." The Vedas began to appear in written form after 1500 B.C.E. but are thought to have existed in oral form as far back as 4500 B.C.E. The oldest is the Rig-Veda, which includes over 1,000 hymns and stories about the gods.

Hinduism itself began to take shape after 900 B.C.E. New texts appeared, particularly the Upanishads (written between 900 and 500 B.C.E.), essays and poems outlining Hinduism's basic concepts. Also influential was the **Law of Manu** (compiled between 200 B.C.E. and 200 C.E.), best known for its support of the caste system.

Along with new scripture, literary texts with religious themes appeared. One such story was the Ramayana (ca. 350 B.C.E.), a tale describing the adventures of Rama, the seventh incarnation of the god Vishnu. Equally important is the Mahabharata (composed between 200 B.C.E. and 200 C.E.), a grand epic of 90,000 stanzas, making it perhaps the longest poem in the world. The Mahabharata depicts a great war between two royal houses. Its most famous section is the **Bhagavad-Gita** ("Song of the Lord"), a poetic dialogue between the young prince Arjuna and the demigod Krishna, who lectures Arjuna on the concept of moral duty.

Hindu Doctrine

The basic concepts of classical Hinduism were in place no later than the 200s B.C.E., after the Vedic and Upanishadic traditions merged and spread throughout India.

At the center of time and space is the World Soul, or Brahman. All things that exist are reflections of the Brahman's perfection. Every living creature has its own soul, known as atman. However, the material world is an illusion (maya). It causes suffering and prevents the individual soul from perceiving or being connected with the World Soul. The goal of existence is to rejoin one's atman with the Brahman, allowing oneself to be absorbed into perfection.

Union with the Brahman is accomplished by undergoing a cycle of life, death, and rebirth called the wheel of life (samsara); spiritual perfection is attained by this process of **reincarnation**. According to the law of deeds (**karma**), a person's actions in one life will have consequences in a future life. When a person has achieved a sufficient understanding of moral duty (dharma), he or she gains release (moksha) from samsara. Liberated from the cycle of life and death, the atman is free to join with the Brahman.

Union with the Brahman can be attained in a number of ways. Early Vedic scriptures placed great value on ritual obedience to the gods and the priestly class (brahmins). The Upanishads argued that ordinary men and women could take greater responsibility for their own spiritual development.

Hindu Deities

In addition to the Brahman, Hinduism recognizes hundreds of gods and goddesses, making it a polytheistic religion. By the 200s B.C.E., three gods in particular gained the largest followings: Brahma, Vishnu, and Shiva. Technically the most important is **Brahma** the Creator, the masculine personification of the Brahman, or World Soul.

Vishnu the Preserver is a savior figure, a great friend to humanity. In various avatars, he appears in literary works such as the Ramayana and the Bhagavad-Gita. **Shiva** the Destroyer is the god of creation and destruction. He reflects the duality of life and death; he is depicted in paintings and sculptures as a dancer.

Goddesses are important in Hinduism. All female deities are considered incarnations of the great mother goddess, **Mahadevi Shakti**. Her most famous avatars are Parvati (wife of Shiva), Durga (a warrior goddess), Lakshmi (Vishnu's wife), and Kali (a goddess of death).

The Caste System and the Place of Women

The Indian **caste system** was given religious justification by Vedic thought and Hindu theology. Its origins date back to the Aryan invasion of India. The Aryans relegated menial tasks and manual labor to the darker-skinned natives. From the 800s to the 600s B.C.E., this scheme grew into a rigid system of social stratification involving four distinct classes. At the highest level were the priests (brahmins). Near the top were the warriors and political rulers (kshatriyas). Commoners (vaishyas), such as farmers and artisans, were next. Servants, serfs, and members of the lower class (shudras) made up the lowest of the four main castes. As time went on, another category, the untouchables—who performed degrading tasks such as the handling of human waste and burial of the dead—was formed. Over the centuries, the caste system grew increasingly complex.

In the Hindu hierarchy, males were thought superior to women (although the Hindu code of behavior required that women be treated with respect, and women played a vital role within the family). Men performed the family rituals, had a monopoly on education, and were allowed to own property. Women were considered legal minors even as adults and could not own property. Many women married in childhood, and divorce was rare. The most extreme form of female subservience to men was the **sati ritual** (also known as suttee), by which wives were required to throw themselves on the funeral pyres of their dead husbands. This practice was discouraged by India's colonial masters, the British, during the nineteenth century. It was outlawed by the Indians themselves in the twentieth century.

The Practice of Sati.
The ritual of sati (or suttee) was a long-standing Hindu tradition. When a man of high caste died, his widow was expected to be burned to death on her husband's funeral pyre. Only in the twentieth century was this practice fully abolished.

Acceptance of one's social situation was considered virtuous. Performance of caste duties was an essential part of dharma, or moral duty. Good behavior as a member of a lower caste in one life would result in good karma, increasing the likelihood of being reborn into a higher caste. The Law of Manu is the most famous expression of Hinduism's religious argument in favor of the caste system.

BUDDHISM

Originating in India, the numerous forms of **Buddhism** have spread worldwide. This complex religion is followed throughout Asia. Although the foundations of Buddhism are associated with the teachings of one person, the variety of beliefs and theologies that fall into the category "Buddhist" is staggering. Broadly speaking, there are two major schools of Buddhist doctrine: Theravada (also known as Hinayana) and Mahayana.

Religious Transition in India

Buddhism was one of several movements born in India during the 500s B.C.E., as the long transition from Vedism to classical Hinduism stirred up religious debate. During this century of spiritual ferment, many teachers experimented with various ways of achieving union with the World Soul. One religious path that emerged during this time—and might have grown into a larger faith, if not for the simultaneous appearance of Buddhism—was Jainism, established by Mahavira (ca. 540–468 B.C.E.), who preached a doctrine of nonviolence and self-denial.

Siddhartha Gautama and the Birth of Buddhism

The individual who founded Buddhism was **Siddhartha Gautama** (ca. 563–483 B.C.E.), born into a noble family from northern India. At the age of twenty-nine, Gautama ventured outside his palace, only to be appalled by the pain and poverty experienced by the common people. In shock, he abandoned his aristocratic life to seek an answer to the question of human suffering. Having been born into one spiritual extreme—sensuality and a love of worldly things—Gautama sought his answers in the opposite extreme: fasting and self-deprivation. Deciding that neither extreme led to salvation, he chose instead a "middle way" of moderation and peace.

While following this middle way, Gautama is said to have achieved enlightenment. He took the name Buddha, "the awakened one," and began to preach. A community of followers spread his teachings; and, after his death, his creed went beyond the borders of India to the rest of Asia.

Buddhist Doctrine

In its earliest form, Buddhism was less a religion than a philosophy. At no time did the Buddha claim divinity. Instead, he wished to correct what he saw as the worst features of Vedism and Hinduism. He also intended to purify concepts such as karma and reincarnation by reducing the role of the priestly brahmins and their rituals. As a result, his teachings either draw on or depart from the fundamental ideas contained in Hindu theology.

Like Hinduism, Buddhism postulates that souls evolve toward spiritual perfection by means of samsara, the wheel of life. However, the Buddha rejected the caste system and argued that any person could achieve liberation, without the aid of priests or rituals. All that was necessary to attain enlightenment was to realize the Four Noble Truths and to follow the Eightfold Path of good conduct (as well as the Five Moral Rules).

By following this moral code, any person can reach enlightenment. In Buddhist terms, liberation from samsara is called **nirvana**, the literal meaning of which is "to extinguish." According to the original teachings of the Buddha, the result of nirvana is not a union of the individual soul with the World Soul. Instead, nirvana leads to a state of superconsciousness, in which one's self is dissolved into the all-encompassing life spirit that transcends place and time.

> **NOTE**
>
> The Four Noble Truths are as follows:
> (1) human existence is inseparable from suffering;
> (2) the cause of suffering is desire;
> (3) suffering is extinguished by extinguishing desire;
> (4) desire may be extinguished by following the Eightfold Path (know the truth; resist evil; do nothing to hurt others; respect all forms of life; work for the well-being of others; free your mind of evil; control your thoughts; practice meditation). In addition to the Eightfold Path, the Buddha described Five Moral Rules (do not kill any living being; do not take what is not given to you; do not speak falsely; do not drink intoxicating drinks; do not be unchaste).

Theravada and Mahayana Buddhism

After the Buddha's death in 483 B.C.E., the tradition he founded split into various denominations, roughly divided into two large movements. The older is Theravada Buddhism ("Way of the Elders"), also referred to as Hinayana ("Lesser Vehicle"). Prominent in South and Southeast Asia, Theravada remains closer in spirit to the Buddha's actual teachings. It emphasizes simplicity, meditation, and an interpretation of nirvana as the renunciation of the self. Gods and goddesses have little place in Theravada, and the Buddha himself is not considered a deity.

The second and newer movement, Mahayana ("Greater Vehicle") Buddhism, is widespread in northern and northeastern Asia, especially in Japan, Korea, Tibet, and parts of China. Mahayana forms of Buddhism tend to be elaborate and complicated, involving more ritual and symbology than the Buddha intended. Part of this change resulted from the fact that Buddhism, upon reaching new lands, often blended with local religions. Moreover, many later Buddhists found the original teachings' austerity to be of little spiritual comfort, and began to argue for means of salvation that the Buddha himself had not spoken of.

In some Mahayana denominations, the concept of nirvana came to resemble traditional ideas of heaven. Concepts of hell appeared, and adherents of Mahayana created complex pantheons of gods and bodhisattvas (souls who had achieved nirvana but chose to remain in the earthly realm in order to help living humans reach salvation). The Buddha came to be seen as divine, and worshippers came to rely more heavily on priests, ceremonies, and new scriptures. The obvious irony is that many of these additions were very much like those aspects of Hinduism of which the Buddha himself had disapproved. Nonetheless, Mahayana traditions flourished.

DAOISM (TAOISM)

Daoism appeared in China during the 500s B.C.E. Like Buddhism (in its original form), Daoism was less a religion and more a philosophical system, whose founding figure made no claim to divinity. However, Daoism's mystical strain grew more pronounced as time passed.

The Founders of Daoism

Traditionally, the founder of Daoism is considered to be **Laozi** (Lao-tse), the "Old Master" (ca. 604 B.C.E.), who may or may not be an actual historical figure. He is also said to have written Daoism's central text, the **Tao-te Ching**, although most scholars believe this collection was compiled in the 300s or 200s B.C.E. Another figure associated with the development of Daoism is Zhuangzi (Chuang-tse), known to have lived approximately from 369 to 286 B.C.E.

Following the Dao

To follow Daoism is to follow "the way," or "the path," the two most common translations of **dao**. Daoist belief maintains that the universe is governed by an invisible, yet irresistible force that can be sensed intuitively. Daoism is deliberately antirational, using parables to train the worshipper to perceive the world in nonlogical ways. (The most famous Daoist paradox is found in the writings of Zhuangzi, who asks himself if he is a man who has just awoken from a dream that he was a butterfly, or a butterfly still dreaming that he is a man.)

A Daoist seeks wisdom in nature, poetry, and spontaneous behavior. He or she is not concerned with politics, money, or material possessions, because all of these are illusory and meaningless. Daoism places an emphasis on individuality, since each person pursues the dao in his or her own unique way.

Daoist Ritual

After a time, Daoism became associated with mystical and magical practices, such as alchemy and fortune-telling. The **I-Ching**, or "Book of Changes," is a Daoist text used in reading the future. Daoism's most famous symbol is the **yin-yang**, a circle whose black and white halves are divided by a double-curved line, serving to illustrate that nothing is absolute, and that opposites flow into each other.

A flexible religion, Daoism has traditionally coexisted with other faiths. It is not uncommon for a worshipper to blend Daoist worship with Buddhism and Confucianism. Since Daoism and Confucianism arose in China at approximately the same time, the relationship between the two has generally been a tight one, even though their philosophical outlooks are, for the most part, diametrically opposed.

Daoism spread throughout its native China. Certain elements were transported to parts of Asia where China had a strong cultural influence, especially Japan and Korea.

CONFUCIANISM

Confucianism: Religion or Philosophy?

Of the world's major belief systems, **Confucianism**, which developed in China during the 500s B.C.E., is the least religious, lacking any objects of worship or clergy. Confucianism's founders believed in the existence of gods and spirits but gave little place to them in their philosophical system. They argued that a morally concerned person should be interested in how he or she acted in the material world. What happened beyond one's physical life was of less importance.

Confucian Texts

Confucianism grew out of the teachings of the sage **K'ung Fu-tzu**, better known as **Confucius** (ca. 551–479 B.C.E.), a minor aristocrat who lived during the politically chaotic Zhou dynasty and served as a government official. Upon retiring from state service, he pondered the nature of the relationship between the individual and society, and his followers captured his thoughts on paper. Although K'ung Fu-tzu is traditionally considered to have authored books on history, divination, ritual, and poetry, he left behind no works of his own. His *Analects* ("Selected Sayings") are recordings of conversations with his students. A second Confucian theorist was Meng-tzu, or Mencius (371–289 B.C.E.).

Confucian Principles

Confucianism proposes that a harmonious society can be created by a combination of benevolent rulership from above and good behavior from below. The well-being of the group comes before that of the individual. Order and **hierarchy** are paramount. Good government is the responsibility of the ruler, and as long as the ruler performs his duties well, his people have an obligation to obey him. Meng-tzu taught that a just ruler possesses the **Mandate of Heaven**, a moral justification for his authority. Unjust rulers who abuse their power lose the Mandate of Heaven, and can therefore be removed by their people.

Ideally, society operates as a model family, with junior members paying respect to their elders. If the home is blessed by **filial piety**, society at large is healthy. This vision is reflected in the five relationships K'ung Fu-tzu described as most important to social tranquility: the ruler should be just, those who are ruled should be loyal; the father should be loving, the son respectful; the husband should be right-eous, the wife obedient; the older brother should be genteel, the younger brother humble; the older friend should be considerate, the younger friend deferent.

Confucianism also established the female as the subservient sex. Men ruled society, fought wars, and acted as scholars and ministers. They could keep more than one wife and divorce any wife who failed to produce a male heir. Women were exclusively homemakers and mothers. Laws prohibited women from owning prop-erty, and they were not provided financial security through a dowry system. However, Confucianism allowed women to have a limited education.

Implicit in these relationships are the concepts of reciprocity and mutual respect. Those who are superior may expect deference, but only if they treat those below them well. Likewise, those who are inferior may expect good treatment from those above, but only if they are properly deferential. Central to Confucian thought is a "golden rule" similar to the one found in Christianity: in the *Analects*, K'ung Fu-tzu declares, "Never do to others what you would not like them to do to you." Confu-sianism's assumption that people are inherently good contrasted with the logic behind a rival doctrine, Legalism, which viewed people as innately immoral, and advocated harsh punishments as the only way to control them.

Confucianism, Neo-Confucianism, and Chinese Political Life

Confucianism coexisted with and at times competed with Daoism and Buddhism. Several times, it gained, lost, and regained its status as an official, imperially sanc-tioned code of conduct. By the 600s C.E., a newer variation of the creed, called Neo-Confucianism, appeared. Even when it was not in official favor, Confucianism's influence persisted. China's traditional emphasis on filial piety, social hierarchy, and respect for authority stems in large part from Confucianism and has persisted into the modern era, even under the Communist regime.

CHRISTIANITY

The Judeo-Christian Tradition

Historically and philosophically, **Christianity** is a child of Judaism. The relationship between the two faiths has often been troubled, but always intimate. Both religions, in the form of the **Judeo-Christian tradition**, have formed the bedrock of Western culture for two millennia.

The Life and Ministry of Jesus

The founder of Christianity was **Jesus of Nazareth** (ca. 4 B.C.E.–29 C.E.), later known as the Christ (from the Greek translation of the term *messiah*). Details about Jesus come from the Gospels, the first four books of the Bible's New Testament. Jesus was born into a Jewish family of humble background. As an adult, he became a wandering teacher and gathered an inner circle of disciples.

Jesus spoke of upholding Jewish laws and traditions but also sought to reform them. To him, obeying rabbis and observing customs were not enough to please

YHWH (in later Christian usage, God). Jesus taught that the sincerity of one's belief mattered more than giving large offerings of money, wearing proper dress, or following dietary guidelines. He maintained that charity, compassion, and forgiveness were of paramount importance. He reinforced this message in the **Sermon on the Mount** ("Blessed are the poor in spirit . . .") and in what came to be known as the **Golden Rule** ("Do unto others as you would have them do unto you").

During his ministry, Jesus claimed to be the Christ, or the Messiah foretold by Hebrew prophecy. Although many Jews expected the Messiah to be a political ruler who would restore the Hebrew state, Jesus had a heavenly kingdom in mind instead. He spoke of himself as the "Son of God," whose teachings would redeem those who followed his words.

The teachings of Jesus proved immensely popular, especially among the common people and the poor. On the other hand, his claims to be the Messiah and his questioning of tradition angered conservatives within the Jewish religious establishment. Also, rumors that Jesus had assumed the title King of the Jews (a misinterpretation of what he meant by being the Messiah) made Roman authorities suspicious. According to the Gospels, when Jesus preached in Jerusalem during the Passover season, Jewish religious authorities demanded that the Roman procurator, Pontius Pilate, arrest him. Pilate, fearing the political repercussions of Jesus's ministry, agreed. Jesus was tried for blasphemy and treason. Found guilty, he was put to death by the Romans. The method of execution was crucifixion, and the instrument of Jesus's death—the cross—is the Christian faith's most important symbol.

The Early Christian Church

Before his arrest, Jesus had claimed he would return from the dead before returning to God, his Father, in heaven. After his crucifixion, Jesus's closest followers began to preach that he had indeed been resurrected (an event celebrated during Easter, Christianity's central holiday). This veneration of the risen Jesus, which soon came to be known as Christianity, was carried on at first by his closest disciples, such as **Peter** (considered to be the first pope) and the authors of the Four Gospels (Matthew, Mark, Luke, and John). Other adherents of the new faith spread the words of Christ as well. These figures, instrumental in establishing the early Christian church, are known as the apostles, who told the story of Christ's Crucifixion and Resurrection. They also foretold the Second Coming, when the physical world would come to an end, the Kingdom of Heaven would be established, and all souls would be subjected to a Day of Judgment. Good Christians would live with God and Christ in heaven; evildoers and nonbelievers would be damned to hell.

Roman law made early Christianity illegal. Despite those obstacles, Christianity gained a large following over the next three centuries, not just in Judaea, but throughout the Middle East and the Roman Empire. Playing a crucial role in the early church's organization was the apostle **Paul**. Born Saul of Tarsus, Paul, originally a persecutor of Christianity, changed his name after a sudden conversion to the new faith. With Peter, Paul worked from approximately 45 to 64 C.E. to establish new centers of worship. His greatest contribution was to widen the appeal of Christianity beyond the circle of its original Jewish worshippers. By decreeing that

Christians did not have to observe Jewish law (including dietary restrictions and the circumcision of male believers), Paul made it easier to convert Greeks and other non-Jewish peoples. This flexibility allowed the new religion to expand faster.

Christianity caught on among many groups, especially those who felt powerless in Roman society: noncitizens, slaves, the poor, commoners, and women. The new religion was open to all, and it held out the hope of a happy afterlife to those whose lives in the present were drab or miserable. Although organized Christianity later became male-dominated, the early church gave women a sense of belonging and, within limits, influential roles within apostolic communities. But as time passed, a strict interpretation of the story of Adam and Eve assigned women the blame for humanity's "original sin." Paul's writings on women put them in a secondary position. They were to obey men, and they were not allowed to occupy the positions of highest leadership within the church (including priesthood). Cultures that adopted Christianity were affected by this worldview for centuries to come.

Roman Persecution of Christianity

In spite of Christianity's appeal and organizational success, to worship as a Christian remained dangerous for more than three hundred years. Christians devised secret codes and held services in hidden places. Roman persecution was a constant peril, and many Christians were arrested and executed. Worshippers who died for their faith were known as martyrs. Ironically, the campaigns of persecution, rather than destroying the new religion, only strengthened the followers' resolve. Moreover, their bravery and dignity often attracted new converts.

Legalization and the Formal Organization Of Christianity

In 313 C.E., legal status was granted to Christianity by the **Edict of Milan**, handed down by the emperor Constantine. In 380 C.E., Christianity became the official religion of the Roman Empire, and in 392 C.E., it was proclaimed the empire's only legal faith. Free from persecution, the church set up a formal hierarchy of priests and bishops, with the pope (the bishop of Rome) at the top. Only men could serve as clergy. The church also found it necessary to establish a body of dogma, an officially agreed-upon set of beliefs. Important issues included the nature of Christ (considered to be both fully human and fully divine) and the doctrine of the Trinity (the belief that God exists in the three persons of God the Father, Christ the Son, and the Holy Spirit). Beliefs not included as dogma were condemned as heresy.

Another task was to compile the books of the **Bible**, which came to consist of two main parts: the Old Testament (the Hebrew Torah, stories from Jewish history, and the writings of Hebrew prophets) and the New Testament (the Four Gospels, episodes from the history of the early Christian Church, and letters written by the Apostles). Decisions about dogma and the Bible were made at a series of councils held during the 300s C.E. and afterward. The priests and scholars who attended the councils or clarified and defended the councils' decisions are referred to as the church fathers. Among the most famous are Jerome (347–420 C.E.), whose Vulgate Bible was the first Latin translation of the holy book, and Augustine (354–430 C.E.), whose *City of God* laid the intellectual foundation for further Christian doctrine.

Christianity After the Fall of Rome

With the Roman Empire's collapse during the 400s C.E. came a new era for the Christian Church. In the Middle East and North Africa, where the Roman legacy was carried on by the Byzantine Empire, metropolitan centers such as Antioch, Alexandria, and Constantinople were the great centers of Christian worship. In the west, where Europe was collapsing into political confusion, the headquarters of the Christian Church was Rome.

Although the Christian Church called itself catholic, or universal, it was, in reality, divided. Doctrinal disagreements, geographic separation, and the passage of time caused the Western and Eastern churches to grow apart after the 500s C.E. In the Great Schism of 1054 C.E., the Western and Eastern churches broke with each other formally. **Eastern Orthodoxy** remained the faith of the Byzantine Empire, and was adopted by most Christians in the Middle East, Russia, Ukraine, and much of eastern Europe. **Roman Catholicism** remained the favored form of Christianity in western Europe. During the Middle Ages, the Roman Catholic Church provided Europeans with a sense of religious unity, preserved Latin manuscripts from the Roman era, and exerted a tremendous sway over secular and political affairs. Splits within the Western Christian church would come later, during the 1500s and 1600s C.E. During the medieval era, its influence remained paramount.

ISLAM
The Origins of Islam

The youngest of the world's major religions (and not actually established during this "Foundations" period), **Islam** transformed itself with amazing speed from a local faith into a cultural and political force of global dimensions. A monotheistic form of worship that originated in the Middle East, Islam is linked with Judaism and Christianity in many ways, and their relationships have frequently been stormy, even tragic. Nonetheless, the three faiths contain many similarities and possess an eventful shared history.

Islam arose in the Arabian Peninsula during the 600s C.E., a time when Arabia was sparsely populated and its desert interior largely unexplored. Arabia's few major settlements were built up around oases and coastal towns serving as centers of the caravan trade that linked the region with the rest of the Middle East. From Arabia, the new religion spread rapidly throughout the eastern Mediterranean. By 1000 C.E., its influence stretched from Spain and Africa's Atlantic coast to the borderlands of India in the east.

Mohammed and His Teachings

The founder of Islam was **Mohammed** (also Muhammad), a merchant from the Arabian town of **Mecca**. Born in 570 C.E., Mohammed began to meditate in the mountains near Mecca when he turned forty. In 610 C.E., he experienced a profound vision. According to Mohammed, the archangel Jobril ("Gabriel" to Jews and Christians) appeared to him, delivering the word of **Allah** (Arabic for "God").

With the help of family members such as Ali (his cousin and son-in-law), Aisha (his favorite wife), and Abu Bakr (Aisha's father), Mohammed preached and gathered a religious community. In 622, he and his followers were forced out of Mecca by local religious authorities, fleeing to the city of Medina. This flight—the **Hegira**—remains a key event in the early history of Islam, and it marks the beginning of the Islamic calendar. Mohammed's community flourished in Medina, and by 630, he and his followers returned to Mecca and converted the city. In 632, Mohammed died, but the religion he had founded grew.

The Principles of Islamic Faith

Mohammed's faith drew directly upon Judeo-Christian images and concepts. He taught that there is one god, Allah. He believed in an afterlife and a final judgment in which believers go to heaven and nonbelievers to hell. Islam pays respect to figures from Jewish and Christian faith. Arabs, like the Hebrews, consider Abraham their patriarch and Abraham's son Ismail (Ishmael) their direct ancestor. Prophets of Allah include Adam, Noah, Moses, David, Solomon, John the Baptist, and Jesus. Islam instructs Muslims to respect Jews and Christians as "**people of the book**."

Still, Mohammed formulated his own tradition. He claimed to be the last of twenty-eight prophets sent by Allah to reveal His teachings to humankind, and the only one to receive Allah's full and perfect message. The name of the religion itself, *Islam*, comes from the Arabic phrase "to submit to God." Likewise, the term *Muslim* means "servant of God," or "one who has submitted to the will of God."

Submission to Allah involves living by the five **Pillars of Islam** described by Mohammed. These are to declare that "there is no god but Allah, and Mohammed is his prophet"; to pray five times daily, facing in the direction of Mecca; to fast during the holiday of Ramadan; to give alms to the poor; and to make a pilgrimage (hajj) to Mecca at least once in one's lifetime.

Other Islamic traditions include abstinence from alcohol and pork; avoiding the portrayal of human or animal figures in art; and polygamy (Muslim men are allowed to take up to four wives). There are also restrictions on how women are allowed to dress or appear; a strictly observant Muslim woman is to guard her modesty and veil herself when in public. Many modern Muslims have become more secular and allow a less stringent observance of these practices. Even in earlier times, male domination of women in Islamic societies was offset by the command that men treat women with respect. Women also enjoyed the right to inherit, have dowries, and own property.

The teachings of Mohammed are contained in the **Qur'an** (Koran), or "Recitation." Muslims consider the Qur'an to be the word of Allah, transmitted directly by Mohammed, so every word is considered sacred. The Arabic spoken by Mohammed is the holy language of Islam. Other important texts are the Hadith, a collection of the proverbs of Mohammed, and the **Sharia**, a codification of traditional Islamic law.

The Expansion of Islam

The expansion of Islam during the 600s, 700s, and 800s C.E. went hand-in-hand with military conquest and political domination. Early Islam made no distinction between political allegiance and religious affiliation; to be a Muslim meant also to belong to a political and social community (*umma*) linked by religious belief. After Mohammed's death in 632, it was decided that the **umma** was to be governed by a **caliph** (*khalifa*), or "successor," who was both a religious and political leader. The first caliph was Mohammed's father-in-law, Abu Bakr.

Before Mohammed's death, most of Arabia had converted to Islam. The first three caliphs—Abu Bakr, Umar (Omar), and Uthman—broke out of Arabia and brought Islam to the rest of the Middle East and beyond. By the end of the 700s C.E., Muslim forces had swept through the Middle East, destroying the Persian Empire, threatening Byzantium, and bringing under Islamic rule Iraq, Syria, Palestine, Egypt, most of north Africa, parts of the Caucasus Mountains, the region that is today Pakistan, Spain, and parts of Italy. From the 600s to the 1200s C.E., this vast territory was ruled over by two Islamic states, or caliphates: the Umayyad Caliphate (661–750 C.E.), centered at Damascus, and the Abbasid Caliphate (750–1258 C.E.), whose capital was Baghdad. The zenith of Islamic civilization as a single political and religious entity came during the first 300 years of the Abbasid Caliphate, roughly the years between 750 and 1050 C.E.

Islamic Denominations

Triumph and expansion did not prevent major splits. From 656 to 661 C.E., disputes among Mohammed's family led to civil war. The final result was the establishment of the Umayyad Caliphate, under Muawiyah (661–680 C.E.). The majority of Muslims accept Muawiyah and his successors as legitimate, referring to themselves as **Sunni**, the "people of tradition and community." More than 80 percent of all Muslims are Sunni. However, the followers of Mohammed's son-in-law Ali (who was killed in the war) considered the Umayyads to be usurpers. They formed a minority denomination known as the **Shiites**, from *Shi'at Ali*, or "party of Ali."

Another Islamic movement is **Sufism**, a mystical tradition that appeared during the 700s and 800s C.E. Sufism places a premium on fasting, prayer, and meditation as ways to grow closer to Allah. It is especially prominent in Iran.

The Geography of Islam

Several holy places are connected to Islamic worship. One of them, Jerusalem, is also shared by Judaism and Christianity, a fact that has led to considerable friction. According to Islamic tradition, Mohammed ascended to heaven from Jerusalem. The holiest site in the Islamic faith is Mecca: Mohammed's birthplace and home to the shrine known as the Kaaba, or Black Rock. Making a pilgrimage, or hajj, to Mecca is one of Islam's five Pillars of Faith. Observant Muslims pray to Mecca five times a day. Medina, to which Mohammed fled during the Hegira, is also a key center of faith.

Islam is most famously associated with the Middle East, and the vast majority of the people who live there are Muslim. However, as a legacy of Islam's rapid and extensive spread during its first three centuries, there are Muslim communities worldwide. Countries with Islamic majorities include most of the nations of North Africa, Pakistan, Indonesia (the country with the largest Muslim population), and others. Sizable Islamic minorities can be found around the globe.

TIP

Islamic theology divides the world into two states: dar al-Islam ("house of peace") and dar al-Harb ("house of war"). The former includes those lands where Islam is the dominant faith. In early times, the expansion of dar al-Islam was encouraged. Many moderate Muslims now consider dar al-Islam to be a wider community including all places where their religion can be practiced freely.

Unit Two: Review Questions

SAMPLE ESSAY QUESTIONS (CCOT AND COMPARATIVE)

CCOT 1. Analyze the political changes and continuities in ONE of the following civilizations before the 600s C.E.

China
Rome
Mesopotamia

CCOT 2. Analyze the changes and continuities in the status of women between the Stone Age and the emergence of the first civilizations.

COMP 1. Compare and contrast the way religion justified social hierarchies and gender relations in TWO of the following regions before the 600s C.E.

India
China
Rome

COMP 2. Compare and contrast how environmental factors affected the development of civilizations in TWO of the following areas before the 600s C.E.

Egypt
sub-Saharan Africa
Mesoamerica

MULTIPLE-CHOICE QUESTIONS

1. Which of the following is least likely to encourage the growth of an advanced civilization?

    (A) the presence of a nearby river
    (B) surroundings dominated by steep mountains
    (C) temperate climatic conditions
    (D) proximity to a lakeshore or seacoast
    (E) rich metal deposits in the neighboring hills

2. Which of the following is an example of resource extraction?

    (A) the sowing of crop seed
    (B) building a dam
    (C) the planting of trees
    (D) mining for iron ore
    (E) digging a canal

3. What do the Code of Hammurabi and Roman law have in common?

    (A) They derived mainly from religious principles.
    (B) They represented a step away from the arbitrary exercise of power.
    (C) They operated on the retributive principle of "an eye for an eye."
    (D) They provided all social classes with equal treatment.
    (E) They allowed all male citizens to participate at least somewhat in politics.

4. How were women generally treated in Stone Age societies?

    (A) Most Stone Age societies revered women and gave them positions of superiority.
    (B) Equal treatment of both genders was common.
    (C) Although not as pronounced as it would later become, gender division of labor was the norm.
    (D) The majority of Stone Age societies have been proven to be matriarchal.
    (E) They regularly went on raids and hunting parties with men.

5. Which of the following would NOT be associated with the Neolithic revolution?

    (A) the discovery of techniques to refine steel
    (B) the domestication of many types of animal
    (C) the widespread adoption of agriculture
    (D) the emergence of the first cities
    (E) the rapid growth of global population

6. Which of the following inaccurately describes agricultural societies?

    (A) Agriculture allowed humans to manipulate their environment as never before.
    (B) Women are thought to have played a key role in the transition to agriculture.
    (C) Agriculture promoted the formation of permanent settlements.
    (D) People began producing their own food approximately 12,000 years ago.
    (E) Agricultural societies were less organized than hunter-gatherer societies.

7. In an oligarchy

   (A) one ruler controls an entire nation.
   (B) a small elite group holds political power.
   (C) people decide key questions by means of a direct vote.
   (D) an elected parliamentary body governs alongside a monarch.
   (E) military commanders dominate the government.

8. Why are rivers considered so important for the development of early civilizations?

   (A) They encourage the development of large navies.
   (B) They allow for the factory production of manufactured goods.
   (C) They make full-scale agricultural production easier.
   (D) They discourage hunting and herding.
   (E) They in fact have little impact on the development of civilization.

9. Which of the following is true of slavery?

   (A) Monotheistic societies tended to forbid it.
   (B) Slaves were used exclusively for agricultural labor.
   (C) Slaves tended to have more rights and freedoms than serfs.
   (D) Slave trades prevailed in Africa, Eurasia, and the Americas.
   (E) Slavery ended worldwide during the 1600s.

10. In what way are the histories of the Bantu and the Polynesians similar?

    (A) Their migrations led to the dispersal of a single ethnocultural group over vast distances.
    (B) They both cultivated corn and potatoes before most other civilizations.
    (C) They were both among the first to develop monotheistic religions.
    (D) They domesticated the horse and became skilled at cavalry warfare.
    (E) Their military prowess allowed them to conquer large empires.

11. According to the map on page 75, to which of the following areas did the main African-Eurasian trade routes NOT extend?

    (A) Central Asia
    (B) Siberia
    (C) China
    (D) North Africa
    (E) Spain

12. What is a major similarity between Hinduism and Buddhism?

    (A) Both support a caste system.
    (B) Both justify violence in the conversion of new worshippers.
    (C) Both embrace the Four Noble Truths.
    (D) Both rest on a belief in karma and reincarnation.
    (E) Both are rigidly monotheistic.

13. What is diffusion, in the context of early societal development?

   (A) the assimilation of minority ethnic groups by a larger population
   (B) the prevention of cultural exchange between neighboring peoples
   (C) the conquest of one civilization by a more powerful one
   (D) the gradual vanishing of a society because of environmental factors
   (E) the spread of goods, ideas, and inventions from one people to another

14. Which of the following is an accurate statement about the Indian caste system?

   (A) The "untouchables" formed its top stratum.
   (B) Jainist doctrine was used to justify it.
   (C) It allowed a high degree of social mobility.
   (D) Aryans tended to fall into the lower categories.
   (E) It permitted virtually no social mobility.

15. What do many researchers now think caused the fall of the Indus River civilization?

   (A) fighting between Hindus and Sikhs
   (B) migratory pressures from Mesopotamia
   (C) environmental factors
   (D) population growth
   (E) the Aryan invasions

16. Which of the following do Shinto and Egyptian sun worship have in common?

   (A) They both justified human exploitation of the environment.
   (B) They both legitimated the authority of a powerful monarch.
   (C) They both venerated nature spirits.
   (D) They both discouraged polytheistic worship.
   (E) They both made extensive use of human sacrifice.

17. In what way did the Olmec and the first Andean civilizations develop along similar lines?

   (A) Both invented the wheel without outside influence.
   (B) Both arose without the benefit of a major river nearby.
   (C) Both learned the secret of metalworking from the Anasazi.
   (D) Both built advanced societies in the midst of thick jungle conditions.
   (E) Both domesticated llamas as a source of wool.

18. Early Islamic political thought included the belief that

   (A) Jews and Christians deserved to be treated with violence.
   (B) Women should be equal in status to men.
   (C) Church and state should be kept scrupulously separate.
   (D) The Islamic political and religious community should be identical.
   (E) Slavery was abhorrent in the sight of Allah.

19. Which of the following was NOT one of Rome's cultural legacies?

   (A) respect for and preservation of Greek culture
   (B) roads and fortifications that lasted for centuries
   (C) the adoption of Islam as an official faith
   (D) a legal code whose influence persists today
   (E) sophisticated engineering and construction skills

20. "The ruler should be just, those who are ruled should be loyal. The father should be loving, the son respectful."

    This principle is likely part of which belief system?

    (A) Confucianism
    (B) Hinduism
    (C) Daoism
    (D) Buddhism
    (E) Christianity

Answers

1. **(B)** Although civilizations can form in nearly any climatic or topographical conditions, nearby bodies of water are helpful for transport, agriculture, and the provision of food and water for large populations. Natural resources and pleasant climates are helpful. Mountains have not prevented civilizations such as the Inca from developing, but they are nonetheless the least advantageous of the five choices available here.

2. **(D)** All of these answers provide examples of human impact on the environment. Only mining, however, involves taking resources from the earth.

3. **(B)** Answers D and E are applicable to later codes, and because the laws of Rome and Babylonia were fundamentally secular, A does not apply. Answer C fits one of the codes (Hammurabi's), but not Rome's, making B the one feasible possibility.

4. **(C)** Answers A and D describe positions more positive than women are thought to have been in during the Stone Age (although a scholarly minority has theorized that preagricultural societies were wholly or mostly matriarchal). Answer B applies only in modern times, and not in all societies (and arguably does not yet apply at all). Simple understanding of gendered divisions of labor is enough to eliminate E.

5. **(A)** Answers B through E correctly describe hallmark features of the Neolithic revolution. But even working in iron, not to mention steel, was beyond Neolithic peoples, making A incorrect.

6. **(E)** Adopting agriculture invariably leads to greater complexity and a higher degree of organization. Even if one is not sure when plant domestication began (as in D), the obvious falseness of E makes it the best response.

7. **(B)** Oligarchy, meaning "rule by the few," was quite common in the ancient world. Answers A and E describe even more restrictive forms of government (monarchies and military dictatorships), and C and D speak of democratic and parliamentary systems.

8. **(C)** You can logically eliminate A and B because navies are generally ocean-going, and factory production was not part of economic life anywhere until centuries later. Knowing that four of the world's earliest civilizations formed along major rivers allows you to strike E. In choosing between C and D, it should be common sense that the presence of a river does nothing to impede herding or hunting (and would in fact make herding easier).

9. **(D)** Slavery was so universal, so multipurpose, and so durable that the only correct response is D, which speaks of its wide geographical spread. Technically, serfs fell into a slightly higher category, but they were often abused just as badly as slaves.

10. **(A)** Answers B and D can be readily discarded, because corn and potatoes were not available outside the Americas until the Columbian Exchange of the 1400s C.E., and horses were not domesticated by either group. Although both fought wars, neither is known for great conquests, and both were polytheistic.

11. **(B)** This question tests elementary map-reading skills. The map itself shows the extensive network of trade routes linking Africa and Eurasia. One of the few places those routes did not reach was the Siberian subcontinent.

12. **(D)** Because Buddhism grew out of Hinduism, the two share many common beliefs, but the Four Noble Truths belong only to Buddhism, which also rejects the caste system. Both are polytheistic, and neither formally approves of violence (Buddhism explicitly rejects it).

13. **(E)** Discoveries, innovations, and new cultural developments can arise because of independent innovation or because of cultural diffusion, which means the exchange of ideas and practices between different societies.

14. **(E)** Jainism emerged after the development of the caste system. The Aryan invaders, who did much to create the system, were at the top, not the bottom—which is where the "untouchables" found themselves. The Indian caste system was one of world history's most rigid social hierarchies, greatly restricting mobility.

15. **(C)** For decades, scholars attributed the collapse of the Indus River civilization to the Aryan invasions. But the actual date of the Aryans' arrival remains uncertain, and recent archaeological discoveries point to some kind of environmental crisis as a likelier cause for the downfall.

16. **(B)** Answers D and E can be readily eliminated; both faiths were polytheistic (except for a brief monotheistic experiment in Egypt), and neither was associated with human sacrifice. Whereas the book of Genesis has often been used to justify "man's dominion" over nature, Egyptian sun worship and especially Shinto (which venerates nature spirits) have not. Both lent their support to political rulers claiming semi-divine status: pharoahs in Egypt, emperors in Japan.

17. **(B)** The wheel never appeared in the early Andes, and the llama was unknown in the north. Andean peoples are not known to have had contact with the Anasazi, who may or may not have known the secret of metalworking. The Andes are not covered with jungle, but what does link the Olmec with the Andean peoples is how they grew into civilized societies without having major river basins nearby, as the Egyptians, Chinese, Mesopotamians, and Indus River people did.

18. **(D)** The concept of the *umma*, a community united by a single religious and political authority, was a key ideal motivating the Islamic world's early caliphates (and making C obviously incorrect). Fellow "people of the book," such as Christians and Jews, were not supposed to be treated with violence (although they often were in practice). Women were not treated as equals, and slavery was permitted (although Muslims were not allowed to enslave fellow Muslims).

19. **(C)** Rome left behind a huge cultural inheritance, including everything described in A, B, D, and E. The religion it adopted shortly before it fell, though, was Christianity, not Islam.

20. **(A)** Daoism and Buddhism are not known for placing a premium on social hierarchy. Hinduism's caste system does so, but fails to emphasize reciprocity as this quotation does. Left to choose between Christianity and Confucianism, one should remember the latter's fondness for familial relations as a metaphor for the proper functioning of society.

UNIT THREE

WORLD CULTURES MATURING
(600–1450)

Unit Overview

GENERAL REMARKS

Between 600 and 1450, newer world civilizations matured, largely on the foundations of older cultures that had collapsed or faded away. This was also an age when world civilizations came into ever-increasing contact with each other.

Many of the world's classical civilizations failed or fell into decline between the 200s and 600s C.E., including the Roman Empire (with the Greek influence it had kept alive), Han China, and India's Mauryan and Gupta empires. The same process continued up to about 1000 C.E., as other societies considered "classical"—such as Tang China, Heian Japan, and the Abbasid Caliphate—weakened or collapsed.

New civilizations were created on the foundations of these classical cultures. In some cases, as in Europe after the fall of Rome, a lengthy period of backwardness, decentralization, and chaos followed the collapse of a classical civilization. In others, as in China, the transition was less traumatic or lasted a shorter time. Whatever the case, sophisticated, advanced cultures—many of them building on the legacy left behind by classical predecessors—appeared throughout the world during the period between 600 and 1450.

One important historical question is whether these civilizations are best studied as **nation-states** (countries as formally defined political entities, in the modern sense of the word) or **cultural units** (defined less by political boundaries, and more by shared traditions, religion, ethnicity, government by a larger imperial or regional authority, and sometimes language). Examples of the latter include the Islamic world, European Christendom, sub-Saharan Africa, and Mesoamerica.

Another general trend was increased communication between world cultures. Although the Americas remained isolated, vibrant systems of interaction appeared among the civilizations of Africa, Europe, the Middle East, Central Asia, Southeast Asia, and the Far East. Trade, religious influence, technological, and cultural exchange all marked this era. The movement of nomadic and migratory peoples, such as the Vikings and Mongols, greatly affected settled societies. (A key question on the AP exam will be how **nomadic movement** as a cause of historical change compares to the importance of **cities** during this period.) Even though the world was not as joined together as it would later become—with the Europeans' encounter with the Americas and greater improvements in communications and transport technology—extensive systems of global interaction were emerging between 1000 and 1450.

BROAD TRENDS

Global Power and International Relations

- With the exception of the Americas, the major civilizations of the world were coming into increased contact with each other.
- Nomadic and migratory populations (especially the Vikings, Mongols, and Polynesians) continued to have a profound impact on large parts of the world.
- The most advanced and politically influential civilizations during these years were China (especially during the Tang, Song, Yuan, and Ming periods) and the Ottoman Empire.
- Nations of medieval Europe, particularly in the west, gained in power and sophistication.
- Major states and empires—such as Mali, Ghana, Great Zimbabwe, the Delhi Sultanate, the Aztecs, and the Incas—flourished, but for a comparatively short time.
- During the 1200s and 1300s, the Mongols radically altered the balance of power in Eurasia. Their empire, one of the largest in history, brought together vast portions of Europe and Asia. For a time, the Mongols imposed not just political unity but a measure of economic and cultural connectedness not seen since the days of ancient Rome or Han China.
- The invention of gunpowder started to change the equation of world power.

Political Developments

- Most forms of government remained nonrepresentative. Monarchies and oligarchies were most common.
- A few nations managed to place formal restrictions on the power of the monarch—concrete legal systems or lawmaking bodies that shared governmental authority—and still remain centralized. England, with its Magna Carta and Parliament, is an excellent example.
- Most states were not nations in the modern sense of the word. Many were decentralized. Others were multicultural empires joined only by the fact that a single civilization had conquered them all.
- Feudalism became a common form of political (as well as economic) organization in decentralized areas. The best-known examples are medieval Europe and the Japanese shogunates.
- Urban centers played a larger role in the political life of most cultures.

Economic and Environmental Developments

- Most societies remained fundamentally agricultural. The vast majority of people resided in the countryside and made their living by farming.
- However, artisanry and craftsmanship were becoming increasingly important.
- This helped give rise to a slow (but steady) trend: urbanization, or the growth of cities.
- Trade and commerce—even banking—became a basic part of economic life in developed societies.

- The growing importance of trade and commerce made merchant classes larger and more influential.
- Trade and commerce led to the creation of intercultural and international trade networks. Among the most important were the Mediterranean, the Hanseatic League, the Silk Road, trans-Saharan caravan routes, the gold trade along the Niger River, Indian-Persian economic exchange, the Indian Ocean, and Pacific trade networks.
- Certain cities became important centers for intercultural and international trade. They include Venice, Cairo, Mombasa, Zanzibar, Samarkand, Canton (Guangzhou), Malacca (Melaka), Timbuktu, and Calicut.
- Massive epidemics (pandemics), struck Eurasia. Most famous was the wave of bubonic plague that swept China, the Middle East, and Europe (the "black death") in the 1300s.

Cultural Developments

- Distinct artistic and cultural traditions developed in each major region of the world.
- The civilizations possessing the greatest degree of scientific knowledge and cultural sophistication were China, the Middle East, Japan, and Muslim Spain.
- Europe underwent great cultural development, especially during the Renaissance.
- China and India exerted a tremendous cultural and religious influence over their neighbors. Buddhism, Hinduism, and art and architectural styles spread from these countries to Southeast Asia, Korea, Japan, Tibet, and elsewhere.
- The Middle East played a large role in spreading knowledge, scholarship, music, art, and architecture to North Africa and Europe. Middle Eastern cultural influence on medieval and Renaissance Europe was considerable.
- Travelers and explorers created links between societies and increased geographical and cultural knowledge. Examples include Zheng He (Cheng Ho), Marco Polo, and Ibn Battuta.
- The invention of block printing in China (perhaps Korea) began to alter cultural life not only in Asia but elsewhere as this new innovation spread.
- Even more dramatically, the invention of the movable-type printing press in Europe during the 1430s led to an information explosion, the rapid spread of knowledge and ideas, and a revolution in intellectual life.

Gender Issues

- Women continued to occupy a secondary role in most societies. Women's political rights were minimal or nonexistent.
- Women had sharply defined occupational roles. They were largely assigned to the domestic sphere and viewed primarily as childbearers and homemakers. Most work women did outside the home—such as weaving, food gathering, or farm chores—was seen as low status.
- However, in most places, women possessed at least some freedoms, including legal and economic rights: for example, the right to divorce abusive husbands, the right to a dowry, the right to inherit and own property.

- In many societies, women played informal, but important, roles. They managed households and family finances, supervised the education of children, and influenced their husbands.
- Being in certain occupations or classes allowed women some respect or escape from male domination. Noblewomen played influential roles in most societies, often as cultural patrons, sometimes as political advisers to their husbands. Priestesses and nuns often enjoyed high status as well as an intellectual life, although their conduct was strictly regulated.
- In some African societies, women enjoyed a great deal of respect, and family trees were matrilinear (traced through the mother), rather than patrilinear.
- In most societies, upper-class women lived easier lives but found themselves more constrained by religious and cultural restrictions on their behavior. Lower-class women, whose lives were much harder, were often less bound by those restrictions because the rules of "proper" behavior applied less to them.
- Societies that feared magic or witchery tended to blame women disproportionately for such things.

QUESTIONS AND COMPARISONS TO CONSIDER

- Differences and likenesses of various world trading systems.
- Intellectual and cultural developments in different societies, and the ways in which societies influence each other (for example, the Middle Eastern influence on medieval European culture or India's influence on Southeast Asian religion, art, and architecture).
- How important is the nation-state (as opposed to larger cultural units) as an object of study during this historical period?
- How did political and social development in western Europe resemble and/or differ from that in eastern Europe?
- Comparisons and contrasts between European and Japanese feudalism.
- Comparisons and contrasts between one of the major European states (or western Europe as a whole) and one of the major African states.
- How did Europe's encounter with sub-Saharan Africa differ from and/or resemble the Islamic world's encounter with it?
- The differences and likenesses between the Mongol Empire and earlier conquest states, such as Rome or Han China.
- The successes and failures of the Roman Catholic Church, the Eastern Orthodox Church, and the Islamic caliphates in their attempts to create a large, multinational civilization united by religion.
- Comparisons and contrasts between Islam and Christianity, not just in terms of doctrine, but also both faiths' impact on social and political organization, gender relations, and views of how nonbelievers should be treated.
- The role of nomadic movement as a cause of historical change during these years compared with the role played by the growth of cities during the same time frame.

Europe During the Middle Ages and the Renaissance

- The medieval period (Middle Ages)
- Feudalism and serfdom
- Roman Catholicism and the ideal of Christendom
- Formation of European states
- The Crusades
- Trade, commerce, and urbanization
- The Black Death (bubonic plague)
- Aristotle and Greco-Latin learning
- Scholasticism
- The movable-type (Gutenberg) printing press
- The Renaissance (classicism and humanism)

The medieval period of European history, also known as the **Middle Ages**, lasted from approximately 500 to 1500. Often, the **medieval era** is broken down into three phases: the Early (ca. 500–1000), High (ca. 1000–1300), and Late Middle Ages (ca. 1300–1500). Not all historians, however, use these labels. Also, the question of periodization is complicated by the fact that during the Late Middle Ages, certain parts of Europe—particularly Italy—began to experience the famous cultural rebirth known as the **Renaissance**.

Whatever one calls the various periods of the medieval era, certain trends are clear. The years from 500 to 1000 were a time of political decentralization and overall backwardness. From 1000 to 1300, Europe enjoyed a general revival. Nations became better defined, the economy grew healthier, and the level of technological and cultural knowledge improved. The concept of Europe as a single civilization joined by a common cultural heritage and the Christian religion took greater shape during these years.

The period between 1300 and 1500 was a complex one, marked by crisis and advancement. On one hand, Europe was struck by social unrest, constant warfare, and, in the form of the so-called Black Death, one of the worst epidemics in world history. On the other hand, the Renaissance began, ushering in a period of artistic and intellectual achievement.

FEUDALISM AND THE MANOR SYSTEM

The Origins of Feudalism

In the aftermath of Rome's fall, Europe became politically decentralized. No single ruler was strong enough to provide Europe with central authority, and monarchs typically did not have the power, money, or military strength to govern their lands effectively. The solution was the system of **feudalism**, in which lords and monarchs (lieges) awarded (infeudated) land to loyal followers (vassals). In exchange, the vassals guaranteed that their parcels of land (fiefs) would be governed, that law and justice would be dispensed, that crops would be grown, and that the land itself would be protected. Feudal retainers often subdivided (subinfeudated) their fiefs into smaller units, granting them to people they could rely on. Feudalism remained at the heart of medieval European politics for centuries.

Feudal Nobility, the Manor System, and Serfdom

The retainers to whom monarchs gave large land grants developed into Europe's **noble** (or **aristocratic**) **class**. Structurally, the feudal nobility resembled a pyramid. At the top was the monarch. Below him (or her) were powerful nobles, and below them were lesser nobles. All members of the feudal nobility were theoretically tied to the monarch by bonds of loyalty and landownership, and they were supposed to help provide political leadership.

The feudal nobility also served a military function. One of feudalism's goals was to provide an army of foot soldiers (recruited by nobles) and an elite force of armored cavalry (**knights**) formed by the nobles themselves. Horses and weapons were so costly and the training so specialized that only members of the upper classes could afford to become knights. According to the code of **chivalry**, the knight was to be a virtuous, Christian warrior who served his lord loyally, treated the lower classes with justice, and acted gentlemanly toward women. Songs and legends, such as those of King Arthur's Round Table, provided examples of how real-life knights were supposed to conduct themselves. Chivalry did restrain the knight's most violent behavior, but in actuality, the code was often broken, and it tended to be more myth than reality.

The feudal system involved more than the ruling class. The vast majority of people in medieval Europe were peasants. The basic unit of feudal landholding was the **manor**, which typically included the lord's residence (an estate or castle) and the peasants' village. Surrounding the residence and village were fields for farming, as well as woodland where food would be gathered and animals hunted (generally a privilege reserved for the lord).

Economically, the feudal system relied on the labor of the peasants. Most peasants in Europe during the Middle Ages were **serfs**. Although serfs were not technically slaves, they were legally unfree. They were not allowed to change residence or profession without permission. Most of their work benefited not themselves but the lord. A portion of their own crops and livestock had to be given to the lord. In addition, serfs had to spend a certain number of days per month fulfilling various labor obligations: building roads, clearing forests, gathering firewood, or most commonly, farming the lord's private fields. Serfs had to pay fees to use any of the manor's facilities that were owned by the lord, including the water mill, the bread oven, the cider press, and the smithy. In times of war, serfs also had to fight: lords would recruit foot soldiers from among them. Overall, living conditions were harsh.

A Medieval Tournament.
The military and political backbone of medieval Europe's feudal system was the knight. High-born and trained from youth in cavalry warfare, the knight was the state-of-the-art warrior of his era. Knights also made up Europe's noble class. Knights honed their military skills—and cultivated the arts of chivalry—at tournaments such as the one portrayed here.

The Time Line of Feudalism

Feudalism persisted throughout the medieval period, and its effects were felt long afterward. Ironically, it outlasted its original purpose. Even after political units began to centralize and resemble modern nations, many feudal practices remained in place. Serfdom took centuries to disappear, especially in central and eastern Europe. The knightly class transformed into an aristocratic nobility that remained a permanent part of European politics and society until the 1800s and even 1900s. Feudalism set into place class differences that survived as tensions between the poor and powerless on one hand and the rich and powerful on the other.

THE IDEAL OF CHRISTENDOM

The Unifying Influence of Christianity

One of the few things binding European nations together following the fall of Rome was the Christian faith, which acted as a unifying force throughout the continent, both culturally and politically.

Rome itself was one of the two major headquarters of Christian worship. The other was Constantinople, capital of the Byzantine Empire. By 1054, doctrinal differences and geographical distance led to the Great Schism, which separated Christians into two churches: **Roman Catholicism** and **Eastern Orthodoxy**. The former was dominant in central and western Europe; the latter was prominent in the Middle East and the Greek and Slavic parts of eastern Europe.

The Catholic Church shaped medieval society in key ways. Its monasteries preserved Latin and Greek manuscripts left over from the Roman era. These included scientific and philosophical essays, literary works, and a wealth of learning that otherwise would have been lost. The church also provided the people of Europe with a sense that, despite national and linguistic differences, they were linked by a single faith. This gave a much-needed feeling of cultural cohesion at a time of extreme decentralization.

The Medieval Papacy and the Political Power of the Catholic Church

The leader of the Catholic Church was the pope, technically the bishop of Rome. At the lowest level of church organization was the priest, who served the needs of an individual community. Only men could become priests. Above the priest was the bishop, who presided over a large territory and supervised many priests. Archbishops and cardinals were powerful church officials who advised the pope. Also part of the church hierarchy were monks and nuns.

After 1000, the Catholic Church became immensely powerful politically. (This is in contrast with the Eastern Orthodox Church, which, in general, viewed itself as subservient to worldly authority.) The pope governed a sizable territory in central Italy, the Papal States. Many popes, especially Innocent III (1198–1216), went to great lengths to assert that the authority of the papacy was superior to that of kings and emperors. The popes had moral authority and the right to determine what was **heresy**, exclude worshippers from the Catholic Church (**excommunication**), and issue calls for holy wars (**crusades**). The ultimate goal of medieval popes was to join the nations of Europe into a single Christian community. Referred to as **Christendom**, this community was to be governed by the pope, with kings and emperors subject to his rule. The Catholic Church never realized this ideal, but for several hundred years, the popes heavily influenced how European monarchs ruled their countries.

The Catholic Church owned vast amounts of land. Combined with its right to collect tithes from the general population, this made the church very wealthy. Another way the church exercised worldly power was control over education, thought, and culture. In 1231, the **Holy Inquisition**, a set of special courts with wide-ranging powers, was established to hunt out and punish heresy and religious nonconformity.

> **NOTE**
>
> Most institutions of learning were connected in one way or another with the Catholic Church. It was dangerous for any scholar or artist to write, say, or produce anything counter to Catholic doctrine.

Monasticism

A prominent feature of medieval Christianity (both Catholic and Orthodox) was **monasticism**, the formation of religious communities whose members (monks and nuns) are not ordained as priests. The first European monasteries stressed contemplation and seclusion. This approach (the Benedictine model) remained dominant from the 500s through the late 1100s. In the early 1200s, new orders, such as the Dominicans and Franciscans, were established to carry on the work of the Catholic Church in the wider world.

THE WESTERN MONARCHIES AND THE EASTERN FRONTIER

Early Kingdoms and the Carolingian Empire

It took several centuries after the fall of Rome for stable nations to form. Short-lived kingdoms, founded by warlords and barbarian chiefs, rose and fell frequently during the 500s and 600s. Internally, decentralization kept states weak, as did external threats such as Viking raids and Muslim invasions.

One of the earliest European nations was the Frankish kingdom, which, by the 700s, grew into the Carolingian Empire. The Franks were a Germanic tribe who, under their king Clovis (465–511), acquired a large empire, including parts of what is now Germany, France, and the Low Countries. Clovis converted his people to Catholicism, and although the kingdom weakened after his death, it did not die away. It grew powerful again under Charles Martel (688–741), a great military leader who successfully turned back Muslim invaders at the **Battle of Tours** (732), one of the most influential battles of the medieval era. Charles Martel established the Carolingian dynasty, and his son Pepin strengthened the kingdom's ties with the Catholic Church.

Even more successful as a nation-building monarch was Pepin's son **Charlemagne** (768–814), whose name means "Charles the Great." Charlemagne defended Frankish territory against Viking, barbarian, and Muslim attacks. He greatly expanded the kingdom and transformed it into the Carolingian Empire (the pope crowned him Holy Roman Emperor in 800). He was an active supporter of education and culture, much of which he entrusted to the church. By the standards of the day, the Carolingian Empire was strong and well organized. It was still a feudal state, however, and, in 843, Charlemagne's three grandsons divided the empire into smaller parts. The concept of the "holy" and "Roman" empire—a viable state allied with the church and, like Rome before it, able to provide relatively centralized authority—also survived.

Other early nations emerged in the late 800s and 900s. Saxon kings united large parts of England. The Capetian dynasty came to rule the area around Paris and gradually gained control over more of France. The eastern, Germanic portion of Charlemagne's realm reformed itself as the Holy Roman Empire, which ruled most of central Europe for centuries to come.

The Vikings

An important factor shaping the development of early medieval European nations was the appearance of the **Vikings**, expert sailors and fierce warriors from Scandinavia. Owing mainly to overcrowding in their homelands, large numbers of Vikings poured out of the north from the 800s through the 1100s. One of the few peoples of this era who could navigate on the open ocean, the Vikings raided and conquered land throughout most of coastal Europe, as far south as the Mediterranean.

The Vikings colonized Iceland and Greenland. Around 1000 C.E., voyagers led by Leif Eriksson reached what is today Canada. The Vikings also settled in parts of England, Scotland, and Ireland. They created long-lasting kingdoms in northwestern France and Sicily. A group of Vikings established a trade route from Scandinavia to Byzantium, through Russia. In the process, they created the first Russian state.

> **NOTE**
>
> By forcing nations such as England, France, and the Holy Roman Empire to defend against their attacks, the Vikings (though not on purpose) prompted those nations to centralize more than they had during the early medieval period.

England and France

In the west, the most stable states were England and France. For four centuries, the political leadership of both countries was intertwined. In 1066, Normans (descendants of Vikings who had settled in France) led by William the Conqueror, invaded England, defeated the Saxon king, and established their rule there. Because William and his successors were connected to the French throne by blood ties and feudal obligations, there was much competition between England and France over land and political legitimacy until the middle of the 1400s.

The **Norman Conquest** brought French-style feudalism to England and helped create a rich cultural fusion, not only Celtic and Anglo-Saxon but also Latin-based, in the British Isles. By medieval standards, England became quite centralized, and it did so despite the fact that significant checks were put on the power of the king. (Normally, the less powerful the monarch, the less centralized the state.) During the 1100s, the English adopted a single law code (common law) and the concept of jury trials. In 1215, the **Magna Carta**, imposed on the king by his barons, guaranteed the nobility certain rights and privileges, limiting the monarch's might. Later in the 1200s, the English nobility won the right to form a **Parliament**, which eventually became a representative lawmaking body that governed in conjunction with the king. In the 1200s and 1300s, English monarchs extended their rule to Wales and Scotland. Ireland would follow later.

In France, the Capetian kings centralized their nation by increasing their own power (the typical route to premodern nation building). Originally, the Capetians ruled only a tiny part of France. England controlled large territories, such as Aquitaine and Brittany, while large and economically important regions such as Flanders and Burgundy remained independent. Generations of Capetian monarchs expanded the size of the French kingdom, beat the English in a number of wars (including the Hundred Years' War, mentioned below), and gained control over Burgundy and other stubborn regions. By the mid-to-late 1400s, France was large and centralized, and the French kings were among the most powerful in Europe. Unlike their English counterparts, French monarchs were not limited or obligated to share power in any legally meaningful way.

The political event that most affected England and France during the fourteenth and fifteenth centuries was the **Hundred Years' War** (1337–1453). The war's first years coincided with the onset of other European crises, including social uprisings and the Black Death. Until the early 1400s, the English won a number of victories, gaining control over more than half of France. Only after the 1420s did the French king, helped by the warrior maid Joan of Arc, drive the English out. The war ended most of the awkward connections between the French and English royal families.

> **NOTE**
>
> Victory over the English helped the French kings to centralize their power at home.

The Holy Roman Empire and Italian States: Decentralization

Important states formed in central and southern Europe, but they were less centralized. Dominating the middle of Europe was the Holy Roman Empire, a multicultural monarchy in which the crown passed back and forth among a group of German noble families. The empire was founded in the 900s by the heirs of Charlemagne. Its name was inspired by the theoretical ideal of a state that was large and powerful ("Roman") and brought a variety of peoples into a single Catholic ("holy") community. The emperor was supposed to work in partnership with the pope, but in real life, the two clashed more than they cooperated.

The Holy Roman Empire was one of medieval Europe's largest states, but the emperor's powers were comparatively weak. His position was not hereditary—he was chosen by the empire's most powerful noble families. The empire's population was ethnically diverse (German, Italian, Hungarian, Slavic, and more), and the empire itself consisted of dozens of duchies, kingdoms, and principalities (almost 200 in the mid-1300s), with each duke, king, and prince guarding his autonomy carefully. Two things helped the empire to centralize somewhat in the 1300s and 1400s. The Golden Bull (1356) asserted the rights and powers of the various rulers under the emperor, but dramatically reduced the number of states allowed to elect the emperor (from all of them to seven). Also, the **Habsburg** family of Austria emerged as a major player in imperial politics during the late 1200s; by 1438, the Habsburgs gained permanent control over the imperial throne (which remained theirs until 1918).

> **NOTE**
>
> From the 1300s onward, the Holy Roman Empire served as Europe's military bulwark against the long wave of Turkish attacks from the east.

Even more decentralized than the Holy Roman Empire was Italy (during this time not an actual country). Most of northern Italy was under the Holy Roman Empire's control, and many southern areas passed in and out of the hands of other foreigners, including the French, Spanish, Muslims, and Byzantines. The parts of Italy that remained free were governed by dozens of city-states; Italy was one of the most urbanized parts of Europe, with a high cultural level as well (it was the birthplace of the Renaissance). Italy's position in the Mediterranean—which enabled trade with the Middle East and Egypt (and, by extension, the Far East, China, and the Indian Ocean)—allowed its cities to develop strong commercial economies. The chief city-states of medieval and Renaissance Italy were Florence, Milan, and Venice in the north, and Naples in the south. Also important was Rome, the heart of the Papal States. **Venice**, which called itself the "Most Serene Republic," created a rich and powerful maritime and commercial empire.

Spain and Portugal

The medieval development of Spain and Portugal was shaped above all by the fact that they had been taken over by Muslim invaders, known as the Moors, during the 700s. From 1031 onward, the people of Spain and Portugal fought the Moors in a long struggle known as the **Reconquista**. The legend of El Cid, an eleventh-century general and one of Spain's great heroes, grew out of this reconquest. By the end of the 1200s, the Spanish had pushed the Moors into Granada, the southernmost part of the country. For the next 200 years, the Moors held out there, until they were expelled completely in 1492, by the armies of Ferdinand and Isabella.

The effects of the Moors and the war against them were many. Spanish territory was liberated gradually, and each newly freed region remained independent, delaying centralization. By the 1400s, there were about half a dozen Spanish kingdoms, not counting Portugal. Only late in the 1400s, when the rulers of the two largest kingdoms, **Ferdinand of Aragón** and **Isabella of Castile**, married and joined their lands together, did Spain take shape as a single country. Another result of the Reconquista was intense religious intolerance. The war caused Catholic authorities in Spain to be extremely rigid in terms of doctrine and hostile to nonbelievers. Muslims and Jews (whom the Moors had welcomed to Spain) were persecuted, and, by the end of the 1400s, forced to convert to Catholicism or leave the country.

The Moorish presence brought benefits as well. Islamic culture was more advanced than that of medieval Europe, so Spain was able to take advantage of the medical, scientific, and technological knowledge brought there by the Muslim conquerors (as well as the Jewish scholars and professionals who came with them). The Spanish city of **Córdoba** was one of Europe's greatest centers of learning and science, thanks to the long-standing Muslim presence there.

Portugal, an independent principality, began its tradition of world exploration during the 1400s, starting a trend that would sweep the globe. (For more, see Chapter 14.)

NOTE

Spanish art and architecture were also affected by the Moorish style, elements of which still persist today.

Byzantium and Eastern Europe

The farther east, the less centralized European nations became, with the exception of the Byzantine Empire, the crossroads between Christian Europe and the Islamic Middle East. **Constantinople** was a tremendously important trading center, linking Mediterranean Europe with the Middle East and, by extension, the overland routes (such as the Silk Road) and sea lanes that joined the Middle East with China, India, and the East Indies.

Although Byzantium was superior to the rest of Europe in terms of economic and cultural advancement, it entered a long period of political and military decline. In the eleventh century, a new enemy, the Seljuk Turks, appeared on the eastern frontier. From the Battle of Manzikert (1071) onward, the Seljuks, then their more dangerous successors, the Ottoman Turks, slowly but unceasingly stripped territory away from Byzantium. By the 1400s, Constantinople itself was under threat; in 1453, the Ottomans seized it. The Byzantine Empire was destroyed, its capital became the Turkish city of Istanbul, and the Ottoman Empire went on to conquer large parts of southeastern Europe, clashing for centuries with the Holy Roman (Austrian) Empire.

Territories on Europe's eastern and northern fringe tended to be more poorly defined, politically speaking. Much of this had to do with the stress of invasions from the east. Mongol attacks in the mid-1200s and constant pressure from the Ottomans during and after the 1400s took their toll and, in many ways, held back the political development of nations. Countries such as Hungary, Sweden, and Poland were exceptions: they were stable and sophisticated, at least for the time being. More typical were the Russian lands, farther to the east. During most of the medieval era, Russia was a loose confederation of city-states, governed by constantly feuding princes. The Mongol invasions of the 1240s placed the Russians under the domination of the Golden Horde; not until the mid-1400s did Russia become free. Only after that did a Russian nation begin to take shape, under the leadership of the tsars of Moscow.

THE CRUSADES

The Concept and Origin of Crusading

Among the powers of the medieval popes was the ability to request monarchs to provide troops and money for holy wars known as **crusades**. Crusades were fought for a number of reasons: to convert nonbelievers to Catholicism, to crush Christian movements the papacy considered heretical (infamous crusades of this type were fought in southern France during the early 1200s), and to resist attacks by foreigners who were not Christian (especially Muslims).

Many underlying factors motivated the Crusades:

> **NOTE**
>
> The best-known crusades, and the ones generally referred to when the term "the Crusades" is used, are those fought by European Catholics against the Muslims of the Middle East and North Africa from 1095 to 1291.

- Genuine religious fervor on the part of both Muslims and Christians
- Geopolitical conflict between Europe and the Middle East
- The Europeans' desire to become more involved in the international trade network stretching from the Mediterranean to China
- Personal ambitions of Europeans hoping to gain wealth and land in the Middle East
- Racial and religious prejudice

The Crusading Experience

The spark of the **First Crusade** (1096–1099) came in 1095, when the Byzantine Empire asked fellow Christians in Europe for military assistance against the Seljuk Turks, who had recently captured Jerusalem. To increase their chances of receiving aid, the Byzantines exaggerated rumors of Turkish atrocities in the Holy Land. Pope Urban II responded by summoning the **Council of Clermont** and calling upon the knights of Catholic Europe to retake the Holy Land from the Turks. In 1096, a massive army of Crusaders traveled to Constantinople, then through the Middle East, fighting Muslim forces along the way. In the summer of 1099, they reached Jerusalem and placed it under siege. After taking the city, the Crusaders, in one of the bloodiest episodes in military history, butchered almost every Muslim and Jew within its walls (as well as a number of native Christians whom they mistook for Muslims). A key reason for the First Crusade's success was lack of unity among Turks, Arabs, and other Muslim peoples.

After the First Crusade, the Europeans established four Christian states known as the Latin Kingdoms. While they lasted, these served as a military and political foothold in the Middle East. They also enabled Europeans to become involved in the lucrative commercial economy that made the region so wealthy.

The Christians maintained their presence in the Middle East for two centuries. However, the Muslims united their efforts in order to expel the Europeans. The many crusades that followed were generally responses to successful Muslim campaigns. Jerusalem, for example, fell under Muslim control again in 1187. Especially after 1200, European crusades lost their focus (the Fourth Crusade of 1202–1204 turned into a sack of Christian Constantinople) or failed miserably (like the ill-fated Children's Crusades). In 1291, the Europeans abandoned their last major outpost (Acre) in the Middle East.

Effects of the Crusades

Long-term effects of the Crusades include the worsening of the relationship between the Muslim and Christian worlds. Also important was the greater awareness of the wider world, especially the lands of the east, that the Crusades stimulated among the Europeans. Along with this came an increased knowledge of—and desire for—the economic wealth to be gained by greater interaction with the Middle and Far East. Moreover, the crusading ideal—the notion that Christian warriors were fighting a holy war on behalf of a sacred cause—contributed to the powerful myth of knighthood and chivalry that emerged in Europe during the Middle Ages.

URBANIZATION, TRADE, AND SOCIETY

While the early medieval era was a time of social and economic backwardness, significant gains were made during the High and Late Middle Ages. However, the latter period was a time of social crisis as well.

Population Growth, Trade, and Commerce

From 1000 to 1300, population growth in Europe was considerable. Advanced agricultural techniques—such as the three-field system of crop rotation and the invention of better plows—caused the food supply to increase.

   Trade and commerce became a larger part of the European economy. Political stability made **banking**, the movement of goods, and the creation of **markets** safer and more convenient. Because the movement of goods was easier by water than by land, **trade routes** tended to follow rivers and coastlines. One major network, centered on Italy, sprang up throughout the Mediterranean, and did much to connect Europe with the commerce of the Middle and Far East (the Crusades did much to stimulate this). Other important networks formed along the Rhine River, in the North Sea and English Channel (especially between England and Flanders), and throughout the Baltic Sea. Trade in the Baltic was dominated by the **Hanseatic League**, a group whose influence stretched from England in the west to Russia in the east. The relatively new practice of banking made trade more feasible and dependable. Powerful banking houses were run by the Medicis in Italy and the Fuggers in central Europe.

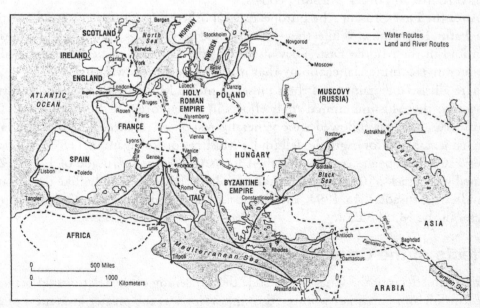

European Trade Routes During the Late Medieval Period and the Renaissance.
European desire for more direct access to the goods of East and South Asia prompted the great wave of exploration that began during the 1400s and continued during the 1500s and 1600s.

Urbanization

Another social trend was **urbanization**. Although the majority of people in medieval Europe remained in the countryside, working as peasants and serfs, an increasingly large number were moving to cities. Existing cities grew larger, and new cities were founded at a great rate. Some parts of Europe, particularly Italy and Flanders, urbanized more quickly than others.

Cities were excellent sites for trade. They attracted artists, writers, and scholars. Because urban populations included shopkeepers, artisans, tradespeople, and laborers of all sorts, the growth of cities also encouraged specialization of labor. Most skilled trades in medieval cities were organized according to the **guild system**. Guilds were labor groups that maintained a monopoly on their respective trades. They restricted membership, established prices, set standards of quality and fair practice, and provided pensions.

Cities were often overcrowded and polluted, and many people lived in poverty. There were benefits to city life, however, including cultural opportunities and the chance to gain greater wealth. A key advantage was immunity from feudal obligations, especially serfdom: typically, if a person left the countryside and lived in a city for a year and a day, he or she was released from status as a serf (as reflected in the popular saying, "city air makes you free").

Social Stress and Black Death in the Late Medieval Period

Although trade and urbanization continued to expand during the Late Middle Ages, these were also years of social stress. A wave of uprisings swept Europe from the early 1300s through the early 1500s (including the peasant Jacquerie of 1358 in France; the Wool Carders' Revolt in Florence, in 1378; and, in 1381, Wat Tyler's Rebellion in England). The causes of such disturbances were many. A general cooling of the climate, referred to by environmental historians as the Little Ice Age, affected harvests and made life in the countryside difficult. More (and longer) wars were being fought, armies were growing larger, and the new gunpowder weaponry of the day was extremely expensive. More peasants were forced into military service (especially during the Hundred Years' War). The taxes of common people also increased. During the last half of the 1400s, religious disagreements and dissatisfaction with the Church sometimes led to rebellion.

Another manifestation of social stress was a sharp rise in the persecution of people thought to be witches. Catholic authorities sought to root out suspected **witchcraft**, issuing a manual in the late 1400s, *The Hammer of Witchcraft*, to aid in spotting and trying witches. Ordinary people were caught up in the hysteria as well. Most of the victims of witch hunts were women.

Social trauma also came in the form of the **Black Death**, the popular name for the bubonic plague. The arrival of bubonic plague in the mid-fourteenth century ranks as one of the greatest medical disasters in Eurasian history. After killing millions of people in China, the disease traveled westward to the Middle East. It reached Europe in 1347 on a ship landing in Sicily.

In 1347 and 1348, the plague ravaged southern Europe. By 1349 and 1350, it spread to central Europe and the British Isles; it was felt in Russia and Scandinavia

NOTE

Many people saw the plague as a sign that the world was coming to an end; others accused Jews of poisoning or bewitching Christians and persecuted them harshly.

from 1351 to 1353. The disease's deadliness and rapid spread caused tremendous panic throughout Europe. This initial bout of the plague killed 25 to 30 million people, roughly one-third the population of Europe. For centuries afterward, the plague recurred periodically in Europe (although no attack was as bad as the first).

Women in Medieval Europe

As a rule, women were subservient to men in all parts of Europe during these years. How much freedom or how many rights a woman enjoyed depended mainly on her social status.

Women of lower classes cared for the household and assisted with farmwork. They bore children and raised them. Women of low birth also worked as servants for upper-class families. One of the few peasant women to leave an individual mark on medieval Europe was the French war leader **Joan of Arc** (ca. 1410–1431).

NOTE

In this era of poor hygiene and limited medical knowledge, many women—as many as 10 to 15 percent—died in childbirth.

In most parts of medieval Europe, women had some property rights. They could own and inherit land and property. They often received dowries (although in some places and times, it was the woman's family that had to provide a dowry to the husband-to-be). Women could separate from their husbands, although obtaining divorces and annulments was difficult, especially for women of the upper classes. Women had protection, but not equality, before the law.

Women could enter religious life; they could not become priests in either the Catholic or Orthodox Church, but they could become nuns. The majority of nuns were from the landed aristocracy. To marry off daughters, noble families had to provide potential husbands with land, money, or a title; an aristocratic family with many daughters was often unable to pay for all of them to get married, and a common solution was to place younger daughters in convents. Women who preferred intellectual pursuits sometimes found safe haven as nuns. For example, **Hildegard of Bingen** (1098–1179), celebrated for her mystical writings and songs, became abbess of a German convent.

Aristocratic women, while not legally the equal of men, could exert informal political and cultural influence. If an aristocratic woman was heir to rich property or a kingdom, she was a desirable match. Noblewomen often managed their husbands' estates and financial accounts. Frequently, the mothers of young kings whose fathers died early served as regents and advisers until their sons came of age.

Some women ruled in their own right, as queens. This situation was not common, and countries whose legal systems were based on tribal Germanic (Salic) law, such as France and the Holy Roman Empire, did not allow women to inherit thrones. However, women would come to rule England, parts of Spain, Russia, and elsewhere. The most famous example of a politically important woman during the Middle Ages was **Eleanor of Aquitaine** (ca. 1122–1204). A dynamic, intelligent woman, Eleanor married Louis VII of France and then Henry II of England. She had much influence over politics in both countries. She was also a great patron of art and music.

MEDIEVAL CULTURE

For many years, it was traditional to view the medieval period as the Dark Ages, an era lacking in culture or sophistication. More recently, it has become standard to recognize the richness of medieval culture, especially during the High and Late Middle Ages. Even so, medieval Europe lagged behind Byzantium and the Islamic world in terms of cultural attainment.

Catholicism and Classicism as Influences on Medieval Culture

The most important factor shaping medieval culture was the Catholic Church, which administered institutions of learning (monasteries, then universities) and was the largest employer of artists, architects, and musicians. Art and ideas that were not in line with church doctrine could be banned—and could lead to severe punishment.

Another influence on medieval culture was the classical learning and literature preserved from ancient Greece and Rome. During the Middle Ages (and long afterward), **Latin** was Europe's language of learning and culture. (Europeans had much less knowledge of Greek until later, when Arab and Jewish translators made materials in that language more accessible.) Medieval scientific thought was dominated by the theories of the ancient Greeks, mainly through Latin translations. Of special importance was **Aristotle**, whose writings on science, philosophy, ethics, and politics were adapted by Christian scholars and placed at the center of the medieval worldview. Greek science taught the Europeans much, but it also encouraged some mistaken ideas, especially the **geocentric theory**, which argues that the sun revolves around the earth.

Eventually, increased familiarity of European artists and scholars with Greek and Roman texts helped give birth to the Renaissance.

> **NOTE**
>
> Ironically, Aristotle had written about the **scientific method** (in which hypotheses have to be tested by observation and experiment), but medieval Europeans tended to ignore this part of his thinking and accepted most Greek science, errors included, as unquestioned fact.

Art, Architecture, and Literature

Most medieval art was religious in nature. Icons, or religious paintings, were largely inspired by Byzantine styles, even in Catholic Europe. Early church music was mainly plainsong (also known as Gregorian chant): human voices unaccompanied by instruments. Over time, arrangements became more complex, and instruments were used by the end of the Middle Ages. The greatest achievement of medieval architecture was the cathedral, which required skill, money, and decades to build. The prevailing styles were **Romanesque** (thick walls, small windows, square build) and **Gothic** (tall, slender spires; large stained-glass windows; ornate carvings; flying buttresses).

In the secular sphere, the medieval Europeans were great builders of castles (although many were modeled on Byzantine and Middle Eastern designs). Troubadours and minstrels appeared in the eleventh and twelfth centuries and popularized nonreligious music (favorite songs were about love, as well as legends of King Arthur, Charlemagne's knight Roland, and El Cid of Spain).

One trend encouraged by troubadours and minstrels—then later authors like Dante Alighieri of Italy (1265–1321), the English poet Geoffrey Chaucer

(1340–1401), and Christine de Pisan (1364–1410), who wrote in French and Italian—was the increased use of native, or **vernacular**, languages. Although Latin remained the language of the educated elite, it became more acceptable to write serious poetic and literary works in the vernacular. This stimulated a growth in literacy and made literature available to a wider range of people.

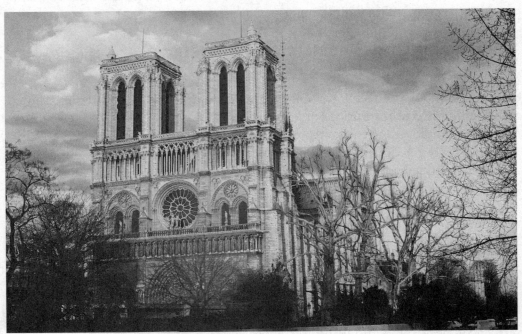

Cathedral of Notre Dame, Paris, France.
One of the best-known landmarks of Paris, the Cathedral of Notre Dame provides a quintessential example of the Gothic style of church architecture.

Philosophy and Intellectual Life

The principal school of philosophy in medieval Europe was **Scholasticism**, which attempted to reconcile reason (logic, the senses, and the learning of ancient Greeks and Romans like Aristotle) with faith in God and Christianity. The greatest of the Scholastics was the Italian monk Thomas Aquinas (1225–1274).

The overall level of learning in Europe was boosted by the appearance of **universities**, starting in Italy during the 900s. Although they were at least partly under church influence, universities provided Europe with havens of learning and the exchange of ideas.

The Printing Press

In the late 1430s, a new invention revolutionized European culture and the intellectual life of the entire world. This was the printing press developed by German inventor **Johannes Gutenberg**. The concept of printing by carving images and words into blocks of wood had originated in China (perhaps Korea) centuries before, and was known to the Europeans. However, block printing was costly and unwieldy. Gutenberg created a **movable-type printing press**, in which individual, reusable metal characters could be placed in a frame to form text. The printing press raised literacy rates, spread information, increased the impact of new ideas and scientific theories, and encouraged the expansion of libraries and universities. It played an indispensable role in the Renaissance, the Protestant Reformation, and a general explosion of knowledge that transformed Europe and the West for centuries.

THE RENAISSANCE

The Concept of the Renaissance

During the early 1300s, an important cultural and intellectual revival began in parts of southern Europe, especially the city-states of the Italian peninsula. This revival became known as the **Renaissance**, or "rebirth." By the end of the 1400s, it was spreading from Italy to the rest of Europe. It is considered to have lasted until approximately 1600.

As noted previously, it was common until recently to think of the medieval era as a time of minimal cultural advancement. Consequently, the Renaissance was often viewed as a revolution, a sudden explosion of new ideas and learning. Because historians now have a better appreciation of medieval culture, it has become standard to see the Renaissance more as a gradual cultural and intellectual evolution. Nonetheless, it did represent a significant change.

The Cultural Outlook of the Renaissance

One of the hallmarks of Renaissance culture was **classicism**: a greater understanding of and admiration for Greco-Roman literature and learning. Of course, medieval Europeans were familiar with this heritage. What changed during the Renaissance was that a greater number of people probed more deeply into Latin sources and, thanks largely to translations provided by Jews and Arabs, the learning of the Greeks.

Renaissance thought was more secular than that of the medieval era. The authors and artists of the Renaissance did not ignore religion; even if they had wanted to, doing so would have been dangerous, thanks to the church's influence. Still, Renaissance writings and artworks placed a greater emphasis on worldly matters.

Similarly, another feature of Renaissance culture was **humanism**, a Greco-Roman concept that went hand-in-hand with the classical revival and Renaissance secularism. Humanism, the conviction that to be human is something to celebrate, ran counter to the church-dominated medieval view that to be human was to be tainted with sin and that worldly life was less important than heavenly afterlife.

Causes of the Renaissance

Why did the Renaissance occur first in Italy? One cause was the urban sophistication of the Italian city-states. Another was the commercial strength of the Italian cities, which generated excess wealth sufficient to support a sustained cultural revival. Italy's success in trade and commerce also gave birth to a class of patrons who, though not always of noble blood, were rich, educated, and eager to improve their status by sponsoring artists and writers (the most famous example is the **Medici** family of Florence). Italy's position as a naval and economic crossroads in the Mediterranean brought it into contact with new ideas and advanced knowledge from the outside world more quickly than the rest of Europe.

Major Figures and Trends of the Renaissance

Important figures in the early Italian Renaissance were the poet Petrarch (1304–1374), the author Giovanni Boccaccio (1313–1375), and the painter Giotto (ca. 1267–1337). As the Renaissance matured, key individuals included the architect Filippo Brunelleschi (1377–1446), the political philosopher Niccolò Machiavelli (1469–1527), the artist and scientist **Leonardo da Vinci** (1452–1519), the painter and sculptor **Michelangelo** (1472–1564), and the painters Raphael (1483–1520) and Titian (1477–1576).

Renaissance architects attained a high degree of engineering skill, boosted by a better understanding of mathematics and a deeper knowledge of the techniques of the Greeks and Romans, who had been master builders. Renaissance painters achieved an astonishing level of realism in their work, compared with the art of the medieval era. In painting, as in architecture, increased familiarity with mathematics enabled painters to work out the **laws of perspective**. The result was a convincing depiction of a three-dimensional subject on a two-dimensional surface. Better paints and equipment, the technique of foreshortening, and the effective use of light and shadowing also increased the quality of Renaissance paintings.

The Spread of Renaissance Culture

By the 1400s, the Italian Renaissance was exerting its influence on the rest of Europe. Travelers, especially northern students attending Italian universities, carried with them techniques drawn from the art and literature of the south. The invention of the movable-type printing press in the 1430s dramatically increased the speed and scope by which information could be produced and transmitted throughout Europe, and the printing press deserves much of the credit for spreading the ideals of the Renaissance beyond Italy. The Renaissance took hold in southern France, and then all of France, as well as England, Spain, the Holy Roman Empire, Poland, Hungary, and elsewhere. By the late 1400s, it was possible to speak of a northern Renaissance. This northern Renaissance had a profound impact on the rest of Europe, especially with regard to the religious controversies of the 1500s that led to the Protestant Reformation.

Islam in the Middle East and Africa

CHAPTER 7

- The Sunni-Shiite split
- The Abbasid Caliphate
- Trans-Saharan caravan routes
- The Arab slave trade
- Mali and Timbuktu
- The Seljuk and Ottoman Turks
- The conquest of Constantinople
- Ibn Battuta

Prior to 600 C.E., the dominant civilizations in the Middle East were the Byzantine Empire and Persia. Suddenly, the political and religious landscape of the Middle East was transformed by the appearance of Islam.

During the 600s and 700s, military conquest carried the new faith out of Arabia, where it was born, to Spain and Morocco in the west, and the borderlands of India in the east. The Islamic caliphate aspired to unite all worshippers into a single political community called dar al-Islam (much as popes strove to do in Christian Europe). The golden age of classical Islam lasted from the middle of the 900s to about 1000, and is associated with the Abbasid Caliphate.

Although the Abbasids retained theoretical control over the Islamic world until the Mongol conquest of 1258, their power started to wane before that. Islamic culture remained advanced, but, politically speaking, the years after 1000 were a period of decline.

> **TIP**
>
> The key tenets of Islam, as well as the place of women in the Islamic world, are discussed in Chapter 5.

Another characteristic of these years was political confusion. From 1000 to the 1400s, many Islamic states rose and fell. Other Middle Eastern peoples, such as the Persians and Turks, rivaled the Arabs as forces in the Islamic community. Outside enemies and invaders added to the chaos. Finally, by the end of the fifteenth century and beginning of the sixteenth, the Islamic world—at least the Middle East and North Africa—was reconsolidated under the Ottoman Turks. However, even under the Ottomans, Islam was never again united as it had been under the Abbasids.

THE EXPANSION OF ISLAM AND THE FIRST CALIPHATES

As described in Chapter 5, Mohammed and his followers spread Islam throughout Arabia in the 620s and 630s. Later in the 600s, Muslim forces conquered Sassanid Persia, weakened the Byzantine Empire, and converted most of the Middle East to Islam. By the early 700s, the Muslims had brought under their sway Iraq, Syria, Lebanon, Palestine, Egypt, most of North Africa, Spain, parts of Italy, Central Asia, and India's western frontier (present-day Pakistan).

Muslim territory was ruled by the **caliph** ("successor"), the title assumed by the new religion's leaders after Mohammed's death in 632. The caliphate was theocratic, with political and religious authority combined. Three caliphs (Abu Bakr, Umar, and Uthman) reigned before the **Sunni-Shiite split** (656–661). After that, power passed to the Umayyad Caliphate (661–750), which governed from Damascus, in Syria, and continued Islam's military expansion. The Umayyad caliphs made Arabic the official language of the Muslim world and imposed a tax on those who did not convert to Islam. A series of rebellions led to the Umayyads' decline.

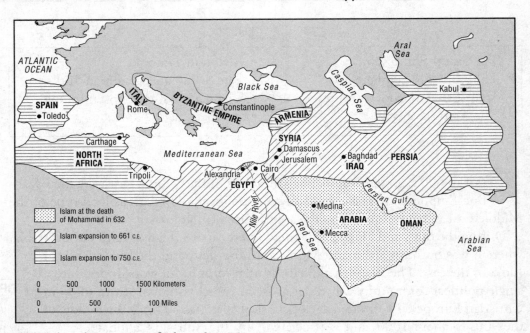

The Birth and Expansion of Islam, 632–750.
Born in Arabia, the dynamic new faith of Islam triumphed throughout the Middle East, where it is still dominant. It then continued to expand, both eastward and westward.

The Abbasid Caliphate

Following the Umayyad dynasty was the **Abbasid Caliphate** (750–1258), which established a great capital at Baghdad and presided over the golden age of classical Islamic culture.

The caliphs were strong and provided peace and stability throughout the Islamic empire. Economic unity prevailed (as it had throughout the empires of Persia, Rome, and Han China), and Abbasid trade networks linked the Middle East with Europe, Africa, the Indian Ocean, and Asia. Just as European bankers facilitated trade there, the concepts of credit and a single currency made possible by Abbasid stability stimulated commerce in the Islamic Empire. Muslim manufacturers were among the most skilled in the world (especially at the production of steel), and, as described at the end of this chapter, the level of cultural advancement was high. The most famous and best loved of the Abbasid caliphs was **Haroun al-Rashid** (776–809).

Abbasid political unity began to disintegrate during and after the 900s. Geographic overextension, the difficulty of ruling millions of people of such diverse ethnicities, and the Sunni-Shiite split all contributed to the caliphate's gradual breakup. Nomadic movements in North Africa, Syria, and Iraq destabilized it as well. As early as 875, Persia and Central Asia came under control of a non-Arabic dynasty (the Samanid). In 909, a Shiite caliphate (the Fatimids) rose up in Egypt and ruled there till 1171. Spain achieved independence briefly from 929 to 976.

At the same time, Baghdad itself was under military threat. It fell to several conquerors, including the Seljuk Turks, who kept the Abbasid caliph in place as a figure-head. Military stress continued, tearing the caliphate apart. (Abbasid weakness largely accounts for the European crusaders' success in seizing Middle Eastern territory.)

The final blow came from the Mongols, who invaded the Middle East in the mid-1200s (for more, see Chapter 10). In 1258, the Mongols captured Baghdad and killed the last Abbasid caliph. Afterward, the Middle East splintered into many separate states. It was reunited, but only partly, by the Turks.

ISLAM IN SAHARAN AND SUB-SAHARAN AFRICA

The Spread of Islam to Africa

Islam reached the eastern parts of North Africa (especially Egypt) in the 600s and 700s. Over the next few hundred years, it spread through the Sahara and to sub-Saharan Africa. Some of northeastern Africa remained Christian: the Nubian kingdoms of Kush and Axum (until the 1300s and 1400s), Ethiopia, and the Coptic Christians of Egypt. However, most converted to Islam.

Islam was brought to Africa by **Arab traders**—either overland (along the **trans-Saharan caravan routes** or by sea, along the continent's Indian Ocean coastline. Conversion was mostly peaceful, although it was sometimes carried out by force. In addition, much of the commercial activity that brought Islam to southern Africa was connected with the extensive **Arab slave trade**. Trade northward consisted of slaves, salt, ivory, and animal skins. Trade southward included manufactured goods like glass, metalwork, and pottery.

As for the west, Islam took root not just in the Sahara, but also sub-Saharan Africa, during the eleventh century. Here, the most dedicated converts were the **Berbers**, desert nomads and hardened warriors. From Marrakesh, in present-day Morocco, Berber clans extended Muslim authority far to the south.

> **NOTE**
>
> Many of the Swahili city-states of Africa's east coast were home to large Muslim communities. After the 1100s, Middle Eastern culture was one of the many elements contributing to the incredible diversity of East African civilizations.

Mali

By the 1300s and 1400s, Islamic states in western sub-Saharan Africa included Songhai, Kanem-Bornu, and many Hausa city-states. The biggest and most powerful was **Mali** (ca. 1250–1460), along the Niger River basin, an important north–south trade route for centuries. Founded in the mid-1200s by the conqueror Sundiata, and blessed with sizable deposits of gold and metal ore, Mali became a key center for trade in western and northern Africa.

Conversion to Islam proved beneficial. Politically, it enabled good trade relations with Arab states to the north. It also created a group of educated scholars who acted as public servants.

Mali's products were highly valued. They included gold, salt, ivory, animal skins, and slaves. The chief commercial outpost (though not the capital) was **Timbuktu**, a stopping point for caravans and traders traveling in all directions. The main commodity here was salt. Timbuktu was also a renowned center of religious studies and Islamic scholarship.

Mali's most powerful ruler was **Mansa Musa** (1312–1337), famous throughout Europe and Africa as one of the world's wealthiest monarchs (a Spanish map of 1375 referred to Mali as home to the "richest and noblest king in all lands"). Mansa Musa more fully systematized the government. By the early 1400s, Mali was under foreign attack, and its territory was steadily shrinking. Its might collapsed by the end of the century.

Culturally speaking, Mali (like most parts of Africa) was home to a strong tradition of oral storytelling and song making. One of Africa's most famous epic poems from this period comes from Mali, the *Son-Jara* (also known as the *Sundiata*). It dates from the 1200s, and it tells of the many exploits of the chieftain Son-Jara (Sundiata), founder of the Mali state.

THE RISE OF THE TURKS

Originating on the open steppes of Central Asia, the nomadic tribes known collectively as the Turks began to exert a signficant influence on the Middle East, starting around 1000 C.E. By the 1400s, the Ottoman Turks would be the dominant political force there.

Mamluks and Seljuks

Most Turkish tribes were adept at horse combat, and many Turks were brought to the Middle East to serve in Arab armies. These cavalry warriors were called **Mamluks**. They became dedicated converts to Islam and were among the best soldiers in the Middle East. By the eleventh century, there were many Mamluks in Asia Minor (present-day Turkey). In 1250, a large group of them migrated to Egypt and established a kingdom there.

In the eleventh century, the **Seljuk Turks** moved westward. They captured Baghdad in 1055 (but kept the Abbasid caliph in place as a figurehead). In 1071, the Seljuks defeated the Byzantine Empire at the Battle of Manzikert. They then took most of Asia Minor, Syria, Lebanon, and Palestine (including Jerusalem). Seljuk successes crippled the Byzantine Empire and ushered in its long period of decline. However, Turkish victories prompted European Christians to begin the Crusades in 1095.

Crusaders and Mongol Assaults

The early **Crusades** and the establishment of the Latin Kingdoms (see Chapter 6) threw the Middle East into political confusion. Until the mid-1100s, neither the weakened Abbasids nor their many political rivals proved capable of organizing effective resistance. One of the Middle East's great leaders during this time was the Kurdish general **Saladin**, who recaptured Jerusalem in 1187 and drove back the Third Crusade (1189–1192).

By the 1200s, the Mamluks, Arabs, and Seljuks had gotten better at fighting the crusaders. The Latin Kingdoms shrank steadily, and the Europeans were expelled by the end of the century.

However, an even greater crisis emerged in the form of the **Mongols** (see Chapter 10), who moved into the Middle East in the mid-1200s, seizing Baghdad in 1258 and destroying the Abbasid Caliphate. Only in 1260 was the Mongol advance halted, as a Mamluk army defeated the Mongols at the Battle of Ain Jalut (Goliath Springs) in Syria. The Mongols took no more territory but established a state (the Il-Khan Empire) that lasted until 1349. For a long time, no single state—Mamluk, Seljuk, or Mongol—was strong enough to centralize the Middle East.

The Ottomans

The group that eventually dominated the Middle East, the **Ottoman Turks**, rose to prominence in the 1300s and 1400s. As early as the 1200s, the Ottomans, who served the Seljuks as vassals, settled northwestern Asia Minor. By the century's end, they had their own independent state, founded by the sultan Osman I (1280–1326).

The Ottomans conquered southeastern Europe and what remained of the Byzantine Empire. Attacks on the Balkans began in the late 1300s, and the Ottoman fleet of galleys (oared warships, often rowed by prisoners or slaves) captured many ports and islands in the eastern Mediterranean. Finally, in 1453, Ottoman armies under Sultan Mehmet II, using the world's largest and most advanced gunpowder artillery, captured Constantinople. The **fall of Constantinople** ended the 1,100-year history of the Byzantine Empire and set the stage for a long, intense struggle against Christian Europe during the late 1400s and 1500s.

ISLAMIC CULTURE

For all its political failures, the Abbasid Caliphate presided over the golden era of Islamic culture. Compared with its neighbors—Europe, sub-Saharan Africa, the steppes of Central Asia—the Islamic world was far more culturally advanced during the 700s through the 1200s. Its only cultural and intellectual rivals during these years were India and China.

Mathematics and Science

The mathematical and scientific aptitude of the Muslims was great. Under the Abbasids, the use of so-called Arabic numerals (which actually originated in India) became widespread. Islamic scholars were also adept at medicine. In the 900s, the physician Razi compiled the *Hawi*, the most thorough medical encyclopedia of its time. Even more famous was the Persian scientist Ibn Sina, known to the West as **Avicenna** (980–1037), whose *Canon of Medicine* remained in wide use until the 1600s, both in Europe and the Middle East. The fact that many stars in the night sky bear Arabic names attests to the skill of Muslim astronomers. One reason for the Ottomans' great military successes was a high degree of expertise with gunpowder weaponry, which required a good working knowledge of metallurgy and chemistry.

> **NOTE**
>
> The term *algebra* comes directly from Arabic, and the Muslims were equally expert at trigonometry.

Philosophy

The Islamic world produced many philosophers: some Muslim, some Jewish (but accepted as citizens and recognized for their accomplishments). Like the Scholastics of medieval Europe, Islamic philosophers investigated the relationship between human reason and religious faith.

The two most famous thinkers came from Muslim Spain. Ibn Rushd, better known as **Averroës** (1126–1198), played an indispensable role in Islamic and European cultural life. A celebrated doctor, Averroës translated and analyzed the works of the Greek philosopher Aristotle, reintroducing his ideas to Europe. A second philosopher was **Maimonides** (1135–1204), a Spanish rabbi. Maimonides wrote commentaries on Jewish scripture and, like Averroës, encouraged the dissemination of Aristotle's ideas throughout Europe. His most famous work, *Guide to the Perplexed*, attempted to reconcile the rationality of Greco-Roman thought with Jewish theology (as Thomas Aquinas would do with Christian thought).

Islam's Influence Over Culture

As in Christian Europe, religion played a large cultural role. Muslim authorities controlled what was acceptable art or literature. Because the **Qur'an** forbids the worship of graven images, Islamic art during these years tended to feature geometric patterns and shapes rather than human or animal figures (although this was not a hard-and-fast rule). Religious colleges (madrasas) provided centers of learning. Much intellectual activity in the Islamic world involved debates and commentaries on the Qur'an, the sayings of Mohammed, and Islamic law (**Sharia**).

Islamic Literature

Among the classics of Islamic literature from the Abbasid years is *The Thousand Nights and a Night*, known in the West as *The Arabian Nights*. The work includes the tales of Sindbad the Sailor, Ali Baba, and Aladdin. Also important is the *Rubaiyat* of **Omar Khayyám** (ca. 1038–1131). Famous as a mathematician and astronomer, Khayyám composed this collection of bittersweet, meditative poems in the early 1100s.

Another masterpiece was *Travels*, the journal of **Ibn Battuta** (1304–1368), the Islamic world's greatest explorer. Born in Morocco, Ibn Battuta spent 30 years visiting Mecca, Persia, Mesopotamia, Turkey, Central Asia, Spain, Timbuktu, India, China, and Sumatra, a journey covering more than 75,000 miles.

From Persia came **Sufism**, a mystical strain of Islam that places an emphasis on attaining union with Allah by means of ritual disciplines and spiritual exercises (especially chanting and dancing). The best example of Sufi thought and belief can be found in the poetry of Rumi (1207–1273).

> **NOTE**
>
> Arabic was both the holy language of Islam and the principal language of cultural and intellectual life, just as Latin was for the Christians of medieval Europe. However, starting in the 800s and 900s, Persian joined Arabic as a major language in Islamic thought and literature.

China, Japan, and East Asia

CHAPTER 8

- The Tang dynasty and Song Empire
- The silk industry
- The Silk Road and the Indian Ocean trade network
- The Grand Canal
- Canton and Chinese urbanization
- The invention of gunpowder
- Neo-Confucianism
- Foot binding
- Kublai Khan and the Yuan Empire
- Marco Polo
- The Ming dynasty
- Zheng He
- Nara and Heian Japan
- The shogunates and the samurai class
- Rice-paddy farming
- Block printing

After the Han dynasty's fall in 220 C.E., China alternated between periods of political unity and fragmentation. Imperial collapse in China tended not to be as traumatic as the fall of Rome was for Europe, but it did cause turmoil. Between 589 and 906, China enjoyed a political revival under the Sui and Tang dynasties. However, after the fall of the Tang, it once again split into various empires and states. This disunity lasted for several centuries, until the late 1200s.

During the 1200s, China, like the rest of Eurasia, was rocked by the explosive military expansion of the Mongols. It was conquered by the Mongols, who played a significant part in the country's reunification. After the mid-1300s, China underwent even greater centralization under the Ming dynasty. Whatever the political situation, the growth of China's cities—among the largest and wealthiest in the world—continued.

Other countries of East Asia, especially Japan, Korea, and Vietnam, passed in and out of the Chinese political orbit. At times they were under China's direct control, at others they were free. China also exerted a strong artistic and religious pull on them. As time passed, all three became more independent politically and culturally.

THE SUI AND TANG DYNASTIES

The first strong dynasty to emerge after the fall of the Han was the Sui (589–618). Despite its short life, the Sui reunified China and expanded its borders in a burst of military conquest.

Even stronger was the **Tang Dynasty** (618–906). Under the Tang, China became larger than ever before. Emperors like Xuanzong (712–755) extended China's rule to parts of Central Asia, Mongolia, Manchuria, Tibet, and the Pacific coast. Like the Han Dynasty, Tang China forced many of its neighbors into a **tributary system**, in which Korea, Vietnam, Japan, and others had to make regular monetary payments to avoid punishment.

The Tang economy grew strong thanks to an advanced infrastructure (good roads, waterways, and canals—especially the **Grand Canal**, which the Sui dynasty created to link the Yellow and Yangzi rivers, and the Tang rulers expanded). Increased trade stimulated the Tang economy. In particular, the **silk industry** made the Chinese (who kept the secret of silk production to themselves for centuries) exceptionally wealthy. Greater control over the southern coast allowed China to take greater part in the **Indian Ocean trade network**. The Chinese also traded with the Middle East and the Mediterranean by means of the 5,000-mile **Silk Road**.

The Tang rulers were cultural patrons. Emperor Xuanzong sponsored the creation of the Han Lin Academy of Letters, a key institution of learning. The Tang exerted a strong artistic and religious influence over its neighbors, including Korea and Japan.

During the 800s, a series of peasant rebellions and military disasters weakened the Tang. In 906, the dynasty collapsed completely, and several centuries of disunity followed.

SONG (SUNG) CHINA

The Song Empire and Its Rivals

Following the Tang breakdown, China fragmented into separate states until the late 1200s. The largest and longest lasting was the **Song (Sung) Empire**, which ruled east-central China, from the Yellow River in the north to the Vietnamese border in the south. The Song lasted until 1279 but lost land steadily, because of war with its neighbors.

Until 1121, the primary threat to the Song was the Liao Empire to the north. The Song paid a tribute of silk and cash to the Liao, but then destroyed them with help from the Jurchen, who lived even farther to the north. Unfortunately for the Song, the Jurchen proclaimed their own empire (the Jin) and turned on the Song. The Song gave up much territory, withdrawing to the south. This smaller Song state survived until the Mongol conquest of the 1270s.

Song Society and Economics

Despite its political troubles, the Song Empire was culturally and economically impressive. It enjoyed steady population growth and **urbanization**, becoming the world's most heavily urbanized society—home to the largest cities on earth, several of them with a million or more inhabitants. Although its economic ties with Central Asia and the Middle East lessened, Song China was still connected with the trade routes (such as the Silk Road) that extended to those regions.

If contact with the Middle East lessened, the Song became more involved with the Pacific coast and Southeast Asia. The port of **Canton** (now **Guangzhou**) became one of the world's busiest and most cosmopolitan trading centers. Song China's large trading vessels, known as junks, cruised the eastern seas and Indian Ocean, carrying silk and manufactured goods.

Song Culture and Religion

Song China was the most scientifically and technologically advanced society of its time, with the possible exception of the Abbasid Caliphate. The Song Chinese were excellent mathematicians and astronomers. Song scientists developed accurate clocks, as well as a working **compass** (first used for navigation at sea in 1090). Also during the Song period, the Chinese invented **gunpowder**, pioneered the use of paper currency (which they called "flying money"), and made use of **block printing** (a practice they may have adopted from the Koreans).

> **TIP**
>
> The most striking example of Song China's scientific and technological expertise was the celestial clock of Su Song (built in 1088), an eighty-foot-tall structure that told the time of day, the day of the month, and the positions of the sun, moon, planets, and major stars. It was the first device in world history to use a chain-driven mechanism (powered by flowing water).

Concerning religion, a great revival of Confucius's teachings—**Neo-Confucianism**—took place during the Song period. Neo-Confucianism was an important unifying factor in a politically divided China. It reinforced Chinese culture's tendency toward hierarchy and obedience, and put a premium on education and cultured behavior. Most governmental officials gained their posts by scoring well on rigorous civil service examinations, a Confucian practice. A new form of Buddhism emerged as well: **Chan** (known as Son in Korea and **Zen** in Japan). Chan stressed simplicity and meditation, and became very popular, both in China and abroad.

Women in Chinese Society

Neo-Confucianism, along with Chinese tradition, was used to justify the greater subordination of women, especially upper-class women, whose families were most likely to follow Confucian dictates. Earlier, a husband's family had to produce a dowry for a new bride; now the reverse became the norm. Marriages were arranged, mainly to the groom's benefit.

The best-known aspect of Chinese subjugation of women was **foot binding**. This painful practice, which kept women's feet tiny and dainty but in the process crippled them, was firmly established by 1200, and it continued into the early 1900s.

Women of the lower classes were generally freer than those of the upper classes, but still occupied a secondary status compared with men. On the other hand, women of all classes had inheritance and property rights, and retained control over their dowry after divorce or a husband's death. Still, the social position of Chinese women was decidedly second-class. (One dramatic exception was Empress Wu Zhao, the only woman ever to rule China in her own right. However, even she was forced off her throne in 705.)

THE MONGOL CONQUEST AND YUAN CHINA

As discussed in Chapter 10, almost all of Eurasia was affected in the 1200s by the sudden and successful military expansion of the Mongols. As **Genghis Khan** and his sons began their conquests, the Chinese states were among their first targets.

The Mongols attacked the Chinese states in 1211. They steadily accumulated territory, even after Genghis Khan's death in 1227. By 1234, the Mongols had captured almost all of western and northern China, and they threatened what remained of the Song Empire. The Song continued to resist for several decades.

In the 1260s, Genghis Khan's grandsons quarreled among themselves and began to divide the Mongol Empire. China and Southeast Asia fell to **Kublai (Khubilai) Khan**, who moved his capital from Mongolia to the Chinese city of Beijing and proclaimed the **Yuan Empire** (1271–1368). Kublai Khan conquered the rest of China, including the Song state, which fell in 1279.

Although Kublai Khan called himself the Great Khan of the Mongols, he and the Mongol leadership adapted themselves to Chinese ways: they adopted Buddhism and made Mandarin Chinese their official language. Indeed, Kublai Khan can be considered the reunifier of China as a single state.

Kublai Khan reigned until 1294 and made Yuan China rich and powerful. Most of his military campaigns succeeded, although he was unable to conquer Japan (which he tried to take in 1274 and 1281) or Java (which he fought in 1293). He forced most of China's neighbors to pay tribute, and the Yuan Empire resisted attacks from other Mongol states in Central Asia.

Kublai Khan rebuilt China's bureaucracy and economy. He repaired roads and canals and built new cities (including the resort of Shangdu, famous in the West as Xanadu). Kublai Khan also restored trade with the west. The **Silk Road**, which had fallen into inactivity, emerged again as a vital trade route. The Venetian merchant **Marco Polo** visited Kublai Khan's China in the 1270s.

The Yuan state was not so fortunate after Kublai Khan's death. During the early 1300s, China suffered tremendous population loss (estimated at 30 to 40 percent), owing to the appearance of **bubonic plague** (which traveled west to the Middle East and Europe, where it was known as the Black Death). Economic decline resulted from the population loss. A series of civil wars broke out in the 1340s, and a final rebellion overthrew the Yuan in 1368.

THE EARLY MING DYNASTY

Triumph of the Ming

The rebel who brought down the Yuan Empire, Zhu Yuanzhang, had been a soldier, a bandit, and a priest. After becoming emperor in 1368, he took the name **Hongwu** (1368–1403) and established the **Ming Dynasty** (1368–1644), one of the longest-lasting and most famous in Chinese history. His son **Yongle** (1403–1424) was also a strong ruler.

At home, Hongwu and Yongle recentralized the country and repaired the damage done by the wars of the 1300s. Once again, the population grew, and the economy recovered. To restore imperial legitamacy, Yongle transformed Beijing into a magnificent capital by building the **Forbidden City**, which served for centuries as the imperial residence and seat of government—and still stands at the heart of Beijing.

Abroad, the early Ming rulers expanded China's borders. Like earlier dynasties, they maintained a tributary system. They forged alliances with kingdoms in Vietnam (Annam and Champa) and Korea (the Yi). When the Mongol warlord Timur, who defeated the Delhi Sultanate (see Chapter 11), attacked China, the Ming drove him away.

Not only was Ming China's army large and effective, its navy was for a time a potent instrument of diplomacy and intimidation. From 1405 to 1433, the admiral and explorer **Zheng He** (Chang Ho) made seven long voyages to Southeast Asia, India, the Middle East, and East Africa. He expanded Chinese trade, gained much knowledge about the outside world, and forced fifty states and cities to pay tribute. After Yongle's death, however, the Ming rulers—distracted by the land-based threat of nomads to the north—lost interest in exploration and naval expansion. This can be seen as a global turning point: had the Ming continued to exploit their power at sea, China might have started a wave of worldwide exploration and colonization, as the nations of Europe were on the verge of doing.

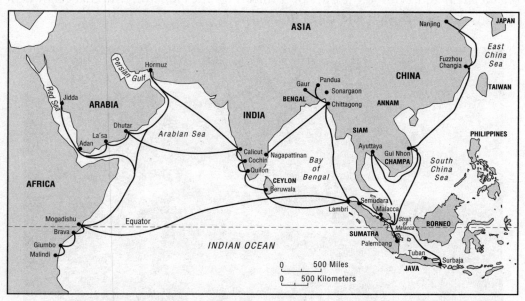

The Voyages of Zheng He, 1405–1433.
China's greatest mariner, Zheng He, sailed several times from China to Arabia and East Africa. He explored, established diplomatic relations, and exacted monetary tribute from weaker states.

Ming Art and Culture

Culturally, the Ming years remain famous as a time of artistic grandeur and intellectual dynamism. Chinese art, religion, and literature continued to exert an influence on countries such as Korea, Vietnam, and Japan (although China's cultural sway over Japan had lessened since the eleventh century).

Confucianism was restored to its place of prominence, rejoining Buddhism as a guiding force in Chinese philosophy and religion. Great works of classical Chinese literature appeared, including a new form of writing, the novel (one example is *The Golden Lotus*, a story about a wicked landowner). Ming artisans produced some of the most exquisite glassware, ceramics, and, especially, **porcelain** that the world has ever seen (it is no accident that the word *china* is synonymous with fine dishware). Another major art form was scroll painting, which depicted landscapes and other scenes on long, vertical rolls of silk and paper.

HEIAN JAPAN

In the 600s C.E., the Japanese imperial family, the Yamato, still ruled from the city of Nara. By the late 700s, however, the emperors wished to escape the political influence of Nara's Buddhist priesthood and shifted their capital to Heian (present-day Kyoto). The classical **Heian period** (794–1185) is a golden age in premodern Japanese history.

The Heian era gave rise to an unusual and complex form of government: the emperor—considered to be the descendant of Japan's Shinto gods, and therefore sacred—lost political power but remained important as a symbolic figurehead. Real power rested with whatever noble family gained the position of chancellor (*kwampaku*) and, with it, the duty of "protecting" the emperor. The chancellor kept the emperor in seclusion and ruled in his name.

Heian Jingu Shrine, Kyoto, Japan.
Kyoto, the old capital of Japan, still contains many of the architectural masterpieces from the Heian era (794–1185), when the city was known by that name. Heian was a major center of Buddhist worship and scholarship, and hundreds of shrines (like the one above) and temples were built there.

From 858 onward, the ruling family in Heian Japan was the **Fujiwara clan**, which gained permanent custody over the chancellorship and imperial family. During the 1000s and early 1100s, the Fujiwara presided over a peaceful, prosperous, and culturally brilliant nation. Japanese painting reached a high level of skill, and one of the classics of world literature, **Lady Murasaki's** *The Tale of Genji*, an epic about love and Japanese court life, dates to this period. Many of Japan's classical prose writers were women. Men considered poetry to be a more elevated art form.

Early in the Heian period, Japanese culture was influenced in many ways by China. Japanese religious life was shaped by the importation of Buddhism and, to a lesser extent, Confucianism and Daoism, all of which coexisted with Japan's native faith, Shinto. China's system of ideograms influenced the Japanese alphabet, and the poetry, painting, and architecture of Tang China had a great impact on Japanese style. After about 1000, the Japanese began to develop a more independent cultural tradition.

Unfortunately for the Fujiwara, their pursuit of cultural refinement and preoccupation with court life led them to neglect military affairs. For decades, the Fujiwara delegated military responsibilities to various warrior clans (from whom the samurai class would emerge). By the 1100s, these clans were quarreling among themselves and, at the same time, with the Fujiwara.

The Heian regime was destroyed by the **Taira-Minamoto war** (1156–1185), fought by two warrior clans who supported rival claimants to the emperor's throne. The Fujiwara were driven from power by 1160. The Taira gained the upper hand at first, but were eventually defeated by the Minamoto, who created a new government known as the shogunate. The conflict marked Japan's transition from classical age to medieval period (as the fall of Rome did for Europe). It also inspired one of Japan's epic works of literature, *Tales of the Heike*.

FEUDAL JAPAN AND THE FIRST SHOGUNATES

Upon defeating the Taira, the Minamoto moved the capital to Kamakura, far from Heian, and established a decentralized military government. As before, the emperor was a symbolically important figurehead, but real power belonged to the **shogun** ("great general").

Two shogunates governed Japan before the country's breakup in the 1500s: the Kamakura (1185–1333) and the Ashikaga (1336–1573), which, after a short civil war, moved the capital back to Kyoto (formerly Heian). The shogunates were feudal systems, in which the shogun shared power with landowning warlords called **daimyo**. Like the knightly aristocracy of medieval Europe, the shogun and daimyo came from a warrior class known as the **samurai** ("one who serves"). To belong to the samurai class was a great privilege.. Just as European knights (in theory) lived by the ideals of chivalry, the samurai followed a strict code of loyalty, honor, and bravery called **Bushido** ("way of the warrior"). Bushido was even more stringent and hierarchical than European chivalry; the most extreme penalty for violating it was ritual suicide (seppuku, or hara-kiri).

The change in government affected the status of upper-class women in Japan. The Heian court had placed great emphasis on cultural brilliance and elaborate manners, and women had a certain social and political influence. The rougher warrior ethic of the shogunates allowed women fewer opportunities. Unlike European chivalry, the code of Bushido did little to encourage respectful treatment of women.

During the 1200s and early 1300s, the Kamakura shoguns kept order in Japan. They even repelled Kublai Khan's two attempts to invade from China (1279 and 1281). The Ashikaga shoguns were politically weaker and allowed greater decentralization. Starting in the mid-1400s, a series of civil wars began tearing Japan apart; by the 1500s, the country was almost completely disunified, with most daimyo ruling their lands independently. Only in the very late 1500s and early 1600s would Japan be reunified.

Under the Ashikaga, trade and commerce flourished in Japan, and an important merchant class emerged. As in China, urbanization proceeded rapidly. New forms of Buddhism arrived, especially **Zen** (**Chan**), which proved popular among the samurai class. Pure Land (Jo Do) Buddhism, which promised a heavenly afterlife, gained a large following among the lower classes. The philosophical simplicity of Zen affected several important cultural practices, such as the *cha-no-yu* tea ceremony, landscaping (rock gardens and bonsai trees), and haiku poetry.

KOREA AND VIETNAM

Like Japan, Korea and Vietnam fell under the cultural and religious (and, at times, political) influence of China. As in China, agricultural production in Korea and Vietnam mainly involved rice cultivation. As with Japan, Korea's and Vietnam's art, literature, and architecture were shaped by China. The writing systems of all three countries—*hiragana* and *kanji* in Japan, *hangul* in Korea, and *chu nom* in Vietnam—were based at least somewhat on Chinese ideograms. From China came Confucianism and various forms of Buddhism.

Korean kingdoms, among them the Gojoseon (Old Choson), formed as early as the 2000s B.C.E. By the 500s C.E., they had developed a long, tangled relationship with China. Silla, for example, the first kingdom to unite the entire peninsula, was a close ally of Tang China and collapsed when the Tang fell. Koryo, the next state, had ties with the Song, then was invaded by the Mongols. It won its freedom by the mid-1300s but collapsed soon after. The kingdom of Joseon, known more commonly in the West as Yi (1392–1910), enjoyed close ties with Ming China. Many scholars speculate that **block printing** was invented in the Koryo state and then passed on to the Chinese. It was also through Korea that much of China's influence on Japanese culture was transmitted.

The Vietnamese had contact with the Chinese as early as the 200s B.C.E. Close ties formed between Tang China and the Vietnamese states of Annam and Champa. At various points after 1000, Annam and Champa were under Chinese rule, paid tribute to China, or allied with China.

The widespread practice of **rice-paddy farming**, or growing rice by means of wet cultivation, originated in Southeast Asia—most likely in Vietnam—around 500 B.C.E. Before this, rice had been grown dry. Wet cultivation led to increased crop yields and spread to other parts of Asia, including China and Japan. In this way, the Vietnamese kingdoms had a profound agricultural and environmental impact on a vast portion of Asia.

South and Southeast Asia

CHAPTER 9

- The Delhi Sultanate
- The importation of Islam to India
- The Indian Ocean trade network (Calicut, Malacca)
- Burma, Thailand, and Annam
- The Khmer Empire and Angkor Wat
- Hinduism, Buddhism, and Islam in Southeast Asia
- Borobudur
- The Polynesian migration

outh and Southeast Asia are regions of remarkable ethnic and cultural diversity. India and the lands that surround it are environmentally and geographically diverse as well. India measures 2,000 miles east to west and 2,000 miles north to south. In the north are mountains and forest. The center is cut by the Ganges and Indus river basins. The southern third is more tropical. The entire climate of the Indian Ocean region is affected twice per year by huge seasonal rainstorms called **monsoons** (which occur in June–July and December–January). Most of Southeast Asia is tropical in climate.

Until the modern era, Southeast and South Asia were often politically fragmented. India in particular was seldom unified as a single state. In other parts of South Asia, kingdoms and states tended to rise and fall rapidly. Culture, tradition, language, and religion served more than politics as unifying factors.

> **NOTE**
>
> By itself, the Indian subcontinent is home to people of several races, dozens of different languages, and many minor and major religions.

INDIA AND THE DELHI SULTANATE

Between 600 C.E. and 1200 C.E., India was disunified. The Gupta Empire, the last state to provide any sort of unity, collapsed in 550 C.E.

The next group to unite a large part of India were Muslim invaders, who reached the northwest frontier (the Indus valley and Afghanistan) in the 700s and converted it to Islam. By the 900s, Muslims were escalating their attacks on the Indian border.

In 1022, Muslim armies, led by Afghan warlords, began the conquest of northern India, a process that continued for the next two hundred years. In 1206, the Muslims captured the city of Delhi, and most of northern India fell into their hands. Muslim generals established the **Delhi Sultanate** (1206–1520s).

The major impact of the Muslim invasions and the sultanate's establishment was to introduce Islam into India. Islam did not displace earlier faiths like Hinduism and Buddhism, but joined them as one of the country's major religions. (One interesting development is that, in India, Muslim women tended to enjoy more property rights than Hindu women, especially those of

> **NOTE**
>
> Technically, the Delhi Sultanate was part of the Abbasid Caliphate (see Chapter 7), but only until the caliphate's destruction in 1258.

low caste; it was also possible for Muslim women in India to divorce and to remarry after their husbands died.)

There were religious conflicts under the Delhi Sultanate. At first, the sultans imposed their new faith harshly. They became less severe over time, but Hindu and Muslim populations did not tend to mix, and tensions—sometimes outright violence and persecution—characterized the relationship. Islam's influence was greatest in the north and along the west coast.

Politically, the Delhi Sultanate grew from the mid-1200s to the mid-1300s, by which point it controlled most of India. Afterward, the sultanate shrank. Many regions in the south broke away. In 1398, the Central Asian warlord **Timur** (see Chapter 10) attacked and captured Delhi itself. When he departed, after a year of plundering, the city was in ruins. The Delhi Sultanate survived, but barely. It grew steadily smaller, then, in the 1520s, succumbed to new invaders from the north.

OTHER INDIAN STATES

Although India's ethnic complexity makes it hard to generalize, for many years, the northern parts of the country were populated by Indo-Europeans (largely descended from the Aryans who invaded ca. 1500 B.C.E.). The south was inhabited by darker-skinned peoples of Dravidian origin.

Independent Southern States

Various states and kingdoms emerged in the south of India, independent of the larger governments in the north. Among them were the Tamil kingdoms on the Indian Ocean coast: they formed around the 100s B.C.E. and survived for 2,000 years.

In the 1300s, even more states emerged in the south, most of them breakaways from the Delhi Sultanate. Bengal became an independent Muslim state in 1338. Gujarat, a Muslim state on the western coast, declared independence from the sultanate in 1390 and flourished as a trading center in the Indian Ocean network. The Vijayanagara Empire (1336–1565) and the Malibar city-states formed Hindu enclaves on the Indian coast. The former controlled many southern ports and the island of Sri Lanka. The latter ruled much of the southwestern coast. The most important of the Malibar cities was **Calicut**.

Indian Ocean Trade

One of the world's most vibrant commercial economies centered on the **Indian Ocean trade network**, which joined East Africa, Arabia, the Persian Gulf, India, the Malay peninsula, Indonesia, China, and Japan. From west to east, this exchange network covered an expanse greater than 6,000 miles.

In the west, a zone controlled largely by Arab traders, goods came from Africa and the Middle East. Africa provided ivory, animal hides, timber, gold, and slaves. From the Middle East came textiles, carpets, glass, and Arabian horses. The middle zone was dominated by Indian cities and kingdoms. India offered precious gems, elephants, salt, and cotton cloth. From Sri Lanka (Ceylon) came cinnamon. Other spices, as well as exotic woods, came from Indonesia. In the east, China traded silk, porcelain, and paper. Japan was a major source of silver.

Major ports in the Indian Ocean network included Sofala, **Mombasa**, and Mogadishu in East Africa; Jidda, Mecca, and Ormuz in Arabia and Persia; the great Malibar metropolis of **Calicut** in western India; and **Canton** (**Guangzhou**) and Hangzhou in China. By means of the Red Sea and Suez isthmus, the Indian Ocean trade network connected to the Mediterranean and the trade networks flourishing there.

SOUTHEAST ASIA

Geographically, Southeast Asia consists of three zones: the mainland; the Malay Peninsula; and the island chains of the Indian Ocean and South China Sea. The climate is tropical, and much of the terrain is mountainous or blanketed by rain forest.

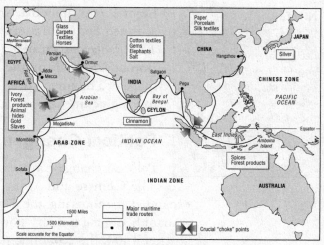

The Indian Ocean Trade Network Before 1500 C.E.
The arrival of Portuguese traders just before 1500, then the massive influx of other Europeans, changed the economic patterns of this region forever.

Between 3000 B.C.E. and 2000 B.C.E., Malays and other peoples arrived, from China, India, and elsewhere. Local inhabitants practiced agriculture by around 2000 B.C.E. The early peoples of Southeast Asia were also skilled bronze workers and navigators (the island peoples traveled great distances in sophisticated outrigger canoes).

Southeast Asian States

Major states emerged in Southeast Asia before and around 500 C.E. These included Burma, the Thai kingdom, and the Vietnamese states of Champa and Annam (see Chapter 8). Most of these states were culturally and economically influenced by China, India, or both. They traded spices (cinnamon, nutmeg, cloves, and pepper), especially for silk from China, and took part in the vast Indian Ocean and Pacific trade networks.

> **NOTE**
>
> Thanks to contact with India and China, most Southeast Asian states adopted Hinduism, Buddhism, and sometimes both. Before 1000 C.E., Islam also appeared in Southeast Asia.

The Khmer and Srivijayan Empires

For years, the two most developed states in Southeast Asia were the Khmer Empire (500s–1454 C.E.) in Cambodia and the Srivijayan Empire (500s–1100s C.E.) of Sumatra.

The **Khmer** civilization emerged in Cambodia and Laos by the 500s C.E. and reached its peak during the Angkor period (889–1454). The Angkor rulers were militarily aggressive, expanding the Khmer state into parts of Burma and the Malay Peninsula. Culturally and religiously, the Khmer were influenced primarily by India. They adopted both Hinduism and Buddhism, building more than 21,000 temples. The Khmer state collapsed in the 1400s, when Cambodia was conquered by neighboring Thailand.

> **NOTE**
>
> The city complex of **Angkor Wat**, with its ornate palaces and pagodas, covers forty square miles.

In the Indonesian islands to the south, the **Srivijayan Empire** took shape. From the island of Sumatra, the Srivijayans expanded, gaining control of the maritime trade routes between Indonesia and the Malay Peninsula by the 600s. They then took over parts of the Malay Peninsula, as well as the Indonesian island of Java. Like the Khmer

NOTE

The Srivijayan Empire declined in the 1000s and 1100s, weakened by outside enemies, then displaced by a new empire. In the 1200s, Islam arrived in the Indonesian islands. It remains a dominant faith there to this day.

Empire in Cambodia, the Srivijayan Empire was influenced by India and accepted both Hinduism and Buddhism (although Buddhism was dominant). The Srivijayans' greatest architectural legacy is the Buddhist temple complex of **Borobudur**, built on the island of Java from 770 to 825. Borobudur is in the shape of a mountain over 100 feet high; every level represents a stage on the path to enlightenment.

Political Changes, 1200s–1400s

Political change came to Southeast Asia from the 1200s through the 1400s. The Chinese and Mongols made repeated attacks from the north. Thailand expanded, conquering the Khmer state in Cambodia. The Vietnamese state of Annam became a military power after the early 1400s, as did Burma in the 1500s.

After 1400, the economic powerhouse of Southeast Asia was the city of **Malacca** (**Melaka**), located on the narrow waterway separating the Malay Peninsula from Sumatra. It connected the Indian Ocean with the South China Sea and was a crucial nexus in the Indian Ocean trade network. Founded in 1400, Malacca was controlled by China, then the Thais. It enjoyed a brief period of freedom before being conquered by European colonists—the Portuguese—in 1511.

THE POLYNESIAN MIGRATIONS

NOTE

In a process lasting over 3,000 years, the Polynesians spread eastward across a 20,000-mile expanse, settling thousands of islands. The region known as Oceania is populated mainly by their descendants.

One of history's most epic journeys was the **Polynesian migration** across the Pacific from approximately 2500 B.C.E. to 900 C.E. Originally from Southeast Asia, the Polynesians left their homes in the Philippine and Indonesian islands around 4,500 years ago.

Early Polynesian Culture

The original Polynesians were root farmers, growing taro and sweet potatoes and supplementing their diet with pigs, chickens, and fish. Their social organization was hierarchical. Tribes were led by powerful chiefs. Polynesian religion was animistic and concerned with avoiding improper behavior, or **taboo** (*tabu* or *kapu* in Polynesia).

Because so much of their life was based on the sea, the Polynesians were expert sailors and navigators. Their **outrigger canoes**, which could sail more than 120 miles per day, allowed them to travel vast distances over open water. Not only could the Polynesians navigate by the sun, moon, and stars, they possessed an intimate knowledge of tides, currents, and wave patterns (creating maps woven from twigs and grasses to represent the ocean's rhythms).

The Migrations

Why the Polynesians began their long migrations is unknown; most scholars speculate that ecological crisis drove them from their homes. Certainly environmental necessity kept them going once they started. When the Polynesians settled an island, the population would grow to such a point that part of the tribe (sometimes all of it) would have to move onward to keep from depleting all the resources.

The first wave of migration took the Polynesians to the island chain of Micronesia, east of the Philippines. Then, around 2000 to 1300 B.C.E., some Polynesians moved to Melanesia, east of New Guinea and Australia and including Fiji.

Another major migration took the Polynesians to the oceanic expanse that now bears the name Polynesia. Polynesia is bounded by an imaginary triangle, with Hawaii at the north, New Zealand to the southwest, and Easter Island to the southeast. By 300 to 400 C.E., Polynesians had settled **Easter Island**, building their famous statues of human heads. By the 1500s, environmental stress and tribal war destroyed the Easter Island civilization. More successful was Polynesian settlement of New Zealand, where the **Maori** culture, established around 800 C.E., survived and prospered. A warrior society, the Maori became the largest single Polynesian subculture by the 1700s.

The Mongol Empires

CHAPTER 10

- Genghis Khan
- The Mongol Empire and the Pax Mongolica
- The Silk Road (Samarkand)
- The breakup of the Mongol Empire
- Kublai Khan
- Timur

During the 1200s, almost all of Eurasia was swept by a whirlwind from Central Asia: the Mongols. United for the first time in their history by Genghis Khan, the Mongols burst out of their homeland in the 1210s, beginning one of the most successful military campaigns of all time. At its peak, the Mongol Empire was the largest conquest state that has ever existed, stretching across most of Asia, parts of the Middle East, and Europe.

By the late 1200s and early 1300s, the Mongol state broke apart into smaller units. The nomadic Mongols were adept at warfare but less so at nation building. This makes for an interesting contrast between their empire and states like Rome and Han China.

Nonetheless, the Mongols had a tremendous impact on Europe and Asia during the 1200s and 1300s. They destroyed and created nations. They shaped the social and political development of many civilizations. Also, for a time, the Mongol states provided a degree of unity—or at least connectedness—to a huge part of the Eurasian landmass. It is increasingly common for historians to speak of the thirteenth century as a period of **Pax Mongolica** (or Pax Tatarica): the "Mongol (or Tatar) Peace." Although the notion of peacefulness may be exaggerated, there is no denying that the Mongols temporarily tamed the vast spaces of Eurasia, affecting many of its great civilizations.

GENGHIS KHAN AND THE RISE OF THE MONGOLS

The Mongols (also Tartars or Tatars) were a group of nomadic tribes from the steppes, or open plains, of Central Asia. They herded livestock. They were excellent horsemen and archers.

The Mongols are frequently perceived as barbaric, even bloodthirsty. This is a stereotype. While they did not have a sophisticated society before their great wave of expansion, they proved adept at **cultural borrowing**. From their neighbors and the people they conquered, the Mongols adoped a law code, a written script, new religious practices, and better technology.

Before 1200, the Mongols, who numbered between 1.5 and 3 million, were divided into more than thirty disunited, often warring tribes. In 1206, the Mongols were united by the warlord Temujin, better known as **Genghis Khan** (also Chingiz, Jenghiz, or Chinggis), which means "ruler of limitless strength." Genghis Khan reorganized the Mongol armies and, shortly after seizing power, led them on their great campaign of conquest.

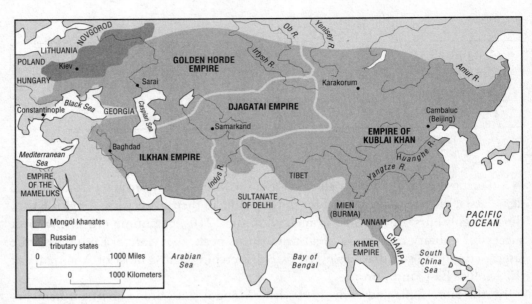

The Mongol Empires, 1294 C.E.
By 1294, the Mongols, a nomadic people, had conquered most of Asia and key portions of Europe and the Middle East. Mongol control over these territories had a major and lasting effect on many parts of Eurasia.

THE FIRST WAVE OF CONQUEST

Mongol conquests began in 1211. The first target was northern China; by 1215, the Mongols had breached the Great Wall and seized the city of Beijing. The Mongols also moved against Central Asia, capturing the great Silk Road trading center of Samarkand. By Genghis Khan's death in 1227, the Mongols controlled a large state encompassing present-day Mongolia, much of Central Asia, and northern and western China. His heirs would enlarge the empire even further.

What accounted for the Mongols' success? It used to be thought—incorrectly—that the main reason was great numbers. The early Mongol armies were large (about 80,000 to 100,000 troops) but not so large that they could have easily overwhelmed such a large territory. Mongol warriors were talented cavalrymen and archers, and they could fire from horseback, galloping at full speed, forward or backward. The Mongols (and their horses) were possessed of great endurance and hardiness. They organized their armies efficiently into tightly knit military units based on groups of ten. The Mongols were also quick to adopt advanced military technology and techniques from their more advanced neighbors. This was especially the case with siege warfare, which the Mongols learned from the Chinese and Central Asian states.

THE SECOND WAVE OF CONQUEST AND THE PAX MONGOLICA

Genghis Khan's heirs continued the wars of conquest. Genghis's third son, Ögödei, ruled the Mongols as Great Khan till 1241. He greatly expanded the empire and built a new capital, Karakorum, for it.

In the east, Ögödei's armies moved farther into China, threatening the Song Empire (which the Mongols defeated in the 1260s). Ögödei also forced Koryo, or Korea, into tributary status.

Ögödei had even more ambitious goals in the west. In 1236, he sent a large invasion force to seize as much of Europe as possible. From 1237 to 1240, the Mongols conquered most of Russia and Ukraine. From 1240 to 1242, they took over parts of Bulgaria, Romania, and Hungary. When they tried to push into Poland and Germany, however, they overextended themselves. Also, Ögödei died in 1241, and succession struggles ended the invasion effort. Russian and Ukraine remained under Mongol rule as tributary states for two centuries.

Commanded by Hulegu, Mongol forces invaded the Middle East in the 1250s, toppling the Abbasid Caliphate in 1258 and advancing until 1260, when they were stopped by a Mamluk army at Ain Jalut.

At their zenith, the Mongols ruled an empire that stretched from Poland in the west to Korea in the east, and from Siberia in the north to Vietnam in the south. Over this massive expanse, the Mongols imposed a single political authority, encouraged economic exchange, made travel conditions safer, and imposed legal order. **Silk Road** trade, which had fallen off, now revived and flourished, and cities like **Samarkand** became crucial economic centers, with merchants, missionaries, and travelers of all professions and ethnicities passing through. Among these was the Venetian merchant and explorer Marco Polo.

Many historians refer to this brief semi-unification of Eurasia as the Pax Mongolica, or "Mongol Peace." It was maintained not just by force but by a surprisingly high level of administrative skill. Helped by their habit of cultural adaptation, the Mongols borrowed a written language (Uighur, a Turkic dialect); their law code (the *yasa*, from China); paper currency (from China); and new religious beliefs (Buddhism and Islam). The Mongols used their own skill with horses to create one of the premodern world's fastest and most efficient postal systems (the *yam*).

BREAKUP OF THE MONGOL EMPIRE

A Chinese proverb is often quoted to describe the Mongol Empire: "One can conquer an empire on horseback, but one cannot govern it from there." Even recognizing their underappreciated political strengths, it must be said that the Mongols were better at conquest than they were at governing. Soon after its size and power peaked, the Mongol Empire, spread too thin, began to break apart.

In 1260, the last khan to rule over a united Mongol empire (Mongke) died. Civil war broke out, and the empire's four largest units became independent states. The homeland, which went to **Kublai Khan**, included Mongolia, China, and territories to the east and southeast. The Golden Horde ruled over Russia and parts of eastern

Europe until the mid-1400s. The Il-Khan Mongols converted to Islam and ruled much of the Middle East until the rise of the Ottoman Turks in the late 1300s. A Mongol state, the Jagadai Khanate, governed Central Asia well into the 1400s. Like the Il-Khans (with whom they often struggled), the Jagadai became Muslims.

A later Mongol warlord was the Jagadai khan **Timur** (also known as Tamerlane). From 1370 to 1405, Timur rose up and attempted to repeat the military triumph of Genghis Khan. Quickly, he conquered Central Asia, Persia, northern India (including Delhi), southern Russia, and parts of the Middle East. The expansion ended with Timur's death, but his descendants ruled over Central Asia—and the Silk Road cities of Samarkand and Bukhara—until the 1500s.

Sub-Saharan Africa

CHAPTER 11

> - The Sahara Desert and Africa's sub-Saharan regions
> - The Bantu
> - Matrilinear societies
> - The Arab slave trade
> - Trans-Saharan caravan routes
> - Ghana and the gold trade
> - Great Zimbabwe
> - The Indian Ocean trade network (Mombasa and Zanzibar)
> - Swahili as a lingua franca

Not just physically, but culturally and politically, Africa is divided by the Sahara Desert. As described in Chapter 7, most of Saharan Africa and the northern continent fell into the orbit of the Islamic world. The story of sub-Saharan Africa is more complex.

A geographical note: The AP World History course subdivides Africa into the following regions: North Africa (covered in Chapters 7, 15, and 23), West Africa, East Africa, Central Africa, and Southern Africa. The latter four are dealt with in Chapters 11, 18, and 26.

INTRODUCTION TO SUB-SAHARAN AFRICA

Factors Restricting the Growth of Major Sub-Saharan States

In sub-Saharan Africa, the development of strong, sizable political units occurred later and more slowly than in other parts of the world. Much of this had to do with the tremendous ethnolinguistic variety there, where more than 2,000 languages and dialects are spoken.

One of the few common threads shared by many—but not all—peoples of sub-Saharan Africa is descent from the **Bantu** tribes. Around 1000 B.C.E., the Bantu began to move out of their homeland in west central Africa. Their descendants settled in almost all parts of the continent south of the Sahara. With the passage of time, each smaller group developed its own distinct language and cultural tradition.

Environmental factors also limited the growth of major states. The fluctuating climate of sub-Saharan Africa and human susceptibility to insect- and animal-borne diseases (especially malaria and sleeping sickness) in sub-Saharan regions were obstacles to population growth.

Basic Features of Sub-Saharan Societies

Most sub-Saharan communities were small. Social life revolved around the village. Food was provided by means of a combination of hunting, herding, and limited agriculture. It appears that most African societies gained the skill of **metalworking** on their own, rather than having it taught to them by outsiders, as was commonly thought until recently.

As in most early civilizations, women in sub-Saharan Africa tended to be subservient to men. Women were often valued, though, for their labor as fieldworkers (while men tended cattle) and for producing heirs. Women also were respected for storytelling abilities and their role in educating young people about moral values and religious beliefs. Interestingly, in Africa, lineage was sometimes **matrilinear**, rather than patrilinear. Women often inherited property, and the husband was required to move into his wife's house. Rules of behavior between the sexes tended to be more informal than in the Middle East, China, or India.

Art and Culture

African tribes possessed a high degree of skill in carving and sculpture, especially in wood and ivory. Metal sculpture became more common over time. By the thirteenth and fourteenth centuries, West African artists were creating masterpieces out of bronze and iron. In Ife, in present-day Nigeria, metalworkers formed bronze and iron statues by first designing molds with melted wax. These sculptures may have influenced the work of metalworkers from the West African state of Benin. Such artists are famous for their sophisticated and detailed bronze, brass, and copper sculptures of heads, ornaments, animal figures, and reliefs depicting court life.

Architecture in Africa varied across regions owing to diverse cultural influences. In sub-Saharan Africa, Great Zimbabwe stood out for its impressive stone buildings and walls. The stones were carefully cut, then set in place without mortar. In Mali, fourteenth-century builders used timber as skeletons in reinforcing mud mosques that still stand today. The architecture of Zanzibar is distinguished by the use of coral to decorate buildings.

African literature of this period was preserved by **oral tradition**. Professional storytellers chronicled history and social custom. They also acted as entertainers and served as advisers to kings. The most famous epic of sub-Saharan Africa from these years is *Son-Jara* (or *Sundiata*), from Mali (see Chapter 7).

Most native African religions were animistic based on the worship of the spirits of animals and ancestors.

Islam and Contacts with North Africa

As time passed, the increased interaction between North Africa and sub-Saharan Africa included trade. Unfortunately, it also included slavery: for hundreds of years, **Arab slavers** penetrated to the south, forcing Africans into bondage. By the eleventh century, some traders in the Sahara owned more than a thousand slaves apiece.

Islam became part of sub-Saharan life, sometimes by force (as in Ghana), sometimes peacefully (as in Mali). Mali's great city of Timbuktu was an important center of Islamic scholarship. Muslims brought religion and trade to the cities of the eastern coast and previously isolated parts of southern Africa. Still, in comparison to North Africa, which became almost completely Muslim, sub-Saharan Africa was less heavily influenced by Islam.

WEST AND CENTRAL AFRICA

Ghana

In West Africa, the state of **Ghana**, founded in the 500s C.E., continued to be strong and prosperous. When Europe began minting coins during the 1200s, Ghana's gold gained in value, and it became a major supplier of gold to the world economy. Koumbi Saleh, one of Ghana's capitals, hosted a prosperous Muslim community of merchants linked to the **trans-Saharan trade route**. Ironically, iron and copper were more useful, and thus more valuable, to Africans than gold was. So caravans carried iron and copper across the Sahara as well.

Over time, Ghana's ecological and demographic conditions weakened its society. As its population grew, food production failed to meet demand in what was by then an extremely arid environment. All of this left Ghana vulnerable to Muslim conquest, the immediate cause of its downfall in 1076.

Central African States and Great Zimbabwe

In Central Africa, a few large city-states became home to advanced civilizations. Among them were Kongo and Benin.

From the 1250s to the 1450s, the most powerful of these states was the one that emerged around the cities of Mutapa and Great Zimbabwe. Politically linked, the two cities controlled seven hundred miles of the Zambezi river basin.

The larger and more important city was **Great Zimbabwe** (ca. 1000–1400). Its name means "sacred graves of the chiefs," and it was crucial as a political and religious center. It was a great walled city, encircling 193 acres and home to approximately 20,000 people.

Great Zimbabwe was immensely wealthy, thanks to large deposits of gold and diamonds. Gold was shipped east to Sofala, where it became part of the East African–Indian Ocean coastal trade complex (see Chapter 9). Archaeologists have found in the ruins of the city gold, jewelry, copper ornaments, birds carved out of soapstone, iron tools, Chinese ceramics, and Persian artworks. Such an assortment shows how extensive trade was in the area at the time.

Rumors of Great Zimbabwe's wealth—and of lost treasures and hidden mines—persisted for hundreds of years, long after the city itself collapsed in the mid-to-late 1400s.

THE EASTERN COAST

East Africa and the Indian Ocean Trade Network

As part of the large **Indian Ocean trade network**, the East African coast was open to a remarkable variety of cultural and economic influences. East Africa gained its wealth from a diverse selection of desirable goods like ivory. Slaves were part of the economy as well. Through trade, African societies had an impact on the outside world. As early as the Roman era, East Africa had commercial ties with India and the Mediterranean. By the tenth and eleventh centuries, African-made goods were reaching China by way of the Indian Ocean trade network. Chinese maritime trade expanded during the early Ming dynasty (see Chapter 8), and many Chinese vessels made their way to the East African coast.

The Diversity of East African City-States

City-states flourished on the East African shore between 1000 and 1500. Nearly forty urban centers were sprinkled along the 1,500-mile stretch of coast running from Mogadishu (in today's Somalia) to the south. They were all multiethnic. Beginning in the 1100s, Persians and Arabs migrated to Mogadishu and pressed southward, mixing with the local Africans. The East African city-states were politically independent. Many were ruled by Arab sheiks, who led rich mercantile families. Key cities included **Mombasa**, Sofala, and **Zanzibar**.

East African cities were also diverse in terms of their populations, which included native Africans; Arabs, Turks, and other Middle Easterners; and Indians and others from South and Southeast Asia. A tremendous amount of ethnic, religious, cultural, and linguistic mixing occurred along the East African coast. Muslims moved in large numbers to the area, starting in the mid-to-late 600s. Islam became important but did not displace local religions. The region's most widespread language was **Swahili**, which became the lingua franca, or common tongue, for much of the entire coast. East Africa was a vibrant area with a booming economy from approximately 1200 to 1500. Even Indonesians, in search of better economic opportunities, crossed the Indian Ocean to settle on Madagascar, an island off the southeast coast of Africa.

By the early 1500s, the arrival of European colonists and explorers would change everything, not just for East Africa but the entire Indian Ocean basin.

> **TRANSNATIONAL LANGUAGES**
>
> Throughout history, certain languages have risen up to allow communication between cultures whose native tongues are very different. The term *lingua franca* is often used to describe them. Examples include Latin; Arabic; Swahili; the sign language used by Native American tribes on the Great Plains; and, increasingly in our own time, English. A language achieves the status of lingua franca for various reasons. In some cases, it is the shared religious language of people who are ethnically different; in others, it is the tongue that most effectively facilitates trade in a multilingual region. Sometimes it is imposed from above by a military or imperial power (like Spanish in Latin America or English in India).

Christianity in East Africa

Christianity existed as a dominant, even official, religion in two parts of northeastern Africa. The Copts, a Christian minority, formed communities in Egypt and Sudan.

Ethiopia (also known then as Abyssinia) was not only the oldest African state but, for many centuries, a Christian kingdom. Rumors about the wealth and Christianity of the Ethiopian monarchs gave rise in Europe to the legends of Prester John: a mythical Christian king in Africa who possessed fabulous wealth. These legends were among the factors that spurred on the age of exploration.

The Americas

CHAPTER 12

- The pre-Columbian era
- The Anasazi
- Cahokia and the Mississippian civilization
- The Olmecs, the Maya, and the Aztecs
- Pyramids and human sacrifice
- Tenochtitlán and Mesoamerican urbanization
- Terrace farming and llama herding in the Andes
- The Incas and Machu Picchu

Unlike the peoples of Eurasia and Africa, who interacted with and influenced each other, the early societies of North and South America developed in isolation. Settled by the descendants of Stone Age travelers who crossed from Asia over a land bridge that joined Alaska with Siberia—then disappeared with a rise in ocean levels—North and South America remained geographically separated from other continents for thousands of years.

By about 9000 B.C.E., the entire length of the Americas, north to south, had been settled. The passage of time, geographical spread, and environmental diversity caused the social groups scattered through the Americas to develop unique cultural, social, and linguistic characteristics.

Major areas of settlement included North America's eastern woodlands, desert Southwest, and open plains; the deserts and jungles of Mexico and Central America; and the Andes Mountains of South America. Before 600 C.E., as discussed in Chapter 3, advanced civilizations emerged in all these areas. Many of these societies are unusual in that they reached an advanced state without developing systems of writing (such as the Incas and the Mississippians) or inventing the wheel.

The geographical isolation of the Americas continued until the end of the 1400s. Only with the voyages of Christopher Columbus did the societies of North and South America come into sustained contact with outsiders. (In the historiography of the Americas, the period before 1492 is referred to as the **pre-Columbian era**.) The arrival of the Europeans changed the Americas beyond recognition. In the meantime, between 1000 and 1450, several major civilizations emerged or reached their peak of development.

NORTH AMERICA

In North America, most Native Americans (known popularly by the erroneous term "Indians") were nomadic or seminomadic hunter-gatherers divided into tribes. Around 1000 C.E., the number of tribes—and the differences between them—increased dramatically and grew until about the 1500s.

The role of women in most North American tribes seems to have been defined relatively loosely. Because most of these groups were not yet fully agricultural, the gender division of labor was not as sharply formed as in the more developed empires of Central and South America. Women tended to gather berries and roots, weave, make pottery, and raise children. However, their status was not necessarily secondary to that of men, at least not formally.

Not counting what is today Mexico, two regions of North America became home to advanced societies. One was the Southwest, where settlement seems to have begun in the 300s B.C.E. Unusually for pre-Columbian North America, many Southwestern cultures were agricultural (learning the practice from more sophisticated societies in Mexico). The most famous Southwestern people were the **Anasazi**, who inhabited the region from about 400 (perhaps earlier) to 1300. They lived in complex dwellings known as pueblos—sometimes built on the open flatland, sometimes high up in the caves of canyons. The Anasazi believed that humans emerged from the earth, so they held religious ceremonies in underground chambers called kivas. This practice was passed on to tribes that later settled in the Southwest. Women in Anasazi communities may have had the right to own property.

To the north and east, sophisticated societies emerged in the Ohio and Mississippi river valleys. These groups built large **earth mounds**, presumably for religious and ceremonial purposes. The first was the Adena culture (ca. 500 B.C.E.–100 C.E.), followed by the larger Hopewell culture (ca. 100–400). After 600, the region's most advanced culture was the Mississippian civilization (ca. 700–1500). Like their predecessors, the Mississippians built great mounds. They also built cities, the largest of which was **Cahokia**, located in what is now western Illinois; by 1200, it had a population of over 30,000.

Between 1250 and 1500, the Mississippian culture was in decline (for unknown reasons, Cahokia was abandoned around 1250). At the same time, Native Americans began to organize themselves into smaller hunter-gatherer groups. These evolved into the major Native American tribes that remain familiar today. The arrival of European settlers and explorers in the late 1400s and 1500s forever changed the lives of all Native Americans.

MEXICO AND CENTRAL AMERICA

It was in Mexico and Central America (or Mesoamerica) that major civilizations in the Americas first developed. Agriculture, in the form of maize (corn) and potato cultivation, was practiced there as early as 5000 to 3000 B.C.E. The region's first dominant society was the **Olmecs** (ca. 1200 B.C.E.–400 B.C.E.), who, like the Sumerians in Mesopotamia, left behind a religious and cultural tradition that profoundly influenced later Central American peoples (see Chapter 3). The Teotihuacán culture (ca. 100 B.C.E.–750 B.C.E.), near what is now Mexico City, created one of the largest urban centers in the world at the time.

Thanks to the pattern set by the Olmecs, there was a high degree of cultural continuity among the peoples of Mesoamerica, all the way through the 1500s C.E. Most Central American societies tended to be hierarchical dictatorships ruled by kings and priests. They were not unified nations but city-states that shared a common culture, interacted economically, and also warred with each other frequently.

Women were subject to rigidly defined gender roles. A few upper-class women gained stature as priestesses or used noble status to exert informal influence. Aztec women could own property and sign contracts independently of their husbands. Still, most women were restricted to roles traditionally assigned to females.

Many of the peoples of Central America—most famously the Maya and the Aztecs—erected large **pyramids** for religious purposes. Unlike the ancient Egyptians, who used pyramids as tombs for the dead, the Maya and Aztecs built pyramids as temples and places of **human sacrifice**.

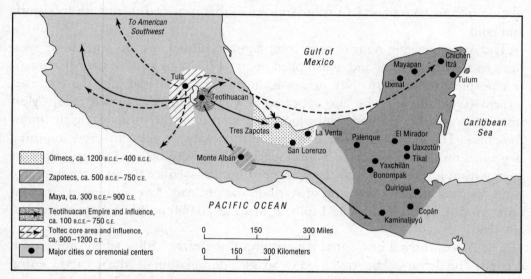

States in Pre-Columbian Central America, ca. 1200 B.C.E.**–1200** C.E.
This map demonstrates that, in Central America, many civilizations developed, rose, and fell in succession. The Olmecs set the pattern for cultural development here, followed by the Maya, Toltecs, and Aztecs.

The Maya

Around 250 C.E., a new culture, the **Maya**, emerged in present-day Guatemala, Honduras, Belize, and southern Mexico. The Mayan lands were governed by approximately forty city-states and rival kingdoms, such as Tikal, Palenque, and Uxmal. At its peak, the Mayan population reached three million.

The polytheistic religion of the Maya, which included human sacrifice and the worship of serpent gods and jaguar deities, derived partly from the Olmec tradition.

The Maya devised an elaborate hieroglyphic script, the most advanced system of writing in the pre-Columbian Americas. Superb astronomers and mathematicians, they invented an ususual but intricate and accurate calendar. They were gifted architects.

The reasons for the Mayan collapse remains a mystery. Theories include land overuse, nearby volcanic activity, disease, and inter-city warfare. Following the Maya were the Toltecs (ca. 968–1156), an aggressive warrior society that conquered central Mexico until civil war and external invasion finished off their civilization.

The Aztecs

The next major group in Central America—and the last before the arrival of the Europeans—were the Mexica, better known as the **Aztecs** (ca. 1300–1520). Their chief city was the metropolis of **Tenochtitlán**, on the site of what is today Mexico City. At the height of Aztec power, Tenochtitlán had a population of half a million, and its marketplace could hold more than 60,000 people.

The Aztecs were even more warlike than the Toltecs before them. During the 1300s, they conquered an empire of more than 125,000 square miles, ruling a population of 5 to 10 million in a tributary system that provided them with foodstuffs and gold.

The Aztecs' religion remains their most famous cultural feature. They built pyramids to serve as temples and worshipped many of the same gods as the Mesoamerican peoples before them. Key deities included the jaguar god and the feathered serpent (Quetzalcoátl, who also appeared as a light-skinned, bearded man). Most important was the sun god, Huitzilopochtli, who took the form of a giant hummingbird. The Aztecs believed that the reappearance of the sun every morning depended on their devotion to Huitzilopochtli. They also believed the sun drew its energy from human blood, so they practiced human sacrifice on an extremely large scale. Victims included prisoners of war but also ordinary Aztec citizens. Historians estimate that, by the end of the 1400s, as many as 20,000 people per year were ritually slain.

The Aztecs thrived in Central America until the early 1500s, when the Spanish arrived. The defeat of the Aztecs led to Spanish domination of Mexico and Central America until the 1800s. The Spanish conquest is described in Chapter 19.

SOUTH AMERICA

The ecological diversity of South America is staggering. Climates range from tropical to cool and arid. Terrain types include jungle, desert, mountains, grassland, and the vast Amazon river basin.

Early Andean Civilizations

The environment in which complex South American societies first developed was mountainous. It was on the west coast, in the **Andes Mountains**, that civilizations first took shape. At first glance, the rugged terrain might seem too inhospitable to encourage the growth of advanced societies. However, that very ruggedness demanded a high degree of cooperation and efficient coordination of human labor, giving rise to a number of major cultures, both before and after 600 C.E.

Most of these societies appeared in the northwest Andes, in what is today Ecuador, Bolivia, and Peru. Among the earliest was the **Chavin** (ca. 850–250 B.C.E.). Later civilizations include the Nazca (100–800 C.E.), the Moche (200–700 C.E.), the Huari (ca. 500–1000), the Tiahuanaco (ca. 500–1000), and the Chimu (ca. 800–1465).

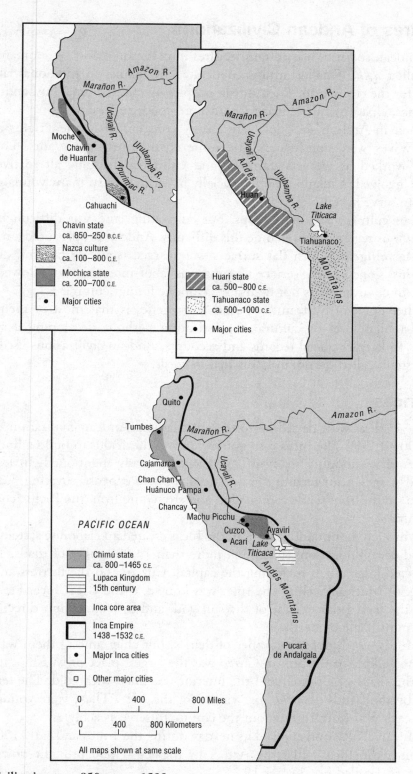

Andean Civilizations, ca. 850 B.C.E.**–1532** C.E.

The earliest major civilizations of South America emerged in the Andes Mountains, on the continent's western coast. The last and greatest was the Incan Empire.

Features of Andean Civilizations

Most Andean societies had certain features in common. Most were organized into clans called *ayllu*. Smaller groups cooperated by taking on rotational labor obligations for the entire clan. The Andean peoples practiced animal husbandry, breeding **llamas**, alpacas, and vicuñas for transport, food, and wool.

Women in Andean societies were greatly constrained in their rights and freedoms. Wives were considered little more than domestic servants. Lower-class women worked as weavers, farmers, and child rearers. One alternative was to become involved in religious life. Especially in Incan society, many young girls were chosen to serve in temples.

Andean cultures also grew crops, but cultivating land was difficult in such a mountainous region. To overcome this difficulty, Andean peoples used a method of **terrace farming**, in which flat surfaces were carved, staircase fashion, out of the mountains' sloped sides. Terrace farming was labor-intensive, but allowed farmers to work in environments not naturally favorable for agriculture.

Another noteworthy feature of Andean societies is that most of them accomplished a high level of cultural sophistication without developing a system of writing. To keep financial records and accounts, Andean civilizations used an elaborate system, called **quipo**, of knots tied in cords.

The Incas

All these features were passed on to the most famous Andean civilization, the **Incas** (ca. 1300s–1536). The Incas rose quickly during the 1300s to build a huge empire in the Andes, subduing many of the peoples already mentioned. In less than a hundred years, Incan territory grew into a massive expanse covering 3,000 miles north to south, from Chile to Ecuador, and stretching from the Pacific coast to the upper Amazon.

Even in such mountainous terrain, the Incas created an elaborate system of transport and communications, including more than 13,000 miles of roads. The Incas constructed large cities, including the capital, Cuzco, and the fortress and temple complex of **Machu Picchu**. The ruler was known as the Great Inca. He was considered the sacred descendant of the sun god, and to look at him directly was an offense punishable by death.

The Incas worshipped a number of deities, but chief among them was the sun god. The Temple of the Sun in Cuzco was the largest place of worship. It was laid out in the shape of a puma, and the interior was lined with gold. The temple was staffed by thousands of *acllas*, or "virgins of the sun." These were young women chosen each year from throughout the empire to serve as acolytes.

The Incan civilization enjoyed its heyday during the 1400s and early 1500s. After that point, the Incas—like the Aztecs in Mexico—were brought down by the Spanish, as detailed in Chapter 19.

Unit Three: Review Questions

SAMPLE ESSAY QUESTIONS (CCOT AND COMPARATIVE)

CCOT 1. Analyze the changes and continuities in the cultural and intellectual outlook of ONE of the following regions between 600 and 1450.

Europe
the Middle East
China

CCOT 2. Analyze the economic and technological changes and continuities in ONE of the following regions between 600 and 1450.

Central Asia
East Africa
South America

COMP 1. Compare and contrast the state-building experiences of TWO of the following political units.

the Mongol Empire
medieval Europe
the Abbasid Caliphate
feudal Japan 1000–1500

COMP 2. Compare and contrast how the arrival of Islam affected TWO of the following regions.

Spain
Sub-Saharan Africa
South and Southeast Asia

MULTIPLE-CHOICE QUESTIONS

1. Which of the following is true of the Japanese shogunates?

   (A) Samurai were not subject to a personal code of obedience or loyalty.
   (B) The merchant class dominated Japanese society during this time.
   (C) Land was held by powerful lords called daimyo.
   (D) The status of women improved relative to what it had been during the Heian period.
   (E) Samurai rejected Zen Buddhism because they considered it overly pacifistic.

2. The Aztecs and Chinese dynasties such as the Tang and the Ming resembled each other in that they

   (A) imposed tributary systems upon neighboring peoples.
   (B) made extensive use of gunpowder weaponry.
   (C) practiced human sacrifice on a huge scale.
   (D) purchased large numbers of forced laborers from Arab slavers.
   (E) cultivated high-yield crops such as corn and the potato.

3. What fate did Russia experience at the hands of the Mongols?

   (A) Its skilled cavalry troops drove off the Mongols' attempted invasion.
   (B) It was conquered, but only for a short time.
   (C) It allied with the Mongols and joined with them in conquering Central Asia.
   (D) It was bypassed by the Mongols in favor of richer lands in the Middle East.
   (E) It was ruled by the Mongols for more than two centuries.

4. The Hanseatic League

   (A) fought in the Middle East during the Crusades.
   (B) dominated regional commerce in the Baltic and North seas.
   (C) traded in diamonds and slaves.
   (D) was a powerful banking house in the Holy Roman Empire.
   (E) competed with Italy for trade in the Mediterranean.

5. Timbuktu was renowned for its

   (A) gold and its role in opposing the Arab slave trade.
   (B) salt reserves and Islamic scholarship.
   (C) large harbor.
   (D) glass and ceramic wares.
   (E) many Romanesque churches.

6. What did Swahili and Latin have in common during the period between 1000 and 1500?

   (A) They were banned by conquering rulers eager to impose their own languages.
   (B) They were both written in pictographic, not alphabetic, form.
   (C) They were the most widely spoken Indo-European languages of the period.
   (D) They allowed communication between diverse populations inhabiting large regions.
   (E) They both died out in favor of vernacular languages during these years.

7. What health-related crisis gravely affected China, the Middle East, and Europe during the fourteenth century?

   (A) the spread of bubonic plague
   (B) crop blights that killed wheat as well as rice
   (C) the outbreak of Spanish flu
   (D) the global cooling known as the "little ice age"
   (E) an early form of the ebola virus

8. Which of the following was NOT a consequence of the Moorish occupation of Spain?

   (A) The Moors brought advanced knowledge of medicine and science.
   (B) The Moors left behind a distinct artistic and architectural style.
   (C) The Moors persecuted Jewish scholars and professionals.
   (D) The Moors withdrew from different regions at different times, delaying political centralization.
   (E) The Moors' presence caused other European states to develop feudal defenses more effectively.

9. Which of the following characterized urban life in medieval Europe?

   (A) Urbanization did little to stimulate the revival of trade.
   (B) City governments fought poverty by creating extensive welfare systems.
   (C) Most professions were organized according to the guild system.
   (D) Cities in western Europe were larger and wealther than those in the eastern Mediterranean.
   (E) The urban poor shouldered the same labor obligations as serfs in the surrounding countryside.

10. The illustration on page 134 (without looking at the caption) most likely exemplifies

   (A) European adaption of Roman building techniques to cathedral construction.
   (B) palace-building as practiced in the Incan Empire.
   (C) regal display on the part of a West African monarch.
   (D) the diffusion of Chinese architectural forms throughout Buddhist Asia.
   (E) the impact on Indian architecture caused by the arrival of the Muslims.

11. Which of the following can most directly be attributed to the Crusades?

   (A) widespread adoption of gunpowder weaponry throughout Eurasia
   (B) European colonization of East African and Southeast Asian ports
   (C) heightened European desire to trade with or control parts of Asia
   (D) a long-term alliance between the Abbasid Caliphate and Mongol armies
   (E) the accelerated eastward spread of diseases such as cholera and smallpox

12. The early Ming emperors

   (A) were culturally brilliant but politically decadent.
   (B) surrendered control over much of their territory to European powers.
   (C) overthrew Mongol rule and reconquered much neighboring territory.
   (D) ignored naval power and the usefulness of overseas exploration.
   (E) neglected art and culture in favor of military pursuits.

13. Which of the following did the Maya and the Aztecs NOT have in common?

   (A) a cultural tradition influenced by the Olmec
   (B) a religion that practiced human sacrifice
   (C) the architectural capability of building large pyramids
   (D) the veneration of similar deities
   (E) strong, centralized rule from a single capital

14. Which of the following is true of the Abbasid Caliphate?

    (A) It presided over the golden age of Islamic culture.
    (B) It forbade Jews and Christians to practice their own religions.
    (C) It provided skilled and firm leadership against the European crusades.
    (D) It imposed sanctions on China and refused to trade with the Far East.
    (E) It established separate Muslim states in Egypt and the western Sahara.

15. Which of the following is an example of China being influenced by its neighbors, rather than the reverse?

    (A) its openness to Buddhist missionaries from Korea
    (B) its borrowing of the compass from Burma
    (C) its adoption of rice-paddy cultivation from Vietnam
    (D) its purchase of the secret of gunpowder from the Khmer Empire
    (E) its adaptation of Japanese ship design in creating the junk

16. A key similarity between women in medieval Europe and in Heian Japan is that

    (A) they could gain educations and respect for their intellectual accomplishments
    (B) patriarchal discrimination barred them from any role in religious life.
    (C) they not infrequently ascended to the throne, ruling as queens and empresses.
    (D) medical advances kept them from dying in childbirth as often as women elsewhere.
    (E) they enjoyed equality before the law, especially with respect to reproductive rights.

17. Which of the following is true about Islam in India?

    (A) Muslim women were just as restricted in their behavior as Hindu women.
    (B) After violent introduction, Islam came to coexist with Hinduism as one of the country's major faiths.
    (C) Islam's influence over India faded away after the Delhi Sultanate's collapse.
    (D) The Delhi Sultanate introduced the new religion peacefully.
    (E) Islam displaced Hinduism and Buddhism almost completely by 1400.

18. One example of the Mongols' skill at cultural adaptation is

    (A) promoting Christianity as a common religion to unite their subject peoples.
    (B) imitating the Europeans' expertise at horseback archery.
    (C) adopting Persian as a written script for their native language.
    (D) borrowing their law code from the Chinese.
    (E) learning from the Russians to build machines for siege warfare.

19. The immediate cause of Ghana's eleventh-century downfall was

    (A) environmental calamity.
    (B) the Crusades.
    (C) Muslim conquest.
    (D) takeover by the Portuguese.
    (E) the Atlantic slave trade.

20. In what way did Islamic and medieval European philosophers think alike?

(A) They understood Jesus Christ to be the son of God.

(B) They attempted to reconcile reason and religious faith.

(C) They considered astrology to be the unfolding of God's will.

(D) They saw monarchy as an illegitimate form of government.

(E) They concluded that religious belief was superior to empirical observation.

Answers

1. **(C)** Answers A and E are false; samurai followed the code of bushido, and they were drawn in great numbers to Zen Buddhism. The merchant class gained more importance over time, but was never dominant even in later years, and the cultural attainments of women, highly celebrated at the Heian court, were not valued by the shogunates.

2. **(A)** Although the Chinese invented gunpowder, their armies were slow to adopt it, and the Aztecs knew nothing of it until the Europeans' arrival. Answer D is true of neither, and C is true only of the Aztecs. Corn and potatoes were unknown outside the Americas until the voyages of Columbus. Both civilizations exacted tribute from nearby tribes and nations.

3. **(E)** The development of the Russian state under Mongol rule (the 1240s through the mid-1400s), during which the city of Moscow rose to prominence, is one of many examples of the Mongol conquests' profound long-term impact on the history of Eurasia.

4. **(B)** The Hanseatic League included cities from England, the Low Countries, the German coast, Scandinavia, and even Russia, and is an excellent example of how wide-ranging trade networks revived in Europe during the high middle ages. It operated in northern Europe.

5. **(B)** Today a synonym for "the middle of nowhere," Timbuktu in Mali was a thriving center of commerce. It was landlocked and Muslim, making C and E incorrect. Choosing among A, B, and D requires knowledge of what the city's chief commodities were, but remembering that few African states actively opposed slavery eliminates A, and remembering its fame in the sphere of religious education points to B.

6. **(D)** Latin and Swahili are lingua francas, or common languages spoken by different peoples living or trading in a large region. In Europe, Latin served for centuries as the language of the educated elite, even as vernacular languages grew in importance. Swahili (not an Indo-European tongue) facilitated trade and communication among the diverse communities of East Africa—and still does so.

7. **(A)** Answers C and E are modern diseases; the former stands out as one of the twentieth century's greatest killers. The "little ice age" came later and did not have as direct a demographic impact as bubonic plague, the correct answer, which is thought to have killed up to a third of the populations it struck in the 1300s.

8. **(C)** During the medieval period, the Muslims were more advanced than the Europeans, making A and B incorrect choices. Likewise, the Moorish threat caused states like the Frankish kingdom to adapt militarily, as at the Battle of Tours, and the Moors' gradual withdrawal did lead to regional diversity in Spain. Spain's Jews were treated far more harshly by Catholic monarchs after the Moors' expulsion than by the Moors themselves.

9. **(C)** The growth of cities had everything to do with trade, and state-sponsored welfare is generally a modern phenomenon, making A and B false. Even the poorest of city people shed serf status ("city air makes you free," as the saying went), and in all respects, western Europe lagged behind the eastern Mediter-

ranean during this period, so E and D are untrue as well.

10. **(D)** Although there are native Japanese elements, this shrine bears the imprint of China's influence. All the other answers refer to national or regional styles clearly not pictured here; as with most image-based questions, basic familiarity with such styles is the key to success.

11. **(C)** The only plausible alternative to C is B, which one could argue resulted in the long term from the exploring impulse stirred up partly by the Crusades. But C is more relevant in the short term.

12. **(C)** Answers A and D apply to the later Ming dynasty, and B describes Qing weakness during the 1800s. While the early Ming rulers were robust conquerers (and sponsored the overseas voyages of Zheng He), they never neglected cultural pursuits, making E incorrect.

13. **(E)** As Mesoamerican civilizations influenced by the Olmec legacy, the Maya and the Aztecs shared many common features. The former, however, were governed by a variety of independent city-states, while the Aztecs ruled from Tenochtitlán.

14. **(A)** Politically weak by the time the Crusades began (eliminating C), the Abbasid caliphs traded widely (making D false) and presided over cultural brilliance. Separate states on the periphery (as in E) broke away from the Abbasids and were not established by them. Jews and Christians were not forced to convert to Islam (as in B), but were taxed if they did not.

15. **(C)** The development of wet rice cultivation led to higher yields and profoundly affected huge parts of East and South Asia. China invented or discovered the junk, the compass, and gunpowder on its own. Buddhism arrived there from India.

16. **(A)** Upper-class individuals such as Hildegard von Bingen and Lady Murasaki received excellent educations and gained cultural fame. Women in both places could become nuns (though not priests). Answer C applies to Europe, but not Japan; deaths in childbirth were quite high in both. In neither case did women enjoy legal equality.

17. **(B)** The Delhi Sultanate converted large parts of India to Islam by means of violence; long after the sultans passed away, the religion remained. Muslim women were not governed by the caste system as Hindu women were.

18. **(D)** Although a few Mongols became Christians, most converted to Islam or Buddhism, and they adopted Uighur, not Persian, as their written script. They learned siege warfare from the Silk Road cities of Central Asia, and their skill at horseback warfare was their own.

19. **(C)** Long-term environmental changes weakened Ghana and left it vulnerable, but the direct cause of its downfall was Muslim invasion from the north.

20. **(B)** Although Muslims respected Christ as a prophet, they did not view him as the son of God. Astrology was widely practiced in the medieval world, but not as part of formal theology. Monarchy was seen as the norm in Europe and the Middle East, and although religion was important to both cultures' intellectual traditions, empiricism was given its due as well. The attempt to strike a balance between reason and faith preoccupied thinkers in both worlds.

UNIT FOUR

WORLD CULTURES INTERACTING (1450–1750)

Unit Overview

GENERAL REMARKS

Between 1450 and 1750, the world's civilizations became truly connected for the first time in history. The most significant trend of this era was the emergence of a fully global system of exchange and interaction. Regrettably, much of this interaction consisted of warfare, exploitation, and slavery. Nonetheless, trade, discovery, cultural interchange, and the faster and easier movement of peoples brought the world's societies into greater proximity.

One of the primary causes of this greater interaction was the massive and sustained effort of the Europeans to explore the rest of the world. Driven by scientific curiosity, the quest for power, the hope of spreading Christianity, and a desire for wealth, European explorers during the 1400s and 1500s sought out oceanic trade routes that would link them directly with China, India, Japan, and elsewhere in Asia. They also encountered the Americas: a "New World" that had, for thousands of years, lain outside the bounds of knowledge of the peoples of Eurasia and Europe.

Within decades, European traders, missionaries, and conquerors had spread throughout the world. The Europeans were the first in history to sail around the globe, and they established a presence in many parts of coastal Africa, Southeast Asia, and the Far East. Most dramatically, European colonizers conquered and transformed the Americas. The opening of the Americas to the rest of the world was done brutally and out of greed, but also played a tremendous role in shifting the world's economic, linguistic, religious, and cultural patterns. It changed forever the environments of the Americas, Africa, and Europe, as new animals, new foods, and new diseases were brought back and forth in a development known as the Columbian Exchange.

Another trend of this era was the rise of Europe. Until the 1400s, Europe had been relatively weak and backward, compared with civilizations such as China and the Ottoman Empire. During the 1500s and 1600s, however, Europe pulled even with China and the "gunpowder empires" of the Islamic east (Ottoman Turkey, Safavid Persia, and Mughal India) in terms of scientific advancement, global power, and wealth. During the 1700s, Europe overtook these other cultures, becoming the strongest, most technologically adept, and richest civilization in the world. By the middle of the 1700s, Europe was well situated to dominate the vast majority of the globe, militarily and economically—and did so in the 1800s.

Technological development and scientific knowledge increased in many parts of the world during this time. Practices that can be considered proto-industrial were appearing in such places as Europe and China. The foundations for the rapid and thorough industrialization of many societies during the late 1700s and 1800s were laid during the 1600s and early-to-mid 1700s.

In addition, agricultural techniques in most societies improved dramatically. In Europe, it is common to speak of an "agricultural revolution." Worldwide, improved agriculture helped cause a significant population increase. The rate of growth was the fastest ever seen to that date, as the world population rose from 350 million in 1400 to 610 million in 1700.

BROAD TRENDS

Global Power and International Relations

- During the first centuries of this era (the 1500s and 1600s), global might was concentrated in China and the Islamic world's "gunpowder empires" (Ottoman Turkey, Safavid Persia, and Mughal India).
- The nations of Europe, especially in the west and north, grew steadily more powerful. By the early 1700s, they were overtaking the civilizations listed previously in terms of military, scientific, and technological aptitude.
- The most dramatic development of the era was the European campaign to explore (and, where possible, colonize) the rest of the world. In particular, the European encounter with the Americas—and the incorporation of the Americas into the global economic system—transformed the world.
- European colonization of the Americas, the African coast, and parts of Southeast Asia set the stage for a massive burst of imperial activity during the 1800s. During the 1700s, European colonization led to the emergence of a truly global economic system. It also created a worldwide system of military competition among European powers for global dominance. Some of the European wars of the 1700s—especially the Seven Years' War (1756–1763), which raged not only in Europe, but also North America and India—can be considered history's first "world wars."
- The increased importance of gunpowder weaponry meant that, from this time forward, technological aptitude and military strength would be intimately connected.

Political Developments

- In many parts of the world, political organization became more centralized and sophisticated. Features of modern government, such as bureaucracies, agencies, admiralties, treasuries, general staffs, state banks, and other institutions, began to appear.
- Nation-states in the contemporary sense of the word emerged. Nation-states were solid political units with relatively fixed borders, a sense of national unity, and populations that were mostly (though never completely) homogenous in terms of language and ethnicity.

- Europe began to experiment with new forms of monarchy: absolutism and parliamentarism.

Economic and Environmental Developments

- Social diversification resulted from the growing importance of nonagricultural ways of making a living. Banking, commerce, trade, shopkeeping, artisanry, and craftsmanship all led to the creation of a middle class (often referred to as the bourgeoisie) in many societies. This middle class was small to begin with, but steadily grew in numbers and importance.

- More economic importance began to be placed on trade, commerce, and money, rather than land (which had been the traditional source and measure of wealth).

- In several civilizations, primarily Europe, proto-industrial modes of production began to appear, especially during the 1700s. By the late 1700s, the concept of capitalism was emerging as well. Both these trends would have a profound impact on the 1800s.

- Europe's exploration and colonization of the Americas created a new major trade network in the Atlantic. This economic system linked Europe, Africa, North America, and South America. Indirectly, it was connected by trade with the Middle East and Asia.

- During the 1500s and 1600s, Spanish and Portuguese extraction of precious metals (especially silver) from the Americas affected economies around the world. This huge and sudden influx of gold and silver coinage into so many economies created a glut of precious metals. Many societies, from Europe to China, experienced severe inflation as a result of this trend during the 1600s.

- The most unfortunate by-product of this era's economic trends was the birth and growth of the Atlantic slave trade, which, from the late 1400s to the late 1800s, resulted in the capture and forced deportation to the Americas of perhaps 12 million Africans. Other slave trades continued as well.

- The Columbian Exchange brought new foods, plants, and animals from North and South America to Africa and Eurasia. The importation of corn and potatoes dramatically altered the diets and agricultural practices of Europe. To North and South America, the Europeans brought new technology, the horse, Christianity, and from Africa, new foods, cultural practices, and religious beliefs. The Europeans also brought diseases, such as smallpox and measles, to which the peoples of the Americas had no immunity. It is estimated that at least 25 percent of the Americas' pre-Columbian population perished within decades from the diseases brought by European conquerors and colonizers.

- World population growth was considerable during these years. From 1400 to 1700, the world's population increased from 350 million to 610 million. The increase was due mainly to improvements in agricultural technique in most world cultures, as well as a general warming of the global climate. The parts of the world that grew the most were Asia and Europe.

Cultural Developments

- Most major societies had well-defined artistic and literary traditions. Increased technological aptitude enabled the production of arts and crafts of high quality.
- The level of scientific knowledge and technological achievement was especially high in civilizations such as China, Ottoman Turkey, Mughal India, and Safavid Persia.
- Europe made exceptional strides in terms of scientific knowledge and technological achievement. The Renaissance, the Scientific Revolution, and the Enlightenment all furthered the intellectual growth of Europe, to the point that, during the late 1600s and 1700s, it overtook the civilizations listed above.
- The steadily increasing influence of the printing press led to the rapid spread of information, scientific knowledge, religious debates, and new ideas. By creating more materials to read—and more incentive to read—the printing press helped to boost literacy rates.
- Europe experienced a religious earthquake, the Protestant Reformation, that profoundly affected not just matters of faith, but cultural life, military and political affairs, and economics. The split between Protestants and Catholics influenced how Europeans spread Christianity to other parts of the world.
- In addition to cultural, religious, and artistic interchange among the societies of Africa, Europe, and Asia, the European encounter with the Americas led to even greater interaction. The movement of Europeans and Africans (mainly slaves) altered the patterns of North and South American ethnicity, religion, language, art, and music.
- As a result of their Age of Discovery, the Europeans established a presence in almost all parts of the world during this era. European colonies and trading missions spread European culture to Africa, Asia, and the Americas.

Gender Issues

- Throughout most parts of the world, women continued to occupy a secondary status in terms of social roles, economic opportunities, and political influence.
- In most societies, marriage remained a primarily economic arrangement. Marriage ties were often a way to gain or transfer wealth and property. Marriage also ensured the inheritance of one's goods and assets by legitimate heirs.
- In a limited, gradual sense, parts of Europe began to develop a greater awareness of the injustice of the position of women.
- Also in Europe, individual women or women of small but important segments of society (from the aristocracy or the emerging middle class, for example) gained educations, became active in business, made scientific discoveries, or became artists and writers.
- In most societies, women developed ways to gain influence or advance their desires in informal, often subtle ways (advising husbands and sons, educating children, running or helping to run businesses, managing household finances, and so on).
- A handful of Europe's most important monarchs during this era—Elizabeth I, Maria Theresa, Isabella, and Catherine the Great, for instance—were female.

QUESTIONS AND COMPARISONS TO CONSIDER

- Compare one or more major European monarchies from this period with an Asian empire (such as Ottoman Turkey, Ming China, or Mughal India).
- Contrast Russia's relationship with western Europe with the way one of the following interacted with the West: Mughal India, the Ottoman Empire, Tokugawa Japan, or China.
- Consider various forms of monarchy during this era and how they were legitimated (divine right, constitutionality, Mandate of Heaven, etc.).
- Compare the growing Atlantic slave trade with other systems of unfree labor (for example, serfdom in medieval Europe, serfdom in Russia, or the Arab slave network in Africa).
- Examine the likenesses and differences between the global economy that emerged after European exploration and the international trading networks that existed beforehand (also compare and contrast both with the globalization of the world economy during the late twentieth and early twenty-first centuries).
- Compare the European Age of Discovery with earlier efforts at exploration, such as Zheng He's or Ibn Battuta's.
- What features distinguish the kingdoms and empires of Africa or the Americas from those in Europe and Asia? What features did they have in common?
- Compare the different approaches of various European nations to colonization (both in the Americas and worldwide).
- How were empires built by Europeans? By African states? By Asian nations?

Europe: Reformation, Absolutism, and Enlightenment

CHAPTER 13

- The Protestant Reformation and Catholic Counter-Reformation
- Absolute monarchies versus parliamentary monarchies
- The movable-type (Gutenberg) printing press
- The scientific revolution and the heliocentric theory
- The Enlightenment (Age of Reason)
- The agricultural revolution and the Columbian exchange
- Urbanization and the appearance of a middle class
- Mercantilism, capitalism, and proto-industrialization
- The Atlantic slave trade

The years between the mid-1400s and late 1700s—often referred to as Europe's **early modern period**—were years of political, religious, intellectual, and socioeconomic transformation. European nations grew stronger and more stable. New Christian churches, the Protestant denominations, were born. Until approximately 1600, the Renaissance spread northward from Italy, affecting all of Europe. Afterward, the scientific awareness and intellectual sophistication of Europe (at least its upper classes) increased by leaps and bounds. The continent's population grew and diversified. Europeans improved their agricultural techniques, their technological aptitude increased, and they took the first steps in building modern industrial and commercial economies.

In addition, Europe's global power skyrocketed. The Europeans did not invent gunpowder weaponry, nor were they the first to use it successfully, but in the long term, they used it most efficiently. Also, as described in Chapter 14, it was during these years that Europe, unlike any other civilization, explored most of the globe, then conquered and colonized a vast portion of it. In the 1400s, Europe was simply one of many major civilizations, and a relatively weak one. By the end of the 1700s, it was among the most powerful, and its military, diplomatic, and economic might would only increase in the 1800s.

THE PROTESTANT REFORMATION AND ITS AFTERMATH

The Crisis of European Catholicism

For more than a thousand years, there had been only one major Christian denomination in most of Europe: Roman Catholicism. (Eastern Orthodoxy was important in Byzantium and eastern Europe.) As described in Chapter 6, the Catholic Church enjoyed an immense amount of prestige, power, and wealth during most of the medieval era.

During the 1300s and 1400s, the church entered a period of long-term crisis. For most of the 1300s, the papacy was transferred by force to the French city of Avignon, making the church look weak. For forty years in the late 1300s and early 1400s, there were rival popes, each claiming allegiance from all Catholics, causing great confusion. The church hierarchy grew notoriously corrupt in the 1400s, selling church offices and granting certificates of forgiveness for sins (indulgences) in exchange for money. As years passed, more people came to see the church as hypocritical and too concerned with money and power. This feeling grew both among ordinary people and scholars, monks, and priests. Until the early 1500s, though, the church was able to crush any opposition.

The Protestant Churches

Real change began in 1517, when a German monk, **Martin Luther**, protested the sale of indulgences in his hometown. In his Ninety-five Theses, Luther launched a general attack against church abuses and certain parts of Catholic doctrine. When the church ordered him to retract his criticisms, he refused and was excommunicated. Quickly, what started as a simple dispute grew into a complete rupture of the Catholic Church. In the 1520s, Luther, now a fugitive, founded a new church, Lutheranism, the first of Europe's Protestant denominations.

With the **Protestant Reformation** under way, other movements soon emerged. The French scholar **John Calvin** established a theocratic community in the Swiss city of Geneva and preached an even more extreme form of Protestantism. Calvinism caught on in France (the Huguenots, an oppressed minority), the Dutch Republic (the Reformed Church), parts of England (the Puritans), and Scotland (the Presbyterians). In England, Henry VIII, previously a staunch defender of Catholicism, declared his country to be Protestant (mainly for political and marital reasons), forming the **Church of England**, also known as the **Anglican Church**.

Many beliefs and practices separated Protestants from Catholics. In the beginning, Lutheran and Calvinist churches favored institutional simplicity, in contrast to the bureaucracy and political power of the Catholic Church. Protestants did not venerate the saints or the Virgin Mary the way Catholics did. Rituals and sacraments were less important to them. Priests were allowed to marry. Most important was the concept of **salvation by grace**, the belief that only God's grace—not good works, observance of rituals, or the power of the pope—could bring a worshipper to heaven. (Calvin's doctrine of **predestination** took the idea further, arguing that whether a person would be saved or not was known to God from the beginning of time.) This belief accounted for the lack of emphasis on sacraments, and it also led Lutherans and Calvinists to emphasize a pure, sincere relationship with God. They were encouraged to read the Bible for themselves (unlike Catholics), making education and literacy important to them.

Not all Protestants thought alike. Calvinist churches tended to be more puritanical and severe. In many ways, the Anglican Church was not far removed from the Catholic Church. During the religious wars of the 1500s and 1600s, Lutherans sometimes fought Calvinists. In England, the Anglican majority persecuted the minority Puritans almost as heavily as it did English Catholics.

The Catholic Counter-Reformation and Religious War

In response to the Protestant Reformation, the Catholic Church underwent change in the mid-to-late 1500s, a process known as the **Catholic Counter-Reformation** (sometimes simply the Catholic Reformation). At the Council of Trent (1545–1563), the church worked to eliminate the worst of its financially and spiritually corrupt practices. To increase its appeal and compete with Protestant churches for worshippers, the church sponsored the creation of impressive religious art and architecture, helping give birth to the Baroque movement. The church also stiffened religious discipline: it reaffirmed the authority of the pope, gave new powers to the Holy Inquisition, and created an Index of Forbidden Books. It also approved the formation of a new religious order, the Jesuits (Society of Jesus), which produced missionaries, teachers, and diplomats to combat Protestantism.

From the 1520s through the 1640s, Europe was plagued by a series of **religious wars**, as the papacy and Catholic monarchs attempted to halt the Protestant tide and, where possible, force Protestants to return to the Catholic fold. The first serious conflicts were in Switzerland (where civil war erupted in the 1520s) and the Holy Roman Empire (Catholic forces won in the 1540s and 1550s, but were forced by political factors to compromise and allow some German states to remain Protestant). Religious violence rocked England and Scotland from the 1530s through the first half of the 1600s. The Dutch war of independence from Spain, which began in the 1560s and lasted eighty years, was motivated largely by the desire of the Dutch to remain Calvinist, even in the face of religious oppression. During the last half of the 1500s, France tore itself apart in a series of bloody civil wars between the Catholic majority and Calvinist (Huguenot) minority. The failed attack of the Armada in 1588 was part of Spain's attempt to defeat Elizabeth I and destroy English Protestantism. The last and deadliest of the religious wars was the Thirty Years' War (1618–1648), which pitted Spain, the Holy Roman Empire, and Catholic German states against the Dutch, the Danes, the Swedes, and Protestant German states (England lent financial support but did not fight). For political reasons, Catholic France sided with the Protestant powers, who won in the end.

> **TIP**
>
> Europe's religious wars were particularly brutal. All sides felt justified by their beliefs in committing horrible atrocities. These wars tended to last a long time and frequently involved women, children, and other civilians. They took place when Europe's armies were growing larger and starting to use **gunpowder weaponry** full-scale, a fact that made them even deadlier. After the Thirty Years' War came to its close in 1648, religious strife did not end, but the age when major wars were primarily about religion was over.

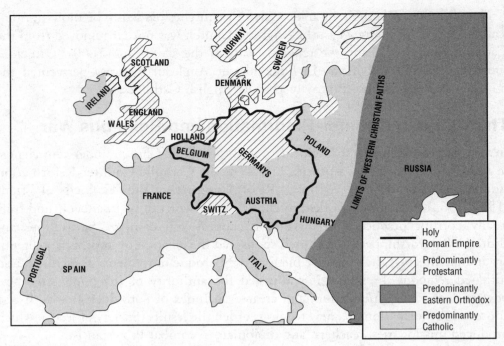

Religious Divisions in Europe, ca. 1600.
For centuries, Christianity had been divided into two large denominations, Eastern Orthodoxy and Roman Catholicism. In most of Europe, the latter had predominated. Starting with the Protestant Reformation in 1517, new religious rifts began to appear. By the end of the 1500s, western and northern Europe were divided into Catholic and Protestant camps, as shown in this map.

ABSOLUTE AND PARLIAMENTARY MONARCHIES

The Fading of Feudalism and the Emergence of European Nation-States

Although traces of feudalism survived, European countries in the early modern period became more like **nation-states** in the contemporary sense: solid political units with fixed borders, a sense of national unity, and mostly (though never completely) homogenous populations in terms of language and ethnicity.

Much of this had to do with the strengthening of central state institutions. During the Middle Ages, institutions had been weak, forcing monarchs to resort to the feudal system. By the 1500s onward, this power structure was changing. Especially by the 1600s and 1700s, European states were developing **bureaucracies**, such as tax-collecting bodies, central banks, general staffs (for the army), admiralties (for the navy), and various ministries and cabinets. Although monarchs and aristocrats still controlled most positions of power, governments were becoming more rational and bureaucratic. Combined with advancements in communications and transport, the development of stronger state institutions allowed monarchs to centralize in a way they had not been able to during the Middle Ages.

Centralizing Rulers

During the late 1400s and 1500s, many rulers went to great lengths to centralize political power. Frequently, this meant competing with the noble (aristocratic) class, which was anxious to keep for itself the feudal privileges it had been granted during the medieval era. Noteworthy state-building monarchs during these years include

- England: Henry VIII (founder of the Anglican Church and booster of English naval power) and Elizabeth I (who secured Anglicanism's place as England's official church, encouraged exploration, repelled the Spanish Armada of 1588, and sponsored Renaissance figures, like Shakespeare)
- France: Louis XI (who conquered Burgundy) and Henry IV (who ended France's religious wars and granted Protestants the right to worship)
- Holy Roman Empire: Charles V (the Habsburg ruler who also governed Spain, encouraged colonization of the Americas, won wars against France and the Turks, and attempted to oppose Martin Luther and Protestantism)
- Spain: Philip II (son of Charles V; although it failed to conquer England in 1588, Spain under Philip II was the most powerful nation in Europe and benefited from its colonial exploitation of the Americas)
- Russia: Ivan III (who threw off Mongol rule and united Russia under Moscow's governance) and Ivan IV (known as "the Terrible" for the extreme violence he used to gain control over his noble class)

By the 1600s and 1700s, two major forms of monarchy emerged. The more centralized form was absolutism, the less centralized was parliamentarism.

Absolute Monarchy

In **absolute monarchies**, there are no legal limitations to the monarch's power (in real life, even absolute monarchs were restricted by informal factors, such as a weak personality, uncooperative nobles, or an unreliable army). Absolutism in Europe was typically justified by the doctrine of **divine right**, according to which the monarch reigns by the will of God. (This is similar to the Mandate of Heaven in China, although divine right theory places no obligation on the monarch to rule justly.)

Europe's archetypal absolute monarch was **Louis XIV** of France, the Sun King who ruled from 1661 to 1715 (he ascended the throne in 1638, but was only five years old at the time). Louis XIV created a highly centralized bureaucracy and national economy. He broke the power of his aristocracy and made it obey him. He built the largest army and navy that Europe had seen in centuries. He turned Paris and his palace of Versailles into grand, impressive centers of power. In many ways, Louis illustrated the strengths and weaknesses of absolute monarchy. He was an intelligent, forceful man who used his extensive powers to make France better-organized, better-run, and mighty. On the other hand, he involved France in too many wars, damaging the economy he had worked so hard to improve. Near the end of his reign, he persecuted French Protestants, to whom his grandfather had guaranteed religious freedom.

France remained an absolute monarchy until the French Revolution of 1789. Other countries created similar regimes. In the late 1600s, the Austrian Habsburgs brought absolutism to the Holy Roman Empire. Leopold I built great palaces around Vienna, centralized his government and economy, and fought wars against the Turks. (In 1683, the Turks nearly destroyed Austria in the **Siege of Vienna** but were turned back; afterward, the Austrians and their allies pushed the Turks steadily to the east.) The constant Turkish pressure on Austria's eastern frontier provided a good excuse for greater imperial control. In the eighteenth century, Maria Theresa and Joseph II carried on Austria's tradition of absolutism.

The small but militarily powerful German state of Prussia became an absolute monarchy during the late 1600s and 1700s. **Frederick the Great** (1740–1786)—a great general as well as a skilled ruler—was one of the most effective monarchs of his time. His victory over Austria, France, and Russia during the Seven Years' War (1756–1763) is considered one of the greatest military triumphs in European history. However, the price Prussia paid for Frederick's talents was greater dictatorship and decreased freedoms.

The largest nation in the world, Russia, also emerged as an absolute monarchy. Thanks to Moscow's tsars, Russia already possessed a tradition of strong central authority. It was, however, economically, culturally, and scientifically backward compared with the West. (One effect of Mongol rule had been to cut Russia off from Europe during the Renaissance.) During the late 1600s and early 1700s, **Peter the Great** not only centralized political power but forced rapid, Western-style modernization on Russia. He also changed Russia's geopolitical orientation. Earlier, Russia had been mainly isolated from Europe and concerned with events in Asia. However, by fighting and winning a long, hard war with Sweden, Peter gained a permanent place for Russia as Europe's great power of the east. It became more European in nature, although never completely so. The other great absolute ruler of eighteenth-century Russia was Catherine the Great, who gained an international reputation for her intellectual achievements and military conquests. Much longer than other European states, Russia kept in place an oppressive system of **serfdom**.

Parliamentary Monarchy

Other governments, such as those in England and the Dutch Republic, took another direction. Even as these states centralized and modernized, the rulers became less powerful. These regimes were known as **parliamentary monarchies**, because the ruler governed in conjunction with some kind of lawmaking body appointed by the aristocracy, elected by some or all of the people, or some combination of both.

During and after their war of independence from Spain, the Dutch wavered back and forth between centralized and decentralized rule. Either way, the *stadholder*—an executive leader who was not quite a king—had to share power with a larger council called the States General.

Even more famous was the system that emerged in England (which joined with Wales, Scotland, and Ireland to form Great Britain in the early 1700s). Since the

1200s, England's monarchs had been compelled to share power with the legislative body known as Parliament. Parliament gradually assumed greater powers until, in the 1600s, the balance of power shifted in its favor. The English Civil War (1640–1649) was partly about religion (Anglican vs. Puritan) but more about power (king vs. Parliament). The forces of Parliament won the civil war, killed the king (Charles I), and established the Commonwealth, ruled by Parliament (then by the general Oliver Cromwell).

When the royal family returned to England in the Restoration of 1660, the rivalry between monarch and Parliament remained (the three-way religious struggle between Catholic, Puritan, and Anglican caused problems as well). Another uprising—the Glorious Revolution of 1688—followed, and another king, William I, also the ruler of the Dutch Republic, was invited to take the throne. The invitation, however, was conditional: William I had to agree not only to an act of religious toleration but also to a **Bill of Rights**, which curtailed the powers of the monarch and made Parliament the dominant partner in English politics. From 1688 onward, Parliament grew steadily stronger, while the monarchy grew weaker and more symbolic.

The advantages of parliamentary monarchy are clear from the English and Dutch examples. Both nations developed strong economies, powerful navies, urbanized societies, and intellectual and cultural outlooks that were relatively open and free from religious persecution. Although poverty and inequality existed in both countries, society was more flexible, and social advancement was more feasible than in absolute monarchies.

THE PRINTING PRESS, THE SCIENTIFIC REVOLUTION, AND ENLIGHTENMENT PHILOSOPHY

The Northern Renaissance and the Baroque

Europe's level of intellectual sophistication rose during these years. The Renaissance, which had begun in Italy during the 1300s, spread to the rest of Europe and continued till approximately 1600. Important figures in this later, **northern Renaissance** included the Dutch philosopher Desiderius Erasmus (known for his debates with Luther, as well as his satirical novel *In Praise of Folly*), the Spanish novelist Miguel de Cervantes (author of *Don Quixote*), the English cleric Thomas More (who invented the term *utopia* in his book of the same name), and, also from England, the poet and playwright **William Shakespeare**.

The cultural style that followed the Renaissance was the **baroque**, which dominated painting and architecture from the early 1600s through the early 1700s. In music, it lasted longer, until the mid-to-late 1700s. Baroque culture emphasized the bold, the dynamic, and the colorful. Another trend of this era was the birth of opera.

The Movable-Type Printing Press and Its Effect on European Culture

A prime cause of early modern Europe's remarkable cultural growth was Johannes Gutenberg's movable-type printing press, invented in Germany in the 1430s.

The spread of Renaissance ideas from Italy to the rest of Europe was due largely to the printing press. The press had even more of an impact on the religious debates that preceded, then caused, the Protestant Reformation. Because an increasing number of people could read the Bible itself, not to mention the hundreds of essays and articles written for and against church reform, religious ideas had a much wider impact than they could have had before.

Renaissance Science and the Heliocentric Theory

Europe's scientific and technological aptitude increased during the early modern period. During the late Renaissance, certain thinkers and scholars were moving away from the intellectual orthodoxy of the Middle Ages, in which a fixed set of ideas from ancient Greece and Rome (especially selected theories from the writings of Aristotle) were combined with Catholic doctrine.

During the mid-1500s, despite the Catholic Church's continued control over European intellectual life, individuals such as the Flemish doctor Andreas Vesalius and the Polish astronomer **Nicolaus Copernicus** began to cross important scientific boundaries. Vesalius did pioneering work in the field of human anatomy. Copernicus provided mathematical proof for the **heliocentric theory**, according to which the earth and other planets revolve around the sun. The Catholic Church favored the geocentric theory, in which the earth—home to what the church considered God's greatest creation, human beings—was at the center of the universe. It took more than another century before the heliocentric theory was accepted as fact throughout Europe.

The Scientific Revolution

The pace of scientific discovery accelerated during the 1600s and early 1700s, which are commonly spoken of as a time of **Scientific Revolution**. Early in the 1600s, thinkers such as René Descartes of France and Roger Bacon of England laid the groundwork for modern formal logic and revitalized the ancient concept of the **scientific method**.

Also in the 1600s, the German astronomer Johannes Kepler and the Italian physicist **Galileo** confirmed and popularized Copernicus's theories. (Kepler also proved that the planets move in elliptical, not circular, orbits.) In doing so, they ran afoul of the Catholic Church; Galileo was tried by the Inquisition and forced to reject his own scientific conclusions in public. (Protestant nations such as England and the Dutch Republic were safer havens for scientific pioneers; only in the 1700s did it become less risky for those in Catholic countries to challenge church doctrine.)

Many of the ideas behind the modern understanding of science were discovered or proven during the Scientific Revolution. They include the states of matter (liquid, gas, or solid), the question of whether light consists of waves or particles, the fact that living creatures are made of cells, the existence of capillaries, the concept of the vacuum, and the science of statistics. Among the scientific instruments invented or perfected during these years were the telescope, the microscope, the pendulum clock, the thermometer, and the barometer.

Isaac Newton (1642–1727) of England represents the Scientific Revolution at its peak. Newton is famous for the laws of motion, his thoughts on the concept of gravity, and his role in inventing the mathematical system of calculus. The publication of his mathematical work *Principia* (1687) is considered one of the most important moments in European intellectual history. Just as important, however, is the fact that Newton, more than any other figure of the Scientific Revolution, understood scientific thought as a totality. He took the discoveries and theories of his day and tied them together into a single system of thought—Newtonian physics—backed up by mathematical proof. Not until Einstein's development of the theory of relativity in the early 1900s would Newton's fundamental principles be seriously challenged or altered.

The Age of Reason (The Enlightenment)

During the 1700s, the educated public of Europe (still a small segment of society, though it was growing) felt it was living in a culturally and intellectually advanced era. Europeans—at least the middle and upper classes—considered themselves to have left behind what they thought of as the intellectual crudeness and superstitious darkness of the Middle Ages and even the 1500s and 1600s, with their wars of religion. They put great faith in the power of human logic and rationality, as well as the recent discoveries of the Scientific Revolution, to solve problems and understand the world around them. Accordingly, it was common to refer to the 1700s as the **Age of Reason** or the **Age of Enlightenment**.

Enlightenment culture valued not just science but also philosophy and ideas about how to make society and government more just, efficient, and humane. Philosophical societies, salons, and literary circles appeared in all the major cities of the Western world during the 1700s, from Boston and Philadelphia in the United States to St. Petersburg in Russia. Among the most important centers of Enlightenment thought were Edinburgh, London, and Paris.

Women played a significant role in the Enlightenment. More women from the upper (and even middle) classes were gaining educations and proving that they were intellectually equal to men. A number became renowned for important Enlightenment writings and activities, including **Mary Wollstonecraft** of England (author of *A Vindication of the Rights of Women*) and Catherine the Great, Empress of Russia. Upper-class women, particularly in France, played a key part in organizing and hosting the salons at which much Enlightenment discussion and debate took place.

Among the most prominent Enlightenment philosophers were John Locke of England, and **Voltaire**, Denis Diderot, and the Baron Charles de Montesquieu (all from France). A later Enlightenment figure was Jean-Jacques Rousseau, also of France. All of these thinkers, as well as others, shared a faith in order and logic. Beyond that, not all had the same ideas about politics and society. All believed that government should be rationally organized and fairly regulated. Most believed in freedom of expression, opinion, and religion. Some, however, were monarchists (they simply felt that the monarch should govern according to law, not tyranny). Others, such as Rousseau, believed in granting more political power to ordinary people, although Rousseau viewed women as inferior to men.

Some Enlightenment philosophers remained Christian (although they opposed religious war). Others, especially Voltaire, opposed organized religion as a flawed human institution, and some became atheists. Nonetheless, their common emphasis on reason and progress bound them together. As described in Chapter 20, Enlightenment ideas played a crucial role in motivating several revolutions at the end of the 1700s, including those in America and France.

SOCIETY AND ECONOMICS

Population Growth and Class Diversification

The 1500s and 1600s were a time of demographic and economic crisis in Europe. Ecologically, Europe experienced a cooling period referred to by historians as the Little Ice Age, and famines were common. The wars of religion not only caused combat deaths but spread disease and caused mass starvation. Agricultural techniques remained relatively primitive. Populations declined or stayed level, depending on year and region.

Many changes came during the 1700s. Environmental conditions improved. New foods from the Americas, especially corn and the potato, revitalized European agriculture (on this **Columbian Exchange**, see Chapters 14 and 19). New ideas and methods for effective food production also emerged; this **agricultural revolution** included soil aeration, the systematic use of manure, the adoption of iron plows instead of wooden ones, and the scientific rotation of crops. The number and severity of famines decreased, and crop yields grew larger.

As a result, Europe's population grew considerably during the 1700s. In addition, it began to diversify. As before, the vast majority were peasants. At the top, royal families and noble classes made up a tiny (but powerful) segment of society. However, a steadily increasing percentage of Europeans made their living as craftsmen and shopkeepers—or even merchants, bankers, and professionals, such as doctors and lawyers. Such people formed a growing (but still relatively small) **middle class**. A related development was increased **urbanization**. All these trends would accelerate in the 1800s.

Mercantilism, Capitalism, and Proto-Industrialization

The economic philosophy that prevailed during most of the early modern period was **mercantilism**, which advocated strict state control over economic activity and the exploitation of colonies (as sources of raw materials and as markets for the home country's manufactured goods).

As part of the Enlightenment, a new economic theory appeared, based on the concept of free trade, competition, and the market forces of supply and demand: **capitalism**. The most famous of capitalism's early supporters was the Scottish economist

Adam Smith, who made a case for it in *The Wealth of Nations* (1776). Capitalism became the Western world's dominant approach to economics in the modern era.

Although true, full-scale industrialization did not occur in Europe until the end of the 1700s, a growing number of people were becoming involved in manufacturing during the early and mid-1700s (and even the late 1600s). They were also making use of machines and methods like cottage industry in ways that can be considered proto-industrial. This **proto-industrialization** was the immediate precursor to the Industrial Revolution of the late 1700s and early 1800s.

A final note about early modern European economics: because of the Age of Exploration, international trade became a key part of European economic activity. A great deal of Europe's wealth during these years was directly or indirectly connected with the **Atlantic slave trade**.

Women in Early Modern Europe

The status and rights of women changed considerably in early modern Europe. On the whole, women of the upper class gained greater access to education and participated more actively in intellectual life. Many women in the emerging middle class became more educated and assumed a greater economic role as business partners, bookkeepers, and operators of various enterprises. Women of all classes gained more control over when and whom they married, as well as divorce, childbirth, inheritance, and similar issues.

In no sense, however, were women considered equal to men, intellectually or economically. Nor did they have equal status or rights. Rates of death during childbirth were still high. Women made up the majority of victims—approximately 75 percent—in the witch hunts of the 1500s and 1600s. Both Catholicism and the new Protestant faiths maintained that women were inferior to and more sinful than men, and both used arguments based on scripture to reinforce these notions.

Women made significant progress in cultural life. Many Catholic nuns maintained a high level of education. Protestantism's emphasis on literacy led upper- and middle-class women to gain at least some degree of learning.

A number of painters were women. Women took part in scientific work, although they were not allowed to become university faculty (except on extremely rare occasions) or join scientific societies. Women also turned to writing and philosophy, especially during the eighteenth century. Like Mary Wollstonecraft and others, they played a crucial part in the Enlightenment.

Some of the most important monarchs of early modern Europe were women. Among them were Isabella of Castile, Elizabeth I of England, Maria Theresa of Austria, and Catherine the Great of Russia.

CHAPTER 14

Age of Discovery, Age of Imperialism: The Western Campaign of Exploration and Colonization

- Exploration, colonization, and the rise of the West
- The compass and improved naval technology
- Gunpowder weaponry
- Trade and missionary activity
- Slavery and resource extraction
- Major explorers and conquistadors
- Trading companies

Between the early-to-mid 1400s and the mid-to-late 1700s, the nations of Europe accomplished what no other civilization had done: they explored the wider world around them, discovered how to sail around the globe, and mapped the planet's major oceans and landmasses.

With this knowledge came might and wealth. The nations of Europe conquered, colonized, and forced open foreign markets. European explorers and generals were aided by superior technology, the vulnerability of many non-Europeans to European diseases, and, in many cases, sheer ruthlessness.

The legacy is mixed. On one hand, exploration gave Europe's nations an unprecedented amount of geographical and scientific knowledge. Colonization made Europe rich and powerful. It was during the years of exploration—and largely *because* of exploration—that Europe started to become the dominant civilization on the planet.

On the other hand, Europe paid a moral and ethical price for the knowledge and power it gained. Exploration and colonization went hand-in-hand with war, greed, prejudice, religious intolerance, and slavery. Many parts of the world remained under European rule for hundreds of years. Even now, the long-standing tensions left over between Western nations and their former colonies continue to have an impact on international relations.

ECONOMIC MOTIVATIONS AND TECHNOLOGICAL CAPABILITIES

Why and how did the Europeans become the first to explore the world? For many centuries, the peoples of Europe had been less technologically and scientifically advanced than their neighbors in the Middle East or countries such as China. Any observer during the medieval era would have thought it unlikely that Europe, only a short time later, would emerge as the leader in world exploration.

Until the 1400s, Europeans' geographic knowledge was limited. They knew the Mediterranean, Baltic, and North seas well. Africa, the Middle East, Asia, and even Russia were poorly known, inaccessible, or impassable. For the time being, the only outlet was the Atlantic Ocean, which was frighteningly unfamiliar.

Economic Motives for Exploration

The Europeans' primary motivation for exploring was economic. During the Middle Ages, the nations of Europe had become aware of the fabulous wealth of other parts of the world, especially to the east. Europeans also knew how desirable many eastern goods were.

NOTE

Mediterranean trade, greater knowledge about the Middle East gained during the Crusades, and the tales of Marco Polo all whetted European appetites for the wealth of far-off places such as China, the Indies, and Japan.

By the 1400s, Europeans were dreaming of silk, metal goods, spices, fruit, jewels and precious metals, and other items unknown or in short supply in their own lands. If they could reach the Far East directly, rather than trading with middlemen in the Middle East, they would be able to make tremendous profits.

New Navigational and Maritime Technology

If Europeans were interested in exploring by the 1400s, they needed the technology and knowledge to do so. Already by the 1300s, Europeans had learned the secret of the **compass** from the Chinese. Better knowledge of the stars (gained largely from the Arabs) and better navigational instruments, such as the astrolabe and sextant, made it possible for European sailors to venture farther from shore without getting lost.

Naval technology improved as well. During the 1300s and 1400s, the Europeans began to build large, long ships, allowing them to sail faster, carry larger food supplies, and cover greater distances. Larger ships were able to crest the huge waves of the open ocean without capsizing or breaking apart. Finally, stern rudders and advanced systems of sails and rigging allowed ships to travel in almost any direction the captain wanted to go, even if the wind was not favorable.

Finally, European nations were beginning to use **gunpowder weapons** by the 1300s and 1400s. Although it was not until the 1500s and 1600s that Europeans invented the huge gunships that let them carry massive firepower to every part of the globe, European sailors and soldiers came equipped with muskets, pistols, and small artillery pieces. Not only could they use gunpowder weapons at sea, but they would be able to use them against less technologically advanced native populations when they reached new lands.

THE IBERIAN WAVE OF EXPLORATION: SPAIN AND PORTUGAL

The first European nations to explore the wider Atlantic world were Portugal and Spain. Both were on Europe's Atlantic frontier. They also had a great deal of maritime experience in the Mediterranean, thanks to trade and a long series of naval wars against the Ottoman Turks.

Portuguese and Spanish exploration during the 1400s and early 1500s proceeded in two ways. First, the Portuguese attempted to reach the lands of the Far East by inching their way down the coast of Africa, rounding the continent, and then sailing across the Indian Ocean to Asia. In the meantime, the Spanish, competing with the Portuguese, attempted to find their own route to Asia by sailing west, around the world. Famously, they found the continents of North and South America instead, as well as an ocean previously unknown to them: the Pacific. Quickly, both countries figured out the relationship between the Atlantic and Pacific.

Henry the Navigator and Portugal's Exploration of West Africa

The Portuguese began Europe's age of exploration thanks mainly to their prince, known popularly as **Henry the Navigator** (1394–1460). He and his successors sent out many voyages to the west and south, attempting to find a sea route to India and the Far East. The Portuguese claimed several Atlantic island groups, including the Madeiras and Azores, and traveled down Africa's western coast, conquering and exploring. They seized the Moroccan port of Ceuta in 1411, and soon afterward, the Cape Verde Islands. The Portuguese continued to expand along Africa's western shore, taking over or domineering areas like Kongo (see Chapter 18). In 1488, Bartholomeu Díaz reached the southern tip of Africa. In honor of the completion of his first leg of the journey to India, the Portuguese named the tip of Africa the Cape of Good Hope.

Spain, Christopher Columbus, and the New World

The Spanish, distracted by the Reconquista (see Chapter 6), were not as quick as the Portuguese to start exploring. Falling behind meant that, if the Spanish wanted their own sea route to Asia, they would have to try something different. The result was the famous voyage of the Italian captain **Christopher Columbus** in 1492, sponsored by King Ferdinand and Queen Isabella.

What Columbus proposed was to sail west to reach China and India. The boldness of his plan lay not in the idea that the world was round, because that was well known to educated Europeans. What made his proposal striking was his belief that the world was small enough that an expedition would be able to sail from Spain to Asia without getting lost or running out of food and water. He set sail in August 1492, and his ships reached the islands of the Caribbean on October 12.

Columbus was convinced that he had found the Indies (hence the mistaken term Indians for Native Americans), but the Spanish and Portuguese realized quickly that what he had found were lands completely unknown to them. The two countries turned to the pope to determine who would be allowed to claim which parts of the

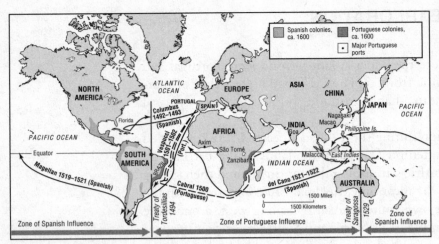

Spanish and Portuguese Exploration, 1492–1529.
The first European nations to colonize the wider world were Spain and Portugal. Their successes are attested to in this map. The north–south lines of demarcation were established by the papacy, to whose authority both nations, being Catholic, submitted.

New World. In **lines of demarcation** agreed to in 1494 and 1529, the pope gave jurisdiction over most of South America and all of North America to the Spanish. The Portuguese received Brazil.

Reaching India and Circumnavigating the Globe

By the end of the 1490s, the Spanish and Portuguese had two worlds to explore and conquer. The Portuguese continued to sail eastward to India from the southern tip of Africa. In 1498, Vasco da Gama became the first European to reach India by sea, and the profit from his voyage equaled sixty times the original investment.

Shortly thereafter, the Portuguese captain **Ferdinand Magellan** (sailing for Spain) led an expedition that tied together all of Spain's and Portugal's previous efforts. Magellan was inspired by the 1513 discovery of Panama by Spanish explorer Vasco de Balboa, the first European to sight the Pacific Ocean from the New World. Hoping to cross both oceans, Magellan's ships left Europe in 1519 and traversed the Atlantic. They rounded South America and made their way through the Pacific, returning to Europe in 1522 (although Magellan himself died along the way).

Spanish and Portuguese Colonization

Having reached Africa, Southeast Asia, and the Far East on one hand and the New World on the other, the Spanish and Portuguese established a colonial presence in all these areas. In the Far East and Southeast Asia, many countries were too strong or too advanced for the Portuguese to conquer, and for the most part they settled for trade. Still, the Portuguese seized some areas, including the Indian port of Goa (1510), the thriving commercial center of Malacca (1511), and the island of Sri Lanka. As they had in West Africa, the Portuguese took over much of the East African coast, setting up strongholds in cities such as Mombasa and Zanzibar.

In the New World, the Portuguese moved into Brazil during the early 1500s. The Spanish built up their power in the Caribbean, using islands such as Cuba, Puerto Rico, and Hispaniola (today Haiti and the Dominican Republic) as bases.

The North and South American mainland fell to the **conquistadores**—generals who brought huge parts of both continents under Spanish control. Florida fell to Juan Ponce de León after 1513. From 1519 to 1521, **Hernán Cortés** waged an effective and brutal campaign against the Aztecs. The Aztec capital, Tenochtitlán, became Mexico City, headquarters of what the Spanish now called New Spain. Later, California, Arizona, New Mexico, Colorado, Texas, Missouri, Louisiana, and Alabama were taken over by other conquistadores, such as Hernando de Soto, Francisco de Coronado, and Álvar Cabeza de Vaca. Farther to the south, in the 1530s, **Francisco Pizarro** destroyed the mighty Incan Empire.

Both in Africa and the New World, Portuguese and Spanish colonies were originally intended to boost their home countries' power and wealth through the exploitation of raw materials. From the start, the Spanish and Portuguese attempted to use Native Americans as slaves. When that effort failed, they brought slaves to the New World from Africa.

THE NORTHERN WAVE: FRANCE, THE DUTCH REPUBLIC, AND ENGLAND

During the 1500s, other European nations began to explore and colonize. The most important were France, the Dutch Republic, and England.

For decades, the Spanish and Portuguese jealously guarded their geographic knowledge and navigational techniques, and were anxious to lock the countries of northern Europe out of Atlantic exploration. At stake were military power, immense wealth, and Catholic-Protestant rivalry.

Only after the mid-1500s were the French, Dutch, and English able to steal enough information, shadow enough Spanish and Portuguese ships, and gain enough knowledge about sea routes to begin their own exploration and colonization. During the 1500s and 1600s, for the French, English, and Dutch to explore and colonize typically meant also fighting the Spanish and Portuguese—either at sea or on land—as the new arrivals tried to take colonial territories away from the older powers.

> **NOTE**
>
> During the early 1500s, the only area that France, the Dutch Republic, and England were able to settle was the northern coast of North America, which the Spanish saw as less desirable. One reason these countries explored here was their hope of finding an alternative route (a "northwest passage") to Asia through the Arctic.

French Exploration and Colonization

In the 1520s, the Italian captain Giovanni da Verrazano, commissioned by the French, surveyed North America's Atlantic coast. From 1534 to 1541, Jacques Cartier traced the course of the St. Lawrence River, the first step in France's settlement of Canada. France established its first cities in Canada in the early 1600s: Port Royal in Nova Scotia (1605) and Quebec, founded by Samuel Champlain (1608).

Later in the 1600s, the French moved southward, exploring the Great Lakes and major rivers. In 1673, Louis Joliet and Father Jacques Marquette, traveling west from the Great Lakes, discovered the Mississippi River and mapped its northern reaches. In 1682, René Robert de la Salle sailed down the entire length of the Mississippi, claiming land for France, even though much of this territory was already under Spanish control. During the late 1600s and 1700s, the French took much of the Mississippi basin and some

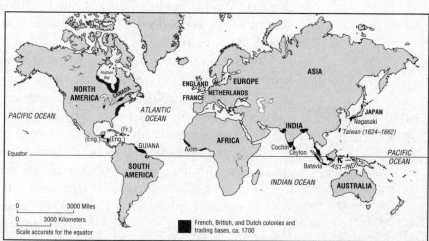

French, English, and Dutch Colonization by 1700.
By 1700, France, England, and the Netherlands had gained many imperial footholds in the Americas, the Caribbean, Africa, and Asia.

of the coast of the Gulf of Mexico away from the Spanish. This large expanse was called Louisiana (different from the state of the same name).

Dutch Exploration and Colonization

Dutch exploration was closely tied to the war of independence against Spain. Dutch strategy in the late 1500s and early 1600s was to fight the Spanish at sea and, if possible, disrupt connections with their colonies. The Dutch did the same to the Portuguese and, by the 1590s, were seizing colonies from them: the Spice Islands in 1595, the Southeast Asian port of Malacca in 1641, the island of Sri Lanka, much of West Africa, and a number of Caribbean islands. To manage their colonies in Asia, the Dutch formed the **Dutch East India Company** (1602). The Dutch also invaded Indonesia, where they maintained a colonial presence for hundreds of years. They ran pepper and spice plantations on the island of Sumatra. On Java, they established the colonial capital of Batavia (1619), now the Indonesian capital, Jakarta.

The Dutch colonized North America as well. In 1609, they commissioned the English sailor Henry Hudson to explore the bay and river that now bear his name.

English Exploration and Colonization

Although England did not begin a major campaign of exploration until after the mid-1500s, it claimed parts of North America as early as the 1490s, thanks to the voyages of John Cabot, who attempted to find an Arctic passage to Asia through Canadian waters. During the mid-to-late 1500s, the English fought a series of naval wars with the Spanish. The English gained much navigational knowledge from these conflicts. Francis Drake, raiding Spanish ports, became the first Englishman to sail around the world (1577–1580).

In the 1600s, the English established their own colonies in North America, from the Carolinas to the Canadian border. Two colonies failed during the 1580s, but the English settlement of Jamestown, led by John Smith, gave the English a foothold in the New World. English Puritans, the so-called Pilgrims, came to America as well, seeking religious freedom. They sailed across on the *Mayflower*, which landed at Plymouth Rock in 1620.

The English made incursions into South Asia as well. Their first expedition to the Indies came in 1591. Shortly afterward, they founded the **British East India Company** (1600) to manage economic—and, later, military—relations with South and Southeast Asia. The English were in northwestern India by 1608 and would gradually take over more of the subcontinent. The English seized the Southeast Asian port of Malacca from the Dutch in 1795.

As with the Spanish and Portuguese, the countries of the northern wave were eager to gain military strength and, especially, economic wealth from their colonies. Exploitation of natural resources—and of the native populations—was the norm. Like the Spanish and Portuguese, the French and English brought slaves to the New World from Africa (see Chapters 18 and 19).

Islamic Empires in the Middle East and North Africa

CHAPTER 15

- The gunpowder empires
- The Ottoman Empire and the sultan
- The capture of Constantinople (Istanbul)
- The janissaries
- Suleiman's conquests
- The siege of Vienna
- The millet system
- The harem

The unity of the single Islamic state, the Abbasid Caliphate, stretching from Spain to India, vanished during the 1200s. Decades of chaos and confusion followed, as Mongol warriors invaded and the Seljuk and Ottoman Turks rose up as regional powers.

Afterward, strong Islamic empires emerged in place of the fallen caliphate: the Ottoman Empire, the Safavid Empire in Persia, and the Mughal Empire in India (the last is described in Chapter 17). All three were highly centralized, technologically advanced, and militarily powerful. They are commonly referred to as the "**gunpowder empires**," because of their mastery of new weaponry and their effective use of it in accumulating regional might.

The grandest and most influential of the Islamic states was the Ottoman Empire. It was also the longest lasting, with a geopolitical role to play on three continents: Africa, Asia, and Europe. Its neighbor to the east, Persia's Safavid Empire, was impressive, but not as strong as the Ottoman state, and it did not survive nearly as long.

THE OTTOMAN EMPIRE

The Ottoman State

The Ottoman Turks, originally nomads from Central Asia, established their own state in 1280. They rose in the late 1300s and 1400s to gain hegemony over most of the Middle East, restoring central authority to the region.

Centralized authority was provided by the **sultan**. He ruled with the help of an elaborate bureaucracy, run by ministers called viziers (*wazirs*), headed by the grand vizier, and provincial governors (beys and pashas). In the early 1500s, Selim I (1512–1520) claimed religious as well as political authority for the sultan, equating the Ottomans' right to rule the Islamic world with that of the Arab caliphates of bygone years.

The sultan's position was hereditary, although the eldest son did not always inherit, largely because the sultan typically did not marry but fathered heirs with a number of

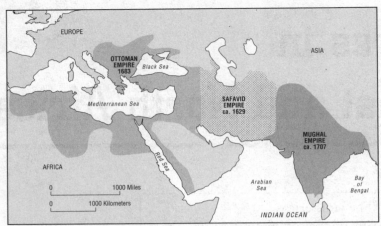

The Islamic World's Gunpowder Empires, ca. 1629–1707.

The Blue Mosque, Istanbul, Turkey.
Officially the Sultan Ahmed Mosque, this seventeenth-century master-piece is popularly known as the Blue Mosque. One of the great land-marks of Istanbul, the Blue Mosque is unusual in having six minarets, rather than the usual four.

concubines. A concubine whose son became the sultan's heir was known as the queen mother and generally enjoyed influ-ence as an adviser to the sultan and her son. When a new sultan came to power, he often killed his brothers to eliminate potential competition. The preferred method of exe-cution was strangling.

The Ottoman Military

The Ottoman Empire was a mighty con-quest state. Under a series of militarily active sultans, it moved into southeastern Europe, and its navies gained sway over the eastern Mediterranean. One of the Ottomans' great triumphs was the destruction of the Byzantine Empire in 1453. That year, the army of Mehmet II **captured the city of Constantinople**, after bombarding it with 26-foot-long cannons that fired ammunition weighing 1,200 pounds. Mehmet turned Constan-tinople into his new capital, **Istanbul**.

Further conquests followed. Selim I moved into North Africa. Ottoman forces pushed farther into Europe, along the Danube River. They seized the Romanian province of Wallachia in 1476, then paused for the next four and a half decades (this time was spent fighting in the Middle East and Africa, as well as consolidating domestic affairs).

A larger and more successful thrust into Europe came under **Suleiman I the Mag-nificent** (1520–1566), greatest of the Ottoman sultans. Suleiman resumed the Ottoman assault on the Danube and Romania, Hungary, and the Holy Roman Empire. By 1529, the Ottomans had reached the outskirts of Vienna, where Christian armies finally stopped them. The Turks were pushed back somewhat, but they now controlled a vast part of southeastern Europe. Moreover, the Turkish fleet enjoyed almost complete supe-riority in the Mediterranean until the end of the 1500s—and remained a deadly enemy even afterward. The Ottoman presence in Europe lingered into the early 1900s.

During the 1500s and first two-thirds of the 1600s, the Ottoman Empire was at its military and organizational peak. As one of the Islamic world's three "gunpow-der empires," Ottoman Turkey was for a time innovative in its adoption of military technology and capable in administering its armies and navies.

The sultans supplemented the traditional cavalry (outdated and not entirely trustworthy) with elite soldiers called **janissaries** (from *yeni cheri*, or "new troops").

They were essentially slaves but given many privileges. The infantrymen were equipped with muskets, and they received advanced training. For many years, the janissary system, although harsh, kept Ottoman Turkey at the forefront of world military affairs.

Diversity and Religious Policy

Also during the 1500s and early 1600s, the Ottomans were efficient at governing their large territory as well as the diverse population that lived there. The Ottomans ruled not only Sunni Muslims, but members of the Shiite minority, Jews, and Christians of the Orthodox, Catholic, and Protestant denominations. Many tongues—especially Turkish, Arabic, and Persian—were spoken in the empire.

Both for political and economic reasons, the sultans practiced relative religious tolerance: non-Muslims were allowed to convert to Islam if they wished but were not forced to do so. They did not have equal rights, they were not permitted to serve in the military, and they had to pay a special head tax. There were occassional abuses. Still, non-Muslims were, on the whole, not treated badly. Ottoman policy kept the peace, and the extra tax revenue was economically beneficial. Each religious group (Muslims included) was grouped into an administrative unit called a *millet* ("nation"): there was one for Jews, another for Orthodox Christians, and so on.

Women in the Ottoman Empire

Among the Ottoman elite, women played influential but informal roles. The sultan's mother (the queen mother) ran the household, controlled marriage alliances, and was sometimes involved in diplomatic relations with foreign officials.

Despite its popular reputation, the **harem** ("sacred place") was not simply a collection of concubines for the sultan's pleasure. It was a complex elite social network. Male members of the harem (mostly eunuchs) were trained for military or administrative positions, while concubines were educated to read the Qur'an, to sew, and to perform music. Members of the harem were ranked by status, and some could leave the harem to marry officials. Few of the women in the imperial harem were used for sexual purposes; most were members of the sultan's extended family. These women also gained influence over male rulers by raising them as boys and training them to respect their guidance.

Outside the imperial family, women on the whole were not seen in public. However, they had the right to own property, retain it after marriage, and could buy, sell, and inherit real estate. They could also testify for themselves in court.

The Long Decline of the Ottoman Empire

The last truly gifted Ottoman sultan was Suleiman the Magnificent. In addition to being a talented commander, he was an excellent domestic ruler. Because of his gift for governance, he is often referred to as Suleiman the Lawgiver. Few of the sultans who followed had Suleiman's qualities, and many were mediocre or worse.

In the late 1600s, the Ottomans made one last attempt at a major European offensive. The attack almost succeeded but was turned back in 1683. That year, the Turks, as they had in 1529, reached Vienna, capital of the Holy Roman Empire. The **siege of**

NOTE

By the 1800s, the Ottoman Empire was, in a bit of black humor, routinely referred to as the "sick man of Europe."

Vienna was seen at the time as a great turning point; had the city fallen, even more of Europe would have been open to Muslim conquest. At the last minute, Vienna was saved by a massive Austrian counteroffensive (greatly assisted by other Catholic allies, especially the Poles, whose cavalry played a key role in the battle). Afterward, the Europeans pushed the Ottomans back to the east. The Turks were not expelled from Europe, but lost much territory from 1683 to 1718.

During the 1700s, the Ottomans fought the Europeans—especially the Austrians and Russians—frequently. However, they never again seriously threatened Europe, and their power declined steadily during the 1700s and 1800s.

Ottoman Culture

The culture of the Ottoman Empire was sophisticated. Its level of intellectual advancement was high. However, after the 1500s and early 1600s, complacency caused the Ottomans to lose the scientific and technological advantages they had enjoyed over the Europeans, who were experiencing their own scientific revolution.

Nonetheless, the Ottomans were skilled at art, literature, music, and architecture. The best-known Ottoman architect is Sinan: during the mid-1500s, he designed eighty-one mosques with large domes and tall, thin minarets. The Turks were also renowned for their mosaics.

NORTH AFRICA UNDER THE OTTOMAN EMPIRE

Just as North Africa had converted to Islam from the late 600s onward, much of the region fell to the Ottomans. In the early 1500s, Selim I conquered Egypt and claimed authority over all Muslims in North Africa.

The Turkish presence in North Africa was mainly restricted to the coast. To the south, the Ottomans gained control over the trade routes crossing the Sahara. They also supervised trading towns along the Niger River and other waterways. Beyond that, the Turks ruled relatively lightly, leaving day-to-day government to local governors called pashas.

THE SAFAVID EMPIRE IN PERSIA

Since Islam's early days, the land of Persia (now Iran) had been an important part of the Muslim world. It had been absorbed by the Arab caliphates and, from the 1200s to the 1400s, controlled by various Mongol and Turkic warlords. At the beginning of the 1500s, under a new empire, it regained its independence.

NOTE

Moving westward from Egypt, the Ottomans took most of Africa's northern coast. They captured the ports of Tripoli, Tunis, and Algiers, as well as many other cities.

In 1501, a fifteen-year-old boy rose to power in Persia, took the ancient title of shah, and proclaimed the Safavid Empire. Devoted Shiites, the Safavid shahs converted the majority of the Persian population to that denomination. Safavid Persia was commercially vibrant; the beautiful city of Isfahan was a great center of trade for silk, ceramic tile, and Persian rugs.

Militarily, the early Safavids were innovative and well organized. Like Ottoman Turkey and Mughal India, Safavid Persia was one of the Islamic world's gunpowder empires. Abbas I the Great (1587–1628) added gunpowder infantry (similar to the Ottoman janissaries) to his army.

Like the Ottoman Empire, Safavid Persia declined in the late 1600s and 1700s. The dynasty fell in 1723.

China, Japan, and East Asia

CHAPTER 16

- The Ming dynasty
- The Manchu conquest and the Qing dynasty
- The European arrival in East Asia
- Silk and tea production
- Canton and trade protectionism
- Daimyo, samurai, and Japanese feudalism
- The reunification of Japan
- The Tokugawa Shogunate
- Social stratification versus urbanization and the merchant class
- Nagasaki and Japanese isolationism

Between the 1400s and 1700s, China and Japan consolidated their position as the dominant powers of East Asia. Under the Ming dynasty, established in 1368, China reached a peak of cultural grandeur and elegance. After 1644, when a younger dynasty, the Qing (Manchu), arose, the Chinese continued to enjoy a high level of artistic and intellectual sophistication and even greater military and political prominence in Asia.

Japan began this period disunited and divided. For more than two centuries—the mid-1300s through the late 1500s—it tore itself apart in feudal wars and civil conflicts. Finally, during the late 1500s and early 1600s, Japan reunified. The regime that completed the reunification, the Tokugawa Shogunate, established strict control over Japanese politics and society, and ruled till the mid-1800s.

In the international context, the Chinese and Japanese remained only dimly aware of a major change: despite their cultural advancement and political consolidation at home, both countries slipped in terms of global power, losing the scientific and technological advantages they had possessed during the period between 1000 and 1450. This power shift, resulting from a certain stagnation, left both countries, especially China, vulnerable to foreign influence and domination during the 1800s.

MING CHINA

In 1450, the **Ming Dynasty** was almost a century old. From its foundation in 1368 to the early 1400s, Ming China had been a politically dynamic and militarily active state, conquering neighbors and exploring faraway lands. It was economically prosperous. Its population grew steadily during the late 1300s and 1400s, recovering from the wars and diseases of the late Yuan period.

Although Ming China remained powerful during the 1500s and early 1600s, its principal strengths during these years were cultural. As described in Chapter 8, the artistic and intellectual achievements of the Ming were impressive: literary masterpieces, fine porcelain ("china"), architecture, and the revival of Confucianism.

During the Ming period, the first European explorers began to arrive. As Portuguese traders and captains arrived in Asia, they established commercial ties with the Ming. The Spanish and Dutch arrived later. Because China was too large and powerful for the Europeans to conquer, they established embassies and trading houses there. Catholic (particularly Jesuit) missionaries were important as well.

The 1600s were a time of rapid decline. The late Ming rulers were weak and allowed the government to decentralize and then unravel. The Portuguese and Spanish traded with silver from North and South America, and the sudden, massive influx of precious metal triggered inflation, then economic breakdown. At the same time, agriculture yields shrank (perhaps because of a worsening of soil quality or a general cooling of the climate). The population grew more quickly than the land's ability to support it, and famines occurred regularly.

Finally, revolution and war drove the Ming to collapse. Serious military threats came from nomads and other invaders from Central Asia, Mongolia, and Manchuria. The huge cost of defending China's borders drained the economy. A massive peasant revolt, lasting from 1636 to 1644, toppled the dynasty. The last Ming emperor committed suicide, after first trying to kill his family.

The peasants' victory, however, was short-lived. Within weeks, enemies from the north, the Manchus, swept into northern China, took Beijing, and established a new dynasty.

THE QING (MANCHU) CONQUEST OF CHINA

The Manchus and the Establishment of the Qing Empire

The **Manchus** were from Manchuria, the large region northeast of China. Although related to the Chinese, the Manchus were ethnically distinct. For many years, the Manchus (who made up less than 5 percent of the population) created an ethnically based system of social stratification, in which the Chinese, as subjects, had to wear certain clothing and tie their hair in long braids, or queues. Males had to shave their foreheads, as reflected in a proverb of the time: "lose your hair or lose your head."

The empire established by the Manchus was called the **Qing** (or Ch'ing, 1644–1911). It included Manchuria and, after 1644, northern China. Skilled warlords, the Manchus continued their conquests. By 1683, they had taken southern China and the island of Formosa (now Taiwan).

The Manchus also controlled or added to their tributary system areas such as Mongolia, Tibet, Nepal, Burma, Vietnam, and much of Central Asia. Qing expansion to the north brought the Chinese into contact with Russia, which was moving deeper into Siberia by the 1600s and 1700s. It took much negotiation for the Chinese and Russians to arrive at a mutually acceptable boundary.

Qing Economics and Foreign Contacts

Full-scale trade with European nations began under the Qing, during the 1690s. Foreign trade was closely regulated by the state, and by the 1750s, most of it was allowed to take place only in one city, the port of **Canton**. Along with silk and porcelain, China's most important commodity was **tea**. While the Qing Empire sent a high volume of exports to other nations, it allowed few imports. This policy of **trade protection** gave China a highly favorable balance of trade.

The Qing regime sharply limited foreign contacts, economic or cultural, with ordinary Chinese, and strove to prevent the population from developing an appetite for foreign goods. Also suspicious of outside influences (and because of their strong support of Confucian ideals), the Qing banned Christianity in 1724. Another reason for limiting foreign contacts was cultural arrogance: like the Ming before them, the Qing considered China to be the center of the world and superior to all nations. In their eyes, Europeans were barbarians.

Emperors Kangxi and Qianlong

During the late 1600s and early 1700s, the Qing emperors were capable rulers, good administrators, and strong centralizers. The Emperor **Kangxi** (1662–1722) is widely considered one of the greatest monarchs in Chinese history: a skilled general, a just lawgiver, and a sponsor of culture and learning. Kangxi bolstered the imperial authority of the Qing by patronizing Confucianism, with its emphasis on respect for authority. Unlike many of the rulers who followed, he appreciated the importance of the West's growing technological aptitude. A later ruler, Qianlong (1735–1796), was the last dynamic ruler the Qing had. He strengthened China's borders, fostered economic growth, and promoted scholarship and art.

After Qianlong, the quality of the Qing rulers declined. They grew more complacent and less active. Also, as during the late Ming period, the Chinese population grew much faster than the economy, partly because of the introduction of New World crops like corn and the potato (population surpassed 300 million by 1799). Over time, national wealth was barely sufficient to support the population. For all but the upper classes, poverty worsened. Despite its strength as a regional power, Qing China was slipping backward in terms of technological innovation, scientific advancement, and global power—a danger the emperors succeeding Kangxi and Qianlong failed to perceive properly. By the 1800s, China would be increasingly open to European and American influence, then domination.

FEUDAL WAR AND REUNIFICATION IN JAPAN

As discussed in Chapter 8, Japan was governed after 1185 by military rulers called **shoguns**, who held power on behalf of the emperor, whose position was essentially symbolic. Although the shoguns preserved order and kept the country relatively unified in the late 1200s and early 1300s, decentralization became an increasingly serious problem in the late 1300s and 1400s. In theory, the Ashikaga Shogunate (1336–1573) ruled the country. In reality, Japan was becoming steadily more feudal, breaking down into semi- or wholly independent states ruled by the landed aristocracy, or **daimyo**. As most feudal nobles in Europe had been knights, most Japanese daimyo belonged to the **samurai** elite.

In the 1460s, Japan descended into an even more chaotic period of anarchy and civil war that lasted till the late 1500s. During this **Era of Independent Lords**, the shogun was weak, daimyo fought daimyo, and samurai who lost or left their masters (*ronin*) became mercenaries or turned to banditry. The economy suffered, and crime rates rose. Starting in the 1540s, Portuguese, Spanish, and Dutch traders, as well as Catholic missionaries (including the Jesuit **Francis Xavier**, who did much to promote his faith in Asia), arrived. The shoguns' political weakness allowed foreigners and their Christian beliefs to gain substantial influence. The Europeans also introduced gunpowder weaponry.

The **reunification of Japan** took more than fifty years (1560 to 1615) and involved the military and diplomatic efforts of three warlords. Oda Nobunaga, one of the first Japanese generals to use gunpowder weapons (especially at Nagashino in 1573), conquered east and central Japan but was assassinated in 1582. Following him was Toyotomi Hideyoshi, who rose from humble origins to reunify almost the entire country. A clever politician, he centralized power from his capital, Osaka, and restored order (at the cost of harsh social stratification). In 1598, when he died, his son was only a child, and civil war broke out once again. The victor was **Tokugawa Ieyasu**, a brilliant, ruthless commander. He appointed himself shogun in 1603 and completed the full unification of Japan in 1615 (a process that included forcing Hideyoshi's son to kill himself). The Tokugawa shoguns would rule Japan for two and a half centuries.

THE TOKUGAWA SHOGUNATE AND THE CONSOLIDATION OF JAPAN

The Tokugawa Shogunate lasted from 1603 to 1868. After so many years of disunity, order and stability were its main priorities. The Tokugawa era is also known as the Great Peace (or the Pax Tokugawa).

Centralization, Dictatorship, and Social Stratification

As Hideyoshi had done before him, Ieyasu centralized the country. He established a new capital at the city of Edo (modern-day Tokyo). As before, the emperor remained a figurehead. Peace came at the price of dictatorship, as well as increased **social stratification**. Japan's class system became more rigid than ever before, and until the mid-1700s, it was almost impossible for a person to move from one class or profession to another. One tool the Tokugawa used to enforce this policy was a renewed emphasis on Confucianism. Ordinary citizens were forbidden to own weapons; the samurai retained the privilege of owning swords. The Tokugawa maintained a strict monopoly on gunpowder technology and kept the number of guns in Japan as small as possible.

Under the Tokugawa, women lived under increased restrictions, particularly if they belonged to the samurai class. Wives had to obey their husbands or face death. They had little authority over property and received less education than men, although they were encouraged to follow artistic and cultural pursuits. Among the lower classes, gender relations were more egalitarian. Peasant men and women both worked in the fields, and women gained respect as homemakers and mothers. Even so, as in earlier eras, girl children were less valued and sometimes either put to death or sold into prostitution. Some women gained status as **geishas**, special courtesans who were highly valued for their musical, artistic, and conversational skills.

Japanese Isolationism

Many Portuguese, Spanish, and Dutch traders and missionaries entered Japan in the late 1500s, and Christianity became quite popular. However, many Japanese, like the Chinese, considered Europeans barbaric. More important, Japanese authorities suspected foreign ideas, including religious ones, and feared the possible effects of uncontrolled importation of gunpowder weaponry. Both Nobunaga and Hideyoshi started the process of restricting foreign access to Japan, even persecuting (and crucifying) Christians on several occasions.

The Tokugawa shoguns continued this policy of **isolationism**. Christianity was officially discouraged. A national seclusion policy was instituted in the 1630s, and from 1649 until the 1720s, foreign traders were allowed entry only into one city, the port of **Nagasaki**. A brief period of openness followed, and then Japan sealed itself off again until the 1850s.

Economics, Society, and Culture

Despite the Tokugawa regime's oppressive nature, it had many accomplishments to its credit. It restored and kept the peace. The population grew rapidly. Rice and grain production more than doubled between 1600 and 1720. Tokugawa Japan became highly urbanized (Edo was one of the world's largest cities), and the shoguns built an elaborate network of roads and canals. Economic growth was impressive: the Japanese became great producers of lacquerware, pottery, steel, and quality weapons.

During the 1600s, and especially the 1700s, the **merchant class** became increasingly wealthy and powerful (an exception to the general rule of social stratification). As for the samurai class, peace brought with it difficult transitions. At the price of obedience, samurai kept their social prestige, but in a modernizing society not at war, there was little need for a warrior elite with traditional combat skills. Some samurai were released from service by their daimyo lords; others found that the value of their land decreased as the country's economic center of gravity shifted to the cities. Masterless samurai (ronin) sometimes turned to crime, and there were occasional samurai uprisings. Most samurai, however, remained loyal, even if their traditionalist mindset kept many of them from embracing social and economic change.

In the cultural sphere, the samurai class maintained many of the traditions and styles mentioned in Chapter 8. There was some European influence on architecture (especially castle building, which had to adapt to the introduction of gunpowder) and painting (more emphasis on the laws of perspective). Among the urban classes, a new form of drama, **kabuki theater**—which featured acrobatics, swordplay, and scenes of city life—became popular. It was very different from the older, more refined Noh drama favored by the upper classes.

South and Southeast Asia

CHAPTER 17

- Gunpowder empires
- The Mughal Empire
- The Indian cotton trade
- The Indian Ocean trade network
- Sati
- The rise of Sikhism
- The European arrival in South and Southeast Asia
- The British East India Company
- The Maori and the Aborigines

Between 1450 and 1750, South and Southeast Asia experienced, on the whole, greater political centralization. These areas were also confronted by the sudden appearance of European explorers and merchants in the late 1400s and early 1500s. Both developments changed the region considerably.

The largest and most powerful states in the region were in India. In 1450, India was ruled by the Delhi Sultanate, which was declining rapidly. In the 1520s, invaders from the north destroyed the sultanate and established in its place the even stronger state: the Mughal Empire, which survived into the mid-1700s.

As before, India and the rest of South and Southeast Asia were characterized by an incredible diversity of ethnicity, language, and religion (major faiths included Hinduism, several forms of Buddhism, Islam, and more). In many ways, this diversity enriched India and its neighbors. However, it also created deep social and cultural divisions, which often caused conflict and strife.

MUGHAL INDIA

As detailed in Chapter 9, the Delhi Sultanate had been weakening steadily during the 1300s and 1400s. The final blows against it came in the early 1500s.

Babur the Tiger and the Mughal Empire

Starting in 1520, **Babur**—a Mongol warlord in the tradition of Genghis Khan and Timur—launched a full-scale invasion of India from the north. Known as the Tiger, he quickly defeated the Delhi Sultanate.

In 1526, after the battle of Panipat, Babur established his own government, the **Mughal Empire**, which he ruled until his death in 1530. His successors conquered most of the rest of India, and the empire continued for the next 200 years. Its name comes from the Persian word for *Mongol* (the word *mughal* is often spelled *mogul*, which, in English, still refers to any rich or powerful individual).

Like the Delhi sultans, the Mughals were Muslims, making their state one of the three great Islamic empires of the era, along with the Ottoman Empire and Safavid Persia (see Chapter 15). Like the Ottoman and Safavid states, Mughal India was a **gunpowder empire**, using military force and advanced weaponry to maintain power, both at home and abroad.

In its prime, the Mughals expanded steadily southward, ruling India from their famous Peacock Throne. Their first capital was Agra; later, the capital moved to Delhi, which was restored to its former glory. The Mughal rulers centralized India. The economy thrived thanks to a boom in the Indian **cotton trade**. The early Mughals were religiously flexible, allowing Hindus and Buddhists to practice their own faiths, even under Muslim rule. Only during the last years of the empire did this approach change.

Mughal India was culturally vibrant. Its architectural brilliance is illustrated by India's most famous landmark, the **Taj Mahal**, the white marble mausoleum built in Agra by Shah Jahan in memory of his wife. In painting and literature, there was a fusion of Persian and Indian styles.

Women in Mughal India

The effect of Mughal rule on women was mixed. On one hand, the Mughals allowed women certain rights. Female aristocrats were awarded titles, earned salaries, owned land, and ran businesses. Some received an education and expressed their creative talents openly. Women of all castes were permitted to sell their woven products. They could inherit land.

However, the Mughals restricted women's rights through **Sharia**, or Islamic law. These practices tended to coincide with restrictions that Indian society had already placed on women, such as cloistering women inside the home, as in the case of Hindu upper-class women. The Hindu practice of **sati** remained legal (although Akbar the Great attempted to outlaw it), and women were instructed to serve their husbands.

Akbar the Great

Mughal rule reached its peak under **Akbar the Great** (1556–1605), grandson of Babur. Akbar completed the conquest of India. A great commander, he used gunpowder weapons to gain control over most of the subcontinent.

Akbar created an efficient nationwide bureaucracy. The tax codes and legal system operated fairly. His reign was one of prosperity.

Akbar was also famed for religious tolerance. He allowed non-Muslims to worship as they wished, abolished the tax paid by non-Muslims, and encouraged friendly relations among Muslims, Buddhists, and Hindus. He even sought advice from the Catholic priests who arrived with European traders. Akbar ensured that a specific percentage of government officials were Hindu, and he married a Hindu princess.

Decline of the Mughal Empire

The Mughals' fortunes took a downward turn during the late 1600s and early 1700s. Akbar's great-grandson, **Aurangzeb** (1658–1707), a militant Muslim who abandoned the policy of religious tolerance, reimposed the tax on non-Muslims and forced thousands to convert to Islam against their will. His policy caused tremendous civil strife which, in turn, adversely affected the economy. Aurangzeb's intolerance also turned one religious minority, the **Sikhs**, into a rebellious and warlike group. The Sikhs' religion, which stressed the power of prayer and meditation, had been founded in the 1400s by the teacher Nanak. During the 1500s and early 1600s, the Sikhs had been peaceful. When Aurangzeb killed their leader in 1675, they revolted, founded their own state in Punjab, and developed a strong warrior tradition.

The Mughal state declined during the 1700s. The social and economic effects of religious struggle continued. Provinces broke away and became independent. In 1739, an Iranian marauder sacked Delhi and carried away the Peacock Throne, the symbol of Mughal glory.

Arrival of the Europeans

European interference in Indian affairs increased. The Portuguese trader Vasco da Gama arrived in 1498 (see Chapter 14). More Portuguese, then Spanish, came to South Asia. They were followed by the Dutch, the French, and the English, who arrived in the 1600s. During the 1500s and early 1600s, the gunpowder empire of the Mughals was strong and technologically advanced enough to keep the Europeans in their place.

During the 1600s, however, the balance of power shifted. The English built textile factories at Fort William (near Calcutta, in the northeast) and Madras. The western gateway port of Bombay (now Mumbai) was ceded to the **British East India Company** (one of the most politically powerful corporations in world history) in 1661. The Dutch East India Company established bases in Ceylon (now Sri Lanka). The French created a great garrison and trading center at Pondicherry, on the east coast. The Europeans profited by gaining control over the trade of Indian cotton for spices from the East Indies.

European, particularly English, control over India increased during the 1700s. Until after the 1750s, the European presence was concentrated mainly on the coastline. Starting in the 1740s, though, large numbers of French and British troops were fighting each other in India, for the "right" to colonize the entire subcontinent. By the 1750s, the English had defeated the French; they then turned to the conquest of India itself. They triumphed over the Mughal state easily, although they kept Mughal rulers in charge of certain parts of India as puppets. In a short time, one of the world's mightiest empires had been transformed into a weak colonial possession.

SOUTHEAST ASIA

Kingdoms of Southeast Asia

Like India, the nations of Southeast Asia solidified politically. They also faced the arrival and constant encroachments of European explorers and colonizers.

Strong states in the region during these years included Thailand (which conquered the neighboring Khmer state in Cambodia), the Vietnamese nation of Annam, and Burma (which maintained the largest army in Southeast Asia). Vietnam and Burma became tributary states of Qing China. The islands of Indonesia were politically and economically important, until they submitted to Dutch colonial control.

Buddhism and Hinduism were dominant religions. Islam was important as well, especially in Indonesia, where it became the majority faith.

The European Presence in Southeast Asia

Europeans arrived in Southeast Asia after 1498, when Vasco da Gama reached India. The Portuguese quickly took over whatever parts of Southeast Asia they could: Malacca, Goa, Sri Lanka, and more. Where they could not conquer, they traded. The same was true for the Europeans who followed: the Spanish, Dutch (who took over Indonesia), French, and English. Because they were smaller and less advanced than India, it was harder for the nations of Southeast Asia to remain free from European colonization—although many managed to do so, at least until the 1800s, when European imperialism became even harder to resist. The Jesuit priest **Francis Xavier** came to Southeast Asia in the 1540s and spent the rest of his life cementing a Catholic foothold throughout Asia.

Australia and Its Neighbors

Farther to the south, the English encountered the continent of Australia. In 1770, the British mariner and explorer **James Cook** charted the east coast of Australia and claimed the continent for his country. The nearby islands of New Zealand (home to the Polynesian **Maori**) and Tasmania came under English control as well.

Full-scale settlement of Australia began in 1788. For years, the population consisted mainly of soldiers, government officials, and criminals "transported" to the colony as punishment. In 1830, Britain claimed the entire continent of Australia. The rate of settlement increased, as free settlers joined the colony seeking their fortunes. Mainly sheep farmers, Australians pushed into the interior and displaced the original inhabitants, the **Aborigines**, who had lived there for tens of thousands of years. The confrontations between colonists and Aborigines were often violent and one-sided, ending with the dispossession and ill treatment of the natives.

Sub-Saharan Africa

CHAPTER 18

- The Songhai state
- The kingdom of Kongo
- The Asante (Ashanti) kingdom
- The Zulu
- The gold and ivory trades
- The Indian Ocean trade network
- The Boers (Afrikaners) and the apartheid system

- Abstraction in African art
- The Arab slave trade
- European exploitation of Africa
- The Atlantic slave trade, the Middle Passage, and triangular trade

Starting in the early 1400s, Africa came under the increased influence of the exploring powers of Europe. Along the western and eastern coasts, Portugal, then other European nations, seized cities, built fortresses, and established permanent colonies. For centuries, Europeans exploited Africa economically, taking gold, spices, ivory, and other resources through trade and by force. Most shameful was the **Atlantic slave trade**, which began in the 1400s, as Portugal started transporting Africans overseas for use as forced labor. Quickly, more nations became involved, and the size and number of slave shipments grew astronomically, with the slave trade persisting well into the 1800s. Its effect on Africa, the Americas, and the economies of Europe was profound.

For the time being, however, the interior of Africa remained largely free from European control. Not till after the mid-1800s would Europeans penetrate much beyond the coasts. Certain African nations grew strong and thrived. On occasion, Africans were able to defeat European forces and stop colonists and slavers from moving deeper into the continent. Nonetheless, the economic impact of European imperialism was felt even in the interior, as were the effects of the slave trade.

WEST AND CENTRAL AFRICA

The Songhai State and Kongo

By the mid-1400s, the previously dominant power in West Africa, Mali, was fading. In its place, the Muslim kingdom of **Songhai** (previously a part of the Mali Empire), rose up. The first of its powerful kings, Sunni Ali, conquered neighboring territory in the 1460s and asserted control over many trade routes and the key city of Timbuktu. Songhai's most famous ruler, **Askia Mohammed** (1493–1528), came to the throne by deposing the last Sunni ruler (the name *askia*, which he adopted after coming to power, means "usurper"). A skilled general, Askia Mohammed continued to expand Songhai's boundaries. He centralized power by creating a complex bureaucracy, and he sponsored art, scholarship, and the building of many mosques. He encouraged trade, and the growing merchant class generated wealth by exchanging salt for gold. A fictionalized account of his reign, *The Epic of Askia Mohammed*, is one of the classics of the West African oral tradition. Songhai prospered until the late 1500s. Civil war followed the peaceful reign of Askia Daoud, and Morocco conquered the divided kingdom in 1590.

Taking shape around 1400, the kingdom of **Kongo** grew out of Bantu-descended communities that had existed since 1000 B.C.E. The state extended from the Atlantic coast to the western edge of what is now the modern state of Congo. Prior to European contact, its economy was based on ivory, cloth, pottery, and metal.

In 1483, the Portuguese arrived in force, and although they did not conquer Kongo outright, they compelled it—largely by taking hostages—to enter into a long and complex relationship with Portugal. The king converted to Catholicism and took the name João I. Later monarchs followed the same example, adopting European names and the Christian faith. For many years, Kongo existed not as a colony, but as a state forced into economic and political partnership with an outside power. This relationship cost Kongo some of its autonomy, but also helped make it powerful. (Much the same is true of the Asante kingdom, discussed below.) During most of the 1500s, Kongo expanded and centralized, establishing an elaborate system of provinces and duchies to govern its population of approximately 500,000. Its large army acquired modern weaponry—and many mercenaries—from Portugal. Kongo helped to satisfy Portugal's growing appetite for African slaves, mainly by using its army to fight its neighbors and enslave thousands of prisoners of war.

Internal disputes and succession struggles weakened Kongo in the late 1500s and early 1600s, and again in the mid-1600s. Even so, Kongo managed to reduce Portuguese dominance: in 1622, with help from the Dutch, it expelled the official Portuguese presence. Periodic conflicts followed until Kongo's decisive defeat of Portuguese armies in 1670. The country went through various phases of unity and disunity throughout the 1700s and most of the 1800s, until, near the end of the century, it was fully colonized.

The Europeans and West and Central Africa

All of West Africa was affected by the arrival of the Europeans in the 1400s. First the Portuguese and then the Dutch, English, and French landed on the African coast, began trading, and built permanent outposts. The original purpose of the Portuguese had been to find their way south and east to India. As they became interested in Africa for its own sake, the Europeans sought to gain control over the **gold** and **ivory trades** that extended throughout West and Central Africa and the upper Zambezi River.

Women in West and Central Africa

As mentioned in Chapter 11, several African groups, particularly in West Africa, were **matrilineal** in organization, and women took part in leadership. In some instances, women became rulers. For example, **Queen Nzinga** (1582–1663) ruled the Mbundu peoples in what is now Angola. She was respected for defending her people against the Portuguese.

In West African trading villages, women took part in market activities. Sometimes women's councils administered the markets.

In North African cities, where Islam dominated, upper-class women were more likely to be cloistered and made to wear veils. However, economic necessity compelled lower-class women to work outside the home.

The Emergence of the Slave Trade

From the late 1400s onward, the development of African nations, the patterns of African trade, and the history of entire tribes were shaped by the growing European presence. The strongest states in West Africa—Oyo, Benin, Dahomey, Kongo, and Asante—were those that cooperated with the European slave trade, by warring on and imprisoning other African tribes, and then selling the captives to European slavers.

In particular, the **Asante (Ashanti)** kingdom, founded by Osei Tutu in 1680, became immensely powerful because its leaders sold gold and slaves to Europeans in exchange for muskets and gunpowder. West Africa was nicknamed the Gold Coast in recognition of the lucrative exchange of gold for slaves. Asante was one of the few parts of Africa where both minerals and agricultural resources were found in abundance.

Even states and tribes in Equatorial Africa, beyond the direct impact of Europeans on the coast, were affected. The trade networks connecting Equatorial Africa with the west coast were redirected or destroyed by the Europeans. Some West Africans began to raid Equatorial Africa for goods to trade with Europeans. Worst of all, the Europeans' desire for slaves frequently led West Africans to fight their neighbors in Equatorial Africa in search of prisoners to sell into slavery.

SOUTHERN AFRICA

Before the arrival of the Europeans, the southern tip of Africa had been settled by various tribes, mainly descended from the Bantu (see Chapter 3). The Portuguese rounded the tip of Africa in 1488, establishing an outpost on what they called the Cape of Good Hope.

During the 1600s, control of the region passed from the Portuguese to the Dutch. Dutch settlers known as **Boers** (also Afrikaners) arrived in 1652 and became firmly established as farmers and traders; their language evolved into a dialect called Afrikaans. Even more so than most white Europeans, the Boers possessed a strong sense of racial superiority and looked upon Africans and other peoples of color as inferior. Over the centuries, the Boers' harsh treatment of native Africans developed into the infamous system of **apartheid**.

The Boers enslaved the nearest African tribe, the Xhosa, a peaceful herding people. As the Boers expanded to the north, they encountered a stronger and more warlike people, the **Zulu**. Many wars broke out between the Boers and the Zulu. By

---

WOMEN IN POWER

Many women throughout history have held political power on an individual basis. Examples include Cleopatra, Elizabeth I, Catherine the Great, Nzinga, Cixi, Golda Meir, Indira Gandhi, and Margaret Thatcher. Matrilineal societies, like those found in parts of West Africa, often afforded women more respect and authority than elsewhere. An interesting question, however, is whether this means that women are treated *equally*. Many queens and empresses come to power only because male alternatives are not available, and it does not necessarily follow that they can (or even want to) use their position to improve the overall condition of women. Even in modern democracies, women tend to be underrepresented as elected officials. In discussing how women have influenced historical developments, be sure not to overgeneralize from the often atypical experiences of powerful individuals. Until very recently, sexism and inequality have been the norms in most times and places.

the early 1800s, the entire region came under British control, although the Boers continued to live there. This awkward, three-way situation caused much conflict during the 1800s.

EAST AFRICA

As discussed in Chapter 11, the towns and states of East Africa were part of the vibrant, cosmopolitan **Indian Ocean trade network**. From the 1400s onward, this system continued to exist, although the arrival of European merchants and conquerors changed conditions considerably.

The Portuguese, the first to arrive, originally viewed East Africa as a platform for reaching the Indies. For example, in 1498, the East African port of Malindi was Vasco da Gama's jumping-off point to Calicut, in India. Soon, however, the Portuguese realized the advantages of having permanent bases in East Africa. Not only would this allow them to reach India more efficiently, it would give them tighter control over trade in the Indian Ocean basin, especially in spices.

In the early 1500s, the Portuguese conquered a chain of cities along the East African coast, turning them into colonies. These included Malindi, Sofala, Mozambique, and Mombasa. Arabs expelled the Portuguese from Mombasa in 1728, but Portugal's presence in the region remained strong for hundreds of years. Others, including the English, later colonized East Africa as well.

AFRICAN CULTURE

Africa did not have a unified approach to art, although it is possible to make some generalizations. **Sculpture** was its most dominant medium. African art was also concerned with human adornment, as in masks and elaborate beadwork. Moreover, much of African art has been **abstract**, or not made to recreate visual reality (long before abstract art became a popular concept in the West).

Between 1450 and 1750, artists continued to produce wood carvings, sculptures, metalwork, and paintings. European traders brought home with them carved **ivory** pieces and textiles, which were admired by distinguished art patrons. **Textile arts** were prevalent in places like the West Congo basin. While textiles were considered prestige objects, owned by the elite, they were also sold to people of the lower classes.

Finely woven **basketry**, often done in intersecting geometric patterns, was treasured by royal families in East Africa. Basketry of high value was produced in Rwanda and Burundi. In the seventeenth and eighteenth centuries in Christian Ethiopia, kings commissioned artists to produce churches with brightly colored wall paintings of holy events. One of the most famous of these churches is the Church of Debre Berhan Selassie in Gondar, Ethiopia.

African architecture was influenced by Arabs and European colonists, who built fortresses and residences in East and West Africa.

THE ATLANTIC SLAVE TRADE

As in most parts of the world, slavery had existed in Africa for many years. African tribes often enslaved members of other tribes. In addition, the large **Arab slave trade** had for a long time extended throughout the Sahara and southward.

The Origins of the Atlantic Slave Trade

The arrival of the Europeans changed the character of slave trading in Africa. The Portuguese began this process, but other European nations followed suit. Over time, the Atlantic slave trade became a central part of the European economy and a primary factor in Europe's ability to generate such great wealth from the 1500s onward.

Starting in 1441, the Portuguese began to enslave Africans, taking them to Portugal and selling them in Europe. The number of slaves brought directly to Europe was relatively small. During the 1500s, however, slaves began to be taken to the Americas, and the numbers grew.

This new slave trade involved important changes. It took Africans farther from home. It became far greater in scale. Also, while unjust, earlier forms of slavery had not always involved hard labor, and owners took some care of slaves, at least as pieces of property. The Atlantic slave trade involved a greater degree of manual labor, and treatment of slaves tended to be harsher.

Reasons for the Expansion of the Atlantic Slave Trade

Several factors increased the demand for African slaves. One was the labor-intensive nature of planting, harvesting, and refining sugar. During the 1500s, Portuguese and Spanish colonies in Brazil and the Caribbean became major centers of **sugar production**, and the desire for slave labor there became more intense.

Also during the early 1500s, it became clear to the Spanish and Portuguese that, in the New World, Native Americans were not well suited as slaves. In addition, by 1542, the Catholic Church had abolished the system that allowed the Spanish to enslave Native Americans (see Chapter 19). If the Spanish and Portuguese wanted a source of slave labor—not just for sugar cultivation but also for **mining**, agricultural work, and menial labor—they had to turn elsewhere. Africa seemed an ideal source.

The Growing Scope of the Atlantic Slave Trade

Roughly 1,000 slaves per year were taken from Africa in the late 1400s, and more than 2,000 per year in the 1500s. It is estimated that at least 325,000 Africans were enslaved by Europeans in the 1400s and 1500s.

The Atlantic slave trade mushroomed in scale during the 1600s and 1700s. More than a million slaves were transported from Africa in the 1600s, and at least 6 million were taken in the 1700s. It is thought that, in total, no fewer than 12 million Africans became slaves in the New World between the mid-1400s and the late 1800s. Thirty-seven percent went to Brazil (the largest slaveholding country), 15 percent to Spanish America, 41 percent to non-Spanish parts of the Caribbean, and 5 percent to the southern colonies of British North America, where they grew crops such as cotton and tobacco.

The Middle Passage

Slaves were captured and shipped to the Americas under notoriously appalling conditions. Many were captives or prisoners of war, herded like animals to the coast and sold to European slavers by other Africans. Most were separated from their families;

many were mixed in with members of other tribes, who spoke different languages and followed different customs.

On the West African coast, slaves were loaded onto ships to make the infamous **Middle Passage** across the Atlantic. The more slaves a ship could carry, the greater its profits, so slaves were packed into boats as tightly as possible. Chained, lying on their backs, surrounded by hundreds of other bodies, all in darkness, slaves endured a nightmarish sea journey for weeks. Upon arrival in the New World, they would be taken to slave markets and sold. In the early years, up to 25 percent of slaves perished during the Middle Passage. During the 1700s and 1800s, slavers cut the average death rate to 10 percent or less—not for humane reasons but because each dead slave was a financial loss.

Atlantic Slavery, the Triangular Trade, and the World Economy

By the 1700s, African slavery had become a crucial element in European economic life and global trade. Until the early 1800s, no major nation made slavery or the slave trade illegal. Moreover, slaves were an integral part of the economic system known as **triangular trade**. European manufactured goods (metalware, cotton textiles, processed alcohol such as gin and rum, firearms) would be brought to Africa and exchanged for gold, ivory, timber, and slaves. The gold, ivory, and timber would be brought back to Europe, while slaves were sold in the Americas.

The Middle Passage therefore comprised the second leg of this triangular trade. In the Americas, slaves would be traded for furs and other materials, such as tobacco, raw cotton, sugar, and silver (typically grown or mined by slaves—and thus, slaves were not only commodities in the triangular trade network but unwilling producers in it as well). These materials would be brought back to Europe. This system was paramount in the growth of European wealth.

The Americas as "New World"

CHAPTER 19

- The conquistadors and New Spain
- Gunpowder weaponry and horse warfare
- The importation of smallpox and measles
- Seville's House of Trade and the viceregal system
- The encomienda system
- Silver mining and sugarcane cultivation
- Plantation monoculture
- The Atlantic slave trade
- The North American fur trade
- The French and Indian Wars
- Indentured servitude and "transportation"
- The Columbian Exchange

As described in Chapter 14, North and South America, which had existed in a state of isolation for thousands of years, came into contact with the rest of the world after the middle of the 1400s. European explorers arrived, considering themselves to have discovered what they thought of as the New World. Of course, the concepts of "discovery" and "New World" were meaningless to the Americas' original inhabitants. Equally meaningless was the name given to them by the Europeans: "Indians" reflected Columbus's mistaken belief that he had reached Asia during his voyages of the 1490s.

During the 1500s and afterward, the Spanish and Portuguese, then other Europeans, turned the Americas into their own spheres of influence. The Europeans also brought the Americas into contact with the rest of the world, economically, culturally, ecologically, and politically.

Most notably, the Europeans made North and South America part of a network of trade and exchange that was expanding literally around the world. Traders, settlers, explorers, and slaves came to the Americas, as did new technology, knowledge, and cultural traditions. The environment of the Americas changed forever, thanks to the Europeans' exploitation of the continents' resources—and their introduction of new diseases, plants, and animals. Conversely, the new foods and natural resources (especially precious metals) extracted from the New World had a significant impact on civilization worldwide—not just in Europe but also Asia and Africa. This so-called **Columbian Exchange** proved to be one of the most significant global developments during the period from 1450 to 1750.

NEW SPAIN

After the 1492 voyage of Columbus, the papal **lines of demarcation** granted jurisdiction over the entire New World to Spain, with the exception of Brazil, which went to Portugal.

NOTE

Starting in 1535, New Spain was governed as a viceroyalty (*viceroy* means "in place of the king"). By the 1700s, three new viceroyalties—Peru, New Granada (northern South America), and La Plata (southern South America)—had been added.

The Spanish first established themselves on the islands of the Caribbean. Military expeditions led by **conquistadores** led to the creation of New Spain on the mainland of North and South America. The conquistadores took over Florida and most of what is today the southern and southwestern United States, including Texas and California. Their most striking victories were the conquest of Montezuma (Moctezuma) II and the Aztecs by **Hernán Cortés**, from 1519 to 1522, and the destruction of the Incan Empire between 1531 and 1536 by **Francisco Pizarro**. The former allowed the Spanish to turn Mexico City (built on the site of the Aztec capital, Tenochtitlán) into New Spain's principal headquarters. The latter opened up South America for future conquests.

Reasons for Spanish Success

Even with very small forces, the Spanish defeated large and powerful cultures in the Americas quickly and decisively. With their **horses** and **gunpowder weapons**, conquistadores such as Cortés and Pizarro enjoyed a military advantage that outweighed their lack of numbers. The Spanish (especially Cortés) were also adept at **divide-and-conquer tactics**, whereby they stirred up rivalries among native tribes and allied with some against others.

What most enabled the Spanish conquest was disease, particularly **smallpox** and **measles** (the same was true of the Portuguese in Brazil). Having no immunity to these new illnesses, native peoples died in massive numbers. Anywhere from one-quarter to one-half of the original population perished—some historians think even more—and the survivors were even more vulnerable to Spanish invasion.

Exploitation, Forced Labor, and Slavery

The conquistador Cortés famously stated that he had come to the Americas for "God, gold, and glory." Although converting Native Americans to Catholicism was considered important (especially to offset the loss of worshippers to Protestant churches in Europe), Cortés's second motivation—economic exploitation—was Spain's highest priority in the New World.

At first, the conquistadores governed the territory they conquered, sending one-fifth (*la quinta*) of their profits back to Spain. The viceregal system placed the New World colonies under Madrid's direct control. All colonial economic activity was run by the **House of Trade** in Seville.

Above all, the Spanish extracted precious metals from the Americas: gold and, even more important, **silver**. The largest silver mines were dug near Mexico City and at **Potosí**, Bolivia's "mountain of silver." Agriculture was important as well. Chief crops included coffee, bananas, tomatoes, corn, potatoes, and most crucial, **sugarcane**, which was turned into rum and molasses. The Spanish (and Portuguese) made use of **plantation monoculture**: the intensive cultivation of a single crop on large estates (known as haciendas, estancias, or latifundia).

Mining, labor-intensive sugarcane farming, and plantation monoculture required large numbers of manual laborers. At first, conquistadores resorted to the **encomienda** system (which declared all peoples in the Americas Spanish subjects) as a way of forcing Native Americans to work as slaves. This practice ended by the 1530s and 1540s, not only because Native Americans proved unable and unwilling to work as slaves but also because the Catholic clergy protested the cruelty resulting from the encomienda system. The book *Tears of the Indians*, by the monk Bartolomé de las Casas, did much to sway Spanish opinion about the plight of Native Americans. The encomienda was abolished in 1542. The result was to persuade the Spanish (like the Portuguese) to turn to Africa as a source of forced labor, leading to the escalation of the **Atlantic slave trade**.

> **NOTE**
> Plantation monoculture is environmentally damaging (it wears out soil); it leads to long-term economic backwardness (by discouraging countries from diversifying their resource base) and, worst of all, encourages unfair labor practices (including slavery).

Ethnic Diversity and Social Stratification

The arrival of the Spanish increased racial diversity in the Americas. Pure-bred Spanish who settled in the New World were known as *peninsulares*. Those of Spanish descent born in the colonies were criollos (better known as creoles). When Spanish and Native Americans intermarried, their families were known as mestizos, or "mixed." Other mixed races were mulattos (Europeans and African blacks) and *zambos* (Native Americans and African blacks). This intermixing of ethnicities and traditions has made Latin American culture very rich.

Unfortunately, during the centuries of Spanish rule, these groups were organized into a rigid social hierarchy, with European Spaniards at the top and those of mixed blood and native ancestry near the bottom. Slaves were on the lowest rung of the social ladder. (Compare this arrangement with India's caste system.)

PORTUGUESE BRAZIL

Brazil, the one major territory in the New World allotted to Portugal rather than Spain, was discovered by accident in 1500 by Pedro Cabral, whose ship blew off course in a storm. At first, the Portuguese considered Brazil unimportant and established an outpost there only in 1532. By the mid-1500s, the Portuguese came to recognize Brazil's economic potential.

Native populations were decimated by Portuguese conquerors, falling victim to superior technology and new diseases. Portugal's treatment of the natives, a mixture of labor exploitation and mass conversion to Catholicism, was similar to Spain's. Various ethnic mixes of European, Native American, and African emerged. **Plantation monoculture** was dominant.

> **NOTE**
> Many of the same trends found in New Spain applied to Brazil.

Mining was important in Portuguese Brazil, as were the forest industries of the Amazon basin. For years, however, the most important resource was **sugarcane**. The labor-intensive nature of sugarcane cultivation prompted the Portuguese to use African slaves, first on their islands off the African coast and then Brazil. The first boatload of slaves to be brought directly from Africa to the New World arrived in 1518 (although African slaves had been brought there indirectly before then). Brazil was the largest importer of African slaves, and it was the last country in the Americas to outlaw slavery—not until 1888.

DUTCH AND ENGLISH NORTH AMERICA

The Dutch in the Americas

In the late 1500s, the Netherlands and England started breaking the Portuguese and Spanish monopoly on global trade routes and overseas colonization. They began to settle in the New World.

The Dutch took over a number of islands in the Caribbean and seized part of northwestern Brazil from the Portuguese. In 1621, the Netherlands established the Dutch West India Company, twin to the older Dutch East India Company.

Farther to the north, the Dutch founded New Netherlands, in the region explored and claimed by Henry Hudson on their behalf. In 1624, Peter Minuit purchased the island of Manhattan from a local Native American tribe. Here, the city of **New Amsterdam**, capital of the new colony, grew into a thriving commercial center. The colony's leader was Peter Stuyvesant. In 1664, the Dutch lost New Netherlands to the English, who gave New Amsterdam another name: New York.

English Colonies and Permanent Settlement in the New World

Like the Dutch, the English moved into the New World as part of their commercial and military rivalry with Spain. They established a presence in the Caribbean, particularly on the islands of Barbados, Trinidad, and Jamaica.

Successful colonization of North America began at Jamestown, Virginia, in 1606. Economic activity was important, although many colonies were established by religious minorities, especially Puritans and Quakers, fleeing persecution at home. The *Mayflower* Pilgrims' Plymouth colony was founded in 1620; the nearby Massachusetts Bay Colony followed in 1628, and Boston was founded in 1630. The English seized New Amsterdam in 1664, renaming it New York. The colony of Pennsylvania, organized in 1682 by William Penn, was home to the English New World's largest city, Philadelphia.

The English took raw materials from the New World: sugarcane from the Caribbean; timber, corn, and potatoes (which caught on in England's oldest and closest colony, Ireland); and in the southern colonies, tobacco, which proved remarkably profitable. In addition, England, more so than other European nations, viewed the New World as a place to encourage large-scale **permanent settlement**. English colonies in the Americas became politically sophisticated, developed strong systems of local government, and, by the 1700s, felt a deep sense of local, even independent, identity.

Slaves were used by English colonists in the New World, especially in the Caribbean and the southern mainland. English criminals were often punished by "transportation," or exile, to the Americas. One institution that brought labor to the English New World was **indentured servitude**: would-be colonists who could not afford passage across the Atlantic would agree to work for a period of time for the families that paid their way. This was more common in the northern colonies.

> **NOTE**
>
> After the American Revolution, England deported its criminals to Australia.

FRENCH CANADA AND LOUISIANA

The French colonial presence in the New World began in **Canada**, in the 1500s and early 1600s, as Jacques Cartier, Samuel Champlain and other explorers charted the St.

Lawrence River and established outposts like Quebec and Montreal. In the 1600s, the French laid claim to the vast **Louisiana** territory, which included the Great Lakes and the Mississippi basin. In the south and along the Gulf of Mexico, they challenged the Spanish. The main priority of the French in North America was the **fur trade**: French colonists were great hunters, trappers, and woodsmen (*voyageurs*).

> **NOTE**
> The French were more adept than other Europeans at cooperating with Native Americans (especially the Hurons and Algonquins), learning their ways, and adapting themselves to local customs and environments.

The French maintained island bases in the Caribbean, including Martinique, Guadeloupe, and Saint Domingue (today Haiti). Sugarcane production was the economic mainstay here.

By the mid-1700s, France had lost much of its territory in the New World. Its principal enemy was England, although Spain was a foe as well. Despite allying with Native American tribes, French colonists lost several conflicts with English settlers, including Queen Anne's War (1701–1714), King George's War (1740–1748), and the **French and Indian Wars** (1756–1763), an offshoot of the Seven Years' War in Europe.

As a result of the third conflict, the English took over Canada (the province of Quebec retained its French heritage). The Louisiana region was handed over to Spain, although the French got it back briefly in the late 1700s. French culture remains important in eastern Canada, the northern fringe of the United States, and the state of Louisiana. There, the Cajuns are descendants of the Canada's Acadians, who were expelled and forced southward by the English after the French and Indian Wars.

THE RUSSIAN-AMERICAN COMPANY

Europe's least famous colony in North America was Russia's. After conquering Siberia in the 1500s and reaching the Pacific coast in the 1600s, the Russians set their sights on Alaska and other areas. In the 1730s and 1740s, the **Bering expedition**, organized by the Russian government, surveyed the waters separating Siberia from North America. Afterward, Russian hunters and soldiers moved into the Aleutian Islands and Alaska.

> **NOTE**
> At least 80 percent of the Aleutians' native population is said to have perished due to Russian colonization, thanks to violence, the spread of disease, and alcoholism.

The **fur trade** stimulated Russian settlement of North America. The Russians established a colony in Alaska in 1784. They created the **Russian-American Company** and moved down the Pacific coast, building fortresses as far south as northern California. They sold Alaska to America in 1867.

THE COLUMBIAN EXCHANGE

Europe's encounter with the Americas led to one of the greatest demographic and ecological transformations in world history, known commonly as the **Columbian Exchange**.

The exchange of foods, plants, and animals shaped the environments of Old World and New World alike. From Europe came sheep, goats, cattle, and pigs, which increased the meat and milk supply in the Americas. The Europeans also brought the **horse**, which provided labor and transport and radically changed the lifestyle of Native Americans who lived on plains and grasslands. **Coffee**, which came from Arabia and Turkey and had already been transplanted to Africa, was found to flourish in South America. The southeastern part of North America joined Egypt and

NOTE

Among the effects of this exchange was the mass transfer of populations. Millions of slaves and hundreds of thousands of colonists came from Africa and Europe to the New World. Once in the Americas, their interaction with the indigenous peoples led to complex and rich ethnic and cultural mixing.

India as one of the world's great sources of **cotton**. Wheat, olives, and grapevines were brought to the Americas as well.

From the Americas came manioc (which became a staple in Africa), squash, sweet potatoes, peppers, beans, peanuts, and vitamin-rich tomatoes. Caribbean **sugarcane** displaced the Old World's sugar beet as a primary source of sugar and became central to the world economy (and the Atlantic slave trade). **Tobacco** and cacao (for making chocolate) became eagerly sought luxury goods in Europe. Because they were easy to grow and yielded many calories per acre, **corn** (maize) and **potatoes** were the New World crops that most affected Eurasia and Africa.

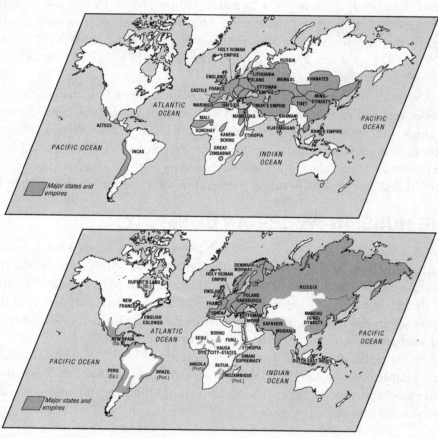

World Boundaries in 1453 and 1700.
In 1453, major states and empires were concentrated in Eurasia and small territories in Africa and the Americas. By 1700, large civilizations had spread into Russia, more portions of the Americas, and deeper into Africa.

NOTE

The death rate caused by European diseases is thought to have been at least 25 percent of the Americas' pre-Columbian population; some estimates run higher than 50 percent.

Tragically, the transfer of diseases, such as **smallpox** and **measles** from Europe—and malaria and yellow fever from Africa—was part of the Columbian Exchange. Environmentally isolated from Eurasia and Africa for so many centuries, the inhabitants of the Americas had no immunity to these new illnesses. The one disease Europeans may have brought back from the New World is the sexually transmitted disease syphilis (although there is much scholarly debate about the origins of this disease).

Unit Four: Review Questions

SAMPLE ESSAY QUESTIONS (CCOT and COMPARATIVE)

CCOT 1. Analyze the changes and continuities in the level of scientific and technological advancement in ONE of the following between 1450 and 1750.

China
Western Europe
Ottoman Turkey

CCOT 2. Analyze the political changes and continuities in ONE of the following between 1450 and 1750.

India
Russia
Japan

COMP 1. Compare and contrast the experience of TWO of the following civilizations as they encountered the Europeans between 1450 and 1750.

Kongo
Mughal India
the Aztecs
China

COMP 2. Compare and contrast the characteristics of TWO of the following labor systems.

the *encomienda* system
Russian serfdom
proto-industrialization in Europe
the Atlantic slave trade

MULTIPLE-CHOICE QUESTIONS

1. Why did China find itself more vulnerable to foreign influence after the late 1700s?

   (A) It had slipped backward in terms of scientific and technological innovation.
   (B) Its rulers encouraged too many imports and generated a negative balance of trade.
   (C) It became overly dependent on Great Britain for military assistance.
   (D) It undermined its social cohesion by allowing too many immigrants to settle there.
   (E) It allowed Christian missionaries to gain too much influence over the population.

2. Which of the following is MOST true of eighteenth-century European society?

   (A) A majority of the population moved into the relatively new middle class.
   (B) Proto-industrialization had little or no impact on economic life until the 1800s.
   (C) The majority of people continued to live in the countryside and work as peasants.
   (D) The rate of population growth fell off sharply.
   (E) The cause of women's suffrage gained great momentum in western Europe.

3. The tendency of the Muslim "gunpowder empires" to innovate technologically in the 1500s and 1600s, and then stagnate, is best illustrated by

   (A) a decline in the quality of carpets manufactured in Safavid Persia after the mid-1600s.
   (B) the transformation of the janissaries into a pampered but obsolete musketeer corps.
   (C) the flawed engineering methods used to build the otherwise beautiful Taj Mahal.
   (D) the Ottoman Empire's failure in the 1700s to create a steamship navy.
   (E) Mughal India's decision to abandon railway construction projects begun around 1750.

4. This commodity played the chief role in motivating French exploration of Canada and Russian exploration of Siberia:

   (A) coffee
   (B) gold
   (C) fur
   (D) tobacco
   (E) diamonds

5. Which of the following negatively affected economic life in Ming China during the early 1600s?

   (A) a decrease in the supply of precious metals, especially silver
   (B) a failure of economic growth to keep up with population growth
   (C) a decline in productivity caused by the addiction of Chinese workers to opium
   (D) a series of wars with Russia on the Siberian frontier
   (E) an unwillingness to grow new foodstuffs from the Americas, such as corn

6. Which of the following can be considered true of Japanese geishas and the women of the Ottoman harem?

   (A) In both cases, they were employed only by the royal family.
   (B) In neither case were they expected to display musical or artistic talents.
   (C) In both cases, their services could be purchased by members of any social class.
   (D) In both cases, they often advised rulers and served as regents.
   (E) In neither case was their exclusive role to provide sexual pleasure.

7. What resulted from Portuguese exploration of West Africa in the 1400s?

   (A) The Portuguese gained control over trade in gold and ivory.
   (B) The Portuguese destroyed existing states like the Asante kingdom.
   (C) The Portuguese used the region as a base from which to conquer Egypt.
   (D) The Portuguese went on to discover new routes to the West Indies.
   (E) The Portuguese expelled nearly all the Muslims living in the region.

8. Which is an example of the changes brought about by the Columbian Exchange?

   (A) the importation of coffee to Africa from South America
   (B) the European encounter with the horse in the plains of North America
   (C) the extraction of silver from Brazil by the Spanish
   (D) the introduction of corn and potatoes to Europe from the Americas
   (E) the spread of smallpox from North America to Europe

9. What did Europe's so-called Scientific Revolution accomplish?

   (A) It successfully promoted the geocentric theory.
   (B) It reconfirmed the teachings of Galen and Aristotle.
   (C) It put into practice Descartes's and Bacon's revival of the scientific method.
   (D) It immediately swept away the Catholic Church's authority over intellectual affairs.
   (E) It provided universal education for people of all classes.

10. The map on page 186 (without looking at the caption) relates to

    (A) patterns of large-scale migration from Spain and Portugal to other parts of the world.
    (B) the Papal Lines of Demarcation that assigned claims to new lands to Spain and Portugal.
    (C) Spanish and Portuguese shipments of tobacco and silver from Africa to Asia and the Americas.
    (D) epidemiological vectors showing how New World diseases affected Spain and Portugal.
    (E) the roles played by Spain and Portugal in the early stages of the Atlantic slave trade

11. This New World region imported the largest percentage of African slaves:

    (A) the Carolinas
    (B) Haiti
    (C) Canada
    (D) Brazil
    (E) Cuba

12. Forced migration in the form of "transportation"—a punishment often handed down by British courts in the 1700s and 1800s—was the primary cause of population growth in which colony?

    (A) Barbados
    (B) India
    (C) Australia
    (D) Jamaica
    (E) South Africa

13. How is the religious policy of the Ottoman sultans best described?

    (A) They gradually converted from Islam to Christianity.
    (B) They expelled Catholics and Protestants, but not Orthodox Christians.
    (C) They allowed a degree of toleration but taxed religious minorities.
    (D) They gave full equality to all worshippers, regardless of faith.
    (E) They ruthlessly suppressed Jews and Christians.

14. What was a major consequence of plantation monoculture?

    (A) It created fewer incentives to rely on slave labor.
    (B) It tended to enrich the lower and middle classes.
    (C) It encouraged the harvesting of a larger variety of crops.
    (D) It left farmers more susceptible to new diseases.
    (E) It led to severe environmental degradation.

15. Which art forms were most prominent in sub-Saharan Africa before 1750?

    (A) painting and composed music
    (B) sculpture and basketry
    (C) written literature and painting
    (D) basketry and written literature
    (E) sculpture and composed music

16. In what way did Qing China's social policies resemble those of the Tokugawa Shogunate?

    (A) Both relied on systems of rigid social stratification.
    (B) Both wished their populations to have greater exposure to foreign goods and ideas.
    (C) Both supported the concept of universal access to education.
    (D) Both boosted the rights and privileges of the growing merchant class.
    (E) Both persecuted ethnic and religious minorities.

17. How does capitalism differ from mercantilism?

    (A) Capitalism emphasizes state-controlled accumulation of wealth, whereas mercantilism gives greater commercial power to merchants.
    (B) Capitalism arose earlier than mercantilism.
    (C) Capitalism shows greater sympathy to socialist ideals than mercantilism does.
    (D) Capitalism places a premium on free trade and market forces, whereas mercantilism favors state control over economic activity.
    (E) Capitalism is more concerned with land-based economic activity, whereas mercantilism is more associated with maritime trade.

18. What effect did the Portuguese presence have on the kingdom of Kongo between the late 1400s and early 1600s?

    (A) The Portuguese forced Kongo's rulers to convert to Catholicism.
    (B) The Portuguese persuaded the people of Kongo to stop enslaving their neighbors.
    (C) The Portuguese conquered Kongo outright during the 1500s.
    (D) The Portuguese protected Kongo from Dutch encroachment.
    (E) The Portuguese enslaved most of Kongo's population by 1600.

19. Russia's colonization of the Aleutian Islands and Spain's conquest of its American territories are similar in that

    (A) large armies were required in both cases to outnumber huge native forces.
    (B) both nations were motivated principally by the desire to convert the natives to Catholicism.
    (C) the economic commodity most sought in both cases was gold.
    (D) a large percentage of both native populations died because of exposure to new diseases.
    (E) both colonizing powers established large cities to govern their new territory.

20. The Mughal Empire grew wealthy in the 1600s and 1700s because of a boom in the global demand for this commodity:

    (A) nutmeg
    (B) cotton
    (C) coffee
    (D) wool
    (E) cloves

Answers

1. **(A)** Remembering that China's rulers minimized contact with non-Asians as much as possible during these years eliminates C, D, and E. Regarding trade, they deliberately exported more than they imported. Like the Safavid, Ottoman, and Mughal empires, Qing China fell behind the West in terms of technological know-how.

2. **(C)** Answers A and E apply to the nineteenth century, not the eighteenth. Answers B and D are exactly opposite to the truth; population grew steadily in the 1700s, and proto-industrialization became increasingly important. Not until well into the 1800s did the majority in any European nation leave agricultural work behind.

3. **(B)** Industrial efforts like the ones described in D and E were not feasible until the 1800s. Persian carpets remained among the best in the world during this period, and the Taj Mahal is an engineering as well as an aesthetic marvel. The janissaries began as one of the world's most effective gunpowder forces, but became corrupt and disobedient over time.

4. **(C)** Each of these commodities motivated some sort of colonial effort. Expansion into Canada and Siberia, however, was driven above all by Europe's ever-growing appetite for fur.

5. **(B)** Like many parts of the world, Ming China suffered a glut, not a shortage, of silver during this time, because of Spanish exploitation of New World precious metals. It also grew corn and potatoes once they were discovered in the Americas. Defense costs were a heavy burden during these years, and China was wary of Russia, but it was not the main foe compared with nomads, warlords, and bandits. Opium was not introduced until the 1700s. Several times over, the pressures of population growth strained China's economy.

6. **(E)** A great deal of myth surrounds the popular understanding of harems and geishas. Harems were complex sub-societies, many of whose members had nothing to do with the ruler's sexual pleasure, and geishas were entertainers and culturally sophisticated companions more than they were courtesans. A key difference is that the harem existed solely for the benefit of the royal family.

7. **(A)** The Portuguese did none of the things described in B through E. They also began the practice of enslaving Africans, a fact not touched on by this question.

8. **(D)** Corn and potatoes, with their high-calorie yields, changed the diets of people around the world forever. Spain did not colonize Brazil (and silver was known to Europeans in any event). The other answers were all involved in the Columbian Exchange, but the direction in which they exerted their influence is reversed or mistaken.

9. **(C)** Answers A and B involve ideas done away with or modified by the scientific revolution, and E belongs to a later time. Not only did the scientific revolution last many years, but Catholicism's influence over intellectual life never disappeared altogether, so D is false as well. Descartes and Bacon resurrected the logic behind scientific problem-solving that Aristotle had spoken of long ago, but that had tended to be ignored by the medieval Europeans who accepted his often flawed empirical observations as fact.

10. **(B)** The names of explorers and the map's discussion of spheres of influence should be enough to exclude the false clues, even without much historical knowledge of the expeditions depicted by the map.

11. **(D)** Although African slaves were first used in large numbers in the Caribbean, and although the slaveholding experience in the U.S. South is the one most familiar to American readers, the largest proportion of slaves brought to the New World went to Brazil—which was also the last country in the hemisphere to ban slavery.

12. **(C)** Until the American Revolution, many of those sentenced to "transportation" were sent to North America.

13. **(C)** Like many empires—Rome's, Alexander's, and Akbar the Great's, for example—the Ottoman state found it useful to show some respect for religious minorities. It made subject peoples easier to govern, and if one taxed them if they refused to convert (as the Ottomans did), the practice was profitable as well. People of the same religion were grouped into social units called *millets*, an institution worth comparing with the Indian caste system.

14. **(E)** Farmers might not get sick because of monoculture, but lack of variety made the areas they farmed more susceptible to having all their crops wiped out by one plant disease. Plantation monoculture favors rich landowners and not the middle or lower classes, and it lends itself readily to unfair labor practices, slavery included. It tends to wear out soil and cause massive deforestation.

15. **(B)** Oral traditions tended to be stronger than written ones in sub-Saharan Africa. Painting and composed music were not unknown, but textiles, basketry, carving, and sculpture were much more common. The abstract nature of many of these works was discovered and eagerly appropriated by Western artists in the late 1800s and early 1900s.

16. **(A)** Although Japan's social system was arguably more stratified than China's, both were extremely hierarchal—with Confucianism providing justification, especially in China. Merchant classes grew in importance, but were not particularly respected by either state.

17. **(D)** Capitalism emerged after (and partly as a reaction against) mercantilism. Socialism, in turn, is largely a reaction against capitalism. Capitalism favors free trade above state control.

18. **(A)** During these years, Kongo was a puppet state under Portugal's control, adopting Catholicism, accepting weapons and new technology from Portugal, and taking prisoners from neighboring tribes for the Portuguese to use as slaves.

19. **(D)** European conquerors tended to have much smaller armies than those they defeated. Although military violence and other forms of abuse led to many native deaths at the hands of European imperialists, disease did the most damage by far. Most scholars estimate that 25 to 50 percent of the pre-Columbian population of the Americas died, mainly because of disease—but some argue that the percentage was much higher still. Answer E is true of Spain, but not of Russia. The Russians were not Catholic, and in the Aleutians, they were principally interested in territorial acquisition and seal pelts.

20. **(B)** India, Central Asia, Egypt, and the U.S. South were among the world's great producers of cotton. Great Britain especially desired to control India (and, later, Egypt) in order to supply its rapidly growing textile industry.

UNIT FIVE

WORLD CULTURES
IN THE MODERN ERA
(1750–1914)

Unit Overview

GENERAL REMARKS

During the 1750–1914 period, the world entered the modern age. In this, it was led by the nations of the West, consisting of Europe and the United States.

Exactly what defines **modernity** is a question of debate among historians. In popular terms, the word *modern* is used as a synonym for "contemporary" or as a way to describe one's own times. In historical terms, it describes an era characterized by certain features. Different scholars outline modernity's features in different ways, but most agree on the following:

- In politics, there is a move from traditional monarchy toward greater political representation. The end result in most societies is some form of democracy or at least the appearance of democracy.
- In economics, industrialization becomes a driving force. There is a shift from feudalism and mercantilism to capitalism. Rather than being based primarily on agriculture, economies are based increasingly on industry and commerce.
- In society, there is class transformation, as old aristocracies fade away in favor of new elites whose status derives from wealth. New classes expand or emerge, especially the middle class and industrial working class. As agriculture gives way to industry, societies urbanize. Population growth accelerates.
- In culture, a scientific, secular worldview becomes dominant. Artistic and literary styles change more rapidly and radically than ever before.

In all these things, Europe, with the United States, moved forward first. Great political upheavals such as the **American Revolution** and the **French Revolution** began the long process of expanding political representation and giving more people a greater voice in politics. It was in Europe that the **Industrial Revolution** began, and it was there that capitalism emerged. Both transformed the economies of the world. Population growth, class diversification, and urbanization were hallmarks of Western social development during the late 1700s and throughout the 1800s. The foundations for modern culture and intellectual life had been laid in Europe during the 1700s, during the Scientific Revolution and the Enlightenment.

To varying degrees, modernization reached the rest of the world in the nineteenth and early twentieth centuries. A few non-Western nations adapted well and quickly, such as Japan. Some, including the Ottoman Empire, China, and the nations of Latin America, modernized slowly or partially. Other civilizations, most notably those of Africa and Southeast Asia, lagged farther behind. No matter the pace, however, change came to all these regions.

Another overarching development between 1750 and 1914 was the **rise of the West** as the world's dominant civilization. Not only did industrialization and modernization make the West prosperous and technologically advanced, they made it powerful as well. European (and American) imperialism resulted in control over most of the world's habitable territory. Many areas that had originally been colonized during the Age of Exploration—such as North and South America—became free during the late 1700s and early 1800s. However, a **new imperialism** swept over Asia, the Middle East, the Pacific, and Africa during the 1800s and early 1900s. Seeking markets and raw materials, armed with industrial-era weaponry, the nations of the West established control over a vast portion of the globe. Never before in history had a single civilization become so powerful. But as impressive as imperialism was practically, it carried a steep moral and ethical price. Imperialism was inextricably bound up with warfare, racial prejudice, economic rapacity, and slavery. Many of the harmful effects of Western imperialism are still felt to this day.

By the end of the nineteenth century, Europe had reached the peak of its power, but would soon fall from that pinnacle. The young United States was overtaking Europe in economic and military strength. New philosophies, scientific theories, and cultural movements were calling into question the traditional certainties and values of the Western world. Most important, Europe was moving toward war. The conflict resulting from the diplomatic tensions of the late 1800s and early 1900s—World War I—was the worst ever fought to that date. It did much to start and then speed up the process of European decline.

BROAD TRENDS

Global Power and International Relations

- The technological, economic, and military rise of the West—Europe and the United States—completely altered the balance of global power. World affairs were increasingly determined by foreign-policy and military developments in Europe, especially during the 1800s.
- The United States broke away from English rule during the late 1700s. During the 1800s, it dominated the North American continent and became a world power.
- The Spanish and Portuguese colonies of Latin America freed themselves from European rule during the early 1800s.
- In North Africa, the eastern Mediterranean, and the Middle East, the gradual collapse of the Ottoman Empire presented the nations of Europe with a troubling and destabilizing diplomatic issue known as the Eastern Question.
- European (and U.S.) imperialism—the "new imperialism" of the mid-to-late 1800s—gave the nations of the West unprecedented global dominance. In

1815, the nations of the West controlled 35 percent of the world's habitable territory. In 1914, they controlled 85 percent.

- The one non-Western nation that developed a modern colonial empire in the late 1800s and early 1900s was Japan.
- In Europe, the new nations of Germany and Italy appeared.
- By the end of the 1800s, diplomatic tensions, nationalism, and competition over colonies made it increasingly likely that the nations of Europe would go to war. An alliance system formed. The level of aggression rose steadily. World War I resulted in 1914.

Political Developments

- The hallmark of modern political life is greater popular representation.
- This trend first got underway in the West. It began in the late 1700s, primarily with the American and French Revolutions.
- During the 1800s, especially after the 1848 revolution, politics in Europe and the West became increasingly representative. By the end of the century, Great Britain, France, and the United States, along with a few smaller countries, had become democracies (although women could not yet vote). Even in nondemocratic states, bureaucracies and parliamentary bodies became an increasingly important part of government, even more so than the will of individual rulers and monarchs.
- Other parts of the world tended to be slower in moving away from traditional autocracies or monarchies. A few, such as Japan and the Ottoman Empire, did so, developing parliamentary forms of monarchy by the start of the twentieth century. The nations of Latin America developed parliamentary governments in theory, but many of those slipped into dictatorship or military rule.
- Much of the non-Western world spent most of the nineteenth century under European (in some cases, U.S.) colonial domination.

Economic and Environmental Developments

- Economic life was transformed by the phenomenon of industrialization, which displaced agriculture as the largest and most important sector of the economy. Industrialization swept Europe in the late 1700s and early 1800s, then spread to the rest of the world. The Industrial Revolution began in England.
- The dominant mode of economic organization in the West became free-market capitalism. Along with industry, commerce and banking—the foundations of a money-based economy (as opposed to a land-based one)—grew in importance.
- Industrialization transformed class structures. The traditional aristocracy, with its status based on land and family prestige, faded. Among the lower classes, the proportion of peasants and farmers shrank. The middle class expanded, gained great wealth, and diversified. A new lower class, the industrial working class, was born.
- Industrialization led to urbanization. Cities grew in size, and more cities were established.

- For any society, the first decades of industrialization were typically painful for the lower classes. Working conditions were poor, and wages were low. Over time, industrialization greatly raised the average prosperity of a society's population, and even the lower classes benefited after some time.
- The non-Western world adopted industrialization at varying speeds and in different ways. Sometimes, European imperial powers introduced it to their colonies. In other cases, rulers of free non-Western nations imposed industrialization from above.
- One of the bedrocks of the world economy during the late 1700s and most of the 1800s was slavery. Africa was the primary victim of slave trading. The East African and Atlantic slave trades continued into the 1870s and 1880s.
- Industrialization vastly increased humanity's impact on the environment. Pollution levels rose.

Cultural Developments

- Starting in the West, a scientific, secular worldview became paramount. The technological and scientific advancements of the Industrial Revolution, as well as the theories of scholars such as Charles Darwin, accelerated this process.
- Greater access to public education became a normal part of life in North America and northern and western Europe throughout the 1800s. Literacy rates rose as a result. The same is true for many other parts of the world during the late 1800s.
- There was a tremendous movement of peoples during this period. In particular, there were massive waves of emigration from Europe and China to the Americas during the mid-to-late 1800s and early 1900s. The United States was the preferred destination, but Canada, Argentina, and Chile took in many immigrants as well.
- Nationalism became a powerful political and cultural force in Europe and then elsewhere. By the end of the 1800s, nationalist movements became prevalent in non-Western parts of the world dominated by foreign colonial rule.
- The non-Western world began to adopt many of the artistic and literary forms of the West, especially print culture and writing styles, as well as architecture. Conversely, styles from Asia, Africa, and the Middle East had an influence on Western culture, particularly in painting, sculpture, and décor.
- In Europe and the Americas, the pace of cultural change sped up. By the end of the 1800s and the beginning of the 1900s, new artistic and literary trends were emerging at a rapid rate. Increasingly, these were about breaking rules and defying conventions.

Gender Issues

- Although in most societies, the status of women remained secondary, the 1750–1914 period saw great changes in gender relations.
- In the West, a greater awareness of the unequal treatment of women began to spread, starting around the late 1700s. This was stimulated partly by the theories of Enlightenment philosophy, as well as the active role played by women in the American and French revolutions.

- During the late 1700s and early 1800s, the Industrial Revolution profoundly altered the conditions under which women worked. It shifted the workplace away from the farm, where men and women both lived and worked, to mines, factories, and other spaces away from the home. This shift created a domestic sphere and a separate working sphere away from the home.
- In Europe and the United States, women of the lower classes were generally compelled to enter the workplace (most frequently textile factories). These women also bore the double burden of serving as the primary homemakers and caregivers for their families.
- After the mid-1800s, the number of working women in Europe and North America declined. Women of the middle and upper classes had rarely worked to begin with. As wages for industrial workers rose (making those jobs more desirable to men) and as laws restricting the number of hours women and children could work were passed, the number of lower-class working women fell. A cult of domesticity, stressing that a woman's place was in the home and a man's in the workplace, dominated Western culture—especially among the middle and upper classes—during the mid-to-late nineteenth century.
- Certain occupations were open to women, such as child care (governesses), teaching, domestic household work (servants and maids), nursing, and artisanry.
- Strong and vigorous women's movements appeared in Europe, Canada, and the United States. They agitated for suffrage (the right to vote), equal opportunity to work, equal pay, temperance, and other causes.
- A handful of European nations—but no major ones—gave women the right to vote before World War I.
- The move toward women's equality tended to be slower in non-Western societies. In some, however, the educational level of women rose, as did the extent of property rights. As in the West, women worked, especially in certain occupations, such as agricultural labor, domestic service, and nursing. As non-Western parts of the world industrialized, lower-class women tended to enter the workplace, as in the industrial West.

QUESTIONS AND COMPARISONS TO CONSIDER

- Compare revolutions in two or more of the following countries: America, Haiti, France, Mexico, and China.
- Discuss the response of non-Western parts of the world such as China, India, Japan, and the Ottoman Empire to imperial encroachments and foreign pressures (especially from Europe and the United States) during this period.
- Compare the status of women in the West and that of women in other parts of the world. Also, in western Europe, compare the roles and conditions of upper- and middle-class women with those of the peasant and working classes.
- Describe the various approaches taken by various Western powers to colonization. Also, how does the late-nineteenth-century wave of imperialism (the "new" imperialism) compare to earlier waves of colonization?
- Discuss various ways in which non-Western states attempted to modernize and adopt industrial practices. How important is the question of whether industri-

alization was imposed on a society from above, by the ruler, or emerged from below?

- Take a close look at Japanese industrialization and European industrialization. How were they alike, and how did they differ?
- How did Western intervention in Latin America differ from Western intervention in Africa during the 1750–1914 period?
- Examine nationalist and anticolonial movements in non-Western parts of the world. Compare and contrast their methods and their successes and/or failures.

The Europeans at Home: Revolution, Reaction, and Reform

CHAPTER 20

- The Atlantic revolutions and the French Revolution
- The Napoleonic wars, the Congress of Vienna, and reaction
- The Industrial Revolution
- Increased representation (reform versus revolution)
- Women's movements and female suffrage
- Nationalism and the unifications of Italy and Germany
- Anti-Semitism (pogroms; the Dreyfus Affair)
- Romanticism, realism, and artistic modernism
- Charles Darwin and the theory of natural selection
- Albert Einstein and the theory of relativity
- Sigmund Freud and psychology

From 1750 to 1914, the European political order changed dramatically. In the mid-1700s, all of Europe's major nations were monarchies. Although a handful were parliamentary, allowing for some level of popular representation, most were absolute—meaning that, in theory, the monarch had few if any restrictions on his or her power. In general, monarchs shared power only with aristocratic noble classes. In any given country, the nobility made up an extremely small proportion of the overall population but controlled most of the country's wealth, owned most of the nation's land, and enjoyed virtually all influence over politics.

From the 1770s through the 1810s, this state of affairs was shaken apart by a wave of **Atlantic revolutions**. The most famous took place in Britain's North American colonies (see Chapter 27) and France, but there were others as well. Although not all their goals were met, the revolutions dealt a death blow to absolute monarchy in most of Europe. Another effect was that an ever-increasing number of people began to dream of—and fight for—social and political systems that treated them fairly and gave them more voice in government. Another factor that changed ordinary Europeans' social and economic aspirations was the **Industrial Revolution**, which happened at the same time as the political revolutions in America and France and is described in Chapter 21.

Although a conservative backlash, known as **reaction**, settled over Europe in the decades following the French Revolution and its Napoleonic aftermath, the desire for more representative government never died. Each nation, its rulers and its people, struggled with this issue in different ways and at different paces. The general trend, however, was for governments to liberalize and democratize over time. This was especially the case after the **revolutions of 1848**. During the second half of the century, reform movements helped to accelerate political change, as well as social and economic progress.

By the late 1800s and early 1900s, most countries in Europe were more or less representative, and a few were, by the day's standards, democratic. Most European economies were fully or partially industrialized. As described in Chapter 22, European powers, thanks to their imperial successes, dominated a vast amount of the rest of the world. These years marked the peak of Europe's global might. Underlying diplomatic and strategic tensions, however, gave rise to World War I (1914–1918): the huge cataclysm that began the process by which Europe toppled from its position of world power.

THE FRENCH REVOLUTION AND THE NAPOLEONIC ERA

Long-term Causes of the French Revolution

The causes of the **French Revolution** (1789–1799) are many and complex. Long-term factors included

- The wide social and economic gap between ordinary citizens (known as the Third Estate) and the country's elite, the Catholic clergy (First Estate) and the aristocracy (Second Estate)
- The unfair tax system, from which the wealthy First and Second Estates were exempt
- The frustrated ambitions of the middle class, who had wealth and education but, because they belonged to the Third Estate, were barred from social advancement
- The influence of the Enlightenment (see Chapter 13), whose philosophers, many of whom were French, made powerful arguments in favor of fair government, equal treatment of citizens, the separation of governmental powers, and civil rights

Added to these causes were the political ineptitude of the last two absolute monarchs of France, Louis XV and Louis XVI, and a long-standing financial crisis in France. Another ingredient was the American Revolution (1775–1783), which France supported (adding to its financial troubles) and which the French people admired. Little did the French government realize that by helping the American revolutionaries, it would encourage revolution in its own country shortly afterward.

The Estates General and the Early French Revolution

The immediate cause of the French Revolution was the impending bankruptcy of the government. Saddled with debts piled up by the previous king, having spent even more money on America's revolution, unable to tax the rich First and Second Estates, and burdened with a wife, Marie Antoinette, who spent lavishly, **Louis XVI (1774–1792)** could not solve France's financial crisis. By 1787 and 1788, inflation, unemployment, food shortages, and rising prices were tormenting the entire country.

In May 1789, desperate for a solution, Louis XVI summoned the **Estates General**: a national assembly of delegates from each estate. The delegates of the Third Estate—mainly middle-class lawyers—came to Versailles expecting to negotiate seriously about changing the tax system and granting equal rights to all classes. By June, however, it was clear that neither Louis XVI nor the First and Second Estates were prepared to compromise. This clash of wills sparked ten years of revolution.

In late June, the delegates of the Third Estate, with liberal members of the First and Second Estates, formed a new governmental body, the National Assembly, and vowed not to leave Versailles until the king granted them a constitution. In July, the people of Paris and other cities rose up in support of the assembly, as did peasants in the countryside. The Paris revolt, **Bastille Day**, is celebrated as the moment France liberated itself from absolute monarchy. Over the summer, the assembly assumed power in Paris.

The first two years of the revolution were a relatively moderate time. Louis XVI was allowed to remain king, but with the reduced powers of a parliamentary monarch. Guided by Enlightenment ideals and the American Declaration of Independence, the assembly guaranteed civil liberties in the **Declaration of the Rights of Man and the Citizen**. Future assemblies were to be elected by popular vote. Aristocratic status and privileges (especially exemption from taxes) were done away with, lands owned by the Catholic Church were nationalized, and church and state were separated. Policy was guided by the motto Liberty, Equality, and Fraternity.

There were, however, problems. At first, the rights proclaimed by the revolution, including the vote, applied only to white, Catholic, adult males. Only with time did Jews, Protestants, and blacks gain those rights, and women, despite the roles they played in toppling the absolutist regime, never did. Slavery was not ended in France's colonies until 1794. Also, the assembly failed to solve worsening economic problems. Louis XVI, encouraged by Marie Antoinette, secretly plotted **counter-revolution**, as did many former aristocrats. Other countries, fearing that their people would follow the French example if the revolution succeeded, threatened war.

Moreover, the victorious revolutionaries could not agree on how to change France. Liberal nobles and clergy, with much of the middle class, were satisfied with parliamentary monarchy and moderate change. The rural population, happy to have equal rights and to limit the power of the king, wanted economic relief but not deeper social change. The urban lower classes (known as sans-culottes) and certain middle-class idealists were more radical. They wanted to end the monarchy altogether, drive out or persecute former aristocrats (even liberal nobles), change society more thoroughly (some favored abolishing Catholicism), and export the revolution to other countries by force. Resolving all these desires would prove impossible.

Radicalism, the Reign of Terror, and the Directory

From the spring of 1792 through the summer of 1794, the French Revolution took a sharply radical turn. In April 1792, France went to war with Austria and Prussia; other countries, including Britain, joined in, and France would remain at war for almost the entirety of the next quarter century. The economy worsened, and early military failures caused mass hysteria. Remaining aristocrats and political moderates fell under suspicion, as did the royal family. Radical parties became more influential.

In the fall of 1792, a new constitution created a new legislature (the National Convention), stripped the king of all powers, and proclaimed the French Republic. Elections brought the radical parties to power. Most important were the **Jacobins**, led by Maximilien Robespierre, a fanatically idealistic lawyer. In January 1793, Louis XVI was executed for treason (Marie Antoinette was killed in October). The Jacobins created an executive body, the **Committee of Public Safety**, which assumed dictatorial powers, persecuted enemies, and attempted the radical transformation of French society. It expanded the war effort, mobilized the economy for combat, and carried out the modern world's first national draft. Civil war erupted in the countryside (especially the Vendee), as peasants rebelled against conscription and the radicals' efforts to eradicate Catholicism.

Between the summer of 1793 and the summer of 1794, Robespierre and the Committee, supported by the urban sans-culottes, carried out a **Reign of Terror**, searching for counterrevolutionaries and traitors. In this panicked, witch-hunt atmosphere, civil liberties were largely ignored. More than 300,000 people were arrested without warrant and tried without jury or appeal. Between 30,000 and 50,000 were killed, many beheaded by the guillotine. In July 1794, a coup within the committee overthrew Robespierre (who was guillotined) and ended the Terror.

For the next five years, a more moderate government called the Directory ruled revolutionary France. The military situation stabilized, and the Directory attempted to restore order after the chaos caused by the Terror. However, the middle-of-the-road Directory was unpopular, and it was overthrown in 1799, bringing an end to the revolution.

Napoleon Bonaparte

Among those who ousted the Directory was a talented and popular general, **Napoleon Bonaparte**, who quickly seized power for himself. Napoleon claimed to follow the ideals of the French Revolution, but in reality, created a dictatorship stronger and more efficient than the absolute monarchy had been. Indeed, in 1804, Napoleon crowned himself emperor of France.

Evaluating Napoleon's reign is difficult. He was arrogant and autocratic, with little respect for democracy or constitutional rule. His wars lasted for years, cost untold amounts of money, and killed millions of people. On the other hand, he modernized France in many ways, creating institutions that still exist today, such as the **Bank of France** and the **Civil Law Code** (known then as the **Napoleonic Code**, still the foundation of modern French law). Until his wars went badly in 1812, his military skills made France immensely rich and powerful.

Napoleon is best known for his military career. After coming to power, he continued the wars France had begun during the revolution. His chief enemies were

Britain, Austria, Prussia, and Russia. From 1805 through 1811, his victories made France the most powerful nation in Europe: the only major nations not under his control were Britain and Russia.

Several factors brought about Napoleon's downfall: his inability to counter British naval power, a guerrilla war in Spain and Portugal, and, finally, an overambitious invasion of Russia in 1812. He was defeated, captured, and exiled in 1814. In 1815, he escaped and had to be beaten again at the Battle of Waterloo. After years of captivity, he died in 1821.

Successes, Failures, and Long-term Effects of the French Revolution

What made the French Revolution and its Napoleonic aftermath so important? After all, in many ways, the revolution failed. The dream of a popularly elected government faded, only to be replaced by the harsh Committee of Public Safety, the semidictatorial Directory, and the unmistakably dictatorial Napoleon. After Napoleon's defeat, the old royal family was restored to power. Moreover, it is hard to argue that liberty, equality, and fraternity were achieved by means of Jacobin terror and the guillotine.

On the other hand, the French Revolution did away with absolute monarchy. Kings, queens, and emperors continued to sit on European thrones, but in no major country, with the exception of Russia, were they all-powerful. As time passed, monarchs yielded more of their power to ministries, parliaments, and legislatures.

Also, the French Revolution (like the American Revolution before it) sparked other **Atlantic revolutions**. Uprisings in Ireland, Belgium, the Netherlands, and Poland followed the American and French examples. They failed, but revolutions in Haiti and Latin America succeeded (see Chapter 27). Even Napoleon spread revolutionary ideals through Europe by writing constitutions for the countries he conquered. Much later, the Mexican (1910), Chinese (1911), and Russian (1917) revolutions were inspired in large part by France's.

In the end, the greatest legacy of the American and French revolutions was to cause people to demand greater popular participation in government and to force nineteenth-century governments to be more attentive to those demands. The rulers of the 1800s might not give into all of their subjects' desires, but they could no longer ignore them as they had before. As time passed, ordinary people became more successful in getting their voices heard and their demands met. The story of European politics during the 1800s and early 1900s is primarily *this* story.

REACTION AND REFORM: POLITICS IN EUROPE, 1815–1914

The Congress of Vienna and the Principle of Reaction, 1815–1848

Real change had to wait for several decades. After the defeat of Napoleon, the leaders of Europe gathered at the **Congress of Vienna** (1814–1815) to settle the peace. Not only did they redraw the map of Europe, but Britain, Austria, Prussia, and Russia restored prerevolutionary governments wherever possible (including in France) and agreed to cooperate in preserving the **diplomatic balance of power**. The experience of the French Revolution and the Napoleonic wars convinced most politicians that any kind of liberalism led automatically to political chaos and war; to them, the best way to maintain order was to oppose any kind of democratic change. This arch-conservative stance was called **reaction**, and its principal spokesman was the Austrian statesman **Klemens von Metternich**, who hosted the congress.

The resulting Congress System helped to keep the peace in Europe until the early 1850s. However, stability came at the price of stifling political change and civil liberties. Although monarchies were no longer absolute, freedom of expression and freedom of the press were restricted, secret police forces became common, and censorship was heavy. Trade unions and workers' associations were illegal (just as the industrial working class was expanding), and political parties were outlawed in many countries.

Even in western nations such as Britain and France, political controls tightened. Less than 5 percent of the British population could vote or run for Parliament, and the Congress of Vienna brought the kings back to France. Change in both countries was slow. In Britain, it took place by means of gradual reform. (In 1832, the First Reform Act slightly expanded the vote and improved the electoral system's districting and operation. In the 1820s and 1830s, the home minister, Robert Peel, ushered in a series of limited social and political changes.) France lurched forward by means of periodic revolution (in 1830, 1848, and 1871).

In central and eastern Europe, the level of repression was much greater. On behalf of his emperor, Metternich ruled Austria with an iron hand. Prussia, now a leading German state, was militaristic and authoritarian. Russia remained an absolute monarchy; there were no meaningful checks on the tsar's power. In addition, Russia continued the practice of **serfdom**, the system of unfree agricultural labor that had died away elsewhere in Europe decades, if not centuries, before. In addition to being inherently unjust, serfdom was inefficient and kept Russia socially and economically backward.

The Revolution of 1848

The **Revolution of 1848**, which shook almost every country on the continent to its political roots, is a great dividing point in nineteenth-century European history. Underlying causes include

- popular impatience with over three decades of reactionary rule
- social and economic pressures caused by the **Industrial Revolution** (see Chapter 21)
- the growing strength of **nationalism**
- a long series of economic downturns and bad harvests that caused the decade to be known as the "hungry forties" (the Irish Potato Famine is the best-known of these crises)

The 1848 revolution began in France, where the king was deposed, and Napoleon's nephew (Louis Napoleon, later Napoleon III) became president. It spread to the rest of Europe, prompting Metternich's famous quote about revolution: "Every time France sneezes, Europe catches cold." Only Britain (which was flexible enough to avoid revolution) and Russia (which punished liberals and radicals harshly enough to make revolution too dangerous) remained immune. Uprisings broke out in Prussia, Austria, most of the German states, and many parts of Italy. Nationalism caused a number of areas ruled by the Austrian Empire (Italian cities, Czech Bohemia, Croatia, and Hungary) to rise up.

By the end of 1848 and early 1849, all the revolts were crushed or faded away. Historians often speak of 1848 as "the turning point that did not quite turn." Still, the revolutions of 1848 had their effects. They compelled Prussia and Austria to grant constitutions. They demonstrated the growing political importance of nationalism and laid the foundation for the later unifications of Italy and Germany. They inspired **Karl Marx** to write *The Communist Manifesto*. Most of all, they hammered home for good the lesson of the French Revolution: that the political, social, and economic demands of ordinary people had to be taken seriously, if not met.

Representative Government and Unifications, 1848–1914

During the second half of the century, most European countries moved closer to representative forms of government. Britain and France became democracies (defined by **universal male suffrage**, or a politically meaningful vote for all adult males). Even in less representative regimes, political power spread outward to larger numbers of governmental advisers, ministries, and agencies.

Britain under Queen Victoria gradually extended the vote to the middle and lower classes by means of the **Second** (1867) and **Third** (1885) **Reform Acts**. Under prime ministers Benjamin Disraeli and William Gladstone, the Conservative and Liberal parties took turns granting economic concessions and fairer labor laws to the lower classes. By the early 1900s, the working class had enough political influence that a new party, Labour, was founded to serve its interests. Britain in the late 1800s had the world's greatest empire and was extremely prosperous. It wrestled, however, with the questions of women's suffrage and Irish nationalism.

France's progress toward democracy was less consistent and less gentle than Britain's. In the republic that existed for a short time after 1848, all adult males could vote. In 1851, however, the president, Louis Napoleon, staged a coup and crowned himself Napoleon III. He was not an absolute dictator (although he increased censorship), and he helped to modernize Paris and industrialize the country. He abdicated after losing the bitter **Franco-Prussian War** (1870–1871). From that time, France remained a democratic republic—although, democracy did not solve all of its problems. France was rocked by corruption and financial scandals, and worst of all was the **Dreyfus Affair** (1894–1906), in which the army and government falsely blamed a Jewish officer for the leaking of military secrets to Germany. The controversy divided the left (which maintained Dreyfus's innocence) from the right (which was convinced of his guilt) and exposed the ugly streak of **anti-Semitism** in modern European society.

Nationalism profoundly affected politics in Italy, Germany, and Austria. The **unification of Italy** took place in the 1860s thanks to a combination of clever diplomacy by the statesman Camillo Cavour, the military leadership of Giuseppe

Garibaldi, and popular patriotism. Under Victor Emmanuel II, Italy became a constitutional monarchy.

The **unification of Germany** was spearheaded by Prussia under the leadership of **Otto von Bismarck**, one of the century's most skilled diplomats. Nationalist sentiment spurred unification, as did a series of short, decisive wars against Denmark (1864), Austria (1866), and especially France (1870–1871). War with Austria made Prussia paramount in the German-speaking world; victory in the **Franco-Prussian War** removed all obstacles to unification. The new German state had a parliament (the Reichstag), and all adult males technically had the vote, although the electoral system was heavily stacked in favor of the upper classes. Germany rapidly became a strong, modern, industrialized state, but under Bismarck, it was very conservative politically. Craftily, Bismarck offered the lower classes generous economic concessions (pensions, insurance, shorter workdays) to keep them from being attracted to trade unions or socialism.

After 1848, the Austrian emperor was forced to liberalize somewhat, and a parliament was established in 1861. A multinational empire, Austria had to confront many ethnic tensions throughout the late 1800s and early 1900s, as the nationalist aspirations of minority populations such as Czechs, Poles, Slovaks, Croats, Serbs, Hungarians, and others mounted. In the **Augsleich** ("Compromise") of 1867, the Hungarian minority, Austria's largest, won equal status, and the country was renamed the Austro-Hungarian Empire. As in other parts of Europe, **anti-Semitism** became an ugly part of political life; at the turn of the century, the mayor of Vienna ran several successful campaigns on an openly anti-Jewish platform.

Even autocratic Russia was forced to change somewhat. Defeat in the Crimean War prompted Alexander II, a moderate liberal, to modernize the country with a series of "great reforms." The most important of these was the **emancipation of the serfs** (1861), which ended a morally reprehensible practice and allowed some economic progress. Sadly, Alexander II was assassinated by terrorists, and the extremely conservative rulers who succeeded him, including the last tsar, Nicholas II, undid many of his reforms. A serious uprising in 1905 almost overthrew Nicholas II; he survived but was forced to create and share power with an elected, semiparliamentary body called the Duma. However, he kept the Duma weak and took every opportunity to avoid cooperating with it. Anti-Semitic persecution escalated in Russia, and **pogroms** (violent raids on Jewish settlements) became increasingly common.

Women's Movements

The English author **Mary Wollstonecraft** is considered the founder of modern European feminism. Her 1792 treatise, *A Vindication of the Rights of Women*, insisted that women, like men, possessed reason and were therefore entitled to equal rights. During the French Revolution, the playwright Olympe de Gouges argued in her "Declaration of the Rights of Woman and the Citizeness" that women should have the same rights as men. The government dismissed her proposal, and she died during the Reign of Terror.

Larger women's rights movements emerged in the 1830s in Europe and the United States. Early on, they focused on reforming family and divorce laws to allow women to own property and file for divorce. This initial effort did not reap quick results, as women did not gain full property rights in Britain until 1870, Germany until 1900, and France until 1907.

Soon, feminists were seeking better access to higher education and jobs. The first professions open to women (beyond domestic servitude, already dominated by women) were teaching and nursing. Women also led the way in campaigning for temperance, the abolition of slavery, and aid for orphans and the poor.

By the middle of the nineteenth century, women began to seek political rights, most notably suffrage, the right to vote. As a rule, European and American **suffragette movements** were led by women of the upper classes. The most vocal women's movement was Britain's, led by Emmeline Pankhurst. Major figures in the U.S. movement were Susan B. Anthony and Elizabeth Cady Stanton. American and Canadian women not only called for the right to vote, they agitated for better working conditions for women, child welfare, and temperance (in the early 1900s, Margaret Sanger began her controversial campaign for public support of birth control). Almost no countries gave women the vote until late in World War I or afterward. Exceptions include Norway, Finland, and a handful of U.S. states.

INTELLECTUAL AND CULTURAL CURRENTS

In contrast to long-lasting cultural and intellectual movements such as the Renaissance and the Enlightenment, trends and styles in the 1800s and 1900s changed constantly. Such rapid evolution has been a hallmark of modern Western culture.

The principal cultural movement of the late 1700s and early 1800s was **romanticism**. A backlash against the rational Enlightenment, romanticism emphasized emotion, heroism, individuality, and the imagination.

In the mid-1800s came numerous scientific discoveries that changed the outlook of the Western world. The most important was the work of English naturalist **Charles Darwin**, who explained the biological process of evolution with his **theory of natural selection**. In *On the Origin of Species* (1859), Darwin caused a scientific and cultural storm by arguing that evolution is a random process in which physical changes that increase an animal's chance for survival are passed on to that animal's offspring. In *The Descent of Man* (1871), he applied the principles of natural selection to human beings and postulated that humans and apes share a common evolutionary ancestry. Darwin's ideas, along with discoveries in other sciences, including geology and archaeology, did much to erode faith in traditional religion and encourage a more secular worldview in the West.

> **TIP**
>
> Famous romantics include Lord Byron, Ludwig van Beethoven, Victor Hugo, Richard Wagner, and Pyotr Tchaikovsky. Around the 1840s, romanticism, while it did not die away, yielded its place of prominence to **realism**. Realists were concerned with everyday life, social problems (such as poverty), and the psychology of their characters. Realist authors include Charles Dickens, Gustave Flaubert, Leo Tolstoy, and Fyodor Dostoevsky.

The culture of the late 1800s and early 1900s was characterized by diversity and innovation. Turning away from realism in the 1870s, **modernist** artists and writers (including Vincent van Gogh, Paul Gauguin, Vasily Kandinsky, and a young Pablo Picasso) broke the rules of traditional culture and experimented with a dazzling array of new styles: symbolism, impressionism, post-impressionism, and on the eve of World War I, expressionism, cubism, and abstraction. Asian and African art powerfully influenced this generation of artists.

During most of the 1800s, Western culture was characterized by faith in progress and excitement about new technology and science. For the most part, especially among the general public, this sense of optimism continued until the eve of World War I. In some ways, however, this was a time of intellectual crisis and uncertainty. German philosopher Friedrich Nietzsche proclaimed famously that "God is dead," and argued that all systems of morality were valueless in the materialistic modern age. Quantum theory and **Albert Einstein's theory of relativity**, elaborated in 1905, opened up new (and unsettling) questions in the field of physics for the first time since the days of Isaac Newton. The early theories of the Austrian physician **Sigmund Freud** about dreams and the subconscious advanced the new science of psychology, but his insights made many people uneasy, both before and after World War I.

Aristide Bruant at Les Ambassadeurs (1892), by Henri de Toulouse-Lautrec.
French painter and poster artist Henri de Toulouse-Lautrec (1864–1901) was one of many artists who, during the late 1800s, departed from the strictly realist styles of the early and middle nineteenth century. Like many of France's impressionist and post-impressionist painters, Toulouse-Lautrec was influenced by foreign art, most particularly Japanese prints.

Industrialization and Worldwide Economic Trends

CHAPTER 21

- Industrialization and the Industrial Revolution
- Proto-industrialization versus traditional artisanry
- The steam engine and the mining and textile industries
- Steamships, railroads, and the telegraph
- The gradual application of electric and petroleum power
- The factory system and interchangeable parts
- Rise of the middle (bourgeois) and working (proletariat) classes

- The stimulation of population growth and urbanization
- Effects on women
- Capitalism (Adam Smith)
- Trade unionism
- Socialism and communism (Karl Marx)
- Global ramifications of Western industrialization
- The cotton gin's impact on the Atlantic slave trade

Until the end of the 1700s, the economies of the world's major civilizations were principally agricultural, and their societies rural. Over the centuries, trade and commerce, as well as arts and crafts, had become increasingly important—but compared with agriculture, remained relatively minor.

In Europe and the United States, this state of affairs changed dramatically during the end of the 1700s and the 1800s. The mass production of goods by means of machine power—industrialization—became a key part of Western economies. The importance of trade and commerce skyrocketed, and a growing number of people moved from rural areas to the city. Capitalism became the dominant economic system. Taken together, these changes form what is commonly known as the **Industrial Revolution**, whose first stage coincided roughly with the political revolutions taking place in America, France, and the Atlantic world. Although industrialization was a "revolution" only in a metaphorical sense—it lasted decades and had no clear-cut beginning or end—it changed life in Europe and the rest of the world as thoroughly as the political revolutions did. It placed new machines and inventions at the disposal of ordinary people. It affected old social classes and created new ones. It changed the way millions worked, where they lived, and how they understood political problems. By 1900, the United States and northern and western Europe had industrialized and urbanized. Many other parts of the world were starting to follow suit.

THE INDUSTRIAL REVOLUTION

Background to Industrialization

The Industrial Revolution is considered to have begun in England in the 1780s with the successful application of the **steam engine** to two sectors of the economy: **mining** and **textiles**.

Many things combined to spark industrialization in England. Already from the late 1600s, proto-industrial practices (methods more productive than traditional artisanry and craftsmanship) had been in place. Machines such as the flying shuttle and the spinning jenny, which sped up the manufacture of cotton, were invented as early as 1733 and 1764. England was already relatively urbanized, and a set of harsh agricultural laws, the **Enclosure Acts**—which, in favor of wealthy landowners, fenced off large amounts of farmland that had once been common property—impoverished many farmers and forced them to relocate to the cities, creating a large pool of available labor. Environmental change played a role as well: the depletion of forests in England and Ireland (timber was used both for fuel and to build ships for the Royal Navy) increased dependency on coal, and efficient coal mining required machine power, especially to pump water out of mine shafts. Other factors working in England's favor were an excellent system of roads and canals and a strong tradition of trade and commerce.

Steam Power and Beyond: The Industrial Era Begins and Matures

What was needed by the end of the 1700s was a power source greater and more reliable than wind, water, or muscle to drive new machines in factories and mines. In 1782, the Scottish inventor **James Watt** patented a steam engine that was both powerful and cost-effective. The first stage of the Industrial Revolution involved the integration of Watt's steam engine into the textile and coal-mining industries.

The next stage of the Industrial Revolution, which lasted roughly until the middle of the 1800s, involved the universal application of steam power—and, more slowly, electricity—to all areas of economic activity. Industrialization also spread to other parts of Europe, as well as to North America. Key trends include

- The modernization of transport, thanks to **steamships** (1807) and **railroads** (the 1820s)
- The modernization of communications, beginning with the **telegraph** (1837)
- The **factory system**, which systematized, mechanized, and increased the scale of production
- The concept of **interchangeable parts**, pioneered by two Americans, the inventor Eli Whitney and a gunsmith, Samuel Colt

Although the Industrial Revolution is considered to have ended around the mid-1800s, the **industrial era** continued throughout the rest of the century and gave birth to a huge wave of invention. Crucial innovations include the vulcanization of rubber (1839); the **Bessemer process** (the 1850s), which made steel production cheaper and easier; the wider use of **electricity** (Thomas Edison's lightbulb came in 1879); the commercial use of **petroleum** (starting in 1859); the birth of chemical industries; the

internal combustion engine (1866–1885), which led to the automobile; the **telephone** (1876–1879); the **radio** (1895–1901); and the **airplane** (1903). Warfare industrialized as well, with modern rifles, better artillery, and the machine gun. In the countryside, the **tractor** helped cause an agricultural boom.

Industrialization occurred first and most thoroughly in western Europe (especially Britain, the Low Countries, France, and Germany), as well as the United States. Southern and eastern Europe lagged behind. Britain led the world in industrial production for most of the 1800s. By the end of the century, Germany and the United States were catching up to, then surpassing, Britain.

The Social and Environmental Effects of Industrialization

The Industrial Revolution and its aftermath vastly transformed Western society. Especially between the 1780s and 1840s, the effects were as traumatic as they were important. For the lower classes, the industrial era's birth pangs were extremely painful.

The economic clout of the traditional aristocracy, whose wealth had been based primarily on land, was diminished by industrialization. The class that benefited most was the **middle class** (or bourgeoisie), especially bankers, merchants, and factory owners who drew direct profits from industrial growth.

The Industrial Revolution astronomically expanded the size of the **working class** (or proletariat). During the first decades of industrialization, this class bore the heaviest economic burden. Their labor allowed the Industrial Revolution to move forward, but until the second half of the 1800s, they were badly treated and barely compensated. Workers received low wages, lived in squalid and crowded housing, worked long shifts (fourteen hours a day, six days a week, was not unusual), coped with unsafe working conditions (risk of fire, dangerous machines, exposure to poisonous or harmful substances), and had no pensions, safety laws, or insurance. Child labor was common.

In the countryside, industrialization caused new social divisions. More land came to be owned by well-off farmers and homesteaders who were essentially middle class. Under them were poor agricultural laborers who formed a rural working class of sorts. (In Russia until 1861, the system of **serfdom** still prevailed, and **slavery** persisted until 1865 in the southern United States.)

Only after the 1840s is industrialization considered to have brought about meaningful improvements for large numbers of Americans and Europeans. Especially after the **1848 Revolutions** (caused partly by the socioeconomic stress of early industrialization), various laws and measures began to give relief to the working class—although completely fair treatment and full political equality were still distant goals, achieved only after hard effort and not until the late 1800s or even 1900s. The overall standard of living rose during the second half of the 1800s, even for the lower classes. At least in major cities, many features of modern life became available after mid-century, including bus service, streetlights (gas, then electric), citywide sewage systems, icebox refrigeration, indoor plumbing, steam heating, canned food, and medical advances (vaccination, germ theory, antiseptic surgery, anesthesia).

Related social trends are massive **population growth** and **urbanization**. Europe's population grew from 175 million (187 million, by some estimates) in 1800 to 266 million in 1850 and 423 million by 1900. Similar growth took place in the United States. Such growth was not the product of higher birth rates, but declining death rates caused by gradual improvements. European cities that existed grew larger; in 1800, London reached the 1 million mark, as did Paris in the 1830s. Many new cities sprang up, such as Liverpool and Manchester, precisely because of the Industrial Revolution. By the mid-1800s, England and Wales were urban societies, meaning that 50 percent or more of the population lived in cities. At that time, the level of urbanization had reached 25 percent in France and the German states, and it continued to grow, as in the Low Countries and the United States. Urbanization is generally associated with social advancement, but it had its seamier side during the industrial era: cities were typically polluted and crowded, and the lower classes lived in slums or shantytowns where sewage was primitive or nonexistent. Diseases such as **cholera**, **tuberculosis**, and typhoid ran rampant in such conditions.

Population growth and urban concentration affected the environment, as did the industrialized nations' voracious appetite for resources and raw materials (wood, coal, metals, and petroleum). Pollution reached unprecedented levels, and, unlike today, there were few laws to combat it. As non-Western parts of the world industrialized, they repeated this pattern. The early stages of human-caused climate change (global warming) are thought to date to the nineteenth-century industrial takeoff.

Women and Industrialization

Before the Industrial Revolution, European women of the lower (and sometimes middle) class worked with men on the farm or in the family business, so motherhood and homemaking were not full-time pursuits. The Industrial Revolution altered that reality, turning husbands into wage earners and wives into homemakers. By the late 1800s, it had created a sharply defined **domestic sphere** for women.

This evolution took time. In the early 1800s, husbands and wives (and often children) in working-class families had to labor in factories or mines to make ends meet. Before 1870, women made up 50 percent of the textile workforce. Ironically, this meant that lower-class women had more opportunity to work than those of the middle and upper classes, but this was not a matter of privilege or right. It was economic necessity, and working women earned much lower pay than men.

Throughout the 1800s, most working women remained in traditional types of female labor, such as domestic service or agricultural work. Most were single, not married. Some single women, desperate for jobs, left Europe for Australia, the United States, or Canada. By the late 1800s, large numbers of poor women worked outside the home.

Increasingly, though, as salaries improved in industry (making these jobs more desirable to men) and laws restricted the number of hours women could work, more working-class women stayed at home. Fewer middle-class (and almost no upper-class) women worked.

Around the turn of the century, with the rising standard of living, a mass consumer society began to emerge. Products such as sewing machines and cast-iron stoves freed up time for women of all classes to pursue activities outside the home. Medical advances reduced infant mortality and the number of women who died in childbirth.

ECONOMIC THEORIES AND MOVEMENTS

Industrialization coincided with the rise of **capitalism** in the West. **Adam Smith's** *The Wealth of Nations* appeared in 1776, just before the Industrial Revolution began. Capitalism encouraged free trade and political liberalism (at least for the middle classes), and it led to the creation of great wealth in the Western world. On the other hand, it was based on competition and, left unregulated, could be cruel to those who lost (like the early working class).

Smith and the other classical economists who favored capitalism argued that the laws of supply and demand—the **"invisible hand,"** to use Smith's metaphor—should operate freely, with minimal government intervention. (Germany, where state control of the economy was pronounced, broke this rule and still became an industrial power-house.) Smith himself insisted that governments should take measures to fight extreme poverty, a point often forgotten today. Other economic thinkers of the day maintained that little could be done about poverty. Thomas Malthus of England wrote in his influential *Essay on Population* (1799) that poverty was one of the inevitable consequences of population growth. David Ricardo's **"iron law of wages"** was even more pessimistic: employers, he said, will naturally pay workers no more than what is needed to allow them to survive. To force them to pay higher wages, Ricardo predicted, would cause them to fire workers, who would then starve. Such theories caused economics to be nicknamed the "dismal science" and were used for a long time by middle- and upper-class industrialists to justify oppressive labor practices.

After the **1848 Revolutions**, it was clear that pure, dog-eat-dog capitalism could not remain as it was without causing severe social and economic stress. But how should it be changed? Liberals and reformers sought to soften capitalism's hard edge by agreeing to fairer labor laws and social welfare measures. For workers, a more radical option (by the standards of the day) was the **trade union** movement. In the early 1800s, unions were illegal in Europe and the United States, and workers risked injury and arrest if they joined unions or went on strike. Still, the union movement gave them a way to struggle for political rights and better treatment in the workplace (higher wages, five-day work week, shorter hours, safety regulations, pensions, and employee insurance). In the late 1800s and early 1900s, unions earned legal status in most countries and gained greater economic and political strength. Political parties dedicated to the needs of workers, such as Labour in Britain, formed.

Even more extreme were **socialism**, which rejected capitalism and denied the validity of private property, and anarchism, which rejected all forms of government. Many varieties of socialism appeared in the 1800s, all sharing the belief that economic competition is inherently unfair and leads to injustice and inequality. The most influential form of socialism is **communism**, originated by the German philosophers **Karl Marx** and Friedrich Engels and most famously outlined in *The Communist Manifesto* (1848) and *Das Kapital* (1867–1894). Marx and Engels argued that all historical development was driven by a **class struggle** between the upper class (which controls capital, or the means of economic production) and the lower class (which is forced to labor for the upper class). They predicted that the age of industrial capitalism, with its struggle between bourgeoisie and proletariat, was the final stage of human history before the realization of socialism. Society would then move on to communism, an economic state of perfect justice, equality, and prosperity. To achieve socialism, however, Marx and Engels believed that revolution would be needed, so they advocated the overthrow of capitalism, by force if need be.

THE GLOBAL IMPACT OF INDUSTRIALIZATION

Industrialization and Imperialism

Western industrialization and imperialism (see Chapter 22) were intimately connected in several ways. First, industrialization gave Western nations the wealth, technological aptitude, and scientific knowledge to conquer and colonize other parts of the world. Particularly, it placed new weapons in the hands of Westerners: gunboats, artillery, quick-firing and accurate rifles, and machine guns, all of which made Western imperialism difficult for poorly armed native forces to resist.

Second, if industrialization gave the West greater ability to conquer and colonize, it also provided more motivation. Industrialization required ever-greater amounts of raw materials: iron ore, coal, rubber, metals, timber, and chemicals, all of which could be stripped from other parts of the world. The growing importance of steamships made it necessary for Western nations to maintain naval bases and refueling stations around the globe. Moreover, as Europe and America produced more manufactured goods, they needed overseas markets to sell them to. All these needs spurred the Western nations' intense burst of imperial activity during the 1800s, especially the second half.

The Influence of Industrial Nations over Nonindustrial Nations

Even in parts of the world that Europe and America did not conquer or colonize, industrialization had a profound effect. In Africa, Asia, and Latin America, Western businessmen and industrialists struck deals with aristocrats or the political elite to exploit local resources. These bargains typically involved the large-scale growth or extraction of a small set of crops or natural resources. This kind of **monoculture** generally damages the environment and retards the development of a healthy, diverse economy. It also exploits these countries' native workers: foreign payments or investments end up in the pockets of a small number of local elites, rather than adding to the national well-being.

> **NOTE**
>
> In the tropics, the derogatory slang for countries with monoculture economies is "banana republic."

In the long term, most non-Western parts of the world came to imitate industrial methods of production. Western colonizing powers exported industrial practices to their imperial possessions. Political leaders in free nations came to see industrialization as a way to gain wealth and power. In such cases, industrialization was typically imposed from above by the ruler. The worldwide adoption of industrialization worldwide continued through the twentieth century and continues today.

Industrialization and the Atlantic Slave Trade

Another global effect of early industrialization concerns the **Atlantic slave trade**. The 1793 invention of the **cotton gin** by the American engineer Eli Whitney transformed the international textile trade. One of the factors limiting growth in the textile trade was the fact that raw cotton still had to be cleaned by hand. The cotton gin changed this situation, enabling the industry to be fully mechanized, which phenomenally boosted England's demand for raw cotton. Although Egypt was a major source of cotton, an equally important supplier was the American South, where cotton was grown and harvested mainly by slaves. Most economic historians argue that, before the 1790s, slavery was becoming less profitable in the American South and might have died away relatively quickly and easily. The advent of the cotton gin, combined with increased English demand, revived the profitability of slave-based production. Therefore, slavery in America was prolonged for decades—necessitating civil war to end it—largely because of the textile trade's industrialization.

The Europeans Abroad: Imperialism, Nationalism, and Foreign Policy

CHAPTER 22

- The new imperialism
- Social Darwinism and the "white man's burden" concept
- The Monroe Doctrine and manifest destiny
- The British East India Company and the Indian Mutiny
- Foreign concessions in China and the Boxer Rebellion

- Japanese imperialism and the Russo-Japanese War
- The Great Game
- The Eastern Question
- The Scramble for Africa and the Berlin Conference
- Nationalism, competition for empire, and the European alliance system

One of the most astounding facts of the nineteenth century is that, while, in 1815, the nations of the West—Europe and America—controlled 35 percent of the world's habitable territory, they controlled 85 percent by 1914. The nineteenth century was an age of empire, in which the West came to achieve dominance over a larger portion of the globe than any civilization had before.

Western imperialism was nothing new. European powers had been conquering other parts of the world since the 1400s. From the 1700s onward, the United States had grown "from sea to shining sea" by means of warfare and subjugation of the native population. From the mid-1800s to the early 1900s, however, imperialism took on a more aggressive and systematic character, and many historians refer to this as the **new imperialism**.

Imperialism remains one of the Western world's longest-lasting and most controversial legacies. As a practical undertaking and a military enterprise, the West's domination of the world was impressive, and it made Europe and America powerful and rich. On the other hand, imperialism was inseparable from bloodshed, racial prejudice, and slavery. As the English-Polish author Joseph Conrad wrote in the novel *Heart of Darkness*—one of the classic literary depictions of European imperialism—"The conquest of the earth, which mostly means the taking it away from those who have a different complexion or slightly flatter noses than ourselves, is not a pretty thing when you look into it too much." Moreover, Europe's and America's campaigns of colonization left deep political scars around the globe, many of which have not yet healed even in the twenty-first century.

Whether abroad or at home, European foreign policy became increasingly aggressive. During the first half of the 1800s, the balance of power achieved by the Congress of Vienna largely kept the peace. After 1850, however, several wars broke out among the European powers: the Crimean War (1853–1856), in which Russia fought France and Britain; the wars of Italian unification, which entangled France, Austria, and several Italian states; and the three wars Prussia fought to unify the German states, especially the Franco-Prussian War (1870–1871).

Much of this aggression was caused by the growing intensity of **nationalism,** a relatively new cultural phenomenon that placed a premium on patriotic sentiment. Another cause was competition over imperial possessions, especially as the century drew to a close and the amount of desirable territory left to be conquered shrank. On the surface, relative stability was maintained from 1871 to 1914, a period in European history known as the Long Peace. But underneath, the potential for conflict grew with every passing year. The **European alliance system** emerged during the 1890s and early 1900s as a result of this growing sense of foreign policy crisis. It was a principal factor in the complex background of World War I.

CAUSES OF IMPERIALISM

A variety of interrelated factors enabled and motivated the new imperialism of the 1800s. They apply to the nations of Europe and, to a degree, the United States.

One set of factors was economic. Industrialization gave the West the ability to conquer and more reasons to do so. It made Western economies hungry for **raw materials,** many of which could be seized from less powerful nations by force. Also, Western nations needed **markets** for the goods they produced and thought colonies would serve well (in retrospect, economic historians have determined that this was a mistaken belief and that colonies were less suitable as markets than other industrialized countries).

A second factor was **military superiority.** Industrialization gave Western armies and navies ocean-going fleets powered by steam (and, later, petroleum), modern rifles, machine guns, rapid-fire and long-range artillery, and more. Only rarely could native populations resist Western military forces. Also, because modern ships required elaborate repair bases and fueling facilities, Western navies needed control over islands and ports around the world to maintain **sea power.**

A social factor prompting imperialism was Europe's rapid **population growth** during the 1800s. One outlet for excess population growth was emigration to the Americas, and millions of Europeans made that choice. Another option was to leave the homeland and go to the colonies.

Scientific and technological aptitude were also instrumental. In this case, knowledge was power. A new wave of exploration during the 1700s and early 1800s added to Western nations' understanding of Africa, Asia, the polar regions, and the Amazon basin. Better maps and geographical familiarity made it easier for Westerners to conquer these areas. Medical advances made it possible to penetrate tropical regions more deeply. Previously, diseases such as sleeping sickness, yellow fever, and **malaria** had prevented Westerners from controlling the interior of Africa and Southeast Asia. The development of effective treatments for these illnesses (especially **quinine**, which relieved the symptoms of malaria) changed this situation.

Finally, a complex set of cultural factors motivated the West to build empires. A sense of racial superiority was widespread among white Europeans and Americans, who believed they were entitled to conquer and colonize "backward" or "primitive" peoples. Cecil Rhodes, who did much to colonize Africa, said famously of his British homeland, "I contend that we are the finest race in the world, and the more of it we inhabit, the better it is." In some cases, this belief was "justified" by crude prejudice. A more sophisticated but still misguided doctrine of **social Darwinism** was also used to argue in favor of imperialism. Social Darwinists implied that it was natural for technologically advanced peoples to conquer those who were less so. (Darwin himself denounced this idea as a perversion of his theories.)

Yet another cultural impulse behind imperialism was a conviction that white Westerners had a duty to teach and modernize the darker-skinned, supposedly primitive peoples of Africa and Asia. The English poet Rudyard Kipling gave this sentiment its most famous label: the **White Man's Burden**. The French spoke of their civilizing mission (*la mission civilisatrice*). This attitude was well-meaning and heartfelt, but also condescending. European and American missionaries, doctors, scientists, and colonial officials sometimes did much good in the places they visited. However, they did so out of at least a subconscious sense of racial superiority, and they often trampled on or eradicated native cultural practices and beliefs.

EUROPE'S OVERSEAS EMPIRES

Western Approaches to Imperialism

Almost the entire non-Western world was colonized during the nineteenth century or fell under the influence of Western nations. By far the largest and most widespread empire was Britain's. (A famous motto of the time: "The sun never sets on the British Empire.") France had a sizable empire, as did Belgium and the Netherlands. Although Austria is not commonly thought of as a colonizing power, its empire was in eastern and southeastern Europe. Russia conquered Siberia, much of Central Asia, and for a time, parts of North America. After 1870, new countries such as Germany and Italy began to build overseas empires, in an attempt to catch up with older imperial powers like Britain and France.

Different powers treated their empires differently. The British are considered to have had the most enlightened approach, relatively speaking. Although they took their colonies by force and exploited them economically—and were prone to the same sense of racial superiority as other Westerners—they interfered less with local customs than other colonizers. In keeping with their sense of the White Man's Burden, they introduced positive social reforms and useful scientific and technological knowledge. Likewise, the French subscribed to the notion of *la mission civilisatrice*, but were less consistent about it. The Portuguese and Belgians were known to be especially harsh masters, particularly in Africa, and Germany and Italy (which used poison gas in parts of North Africa) were arguably more brutal yet.

The Americas

North America fell mainly under the sway of the United States, which conquered the entire Western frontier during the nineteenth century. Motivated by the doctrine of **manifest destiny**—the belief that it was entitled to the entire landmass between the Atlantic and Pacific—the United States fought Mexico, negotiated borders with British Canada, and warred on Native Americans, driving them to defeat and onto reservations. This was no less an imperial campaign than what European nations did in Africa or Asia. The Spanish lost their empire in North America when Mexico launched a revolution in the 1810s and 1820s. The Russians gave up their North American possession, Alaska, to the United States in 1867.

The **Latin American wars of independence** freed Mexico, Mesoamerica, and South America from Spain and Portugal in the early 1800s. However, much of Latin America came under the sway of the United States, which did not conquer the region but considered it part of the U.S. sphere of influence. The **Monroe Doctrine**, issued in 1823, formally stated that the United States would not permit European interference in the Western Hemisphere. U.S. economic and political influence over Central and South America increased throughout the 1800s. At the end of the century, in 1898, the **Spanish-American War** gave the United States control over Cuba, Puerto Rico, and the Virgin Islands, making it an imperial power in Latin America.

Southeast Asia

The vast expanse of Asia was colonized and influenced by a variety of powers. The region that had been longest under European control was Southeast Asia. The Dutch tightened their grasp over Indonesia. France took over Indochina, the area that is today Laos, Cambodia, and Vietnam. By the mid-1880s, the British controlled Burma, the Malay Peninsula (with the trading center of Singapore), and northern Borneo. Farther to the south, Britain reigned over the continent of Australia. The Philippines had belonged to Spain since Magellan's voyage of 1521, but the United States took them in 1898, following the Spanish-American War. Later in the century, Germany seized a number of Pacific islands for use as naval posts.

India

The heart of the British Empire was India. Britain and France quarreled with each other over hegemony in India during the 1700s. At the battle of **Plassey**, in 1757, the British won a major victory over the Mughal Empire, enabling them to consolidate their military presence in India and leading to a decline of French influence. Over the next decades, the British went on to conquer most of the subcontinent. Until the late 1850s, India was not administered directly by the British government but by the semiprivate **British East India Company**, one of the richest and most powerful business ventures in world history. In 1857, however, the **Indian Mutiny** (also known as the **Sepoy Rebellion**)—which failed but shocked the British badly—persuaded the government to assume full control over the colony. India was exceptionally important to Britain, in terms of national pride, strategic position, and economic benefit. During the late 1800s, one-quarter of the wealth generated by the British Empire came from India.

China

Qing China, despite its vast size and immense population, fell victim to almost every European nation, as well as to the United States. China was not technically colonized. However, thanks to military defeat at the hands of the British and other foreigners during the middle of the 1800s, it was compelled to open its borders and trade with other countries at highly disadvantageous terms. It gave up pieces of territory such as **Hong Kong** (a British colony from 1842 until 1997, when it returned to Chinese rule), as well as Manchuria and Korea. The British, French, Americans, Germans, Russians, and others were allowed to establish **foreign concessions**: large districts in coastal cities where Western, not Chinese law, prevailed. Foreign ships were allowed to sail as far up Chinese rivers as they pleased. The balance of trade was lopsidedly in favor of the foreigners. The Chinese rose up to resist foreign domination in the failed **Boxer Rebellion** of 1900. In 1911, the Qing Dynasty collapsed, its weakness due in large part to foreign meddling.

Japan Resists Western Imperialism

Unlike most Asian nations, Japan resisted Western imperialism, becoming an imperial power itself. Isolated until 1853, when the U.S. Navy forced it to resume diplomatic and economic relations with the wider world, Japan chose to adopt the science, technology, and military know-how of the West, especially under **Emperor Meiji**. Not only did Japan avoid foreign takeover, it began to build its own Asian empire. It defeated China in 1895, taking the island of Taiwan and occupying Korea. More shockingly, Japan dealt Russia a humiliating defeat in the **Russo-Japanese War** (1904–1905), gaining control over more of the Asian mainland, as well as a number of islands.

Central Asia and the Great Game

Much of Central Asia—the wide expanse of desert and mountains through which the Silk Road had run—fell to Russia, which felt the need to protect its southern frontier. Because Russia lacked **warm-water ports**, it hoped to drive to the Indian Ocean and gain an outlet to the sea. The Islamic khanates and cities of Turkestan, Bukhara, Samarkand, and the Afghan border were taken by the Russians between the 1820s and 1880s. Russian imperialism in this region greatly disturbed Britain because it placed the Russians within striking distance of the Middle East, much of which was in the British sphere of influence. More important, Russian encroachments on Central Asia threatened the lines of communication between Europe and India, which the British were determined to protect at all costs.

For most of the 1800s, Britain and Russia were locked in an intense campaign of espionage and diplomatic intrigue known as the **Great Game**, a term coined by the poet Rudyard Kipling (Russians called it the Tournament of Shadows). The Great Game never resulted in outright war, but created a deep rivalry between Britain and Russia until shortly before World War I.

The Middle East and the Eastern Question

For centuries, the Middle East and most of North Africa had been in the hands of the Ottoman Empire. However, the Ottoman Empire was collapsing, and the **Eastern Question**—how to fill the power vacuum caused by the Ottomans' decline—became a central issue in global politics. During the last half of the 1800s, large portions of this region were seized by Europeans, especially the French and British. Algeria, Tunisia, and most of Morocco became French. Part of Morocco fell to Spain, while Italy captured Libya.

> **TIP**
>
> The global importance of the Middle East—based largely on its geographic position between Europe and Asia—increased dramatically with the **discovery of petroleum** there in 1908. Middle Eastern oil still plays a key role in modern geopolitics.

The most important territory was Egypt, which became a British protectorate in the 1880s. During the 1870s, Egypt, an autonomous part of the Ottoman Empire, had fallen under French and British influence. Both countries financed the construction of the **Suez Canal**, which opened in 1869. Control over the canal—a vital link between Europe and the Mediterranean on one hand and the Red Sea and the Indian Ocean on the other—was crucial, and the British used economic pressure to gain political control over Egypt. They also established control over the Sudan, and both countries became part of the Anglo-Egyptian Administration. To the east, Persia, which had remained independent of Ottoman rule, was divided into two spheres of influence by Russia and Britain.

The Scramble for Africa

Africa experienced the most intense burst of European imperialism near the end of the century. Until the 1880s, only Africa's coastlines had been directly colonized or exploited. Gold, ivory, foodstuffs, and especially slaves had been wrested from Africa, either by military force or economic pressure. Although slavery and the slave trade had been made illegal by most Western nations following the French Revolution and Napoleonic Wars, both institutions continued throughout the 1800s. Slavery was practiced in the United States until the Civil War of the 1860s, and even afterward, it continued in parts of the Caribbean and South America. Not until Brazil outlawed slavery in 1888 did the **Atlantic slave trade** end completely. More than 2 million slaves were transported from Africa during the 1800s, bringing the likely total of African slaves captured from the late 1400s to the late 1800s to at least 12 million.

The character of African colonization changed remarkably after 1880. From then until the 1910s, European nations raced to take over territory in Africa. Thanks to better maps, industrial-era weapons, and effective tropical medicines, European colonizers penetrated every part of what the West thought of as the "dark continent." This so-called **Scramble for Africa** became so intense that, several times, it almost sparked war in Europe. The **Berlin Conference** (1884–1885), presided over by Otto von Bismarck, laid down guidelines for African expansion and, for a time, preserved peace. Still, competition over African territory caused diplomatic crises among the European powers during the early 1900s, especially the **Boer War** (1899–1902). For the Africans, the sudden and overwhelming influx of Europeans spelled disaster. By 1914, only two nations in Africa remained free: Liberia, whose independence was guaranteed by the United States because it had been founded by freed American slaves, and Abyssinia (Ethiopia), which armed itself with modern weapons and drove off Italian efforts to conquer it. Within three decades, the rest of the continent had been brought under Europe's imperial sway.

The Balkans

Even parts of Europe were vulnerable to imperial predation. Southeastern Europe—the **Balkans**—lay at the crossroads of several empires. Although this area was the most economically and culturally backward of Europe, the imperial ambitions of Russia, Austria, Italy, and the deteriorating Ottoman Empire all centered on it. The level of competition among these powers steadily escalated. Complicating the situation was the intense wave of **nationalism** that swept most of southeastern Europe during the nineteenth century. Starting with the **Greek war of independence** in the 1820s, the various minorities ruled by the Ottomans, Austrians, and Russians constantly agitated for greater independence—and, if they had independence, they craved more territory. To realize their goals, many of these peoples were willing to risk war. By the early 1900s, the nationalist ambitions of many Balkan peoples, especially the Serbs, had become a destabilizing force in European politics. Not only were two Balkan wars fought in 1912 and 1913, but the events that triggered World War I took place there.

AGGRESSION AT HOME: NATIONALISM, WARFARE, AND ALLIANCE SYSTEMS
The Balance of Power in Nineteenth-Century Europe

As noted above, the European **balance of power** had been maintained during the first half of the 1800s. Even the wars of the mid-1800s were short and limited in intensity. Ironically, it was during the Long Peace of 1871 to 1914 that tensions worsened. Although this era gave birth to the modern Olympic Games (starting in 1896) and the Nobel Peace Prize (first awarded in 1901), the turn of the century was marked by saber-rattling, **jingoism** (a British nickname for belligerent patriotism), and **brinksmanship** (a diplomatic term referring to a country's willingness to risk war in order to get its way).

Factors Destabilizing the European Balance of Power

Several factors upset Europe's diplomatic stability in the late 1800s and early 1900s. One was the force of **nationalism**, which in most countries transformed patriotic sentiment into aggressive tendencies. Another was **competition over empire**: as the 1800s came to an end, there were fewer places for European nations to expand. Especially in Africa, the jostling for new conquests came close to starting war several times in the early 1900s. A third destabilizing force was the ambitious nature of German foreign policy. An economic and military powerhouse, despite having been united only in 1871, Germany came to believe that it deserved what it called "a place in the sun": equal military and imperial status with older nations such as Britain and France. This was the case especially under **Wilhelm II**, who came to the throne in 1888 and dismissed the skilled and cautious diplomat **Otto von Bismarck** in 1890. Under Wilhelm II, Germany became openly aggressive and forceful, unnerving the rest of Europe.

The Creation of Europe's Turn-of-the-Century Alliance System

From the 1880s to the 1910s, the **European alliance system** took shape, dividing Europe into two armed camps. Germany and Austria formed an alliance in 1879; joined by Italy in 1881, they formed the Triple Alliance. (Italy dropped out of this coalition in World War I, but the Austro-German partnership held firm.) In response, France, bitter about defeat in the **Franco-Prussian War** (and the resulting loss to Germany of the border provinces Alsace and Lorraine), allied in 1894 with Russia, which viewed Austria as a threat in the Balkans. Geographically, France and Russia had their rivals surrounded.

Until 1907, Britain remained unaligned. Thanks to the **Great Game**, it viewed Russia as an enemy, and it had little affection for France. After 1890, though, it felt increasingly alarmed by Germany. Wilhelm II's aggressive imperialism and his expansion of the navy (which menaced the root of Britain's global power, control of the seas) soured Anglo-German relations and shifted British strategy. In 1907, the British informally joined the Franco-Russian alliance, forming the Triple Entente ("understanding").

At this point, any crisis between two countries could potentially involve all of Europe's major powers, the likelihood of war increased. Worsening the problem was Germany's strategy in case of war, the **Schlieffen Plan**. Facing the dilemma of a two-front war, German generals planned a rapid, massive attack against France. Once France was defeated, the Germans and Austrians could deal with Russia at their leisure. To work, the Schlieffen Plan would have to be executed with lightning speed. In the event of a crisis, Germany would have little time to make decisions or resort to diplomacy, and thus, the outbreak of war became even more probable.

The Middle East

CHAPTER 23

- Decline of the Ottoman Empire
- The janissaries
- The Tanzimat Reforms
- The Greek war of Independence and Balkan nationalism
- Muhammed Ali's uprising
- The Eastern Question
- The Suez Canal
- The Balkan Crisis and the Congress of Berlin
- Enver Pasha and the Young Turks
- The Madhi
- The Great Game

The Middle East, with Islamic North Africa and Central Asia, underwent a fundamental transformation between the early 1700s and early 1900s. Before 1700, the Ottoman Empire, feared and respected throughout Eurasia as a great power, reigned supreme over most of this region. Where it did not, states such as Persia and the khanates of Central Asia stood strong and free.

After 1700, military setbacks at the hands of European enemies weakened the Ottoman Empire. Its European possessions gradually slipped away. Internal decay allowed outlying territories in North Africa to gain autonomy. Those territories were then taken into British, French, and Italian empires, further eroding Ottoman power. By the nineteenth century, the failing Ottoman Empire had earned an unflattering nickname: the "sick man of Europe." Periodic reform efforts kept the state alive during the 1800s but did not stave off decline. More reform came at the beginning of the 1900s, but World War I destroyed the Ottoman Empire, which was then transformed into the modern Turkish state.

In the meantime, how to deal with the steady collapse of the Ottoman state and still maintain the European balance of power became one of the crucial foreign policy issues of the 1800s. This Eastern Question perplexed diplomats for decades.

European imperialism also dealt blows to other states in the Middle East and neighboring regions. Egypt, the Caucasus, Persia, and Central Asia came under European—mainly British and Russian—control during the 1800s.

THE DECLINE OF THE OTTOMAN EMPIRE

The Ottoman Empire sustained a heavy set of blows in the late 1600s and early 1700s. In 1683, the Turks nearly succeeded in capturing Vienna, capital of the Austrian Habsburgs. They failed and, in the next three and a half decades of fighting, lost battle after battle and much territory, including Hungary and Transylvania. The treaties of Karlowitz (1699) and Passarowitz (1718) left the Turks greatly diminished in Europe.

Occasional conflicts with Austria continued to sap Ottoman strength. Even worse were the periodic wars the Turks fought with Russia, especially against Peter the Great in the 1710s and Catherine the Great in the late 1700s. With each new struggle, the Turks lost more territory.

Internal Decay and Attempted Reform

Internal troubles also damaged the Ottoman state. Mediocre rulers and governmental corruption had weakened the political system during the 1600s and continued to do so in the 1700s. The dilemma was that sultans who wished to improve or modernize the system met with opposition from influential groups and officials with vested interests in the traditional way of doing things.

This was especially the case with the armed forces. The **janissaries**, who had been so innovative and effective in the 1500s and 1600s, became backward and complacent in the 1700s and early 1800s, refusing to adapt to new technology and tactics. Unfortunately for the empire, the janissaries were, until the 1820s, powerful enough to prevent any change for the better. For example, when Selim III tried to reform the bureaucracy and modernize the army and navy, the janissaries, fearing the loss of their privileged position, assassinated him in 1807.

Later sultans were more effective at changing the system. From the 1820s onward, the Ottoman leadership made some progress in modernizing the political system, the economy, and the military. The sultans boosted Western educational principles, scientific knowledge, and technological expertise. To a degree, they also secularized, against the protests of the traditional Islamic clergy. In the late 1820s, Mehmet III created a professional, European-style army and navy and then subdued the janissaries.

From 1839 through 1876, the Ottoman government introduced a wide-ranging set of changes known as the **Tanzimat reforms**. These reforms emphasized greater religious tolerance for the non-Muslims *millets* (social groups categorized by religion) living in the empire, reform of the legal system, the creation of schools that would teach Western science and technology, the establishment of national telegraph and postal systems, and more. The Tanzimat reforms even included discussing the possibility of a constitution. Another effect of the reforms was to give women greater access to education. Public schools were founded for women, and more of them (although still a small number) began to enter public life in the late 1800s.

Still, such limited change was not enough to solve the empire's deep-seated internal and external problems. The Tanzimat reforms and other such measures alienated conservatives and traditionalists, who found them too extreme. Yet they did not do enough to satisfy the growing numbers of forward-looking politicians and military officers who wanted more change than the sultan was willing to make. By the early 1900s, this generation of modernizers, known as the **Young Turks**, would, from within the regime, play a decisive role in ending the sultan's rule.

Revolts, Rebellions, and the Gradual Disintegration of the Ottoman Empire

Long before this, external problems such as rebellion and war were disintegrating the Ottoman Empire. In the early 1800s, an upsurge of nationalism, combined with political turmoil caused by the Napoleonic Wars, led to many uprisings in Turkish-controlled Europe. Serbia revolted in 1807, and even though the revolt failed, the Serbs remained restless.

More seriously, the **Greek war of independence** began in 1821. By 1827, France and Britain, responding to Christian Europe's outpouring of sympathy for the Greeks, aided the rebels (earlier, the poet Lord Byron had helped turn the war into an international cause by leaving England to fight and die on the side of the Greeks). Russia, sharing Greece's Eastern Orthodox faith, also joined the war. Defeated by this coalition, the Ottomans were forced to recognize Greek independence in 1832. At the same time, the Ottoman government had to cope with the rebellion of **Muhammad Ali** in Egypt and the growing autonomy of possessions in western North Africa.

The Eastern Question

From the 1820s onward, the steady collapse of the Ottoman state presented the nations of Europe with a geopolitical challenge known as the **Eastern Question**. Although the Turks had been Europe's enemies since the 1300s, the Ottoman Empire was now seen as a satisfactory regime to have in place in the Middle East. It was no longer a real threat, it was predictable, and, for the time being, it held together many volatile parts of Asia and Europe. To destroy it or allow it to fall apart quickly might cause chaos or give birth to a new state that was strong and hostile.

Another aspect of the Eastern Question was that the nations of Europe did not wholly trust each other. The Ottoman Empire sat at a geographically crucial juncture: the crossroads of Europe and Asia, the joining of the Black and Mediterranean seas, and the Suez isthmus, which linked the Mediterranean with the Indian Ocean and Asia. If one European country seized too much territory from the Ottomans at one time, it would upset Europe's fragile **balance of power**. Informally, the nations of Europe agreed to solve this part of the Eastern Question by not acting too suddenly or decisively in the region. The Ottomans' decline was to be managed carefully and slowly. If necessary, the European powers would prop up the empire if it seemed in danger of immediate collapse.

The complexity of the Eastern Question was illustrated many times. The Europeans took so long to help Greece in the 1820s because they feared causing too much damage to the Ottoman Empire at once. Soon after joining the Greeks *against* the Turks, Britain and France gave aid *to* the Turks by helping contain Muhammad Ali's revolt in Egypt; they worried that he would be too formidable an enemy if he toppled the Ottoman sultan. Sometimes the Eastern Question pitted the Europeans against each other; when Russia annexed Ottoman territory in the early 1850s, Britain and France fought alongside the Turks in the Crimean War (1853–1856), the first time since Napoleon's defeat that European powers clashed with each other.

Tensions worsened after 1870. The construction of the **Suez Canal** in 1869 increased the strategic and economic importance of Egypt, as well as Britain's and France's interest in the region. Italy's unification in the 1860s meant yet another European power with ambitions in the eastern Mediterranean. Moreover, Balkan **nationalism** intensified in the late 1800s. The **Balkan Crisis** (1876–1878) nearly destroyed the Ottoman Empire: when Romania, Bulgaria, Serbia, and Montenegro revolted against the Ottomans, Russia went to war on their behalf, beat the Turks, and imposed a harsh treaty. The rest of Europe, not wanting Russia to defeat the Turks too decisively, intervened. At the Congress of Berlin (1878), the four rebel nations gained their freedom, but the European powers compelled Russia to offer a more generous treaty to the Turks. Once again, the Eastern Question was dealt with through a combination of opportunistic land-grabbing and balanced management.

The Ottoman Empire's Final Years

Domestically, the Ottoman Empire, steadily losing territory and constantly interfered with by the powers of Europe, suffered great difficulties as the 1800s came to an end. As the twentieth century began, the sultan's days were numbered. A group of pro-Western army officers, with a modern, secular outlook, began to form. They called themselves the **Young Turks**, and they were deeply dissatisfied with the sultan's failures to reform and strengthen the Empire. Led by Enver Pasha, the Young Turks seized control in 1908, neutralizing the last sultan and establishing a parliamentary government. The Young Turks modernized the military, aligned themselves with Germany, and began a series of social, economic, and political reforms.

However, they could not save the Ottoman Empire. Between 1911 and 1913, the Italians seized the Ottomans' last provinces in North Africa, and a coalition of Serbia, Greece, and Bulgaria defeated the Ottomans in two Balkan Wars. Finally, during World War I, the Young Turk government sided with the Germans. Defeated by the Allies in 1918, the Ottoman Empire collapsed altogether, and its Middle Eastern possessions rebelled or were stripped away by the French and British. The empire was replaced by the modern Turkish state during the 1920s.

EGYPT AND NORTH AFRICA

At its peak, the Ottoman Empire ruled most of Islamic North Africa. Even before the late 1700s, the empire's grip here was weakening owing to distance and the desire of cities such as Tripoli, Algiers, and Tunis for greater autonomy.

Things worsened with the Napoleonic Wars. In 1798, France sent Napoleon to capture Egypt and the Suez isthmus. He easily defeated Egyptian and Turkish armies, temporarily deposing the Mamluks who ruled Egypt on the Ottomans' behalf. Although the English restored the regime, Ottoman authority in Egypt was badly damaged.

The Revolt of Muhammad Ali

In 1805, the rebellion of **Muhammad Ali** freed Egypt from Ottoman rule. An officer in the Turkish forces, Muhammad Ali seized power and began to modernize Egypt until his death in 1839. He created a Western-style military, modernized agriculture (especially cotton), boosted industrialization, and recruited large numbers of European professionals to work for him and teach his people new skills. Muhammad Ali transformed Egypt into one of the world's greatest suppliers of cotton, although he worked his peasants oppressively to do so.

Muhammad Ali threatened the Ottomans even more seriously when he tried to expand his borders. He took the Sudan, then went east, capturing the Sinai, Syria, parts of Arabia, and northern Iraq. He threatened the Ottoman capital, Istanbul. Afraid that he would topple the Ottomans completely, France and Britain stepped in. Recognizing Muhammad Ali as the hereditary prince (khedive) of an autonomous Egypt, the Europeans convinced him not to expand further—and in so doing, saved the Ottoman Empire. Even so, the empire had been badly injured.

European Imperialism in North Africa

As the 1800s passed, the western parts of North Africa, now cut off from the Ottoman Empire by Egypt, fell out of the Ottomans' hands and into those of European imperialists. The French seized Algeria in 1830; more than 150,000 French settled there by the mid-1850s, and France considered Algeria to be as important to it as India was to Britain. Later, the French established a protectorate over neighboring Tunisia. Morocco fell to the French and Spanish late in the century. Libya was conquered by Italy during the Italo-Turkish War (1911–1912). This was the first war in which airplanes flew in combat, and the Italians used poison gas as well.

The Suez Canal and English Dominance over Egypt and Sudan

Egypt fell out of the Ottoman orbit only to be sucked into the European sphere of influence. Muhammad Ali's grandson Ismail, also a reformer, decided to build a canal across the Suez land bridge that linked the Mediterranean with the Red Sea. Ismail's other modernizing efforts, which included building schools and hospitals, were helpful to Egypt. In the short term, building the Suez Canal led to European domination. A French engineer, Ferdinand de Lesseps, designed the canal, and British and French companies supervised the construction, which lasted from 1854 to 1869. The **Suez Canal** was a marvel of modern construction, and it revolutionized international shipping. However, thousands of Egyptians died during the construction, and the French and British held most of the shares in the company that owned the canal. The British bought up many French shares and, in 1875, all of Egypt's. This gave Britain an excuse to interfere in local politics. In 1881, the Egyptian military revolted against the khedive. Under the pretext of protecting their investment in the canal, the British assumed control over the region, establishing a protectorate called the Anglo-Egyptian Administration. Although the khedive technically ruled Egypt, the British controlled the government. (For other examples of Western economic dominance over regions that were not technically colonies, see Latin America and China during the late 1800s and early 1900s.)

The British extended the Anglo-Egyptian Administration southward, bringing the Sudan under its control. In the 1880s and 1890s, British authority was opposed by a religious leader and Islamic rebel known as the **Mahdi** (Arabic for "one who is rightly guided"). In 1885, the Mahdi's army massacred a British force at Khartoum, one of Britain's most stunning imperial defeats. In 1898, the British beat the Mahdi at Omdurman in a classic imperial battle in which a small European army, armed with modern rifles and machine guns, mowed down a much larger but poorly armed indigenous force.

From the late 1800s until after the end of World War II, Egypt and North Africa remained in European hands.

PERSIA, THE CAUCASUS, AND CENTRAL ASIA

Much the same pattern that applied to the Ottoman Empire and North Africa was repeated in the rest of the Middle East.

The Decline and Partition of Persia

Like the Ottomans, the Persians had created a mighty gunpowder empire, the Safavid state. It remained strong through the early 1700s, but then found itself at the mercy of outside powers. To the north was Russia, which, as it modernized and Westernized, seized Persian territory in a number of wars. In the late 1700s and 1800s, Russia took portions of the Caucasus Mountains, which lay between the two countries, absorbing Armenia, Georgia, and Azerbaijan. The first two, Christian states living under the Islamic Persians, had asked Russia for help (but had not wanted to become part of the Russian Empire as they did).

The Qajar Dynasty, which ruled Persia from 1794 to 1925, was unable to resist foreign control, even though it technically ruled the country. (In this, its situation resembled China during these years.) In the 1800s, Britain and Russia cynically divided Persia into spheres of influence, allowing them to balance their rivalry in the region and flank the Ottomans. The northern zone went to Russia, the southern zone to Britain. This arrangement lasted until after World War II. British investment in Persia was heavy, especially after the discovery of oil reserves 1908.

The Russian Conquest of the Caucasus and Central Asia

From the 1820s through the 1880s, the Russians waged long, intense campaigns of conquest and colonization in the Caucasus and Central Asia, home to the Silk Road khanates. The Russians conquered these regions for several reasons: nationalistic pride, natural resources (Central Asia is a great cotton-producing region), strategy (the Russians feared having a long, open southern frontier), and the hope, never realized, of driving to the Indian Ocean to establish warm-water ports. In long, bloody wars of pacification, the Russians crushed Islamic tribes in the Caucasus. Further to the east, they took Tashkent (1865), Samarkand (1868), and Bukhara (1868), driving all the way to the Afghan border.

As discussed in Chapter 22, Russian ambitions here distressed the British: Russia threatened Britain's lines of communication to India and drew near to India itself. The resulting **Great Game** of espionage and diplomatic maneuver caused much Anglo-Russian rivalry until the early 1900s.

China and Japan

CHAPTER 24

- The decline of Qing China
- The tea and opium trades
- The Opium Wars, the concessions system, and the Open Door Policy
- The Taiping Rebellion
- The Dowager Empress Cixi and the Boxer Rebellion
- Sun Yat-sen and the Nationalist Party
- The Tokugawa Shogunate
- Matthew Perry and the opening of Japan
- The Meiji Restoration and Japan's industrial modernization
- The Russo-Japanese War

As with the rest of the globe, the European presence in East Asia increased dramatically from the late 1700s through the early 1900s. The major states there, China and Japan, reacted to this development in different ways.

Famously, Napoleon Bonaparte referred to China as a sleeping dragon. By that, he meant that with its huge population, vast size, and rich resources, China had the potential to become one of the world's mightiest nations. However, under the rule of the Qing (Manchu) emperors, China continued to slumber, and its power decreased rather than increased. Deluded by a sense of its own grandeur, based on past accomplishments and old traditions, the Qing leadership did little to modernize or industrialize. This backwardness left it vulnerable, and, during the 1800s, China suffered repeated defeats at the hands of Western powers. Although China was not actually conquered and colonized, it was forced to grant so many privileges and economic concessions to outside powers that its integrity as an independent nation was compromised. The Qing state weakened internally in the late 1800s and collapsed in 1911.

By contrast, Japan responded effectively to the challenge posed by the West. When the United States and the nations of Europe forced its markets open to the world in the 1850s, Japan chose to learn from them. From 1868 onward, under new leadership, the Japanese modernized, industrialized, and militarized. They preserved their independence. By the 1890s and early 1900s, Japan was itself an imperial power, expanding its sphere of influence in East Asia. As several wars during these years proved, Japan became the first non-Western nation in the modern era capable of rivaling Europe and America in military ability and strength.

QING (MANCHU) CHINA IN DECLINE
The Peak of the Qing Dynasty

The Qing, or Manchu, rulers who had conquered China from the north in 1644 had been mighty, ruthless leaders. The dynasty's peak, however, had been the long reign of Kangxi (1662–1722). Emperor **Qianlong** (1736–1795) was the Qing's last strong, competent ruler.

During the last half of the 1700s, Qianlong defended China's long borders, kept the empire's far-flung regions under control, improved economic growth, and sponsored art and learning. During his reign, one of the greatest novels in Chinese literary history appeared: Cao Xuequin's *Dream of the Red Chamber* (1791), which narrates the tragedy of two young lovers caught up in the decline of a wealthy and powerful clan.

Internal Decline of the Qing

Unfortunately for the Qing, several negative trends weakened China after Qianlong's death. The quality of leadership steeply declined, as weak, incompetent emperors took the throne.

More widely, the government became riddled with corruption. The cost of maintaining border defenses along the northern and western frontiers became increasingly burdensome. The economy worsened, and population growth was too rapid (China had 300 million people at the beginning of the century, and 400 million by the end). Popular discontent with the Qing and bad economic conditions broke out into open revolt several times. One such occasion was the White Lotus Rebellion (1796–1804), which took years for the authorities to suppress.

Chinese Foreign Trade Before the 1830s

At the same time, an external problem made itself felt: increased economic and diplomatic pressure from the West, particularly from Britain. As late as the 1810s, the Chinese had the upper hand in their relationship with the West. China was too strong to conquer, and it enjoyed an enormous advantage in its balance of trade.

Europeans could trade with China only in a small number of designated ports and cities (including Kiakhta in the north and **Canton** on the southern coast). The Chinese accepted only a tiny selection of Western goods in trade. In return, they sold the nations of the West silk and porcelain. The most profitable commodity was **tea**, which the Chinese sold in immense quantities to the outside world, especially Russia and Britain. In exchange, the West paid China vast amounts of silver bullion.

For years, Westerners complained about these conditions and requested the Chinese to let them sell more goods in China. In 1793, a British delegation led by Lord Macartney made such a request, but it was denied. Famously, Macartney, in order to meet the Emperor Qianlong, was compelled to lower himself onto one knee, and he was referred to by the Chinese not as an ambassador, but as a tribute-bearer. When Macartney asked that the British be allowed to sell more of their goods to China, Qianlong replied, "Your country has nothing we need." In 1816, a similar mission under Lord Amherst received much the same response.

Tea Harvesting in China.
For hundreds of years, silk, then porcelain, had been China's chief trade commodities. During the 1600s and 1700s, however, tea overtook both in importance. The tea trade played a great role in global economics during the 1700s and 1800s. During those centuries, "all the tea in China" became the most popular slang phrase to describe unimaginable wealth. Shown here is the traditional method of harvesting and processing tea in China.

The Qing's refusal to bargain was partly tough business sense. However, it also had to do with feelings of superiority: the Qing believed that the emperor was the Son of Heaven, that China was the **Middle Kingdom** and the center of the universe, and that all outsiders were barbarians. What the Qing failed to realize, however, was that the Western "barbarians" were, by this point, much more scientifically and technologically advanced than the Chinese—and had stronger navies, better weapons, and more effective armies. The days when the Chinese could intimidate foreigners into accepting such an embarrassing and unprofitable imbalance of trade were about to end.

The Opium Wars and Foreign Domination of Qing China

Meanwhile, the British, followed by other Europeans, found a clever, if unethical, way to break into Chinese markets: the **opium trade**. Opium was known in China, but not widely available, in the 1700s. In the early 1800s, the British began flooding China with opium grown in northeastern India. With lightning speed, opium became the drug of choice among Chinese of all classes. The British made fantastic profits, and the balance of trade swung suddenly in their favor. Over time, other countries—including France, Portugal, and the United States—sold opium to China, but Britain controlled 80 percent of the trade.

The Chinese government was outraged. The trade was illegal. It reversed the balance of trade, and silver bullion, instead of flowing into China, flowed out at an alarming rate. Moreover, opium addiction was so widespread that it affected economic productivity: on any given day, millions of farmers and workers were so incapacitated by the drug that they could not work. The Chinese protested to the West. One official lamented, "The foreigners have brought us a disease which will dry up our bones, a worm that gnaws at our hearts, a ruin to our families and persons. It means the destruction of the soul of our nation."

The Qing government tried to strike back by arresting dealers, seizing opium supplies, and intercepting boats carrying the drug. The problem for the Chinese was that aggressive action risked giving the foreigners an excuse for war. This happened in 1839, when the Chinese navy blockaded Canton, one of the few ports where foreigners were allowed to trade, sparking the first **Opium War** (1839–1842). The British won easily, then forced the humiliating Treaty of Nanking on the Chinese. The Qing government had to open five more ports to foreign trade, lower tariffs on British goods, and grant extraterritorial rights to areas in China where the British lived and worked (British, not Chinese, law prevailed in these areas). In addition, China surrendered **Hong Kong** to Britain.

Further trade conflicts, including a second Opium War (the so-called Arrow War) and a Franco-British expedition to Beijing, took place between 1856 and 1860. New treaties legalized the opium trade, opened more ports to foreign trade, and granted greater powers to the Portuguese, French, British, Americans, and Russians, who set up **economic concessions** on Chinese territory. Later in the 1800s, China grew weaker and had to give more privileges to foreign traders. Japan, Germany, and Italy gained concessions as well. Much territory along the Chinese coast was extraterritorial: legally under foreign, not Chinese, control. By 1898, foreign vessels were allowed unrestricted travel up the rivers of China.

The Taiping Rebellion

Serious internal problems dogged the Qing at the same time. The worst was the **Taiping Rebellion** (1850–1864), the costliest and most devastating civil war in world history. The Taiping Rebellion lasted almost a decade and a half and claimed between 20 to 30 million lives, making it the second deadliest war in history, next to World War II.

The uprising was started by Hong Xiuquan, a Cantonese clerk educated partly by Protestant missionaries. An aspiring government official, Hong failed his civil service examination. The shock caused him to have visions, in which he became convinced that he was Jesus Christ's younger brother, destined to establish a "heavenly kingdom of supreme peace"—the meaning of the word *taiping*—in China.

Hong's rebellion began in 1850. An extraordinarily magnetic leader, Hong attracted several followers capable of organizing an effective modern army. His vision of a new China also appealed to millions of ordinary Chinese who resented the Qing's high taxes, its arbitrary and oppressive rule, and the fact that the Manchu emperors were essentially foreign rulers. At their peak, Hong and the Taiping leaders controlled one-third of China.

The Taiping Rebellion waned after 1860. Competent generals took over the Qing war effort, and the government was assisted by a foreign force—the Ever-Victorious Army—commanded by an American soldier of fortune, Frederick Townsend Ward, and then the English general Charles "Chinese" Gordon. Quarrels among the Taiping leadership hurt the movement as well. By the early 1860s, the Taiping forces were in retreat. Hong committed suicide by taking poison in 1864, and the remaining Taiping leaders were captured and executed.

The Leadership of Dowager Empress Cixi

The Taiping Rebellion left China in ruins, and the Qing government was thrown into chaos. A limited reform—the "self-strengthening movement"—was attempted in the 1860s, but had little real impact. Not until 1878 did a strong leader emerge—unfortunately, one who adamantly opposed modernization. The dowager empress **Cixi** "ruled" China from 1878 to her death in 1908. A concubine to the emperor in the 1850s, Cixi became a major figure at the Qing court. In 1878, she placed her nephew Guangxu on the imperial throne and gained the position of regent. She did not rule China in her own right, but controlled her nephew—and the government—long after Guangxu became an adult.

Under Cixi's influence, Qing rule became more oppressive. China's outlying possessions—Tibet, Mongolia, Chinese Turkestan—began to slip away, gain greater autonomy, or fall into foreign hands. At home, Cixi opposed all reform, which she regarded as pro-Western treason. In 1898, when her nephew, the emperor, began listening to reform-minded advisers, she acted harshly. When Guangxu launched his short-lived Hundred Days' Reform, Cixi placed him under house arrest and executed the reformers.

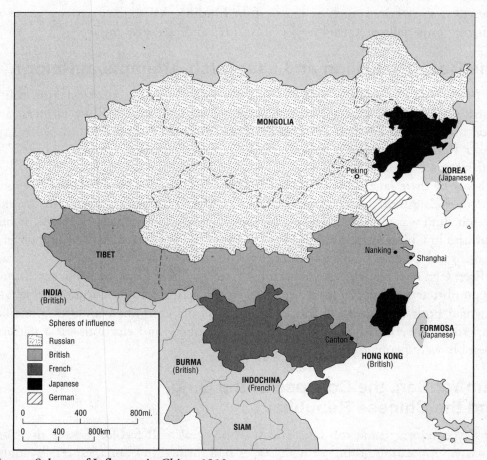

Western Spheres of Influence in China, 1910.
Starting in the early-to-mid-1800s, Great Britain, then other Western nations, pressured China into opening its markets and yielding up economic and political control over much of its coast. These concessions grew in size and number during the 1800s and early 1900s, reaching their peak just before the Qing dynasty's collapse in 1911.

The Sino-Japanese War and the Open Door Policy

All this time, foreign domination of China increased, especially as the new nations of Germany and Italy pushed for a greater share of Chinese trade. Germany took the major port of Tsingtao. Japan defeated China in the Sino-Japanese War (1894–1895). In 1898, the United States, with its **Open Door Policy**, arranged for all Western nations to have equal access to Chinese markets. Such a policy reduced much of the pressure that European nations were placing on China to open up further, but it also meant that foreign control continued.

Missionaries in China

Another result of increased foreign influence in China was a rise in the level of missionary activity there. From the late 1800s through the mid-1900s, it became more common for Protestant and Catholic clergy and volunteers to travel from Europe and the United States to China in order to spread Christianity and teach Western languages. In this way, they interfered with and even eroded traditional Chinese culture.

However, missionaries also brought scientific and technological knowledge, treated diseases and ailments with modern medicine, and helped eliminate oppressive cultural practices, such as female **foot binding**. Missionary activity serves to illustrate imperialism's mixed legacy of positive and negative impact.

The Boxer Rebellion and Last-Ditch Attempts at Reform

In 1900, Chinese anger at foreign influence burst out of control. Making things worse were a severe drought, which damaged agriculture and hurt farmers, and widespread unemployment in the cities. What followed during the summer was the **Boxer Rebellion**, so called because many of the rebels were Chinese "boxers," or martial-arts experts.

Most of their rage was directed at foreigners, especially in the capital, Beijing, where rebels attacked foreign residents and besieged foreign legations. In the end, the rebellion was put down, mainly by foreign troops. In revenge, the foreign communities in China burned a number of temples. They also forced the Qing government to pay a heavy financial penalty.

Even Cixi now recognized the need for at least some reform. In 1905, she formed a committee to investigate the possibility of writing a constitution. She and Guangxi both died in 1908, but the reform effort continued under China's last emperor, Henry Puyi. Local assemblies were formed, and elections for a national assembly were planned for 1910.

Sun Yat-Sen, the Collapse of the Qing, and the Chinese Republic

However, reform came too late, and was too weak and feeble, to save the Qing dynasty. Opposition groups of many types had formed in China, especially among younger Chinese who opposed Manchu domination of their race and favored Western-style modernization. The most important of these revolutionaries was **Sun Yat-sen** (1866–1925), who lived and traveled widely in America and Europe. Sun united a number of opposition groups into a movement called the Revolutionary Alliance and promoted three "people's principles": nationalism (opposition to Manchu rule and Western imperialism), democracy, and livelihood (a semi-socialist, but not Marxist, concern for people's welfare). Although he supported using force to remove the Qing, Sun hoped to unite all of China's people in equality under a constitutional democracy. In many respects, his ideals were similar to those of France's revolutionaries in 1789. Unlike them, however, he supported universal suffrage for women as well as men.

The Qing regime collapsed in the fall of 1911, because of a major uprising in the Chinese region of Wuhan. Although Sun was in the United States at the time, his movement was at the rebellion's forefront, and as the revolution spread, he returned from America. A Chinese Republic was founded in early 1912, with Sun as its president. His party now called itself the **Nationalist Party** (**Kuomintang**). For the first time in recorded history, China was ruled not by an imperial dynasty or foreign conqueror, but a politician brought to office by popular action.

But as in revolutionary France, political idealism was no match for ideological disagreements between left and right (with Sun in the middle), economic crisis, and the breakaway of frontier provinces. Shortly after coming to power, Sun was forced to step aside as president in favor of military officers who governed more from the right (a point of similarity between China's revolution and Mexico's, which began in 1910). Decentralization and civil war characterized the 1910s through the 1940s. Sun died in 1925, with China still in chaos. In 1949, his successor, Chiang Kai-shek, was defeated, and a communist government seized power.

ISOLATION AND PARTIAL MODERNIZATION IN TOKUGAWA JAPAN

The Tokugawa Shogunate in the Eighteenth Century

In the 1750s, Japan was ruled by the **Tokugawa Shogunate**, which had taken power in the early 1600s. As before, supreme authority technically rested with the emperor, but real power belonged to the shogun, who ran the country in the emperor's name. Under the shogun were the remnants of the **samurai** class, the warrior aristocracy from Japan's feudal era.

In the 1600s and early 1700s, the Tokugawa shoguns were dynamic rulers. They had centralized Japan and transformed it from a constantly warring collection of disunified states into a single country at peace. The Tokugawa shoguns were highly dictatorial, creating a rigidly stratified society that restricted social mobility, kept ordinary citizens out of politics, and allowed few personal freedoms. Tokugawa Japan also isolated itself from the rest of the world. By the 1720s, the only country Japan had formal relations with was Korea. Informal ties were maintained with China, and the government allowed some foreign trade at the port of **Nagasaki**.

Partial Modernization in Tokugawa Japan

In the late 1700s and early 1800s, Tokugawa Japan partially modernized, both economically and socially. Population growth was steady. Japan, already a society of cities, experienced even more urban growth. Kyoto and Osaka were major centers, and the capital, Edo (present-day Tokyo), had a population of well over a million. Agriculture practice was rationalized, allowing fewer people to grow more food. This reform led to further urbanization and freed up a labor force just as proto-industrialization began in Japan.

Trade, commerce, and manufacturing became increasingly important. A national infrastructure—more roads, canals, and ports—began to emerge. The **merchant class**, soon to be a modernizing middle class, grew in number, wealth, and influence. Despite the country's international isolation, some Japanese gained an awareness of Western science and technology.

Partial modernization placed the shogun and the samurai in a dilemma. It made Japan more prosperous and more advanced. On the other hand, the spread of new foreign learning, the movement of people from countryside to city, and the increased social and economic clout of the merchant class undermined the power and land-based wealth of the traditional aristocracy.

Therefore, the regime allowed some modernization, but not as much as Japan was capable of. In particular, members of the samurai class—whose military prowess was based on skill with traditional weapons, such as swords—were anxious to preserve the state's monopoly on gunpowder weaponry. How long the Tokugawa leadership would have kept up this approach is impossible to say. In the early 1850s, however, external forces compelled Japan to change.

The Opening of Japan and the Overthrow of the Shogunate

In 1853, American gunships appeared off the Japanese coast. Their commander, **Commodore Matthew Perry**, requested Japan to open its economy to foreign trade. Although the Americans' words were friendly, the threat of naval bombardment lay behind them. After some debate, the shogun agreed to end his country's decades-long isolation. Over the next five years, European nations persuaded the Japanese to open up to them as well. For a time, it appeared that Japan might fall victim to the same kind of Western economic pressure that was crippling China.

Painfully aware of what was happening to China, certain samurai leaders, particularly from the southern provinces of Satsuma and Choshu, urged the shogun to stand up to foreign intimidation. This Sat-Cho Alliance gained a following at the Edo court and pressed for the severance of all ties with the West. It also took matters into its own hands. In 1867, a Choshu coastal fortress fired on Western ships, and the ships fired back. The resulting scandal gave the Sat-Cho Alliance the pretext it needed to move against the last shogun, who had just come to power. In January 1868, the Sat-Cho staged a military uprising and overthrew the shogunate. Meiji, who had ascended to the throne only in 1867, and was the first emperor in nearly a thousand years to enjoy full imperial powers.

THE MEIJI RESTORATION AND JAPANESE ASCENDANCY

The **Meiji Restoration** of 1868 began Japan's modern age. Although the rebellion that brought Meiji to power was initially anti-Western, even the most xenophobic members of the new government realized that, in order to avoid Western domination, Japan would have to adopt Western learning, economics, and military methods. In addition, the emperor himself was personally inclined toward Westernization. What followed was a revolution from above, in which Meiji's government radically altered Japanese politics, economics, and social organization.

From Feudalism to Constitutional Monarchy

In 1871, Meiji abolished feudalism. Although individual samurai continued to serve in positions of power, hereditary privileges were done away with. Government stipends to the samurai, a privilege of the past, were eliminated. Former samurai were forbidden to wear swords, their traditional symbols of authority, in public.

The rigid social hierarchy of the Tokugawa regime ended. Modern laws (the Civil Code of 1898) were drawn up. The Constitution of 1890 created an elected parliament, the Diet. Owing to property qualifications and other restrictions, suffrage was quite low, around 5 percent, and the emperor had a great deal of power over the Diet. The civil code and constitution also made little room for the rights of women, who were largely confined to a secondary status (industrialization gave many lower-class women jobs, but these were low-paying, low-status positions). In effect, Meiji and his successors created an oligarchy (rule by the few) that was less repressive and restrictive than the Tokugawa regime but hardly representative.

Industrialization and Economic Modernization

Meiji and the emperors who followed him altered the economy beyond recognition. Agricultural productivity increased. The major change, however, involved industrialization. Meiji sent young members of the upper class to visit or study in Europe and America, to learn engineering, economics, and military science. He created a Ministry of Industry in 1870 as well as state banks to finance his industrialization campaign. New railroads, steamships, ports, and canals were constructed every year. Huge corporations called *zaibatsu*, sponsored largely by the state, came to dominate the economic landscape. The government encouraged not just large-scale industry but also private enterprise, spurring the growth of a larger middle class.

Economic growth came at a price. For farmers, taxes increased. Working conditions for the industrial lower classes were oppressive, just as they had been during the first decades of Europe's Industrial Revolution. Sweatshop environments, low wages, and unsafe labor practices prevailed, especially in textile mills and coal mines. In one mine near Nagasaki, workers toiled in temperatures of up to 130 degrees Fahrenheit, and were shot if they tried to escape. Unions of any type were forbidden.

Social and Class Transformation in Japan

Social transformation was a major part of the Meiji Restoration. The traditional privileges of the samurai class were taken away. Access to political positions was increasingly dependent on merit, competence, and civil service examinations. Meiji's reforms and Japanese industrialization increased the size and power of the merchant and middle classes, much as industrialization did in the West. The feudal prejudice against trade and artisanship faded away.

Things changed for the lower classes as well. The farming population decreased, while the industrial working class grew. Taxes increased considerably for both, and the lower classes were barred from full political participation by the Constitution of 1890. However, they also benefited in some ways from the Meiji reforms. The new tax system of 1872 funded a national educational system. Commoners, who previously had not been allowed to handle or learn how to use weapons, were now allowed to serve in the military. Overall, Japanese society adopted Western dress, fashions and manners, the Western calendar, and the metric system. The population boomed, growing from 35 million in 1873 to 55 million in 1918—although this badly strained the economy.

Japanese Militarism and the Russo-Japanese War

Meiji Japan became increasingly militaristic. Nationalist sentiment ran high during the late 1800s and 1900s, spurring the desire for empire building. The government-sponsored religion of **State Shintoism**, a modern revival of Japan's ancient faith, emphasized Japanese superiority and veneration of the emperor as a descendant of the gods. Japan wanted markets for its manufactured goods. A resource-poor island, Japan also needed raw materials to continue industrial growth.

Japan's expansion began in the 1870s. It forced Korean ports open to trade, much as the West had done with China and Japan itself. From China, it took the Ryukyu Islands, which include Okinawa, the most cherished of Japan's overseas possessions. In the 1880s and early 1890s, Japan modernized its navy and drafted a well-drilled and well-equipped army.

More military successes followed. The Sino-Japanese War (1894–1895) resulted in Japan's occupation of Taiwan and Korea (annexed in 1910). An even more impressive triumph was the **Russo-Japanese War** (1904–1905). Competition over influence in Manchuria caused great tension between the two countries. Russia's rapid expansion and its construction of the Trans-Siberian Railroad, the longest in the world, interfered with Japanese ambitions. The Japanese opened the war with a surprise attack on Russia's Pacific naval base at Port Arthur. Tiny compared to Russia, Japan was nonetheless better prepared for war and had the advantage of fighting close to home. When the war ended, Japan was victorious. It annexed land near Korea, the southern half of Sakhalin Island, and the Kurile Islands.

The Russo-Japanese War (which helped cause Russia's 1905 Revolution) marked the first time in the modern era that a non-Western nation had defeated a European power in a full-scale military conflict. It was an early warning signal that, before too long, Europe's peak as the world's dominant civilization would eventually pass— and that its empires would slip away. As for Japan, it entered the new century as a modern, industrial nation and a regional power with a growing empire. Japan would continue to modernize. Unfortunately, its militaristic, nationalistic streak would widen as well, and its imperial ambitions would spin out of control.

India and Southeast Asia

CHAPTER 25

- The decline of Mughal India
- The British East India Company and the battle of Plassey
- The Indian cotton industry
- The zamindar system
- Sepoys and the Indian Mutiny
- National liberation movements and the Indian National Congress
- The Dutch East India Company and Indonesia
- Singapore and Hong Kong
- French Indochina and *la mission civilisatrice*
- Thailand's continued independence
- The Spanish-American War and U.S. annexation of the Philippines

The proverbial jewel in the crown of the British Empire was India. The conquest and ownership of this country, one of the largest and most populous regions on earth, by a small island nation 5,000 miles away was one of the central facts of nineteenth- and early-twentieth-century life. Throughout the 1800s, British control over India affected global economics, the movement of navies, international relations, and the balance of world power. It gave Britain immense wealth and prestige, and it affected the course of Indian history, changing politics, economic development, social practices, language, and virtually every aspect of Indian culture.

Likewise, the great arc of Southeast Asian nations and islands that stretched between British India and China came under increased Western control in the 1800s. By the end of the century, only a tiny portion of Southeast Asia remained free of foreign domination.

On the other hand, **national liberation movements** were beginning to form by the late 1800s, both in India and the rest of Southeast Asia. For the time being, they were unable to dislodge their foreign masters, but they lay the foundation for the movements that successfully expelled European colonists after World War II.

FROM FOOTHOLD TO MASTERY: THE BRITISH IN LATE-EIGHTEENTH-CENTURY INDIA

During the last half of the eighteenth century, most of India was technically ruled by the once-mighty **Mughal Empire**. However, the Mughals' political fortunes had declined badly since the glory days of the 1500s and 1600s. Many parts of the subcontinent had slipped out from under Mughal rule, becoming independent kingdoms or city-states. Also by the 1700s, increased pressure from European outsiders destabilized what was left of Mughal power.

Anglo-French Competition over India

In the early 1700s, the Portuguese and Dutch still maintained small settlements along India's coasts. The Europeans most intent on controlling India, however, were Britain and France, who took advantage of growing Mughal weakness. For the time being, Britain's interests were represented by the **British East India Company**, which financed the military takeover and economic development of India.

From the southeastern ports of Pondicherry and Madras, which they captured temporarily from the British, the French tried until the late 1750s to grapple with the British East India Company for hegemony over India. However, French colonial administrators did not get adequate support from the home government in Paris.

At the end of the decade, the British East India Company, under Sir Robert Clive, enlarged its power by scoring key military successes against the Mughals. When Indians attacked the British population of Bengal and jailed soldiers and civilians alike in a horrible underground prison known as the **Black Hole of Calcutta**, the British used the event as a pretext for military action. In 1757, at the crucial battle of **Plassey**, Clive defeated a Mughal force more than ten times the size of his own. By 1764, all of Bengal was in Clive's hands, and the Mughals granted such extensive military and economic concessions that British superiority on the subcontinent was permanently ensured. The French zone of control shrank to the coastal territory surrounding the port of Pondicherry.

Britain's Gradual Conquest of India

Even in 1800, the British held only a comparatively small part of India. Major centers of control were Bombay, the gateway port of the west coast; Madras, a cloth-making center on the southeast shore; and Fort William, near Calcutta, in the Bengal region of the northeast.

The British East India Company used military and economic power to expand its control and pressure the Mughals to grant it ever-widening tax-collecting rights and administrative powers. At first, the British had footholds only on the coasts, but they gradually extended their reach into the interior, especially up the Ganges River in the north. In some regions, the company governed directly. In others, it ruled through the authority of local Mughal officials or friendly natives.

Between the 1760s and 1810s, the company fought a number of campaigns. Major foes included Haidar Ali, who led guerrilla armies in the south; Tipu Sultan, who fought on central India's Deccan Plateau; and the Maharatta princes. Many British generals who became famous in other conflicts—such as Cornwallis, who lost to the Americans at Yorktown, and Wellington, who defeated Napoleon at Waterloo—saw service in these wars.

By 1810, the company controlled almost one-fourth of India, and most of Ceylon (now Sri Lanka).

British Administration of India Before 1800

Before 1800, the British East India Company's administration of British India was heavy-handed, even clumsy. Initially, the main goal was to create a local **cotton industry**. The British would process the cotton into cloth and sell it to the East Indies for spices, which were sent back to Britain.

In the beginning, British rule harmed the local population in several ways. Profits generated by Indian raw materials went to Britain, rather than benefiting the local economy. The size and efficiency of British-built textile mills drove local textile enterprises, often run by women, out of business. Also, British tax law allowed local authorities to confiscate land from peasants who could not pay their taxes. The British thought they had created a fair taxation system by leaving collection to native officials called **zamindars**. However, the zamindars lost no time in overtaxing their countrymen and then making themselves rich by using British law to seize land from peasants. Such confiscations became so common in the 1770s that famines struck the countryside, killing approximately one-third of the Indians— mainly peasants—living under British control.

INDIA UNDER BRITISH RULE: THE 1800s

During the first half of the 1800s, the British extended their control over India. They moved from the coastline and the Ganges River valley into the interior, gaining authority—whether direct or indirect—over the entire country. The British also took outlying northwestern areas, such as Punjab and parts of Afghanistan, after a series of conflicts with skilled warriors like the **Sikhs** and mountain peoples like the Pathans.

Methods of British Control

British colonial authority—referred to popularly as the **Raj**—was complex. Although the British crown became more involved, the British East India Company still assumed primary responsibility for administering and exploiting the expanding colony. Cities such as Bombay and Calcutta were directly governed by the Raj, as were the coasts and large swathes of the interior. In some parts of the interior, the British ruled indirectly, allowing obedient rajas and maharajas to stay on their thrones. In this way, the British ruled some areas at less cost and effort.

Positive and Negative Effects of British Colonial Rule

The British got better at colonial administration than they had been during the 1700s. They were guided by a combination of selfishness, a desire for efficiency, and the well-meaning but condescending sense of superiority that poet Rudyard Kipling later called the **White Man's Burden**. British economic interests in India, formerly restricted to cotton, now became multifaceted. A wide variety of resources was now sought and exploited. To make their own lives in India more comfortable and because they felt it would be better for the native Indians, British colonizers modernized the country in many ways. They created roads and railroads (which reduced the number of famines by improving food distribution), a telegraph system, and a postal service.

The British also affected India's cultural life. They put into place a quality educational system, partly to raise the level of scientific and technological knowledge, partly to create a group of Western-educated natives who would be loyal to Britain and assist in governing a pro-British India. In the words of the historian Thomas Macauley, who helped create this system, the goal was to educate a native elite that was "Indian in blood and color, but English in taste, in opinion, in morals, and in intellect." For the same reasons, the British created a civil service examination system

NOTE

The English, simply to keep order, reduced the level of sectarian strife between Muslims and Hindus.

for Indians who wished to work in the government. The Raj officially discouraged the conversion of Indians to Christianity (although individual British officials sometimes violated this policy). Still, the British sometimes eliminated cultural and religious (particularly Hindu) practices they felt were inhumane, including **sati** (or suttee) the practice of burning a widow alive at her husband's funeral; *thuggee* (the ritual assassination of travelers in the name of the goddess Kali); and the **caste system's** harsh treatment of so-called untouchables.

Native Officials and Sepoy Troops

The British went to great lengths to instill loyalty within their native subjects. Their comparatively light touch in religious and cultural practices helped greatly. Whenever possible, the British delegated local political authority to Indians. The British East India Company also trained large numbers of native troops called **sepoys**. Using native troops made it easier for Indians to accept foreign rule; as well, it saved the British a great deal of money and kept them from having to draft large numbers of their own citizens to serve far from home. The number of actual British soldiers and officers in India was quite low.

The British Approach to Colonial Rule

The British method of imperialism in India—which they tended to follow in other colonies in Asia and Africa—is difficult to evaluate. British rule brought many benefits and new learning to the non-Western world, and compared with other imperial nations, British colonial practice was relatively humane. However, British rule was established by conquest, supported by military might, preserved by divide-and-conquer politics, and done for the purpose of economic exploitation. Even when they did good, it was out of a belief that they were civilizing a "lesser" race.

The Indian Mutiny (The Sepoy Rebellion)

Tensions between the British and Indians were present throughout the 1800s. On one occasion, those tensions exploded suddenly and violently: the **Indian Mutiny** (1857–1858), also known as the **Sepoy Rebellion**, ranks as one of the most traumatic events in modern Indian and British history.

Within many sepoy regiments, underlying resentment of British rule broke out into open revolt, owing to rumors that British officers were deliberately trying to undermine Hindu and Muslim religious practices. Legally, the Raj was allowed to require sepoys to serve overseas. In the case of Hindus, crossing large bodies of water would break their caste. Hindu sepoys were not, in fact, sent overseas, but fear that they might be stirred up trouble. The perceived violation of Muslim and Hindu dietary restrictions actually triggered the rebellion. New rifles with greased cartridges were issued to sepoys in 1857. The false rumor that the grease was made from pig and cow fat—unclean to devout Muslims and Hindus, respectively—caused great outrage.

With lightning speed, the initial disturbances became a massive wave of nationwide revolt. Hundreds of thousands were killed: British soldiers, British civilians, loyal Indian troops, rebels, and Indian civilians. Massacres and atrocities were committed by both sides.

By 1858, after great effort and a tremendous amount of anxiety that India would be lost altogether, British troops, along with natives who continued to serve the Raj, put down the rebellion.

The British Crown Assumes Control

For the rest of the century, British rule over India remained solid. One important change was that the British crown took from the British East India Company all authority over the subcontinent. The British government now oversaw politics, ran the army, and supervised the colonial economy. In 1877, Victoria, queen of England, took the title empress of India.

> **NOTE**
>
> The British were fortunate that the rebels had no clear plan or single leader. Moreover, Hindu and Muslim rebels often failed to cooperate with each other—and sometimes fought each other.

Nationalist Movements in Turn-of-the-Century India

Even though British control grew more secure, problems simmered under the surface. The British strategy of educating a native elite in the Western style was generally successful, but in some cases backfired. Larger numbers of these educated young people used their knowledge to agitate for freedom. Education exposed many of them to liberal or radical ideas and convinced them that it was hypocritical of the British—with their long tradition of civil liberties and representative government—not to apply those liberties to nonwhite races.

Eventually, the most famous and influential member of Congress was **Mohandas K. Gandhi**. Trained as a lawyer in London, he lived in South Africa from 1893 to 1915, defending the rights of Indian workers living under the system of apartheid. After returning to India in 1915, he started to preach nonviolent resistance to British rule.

> **NOTE**
>
> The most important of the new nationalist groups was the **Indian National Congress**, formed in 1885. Most members were English-speaking, educated members of the native upper classes.

SOUTHEAST ASIA

Like India, Southeast Asia found itself increasingly in foreign hands during the late 1700s and 1800s. Before 1800, the only large areas firmly under European control were **Indonesia**, or the Dutch East Indies, and the Philippines, which belonged to Spain. By 1786, the British also had a presence in the Malay Peninsula. The Portuguese retained parts of the island of Timor, a tiny remnant of the Indonesian colony the Dutch had taken from them. Dutch rule over Indonesia was the responsibility of the **Dutch East India Company**, which handed much responsibility over to upper-class natives, trained and educated in the Western style.

Malaya and Singapore

As the British tightened their grip on India during the early 1800s, they made parallel advances into nearby Southeast Asia. In exchange for giving up claims on Indonesian territory, the British were allowed by the Dutch to absorb the Malay Peninsula, which was rich in rubber, tin, oil, copper, iron, and aluminum ore (bauxite). In 1819, British official Stamford Raffles established a British outpost on **Singapore**, an island at the peninsula's tip. Quickly, Singapore became an important

NOTE

The French placed more emphasis on religious conversion than the British.

trading center and fortress; with the advent of steamships, it became a key naval base and one of Britain's prized possessions in Asia.

The French Conquest of Indochina

The European incursion into Southeast Asia never ceased. Britain took over Burma, formerly a major power, in 1826. To prevent the British from having an unbroken chain of colonies stretching from India to the South China coast, France moved into **Indochina**, the territory that now encompasses Vietnam, Cambodia, and Laos.

From 1857 to 1859, France pressured Vietnam into accepting foreign rule. Cambodia followed in 1863, and Laos in 1893. Indochina was the source of many raw materials, but most profitable to the French were chrome, oil, bauxite, tin, and rubber.

The French model of imperialism was similar but not identical to that of Britain's. The French exploited the economy, but in accordance with their ideal of *la mission civilisatrice*, they also brought modern science and technology to their colonies in Southeast Asia. They educated—and often converted to Catholicism—a local elite of upper-class, Westernized natives. On average, the French resorted more readily to repression and violence to maintain order and carry out policy.

Modernization and Freedom in Thailand

The only state on the Southeast Asian mainland that remained independent throughout the 1800s was Thailand, owing to good leadership and good luck. Like Emperor Meiji in Japan, King Mongkut and his successor, King Chulalongkorn (both made famous in Anna Leonowens's memoir, *Anna and the King of Siam*, grossly distorted by Broadway and Hollywood), were modernizing monarchs, introducing industrialization and Western-style reform into their country. Thailand's geographic setting was also fortunate. The country lay between British-controlled Burma and French-dominated Indochina, and both European powers agreed informally to let it serve as a buffer zone between their colonies.

U.S. Annexation of the Philippines

The last major colonial takeover in Southeast Asia was the 1898 **annexation of the Philippines** by the United States, as a result of victory in the **Spanish-American War**. Although the conflict centered on Cuba, the United States sent a fleet under George Dewey to neutralize the Spanish naval forces based at Manila Bay. Then, with the assistance of native Filipinos (who, at first, saw the Americans as liberators), U.S. troops landed, defeated Spanish ground forces, and occupied the islands.

American victory resulted in Spain's being stripped of its colonies. This action raised the question of what to do with the Philippines. After great debate, the U.S., wishing to keep the Philippines from falling into the hands of the Japanese, chose to take possession. The islands also provided the United States with a superb naval base in the Pacific and a way station for trade with China. Moreover, the Americans felt a "moral" obligation, similar to the **White Man's Burden**, to civilize the Filipinos. The tragedy was that American colonization had to be imposed by means of a savage jungle war, as a Filipino guerrilla force led by **Emilio Aguinaldo** resisted the American takeover until 1901.

NOTE

The English poet Rudyard Kipling wrote the poem *White Man's Burden* to commemorate the U.S. victory over the Spanish.

Sub-Saharan Africa

CHAPTER 26

- Kongo
- The Asante (Ashanti) kingdom
- The Boers (Afrikaners) and the Great Trek
- The Zulu
- The diamond industry in South Africa
- Zanzibar and the Arab-East African slave trade
- The Atlantic slave trade
- The Scramble for Africa and the Berlin Conference
- The Belgian Congo and the rubber industry
- The Herero Wars
- The Boer War

Like most of the non-Western world, sub-Saharan Africa fell under the increased sway of European imperialism from 1750 to 1914. Already for several centuries, Africa had been victimized by the **Atlantic slave trade**. Europeans had plundered gold, ivory, and countless other goods. They had established outposts, naval bases, and small colonies on the east and west coasts of the continent.

Nonetheless, Europe's direct influence, especially south of the Sahara, was comparatively limited until late in the 1800s. After the Napoleonic Wars, the slave trade was made illegal in most Western countries. Although it continued for decades unlawfully, the Atlantic traffic in slaves tapered off and faded away. Moreover, strong African states resisted foreign domination for much of this period (in a sad irony, much of this strength was due to profits made by cooperating with the slave trade). Although the Europeans found it relatively easy to take control of North Africa and parts of the coastline, the central and southern interior remained for a long time difficult to penetrate.

Great changes came after 1880. Before then, outside powers controlled approximately 10 percent of Africa. Less than three and a half decades later, in 1914, foreigners controlled the entire continent, with the exception of two small countries. By the middle of the 1800s, explorers and missionaries had gained precise geographical knowledge of the African interior. Better medicines enabled larger numbers of soldiers and settlers to travel to and live in Africa's tropical zones. Industrial-era weaponry increased the Europeans' military superiority. During the 1880s and 1890s, they voraciously carved up African territory while there was still room to expand. This **Scramble for Africa** subjugated virtually the entire continent. It also stirred up the combative passions of the Europeans and contributed to the diplomatic tensions behind World War I.

FREEDOM'S TWILIGHT: AFRICAN STATES FROM THE LATE 1700s TO THE MID-1800s

African States During the Late 1700s and Early 1800s

European hegemony over Africa was a long time in coming. During the late 1700s and early 1800s, a number of states were strong enough to resist foreign domination. Others were useful and cooperative enough that it was worthwhile for the Europeans to work with them rather than fight them. Some of these states, such as Benin, Oyo, Dahomey, **Kongo** (see chapter 18), and Asante (Ashanti), played large roles in the Atlantic slave trade. They helped European traders and slavers capture and transport their fellow Africans.

In the west, a number of states remained independent well into the 1800s. These included the Hausa, Fulani, and Yoruba states. These Muslim theocracies formed, broke apart, and reformed, constantly fighting each other in costly civil wars.

The Asante (Ashanti) Kingdom

The strongest and most unified of the West African states was the **Asante** (**Ashanti**) kingdom, one of the last to survive as an independent state. Founded in the late 1600s, Asante took part in the flourishing trade in gold and slaves on Africa's west coast. Using profits to buy guns, it became a strong military power.

Asante's might increased dramatically during the late 1700s and early 1800s, especially as its African neighbors fought each other or came under foreign control. A large military buildup began under Osei Kojo (1764–1777). During the early 1800s, the Asante threatened European outposts and trade routes along the Gold Coast. They also resisted British, French, and American attempts to destroy the slave trade in the 1820s. By 1823, Britain found itself locked in a series of Asante wars that lasted until the end of the century, when it finally subdued the kingdom.

South Africa, the Boers, and the Zulu

South Africa had been colonized by the Dutch in the mid-1600s. For a century and a half, these Afrikaner **Boers**, as they called themselves, displaced or conquered native Africans. When the British assumed control over South Africa during the Napoleonic Wars, the Boers were themselves displaced. In the 1830s, they made their **Great Trek** to the north and east and, in the 1850s, founded the Orange Free State and the South African Republic (Transvaal), both of which bordered British South Africa. In the meantime, they and the recently arrived British came into contact with a new native power: the Zulu tribe.

The **Zulu**, a Bantu-speaking people, were relatively quiet and peaceful before 1800. But around 1816, a new chieftain, **Shaka**, seized power and united Zulu clans into a single tribe. A gifted military leader, Shaka has been called the Black Napoleon, and even after his death in 1828, the Zulu remained warlike.

The Zulu defeated neighbor after neighbor, causing a significant wave of tribal migration throughout the southern part of the continent. The Zulu also fought the Boers and British, and it took several wars for the Europeans to pacify them. The last major conflict, in 1879, was provoked by British officials who hoped to move into the Zulu lands because diamonds had recently been found there.

The discovery of these **diamond fields** heightened tensions in South Africa. Gold deposits were also found. The sudden emergence of such great potential wealth destabilized things by making parties more willing to fight over territory. The British began annexing diamond fields in 1871. Diamond mines cruelly exploited African labor. Workers were rigidly segregated by race.

East Africa

The East African coast, which had come under Portuguese domination between the late 1400s and late 1600s, enjoyed a period of strength and independence, at least from European control, during the late 1700s and early-to-mid 1800s. For the time being, the large island of Madagascar remained free, as did the Batutsi state in what is today Rwanda.

The Coptic Christian kingdom of Ethiopia, which earlier had allied with Portugal against Muslim conquerors, expelled the Portuguese, largely over questions of religious doctrine, in 1632. For the next two and a half centuries, Ethiopia went into isolation, then modernized under Theodore II, who came to the throne in 1855. As for the rest of the coast, the new power was not European but Arab. In 1728, Arabs drove the Portuguese from the port of Mombasa. Portugal's strength in the region then waned, although it retained footholds along the coast.

By the early 1800s, Omani Arabs had gained tremendous political influence in East Africa, and also controlled the flourishing trade between the East African coast and India. The most important East African port was **Zanzibar**, on a small island off the coast of Tanganyika. Its role as an economic powerhouse was demonstrated by the fact that the Omani sultan made it his capital in 1840. Zanzibar's primary trading partner was Bombay. This fusion of Arab, African, and Indian stimulated not just economic interaction but cultural interchange as well. Zanzibar's Arab masters extended their economic influence into Africa's interior, to the west and north.

Among the principal resources that flowed through Zanzibar were cloves, spices, sugar, and ivory. An even more important part of Zanzibar's economy was slavery. Ironically, just as the demand for slaves in the Atlantic was finally withering away, there was a major resurgence in the **Arab–East African slave market.** This had much to do with the growth of plantation agriculture in the area, fueled by the increased demand for sugar and spices. Between 1875 and 1884, the peak of the East African plantation economy, 44 percent of the total population was made up of slaves.

THE END OF THE ATLANTIC SLAVE TRADE
The Atlantic Slave Trade Becomes Illegal

One of the great changes coming to Africa during the 1800s was the gradual end of the **Atlantic slave trade**. Its demise resulted partly from economic and practical considerations. It was becoming more difficult and therefore more expensive to obtain slaves. Equally

NOTE

Zulu armies, led by Cetewayo, eventually lost the **Zulu War of 1879**. This took eight months for the British to win, and one of the early battles, Isandhlwana, in which a British force was massacred to the last soldier, was one of the worst military defeats suffered by a European force in Africa.

NOTE

It took decades for the Western powers to eliminate the East African slave trade. Abolition came about as a result of popular outrage, missionary activity (a key figure was the Scottish explorer and humanitarian **David Livingstone**), and military action. The great slave market in the center of Zanzibar was shut down in 1873. The British took over the city later in the century.

important was the growing revulsion that slavery caused in many Western countries. For moral, ethical, and religious reasons, an ever-greater number of citizens and politicians were unwilling to continue basing their nations' economies so squarely on slavery. Countries like revolutionary France, the Netherlands (1795), and Denmark (1803) began to make slavery illegal.

The major turning point came when Great Britain, in 1808, resolved to make the slave trade illegal (slavery was banned in all parts of the British Empire in 1834). During the peace settlements that followed the Napoleonic Wars, the British convinced almost all of Europe and the Americas to outlaw slavery and the slave trade. With the exception of Spain and Portugal, Europe agreed (Russia relied on **serfdom** till 1861, but this was a different question). For the most part, the Americas went along as well. Canada (still part of the British Empire) and most of Latin America outlawed slavery. The holdouts were Cuba and Brazil, which did not end slavery until 1883 and 1888. The United States, split between the slaveholding South and the nonslave North, agreed to make the slave trade illegal. The government also worked to restrict the spread of slavery within the United States as the country expanded. Not until after the U.S. Civil War (1861–1865) was slavery made illegal throughout the country.

The Atlantic Slave Trade Continues Illegally

The continued survival of slavery in the Americas meant that the Atlantic slave trade, illegal or not, went on during a good part of the 1800s. It has been calculated that 2 million Africans were transported to Brazil, Cuba, and the Caribbean during the 1800s. A small percentage of these were smuggled into the United States. The best estimate of the number of Africans enslaved by the Atlantic slave trade between the late 1400s and the 1800s is approximately 12 million.

As noted above, a market in African slaves flourished in Zanzibar during the 1800s, not ending until 1873. According to some sources, at the end of the nineteenth century, the number of slaves in the Islamic states of West Africa stood at nearly 5 million.

Foreign powers did more than legislate against the slave trade. **Abolition movements**, especially in Britain and the northern United States, pressured their governments to fight slavery actively. Canada served as a haven for slaves escaping from the southern United States. **Missionaries** in Africa, especially those from Britain, campaigned against slave raids and slave markets—both on the Atlantic coast and in East Africa and Zanzibar.

The British founded special colonies in Sierra Leone and the Gold Coast for freed blacks. Similarly, a group of American blacks and freed slaves settled the nation of Liberia, on the West African coast, with sponsorship from the U.S. government.

In the early 1800s, the British government dispatched the Royal Navy to blockade the West African shoreline, hunt down slave ships, and bombard the coastal forts of African states that continued to support the slave trade. Less enthusiastically, France and the United States joined in these expeditions.

Effects of the Slave Trade on Africa

The slave trade took an immense toll on Africa. Obvious effects included human suffering, population loss, dependence on foreign goods (as opposed to indigenous production), the stirring up of tribal warfare, and the disruption of traditional trade networks and economic practices.

It is equally obvious how the ending of the slave trade benefited Africa. However, there were also unforeseen, less positive consequences. One was a sharp economic slump—because, however heinous, the slave trade had been extremely lucrative. Economic weakness left African states more vulnerable to foreign takeover in the late 1800s. Moreover, the antislavery intervention of Great Britain and other nations, however well-intentioned, gave Europeans a pretext for involving themselves in Africa's affairs and thinking of military action as legitimate. This helped pave the way for the rush to conquer all of Africa at the end of the century.

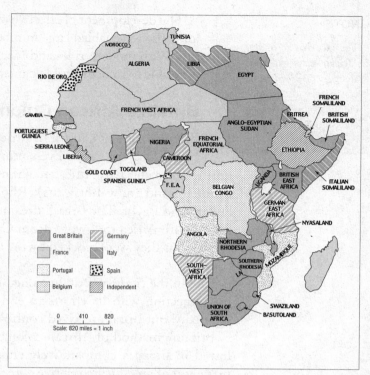

European Imperialism in Africa, 1914.

EUROPEAN IMPERIALISM AND THE "SCRAMBLE FOR AFRICA"

Approximately 10 percent of Africa was under foreign control before 1880. Most of this territory lay north of the Sahara or along the coastlines. Suddenly, between 1880 and 1914, the states of Europe were caught up in a breathlessly rapid "**Scramble for Africa.**" On the eve of World War I, only two countries—Ethiopia and Liberia—remained free.

Reasons for Europe's Late-Nineteenth-Century Domination of Africa

Many factors motivated and enabled the Scramble for Africa. First, a series of geographic expeditions from the 1770s through the 1860s gave the Western world an unprecedented amount of information about the African interior. Mungo Park of Scotland traced the entire Niger River from 1795 to 1805. The missionary David Livingstone, who arrived from Scotland in 1841 and fought the East African slave trade, also found time to explore the Zambezi basin and discover the Victoria Falls (1855). Anglo-American adventurer Henry Stanley explored the Congo, while England's John Speke unraveled one of Africa's greatest geographical mysteries by locating the source of the Nile in 1863.

NOTE

The fact that so many African states were torn apart by civil or intertribal conflicts made them vulnerable to European takeover. So did economic backwardness.

The development of effective treatments for tropical diseases—such as **quinine** for malaria—enabled large numbers of Westerners to move into the African interior. With modern rifles and machine guns, small numbers of European soldiers were able to inflict horrible damage on native warriors, even when outnumbered.

Britain's African Colonies

Britain's zone of control in Africa included the Gold Coast, Sierra Leone, and Nigeria in the west. Even more extensive was its collection of colonies in northeastern and East Africa, an almost unbroken chain that included South Africa, Bechuanaland (now Botswana), Rhodesia (now Zimbabwe), Kenya, Uganda, the Sudan, and Egypt. The British dreamed of building a continental railway stretching from South Africa to Egypt ("from **Cape to Cairo**," as the imperialist Cecil Rhodes put it), but they were blocked by the German acquisition of territory on the eastern coast.

Late in the century, Britain gained influence over the rich port of Zanzibar, partly in connection with its efforts to end slavery there. Zanzibar had been claimed by Germany, but Britain received control over it as part of a swap of colonial territories.

Britain's method of African colonial administration was similar to the one it followed in India: a comparatively enlightened **White Man's Burden** approach that made use of an educated native elite, deployed native troops trained in the Western style, and brought new science and industrial technology to the colonies.

The French in Africa

France's African empire was restricted mainly to the Saharan north: Morocco, Algeria, Tunisia, West Africa, and Equatorial Africa. However, it had territories elsewhere, such as Djibouti, part of the Somali coast, and the island of Madagascar. As in Southeast Asia, France acted in accordance with its "civilizing mission" and, for the most part, treated its colonial subjects responsibly.

The Portuguese

Portugal retained control over its longtime possession in West Africa, Angola. On the eastern coast, where it had once reigned supreme, it took Mozambique. Unlike the French and British, the Portuguese were quite harsh with their African colonies.

Belgium and the Congo

Tiny Belgium gained control over one of the largest African colonies: the vast **Congo** basin. In 1876, **Leopold II** of Belgium, with the Anglo-American explorer Henry Stanley as his manager, established a private company for the economic development of the Congo. By 1884, the Congo was fully under the company's control. In his will, Leopold left the colony to Belgium.

Leopold's exploitation of the Congo was brutal, and Belgium's record as a colonizing power was among the worst in Africa. Belgian-owned **rubber plantations** overexploited rubber trees and, worse, brutally forced Congolese villagers to meet production quotas. One vile practice was the policy of some

NOTE

Before the Belgians arrived, the area's population was around 20 million. By 1911, only about 8.5 million remained.

overseers to chop off the right hands of Congolese workers who did not harvest enough rubber. Some workers were simply massacred. Belgian occupation led to massive depopulation.

Italian and German Colonization of Africa

The new nation of Italy had poor luck in Africa. In 1911 and 1912, it seized Libya from the Ottoman Empire in a short war that involved the use of aircraft and poison gas. Before that, in 1896, the Italians had attempted to conquer Ethiopia. King Menelik II, however, had prepared well by purchasing modern rifles for his army and hiring Western mercenaries to train his troops. The Italians were prevented from taking Ethiopia by their humiliating defeat at the Battle of **Adowa**, which ranks as one of the most embarrassing setbacks in the history of European imperialism.

> **NOTE**
>
> Historians estimate that the Germans killed almost 80 percent of the Herero—64,000 of 80,000—by the time they quelled the rebellion.

Also new to the world stage was Germany. In keeping with the military prowess they had shown in Europe, the Germans quickly assembled a sizable empire in Africa. Their possessions included Togoland, the Cameroons, Southwest Africa, and German East Africa (Tanganyika, off of which the island of Zanzibar lay).

Unfortunately, the colonies left for the Germans were those no one else had wanted. Rather than turning a profit, they lost money. The Germans also had to deal with several major uprisings, including the Maji Maji revolt in Tanganyika (1905–1907) and the infamous **Herero Wars** in Southwest Africa (1904–1908). The latter were especially savage, to the point of genocide.

African Women and European Imperialism

One of the major consequences of colonial rule was that many African families were broken up. Husbands went to work in mines or on plantations, while wives and children stayed behind in villages and on reserves. Women were left to grow food for their families for mere survival and to care for the sick and aged. Long separations between spouses led to a rise in the level of prostitution and the spread of sexually transmitted diseases.

In general, African men benefited more than women from the economic changes brought by colonial rule. In regions where colonial officials introduced private property rights, property was given to male heads of households, not women. Most jobs, even those in teaching, were reserved for men, and women were discouraged from running family businesses or selling goods in markets.

Imperialism in Africa and Its Effects on European Diplomacy

The Scramble for Africa stirred up aggression among the Europeans, bringing them numerous times to the brink of conflict.

The German diplomat Otto von Bismarck attempted to cool tensions at the **Berlin Conference** (1884–1885), whose purpose was to agree on boundary lines and set down rules for further expansion into Africa. The lines on the resulting map reflected European desires and had little relation to the traditional territorial boundaries of African tribes or ethnic groups, none of whom were invited to take part.

The Berlin Conference temporarily helped to prevent war over Africa, but tensions rose in the 1890s and 1900s. In 1896, France and Britain almost came to blows as a result of the Fashoda Incident, in which French troops moving eastward into the Nile Valley encountered British soldiers who regarded the region as belonging to them. The French withdrew, but not before a short war scare. In the early 1900s, Germany's naked ambitions in Africa caused more trouble. Its interference with French and Spanish plans for northwestern Africa led to a Morocco Crisis in 1906 and another one in 1911.

Even worse was Germany's public support of the Dutch Afrikaners in the **Boer War** (1899–1902). Here, fighting had broken out between the British and Boers in South Africa. Although the British had a larger, better-equipped army, the Boers were skilled guerrilla soldiers and excellent sharpshooters, fighting on their home territory. The war was a painful one, with the British forced to pacify the Boer civilian population. More than 120,000 women, children, and male noncombatants, many of them black Africans, were placed in **concentration camps** (the twentieth century's first) by the British. Between 26,000 and 28,000 died, causing an international outcry. The Germans made no secret of their sympathy for the Boers. This public favoritism had the result of worsening Anglo-German relations, already strained because of the two countries' naval race and Britain's anxieties about German imperialism elsewhere in Africa (especially German East Africa, which kept Britain from building a continental railroad from Egypt to South Africa). These tensions had profound effects on the alliance system that emerged in the years before World War I.

In this way, the Scramble for Africa backfired on the Europeans. Imperial successes led to diplomatic problems, which, taken together, helped bring about World War I—the conflict that began breaking down European world power.

CHAPTER 27

Revolution and Consolidation in North and South America

- The Atlantic revolutions
- The American Revolution
- The Monroe Doctrine, the Louisiana Purchase, and manifest destiny
- Slavery in America and the Atlantic slave trade
- Immigration to the United States and the Americas
- The Haitian Rebellion

- The Latin American wars of independence
- The Mexican-American War
- Caudillos, monoculture, and dollar diplomacy
- The Spanish-American War
- The Panama Canal
- The Mexican Revolution

During the late 1700s and early 1800s, the colonies of the New World—the possessions of European powers for three centuries—threw off the ties that bound them politically and economically to their home countries. The **American Revolution**, the **Haitian Rebellion**, and the **Latin American wars of independence** were all part of the great wave of revolutions, including the French Revolution, that struck the Atlantic world during this era.

However, their results differed greatly. In the north, the American Revolution created an economic and political powerhouse: the United States, the modern world's first major nation to become a democracy, steadily expanded across the continent. Despite internal troubles, even wars, concerning slavery and the suppression of Native Americans, it grew in size and might. Like the nations of Europe, it industrialized. Already by the early 1800s, the United States was the dominant power in the Western Hemisphere. By the end of the century, it had acquired overseas territories of its own and was on the threshold of becoming a world power.

As for Latin America, revolution brought freedom, but did not create nations as well equipped to deal with freedom as the United States was. Despite high ideals, most of the new Latin American nations were plagued by dictatorial politics, economic backwardness, poverty, racial prejudice, and frequent revolutions and civil conflicts. In addition, the great power to the north, the United States, became increasingly involved in Latin American economics and politics, and not always for the better.

THE AMERICAN REVOLUTION AND THE BIRTH OF THE UNITED STATES

Causes of the American Revolution

The **American Revolution** (1775–1783) resulted from the combination of several trends in the thirteen British colonies in New England and the mid-Atlantic coast:

- A growing sense of patriotism and national identity. In this sense, the "revolution" was less a revolution and more a war of independence.
- Increased resentment of Great Britain's economic mastery. The taxes Britain levied to pay for the army it maintained in North America angered many colonists, especially because they lacked representation in the British Parliament.
- The desire of the colonial merchant (that is, middle) class to better itself. Economic freedom from Britain would allow American merchants to become wealthier, thanks to free trade and the new spirit of capitalism.
- The influence of Enlightenment philosophy. Most of the leaders who carried out the American Revolution and shaped the government afterward had read the works of Enlightenment thinkers such as Locke, Montesquieu, and Voltaire. The **Declaration of Independence** (1776), by Thomas Jefferson, is considered a classic Enlightenment text.

The American Revolution

Whatever the causes, the American Revolution broke out in 1775, with the twin battles of Lexington and Concord. At first, the poorly trained and poorly armed American forces, led by George Washington, struggled against Britain's professional armies. By 1777, however, the tide was turning. Although some colonists, nicknamed Tories, remained loyal to the British, popular support for the revolution was high; most members of all classes—lower, middle, and upper—united behind it. The Americans were fighting on their home territory. Not only did European mercenaries and freedom fighters with military experience arrive to train American troops, the Americans used unconventional tactics and guerrilla warfare to counter the British soldiers' training. The British were fighting far from home, at the end of extremely long supply lines.

After America's victory at Saratoga in late 1777, France, Britain's mortal enemy, lent military and naval aid to the American colonists. The assistance of the French fleet against Britain's Royal Navy was particularly helpful.

By 1781, the British war effort was failing. When the main British force was surrounded at Yorktown, the war was effectively over, although peace talks dragged on until 1783. The Americans were victorious—and had won themselves a new country.

The U.S. Constitution and the Formation of the American Government

The next step was to determine a form of government. There was much disagreement over how closely bound the thirteen colonies would be. Also, who should have power? Should the government be elected? If so, who should be allowed to vote?

What should be done about slavery? These questions and others were decided at the Constitutional Convention of 1787. By 1789, the **United States Constitution** had been accepted by all thirteen states.

The system that resulted was a democratic republic, in which a federal government shared powers with governments in each state. To prevent a dictatorship, power at the federal level was shared among three branches (a concept borrowed from the Enlightenment philosopher Montesquieu): executive (president), legislative (Congress), and judicial (Supreme Court). State governments, as well as the president and members of Congress, were to be elected. However, democracy in this case—as in all cases before the twentieth century—was not all-inclusive. Elections were indirect. Women and Native Americans could not vote; nor could men who failed to fulfill certain property requirements. Moreover, the U.S. Constitution did not outlaw slavery.

Despite its initial flaws, the U.S. Constitution has remained one of the most successful political documents in world history. It is also the product and cause of an international philosophical exchange. Most of the Constitution's ideals and political principles came from England and France, thanks to the influence of Locke, Voltaire, Montesquieu, Rousseau, and others. In turn, the Constitution (and the Declaration of Independence) had an enormous impact on the **Atlantic revolutions** that followed in the 1780s, 1790s, and early 1800s. France's **Declaration of the Rights of Man and the Citizen** drew heavily upon both documents, as did the failed Dutch rebellion of the 1780s. In the early 1800s, the revolutionaries of Latin America tried to adapt the American Revolution's methods and ideals.

The Growing Global Importance of the United States

The domestic history of the United States is beyond the scope of the AP World History examination. A few points, however, should be made about the new country's effect on global affairs during the 1800s and early 1900s:

- *Inspiring freedom*: America's example of representative government and respect for civil liberties (in spite of flaws such as slavery) stood out as an example to people in other countries who wished to bring about similar changes.
- *Sphere of influence*: The **Monroe Doctrine** (1823), in which the U.S. government warned the nations of Europe against intervening in the Western Hemisphere's political affairs, was the first step in creating a sphere of influence. The United States quickly became the dominant power in the Americas. By the end of the 1800s, especially after the **Spanish-American War** (1898), its economic and political influence over Latin America was considerable—and, in some cases, imperial.
- *Expansion*: The rapid growth of the United States, from the east coast to the Pacific, greatly altered the balance of world power. This growth began with the **Louisiana Purchase** (1803) and continued with the **Mexican-American War** (1846–1848). The United States became a huge nation, incredibly rich in natural resources. It was motivated by the ideology of **manifest destiny**, the belief that continental expansion was a natural right.
- *Slavery*: The persistence of **slavery in the American South** was a key factor in allowing the Atlantic slave trade to continue for so long. It was the underlying cause of the U.S. Civil War (1861–1865).

- *Industrial growth*: During the last two thirds of the 1800s, the United States not only followed Europe in industrializing but surpassed it. Many of the era's key innovations and inventions came from the United States. Also, by the end of the 1800s, America was poised to become the greatest economic power in the world. It was overtaking Europe's strongest industrial powers, Britain and Germany, in many economic sectors.
- *Immigration*: America's reputation as a land of freedom and economic opportunity drew millions of **immigrants** from Europe and Asia during the 1800s. Between the 1830s and 1890s, an estimated 17 million people came to settle in the United States. Immigrants continued to arrive during the early 1900s. Combined with the large numbers of Europeans and Asians who emigrated to Latin America during these years, this development had a tremendous demographic effect on the geographic balance of world population.

Developments in Canada

Canada, the other British colony in North America, underwent changes during the 1800s. Although Canada remained loyal during the American Revolution, a desire for greater autonomy made itself felt not long afterward. Armed uprisings took place in 1837 and 1838. Although they failed, they convinced the British that flexibility was called for. In 1840, Upper Canada (now Ontario) and Lower Canada (now Quebec), along with other territories in the east, joined together as the United Provinces of Canada. However, they were not self-governing.

More independence came in the 1860s. Canadian politician John Macdonald became the leader of the country's freedom movement. Thanks largely to his efforts, not to mention British fears that a disgruntled Canada might grow closer to the United States, Britain's government, in 1867, conferred upon Canada **dominion status**, entitling Canada to its own constitution and parliament. The constitution created a confederation of Upper and Lower Canada, Nova Scotia, and New Brunswick.

The British monarch was still the head of state, and, for the time being, foreign affairs were still controlled by Britain. Still, in most respects, Canada was self-governing. John Macdonald became the first prime minister. Over time, confederation was extended to the western provinces, first Manitoba and British Columbia, then Alberta and Saskatchewan. Later, Great Britain used the scheme of dominion status to give similar autonomy to Australia and New Zealand.

THE HAITIAN REBELLION

A key moment in the spread of the Atlantic revolutions to Latin America and the Caribbean was the **Haitian Rebellion** (1791–1804), the only large-scale slave revolt to succeed in the New World. The Haitian Rebellion was inspired in large part by the American Revolution and caused directly by events related to the French Revolution.

The island of Haiti, known then as Saint Domingue, had been colonized by the Spanish and French. Each ruled half of the island, whose economy was based on sugar and coffee. The French half was populated by a mix of French colonists, Creoles (those of French descent but born in the colonies), free blacks (known as *gens de coleur*), mulattos, and half a million black slaves. When the French Revolution began in 1789, it threw French Haiti into chaos, mainly because the white colonists and free blacks, who competed over Haiti's sugar economy, quarreled. Free blacks and mulattos received equal rights in May 1791 (losing them temporarily between September 1791 and March 1792), but slaves, who remained unfree, rebelled in August 1791.

By 1793, **François Toussaint L'Ouverture**, often referred to as the Black Washington, was leading the revolt. L'Ouverture was literate, well-read, and a talented commander. The French government ended slavery in 1794, but L'Ouverture's goal was now full independence and the liberation of slaves on the Spanish side of the island, which he crossed into in 1798. At this point, L'Ouverture hoped to make Haiti a country for free blacks that would be friendly to France but self-governing.

Unfortunately for L'Ouverture, the French had no intention of letting Haiti go free. Over the next four years, the French debated the Haitian question. Then, in 1802, Napoleon Bonaparte decided to send troops to retake Haiti for France. Ironically, while a young officer in France's revolutionary army, Napoleon had been an admirer of L'Ouverture, but now the two men were enemies.

The French captured L'Ouverture and sent him back to France, where he died in prison. However, the French, unused to tropical warfare, failed to conquer the Haitian rebels. Yellow fever killed over 40,000 French troops. In 1804, the French went home in disgrace, and the independent nation of Haiti was born.

The Haitian Rebellion inspired rebellion elsewhere in Latin America and had one other far-reaching effect. Because of his frustration with the fighting in Haiti, Napoleon decided not to maintain major colonies in the New World. To this point, France had been the master of central North America: the large Louisiana territory, stretching from the Great Lakes to the Mississippi Delta. In 1803, Napoleon sold it at a bargain price to the United States President Thomas Jefferson, who, unlike Napoleon, recognized that the **Louisiana Purchase** would allow the United States to control the North American continent. By helping to convince Napoleon to sell Louisiana, the Haitian Rebellion brought about a major shift in global power.

THE LATIN AMERICAN WARS OF INDEPENDENCE

From 1810 to 1825, Mexico, Central America, and South America gained their independence from Spain and Portugal. As with the American Revolution, reasons for the **Latin American wars of independence** included a growing sense of national identity and local resentment of Spanish and Portuguese economic policies. Also important was the frustration that the European-descended, or *criollo* ("creole"), upper and middle classes felt toward the rigid social hierarchy of Latin American societies, which prevented them from realizing their goal of upward social and economic mobility. Even before the revolutions began, tensions were brewing.

The spark that set off the Latin American revolutions was lit by Napoleon back in Europe. Between 1807 and 1809, Napoleon invaded Spain and Portugal, toppling the royal governments there. The Spanish king was placed under house arrest,

THE CAUSES OF REVOLUTION

Understanding how and why revolutions take place is a daunting task for any historian. Social stress and class differences, economic inequality and poverty, incompetent or oppressive political leadership, and intellectual and cultural forces (religion, nationalism, doctrines, ideologies) are almost always at the root of any major revolution. Studying and comparing revolutions involves trying to figure out which of these is more or less important in any given case. Another important distinction has to do with whether forces causing revolution come *from above* (top-down), *from below* (bottom-up), or, as is often the case, both. Who are the actual revolutionaries? Do they continue to cooperate after the initial seizure of power, or do they disagree and quarrel among themselves, leading to further struggle?

while the Portuguese royal family fled to Brazil. These sudden blows to the monarchies had a swift and profound impact on Latin American politics. Brazil's transition to independence was relatively smooth. Spain's possessions, however, rose up in rebellion.

Simón Bolívar and the Liberation of Spanish South America

The most influential revolutionary was **Simón Bolívar** (1783–1830), known throughout Latin America as the Liberator. A member of the creole upper class in Venezuela, Bolívar was inspired by the ideals of the Enlightenment, frustrated by the inefficiency and injustice of Spanish rule, and personally ambitious.

In 1810, Bolívar took control of the independence movement sweeping across northern South America: Venezuela, Colombia, Bolivia, and Ecuador. Unlike many members of the creole elite, who rebelled against Spain for the sake of their narrow class interests, Bolívar realized that no revolt could succeed unless it attracted all classes. In a bold stroke, he promised to fight for the rights of mixed-race Latin Americans, as well as the emancipation of slaves. This pledge turned a small and unsuccessful upper- and middle-class rebellion into a mass war of independence. The military turning point of Bolívar's wars came from 1819 to 1821, when he gained control over Venezuela and Colombia.

At this juncture, Bolívar joined forces with another freedom fighter, José de San Martín, a general turned revolutionary. Between 1816 and 1820, San Martín had freed Argentina, Chile, Uruguay, and Paraguay. Despite political differences—San Martín was more conservative—the two men decided to cooperate, with Bolívar as leader. By 1825, royalists had been cleared out of Bolivia, Ecuador, and Peru, and Spanish South America was now free.

Brazilian Independence

In the meantime, Brazil also became independent. Here, the move toward freedom came from above, rather than below. In 1820, the king of Portugal went back to Europe to reclaim his throne. He left his son, Prince Pedro, as regent. However, he also gave Pedro this advice: "My son, if Brazil starts to demand independence, make sure you are the one to proclaim it. Then put the crown on your own head." Indeed, in 1822, when Brazilians began to agitate for freedom, Pedro declared independence, created a constitutional monarchy, and proclaimed himself Pedro I.

Mexico's War of Independence

Mexico and Central America liberated themselves as well. The **Mexican War of Independence** (1810–1823) was complicated by the inability of various social classes to cooperate. It began in September 1810, when the priest **Miguel Hidalgo**, unfurling the flag of the Virgin of Guadalupe, called for independence from Spain. Hidalgo was killed in 1811, but his fight was carried on by another priest, **José Maria Morelos**. Hidalgo and Morelos fought not just for freedom from Spain but also social justice. They wanted equal rights for Indians, mestizos, and slaves (whom they planned to set free). They wanted constitutional rule. Hidalgo and Morelos's platform gained mass support from the lower classes. Unfortunately, they were opposed not just by the Spanish but many upper-class Mexicans, even those who wanted independence. Like Hidalgo, Morelos was killed, in 1815, by conservative Mexicans, not the Spanish.

Therefore, Mexico's revolt was completed by the elite, not the lower classes. A conservative colonel, Agustín Iturbide, overthrew Spanish rule in 1820–1821. He tried to establish a dictatorship, with himself as emperor, but was quickly overthrown. A Mexican republic was proclaimed in 1823, the same year that the nations of Central America, south of Mexico, established the United Provinces of Central America.

The Caribbean

Only in the Caribbean did Spain retain American colonies. Until its defeat by the United States in the Spanish-American War of 1898, it kept islands such as Cuba and Puerto Rico. Other European countries also held onto Caribbean colonies.

POLITICAL CONSOLIDATION IN LATIN AMERICA
Political Difficulties in Nineteenth-Century Latin America

Before his death in 1830, Simón Bolívar commented pessimistically about the revolutions he had helped to make: "We have achieved our independence…at the expense of everything else." In and of itself, freedom did not bring about good government, social justice, or healthy economies. Throughout the 1800s and early 1900s, Latin America suffered from a number of fundamental problems.

First and most immediate was political breakdown. Bolívar divided Latin America into a handful of sizable states. Almost right away, though, Bolívar's mega-confederations—such as Gran Colombia and the United Provinces of the Río de la Plata—split apart into smaller states.

Second was the failure of constitutional rule in many of these states. Bolívar drafted constitutions for more than a dozen nations. These were influenced by the Napoleonic law code and the ideals of the American and French revolutions (although they favored indirect over direct democracy). But there was little tradition of constitutional rule in Latin America, so civil liberties and political rights had little meaning.

This failing led to a third problem: the prevalence of dictatorial rule. Military or political strongmen, known as **caudillos**, often gained control of Latin American governments. They ruled by means of personal charisma, military force, or oppression. Despite the efforts of reformers and liberals, such as Mexico's Benito Juárez, who led the country from 1867 to 1872, conservative dictatorship, rather than representative government, was the rule in nineteenth-century Latin America.

Economic Backwardness

Another difficulty was economic backwardness. Hundreds of years of Spanish and Portuguese rule had geared Latin American economies to extract raw materials. They generally emphasized **monoculture** or, at best, the development of only a small set of resources. They required large reserves of slaves or cheap labor. These practices continued, as did plantation agriculture. Latin American leaders failed to diversify their economies. Profits benefited only the elite (or foreign investors), while the labor was carried out by large numbers of extremely poor peasants and workers. Latin American economies were comparatively slow to modernize and industrialize.

Social and Racial Divisions

Social inequality persisted. Although constitutions theoretically did away with the rigid social hierarchies put into place by the Spanish and Portuguese, people of mixed race, Indians, and blacks still experienced much prejudice. In many areas, such as Mexico's Yucatán Peninsula, the Argentinian pampas, southern Chile, and Brazil's Amazon basin, racial tensions led to uprisings and guerrilla wars. Another social problem was economic inequality: the gap between rich and poor had always been wide, and it remained so or grew even wider during the 1800s. In Brazil and Cuba, slavery continued to be legal until the 1880s.

Foreign Influence over Latin America

Yet another problem was the increased influence of foreign countries over Latin American economics and even politics. This was especially the case with the United States. During the Texas rebellion of the 1830s and the **Mexican-American War** (1846–1848), the United States took vast amounts of territory from Mexico, including Texas, New Mexico, Arizona, and California.

During the 1860s, Napoleon III of France attempted to install a Habsburg emperor, Maximilian, as the ruler of Mexico.

Slavery in Brazil.
From the mid-1500s to the end of the 1800s, Brazil was the largest single importer of slaves from Africa. In particular, the sugar industry depended on slave labor. Not until the 1800s did Brazil's government make slavery illegal. Shown here are scenes of the sale and punishment of slaves in Brazil.

Less dramatically, foreign investors, especially from Britain and the United States, worked hand-in-hand with Latin American elites to control Latin American economies, then pocket the profits. This "**dollar diplomacy**" gave Britain and, later, the United States a tremendous amount of influence in the region.

Until late in the 1800s, Spain maintained a presence in the Caribbean, retaining control over islands such as Puerto Rico and Cuba. Spanish treatment of these colonies was harsh. Slavery persisted in Cuba until the 1880s. Cuban freedom movements began to appear. The most famous voice for Cuban independence was the poet José Martí. Spain responded by placing political agitators in **concentration camps**, the modern world's first such prisons (borrowed by the British in the early 1900s, during the Boer War). Spain's influence here ended in 1898, with the Spanish-American War.

The United States also exercised political power in the region, viewing the Americas as its sphere of influence. The **Spanish-American War** (1898) gave the United States an empire of sorts in Latin America, by placing Cuba and Puerto Rico under its protection. The United States built the **Panama Canal** in the early 1900s, another sign of its regional dominance.

> **TIP**
>
> When the Pan-American Union formed in 1889 to promote cooperation among Latin American nations, cynics referred to it as the "Colonial Division of the U.S. State Department."

Limited Modernization and Industrialization

Despite all these problems, Latin America modernized somewhat in the late 1800s and early 1900s. Industrialization came late, but it did come, especially in countries like Mexico and Argentina. Countries such as Argentina, Uruguay, and Chile made it possible for women to gain educations (even, in Chile, law and medical degrees), and extended greater rights to them.

Immigration from Europe and Asia swelled the populations of Latin American nations. Although countries like Argentina, Brazil, and Chile did not receive the same numbers as the United States, millions settled there during the last half of the 1800s, adding to what was already a diverse social and ethnic mix.

The Mexican Revolution

From 1910 to 1920, at roughly the same time as China and Russia, Mexico experienced one of the early twentieth century's most significant political uprisings. The **Mexican Revolution** deposed **Porfirio Díaz**, president of Mexico between 1876 and 1910. Díaz did much to modernize and industrialize the country, but, over the years, grew corrupt and abusive. He rigged elections and hired armed thugs (known as *rurales*) to intimidate people into voting for him. When **Francisco Madero** ran against him in 1910, he put Madero in jail.

However, Madero escaped, gathered supporters, and started a mass uprising by pledging to carry out meaningful agrarian reform. In 1911, he defeated the federal armies and forced Díaz to abdicate. He attempted to create a liberal democracy, but as with the moderates in revolutionary France and Sun Yat-sen in China, he was not destined to govern for long. He found himself caught between conservative counterrevolutionaries and radicals like **Francisco "Pancho" Villa**, **Emiliano Zapata**, and Pascual Orozco, who had initially supported him, but wanted him to reform more rapidly than he was willing to. These leaders, with much of the rural population, rose up against Madero. From the right, the military plotted against him as well, and General Victoriano Huerta staged a coup d'etat in 1913. Within a week, Madero was murdered.

Huerta (whose government U.S. President Woodrow Wilson refused to recognize) was replaced in 1914 by Venustiano Carranza, who served off and on again as president until 1920. Although he tried to accommodate many of the radicals' demands, rebels such as Villa and Zapata continued to agitate against him. (Zapata, whose movement included many women, was killed in 1919. Villa, whose incursions into U.S. territory provoked an American military response in 1916, survived till 1923.) Carranza devised the populist Constitution of 1917, which embraced socialist principles, but had little chance to enforce it. Villa's and Zapata's rebellions sapped his strength, and his officers betrayed him. In 1920, Carranza, like Madero, was removed and killed by one of his generals, Álvaro Obregón.

In practical, if not ideological, terms, this moment is generally considered to have ended the revolution. Violence continued into the early 1930s, but order was restored, and the leaders—much like Napoleon or France's Directory—claimed to act in the revolution's name. In 1929, they created a **National Revolutionary Party** (renamed the PRI, or **Institutional Revolutionary Party**, in 1946). Between 1934 and 1940, Lázaro Cárdenas made the first genuine attempt to govern according to the Constitution of 1917, but the PRI regime gradually degenerated into mild authoritarianism.

Unit Five: Review Questions

SAMPLE ESSAY QUESTIONS (CCOT AND COMPARATIVE)

CCOT 1. Analyze societal changes and continuities in ONE of the following areas between 1750 and 1914.

     sub-Saharan Africa
     China
     Latin America

CCOT 2. Analyze the changes and continuities in status of women in ONE of the following areas between 1750 and 1914.

     Western Europe
     India
     the Middle East

COMP 1. Compare and contrast the European experience of industrialization with that of Japan between 1750 and 1914.

COMP 2. Compare and contrast the relations that TWO of the following had with the Western powers between 1750 and 1914.

     China
     Southeast Asia
     Latin America
     sub-Saharan Africa

MULTIPLE-CHOICE QUESTIONS

1. Charles Darwin's contribution to nineteenth-century intellectual life is best summed up as follows:

   (A) He successfully disproved the theory of evolution.
   (B) His theory of natural selection satisfactorily explained how the process of evolution works.
   (C) His cultural relativism cast doubt on Christianity and other traditional value systems.
   (D) He was the first to propose the theory of evolution.
   (E) His understanding of genetic theory unlocked the secret of how evolution worked.

2. How did the leaders of China's Taiping Rebellion and the Madhist revolt in the Sudan resemble each other?

   (A) Both embraced Marxist principles.
   (B) Both supported a program of rapid industrialization.
   (C) Both redistributed land to impoverished peasants.
   (D) Both successfully expelled Western imperialists.
   (E) Both leaders claimed to be divinely inspired.

3. How did industrialization in the early 1800s affect the Atlantic slave trade?

   (A) It increased demand for U.S. cotton and revived the slave trade for several decades.
   (B) Its emphasis on machine production caused the slave trade to experience a rapid downturn.
   (C) It had little or no effect on the slave trade.
   (D) It provided the British navy with the steamships needed to interdict the slave trade.
   (E) It brought an immediate end to the slave trade.

4. The discovery of what resource caused great turmoil in South Africa during the late 1800s and early 1900s?

   (A) bauxite
   (B) oil
   (C) silver
   (D) diamonds
   (E) rubber

5. Which of the following is NOT true of the Meiji Restoration?

   (A) The middle class expanded and gained influence.
   (B) The regime allowed labor unions to form.
   (C) The samurai class lost many of its traditional privileges.
   (D) An industrial working class grew rapidly.
   (E) Commoners were allowed to serve in the military.

6. Which of the following is true of BOTH the French and Mexican revolutions?

   (A) Centrally organized reigns of terror were carried out by each revolutionary regime.
   (B) Rural populations gave wholehearted support to both revolutionary regimes.
   (C) After long struggle, radical social and economic platforms triumphed in the end.
   (D) Early leaders proved unable to keep moderate and radical revolutionaries united.
   (E) Military officers unanimously opposed revolutionary regimes in both cases.

7. Which of the following accurately describes the Tanzimat Reforms and Qing China's "self-strengthening policy"?

   (A) Both embarked on a quick transition to free-market capitalism.
   (B) Both argued that traditional religious belief was superior to Western materialism.
   (C) Both set incremental changes into motion, but failed to achieve significant improvements.
   (D) Both placed greater restrictions on women's career choices.
   (E) both favored rapid industrialization as long as the state controlled economic policy.

8. The map on page 283 illustrates that

   (A) France controlled Cameroon and Tanganyika.
   (B) Britain controlled Madagascar and Mali.
   (C) Belgium was the only European nation to colonize Central Africa.
   (D) Germany controlled the largest amount of territory in Africa, followed by France.
   (E) The only African states not colonized by outside powers in 1914 were Liberia and Ethiopia.

9. "Every time Paris sneezes, the rest of Europe catches cold."

   This observation, offered by Prince Klemens von Metternich, most likely refers to

   (A) the eagerness with which other countries imitated French clothing and culinary fashions.
   (B) the intellectual influence exerted over the continent by the French Enlightenment.
   (C) the tendency of French revolutionary impulses to catch on elsewhere in Europe.
   (D) the frequency with which European epidemics originated in France.
   (E) France's habit of violating the treaties signed at the Congress of Vienna.

10. What political strategy contributed most to the success of the Latin American wars of independence?

   (A) promising freedom to slaves and equal rights to all
   (B) attracting lower-class support by calling for a socialist revolution
   (C) arresting and executing those who remained loyal to Spain
   (D) appealing to the middle classes by promising the vote only to those with property
   (E) securing aristocratic support by pledging to keep slavery legal

11. Who were the zamindars?

    (A) the pro-British merchant class of eastern India
    (B) Muslim troops who allied with the British against Hindu communities in India
    (C) Hindu priests who called for a holy war against British rule
    (D) native officials who administered parts of India for the British East India Company
    (E) British-trained native troops who rebelled against the British occupation of India

12. Great Britain's First Reform Act resembled the Meiji Constitution in that:

    (A) both denied women the right to work.
    (B) both established a system of universal military service.
    (C) both extended the vote to all adult males.
    (D) both allowed trade unions to function legally.
    (E) both permitted only a small fraction of the population to vote.

13. Which of the following did NOT encourage the "new" imperialism of the late 1800s?

    (A) a sense of racial and cultural superiority on the part of Western societies
    (B) a perceived need to compete against the rising industrial economies of Africa and Asia
    (C) the military superiority bestowed by industrial-era weaponry
    (D) the strategic necessity of maintaining naval bases and refueling stations overseas
    (E) new medical treatments for tropical diseases

14. How did Japanese industrialization differ from industrialization in Europe?

    (A) The middle class was less important to Japan's industrial growth than in Europe.
    (B) Female wage earners in Japan were treated with greater respect than in Europe.
    (C) Japanese industrialization was directed more by the government than in most of Europe.
    (D) Industrial growth in Japan was not accompanied by as much urban growth as in Europe.
    (E) Living and working conditions for Japan's working class were much better than in Europe.

15. Which of the following statements would a Marxist most likely oppose?

    (A) Employers should not be compelled to pay workers higher wages.
    (B) Economic competition is inherently unjust.
    (C) Throughout history, the upper classes exploit the labor of the lower classes.
    (D) Free-market capitalism leads to social inequality.
    (E) Violent revolution may be necessary to achieve socialism.

16. During the early 1800s, what aspect of their trade relations with Qing China most upset Western nations?

    (A) China's insistence on selling rice at exorbitantly high prices
    (B) China's refusal to import large amounts of foreign goods
    (C) China's sponsorship of the illegal heroin trade
    (D) China's use of slave labor to harvest tea
    (E) China's reluctance to sell silk and porcelain

17. Which of the following best describes patterns of immigration during the 1800s?

    (A) Large numbers of Europeans and Asians emigrated to North and South America.
    (B) Many Europeans emigrated to North America, but few Asians did so.
    (C) Only the United States allowed immigration; the Latin American nations prohibited it.
    (D) Immigration had little effect on the demographic profile of the United States.
    (E) Thousands of North Americans emigrated to western Europe.

18. The artwork reproduced on page 240 is best described (without looking at the caption) as

    (A) a portrait inspired by the French Romantics' idealization of heroic individuality.
    (B) an excellent example of the influence of African art on French painting and design.
    (C) a typically Realist critique of social inequities in nineteenth-century France.
    (D) a French post-impressionist's blurring of the lines between art and advertising.
    (E) a propaganda poster mobilizing French youth to join the army.

19. Who were the caudillos in the context of Latin American history?

    (A) cattle ranchers who developed the southern pampas
    (B) wealthy plantation owners who dominated agricultural production
    (C) conservative strongmen who established authoritarian regimes
    (D) native warriors who rebelled against several post-independence regimes
    (E) liberal politicians who safeguarded constitutional rule

20. Which of the following is true of Western missionaries in the 1800s?

    (A) They eliminated the sati ritual in India.
    (B) They combated the East African slave trade.
    (C) They encouraged the Chinese practice of foot binding.
    (D) They converted much of Indochina's population to Protestantism.
    (E) They were supported in their proselytizing efforts by the British East India Company.

Answers

1. **(B)** Theories of evolution arose as early as the 1700s; the difficulty lay in finding a scientifically convincing way to explain the process. Darwin's concept of natural selection did, although he had no awareness of genetic theory, which was pioneered by Gregor Mendel. Although Darwinian theory played a role in destabilizing literal interpretations of Christian doctrine, answer C applies more to figures such as Friedrich Nietzsche.

2. **(E)** Whereas the Taiping redistributed wealth in certain ways and claimed to support certain aspects of modernization, as in answers B and C, the Madhi did not. Both failed to expel foreign forces, and neither had a Marxist program. The Madhi claimed to be a messiah figure from Sufi tradition, and Hong Xiuquan claimed to be Jesus Christ's younger brother.

3. **(A)** By mechanizing the way cotton bolls were cleaned, Eli Whitney's cotton gin allowed cotton suppliers to satisfy demand from the thread-spinning and cloth-weaving sectors of the textile industry, which were already mechanized. The industry's capacity exploded in the 1790s, and hunger for raw cotton boosted cotton production in the slaveholding U.S. South—prolonging slavery much longer than most historians believe it would otherwise have lasted.

4. **(D)** All of the commodities listed here inspired imperial efforts on the part of European powers, and rubber and oil are produced elsewhere in Africa. It was diamonds, however, that provoked intense competition among the British, the Boers, and the Zulu over mineral-rich territories.

5. **(B)** The Meiji regime liberalized as much as was necessary to spur modernization, but no more. Industrialization and class change led to the developments listed in A, C, D, and E. However, industrial working conditions were extremely hard in nineteenth-century Japan, and, as in Europe earlier in the 1800s, trade unions were forbidden.

6. **(D)** Answer A applies to France, not Mexico. Both revolutions were opposed by peasant uprisings (Zapatistas and Villa supporters in Mexico, the Vendée rebels in France), but enjoyed the support of liberal and centrist military officers. Neither achieved all their aims, and the problem described in answer D is the main reason.

7. **(C)** These programs exemplify the failure of Ottoman Turkey and Qing China to keep up with a rapidly modernizing and industrializing West, a problem reflected in answer C. Ottoman rulers made a better effort, but were hindered by anti-reformist forces such as the janissaries. After about 1800, the Qing emperors grew almost completely complacent about questions of technology and industry.

8. **(E)** Choosing the right response is a function of simple map-reading skills. All the information needed to answer this question is contained in the map's legend. Some map questions require you to rely on outside knowledge.

9. **(C)** Answers A and B are reasonably plausible answers, but knowing about Metternich's role at the Congress of Vienna and his reactionary opposition to political change of any sort should call to mind how French revolutions in 1789, 1830, and 1848 were imitated throughout Europe.

10. **(A)** Early independence efforts in Latin America tended to stall because they were seen as benefiting merely the interests of the upper classes. Once leaders such as Simón Bolívar began to appeal to a larger cross section of society, independence movements gained the strength needed to throw off Spanish rule.

11. **(D)** Answer E refers to the sepoys. Zamindars did not always act in the interest of their own people (sometimes overtaxing native Indians and skimming revenues off the top before passing the correct amount on to the British). In general, the British made the task of imperial governance easier and cheaper by relying on native troops and administrators whenever feasible.

12. **(E)** The British Parliament and Japanese Diet are examples of how, in the 1800s, elected lawmaking bodies were not necessarily democratic by contemporary standards. In these cases, restrictions on who could vote meant that less than 10 percent of the population could take part in the electoral process. All adult males voted for Germany's Reichstag, but, there, not all votes counted equally.

13. **(B)** All these factors contributed to the "new" imperialism except B. Apart from Japan, no country in Africa or Asia was industrializing to the extent that it could have competed with Europe or North America.

14. **(C)** Although Japan industrialized later and more quickly than Europe, its social and economic experience of industrialization greatly resembled Europe's. One chief difference lay in how Japan's imperial government closely directed the industrialization process, whereas laissez-faire, noninterventionist economics were the rule in Europe. (Bear in mind, though, that in Germany and especially in Russia, industrialization was firmly guided by the hand of the state, a fact that did not

prevent Germany, at least, from becoming an industrial power.)

15. **(A)** All of these are standard Marxist principles, except for A, which is a restatement of David Ricardo's "iron law of wages"—an axiom Marx himself was familiar with but did not recognize as a naturally desirable state of affairs. (Ricardo saw it as an unavoidable evil in economic life.)

16. **(B)** As it does today, China in the 1700s and 1800s went to great lengths to maintain a positive balance of trade, or to export more than it imported. China was happy to sell whatever the Europeans wanted to buy, including silk, porcelain, and especially tea. The British responded by selling opium to the Chinese, who quickly became addicted to the drug.

17. **(A)** Nineteenth-century immigration resulted in one of the largest population transfers in world history. The Americas attracted a great number of immigrants from Europe and Asia—whose populations still grew tremendously, despite losing millions to emigration. Although many traveled to the United States, Argentina, Chile, and Canada were important destinations as well, and remain multicultural societies as a result.

18. **(D)** Basic familiarity with nineteenth-century artistic styles is the best tool for answering this question. The presence of text (even without being able to read the French) helps narrow the likeliest alternatives to D and E, and the absence of any sort of military imagery makes it safer to eliminate E.

19. **(C)** Answers C and E are diametrically opposed, and remembering how fragile constitutional rule tended to be in Latin America makes E a less likely answer. The categories described in the other answers existed, but went by different names.

20. **(B)** Sati was eliminated in India, but by the authorities, and the British East India Company, which had no wish to offend natives on religious grounds, actively restricted missionary efforts. Missionaries discouraged foot binding in China; in Indochina, missionary activity was carried out mainly by French Catholics, not Protestants. Missionaries such as David Livingstone were instrumental in ending the slave trade in East Africa.

UNIT SIX

THE TWENTIETH CENTURY AND CONTEMPORARY WORLD CULTURES (1914–PRESENT)

Unit Overview

GENERAL REMARKS

The twentieth century ranks as one of the most tumultuous eras ever. It was a time of paradox and contradiction, leading one historian to refer to it as the "age of extremes." The largest part of the world to date adopted democratic forms of government (and allowed women to vote), but history's most oppressive dictatorships appeared as well. The 1900s were a time of unprecedented prosperity, but also of striking socioeconomic polarity, as the gap between rich and poor widened. There were tremendous cultural and scientific advancements, but also the worst wars and the greatest arms buildup in human history.

The first half of the century was dominated by two great military conflicts: **World War I** and **World War II**, both of which caused immense devastation. The latter was the bloodiest and costliest conflict humanity has ever experienced, but both led to profound changes in the world balance of power. World War I destroyed several of the nineteenth century's great empires and sapped Europe's strength. World War II completed the weakening of Europe, dislodging it from its position of global mastery.

The interwar years were marked by economic crisis, resulting from the **Great Depression**, which emanated outward from the United States. This period also saw the emergence of powerful dictatorial regimes, such as Soviet Russia, Fascist Italy, and Nazi Germany, and it appeared for a time that **totalitarianism**, not democracy, might be the wave of the future. Starting with the establishment of the Soviet state, **communism** became an influential—although, in the end, seemingly unworkable—alternative to **capitalism** as a form of economic organization.

During the century's second half, sweeping trends affected the entire world. One, following the collapse of Europe's global dominance, was **decolonization** (or **national liberation**). From the 1940s through the 1970s, parts of Africa, Asia, and the Pacific that had been under European (and U.S.) imperial control became free. This wave of national liberation created dozens of new nations. In some cases, decolonization proceeded peacefully. In others, it was attained by force or disintegrated into violence and political chaos.

Another effect of World War II and Europe's decline as a global power was a new diplomatic alignment, the **Cold War**. In the previous century and a half, world affairs had been determined by the workings of the European balance of power. After World War II, political and economic power might was concentrated in the hands of two evenly matched superpowers: the United States and the Soviet Union. This situation of bipolar equilibrium persisted for four and a half decades, dividing most of the globe into two hostile camps.

The twentieth century was an era of modernization. Societies already industrialized when the 1900s began—such as the United States, Canada, western Europe, and Japan—became even more adept at scientific and technological innovation, until, after the 1940s and 1950s, they moved into postindustrial modes of economic organization. Such societies are generally referred to as the **developed world**. A number of other countries, especially in Asia, have similarly modernized. The majority of the world's nations, known as the **developing** or **nondeveloped world** (or, in Cold War terms, the **Third World**), remain in a less advanced stage of economic and technological progress. The gap between poverty and prosperity is perhaps wider today than at any other time in history. All modern soscieities, developed or nondeveloped, have had an immensely greater impact on the environment. The most noticeable effect today is **climate change** (popularly known as global warming).

The 1980s and 1990s saw the collapse of communism in Europe and the USSR, and with that, the end of the Cold War. The same decades witnessed a wave of democratization in many parts of the world, as well as the increased **globalization** of the world economy. The greater ease with which ethnicities and traditions meet and mix has stimulated a high degree of **multiculturalism**, and mass communications have made the world, metaphorically speaking, a much smaller and more connected place. This is especially due to the sudden proliferation of computer technology, which has caused an **information** (or **digital**) **revolution**.

The world's general direction in the early twenty-first century remains unclear. Many trends, such as the end of the nuclear arms race, economic globalization, the worldwide prevalence of American popular culture, and the spread of mass communications and computer technology, seem to be drawing the world closer together. On the other hand, ethnic violence and **genocide**, extreme forms of nationalism, religious fundamentalism, proliferation of **weapons of mass destruction**, potential tensions between China and the West, and ongoing tensions between the West and the Islamic world all threaten to pull the world farther apart. The same is true of the terrorist attacks of **September 11, 2001**, on the World Trade Center and Pentagon—the symbolic beginning of the new century—and the resulting **war on terror**.

BROAD TRENDS

Global Power and International Relations

- During the first half of the 1900s, two world wars profoundly shaped global affairs.
- After 1914, Europe's position of world dominance was weakened by World War I—although, for three more decades, it retained a position of global importance, as well as its overseas empires.
- The United States, after World War I, became the world's richest and most powerful nation.

- World War II completed the dismantling of Europe's global dominance. It left world power divided between two superpowers, the United States and the USSR.

- For four and a half decades after World War II, most of the world was divided into hostile camps, led by the United States and the USSR, in a geopolitical struggle known as the Cold War. Although the superpowers never warred against each other directly, they used other nations as proxies in their struggle. They engaged in a nuclear arms race, the largest and most expensive weapons buildup in world history.

- From the 1940s through the 1970s, a mass wave of decolonization deprived the European powers of their empires. Former colonies in Asia, Africa, the Pacific, and elsewhere became free. Dozens of new nations were formed.

- During the late 1980s and early 1990s, communism in Eastern Europe and the USSR collapsed. This dramatic development helped end the Cold War.

- The only remaining superpower is the United States. A rising power is China, with Russia reasserting itself after a decade of weakness in the 1990s.

- The terrorist attacks of September 11, 2001, began a new global struggle, the U.S.-led war on terror. It sharpened tensions between the developed West and the Islamic world, and sparked wars in Iraq and Afghanistan.

- The gap between high-tech and low-level warfare has grown wider than ever before in history. The most advanced armed forces possess weapons of mass destruction, precision-guided ("smart") weapons, and—thanks to what strategists call the "revolution in military affairs"—digitally integrated systems. Much of the rest of the world fights low-intensity or guerrilla wars, using only small arms and hand-to-hand weapons.

Political Developments

- The level of popular representation in national governments grew in many countries, especially the Western democracies.

- Women gained the vote in most Western nations, and later in most other countries.

- Between the world wars, democracies tended to be politically weak and economically depressed.

- The most dynamic governments of the interwar period were the totalitarian dictatorships, which aimed to control as many aspects of their subjects' lives as possible.

- After World War II, the primary form of political and economic organization in the West (Canada, the United States, and Western Europe) was the democratic state with a capitalist system, although capitalism was modified to varying degrees by social welfare systems.

- A number of regimes, led by the Soviet Union and China, adopted communist economic systems. Their political systems tended to be dictatorial.

- The nations of the so-called Third World, which joined neither the U.S. alliance nor the Soviet bloc during the Cold War, experimented with a variety of political and economic systems.

- During the late 1980s and early 1990s, communism collapsed in Eastern Europe and the Soviet Union. This development ended the Cold War and left China as the world's major communist state.
- The globalization of culture and economics has led some to speculate that the nation-state may fade away or cease to be the primary form of political organization. Whether or not this prediction will prove true, regional alliances and economic blocs, such as the Association of Southeast Asian Nations and the European Union, have become increasingly important in the late twentieth century and early twenty-first.

Economic and Environmental Developments

- During the first half of the century, the West (Europe, Canada, and the United States) fully industrialized. Certain other parts of the world achieved significant degrees of modernization and industrialization (such as Japan, parts of Latin America, and China).
- A number of countries experimented with communist economies (the Soviet Union, Eastern Europe, China, North Korea, Cuba, Vietnam, and others).
- During the 1930s, the Great Depression, emanating from the United States, negatively affected the economies of most of Europe and Latin America, as well as Asia and Africa to a lesser degree.
- World War II consumed a huge amount of the world's economic resources during the first half of the 1940s. It is estimated that, at the war's peak, between one-quarter and one-third of the world's entire productive capacity was devoted directly or indirectly to World War II.
- After World War II, a great split between the capitalist West and the communist Soviet bloc (and China) emerged. This split prevailed until the end of the Cold War.
- Also after World War II, a different split emerged between the developed world, whose prosperity steadily grew (with a few minor regressions, such as the economic crisis of the 1970s), and the nondeveloped and developing (or Third) world, which lagged behind. Because so many nondeveloped and developing nations are located near or south of the equator, this disparity is sometimes referred to as the north–south split.
- After the 1950s and 1960s, Western economies began to move from industrial economies to postindustrial economies, based less on manufacturing and more on service, information, and advanced technology (especially computers). This trend continues.
- During the 1970s, a general economic crisis, characterized by energy (particularly oil) shortages, recession, and unemployment struck the capitalist West.
- A general rise in prosperity took place in Western economies during the 1980s and 1990s. The same was true in China. The Soviet bloc experienced a severe economic downturn.
- The 1980s and 1990s were also an era of greater economic globalization, as international trade, economic regionalization, and the clout of multinational corporations became increasingly important. This trend continues.

- The collapse of communism in Eastern Europe and the USSR forced a number of countries to make a painful transition from communism to free-market economies. Most of these countries continue to wrestle with this transition in the twenty-first century.
- Escalating industrialization, increased energy and resource consumption, massive engineering projects, and the production of toxic, chemical, and nuclear waste have exponentially increased humanity's impact on the environment.
- Environmental awareness in the West grew slowly during the early 1900s, then expanded after World War II. Green movements have grown in size and influence.
- The emission of greenhouse gases (especially carbon dioxide) is thought by most scientists to be causing climate change (global warming). The best-known international effort to cooperate in understanding and reversing the trend is the Kyoto Protocol (1997).

Cultural Developments

- Mass media and mass communications technology transformed the cultural sphere. Cinema, radio, television, and other electronic media have been used to create high art.
- Mass media have also been used to create popular (or mass) culture: music, literature, and so forth aimed at a popular audience for purposes of entertainment.
- The art of the twentieth century was characterized by bold experimentation and the distortion, even abandonment, of traditional norms and conventions.
- During the first two-thirds of the 1900s, largely because of the demoralizing effects of Europe's decline and the world wars, Western high art tended to be marked by uncertainty and pessimism (in contrast to the exuberance and energy of popular, or mass, culture).
- Scientific advancement proceeded at a breathtaking pace and scale. Especially innovative fields were physics, biotechnology, rocketry, electronics, and computers.
- After World War II, Western culture began to move beyond the "modern" period into a newer "postmodern" era.
- Global cultures have begun to mix, interact, and blend to an unprecedented degree. This celebration and acknowledgement of different traditions and styles is generally referred to as multiculturalism.
- Since the 1990s, the proliferation of personal computer technology, particularly access to the Internet and World Wide Web, has led to an information (or digital) revolution.

Gender Issues

- Women's movements began to campaign for greater equality and the right to vote during the late 1800s and early 1900s.
- By moving large numbers of women into the workplace, World War I accelerated the cause of women's equality.

- Most Western nations gave women the vote shortly after World War I.
- Even more so than World War I, World War II gave millions of women the opportunity to work. Many served in the armed forces (mostly in noncombat roles). Women's wartime accomplishments significantly boosted their hopes and chances for more rights and greater equality.
- The development of reliable contraception (especially birth-control pills) gave women with access to it unprecedented control over pregnancy.
- During the 1960s and 1970s, a great feminist movement, agitating for women's liberation and equal rights, swept Canada, the United States, and Western Europe. Since then, women's movements have sought to achieve more than simple legal equality and the right to vote. Their goals have been to reach full cultural and economic equality, changing social norms and behaviors to create a more positive climate for equal gender relations.
- Progress toward equal treatment of women has been uneven in other parts of the world.

QUESTIONS AND COMPARISONS TO CONSIDER

- Discuss the ways different nations and regions modernized during the twentieth century. Were they industrialized before the 1900s? Did modernization efforts come from the population at large, or were they instituted by the government? Did they have to be put into place by force? Has modernization by force proven effective?
- What impact did the world wars have on the non-Western world? Compare different regions, such as Africa and Asia. How did the wars affect women?
- Compare two or more of the twentieth century's major revolutions, such as the Russian, Chinese, Mexican, Cuban, or Iranian. Alternatively, compare one or more of these with revolutions in previous centuries. Compare how each affected women.
- Examine the process of decolonization as it played out in various parts of the world (compare, for example, India and Africa).
- Focus on specific national liberation movements and independence struggles during the period of decolonization. What obstacles did various movements face? How did their approaches to liberation and decolonization differ, and how were they alike? Did they use force? If so, how and why?
- How has the legacy of colonialism affected cultural identity and/or patterns of economic development in Africa, Asia, and Latin America?
- How has nationalism in Europe differed from nationalism in decolonizing or decolonized parts of the world, both in character and in its political effects?
- Compare the effects of the Cold War on the West, the East, and the so-called Third World. How useful are these labels?
- How has the rise of Western consumer society and economic globalization affected different civilizations outside Europe? Compare, for example, China with sub-Saharan Africa, or Japan with Latin America.
- How does ethnic violence in the late 1900s compare with the Holocaust?

- Compare the nation-state with regional groupings (diplomatic, economic, military) that have emerged during the late twentieth and early twenty-first centuries.
- What models for economic development in the developing (or Third) world have been proposed and/or attempted? What social and political consequences have they led to?
- Examine Western and non-Western forms of cultural expression. How have mass media and popular culture affected world culture? Which has become more important: multiculturalism or the Americanization of contemporary world culture?
- Consider how high-tech warfare (nuclear arms and other weapons of mass destruction, "smart" weapons, the so-called revolution in military affairs) contrasts but also coexists with guerrilla warfare and other forms of low-intensity conflict.

World War I

CHAPTER 28

- World War I (Allies versus Central Powers)
- Nationalism and competition over empire
- The European alliance system
- Trench warfare and the Western Front
- naval blockade and submarine (U-boat) warfare
- The Armenian genocide
- Total war
- The home front (rationing, conscription, restriction of civil liberties)
- Women's roles and female suffrage
- The Paris Peace Conference, Treaty of Versailles, and the Fourteen Points
- The League of Nations
- The Balfour Declaration
- The Spanish flu

In the late summer of 1914, the nations of Europe went to war. All of them expected that the conflict would be short and decisive. As the British press proclaimed, "the boys" would be "home by Christmas."

Instead, **World War I** (1914–1918), known to the people who experienced it as the Great War, lasted more than four years. More than thirty nations joined in the fighting. The war killed up to 10 million soldiers. Between 3 to 5 million civilians perished as well, mainly of disease and starvation caused by the war but also as a result of direct military action. Approximately 28 to 30 million people were wounded or disabled. At war's end, Europe's economies lay in ruins, even those of the countries that had won. The treaties that ended the war completely redrew the map of the world.

World War I shattered Europe politically and culturally. Four great empires—the German Reich, Russia's tsarist regime, Austria-Hungary's Habsburg dynasty, and Ottoman Turkey—were destroyed. Russia's suffering led directly to communist revolution; Germany's defeat inspired Adolf Hitler to follow the path of fascism. Even victorious nations like Britain, France, and Italy were exhausted and demoralized. The optimistic faith in progress so prevalent in the nineteenth century vanished, to be replaced by gloom and anxiety, and the Europeans' view of themselves as models of civilized behavior and cultural superiority was exposed as a foolish illusion. The only major nation in the West to escape this malaise was the United States, which remained comparatively undamaged by the war—and profited from it economically.

Far-reaching social changes resulted from or were sped up by the war. These included the final decline of the aristocracy, the rise of the middle and lower classes, the greater democratization of European politics, the complete industrialization and modernization of European economies, and the granting of suffrage to women.

In global terms, World War I caused a fundamental shift in power. Europe had gained tremendous global might during the last half of the 1700s. In the nineteenth century, it had become the dominant civilization on the planet, and it reached the zenith of its power from 1870 to 1914. After World War I, it was clear that Europe would not be able to continue in this position of preeminence for much longer. The United States was becoming the world's military and economic powerhouse. Europe's imperial possessions were increasingly restless, and although countries such as Britain and France held on to their empires for a while longer, the process of decolonization was unavoidable—the question was when, not whether, it would happen.

For all these reasons and more, World War I, rather than the calendar year 1900, is considered metaphorically to be the true beginning of the twentieth century.

BACKGROUND AND BEGINNING

As discussed in Chapter 22, long-term causes of World War I include a potent cocktail of **nationalism**, **competition over empire**, and an unstable **European alliance system** (France and Russia, informally aligned with Britain, against Germany, Austria, and Italy) with the potential to draw all the continent's powers into conflict in the event of crisis.

That crisis came in the Balkans, in Sarajevo, capital of Bosnia: a Slavic province under Austrian authority but with a large Serb population and, therefore, coveted by the young and intensely nationalistic nation of Serbia. On June 28, 1914, a Bosnian Serb student assassinated the heir to Austria's throne, Franz Ferdinand, and his wife.

The assassination caused outrage worldwide but especially in Austria, which blamed Serbia and decided to use the murders as a pretext to humble its troublesome neighbor. In July, Austria issued Serbia an ultimatum, a list of humiliating demands, and threatened war if Serbia did not agree to them. Because of the alliance system and a general sense of nationalist belligerence, this regional quarrel rapidly escalated into a continental conflict. Russia, protective of its fellow Slavs (and unfriendly to Austria) supported Serbia. Germany assured Austria of its support (the infamous "blank check"), even if Russia intervened. France was pledged to aid Russia in the event of hostilities.

On July 28, Austria declared war on Serbia. Russia responded by mobilizing its troops. Like clockwork, the alliance system went into operation (Germany's plan for avoiding a long two-front war required immediate action, a factor that sped up the process). Between July 28 and August 4, Serbia, Austria, Russia, Germany, France, and Britain entered the war. Although guilt for the the war was later assigned principally to Germany, many factors contributed to its beginning, and a number of countries share at least some blame.

COMBAT

The Combatants: The Allies and the Central Powers

The war expanded beyond the original alliance system. The **Allies**, as the Triple Entente now called itself, consisted of Great Britain, France, and Russia. Britain's imperial dominions, including Canada, Australia, New Zealand, and South Africa, also took part. Italy abandoned its former partners and joined the Allies in 1915, because Britain and France promised it Austrian territory. In 1917, the United States would join the Allied war effort; later that year, Russia would drop out of the war. On the other side were the **Central Powers**. These were Germany and Austria, the nations of the Triple Alliance, minus Italy. They were joined by Bulgaria and the Ottoman Empire. Other nations took part in the war, but these were the major combatants.

The Schlieffen Plan, the Invasion of Belgium, and the Battle of the Marne

Germany's **Schlieffen Plan** and its failure shaped the first phase of World War I. Faced with a two-front ground war against France and Russia, as well as the long-term threat of the British navy, Germany made a daring gamble: the Schlieffen Plan sent 75 percent of the German army against France, with the goal of taking Paris in six weeks. The rest of the army, with the Austrians, would defend against Russia. To catch the French off guard, the main attack force would move through Belgium, which was neutral.

The illegal invasion of Belgium, which killed many civilians, stained Germany's reputation badly. It enabled Allied propaganda to argue convincingly that the Germans were aggressors, "barbarians," and "Huns."

By early September, the Schlieffen Plan had failed. Belgium resisted more stoutly than Germany had anticipated. The Russians mobilized more quickly than expected. Although German troops came within sight of Paris, the French army made a heroic stand at the Marne River. The battle there saved Paris, foiled the Schlieffen Plan, and dashed any hope of a quick end to the war.

Trench Warfare, the Western Front, and the Eastern Front

In late 1914, two European fronts, the Western Front and Eastern Front, took shape. They were very different. In the west, stalemate prevailed. Both sides were evenly matched and armed with the latest in industrial-era weaponry. Artillery, machine guns, and modern rifles had made the battlefield so deadly that traditional tactics, which involved charging the enemy, were no longer feasible. Military technology disproportionately favored the defensive. The result was **trench warfare**, one of the most horrific styles of combat in human history. For the next three years, fighting on the **Western Front**, while exceptionally bloody, resulted in almost no movement at all. Actions such as the Verdun Offensive and the Battle of the Somme, both in 1916, rank among

World War I in Europe, 1914–1918.
In Western Europe, the basic dynamic of the conflict was determined quite early. Then, thanks to the stalemate of trench warfare, it changed very little until the last months of war. In the east, fighting conditions were much more fluid.

NOTE

By the end of 1914, 500 miles of trenches, bunkers, and barbed wire, separating the Germans from the Allied forces, stretched from the English Channel to the Swiss border.

NOTE

Not until 1917 and 1918 did tactical changes and new weaponry (such as tanks and airplanes) start to end the painful stalemate of trench warfare.

the most futile operations of all time, resulting in hundreds of thousands of casualties but no useful outcome.

Ordinary life in the trenches could be almost as miserable as combat. Mud, lice, rats, disease, and the smell of dead bodies combined to make the trench experience maddeningly terrible. Eloquent descriptions of trench warfare can be found in literary works such as Erich Maria Remarque's novel *All Quiet on the Western Front*, Robert Graves's autobiographical *Goodbye to All That*, and the work of Britain's so-called "war poets" (Robert Owen, Siegfried Sassoon, Stephen Spender, and others).

Fighting on the Eastern Front was very different. This front was much longer, extending well over a thousand miles, and less entrenched. Serbia fell to the Austrians. After initial setbacks, the Germans and Austrians moved quickly and efficiently against the Russians, killing, wounding, and capturing millions. They also took hundreds of thousands of square miles of Russian territory. From the beginning, the Russians found themselves in terrible trouble. Bulgaria and the Ottoman Empire joined the war on the side of the Central Powers, cutting Russia off from its allies. By 1917, Russia was nearing the end of its capacity to fight.

Naval Warfare and the Use of Submarines

Considering that the naval race between Britain and Germany had been an underlying cause of the war, it was ironic that there were few traditional ship-to-ship battles in World War I. Britain's Royal Navy imposed a blockade on Germany and Austria, causing the starvation of thousands. In response, Germany deployed its most effective naval weapon: the **submarine** (or **U-boat**), which enabled the German navy to do tremendous economic damage to Britain. However, submarine warfare carried with it the danger of destroying neutral ships or killing civilians from neutral countries, so it was diplomatically risky. Over time, Germany's success with submarine warfare would backfire, bringing the United States into the war in 1917.

The Global Dimensions of World War I

The war also took on a global dimension. The war had begun largely because of empire, and its effects spread to Europe's colonies. Britain's imperial dominions, including Canada, Australia, New Zealand, and South Africa, declared war on the Central Powers and took an active part in European and Middle Eastern combat.

France and Britain mobilized native troops in Africa. Although most played a support role, performing construction and garrison duties, some saw combat in Africa against German colonial troops. The French also brought African troops to the Western Front (in a classic instance of prejudice, the Germans feared these soldiers as cannibals). More than 2.5 million Africans (almost 2 percent of the total population) were involved in the war effort in some way. Britain mobilized Indian sepoys, Sikhs, and Nepalese Gurkhas for combat in the Middle East.

The fighting spread beyond Europe. There were clashes in Africa. Japan joined the Allied war effort, then took over Germany's island colonies in the Pacific. Australia seized German New Guinea. The most important non-European theater of war was the Middle East. In 1915, the British, using Australian and New Zealander troops, tried to knock Ottoman Turkey out of the war by landing at Gallipoli, southwest of Istanbul. This campaign proved an utter disaster, resulting in 50 percent casualties.

More successful was the effort of T. E. Lawrence, better known as Lawrence of Arabia, who persuaded Arab princes to rise up against their Ottoman masters. By 1917 and 1918, the British, with their Arab allies, dismantled what was left of the Ottomans' Middle Eastern empire. Before that, however, in 1915, the Ottomans carried out the **Armenian genocide**, using the excuse of potential pro-Russian disloyalty to massacre somewhere between 500,000 to 2 million victims.

The War's Last Stages: 1917 and 1918

The year 1917 was a crucial turning point in several ways. The original European combatants were exhausted by the fighting. Frustrated by the stalemate and its ability to win surface battles at sea, the German navy turned to unrestricted submarine warfare, hoping to starve Britain out of the war. Economically, the U-boat campaign worked: by the spring of 1917, Britain was reduced to a six-week food supply. Diplomatically, however, submarine warfare was a disaster, as it provoked the United States to declare war in April.

On the other hand, Russia was collapsing. The tsarist regime fell in March, and although the new government attempted to continue the war effort, the Russian army was in full retreat and suffering mass desertions. When Vladimir Lenin and the Bolsheviks staged their Communist revolution in October–November 1917, they took immediate steps to pull Russia out of the war. Germany was now free to send large numbers of troops to the Western Front, where the balance of force was already razor-thin.

The last year of World War I—late 1917 to late 1918—was a great military race. The Allies' goal was to get American soldiers across the Atlantic (with German U-boats sinking troop ships) and ready for combat. The German goal was to transfer soldiers from the Eastern Front to the west and use them to knock the weary French and British out of the war before the Americans arrived in large numbers. Whichever side accomplished its goal first would win, and it was not clear until the summer of 1918 who would prevail.

Realizing that time was against them, the Germans launched a massive offensive against Paris in the spring of 1918. As in 1914, this attack was halted by a determined stand at the Marne River. During the summer, American, Canadian, British, and French troops pushed the Germans back. By the fall, the Germans were in full retreat, and strikes and mutinies convinced the Austrian and German governments to surrender. World War I ended on November 11, 1918.

THE HOME FRONT

World War I was a **total war**, requiring nations to involve their populations and mobilize their resources completely in order to carry on the fight. The last such war in the Western world had been the U.S. Civil War (1861–1865). Europe itself had not experienced such a conflict since the days of Napoleon. Against their expectations, the nations of Europe—and, to a lesser extent, the United States—found that World War I affected their civilian populations deeply and directly. The **home front** became a crucial part of every combatant's war effort.

Conscription

The war required mass **conscription**. Already before the war, most European powers had armies of 1 to 2 million men, larger than ever before in history, but those numbers did not suffice. Even in Britain, which had a long tradition of maintaining an all-volunteer army, substantial conscription was called for. Eventually, the belligerent nations of World War I drafted more than 70 million men. Small numbers of women volunteered to serve in Anglo-American forces but did not take active part in combat. Many women served on the front as nurses.

Economic Mobilization and Rationing

Entire economies had to be geared for war. Industrial wartime production required enormous amounts of raw material: iron, steel, petroleum, rubber, cloth, and more. The need for uniforms, weapons, tanks, aircraft, ships, and other wartime necessities was immense. Agricultural production had to be stepped up in order to feed armies and civilians. With so many able-bodied men gone to fight, the strain put on civilians—especially women—to keep national economies functioning was incredible. All major combatants centralized their economies, placing even private enterprise at least somewhat under state control. Food, strategic materials, and consumer goods were rationed, and the **rationing** grew stricter as time passed.

By late 1916 and early 1917, all European nations were suffering terrible shortages. Britain's food supply was almost depleted by Germany's campaign of unrestricted submarine warfare. Germany and Austria experienced the so-called turnip winter in 1916–1917. Russia, cut off from outside help and supplies by Germany and the Ottoman Empire, was so lacking in food and equipment that, by the end of 1916, its soldiers were sent to the front barefoot and unarmed. They were told to scavenge boots and rifles from soldiers who had died in battle.

Restrictions on Civil Liberties

Another domestic effect was the **restriction of civil liberties**, even in democracies such as Britain, France, and America. All countries imposed censorship on the press, the mass media, and the mail. Those suspected of espionage or treason could be arrested, tried, and sentenced without due process. In most countries, political parties agreed to unite behind the war effort and refrain from criticizing the government. Socialist parties and trade unions were supervised and their activities curtailed. Even pessimism or an insufficient display of patriotism could bring a person under suspicion; men who attempted to gain conscientious objector status were often denied, and even if they succeeded, they were harassed or ridiculed. German-speaking immigrants in Allied nations sometimes suffered persecution.

Women and the War Effort

Perhaps the most striking effect on the home front involved the **role of women**. With so many men serving in the armed forces, farms, factories, and workplaces were left understaffed, just as wartime economic pressures required greater production. In all major countries, women stepped up to take the place of men in the workplace, serving as truck drivers, farmhands, factory workers, and munitions workers.

The economic contribution of women to their countries' war efforts was considerable. In Britain, over 1.35 million women who had never worked before took jobs. In the factories of Germany's most important arms producer, Krupp, women made up 38 percent of the workforce. Even France, highly resistant to the notion of giving women equal rights, granted a minimum wage to female textile workers producing uniforms.

NOTE

Once the war was over, many of the jobs that had gone to women were given back to the men who returned.

THE PARIS PEACE CONFERENCE

After the war, peace terms were decided at the **Paris Peace Conference**, which lasted from 1919 to 1920. All decisions were made by the leaders of the victorious Allied nations. Delegates from the defeated Central Powers were excluded. The major players were Woodrow Wilson of the United States, David Lloyd George of Britain, Georges Clemenceau of France, and Vittorio Orlando of Italy. The Allies drew up five treaties, one for each defeated power: Germany, Austria, Hungary, Bulgaria, and the Ottoman Empire. The most important was the **Treaty of Versailles**, the agreement reached with Germany and signed on June 28, 1919.

Diplomatic Disagreements Among the Allied Leaders

The Conference was characterized by a clash between American idealism and the European Allies' thirst for revenge. In his words, Wilson's desire was "to make the world safe for democracy" and prevent war in the future. These goals were reflected in his **Fourteen Points**, which called for freedom of the seas, an end to secret treaties, free trade, arms reduction, **decolonization**, the rearrangement of European borders according to the "self-determination" of national groups, and the establishment of an international dispute-resolution body called the **League of Nations**.

NOTE

All the European victors were opposed to Wilson's goal of decolonization.

By contrast, Lloyd George and Clemenceau focused on making Germany pay for the war and keeping it weak in the future. Italy wanted the Austrian land and German colonies it had been promised by Britain and France.

The Terms of the Treaties

The treaties that resulted were the product of bitter negotiation and compromise. As Wilson wished, the League of Nations was formed. Ironically, since the U.S. Congress did not ratify the Treaty of Versailles, America never joined the League, a fact that weakened it from the start. Many of the other Fourteen Points were discarded or watered down. Taken together, the main points laid out in the five treaties included

- *Dismantling of Austria-Hungary*. The Habsburg Empire was destroyed. Austria and Hungary became two separate states, and each lost territory.
- *New nations*: Out of Habsburg territory, and out of lands lost by Germany and Russia, new countries were created, including Yugoslavia, Czechoslovakia, Poland, Finland, Latvia, Lithuania, and Estonia. This was done in accordance with Wilson's principle of **self-determination**.

- *Italy and Austria*: Italy received some of the Austrian territory it was promised, but not all.
- *Population transfer in the Balkans*: Thousands of Turks living in southeastern Europe were expelled and sent to the Ottoman Empire. Likewise, large numbers of Greeks living in the Ottoman Empire were forced to move to Greece.
- *The Middle East*: The Ottoman Empire was stripped of its Middle Eastern possessions, especially the Arab lands. These were placed under temporary French and British control, according to a **mandate system** (the League of Nations would help supervise these areas, which were to be prepared for eventual independence). This stipulation disappointed the Arabs, who had expected freedom in exchange for their military assistance against the Ottomans. Britain also assumed control over Palestine. In the **Balfour Declaration** of 1917, Britain agreed in principle to the creation of a Jewish homeland in Palestine, but delayed on this question, to avoid antagonizing Arabs throughout the Middle East.

Germany and the Treaty of Versailles

The most important provisions pertained to Germany. The Treaty of Versailles imposed the following terms:

- *War guilt*: Article 231, the **war-guilt clause**, laid chief blame for World War I on Germany (although Germany deserved a good part of the blame, other nations, such as Austria, did much to start it as well).
  - *Loss of territory*: Germany lost approximately 13 percent of its territory. The provinces of Alsace and Lorraine went to France, and other lands went to Denmark, Belgium, and Poland. France and Belgium occupied the resource-rich Saar until 1935. The Rhineland, the borderland between France and Germany, was to be occupied till 1935 and maintained as a demilitarized zone in perpetuity.
  - *Loss of colonies*: Germany's colonies were placed under Allied trusteeship. Only Wilson prevented France and Britain from colonizing them outright.
- *Disarmament*: France and Britain feared a resurgent Germany and disarmed it. The army was allowed a token force of 100,000 soldiers. It was not permitted any military aircraft, submarines, battleships, or heavy artillery.
- *War payments*: Against Wilson's wishes, France and Britain insisted that Germany pay the full cost of the war, calculated to be $32 billion. According to the initial repayment schedule (which was changed several times), Germany was to make war payments until 1961.

> **NOTE**
>
> Article 231 was used to justify the heavy punishments that the Treaty of Versailles imposed on Germany.

The Paris Peace Conference is considered to have produced a flawed peace. Greed and revenge determined many of the terms. Ignorance, especially regarding Eastern Europe and the Balkans, where new regimes tended to be unstable and weak, played a large role in redrawing the world map. Justified or not, the harsh treatment of Germany made the peace unacceptable to most Germans and would be a significant factor in the rise of Hitler and the beginning of World War II. (On the other hand, it cannot be said that the Treaty of Versailles *directly* caused either of these events.)

LONG-TERM CONSEQUENCES

The grim immediate consequences of World War I were obvious: 10 million soldiers killed, somewhere between 3 to 5 million civilians killed, and 28 to 30 million people wounded. Financially, the cost was assessed at $32 billion. Countless people, particularly in eastern Europe, where borders shifted constantly, were made homeless or stateless. As a final injury, a global epidemic of **Spanish flu** struck during the closing months of World War I, killing 20 million people (perhaps more) worldwide.

Long-term consequences were as follows:

- *Destruction of Eastern and Central European empires*: The German, Austro-Hungarian, Russian, and Ottoman empires all fell.
- *Instability in Eastern Europe*: The new nations of Eastern Europe were inexperienced and weak. Nationalist tensions within them ran high. During the 1920s and 1930s, only Czechoslovakia would prosper and remain democratic. The others experienced economic difficulties, became politically authoritarian, and suffered from ethnic strife.
- *Social and political transformation*: World War I did not cause this trend, but helped to accelerate it. Even before the war, the political power and socioeconomic influence of the traditional aristocracy had been vanishing, while that of the middle and lower classes had been rising. In almost all countries of Europe— and elsewhere—World War I did much to complete this transformation.
- *Further industrialization and modernization of Western economies*: War mobilization spurred further industrialization in Europe and North America.
- *Women's suffrage*: Thanks largely to the economic role they played during the war, women gained greater respect not just in the workplace but the public sphere overall. The most important result was **women's suffrage** in most Western nations, during or just after World War I. Scandinavia, the Low Countries, Russia, Britain, Canada, the United States, and others gave women the vote. France and Italy were alone among the major Western powers in resisting this trend; not until the 1940s did women there get the vote.
- *German resentment*: Almost all Germans regarded the Treaty of Versailles as unfair. Many saw it as illegitimate. Anger about the war payments was universal. Years later, this attitude played an important role in the rise of Hitler and the outbreak of World War II.
- *General decline in European economic and global power*: Although the nations of Europe still maintained the appearance of great powers, they had been badly drained. Even the victors' economies were in sad shape, and those of the losers were in shambles. France, Britain, Belgium, Portugal, and the Netherlands still

DISEASE AND WORLD HISTORY

From humanity's earliest days, disease has played an enormous role in how societies interact with each other. Pandemics in the form of bubonic plague (which swept from China to Europe in the 1300s and plagued Eurasia for centuries) devastated numerous societies. The demographic impact of the spread of smallpox and measles to the Americas by European explorers and conquerors in the 1400s and 1500s was nightmarish. Rampant urbanization and overcrowding in the 1700s and 1800s caused massive outbreaks in cholera and tuberculosis. Until the late 1800s, illnesses like malaria and sleeping sickness prevented European imperial powers from penetrating too deeply into the interiors of Southeast Asia and especially Africa. The modern age has brought with it a better understanding of disease, but it has also given rise to much greater global mobility, a factor that makes the widespread outbreak of epidemics and pandemics faster and more likely than before. The Spanish influenza after World War I, the emergence of AIDS (acquired immune deficiency syndrome), and the recent appearance of SARS (severe acute respiratory syndrome) and avian flu are good examples.

possessed their overseas empires, but maintaining control over them would become increasingly difficult during the 1920s and 1930s and even more so after World War II.

- *Sense of uncertainty and anxiety in European culture.* Even before World War I, the prevailing faith in progress that had characterized Europe's cultural life during most of the 1800s had been waning (see Chapter 20). Despair caused by the war, plus the gloom surrounding Europe's political and economic comedown, brought this sense of uncertainty and anxiety to the forefront of European culture.

CHAPTER 29

The Twenty Years' Crisis: The World During the Interwar Period

- The League of Nations
- Democratic weakness in Europe and U.S. isolationism
- The Great Depression and its global impact
- Totalitarianism
- Soviet communism (Vladimir Lenin and Joseph Stalin)
- Italian fascism (Benito Mussolini)
- Nazi Germany (Adolf Hitler) and anti-Semitic policy
- State capitalism (syndicalism)

- Modernization from above in Turkey and Persia
- Oil in the Middle East
- Nationalists vs. Communists in China (Chiang Kai-shek versus Mao Zedong)
- Japanese militarism, war in China, and the Rape of Nanjing
- The Indian National Congress and *satyagraha*
- Latin America, U.S. influence, and dictatorship

Many historians have argued that World War I and World War II were simply two halves of the same conflict, separated by twenty years of temporary peace. Whatever the truth of that observation, it is undeniable that the peace of the 1920s and 1930s rested on a shaky foundation.

This was certainly the case in Europe, where many of the problems stirred up by World War I were not solved by the treaty settlements that followed. Also, the social, economic, and political forces unleashed by twentieth-century modernization were too strong to handle for many governments, especially those that had been damaged badly by the war or newly created by the Paris Peace Conference. Another factor that affected the fortunes of interwar Europe was the **Great Depression**. Starting in the United States in October 1929, the Depression began to affect the economies of Europe (and elsewhere) by 1930 and 1931. It damaged beyond repair many economies that had already been struggling during the 1920s. As a result, dictatorship, often in its most extreme form, **totalitarianism**, became the rule, not the exception, in European politics during the 1930s.

Elsewhere in the world, powerful political developments were underway. Revolution, modernization, and industrialization caught up with many countries that had not experienced those trends during the 1800s. European possessions in Africa,

Asia, and the Middle East began to agitate more actively for **decolonization** and **national liberation**. Nationalism, dictatorship, and militarism became part of political life in much of the non-Western world.

Finally, by the mid-to-late 1930s, the storm clouds of war gathered. Japanese aggression in Asia, along with German and Italian belligerence in Europe and elsewhere (see Chapter 30), made it more likely with every passing year that a major conflict would break out. The failure of the Western democracies to prevent such a conflict demonstrates the weakness of the interwar peace.

POLITICAL EXTREMISM AND ECONOMIC DEPRESSION IN EUROPE

Fragile Peace and the Crisis of Democracy

During the 1920s, peace prevailed in Europe, but it was fragile. Also, at the beginning of the decade, it was incomplete. From 1919 through 1922, there were revolutions, civil wars, and military clashes in Germany, Russia, Poland, Hungary, and the Balkans. Even afterward, peace was preserved mainly by the fact that European nations were too exhausted to fight. The new **League of Nations** provided what little political leadership there was. It was well-meaning and accomplished a great deal of humanitarian work, but it was largely ineffective. It had few powers of enforcement. Also, the United States, now the world's strongest and richest country, refused to join.

Despite treaties during the 1920s intended to outlaw war (such as the Treaty of Locarno and the Kellogg–Briand Pact), there was little political will on the part of liberal democracies to ensure long-term peace. During the 1920s, the absence of any real threat created an illusion that permanent peace had been achieved. That illusion would be shattered during the 1930s.

European democracy did not flourish during the 1920s or 1930s. In 1920, there were twenty-three governments in Europe that could be considered democratic. By 1939, there were only twelve. Most of the new states of Central and Eastern Europe fell victim to political extremism, especially during the 1930s, when inflation and, especially, mass unemployment caused by the Great Depression made it difficult to maintain a healthy form of government. Right-wing dictatorship, as well as ethnic discrimination and class tensions, plagued this part of Europe during these years. As described below, the most famous of these dictatorships emerged in Italy and Germany.

Even in stronger and better-established democracies such as France and Great Britain, times were troubled. During the comparatively easier 1920s, both economies, especially Britain's, were sluggish as a result of World War I's draining effect. Both had borrowed a great deal of money from the United States, and each relied on German war reparations to keep up its own payments. Unemployment, strikes, and deficits became the norm in France during the early 1920s and in Britain during the entire decade.

The 1930s were even worse because of the Depression. By 1932, one British worker in four was out of work. France was not as badly hurt as Britain, but it went through hard times. Particularly during the 1930s, both democracies suffered from a lack of firm political leadership. In Britain, a shaky coalition, the National Government ran Parliament with caution and compromise. Some relief came with the creation of a **modern welfare state**, as social security, pensions, unemployment insurance, and so on, were put into place. In France, elections were frequent, and leadership passed from left to right and back again on a regular basis. During the 1930s, economic weakness and political mediocrity made it difficult for France and Britain to cope with the growing threat of Hitler's Germany.

Communism in the Soviet Union

The general crisis of democracy in interwar Europe meant that the most dynamic regimes tended to be the dictatorships, which grew in number and power during the 1920s and especially the 1930s. The first of the new dictatorships was the Union of Soviet Socialist Republics (USSR), or the Soviet Union, the communist regime that rose to power during World War I, in October–November 1917.

When the tsarist regime of Nicholas II fell in February–March 1917, its place was taken briefly by a moderate Provisional Government that attempted to continue the war against Germany, solve Russia's dismal economic problems, and establish a democratic government. In that its first stage was relatively liberal, the Russian Revolution resembled the French Revolution of 1789.

However, the Provisional Government did not satisfy the desire of the vast majority of the Russian population (80–85 percent of whom were peasants) for economic stability, land reform, and peace. The party that benefited most from popular discontent were the Communists, or Bolsheviks, led by **Vladimir Lenin** and his second-in-command, Leon Trotsky.

In the fall of 1917, Lenin and Trotsky overthrew the Provisional Government. From then until 1921, they pulled out of World War I, formed the Soviet government, and fought and won the terrible Russian Civil War (which pitted the Bolshevik Red Army against their anticommunist enemies, called Whites). From 1921 till his death in 1924, Lenin tightened his grip on power and attempted to modernize the Soviet Union along Marxist lines. One of his major challenges was that, while Marx had predicted that communist revolution would first take place in a mature capitalist society with a large industrial working class, Russia was a backward, barely capitalist nation with a huge peasantry and an extremely small working class. A compromise in 1921, Lenin's New Economic Plan (NEP) took a more gradual approach to socialist development, allowing for limited private trade. It lasted until 1927–1928.

Lenin died in 1924. A half-decade succession struggle followed, during which **Joseph Stalin** defeated Trotsky for control over the Soviet government. Stalin became one of the most oppressive dictators of all time. Overturning the NEP, Stalin rapidly modernized the USSR, starting in 1928. His **Five-Year Plans** were intended to transform the Soviet Union from an agricultural society into a modern industrial state. The **collectivization of agriculture**—the placement of all peasants on state-run farms—was meant to rationalize farming, increase governmental control over the countryside, and harness the labor of the peasants (profits generated by agriculture were used to pay for the Five-Year Plans).

Although the USSR modernized under Stalin, the price was steep. The Five-Year Plans amounted to a state-sponsored industrial revolution, with the same social and economic trauma, but applied with ruthlessness and police brutality. Collectivization resulted in a **Great Famine** in southern Russia, Ukraine, and Kazakhstan that killed approximately 4 million to 6 million people. Later in the 1930s, Stalin carried out a huge campaign of terror, the **Purges**, which resulted in the execution of approximately a million people and the arrest and exile to labor camps (**gulags**) of at least 5 to 7 million. Like most modern dictators, Stalin used propaganda to indoctrinate his subjects and instituted an extravagant cult of personality to glorify himself. The Stalinist experience is an extreme example of rapid modernization, directed from above by dictatorial leadership. In Stalin's case, this approach brought the country far more torment then benefit.

Fascism in Italy

In Italy, dictatorship came from the right. After World War I, Italy was rocked by economic depression and political turmoil. Strikes, communist agitation, and constant governmental turnover brought the country to the edge of chaos. The middle and upper classes, frightened of social breakdown and left-wing revolution, looked for a strong leader to restore stability. They turned to **Benito Mussolini**, the right-wing, anticommunist leader of the Fascist Party.

Fascism, Mussolini's invention, is a difficult political concept to define. It can best be described as right-wing radicalism or revolution from the right, unlike ordinary right-wing conservatism, which seeks to prevent change. Fascism seeks to bring about change. It is anticommunist but also anticapitalist and antidemocratic. Fascism is also often characterized by hypernationalism and a state-sponsored campaign of racial and ethnic bigotry.

In October 1922, Mussolini was placed in charge of the government by the king, who feared the communists. For the next twenty-one years, governing Italy, he became increasingly dictatorial. He coined a new term to describe his style of rule: **totalitarianism**, a twentieth-century form of dictatorship in which the regime, using modern technology and bureaucracy, attempts to control every aspect of its subjects' lives. Compared with other totalitarian rulers, such as Stalin and Hitler, Mussolini was actually mild. Still, he imposed censorship over culture, imprisoned (and sometimes killed) political enemies and dissidents, and used propaganda to create a cult of personality.

On the other hand, Mussolini modernized Italy. He built new highways, sponsored literacy campaigns, fought the Mafia, and brought medicine and technology to backward parts of his country. His chief claim to fame was to have made Italy's notoriously inefficient trains run on time. His economic policy was based on the principle of syndicalism (a form of **corporatism** or **state capitalism**, common in right-wing dictatorships). In fascist economies, corporate leaders, rather than practicing free trade, are required to cooperate directly with the government, and labor unions are suppressed. During the 1920s, Mussolini was considered by many to be an effective, even admirable, leader despite his dictatorial tendencies. During the 1930s, however, the Depression undercut his modernizing efforts. He became more dictatorial and, in foreign policy, more aggressive (see Chapter 30). Also during the 1930s, Mussolini drew closer to the newer fascist regime of Nazi Germany.

Nazism in Germany

Germany's road to dictatorship was longer than Italy's, and the results were infinitely worse. From 1919 to 1933, Germany was governed by a democratic regime, the **Weimar Republic,** which was dogged by economic trouble (hyperinflation during the early 1920s wiped out the value of the German mark), the burden of war payments, widespread resentment of the Treaty of Versailles (which the Weimar regime had been forced to sign), and the rise of extremist political parties.

From the left, the German Communist Party became a powerful threat. From the right appeared **Adolf Hitler** and the **Nazi Party**: an anticommunist, antidemocratic group that, after Mussolini's rise to power in Italy, consciously imitated fascism in many ways. The Nazi Party, also obsessed with the notion of racial purity, hated all minorities, but especially Jews, whom the Nazis viewed as "subhuman" and the source of all of Germany's troubles. In 1923, Hitler and the Nazis made a failed attempt to take over the German government. During the short time he spent in prison, Hitler wrote his infamous memoir, *Mein Kampf* (*My Struggle*).

By the late 1920s, the Weimar Republic appeared to have established a reasonably solid democracy. The Depression, however, ended the calm. Its effects reached Germany in 1930. The economic pain, destroying the Weimar Republic's ability to govern democratically, boosted Germany's extremist parties, the Communists and the Nazis. A series of elections in 1932 made the Nazi Party the largest in Germany. In January 1933, Hitler was appointed chancellor of Germany.

> **TIP**
>
> By 1932, 6 million Germans—almost 40 percent of the workforce—were unemployed.

Having risen to power by legal means, Hitler established himself as an absolute dictator within months. In February 1933, the Reichstag building, seat of the German government, was burned down. Hitler took advantage of the resulting panic to declare a state of emergency and pass the Enabling Act (March 1933), which suspended the Weimar constitution and gave Hitler the power to rule by decree for four years (a limit Hitler had no intention of obeying).

With blinding speed, Hitler outlawed all other political parties (especially his archenemies, the Communists), took control of the press and mass media, banned labor unions, imposed a system of state capitalism similar to Mussolini's, built **concentration camps,** such as Dachau, for political opponents and dissidents, and established a secret police, the Gestapo. He managed to end German unemployment by means of a giant program of public works and highway building, as well as a massive increase in arms production.

The Nazi regime also instituted **anti-Semitic policies** (it targeted other racial "undesirables" as well). Jews were forced out of various professions (such as law, civil service, and university teaching), their businesses were boycotted, and they were physically harassed. Before World War II, the most drastic official measures taken against the Jews were the **Nuremberg Laws** of 1935. These laws stripped German Jews of their citizenship and forbade Jews and German non-Jews to marry or have sexual relations of any kind.

In terms of foreign policy, Hitler pursued a highly aggressive diplomatic line. As described in Chapter 30, Hitler's belligerence was the principal reason that the fragile peace of the 1920s began to shatter in the 1930s.

NATIONALISM AND MODERNIZATION IN THE MIDDLE EAST

Even before World War I, the Middle East had been on the threshold of great change. Modernization was coming gradually to the Ottoman Empire. In those parts of the Middle East controlled by outside powers, the force of nationalism was rising. By toppling the Ottoman Empire, World War I brought even greater changes to the region.

The Birth of Modern Turkey

The transformation of the Ottoman Empire into the modern Turkish state had its roots in the efforts of the **Young Turks**, who had seized power in 1908 (see Chapter 23). These pro-Western, modernizing officers and politicians had already started to carry out reform before World War I. During the war, the Turks joined the Central Powers and shared defeat with them. The Ottoman Empire suffered more than 300,000 casualties and saw their Middle Eastern possessions rise up in revolt. It surrendered in October 1918.

After the war, the Turks lost most of their Middle Eastern territories to France and Britain. Greece, with Allied permission, was threatening to seize Turkey's western provinces. In the midst of this crisis, a new leader emerged: **Mustafa Kemal**, a colonel who had fought bravely against the British landing at Gallipoli in 1915. Kemal formed a new government in the city of Ankara, drove the Greeks from the Turkish mainland, and negotiated a new treaty with the Allies. In 1923, the last sultan fled the country, and the Ottoman Empire was no more. In its place, Kemal established the Turkish Republic, becoming its first president. He took the title **Ataturk**, meaning "father of the Turks."

TIP
To this day, Turkey's status as the most Westernized and most secular state in the Middle East, next to Israel, is a direct legacy of Ataturk's policies.

From 1923 till his death in 1938, Ataturk labored to create a modern, secular state in Turkey. He wrote a constitution and, despite the fact that he was quite authoritarian, made the pretense of acting like a democratic ruler. Industrialization, Western dress, and Western education were encouraged. Turkish was written in the Roman alphabet. Church and state were separated, and Islamic law (Sharia) was replaced by a European law code. Women were no longer required to wear the veil. They received the right to vote in 1934, and they were encouraged to become educated and join the workforce.

Persian Independence and Modernization

Persia went through a change similar to that of Turkey, becoming the modern state of Iran. From 1794 to 1925, Persia was ruled by the Qajar dynasty. In reality, however, the country had been divided into two spheres of influence: Russian in the north, British in the south. After World War I, the British presence in Persia increased, largely because of the oil reserves there. Resentment of foreign domination grew steadily, and a nationalist backlash was inevitable. In 1921, an officer named Reza Khan mutinied against the Qajar rulers and expelled the British. By 1925, he had gained control of the country. He called himself **Reza Shah Pahlavi** and established a new royal dynasty. Like Ataturk in Turkey, Reza reformed his country, which he renamed Iran. Although he was not as much a foe of the Islamic clergy as Ataturk was, he Westernized Iran, boosted education, did away with the veil for women, and, in general, secularized the nation. Like Ataturk, he tended toward authoritarianism.

Egypt, North Africa, and Arabia

The political fate of the rest of the Middle East was mixed. Egypt and North Africa remained in British, French, and Italian hands, although nationalist sentiment there was growing. For the time being, the Arabian Peninsula remained under Turkish control. The other Arab states formerly under Ottoman rulership were now placed under French and British control and divided into **mandates**, to be supervised partially by the League of Nations. Syria and Lebanon were assigned to France, while Iraq, Jordan, and Palestine fell to Britain.

This arrangement angered most Arabs, who had thought that, by helping the British fight the Turks, they would gain full independence. Another thing enraging the Arabs was the **Balfour Declaration** of 1917, which publicly stated the British government's intention to create a Jewish homeland in Palestine—whose population, in the late 1910s, was 90 percent Arab.

Change came to all these areas during the 1920s and 1930s. Despite the fact that the British allowed only limited Jewish emigration to Palestine to keep from provoking the Arabs, thousands of Jews flooded into the region, many of them illegally. By 1939, the Jewish proportion of the population had risen from 10 to 30 percent.

In the early 1920s, an Arab prince named **Ibn Saud** drove the Ottomans out of the Arabian Peninsula and then united Arabia's many tribes. In 1932, he founded the kingdom of Saudi Arabia. As the only major Arab state to enjoy full independence, Saudi Arabia was important in and of itself. After 1938, it became even more important, with the discovery of huge oil reserves. Overnight, Saudi Arabia became wealthy and strategically vital.

MILITARISM AND REVOLUTION IN ASIA
The Chinese Republic

In 1911, revolution in China had overthrown the Qing imperial dynasty. Taking its place was the Chinese Republic, governed by the **Nationalist Party** (**Kuomintang**). **Sun Yat-sen**, often regarded as the father of modern China, was president.

Quickly, however, the republic disintegrated. In 1912, Sun was forced to give up the presidency to General Yuan Shikai, in order to gain the support of the armed forces. In the face of Yuan's growing traditionalism and dictatorialism, Sun and the Kuomintang found themselves in opposition to the government. In 1913, Yuan disbanded the parliament. In response, the Kuomintang began a revolution. It failed, and Sun fled to Japan. Yuan ruled until his death in 1916. Military officers continued to govern in Beijing until the early 1920s.

The rest of China slipped into anarchy. Warlords and bandits took control of vast stretches of the country. In 1920, Sun and the Nationalists returned to the mainland, establishing a base at Canton and throughout southern China. The **Chinese Communist Party** (CCP), founded by radicals at Beijing University in 1921, became a major force. A deadly external threat came from Japan, whose imperial ambitions grew during and after World War I. Japan already controlled Korea and had a sphere of influence in southern Manchuria. Because it had aided the Allies in World War I, Japan also had their blessing to expand that sphere after the war.

Political control was not the only issue over which Chinese parties struggled. During these years, there was a great clash between traditional values and the desire for modernization. The military government in Beijing attempted to revive Confucian principles, while younger students and intellectuals embraced progressive concepts such as democracy, technology, and science. The clearest example of popular activism came on May 4, 1919, when thousands of students came to **Tiananmen Square** in Beijing to protest against the military government. The immediate cause of the May Fourth Movement was the government's willingness to allow Japan to annex Shantung Province. Underlying that specific issue, however, was the desire for political and social reform. As for China's other major political actors, the CCP was progressive in its outlook, while the Kuomintang was torn between the past and the future.

The Chinese Civil War: Nationalists Versus Communists

By the mid-1920s, the main political forces in China were the Nationalists and Communists. From 1923 to early 1927, both parties cooperated to drive warlords and foreign powers out of China. Sun Yat-sen died of cancer, leaving the leadership of the Kuomintang to **Chiang Kai-shek**, a Western-educated officer who leaned farther to the right than Sun had. By early 1927, the Nationalist-Communist alliance had gained control of all China south of the Yangtze River, including the major cities of Shanghai and Nanjing.

In April, Chiang turned against the Communists, murdering thousands of them in Shanghai. Most of the rest of the party was driven far to the north, under the revolutionary **Mao Tse-tung (Mao Zedong)**. Chiang took Beijing in 1928 and founded a Kuomintang regime that combined Westernization with mild authoritarianism. Chiang proclaimed his allegiance to Sun's principles and made some attempts to create a constitutional government and an industrial economy. However, corruption, backwardness, the threat of Japanese imperialism, and warlord anarchy hampered his efforts.

Full-scale civil war against the Communists would soon resume. Against incredible odds, Mao Tse-tung kept the CCP alive, leading it on the Long March (1934–1935), far to the north. At Yenan, the Communists established a base from which to launch military operations against the Nationalists.

Starting in 1931, Japan seized all of Manchuria from China. In 1937, Japanese forces attacked China itself, starting a three-way conflict among the Nationalists, Mao's Communists, and the invading Japanese.

> **TIP**
>
> Mao's central strategy was to make communism appealing to China's vast peasant masses, rather than concentrate on the small industrial working class in the cities.

Japan During the 1920s

In the early 1900s, Japan evolved in some ways toward a democratic parliamentary monarchy. The powers of the Diet increased, and a bill of rights guaranteeing universal male suffrage and other civil liberties was granted in 1925. Freedom of the press expanded. The emperor, Taisho, supported democratic reform. The economy continued to industrialize and modernize.

On the other hand, traditional forces remained in place. The upper class retained its oligarchical outlook. Most of Japan's industrial might was concentrated in the hands of a small number of corporate conglomerates called *zaibatsu*. The effect of this system was to keep wealth in the hands of a tiny number of rich and powerful industrialists and capitalists. Also, because the *zaibatsu* enjoyed such a close relationship with the government, economic policy was largely under state influence, in a way not unlike the system of state capitalism practiced in Fascist Italy and Nazi Germany. There was little economic liberalization to match political democratization; trade unions remained weak, working conditions remained dreadful, and strikes and riots were common. Even before the Depression, social stress was building to a dangerous level. Japan's new emperor, Hirohito, who took the throne in 1926, was easily influenced and poorly equipped to cope with the growing crisis.

Japanese Militarism and the Invasion of Mainland Asia

Imperial aggression and the effects of the Great Depression derailed Japanese democratization during the 1930s. Japan's exports plummeted more than 50 percent. Farmers and workers were badly hurt. Nationalism, bolstered by state Shintoism (a bigoted and politicized perversion of Japan's indigenous faith), skyrocketed, and anti-Western feelings sharpened. The slogan "Asia for the Asians" called for the expulsion of colonizing powers such as Britain and France.

In September 1931, Japan took Manchuria from China, turning it into a puppet kingdom, Manchukuo. Shortly afterward, Japan withdrew from the League of Nations. At home, two prime ministers were assassinated, one in 1930 by left-wing extremists, the other in 1932 by radical rightists. By 1941, the Japanese military, under Hideki Tojo, had gained control of the parliamentary government and dominated Emperor Hirohito.

In July 1937, the Japanese invaded China, committing dreadful atrocities against the civilian population. The so-called **Rape of Nanjing** in December climaxed with the massacre of 200,000 to 300,000 noncombatants, including women and children. Japan's war against China continued throughout the 1930s and World War II. In 1938 and 1939, the Japanese clashed with the Soviets on the Siberian borderland but were turned back. The war then spread to Southeast Asia, as Japan took over French and British colonies and established its own empire, which it referred to as the **Greater East Asian Co-Prosperity Sphere**.

Nationalist Movements in South and Southeast Asia

In South and Southeast Asia, most of which remained under British and French colonial rule, nationalism became widespread. In Vietnam, Burma, Indonesia, and elsewhere, anticolonial agitation escalated. Typically, such efforts involved an uneasy alliance of Western-educated, middle-class modernizers with intellectuals and students inspired by the communist ideals of Marx and Lenin. It was similar to the temporary joining of the Nationalists and Communists in China—and, as in China, these alliances typically broke apart.

Gandhi, Nehru, and the Indian National Congress

The most successful freedom movement appeared in British-controlled India. The moving force here was the **Indian National Congress** (later the Congress Party), founded in 1885. After World War I, the movement's dominant figure was **Mohandas K. Gandhi**. Because it had loyally supported Britain in World War I, India hoped it would gain greater autonomy after the war, perhaps even dominion status, as Canada, Australia, and New Zealand had. However, demonstrations and protests, organized largely by Gandhi, led to clashes with the British. In 1919, at Amritsar, British troops fired on unarmed protestors, killing 379 and wounding 1,137. This massacre led to chaos. The British imposed a strict crackdown, and Gandhi went to prison.

For the rest of the 1920s, India balanced on a political knife-edge. The British began to make concessions, such as the Government of India Act (1921), which allowed 5 million Indians to vote and created a new parliament, two-thirds of whose members would be Indian. However, the earlier repression of the British prompted the Congress Party to demand more. India could easily have erupted into bloody revolution. That it did not was due mainly to Gandhi's political and spiritual guidance.

Whether free or in prison, Gandhi—now known increasingly as Mahatma, which means "great soul"—preached the policy of nonviolent resistance. Based partly on Hindu religious principles, this policy was called *satyagraha* ("hold to the truth"). An example of *satyagraha* in action came when the British imposed a high tax on salt. Rather than protest violently, Gandhi led 50,000 people on a 200-mile march to the seashore, where they began to make salt illegally by drying out seawater. When the British arrived, Gandhi allowed himself to be arrested peacefully.

Gandhi was freed in 1931. He continued to work with the Congress Party but as a guiding force rather than as a politician. The political leader, also Gandhi's working partner, was a younger lawyer and intellectual, **Jawaharlal Nehru**. The spiritual, traditional Gandhi and the modern, secular Nehru pressed the British for greater reform. In 1935, the British granted a constitution that was a long step forward on the path to eventual self-rule. In 1937, Gandhi and Nehru began their Quit India campaign, trying to convince the British to leave altogether. The advent of World War II delayed British withdrawal, but India gained its freedom in 1947, soon after the war.

Muhammad Ali Jinnah and the Muslim League

The Congress Party was not the only force pressing for Indian independence. India's Muslims had their own freedom movement. During World War I, Muslims and Hindus had pledged to work together for greater autonomy from the British, but they went their separate ways during the 1920s. In 1930, the **Muslim League**, led by **Muhammad Ali Jinnah**, formed. It paralleled the Congress Party's independence efforts, but its aims were different. The Muslim League called for the creation of a separate Muslim state called Pakistan ("land of the pure"). The failure of the Muslim League and the Congress Party to resolve their differences peacefully led to great bloodshed when independence was finally achieved in 1947. It also lay the foundation for the bitter Indo-Pakistani rivalry that still persists.

DICTATORSHIP IN LATIN AMERICA

Outside Influences on Latin America

Before World War I, modern nations in Latin America, while politically independent, had been economically dominated by outside influences. British and U.S. investors exercised great control over enterprises in Latin America. Most Latin American nations relied on the export of one or two raw materials or agricultural products. Chile was a source of fertilizer and copper; Peru mined copper as well. Chile and Brazil sold steel. Oil was taken out of Mexico, Bolivia, Argentina, and Peru. Argentina produced wheat and beef. Central America grew bananas and other fruit. As it had for centuries, sugar came from the Caribbean and Brazil. Brazil was the source of 75 percent of the world's coffee supply.

In exchange for foreign capital and industrial know-how, political elites in Latin American countries allowed foreigners much influence over local politics. The great mass of the population did the work and saw very few of the resulting profits.

The U.S. Sphere of Influence in Latin America

World War I increased the U.S. role in Latin America's political and economic life. With their economies weakened by the war, countries such as France and Britain no longer had the funds to invest in Latin America. The United Fruit Company and other U.S. corporations became major forces in Latin America.

Strategically, the United States viewed Latin America as its sphere of influence and had done so since the late 1800s. The United States had gained possessions such as Puerto Rico and the Virgin Islands, as well as a protectorate over Cuba, after the Spanish-American War of 1898. U.S. Marines had occupied Haiti. Just as the British had taken control of the Suez Canal, America established a military presence after constructing the **Panama Canal**. Instability in Mexico convinced the United States to militarize the border. The United States sponsored dictators, such as Vicente Gómez of Venezuela and Fulgencio Batista of Cuba, in order to preserve stability. A sense grew among Latin Americans that the people of the United States—the *yanquis*, or "yankees"—were imperialists.

In the mid-1930s, Franklin Roosevelt attempted to reduce U.S. influence over Latin America. His **Good Neighbor Policy** (1935) was intended to accomplish this goal and thereby improve relations with the region. As a token of goodwill, Roosevelt withdrew U.S. Marines from Haiti. For the first time in three decades, the United States had no troops in Latin America.

The Great Depression's Effects on Latin America

Unfortunately, the United States affected Latin America in yet another way during the 1930s. The effects of the Great Depression on the region were devastating. Since Latin American economies were so dependent on exports to the United States, the inability of the United States to purchase Latin American goods caused tremendous damage. Exports were cut almost in half. As in many parts of Europe, the economic pain caused by the Depression had a negative effect on politics, inclining Latin American governments toward extremism and dictatorship.

As discussed in Chapter 27, there was a long-standing tradition of authoritarian rule in Latin America. This trend continued into the 1920s and 1930s, when there were few if any genuine democracies in Latin America. The three largest and wealthiest nations—Mexico, Brazil, and Argentina—all became dictatorial, to one degree or another, during these years.

Dictatorship in Mexico, Brazil, and Argentina

The revolution Mexico began in 1910 was declared to have ended in 1920, when military officers took charge of the regime. Violence continued till 1929, when power passed to the National Revolutionary Party, which renamed itself the **Institutional Revolutionary Party** (PRI) in 1946 and ruled until the late 1980s. Governed in theory by the Constitution of 1917—which guaranteed universal suffrage (including for women) and the right to strike—Mexico tended in reality toward oligarchy, in which the PRI chose a president every six years and then arranged an election that guaranteed victory to its candidate.

Under this mild form of authoritarianism, the upper classes prospered and the country modernized. But the middle class was small and narrow, while the large lower classes—workers and peasants—lagged far behind the elite. Things improved under **Lázaro Cárdenas**, who became president in 1934. His land reform, in which 40 million acres were taken from the upper class and distributed among the peasantry, made him popular with the lower classes. He also stood up to the United States by nationalizing the oil industry. Roosevelt lived up to his Good Neighbor promises and refrained from intervention. In exchange, Cárdenas compensated U.S. companies for their losses, then formed PEMEX, Mexico's state-run oil enterprise. He transferred power legally to his successor, Manuel Camacho, in 1940.

Brazil became more genuinely dictatorial. Before 1930, the government was dominated by wealthy landowners, most of whom owed their power and riches to the **coffee trade**. The Depression, however, plunged the country into crisis. In 1930, Getúlio Vargas, a cattle rancher, became president and ruled as dictator until 1945. He governed from the far right, imitating Fascist Italy and Nazi Germany. He censored the press and authorized his secret police to torture political opponents. On the other hand, he modernized the economy, diversifying it and freeing it from its dependence on coffee. Under Vargas, Brazil became Latin America's most industrialized nation. He was forced out of office by his army in 1945.

Argentina became a military dictatorship during the 1930s. In 1916, Hipólito Irigoyen of the Radical Party was elected president. His reform measures were intended to improve the lot of the lower and middle classes, and labor unions became more active. However, landowners and the upper class sabotaged Irigoyen's efforts and, in 1930, supported the army as it ousted him. The military government lasted throughout World War II, but its efforts to return to the old export-based economy failed. Labor unrest increased, and the radical lower classes, the *descamisados* ("shirtless ones"), grew louder and more belligerent. Shortly after World War II, in 1946, General **Juan Perón**, with his charismatic wife, Eva, appealed to the lower classes to come to power, then established his own dictatorship.

World War II and the Holocaust

CHAPTER 30

- World War II (Allies versus the Axis)
- Aggression versus appeasement before the war
- Blitzkrieg warfare and the effects of tanks and aircraft
- The Lend-Lease program
- The Greater East Asian Co-Prosperity Sphere
- Pivotal battles (Midway, El Alamein, Stalingrad, the D-Day landings)
- Submarines and the war at sea
- Strategic bombing and the atomic bomb
- War crimes, crimes against humanity, and genocide
- The Holocaust (Final Solution)
- The Cold War

World War II (1939–1945) was and remains the biggest, costliest, and deadliest armed conflict in human history. Beyond that, its long-term global impact continued to be felt in world politics, economics, and diplomacy for five decades.

Before the war ended, sixty-one nations joined the fighting. They were divided into two coalitions, the **Axis Powers** and the **Allied Powers**. The major combatants were

- The Axis Powers: Nazi Germany, Fascist Italy (joined the war in June 1940; left the war in July 1943), and Japan
- The Allied Powers: Great Britain, France (left the war in June 1940), Canada, Australia, New Zealand, the Soviet Union (joined the war in June 1941), and the United States (joined the war in December 1941).

The war was waged over two-thirds of the entire planet. Economically, it has been calculated to have cost $1.6 trillion in 1940s dollars ($4 trillion to $5 trillion in contemporary terms). By the war's midpoint, somewhere between one-quarter and one-third of the world's productive capacity was directly dedicated to war production.

Concerning the grimmest statistic of all, somewhere between 55 to 60 million people were killed during the war. Almost half of those who died were civilians. World War II involved **genocide** as well. Millions of victims—6 million of them Jewish—perished in the German campaign of racial extermination known as the **Holocaust**.

World War II also shifted the balance of global strength completely. World War I had begun the process of toppling the powers of Europe from their position of dominance; World War II finished it. When World War II was over, only two

337

nations, the United States and the Soviet Union, had the military and economic might to affect the course of world events. The great geopolitical struggle between these two new superpowers, the **Cold War**, was the dominant factor shaping global diplomacy, military affairs, and international trade for four and a half decades. World War II also destroyed the imperial might of the European powers. From the 1940s through the 1970s, a massive wave of **decolonization** swept through the non-Western world, and dozens of nations in Africa and Asia became free.

In addition, World War II changed the patterns of international trade, shifted global wealth to the superpowers (especially the United States), spurred a boom in technological and scientific innovation that would be put to civilian use long after the war was over, brought women into the workplace, and had countless other social, economic, and cultural effects. For these and many other reasons, World War II can be considered not only the largest military enterprise in world history but also the most influential.

THE ROAD TO WAR

Unlike World War I, whose origins were quite complex, World War II resulted from a straightforward pattern of aggression on the part of Nazi Germany, Fascist Italy, and Japan. Especially in Europe, major democracies responded weakly and passively. Hamstrung by the Great Depression, anxious to avoid another global conflict, and simply hoping that each aggressive move would be the last, countries such as France, Britain, and the United States did little to stand up to the dictatorships. This policy of letting aggressors have what they want in the hope they will demand no more is known as **appeasement**. The **League of Nations** proved almost useless in dealing with foreign-policy crises. Here is a timetable of what is often referred to as the road to war:

- 1933:
  —Hitler withdrew from the League of Nations.

- 1935:
  —Hitler openly began to rebuild the German army and navy, violating the disarmament clauses of the Treaty of Versailles.
  —Mussolini invaded Ethiopia, causing international outrage. The League of Nations imposed weak sanctions. They did not prevent Italy from taking Ethiopia; their effect was to anger Mussolini and draw him closer to Hitler.
  —The Soviet Union, fearful of Germany, concluded an alliance with France. Both countries agreed to protect Czechoslovakia. France also signed a treaty to protect Poland. This policy of antifascist cooperation was known as **collective security**.

- 1936:
  —Again violating the Treaty of Versailles, Hitler sent troops into the Rhineland, a demilitarized zone. France and Britain protested but took no action. This lack of response set a precedent, in which Hitler would act and the democracies would appease him.

—Mussolini completed his conquest of Ethiopia.

—The Spanish Civil War (1936–1939) began with Francisco Franco's military uprising against the leftist government. Because Franco was allied with Spanish fascists, Mussolini and Hitler assisted him (the Germans took the opportunity to test tanks, airplanes, and new tactics, including terror bombing). Stalin attempted to aid the Spanish government and expected France and Britain to help him do so. He was disappointed when they did not, and his trust in the Western democracies eroded. Aside from the USSR, only a contingent of volunteers, the International Brigades, joined against the rebels. Franco won, became dictator of Spain, and ruled till his death in 1975.

- 1937:

  —In Japan, the military gained control of the government.

  —Germany, Italy, and Japan formed their alliance.

  —Japan invaded mainland China, where the Japanese committed terrible atrocities, including the **Rape of Nanjing**.

- 1938:

  —Germany annexed Austria in the **Anschluss** ("union").

  —Hitler announced plans to seize the Sudetenland, formerly German territory, given to Czechoslovakia after World War I. Mussolini and Hitler met with Neville Chamberlain, Britain's prime minister, and the French premier at the German city of Munich. The Czechoslovaks were not invited; neither were the Soviets, who, with France, had promised to protect Czechoslovakia from aggression. Britain and France let Germany have the Sudetenland in exchange for Hitler's promise to expand no further. Chamberlain claimed to have guaranteed "peace in our time," but the **Munich Agreement** was **appeasement** at its worst. It also destroyed collective security: Stalin, angry and betrayed, chose not to trust Britain and France any further.

  —Japanese and Soviet troops clashed on the Siberian border.

- 1939:

  —Germany took the rest of Czechoslovakia. By doing so Hitler showed the world how foolish France and Britain had been to believe his promises.

  —Germany took western Lithuania.

  —Italy invaded Albania.

  —The Japanese and Soviets fought again in Siberia.

  —Hitler began to make claims on Polish territory that had formerly belonged to Germany. Realizing that this was where Hitler would act next, France and Britain promised to guarantee Poland's safety.

  —Wishing to avoid a two-front war, Hitler sought to reach an agreement with Stalin before invading Poland. In August, Stalin, no longer trusting Britain and France, agreed to sign a nonaggression pact with Hitler. This **Nazi-Soviet Pact** kept the USSR neutral and opened the way for Hitler to invade Poland.

  —On September 1, 1939, Germany invaded Poland and thus World War II began.

THE AXIS ASCENDANT, 1939–1941

During the first half of the war, the Axis powers were triumphant. In Europe, the only major powers opposing Germany were France and Britain. The USSR had agreed to remain neutral, and the United States, sunk into isolationism, stayed out of the fighting as well. In Asia, Japan expanded its war against China to include a greater war of conquest against British, Dutch, and French colonies in Southeast Asia.

New Technology and World War II

In terms of combat and technology, World War II was very different from World War I. In the latter, military technology had favored the defensive, resulting in the hellish stalemate of trench warfare. By the time World War II began, military technology had developed in such a way as to make warfare more rapid and more dynamic.

At sea, naval aircraft, aircraft carriers, new landing craft that allowed marine troops to invade faraway islands and beachheads, and long-range submarines gave the combatants a truly global reach. On the ground, new artillery and, especially, tanks gave armies tremendous offensive punch, as well as the ability to move quickly. In the air, giant strategic bombers were able to fly thousands of miles and drop unheard-of quantities of explosives, further increasing offensive capacity.

This new technology helped make World War II a fast-paced, decisive conflict. It also had the unfortunate effect of making warfare deadlier and involving civilians to a degree never before imagined.

The need to develop better and more effective military technology had a tremendous effect on civilian technology long after the war was over. Among the many wartime innovations that played a large role in postwar life were radar, sonar; jet aircraft, synthetic materials (such as nylon), rocketry, atomic energy, and computer science.

Blitzkrieg, the Invasion of Poland, and Sitzkrieg

The war began with Germany's invasion of Poland, in September 1939 (although it must be remembered that Japan had been fighting China since 1937). The new offensive character of war could be seen right away in Germany's innovative method of **Blitzkrieg** ("lightning war"), which used tanks and airplanes to penetrate deeply and quickly into enemy territory. Within weeks, the fighting in Poland was over—especially because the USSR invaded the eastern half of the country, in accordance with the Nazi-Soviet Pact.

In contrast to Germany's fast action, Britain and France, although they declared war, did very little. With an outdated World War I mentality, the Allies waited for Germany to attack them, believing that, as in 1914, the defense would prevail. While Britain and France marked time, Germany prepared its attack. The winter of 1939–1940 was nicknamed Sitzkrieg ("phony war").

Germany's Invasion of Western Europe and the Fall of France

In April 1940, Hitler launched his assault on Western Europe. The next several months were stunningly successful. Denmark, Norway, Luxembourg, Belgium, and the Netherlands were defeated in weeks, if not days.

Most amazing of all was the fall of France. The Germans attacked France on May 10. By June 22, the largest and most powerful democracy on the European continent had surrendered. The French had been confident that their great chain of border fortifications, the Maginot Line, would protect them. The German Blitzkrieg sidestepped the Maginot Line and sent tanks streaming into northern France. The defeat of France shocked the world. It also left Great Britain in the seemingly hopeless position of fighting Germany and Italy (which joined the war in June) by itself.

The Battle of Britain

From the summer of 1940 to the spring of 1941, Germany concentrated its attention on Britain. Meanwhile, Italy launched attacks in the Mediterranean, trying to take Greece, Yugoslavia, and Egypt (still under British protection). Hitler's attempt to knock Britain out of the war failed. The Royal Navy protected the British Isles from invasion. When Hitler tried to win the war from the air, the Royal Air Force defended England's skies in the **Battle of Britain**.

Britain held out thanks to the skill of its air force, its use of radar, and economic aid from Canada and the United States (although the United States was neutral, the government of Franklin Roosevelt was sympathetic, and its **Lend-Lease program** of economic assistance kept Britain and, later, the USSR well-supplied throughout the war).

Invasions in the East and Operation Barbarossa

In the spring and summer of 1941, Hitler shifted his focus from Britain to Eastern Europe. Mussolini's wars in Greece, Yugoslavia, and North Africa had gone wrong, and Germany had to assist him. One of Hitler's most skilled tank commanders, Erwin Rommel, was sent to Africa to fight the British in Egypt.

Hitler also had a larger plan in mind: the invasion of the Soviet Union, code-named **Operation Barbarossa**. Although the USSR and Germany had carefully observed their pact of neutrality since August 1939, Hitler, having eliminated France from the war, felt confident enough to fight the USSR, even though Britain had not yet been defeated.

On June 22, 1941, Germany invaded the Soviet Union, starting the largest ground war in history. From this point onward, 60 to 75 percent of the German armed forces would fight on this eastern front. At first, it looked as though the USSR would fall as quickly as France had. German forces surrounded Leningrad, the USSR's second largest city, placing it under the worst siege in modern times. They drove deep into Ukraine and southern Russia. They also reached the outskirts of Moscow, the capital. A last-ditch defensive effort in December halted the German advance, but only barely.

Japanese Aggression in Southeast Asia

In the Pacific, fighting between China and Japan continued. Japan's war effort widened in 1940 and 1941, as French, Dutch, and British misfortunes in Europe made their Asian empires vulnerable. When France fell in 1940, Japan began to threaten its colony in Indochina. Japan's eventual goal was to establish its **Greater East Asian Co-Prosperity Sphere** over the entire Chinese coast, all of Southeast Asia, India, Indonesia, and perhaps Australia and New Zealand.

By the summer of 1941, Japan's takeover of Indochina and increased aggression toward Southeast Asia compelled the United States, already upset at Japanese atrocities in China, to impose economic sanctions. Without steel, oil, and other raw materials from the United States, the Japanese war effort on the Asian mainland would be badly damaged. Japan viewed the embargo as an act of war and in late 1941 began to plan a military assault against the United States.

Pearl Harbor and Japan's Assault on the South Pacific

On December 7, 1941, just as the Soviets were halting the Germans outside Moscow, Japan launched its surprise attack on the U.S. naval installation at **Pearl Harbor**, Hawaii. At the same time, the Japanese bombed and invaded U.S. bases throughout the Pacific and on the Philippines.

By the spring of 1942, the Japanese were masters of the South Pacific and Southeast Asia, having captured Hong Kong, Indochina, Thailand, part of Burma, the Malaysian Peninsula (including the great British base of Singapore), the Philippines, Indonesia (the Dutch East Indies), and hundreds of small Pacific islands. However, the effect of the Japanese attack was to bring the United States into World War II, both in the Pacific and in Europe (several days after Pearl Harbor, Germany joined Japan in declaring war on the United States).

Because Pearl Harbor, however devastating, was not a knockout blow, what the Japanese had managed to do was to rouse one of the world's largest countries—with great humanpower resources and the most productive economy on earth—and involve it in the war. In the long term, neither Japan nor Germany would be able to match America's capacity for military industrialization or mass conscription of troops.

THE ALLIED QUEST FOR VICTORY, 1942–1945

The Shifting Balance of World War II

The second half of the war, 1942 through 1945, was very different in character from the first. Most obviously, a different set of countries was involved. France had dropped out, but the USSR and the United States had joined in. Just as important, a different set of factors came into play. The Axis Powers' advantage lay in the skill and quality of Germany's and Japan's armed forces. Allied advantages, especially once the Soviets and Americans became involved, were geographic size, huge reserves of humanpower, large economies, and abundant natural resources.

This distribution of advantages meant that the longer the war lasted, the more likely it was that the Allies would win. Realizing that time was against them, Germany and Japan had been trying to gain decisive victories between 1939 and the end of 1941. Germany's failure to take Moscow and Japan's failure to cripple America permanently with its initial sweep through the Pacific ended the Axis's chances of ending the war quickly. Although Germany and Japan still held the advantage when 1942 began, all the long-term trends were against them.

The Turning Point: 1942

A handful of battles during the summer and fall of 1942 completely changed the tide of the war. If the Axis had won these encounters, they might have been able to force a favorable end to the war. By losing all three, Japan and Germany wasted vast amounts of irreplaceable troops, weapons, and equipment—and lost the strategic initiative they had enjoyed since 1939. These battles were

- **Midway** (June 1942), a naval battle in which the United States destroyed much of the Japanese aircraft-carrier fleet;
- **El Alamein** (July–November 1942), where the British turned back the drive of German tanks toward Egypt and the Suez Canal;
- **Stalingrad** (August 1942–February 1943), a savage clash on the Volga, where the Soviets prevented Germany from capturing south Russia and oil reserves in the east.

With these victories, the Allies had held on long enough for their advantages—larger populations and larger economies—to become decisive.

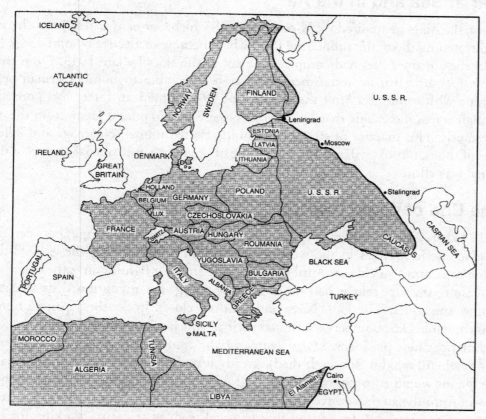

The European and Mediterranean Theaters of Combat, World War II, 1942.
From September 1939 until the autumn of 1942, the Axis Powers—Germany, Italy, and Japan—succeeded in seizing the military initiative and keeping it. By the middle of 1942, Nazi Germany had reached the height of its power. The areas shaded in gray mark territory that was controlled directly by Germany before the war, belonged to its allies, or had been conquered by it during the war. Not long after this point, primarily because of defeats at El Alamein and Stalingrad, the tide of war turned against the Germans and their partners.

The Shifting Tide: 1943 and 1944

In 1943 and 1944, the Allies determined the direction and pace of the war effort. In the Pacific, the Americans pushed the Japanese steadily westward. Australia, India, Burma, and large parts of China remained free and joined in the fighting. Guerrilla uprisings in Thailand, Vietnam, Indonesia, and the Philippines hurt the Japanese badly.

On the European and Mediterranean fronts, Britain and America took control of North Africa and then used it as a platform from which to invade Italy, depose Mussolini's Fascist government, and knock Italy out of the war. From the east, the Soviets pushed the Germans out of their country, into Eastern Europe, and toward Berlin.

In June 1944, in the **D-Day invasion** (technically known as Operation Overlord, or the Normandy Invasion), British, Canadian, and American troops, ships, and aircraft crossed the English Channel and landed on the coast of France. On land, Hitler now faced Allied threats from three directions: the eastern front, the Italian peninsula, and Western Europe.

War at Sea and in the Air

At sea, the Allies neutralized the last weapon with which Germany had any real chance of threatening them: the **submarine fleet**, which became ineffective by mid-1943.

In the air, the Allies had complete control of the skies by late 1943. From that point forward, British and American aircraft were able to bomb German-held Europe with impunity. After the summer of 1944, American forces had gone far enough across the Pacific that U.S. bombers were able to pound Japan from the air constantly. This practice of **strategic bombing** caused immense damage and killed tens of thousands of civilians. It remains one of the most controversial aspects of the Allied war effort.

The End of World War II

In 1945, the Axis surrendered. Germany gave up the fight first. Caught between the Anglo-American Allies in the west and the Soviet advance from the east, Hitler chose to commit suicide on April 30. Germany stopped fighting in early May.

Despite the fact that it had no hope of winning, Japan continued its struggle against the Allies. The U.S. Navy and Marines closed in on the Japanese home islands, while U.S. bombers continued their assault from the skies.

America's new president, Harry Truman (who came to the Oval Office in April 1945, when Franklin Roosevelt died), greatly feared that an invasion of the Japanese islands would cost tens of thousands of American and Japanese lives. He hoped to win from the air, but conventional bombardment did not seem to be forcing the Japanese to surrender. In July, an international team of scientists working for the Allies tested the first operational atomic bomb in New Mexico. Truman chose to use the A-bomb against the Japanese.

After warning Japan's government that the United States had a new weapon of terrible power, Truman acted. On August 6, 1945, a B-29 bomber named *Enola Gay* dropped an atomic bomb on **Hiroshima**. The initial blast killed at least 78,000 people and destroyed the entire city center; tens of thousands more died later, of burns or radioactive fallout. When the Japanese government ignored Truman's next request for surrender, the Americans dropped a second bomb on August 9, on the port of Nagasaki. The following week, the Japanese agreed to a cease-fire. They surrendered officially on September 2.

THE HOLOCAUST AND OTHER WAR CRIMES

War Crimes and Crimes Against Humanity

The most grisly aspect of World War II involved the many war crimes committed during the seventy-three months of fighting. Of the 55 to 60 million people who died during the war, approximately half were civilians. A good number were killed by means that fell outside the bounds established by international law or acceptable military behavior. Many of these atrocities were horrendous enough that the phrase "war crime" seemed inadequate to describe them. It was after World War II, therefore, that the phrase "**crime against humanity**" entered the world's legal vocabularies.

The Axis Powers were not the only nations to kill civilians. The Red Army committed many crimes—rape, plunder, wanton destruction of civilian property—as the Soviets advanced through Eastern Europe and Germany. The American and British policy of strategic bombing, both over Japan and German-held Europe, caused tremendous civilian suffering. Some commentators, including many Germans and Japanese, have argued that strategic bombing can be considered a war crime (it should be noted that this is a minority opinion). America remains the only nation that has ever used an atomic or nuclear weapon in wartime, and the question of whether it was necessary to use it against Japan continues to be a matter of controversy.

Japanese War Crimes

Nonetheless, it was the Axis that committed war crimes and crimes against humanity systematically and on a large scale. In Asia, Japan was guilty of a wide variety of atrocities. Even before World War II, Japanese forces had raped, pillaged, and butchered civilian populations in many Chinese cities, most notably Nanjing in December 1937.

As the Greater East Asian Co-Prosperity Sphere widened during World War II, Japanese soldiers continued to terrorize civilian populations, not just in China but in all of Southeast Asia. On many occasions, Japanese armies killed American, British, and Asian prisoners of war, against all legal conventions pertaining to military conduct. Prisoners of war were also used as subjects for Japanese scientific experiments, especially for testing biological and chemical weapons. Finally, the Japanese military rounded up women from Korea and Southeast Asia and forced them to serve as prostitutes, or "comfort women," for Japanese soldiers. After the war, the U.S. military authorities held a series of Tokyo Trials, during which Japanese civilian and military officials were tried for these crimes.

Nazi Atrocities

More infamous were the crimes against humanity committed by the Germans. Prior to the war, the Nazis operated an extensive apparatus of terror, which included a secret police (the Gestapo) and concentration camps (such as Dachau). Dissidents (including Protestant and, especially, Catholic religious leaders who protested Nazi policy) had been imprisoned, even executed, since the early 1930s.

As the war began and then progressed, the Nazis began to "euthanize" medical patients with incurable diseases, venereal diseases, or tuberculosis. They killed homosexuals, people with mental disabilities, and political dissidents. They performed medical and scientific experiments on human subjects, typically to the point of mutilation and death (Jews and Soviet prisoners of war were used most often).

Nazi Racial Policy and Genocide

Most heinous were the Nazi campaigns of **genocide** (a term devised in the 1940s, by a Jewish lawyer, to reflect the special, premeditated nature of the crime). The Nazis targeted a number of ethnic and cultural groups. Roma (Gypsies) and Slavs were among those they considered to be "subhuman" or "undesirable."

Most of all, the Nazis hated the Jews. After Hitler's rise to power in 1933, the Nazis passed a number of anti-Semitic policies that grew worse over time. The worst had been the **Nuremberg Laws** (1935), which deprived German Jews of their civil rights. Before the war, however, violence against Jews was not yet official policy, even though, in reality, thousands of Jews were harassed and beaten and their homes and businesses vandalized during the late 1930s. In November 1938, on Kristallnacht ("Night of Broken Glass"), thousands of Jewish shops, synagogues, and homes throughout Germany and Austria were attacked or burned in a single night.

It was during the war that Nazi anti-Semitic policy escalated to the point of genocide. There were 11 million Jews in Europe before the beginning of the war. In 1939 and 1940, as the Germans brought more of Europe under their control, Nazi authorities began to round up Jews and detain them, either in **ghettos** or in existing concentration camps, such as Dachau. It was sometime in 1941 that the order for genocide came down from above. Although no written orders survive, it is certain that, ultimately, the command was issued by Hitler himself.

The Holocaust

Nazi genocidal policy is popularly referred to by the name given it by the Jews: the **Holocaust**. The Nazis referred to it as the **Final Solution**. Whatever its name, it evolved as follows:

- 1939–1940:
  - —Jews were forced to wear the yellow star to identify themselves.
  - —Polish Jews were rounded up and placed in ghettos.
  - —Other European Jews were imprisoned in concentration and transit camps.
  - —Some Jews were sporadically executed or died by random violence.

- 1941:
  - —In July, an order "to make preparations for the general final solution of the Jewish problem within the German sphere of influence in Europe" was handed down to the SS (the Nazi security forces).

—The Nazis organized **special action squads** (*Einsatzgruppen*) to follow the German army into the Soviet Union, round up Jews, and execute them by shooting.

—Dissatisfaction with the special action squads grew. This method of execution was considered to be too slow, too wasteful of ammunition, and too hard on the morale of the executioners. Because the squads only buried the bodies instead of destroying them, the danger remained that the victims could later be found.

—Experiments with carbon monoxide and other gases were carried out at various concentration camps in an attempt to find an "efficient" way to kill large numbers of victims. Experimental cremation methods were tested.

—Late in the year, construction of special camps for execution and cremation began.

—A cyanide-based insecticide, Zyklon-B, was chosen as the means of extermination.

• 1942:

—In January, fifteen Nazi officials met in the suburbs of Berlin. Here, at the **Wannsee Conference**, it was decided to use special **extermination camps**, already under construction in German-held Poland, to eliminate Jews and other undesirables. Among these were Majdanek, Chelmno, Belzec, Sobibor, and Treblinka. The largest and most infamous was **Auschwitz-Birkenau.**

—The special extermination camps went into operation.

• 1943–1945:

—Jews from all over Europe were shipped to the extermination camps. Other victims were also taken there. Victims were gassed, their bodies processed, their remains cremated.

—Soviet liberation of camps in Poland began in 1944. Auschwitz-Birkenau was liberated in early 1945.

—Camps in the west were liberated by the British and Americans.

In the end, the Final Solution resulted in millions of deaths. Of Europe's 11 million Jews, approximately 6 million were killed. In addition, many non-Jewish victims (especially Roma) perished.

It was mainly to punish these crimes that the Americans, British, and Soviets organized the Nuremberg Trials (1946), which prosecuted Nazi leaders. During these trials, the term *crime against humanity* was codified as law. In 1948, in a collective effort to avoid such atrocities in the future, the United Nations adopted the Universal Declaration of Human Rights.

The Cold War

CHAPTER 31

- The Cold War
- The Yalta Conference
- The United Nations
- The containment strategy (the Truman Doctrine and the Marshall Plan)
- NATO versus the Warsaw Pact
- Chinese communism and the Sino-Soviet split
- The domino principle
- The Korean and Vietnam wars
- The Soviet invasions of Hungary and Czechoslovakia
- National liberation and decolonization

- Nonalignment, the third world, and proxy wars
- The Berlin Wall and the Cuban Missile Crisis
- The nuclear arms race, deterrence, and MAD
- Détente
- Solidarity and unrest in Eastern Europe
- Perestroika and glasnost
- The fall of the Berlin Wall
- The collapse of the USSR

The end of World War II fundamentally shifted global power. For over 200 years, the constantly shifting balance of power among six or seven European nations had determined the course of world events. With Europe devastated by the war, only two nations possessed true global strength: the United States and the Soviet Union. Because these two nations were orders of magnitude stronger and wealthier than any great power had been before them, they were referred to as **superpowers**.

The popular name given to the state of rivalry that existed between the United States and the USSR from 1945 to 1991 is the **Cold War**. It divided the world into hostile camps—although its bipolar nature was complicated by the eventual breakup of the alliance between Communist China and the Soviet Union. The Cold War gave birth to a nuclear arms race that brought into the world the deadliest weapons ever seen. The great wave of **decolonization** that took place after World War II (see Chapter 32) was deeply affected by the Cold War, because newly free nations often had to choose between allying with one superpower or another. Although the United States and USSR never went to war with each other, dozens of small and medium-size conflicts were fought worldwide between 1945 and the end of the Cold War, killing an estimated total of 50 million people, more than half of them civilian.

The Cold War finally ended in the late 1980s and early 1990s, with the collapse of communism in Eastern Europe and the breakup of the Soviet Union.

WARTIME DIPLOMACY

The wartime alliance between the United States, Great Britain, and the Soviet Union had been a marriage of convenience. Although the United States and Britain were mutually sympathetic, they cooperated with the USSR and its dictator, Joseph Stalin, only because they needed Soviet help to defeat Hitler. Even during the war effort, many tensions arose between Franklin Roosevelt and Winston Churchill on one hand and Stalin on the other. It was clear to all that things would only get worse after the war ended.

The issues concerning the wartime allies were discussed at three summit meetings: the Teheran Conference (November 1943), the Yalta Conference (February 1945), and the Potsdam Conference (July 1945). The questions dealt with included the following:

- *Second front*: The USSR, which fought the vast bulk of the German army, desperately wanted its allies to open up a second front in western Europe as soon as possible. At Teheran, it was decided to invade France in June 1944.
- *Japan*: In exchange for Asian territory, the Soviets agreed to help fight Japan after Germany was defeated. The Americans struck this deal before the atomic bomb was tested.
- *Division and denazification of Germany and Austria*: Germany was to be occupied and divided into four sectors: British, French, U.S., and Soviet. Berlin, which fell into the Soviet zone, was likewise divided, and the western parts of the city were guaranteed highway, air, and rail access to the other zones. Austria was similarly partitioned. Both countries were to undergo a process of denazification, in which former Nazis would be removed from public offices and positions of authority. Germany was to repay $20 billion in reparations. The division of Germany lasted until the end of the Cold War. Austria was allowed to reunify in 1955.
- *United Nations*: Just as Woodrow Wilson had created the League of Nations after World War I, Franklin Roosevelt hoped to establish a new international body, stronger and more effective than the League had been. This body was to be called the **United Nations**.
- *Fate of Eastern Europe*: By far, this was the most sensitive issue. As they defeated Germany, Soviet troops occupied Eastern Europe. It was clear that Stalin hoped to turn this territory into a Soviet sphere of influence. Roosevelt and Churchill were deeply concerned, but Stalin had millions of troops in the region and to press him too hard on this question was to risk having him drop out of the war before Germany was defeated. At Yalta, Roosevelt and Churchill came up with an awkward compromise. They agreed that the USSR would have informal influence in certain East European nations. In exchange, they asked the Soviets to promise to allow free elections throughout Eastern Europe. Stalin agreed and then broke his promises. Some historians see Roosevelt and Churchill as having betrayed Eastern Europe; others argue that there was little they could have done, considering the situation's military realities.

THE COLD WAR BEGINS, 1945–1949

The first stage of the Cold War can be considered to have lasted from 1945 to 1949. Although there were concerns about other parts of the world, such as Japan, Korea, and China, the focus of the Cold War during these early years was primarily European and Mediterranean. For Europe itself, of course, this was a bitter comedown. From being the shaper of world events, Europe—reduced to the superpowers' battleground—was now shaped by them.

The Cold War Division of Europe, 1957.
From 1945 until 1989, the Cold War divided the nations of Europe—with only a few exceptions—into two camps, one dominated by the Soviet Union, the other led by the United States and its European allies. By the mid-1950s, the so-called Iron Curtain had descended over Europe. The nations of the West were joined by the North Atlantic Treaty Organization, a military alliance, and many also joined in the European Economic Community. The Eastern bloc was held together by the Soviet-imposed military alliance known as the Warsaw Pact, as well as COMECON, an economic union led by the USSR.

The Soviet Absorption of Eastern Europe

From 1945 through 1948, the USSR took over Eastern Europe, installing pro-Soviet, communist governments in the eastern half of Germany and in Poland, Czechoslovakia, Hungary, Romania, and Bulgaria. Yugoslavia became communist as well, but under its stubbornly independent leader, Josip Tito, Yugoslavia broke with the USSR in 1948. Albania, also communist, allied with the Soviets until Stalin's death; the mid-1950s, it isolated itself from both superpowers. In March 1946, Winston Churchill warned of the permanent division of the continent in his famous "**iron curtain**" speech.

All of this was a violation of the Soviets' promises at Yalta. In addition, the USSR was threatening Iran and Turkey in 1945 and 1946. The Yugoslavs were sponsoring a communist rebellion in Greece. This brought the Soviet bloc perilously close to the oil fields of the Middle East, as well as the important waterways of the eastern Mediterranean.

Stalin's policy during these years was simple: to gain as much territory as possible without a fight. Although they kept it as secret as possible, the Soviets had been hurt badly by World War II. They had lost 25 million to 28 million dead. One-third of their entire economy had been destroyed. The USSR could not afford to fight the West. On the other hand, Stalin wanted a buffer zone in Eastern Europe, in order to protect his country from suffering again as it had in World War II. Also, because the United States had atomic weaponry and the USSR did not, Stalin felt even more vulnerable. His goal was to push the Americans as hard as he could, up to the point where they pushed back. The clearest example of this came in 1948, during the **Berlin Blockade**. In March, the Soviets suddenly cut off highway and railroad traffic between West Berlin and the western zones of Germany. It was easy to do this without provoking an actual war. When the United States began to fly airplanes to West Berlin, however, Stalin was faced with a choice: allow the flights to continue or shoot the aircraft out of the skies, an act that would certainly start a war. Stalin backed down, having reached the limit of what the United States would allow.

The U.S. Response: Containment

Until 1947, the United States had no coherent strategy for the emerging Cold War. That year, however, as communist takeover threatened Greece and Turkey, President Harry Truman acted. In March, the United States assisted Greece and Turkey, proclaiming the **Truman Doctrine**, which promised "moral and material aid to any and all countries whose political stability is threatened by communism."

Later in 1947, the United States unveiled the European Recovery Plan (or **Marshall Plan**), brainchild of the secretary of state, General George Marshall. Remembering how, during the Depression, economic suffering had driven many European nations to political extremism, Marshall argued that poverty and homelessness in post-World War II Europe might drive governments to communism. The Marshall Plan pumped over $13 billion into Europe for purposes of economic reconstruction. Even the nations of Eastern Europe were invited to take part in the Marshall Plan, but the USSR forbade them to do so.

Finally, in 1949, the Truman Administration made a military commitment to the Cold War with the formation of the **North Atlantic Treaty Organization** (NATO), which bound the United States, Canada, Britain, and nine other Western European states into a formal strategic alliance (the number of NATO members has grown steadily over time).

All these initiatives were elements in the United States's overarching strategy for dealing with the USSR: **containment**. This term was coined by the diplomat George Kennan, who argued that the USSR would expand as far as it could, as long as it did not have to fight. Soviet expansion, therefore, could be halted by "long-term, patient, but firm and vigilant containment."

Containment did not necessarily mean war but could also consist of economic and diplomatic support for countries targeted by the USSR. The advantage was that Soviet expansion could be kept in check without risking combat. There were, however, drawbacks. Containment gave the initiative to the Soviet Union: it acted, then the United States reacted. There was no end in sight, meaning that containment would have to be pursued for years, if not decades. It would cost immense amounts of money, especially as the arms race between the two countries escalated. Moreover, as described below and in Chapter 32, the containment strategy affected—and not for the better—how America chose its allies in the developing (or "third") world of Africa, Asia, and Latin America.

The Soviets resisted containment. In response to the Marshall Plan, the USSR formed its own economic union, the Council for Mutual Economic Assistance (COMECON). It also developed its own military bloc, the **Warsaw Pact**, to oppose NATO.

By the end of the 1940s, Europe was sharply divided between noncommunist and communist camps, with only a few nations remaining neutral. By 1949, however, Europe ceased to be the only battleground—or even the primary battleground—of the Cold War.

THE COLD WAR GLOBALIZES, 1949–1968

Nineteen forty-nine was a key year in the history of the Cold War. NATO was established. That summer witnessed the **first Soviet atomic test**, which eliminated America's edge in military technology and started a four-decade nuclear arms race.

The Cold War in Asia and the Third World

Also in 1949, after years of civil war, **Mao Tse-tung** defeated Chiang Kai-shek's Nationalists, completing the **communist revolution in China**. The Nationalists fled to Taiwan. On the mainland, Mao established the People's Republic of China (PRC) and allied with the USSR (on Mao's domestic policies, see Chapter 32). In a matter of months, the Cold War had expanded dramatically: The two largest nations on the Eurasian landmass were now together under the banner of communism, and one of them possessed atomic weapons.

With the situation in Europe largely stalemated, the Cold War's focus shifted increasingly to Asia, as well as Africa and Latin America. The first sign of this shift was the **Korean War** (1950–1953), which began with an invasion of the noncommunist South by the communist North (with support from Stalin and, especially, Mao). The United States led a United Nations army to defend South Korea. After three years of combat and more than a million deaths, the war ended with the country still divided, exactly where it had been before.

As the Cold War took on a more global dimension, the U.S. policy of containment became more difficult. In Asia, Africa, and Latin America, there was already a so-called **Third World** of nonaligned nations, most of them less economically developed than the West or the USSR, and if the Soviets attempted to win influence there, the Americans had to compete. The post-World War II wave of **decolonization** and **national liberation** added new regimes to the Third World, and because they had just freed themselves from Western imperialism or overthrown dictators supported by Western powers, many were inclined to stay unaligned (like India and Egypt) or seek ties with the USSR (for example, Cuba after 1959). As the Soviets, Chinese, and Cuba tried to spread communism throughout the Third World, the United States responded with its own interventions. Unfortunately, America came to choose its Third World allies based mainly on how anticommunist they were, not how democratic—and thus, it supported many dictatorial and authoritarian regimes.

> **TIP**
>
> American anxieties about the possible global expansion of communism were based on what was popularly known as the **domino principle** (if one country in a region "falls" to communism, the rest will too).

After Korea, key Cold War events in the Third World include the **Cuban Revolution** (1959), which heightened tensions by placing a communist regime and Soviet ally only miles off the U.S. coast. The **Vietnam War** (1954–1975) began with the liberation of Vietnam from French colonization and continued with America's attempt to prop up an unpopular government in South Vietnam against revolution and invasion from the communist north. This was classic domino-principle strategy on the part of the United States, which feared the spread of communism throughout all of Southeast Asia. However, the war took a turn for the worse in 1968, and America withdrew in defeat in 1973. For more on Cuba and Vietnam, see Chapter 32.

Superpower Rivalry and the Sino-Soviet Split

In the United States, presidents of both political parties pursued firm and active foreign policies and followed the policy of containment. In the USSR, Stalin died in 1953, and new leadership caused more noticeable changes. Nikita Khrushchev (1953–1964) was less brutal than Stalin. He denounced the crimes of Stalin and (within strict limits) allowed some liberalization at home and in the Eastern bloc. He declared his willingness to be friendlier to the West and even visited the United States. Leonid Brezhnev (1964–1982), who forced Khrushchev into retirement, was more of a hard-liner but still not as harsh as Stalin.

Even so, Cold War tensions and the arms race continued. During the 1950s and early 1960s, Khrushchev showed that liberalization had its limits. In 1956, when Hungary reformed more than the USSR wished, then tried to leave the Soviet bloc, Khrushchev suppressed the **Hungarian uprising** by force. His foreign policy became unpredictable. Encouraged by the Cuban Revolution and angered by the flight of American U-2 spy planes over the USSR (in May 1960, the Soviets shot down a U-2 and captured the pilot, causing an international crisis), Khrushchev pursued a boldly aggressive course in East Germany and in Cuba. In August 1961, the Soviets built the **Berlin Wall**. To demonstrate U.S. determination, the U.S. president John F. Kennedy visited the city and declared in a rousing speech, "I am a Berliner." A bigger and more dangerous showdown came in 1962, when Khrushchev attempted to install nuclear missiles in Cuba. In October, U.S. spy planes uncovered what the Soviets were doing, and Kennedy answered with a naval blockade of Cuba. The resulting **Cuban Missile Crisis** is generally considered to be the moment that brought the world closest to nuclear war. The Soviets backed down and withdrew the missiles; the failed gamble and the resulting loss of prestige played a major role in the ouster of Khrushchev in 1964. (Another factor was the USSR's worsening relationship with China, discussed below.)

Tensions cooled somewhat during the rest of the 1960s, although relations were not friendly. When Brezhnev came to power, he proved more authoritarian than Khrushchev, but also more predictable. In 1968, when Czechoslovakia began a major reform program, the "Prague Spring," Brezhnev cracked down hard, sending in a Warsaw Pact army to restore Soviet control. He justified the intervention by stating that the USSR had the right to "protect communism" in Eastern Europe (in other words, to control the Soviet bloc as it pleased), a stance that became known as the **Brezhnev Doctrine.** However, Brezhnev seemed less likely to threaten Europe outside the USSR's declared sphere of influence. Of course, proxy struggles in the Third World continued, and the U.S. involvement in Vietnam escalated.

Cold War geopolitics grew more complex with the **Sino-Soviet split**, which began in the 1960s and continued till the collapse of the USSR. Even though both nations were communist, the Chinese resented the Soviets' patronizing "older brother" attitude (they also felt that many Russians, being white, treated them as racial inferiors). The Soviets did not give the Chinese the secret of nuclear weapons. (China finally developed its own atomic bomb in 1964.) Mao was upset with what he saw as the softer line of Stalin's successors. By the early 1960s, tensions between China and the USSR were serious (but not yet understood in the West). As the decade ended, the Sino-Soviet border became a militarized zone, and occasional episodes of violence broke out. The United States would exploit this split in the 1970s.

The Arms Race and Space Race

When the USSR ended the American monopoly on atomic weapons in 1949, a long **nuclear arms race** began. During the 1950s and early 1960s, the United States had more weapons, but its advantage narrowed as time passed. By the mid-to-late 1960s, the superpowers reached a state of nuclear parity: they each had roughly the same quantity of weapons, and they each had the ability to drop nuclear bombs from airplanes, fire nuclear missiles from submarines, and launch nuclear warheads on intercontinental ballistic missiles (ICBMs) directly at each other's countries. Britain, France, and China also possessed small nuclear arsenals.

Nuclear weapons made traditional military thinking obsolete and greatly heightened international tensions. Any quarrel that got out of control (as, for example, the assassination of Franz Ferdinand did in 1914) could result not just in a world war but global devastation. Over time, nuclear weapons became most important for how they were *not* used: their **deterrence** value was seen as a way of preventing war between the superpowers. In theory, as long as each side remained convinced that rash or aggressive action would destroy it as well as its enemy, both sides would avoid doing anything that might trigger a serious crisis. This logic was referred to as **Mutually Assured Destruction**, with the appropriate abbreviation MAD.

Because rocket technology was so intimately connected with the development of nuclear missiles, the arms race had much to do with another form of superpower competition: the **space race**. Ostensibly a peaceful scientific venture, the exploration of space became associated with hyperpatriotic pride and military rivalry. At the start, the Soviets had the advantage: they launched the first human-made object into space, the satellite *Sputnik*, in 1957, and they sent the first human into space, Yuri Gagarin, in 1961. However, the United States pulled ahead, becoming, in 1969, the first (and, so far, only) nation to land a crewed spacecraft on the moon.

THE LATE STAGES OF THE COLD WAR, 1968–1991

Détente During the 1970s

Between 1969 and 1979, the Cold War entered a more peaceful phase known as *détente* (a French diplomatic term referring to the relaxation of tensions). The United States, wearied by the Vietnam conflict and plagued by economic recession at home, was relieved to scale back hostilities. The USSR was motivated by the need for U.S. and Canadian grain shipments, as well as fears that America was growing closer to China—President Richard Nixon skillfully exploited the Sino-Soviet split by visiting China in 1972.

Détente did not mean tensions disappeared completely. Conflicts in Africa, Asia, and Latin America raged, with the United States and USSR sponsoring opposing sides. The arms race continued, and nuclear arsenals grew larger. Still, for almost a decade, the Soviets and Americans established a working relationship and, at times, genuinely cooperated. The United States sold grain to the USSR. Both powers cooperated in the enforcement of the **Nuclear Non-Proliferation Treaty** (1968–1969), whose purpose has been to prevent the spread of nuclear weaponry. The United States and USSR signed the first arms-control treaties, such as SALT (1972) and the Anti-Ballistic Missile Treaty (1972). In the Helsinki Accords of 1975, the Soviet government agreed to guarantee its people basic human rights. The superpowers even cooperated in space, during the Apollo-Soyuz mission (1975).

The Early-to-Mid 1980s: The Cold War Resumes

The spirit of détente ended in 1979. That year, the **Soviet invasion of Afghanistan**, which threatened the oil supplies of the Middle East as well as the Indian Ocean coastline, damaged relations between the superpowers. Another point of tension was the **Sandinista revolution in Nicaragua** (1979), which the Soviets supported. The latest arms-control treaty, SALT II (1979), went unratified. In 1980 U.S. President Ronald Reagan swung American foreign policy far to the right.

In terms of the arms race and the risk of nuclear war, the period between 1979 and 1985 was the Cold War's most dangerous time, with the exception of the Cuban Missile Crisis of 1962. The arms race escalated. Third World brushfire wars, terrorist campaigns sponsored by the USSR and its allies, and covert operations carried out by the CIA or the KGB increased in number. Both superpowers publicly expressed hostility. Each boycotted Olympic Games hosted by the

> **TIP**
>
> The Afghan War lasted ten years and became a Vietnam-like nightmare for the Soviets. It also destroyed détente.

other (Moscow in 1980, Los Angeles in 1984). Reagan referred to the Soviet Union explicitly as the Evil Empire. Because the nuclear weaponry of the 1980s was faster, more accurate, and more destructive than ever before, the chances that a diplomatic crisis could result in a full-scale, civilization-destroying exchange mounted.

Unrest and Reform in the Soviet Bloc

In the meantime, the USSR experienced political stagnation and economic slow-down at home (especially because of the arms race and the cost of the war in Afghanistan). In Eastern Europe, there was growing unrest, especially in Poland, where the 1980 creation of the trade union **Solidarity**, led by Lech Walesa, sparked a decade-long protest movement that united workers, intellectuals, and Catholic clergy (Pope John Paul II, originally from Poland, did much to support anti-Soviet agitation in Eastern Europe). Other important dissidents included the playwright Vaclav Havel of Czechoslovakia and, in the USSR, the physicist Andrei Sakharov, as well as his wife, Elena Bonner.

Real change was impossible under the aging Brezhnev and his immediate successors. In 1985, however, a younger, reform-minded leader rose to power in the Soviet Union: **Mikhail Gorbachev**. Gorbachev understood that inefficency, corruption, and economic weakness were undermining his country. He also knew that the USSR could no longer afford to continue fighting in Afghanistan, keep up with America in the arms race, or even maintain control over Eastern Europe.

During the late 1980s, Gorbachev launched two interrelated reform efforts: *perestroika* ("restructuring") and *glasnost* ("openness"). **Perestroika** involved economic changes similar to the reforms of **Deng Xiaoping** in China (see Chapter 32). Within limits, it reduced central state control over the economy, allowing for some free enterprise and expansion of private property. Such changes worked better in China than in the USSR, partly because of long-ingrained inefficiency in the Soviet system, partly because Deng fought conservative opposition in his government more effectively than Gorbachev did. Another difference was Gorbachev's policy of **glasnost**, which allowed greater freedom of the press, public criticism of political corruption and workplace abuses, and frankness about the USSR's clouded past (especially the Stalin era). He allowed competitive voting, created an elective parliament, and legalized non-Communist political parties. Gorbachev hoped that such freedoms would motivate the Soviet people to work harder to make perestroika succeed. Instead, glasnost made people feel freer to ask for even more change—and to criticize Gorbachev himself when things began to go wrong. (Deng did not permit such social and cultural freedoms in China.)

The Walls Come Down: The Cooling of the Arms Race and the Liberation of Eastern Europe

Gorbachev, hoping to reduce superpower tensions, turned a friendlier face to the West. Although tough discussions lay ahead, the terrible nuclear fears of the previous half decade began to fade. By 1987, Gorbachev and Reagan were negotiating arms-reduction agreements and cooling tensions even further.

Gorbachev also started to loosen the USSR's grip on Eastern Europe. He began economic reform and called for greater observance of human rights. Gorbachev's press secretary joked about the "Sinatra Doctrine," hinting that, instead of upholding the Brezhnev Doctrine, the Soviets would allow East European governments to do things "their way."

In the end, Eastern Europe went free. The key year was 1989. Poland, where Lech Walesa and the Solidarity movement won free nationwide elections, led the way. Hungary followed suit by opening its borders to the West. In Czechoslovakia, Vaclav Havel's dissident movement came to power in the so-called Velvet Revolution. Bulgaria's communist regime resigned. In November, the East German Communist Party collapsed, bringing about the freedom movement's most celebrated, most euphoric event, the **fall of the Berlin Wall**. In December, the deeply repressive regime in Romania was overthrown (in one of the freedom movement's rare moments of violence, the dictator, Nicolae Ceausescu, and his wife were executed). Soon, in October 1990, the map of Europe would be dramatically redrawn by the **reunification of Germany**.

Parallel Freedom Movements

The freedom movement in Eastern Europe inspired or paralleled other freedom movements worldwide in 1989 and 1990. Not all succeeded. In May 1989, the seventieth anniversary of the May Fourth Movement that had demanded progressive reform from the Chinese Republic, Chinese students gathered at **Tiananmen Square** in Beijing. They, too, wanted greater freedoms. The Deng regime refused to grant any concessions and, when the students disobeyed orders to disperse, crushed the demonstrations by sending in tanks. Economic change was allowed but not political change.

The nations of Latin America were luckier. Starting in the late 1980s, they began a wave of democratization that continued into the 1990s. In South Africa, in 1990, **Nelson Mandela**, leader of the African National Congress, was released from prison, where he had been held since 1964. Free elections and the **end of apartheid** soon followed.

The Fall of the Soviet Union, 1989–1991

While Eastern Europe rejoiced, trouble brewed in the USSR. Gorbachev faced two major problems after 1989. At home, perestroika was failing, and discontent with his leadership was rising. Liberals and moderates who had originally supported Gorbachev wanted more change than he was willing to give. On the other hand, he had made enough changes to alienate hard-liners and conservative communists. Abroad, the East European freedom movement encouraged an upsurge of **anti-Soviet nationalism** in the USSR itself. In 1990 and 1991, non-Russian parts of the country (especially the Baltic republics, Georgia, and Ukraine) pushed for greater autonomy or declared independence outright. In one instance, Gorbachev resorted to violence (he sent tanks into Lithuania in 1990), but overall, he did not have the heart to crush independence movements by force. As 1991 progressed, the continued existence of the Soviet nation was in doubt.

A sudden blow came in August 1991, when hard-line members of the regime staged a three-day coup against Gorbachev. Thanks to popular resistance and bold leadership by politicians, including Boris Yeltsin, who rallied people against the coup, the takeover failed. Gorbachev returned to power, but he had been fatally weakened. The breakup of the USSR continued; various republics, including Russia itself, went their own way in the fall and early winter, and Gorbachev was powerless to stop them. In December 1991, Yeltsin (now president of the Russian Republic) and the leaders of Ukraine and Belarus declared the formation of a new, post-Soviet confederation, the Commonwealth of Independent States, which made the USSR irrelevant. Bowing to the inevitable, on December 25, Gorbachev resigned as Soviet leader and declared an end to the USSR itself. Soviet Communism, whose birth in 1917 had been one of the major events of the early twentieth century, did not live to see the twenty-first.

The Fall of the Soviet Union and Formation of the Commonwealth of Independent States, January 1992.
In late 1991, Mikhail Gorbachev was forced to dissolve the USSR. At that time, leaders of the former republics of the Soviet Union, with the exception of Estonia, Latvia, Lithuania, and Georgia, chose to form the Commonwealth of Independent States as a way to maintain ties and attempt a smooth transition from Soviet rule.

CHAPTER 32

Divergent Forms of Development in the Postwar World, 1945–1991

- The developed world and postindustrial (service) economies
- Sovietization versus Westernization in postwar Europe
- European economic union (the European Union)
- The 1968 protests
- The economic slump of the 1970s
- National liberation and decolonization
- The developing (third) world and the north-south split
- The Organization of Petroleum Exporting Countries (OPEC)
- The Arab-Israeli conflict

- The Iranian Revolution
- Apartheid
- Indian and Indonesian independence and nonalignment
- Japan, the "little tigers," and economic growth in Asia
- Communism in Vietnam, Cambodia, and North Korea
- Maoist radicalism versus Deng Xiaoping's reformism in China
- The Cuban and Nicaraguan revolutions
- Dictatorship and democratization in Latin America

While the postwar decades were dominated diplomatically by the Cold War (see Chapter 31), individual parts of the world underwent a variety of political and social changes.

One preeminent trend was economic and technological modernization. However, this trend applied unevenly to different parts of the world. The societies of the West, the United States, Canada, and Western Europe, were already the most developed and industrialized in the world and therefore had the capacity to keep modernizing quickly and thoroughly. They became immensely prosperous and advanced, moving into a **postindustrial stage** by the end of the twentieth century. As for regions such as the Middle East, Africa, Asia, and Latin America, modernization, in most cases, was slower. The labels typically given to these regions—the **developing world**, less developed countries, or nondeveloped world—indicate how they lagged behind the nations of the West.

The postwar world was also an era of **decolonization**. World War II completed the process of weakening the grasp that several European nations still had on their empires. From the 1940s through the 1970s, countries such as Britain, France, Belgium, and the Netherlands were convinced or forced to free their colonies in the Middle East, Africa, and Asia. Moreover, many regions that had not been colonized per se but had been economically and/or politically dominated by outside powers began to assert themselves in the postwar era. This made the so-called **Third World**—the developing or newly liberated nations of Asia, Africa, the Mideast, and Latin America—increasingly important in global politics and economics. Unfortunately for many of these states, decolonization has sometimes caused as many problems as it has solved. Not all newly liberated countries were able to develop healthy forms of government and economic organization. Also, many of them were caught up on one side or the other in the politics of the Cold War, as the United States and Soviet Union dueled for global influence.

To this day, many imbalances and inequities between the West and the developing world still persist from the Cold War era. In particular, the great disparity in technological development and the vast gap between the West's affluence and the ghastly poverty of many parts of the developing world remain in place and continue to cause political and economic tension. The geographical placement of most of the developed or developing world has made it common to refer to their divide as the **north–south split**.

RECOVERY IN POSTWAR EUROPE

Europe found itself in a paradoxical situation during the postwar era. On one hand, World War II had ended its global dominance. It had been divided by the superpowers into a Cold War battleground. It lost its remaining colonies. On the other hand, after repairing the damage caused by World War II, most of Europe came to enjoy an unprecedented level of prosperity. This was certainly the case in Western Europe, which became one of the wealthiest and most technologically advanced societies on earth. Even communist-controlled Eastern Europe, which remained more backward, overcame the devastation caused by the war. Albeit more crudely and more slowly than in Western Europe, Eastern Europe's standard of living and level of modernization rose from the 1950s onward.

World War II's Effects on Europe

Wartime damage had been extensive. Millions were dead. A third of the Soviet economy had been destroyed. German cities lay in ruins. At least 50 million people were homeless, and more than 16 million were refugees displaced persons (DPs) without a country. The migration and dislocation caused by World War II was tremendous. Horrendous poverty, marked by shortages of food, clothing, consumer goods, and housing, threatened to plunge Europe into chaos.

In another blow to European prestige, colonies worldwide began to agitate for and win their freedom during the late 1940s and afterward. These national liberation movements and wars of decolonization caused European governments great stress and strain.

Sovietization in Eastern Europe

Despite these effects of war, economic recovery began surprisingly quickly. In the east, owing to the sheer political will of Stalin and the plundering of its new East European satellites (especially the Soviet-controlled zone of Germany), the USSR recovered to prewar economic levels within a decade. The USSR went on to create Soviet-style economies throughout the Eastern bloc. Economies were nationalized and centrally planned. Massive industrialization campaigns began. Collectivization, while not as brutally implemented as in the USSR during the 1930s, brought agriculture under state control.

In both the USSR and Eastern Europe, there was substantial economic growth after the 1940s and early 1950s. **Social welfare systems**, which provided education, medical care, pensions, and other basic services to all citizens, were put in place. However, East European economic production was characterized by poor quality. Consumer goods were constantly in short supply because so much emphasis was placed on weapons production during the arms race against the United States. Because Soviet and East European production was carried out without any regard for the environment, the ecological damage caused by a half century of East European industrialization was nothing short of catastrophic—and remains a problematic legacy. Moreover, the entire system was maintained by means of political repression. Especially under Stalin, Soviet control over Eastern Europe was harsh. There were periods of liberalization, but they were sporadic and temporary. The price of going beyond what the Soviets were willing to allow was demonstrated by the Soviet invasions of Hungary (1956) and Czechoslovakia (1968). Not until the end of the 1980s would the Eastern bloc experience real freedom.

Recovery in Western Europe

Economic recovery was more dramatic in Western Europe. As a first step, the European Recovery Plan (better known as the **Marshall Plan**) infused more than $13 billion into the economies of Western Europe. This infusion helped to rebuild the war-torn nations of Europe. It helped prevent the spread of communism. It also rewarded the United States, because this first dose of economic aid created healthy markets eager to buy U.S. goods.

Growth continued throughout the next two decades. A particular star was West Germany, which rose from the ruins of war to become Europe's economic powerhouse. Ironically, Great Britain, one of the victors of World War II, took a longer time than most European nations to recover (mainly because it had spent so much money fighting World War II). Industrial growth was high. Technological innovation allowed West European economies to move beyond industrial production to service, or postindustrial, modes of economic activity (the same was true in the United States).

As in Eastern Europe, most West European nations put into place social welfare systems or improved on the ones created during the 1920s and 1930s. Although they were not socialist or communist, many West European nations began to experiment with economic systems that were not purely capitalist either. This blend of capitalist and social-welfare (even mildly socialist) practice began to be called the "**third way**."

Not all developments in Western Europe were positive. Europe was caught in the crossfire of the superpowers' nuclear arms race. For a long time, Germany refused to come to grips with the Holocaust or its Nazi past. Democracies such as France and Italy, mired for decades in widespread official corruption, experienced frequent government turnover. France was rocked by the worldwide wave of **1968 protests** that struck not only Paris but also Mexico City, Prague, and universities throughout the United States. Mild authoritarianism and antiunionism persisted in countries such as Spain, Portugal, and Greece until after the mid-1970s. Great Britain wrestled with nationalist aspirations and, after the late 1960s, terrorism in Northern Ireland.

Economic Union in Western Europe

One way the West Europeans made up for their loss of global might was to devise various forms of union. Over time, the principle of union has enabled Europe to boost its economic strength, increase its diplomatic clout, and (less successfully) work together to prevent the outbreak of war or political extremism.

At first, efforts to unite were economic. In 1952, six nations (Belgium, Luxembourg, the Netherlands, Italy, France, and West Germany) formed the European Coal and Steel Community. In 1957, the same countries agreed to even stronger ties by establishing the European Economic Community, also known as the Common Market. The goal of the EEC was to eliminate internal tariffs and encourage the free movement of money, goods, services, and labor. Eventually renamed the **European Union**, the group expanded (Britain, Ireland, and Denmark joined in 1973, while others were admitted later) and strengthened its ties. By the mid-1990s, it included fifteen members and was moving toward monetary union (see Chapter 34).

Other regional organizations binding Western Europe together include the **North Atlantic Treaty Organization** (NATO, formed in 1949) and the Council of Europe (also 1949).

Economic Crisis During the 1970s

Economic crisis struck the Western world—the United States as well as Europe—in the early 1970s. In 1971, the United States was forced to detach the dollar from the gold standard. This move led to monetary instability across Western Europe, whose trade was so dependent on the U.S. currency. The **oil embargo** of 1973, imposed by the nations of the Middle East (from which Western Europe bought 70 percent of its oil), badly damaged the economies of Europe and the United States.

Both Western Europe and the United States suffered from inflation, recession, and unemployment.

Western Europe During the 1980s and 1990s

During the 1980s, many West European nations moved to the right, in an effort to escape the malaise of the 1970s. The elections of leaders such as Margaret Thatcher in Great Britain and Helmut Kohl in West Germany were part of this general trend. The same is true of the election of Ronald Reagan in the United States. Even France's first socialist president, François Mitterand, was forced to make concessions to the right.

In many West European countries, there was a partial retreat from the social-welfare systems of the past, as Thatcher and other leaders carried out **privatization** of state-run sectors of the economy. Overall, West Europe economies recovered during the 1980s and 1990s. To be sure, unemployment, poverty, socioeconomic inequality, and racial prejudice (stirred up by the large influx of non-European and East European immigration into Western Europe) were problems. Still, by the end of the Cold War, Western Europe was a region in which economic prosperity, healthy democratic government, and technological advancement could be taken largely—although not universally—for granted.

Major leaders of postwar Europe include Charles de Gaulle, president of France during the late 1950s and 1960s. France's most decorated World War II hero, de Gaulle was fiercely independent and resisted American domination of European affairs. Konrad Adenauer, chancellor of West Germany (1949–1963), restored Germany's place in the international community. Willy Brandt (1969–1974), also of West Germany, became famous for his policy of *Ostpolitik* (détente with Eastern Europe). Margaret Thatcher, the first female prime minister of Great Britain (1979–1990), moved British politics and economics to the right, dismantled and privatized much of Britain's nationalized social-welfare apparatus, and worked with Ronald Reagan (and later President George Bush) of the United States in opposing Soviet communism. In France, president François Mitterand (1981–1995) made the socialists, rather than the communists, the respectable voices of the French left wing. Helmut Kohl (1982–1998) of West Germany led his country to economic dominance during the 1980s. His enduring mark on German history is his reunification of East and West Germany in October 1990 after the collapse of communism in Eastern Europe.

DECOLONIZATION AND THE EMERGENCE OF THE DEVELOPING WORLD

One of the most powerful trends of the postwar era was the surge in importance of the **developing world** (also referred to in Cold War terms as the **Third World**). It consisted of nations in Latin America, Asia, Africa, and the Middle East that had lagged behind the countries of the West in economic and political development, had been kept under the political and economic thumb of foreign powers, or had been directly colonized.

Decolonization and National Liberation

Even before World War II, some steps had been taken to decolonize. Britain gave home rule to Ireland in 1922 thanks largely to an armed uprising there in 1916. In 1931, the Statute of Westminster transformed the British Empire into the British Commonwealth, whose members were entitled to varying degrees of autonomy. France and Britain began to allow some of their Middle Eastern mandates and protectorates greater freedom, if not actual independence, during the 1930s.

After World War II, **decolonization** and **national liberation** became major agents of change in Asia, the Middle East, and Africa. World War II pried loose the grip that countries such as Britain and France had kept on their empires even after World War I. From the 1940s through the 1970s, dozens of new nations came into being, having attained freedom from their imperial masters.

Another change in the developing world during the Cold War era was the overthrow (or attempted overthrow) of dictators and oligarchies, many of whom had been installed or supported by foreign governments or economic interests. This was especially the case in Latin America, the countries of which were nominally free but often influenced heavily by the United States. These political conflicts were often referred to as struggles for national liberation, just as actual decolonization campaigns were.

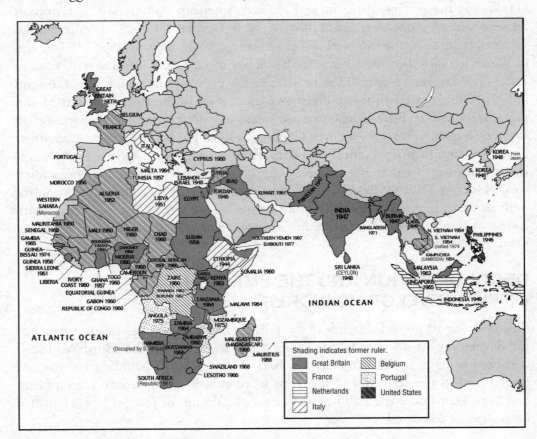

Decolonization and National Liberation in Africa and Asia After 1945.
World War II dealt the final blow to Europe's ability to maintain control over colonial empires. From the 1940s through the 1970s, a great wave of decolonization and national liberation swept Africa and Asia. Freedom was attained in a variety of ways—sometimes peacefully, sometimes by force.

Patterns of Decolonization

The means and results of decolonization varied from country to country. Specific cases are discussed in the geographical sections that follow. There was no set pattern to decolonization. Whether or not a newly liberated nation succeeded in building a healthy political and economic system depended on, among other things, the following questions:

- Did a newly decolonized nation have to fight a war to become free?
- How enlightened had the colonizing power been? Had it educated a native elite, leaving behind politicians, economists, and trained personnel with practical skills? Did the colonizing power assist actively with the transition to freedom? As a rule, Britain had a good record in this respect. To a lesser degree, France did as well.
- Were there serious ethnic, cultural, or religious divisions? In some countries, the colonizing power kept such tensions under control. Decolonization sometimes released them, leading to violence.
- Did a country have natural resources to exploit? Did the government exploit them efficiently? Former colonies that could not compete on the international market often suffered economic difficulties. Also, a newly liberated nation that did not diversify its economy but continued to rely on monoculture or the extraction of a small set of resources tended to recreate the same problems—a gap between rich and poor, economic backwardness, and environmental damage—that colonialism had caused.
- Did a newly liberated country take sides in the Cold War? Often, former colonies turned to one of the superpowers for economic and political support. Because their former masters were typically aligned with the United States and because the Marxist rhetoric of the Soviet Union (and as time passed, China) sounded appealing, many newly liberated countries turned at least for a while to the USSR (or less frequently, China). Superpowers often intervened in the affairs of decolonized nations.

THE MIDDLE EAST
General Patterns in the Postwar Middle East

Developments in the postwar Middle East were dominated mainly by the following factors:

- *The region's strategic and economic importance as the world's key source of petroleum.* Two-thirds of the world's crude oil is produced in the Middle East. The **Organization of Petroleum Exporting Countries** (OPEC), founded in 1960, is dominated by states from this area. Unfortunately, the wealth derived from oil has not led to the elimination of poverty or socio-economic inequality.
- *Contradictions between the urge to modernize and a desire to preserve Islamic tradition.* Long before the September 11, 2001, bombings, **Islamic fundamentalism** had been a force in the Middle East. One of the difficult questions facing the Middle East is how to balance Islamic heritage and Sharia law with progressive social and political practices such as democracy, civil liberties, secular law codes, and gender equality. In particular, how women are treated depends on how this issue is resolved.
- *The destabilizing effect of the Arab-Israeli conflict since 1948.* This remains an intractable, painful, and divisive issue, even into the twenty-first century.
- *Competition between the United States and the USSR for influence in the region during the Cold War.* The Middle Eastern states firmly in the U.S. camp were

Turkey and Israel. All others switched sides, back and forth, depending on where they thought their advantage lay.

- *Authoritarianism.* Dictatorship and human rights abuses have persisted, even in countries that are technically democratic.

Autonomy and Modernization

Even before World War II, the protectorates and mandates of the Middle East had gained freedom or greater autonomy. Saudi Arabia, Iraq, Jordan, Syria, and Lebanon were all free. Egypt and North Africa became independent during the 1950s and 1960s. Egyptian officers staged a coup against the pro-British king in 1952. Libya, taken from Italy by France and Britain during World War II, was also freed in 1952. Morocco and Tunisia gained freedom from France in 1956. Algeria, the African colony France was most unwilling to set free, fought a bitter war of independence from 1954 to 1962.

Turkey and Iran, already independent, continued on their paths toward modernization. More than any other Islamic state, Turkey has remained dedicated to secularism and Westernization. It has integrated itself into European markets, as well as the NATO alliance. Thus, Turkey has served as a gateway between the Western world and the Middle East. Iran did much the same but to a lesser extent and only until 1979, when its pro-Western government was overthrown.

Egypt Under Gamal Abdel Nasser

Independence, oil-based wealth, and geostrategic importance made the states of the Middle East more assertive in the 1950s and 1960s. The most famous example of this new **Arab nationalism** appeared in Egypt, which became an independent republic in 1952. By 1954, Colonel **Gamal Abdel Nasser** had taken control of the government.

A great booster of modernization, Nasser was a proponent of pan-Arabism and tried create a United Arab Republic joining all Arab nations together. This effort failed, but Nasser succeeded in modernizing his country. He also stood up to the West, nationalizing foreign-owned or foreign-controlled industries and businesses.

In 1956, Nasser took the bold step of declaring **Egyptian ownership of the Suez Canal**. This prompted the Suez Crisis, in which French, British, and Israeli troops tried to seize the canal. The United States and USSR, wishing to avoid serious armed conflict in the region, forced the three armies to withdraw, leaving the canal in Egyptian hands. The end result was a blow to British and French prestige, showing how the Cold War diminished European power.

Because Nasser was anti-British, he chose to strengthen ties with the USSR, at least temporarily. Soviet advisers and engineers brought technology and weaponry to Egypt; they also constructed the **Aswan Dam**, the world's largest. However, when the Soviets tried to control Egyptian politics, Nasser expelled them.

Nasser died in 1970. He was succeeded by Anwar Sadat, who drew Egypt closer to the United States and, in 1978, became the first Arab leader to recognize Israel. Sadat was assassinated by Islamic militants in 1981. Since then, Hosni Mubarak has served as president.

The Establishment of Israel and the Arab-Israeli Conflict

One of the most dramatic developments in the postwar Middle East was the **establishment of the State of Israel** (1948) as a homeland for the world's Jews. In 1917, Britain, which gained control over Palestine at the end of World War I, agreed in principle to create a Jewish state there but delayed this decision during the 1920s and 1930s in order to avoid Arab unrest.

After World War II and the horrors of the Holocaust, international sympathy for the Jews, along with strong U.S. support, led to the creation of Israel. Immediately, this stirred up Arab outrage and plunged the Middle East into war. The Israelis had to fight a war in 1948 simply to keep the state that had been given them. This had the effect of displacing Palestinian Arabs, who scattered to Jordan, Lebanon, and throughout the Middle East.

In 1964, the Palestinians gained a semblance of leadership with the foundation of the Palestinian Liberation Organization (PLO), a terrorist group and political movement led by **Yasser Arafat**.

The Arab states fought several wars against Israel, most notably the Six-Day War in 1967 and the Yom Kippur War in 1973. Each time, Israel, with a supremely trained, highly motivated army and strong backing from the United States, defeated the Arab coalitions, taking territory away from Arab states in the process. PLO terrorism was frequent; most infamously, a PLO squad assassinated members of the Israeli Olympic team in 1972.

Not until 1978, when **Anwar Sadat** of Egypt, encouraged by U.S. President Jimmy Carter, agreed with Israeli Prime Minister **Menachem Begin** to recognize Israel in exchange for the return of the Sinai Peninsula, was there an end to outright war in the region. Following Egypt's lead, a number of moderate Arab states began to recognize Israel during the 1980s.

However, problems remained. Throughout the 1980s, the Palestinian population of Israel staged a continuous uprising called the **intifada**. These demonstrations and protests often led to bloodshed. At the same time, terrorist groups acted against Israel as well. Terrorist attacks placed Israel in a difficult position: To avoid a total breakdown of security, it—despite being a democracy, committed to human rights—felt compelled to use violence against civilian agitators, who, while hostile and sometimes dangerous, were poorly armed and often minors.

In 1993 and 1994, the Israelis and Palestinians signed historic peace agreements, one of which called for Palestinian self-rule in parts of Israel. The United States attempted throughout the 1990s to mediate between the two sides and to keep the peace process alive. Nonetheless, tensions remained high, and the peace effort collapsed in 2001, amid violence from both sides.

Iran and Iraq

The most powerful dictatorships in the Middle East were those of Iran and Iraq. Since the 1920s, Iran had been ruled by the secular, modernizing Pahlavi shahs. The last shah, **Mohammad Reza Pahlavi**, ruled from 1941 to 1979. He used Iran's oil wealth to industrialize and modernize. Like the Turkish government, the shah's regime opposed Islamic traditionalism, encouraging Western dress, Western education, the unveiling of women, and the eradication of Sharia law. The shah became an ally of the United States.

Unfortunately, the shah relied on repression to carry out modernization: dissidents were ruthlessly suppressed by the secret police (SAVAK), and the regime was decidedly antidemocratic. By 1979, the shah was in poor health, and his popularity had plummeted; he was seen by many as an American puppet and a disrespecter of Islam. He left the country to seek medical treatment and died of cancer in 1980.

In the meantime, in 1979, the Shiite cleric **Ayatollah Ruhollah Khomeini**, an Islamic fundamentalist the shah had exiled years before, returned to Iran and took control of the country. This **Iranian Revolution** transformed the country into an anti-Western (particularly anti-U.S.), theocratic dictatorship. Famously, the new regime held American hostages captive from 1979 to 1981. At the same time, Iran went to war with neighboring Iraq. The Iran-Iraq War lasted from 1980 to 1988, and devastated both countries. Khomeini died in 1989. The theocracy he created remains in place. Compared with other major revolutions of the modern era, the Iranian Revolution is unusual, if not unique, in being antimodern and religiously based.

Iraq came under the control of **Saddam Hussein** and his Baath Party in 1979. Although his title was president, Hussein became one of the Middle East's most powerful dictators. Originally sponsored by the United States because of his opposition to Iran, Hussein turned his brutality against his own people, his neighbors, and the United States. During his war with Iran, he used poison gas, drafted teenaged children to fight, and killed many civilians. He viciously persecuted Iraq's Kurdish minority.

In 1990, Hussein invaded the oil-rich state of Kuwait and appeared ready to move against Saudi Arabia. In the first major conflict of the post–Cold War era, the first **Gulf War** (1991), the United States led a military coalition to push Hussein out of Kuwait. Between 1991 and 2003, the United Nations imposed trade sanctions, backed by U.S. and allied military action, to prevent Iraq's development of weapons of mass destruction (and to compel Hussein to allow weapons inspections). Hussein's regime was overthrown in a U.S.-led war in 2003.

AFRICA

Decolonization began in Africa mainly during the 1950s and 1960s, somewhat later than in the Middle East or Asia. By the late 1990s, Africa would contain forty-six countries. Security and economic stability in most of them are still affected by the legacy of colonialism.

National Liberation in North Africa

The Islamic states of North Africa became free during the 1950s. Egypt declared independence in 1952, as did Libya. Morocco and Tunisia gained freedom from France in 1956. The long and painful **Algerian War of Independence** (1954–1962) against France completed the process of lifting the colonial yoke from North Africa.

North African states had several advantages over sub-Saharan Africa when it came to decolonization. They were largely, although not completely, homogeneous in terms of religion, ethnicity, and language. They had existed as meaningful political units for a long time, making the transition to nation-state easier. Their colonizing powers also left behind technology and industrial infrastructures (railroads, telegraphs, canals, roads) that proved economically useful, especially in Algeria and Egypt.

Independence in Sub-Saharan Africa

The nations of sub-Saharan Africa had more of a struggle to create successful independent states. Major freedom movements began during the 1940s, in South Africa (the African National Congress); the Gold Coast, or Ghana (Kwame Nkrumah); and Kenya (Jomo Kenyatta).

For the most part, these were nonviolent movements led by intellectuals and labor activists. There were, however, exceptions. The Mau Mau movement in Kenya departed from Kenyatta's approach and killed almost 2,000 people in the 1950s. Violence played a substantial part in the decolonization of Zimbabwe (Rhodesia), South Africa, Rwanda, Zaire (the Belgian Congo), Angola, and Mozambique.

Varying Transitions to Freedom

For the most part, decolonization in the parts of Africa that had been British and French went smoothly. Both Britain and France prepared their colonies for freedom by educating native elites, allowing greater native representation in transitional governments, and minimizing the possibility of interethnic conflict.

Not all went well, however. In Rhodesia, a white-controlled government declared independence from Britain in 1965. It harshly repressed black natives, who responded with violence. Only after a savage conflict was Rhodesia placed under native rule, in 1980, when the country renamed itself Zimbabwe. South African independence from Britain involved serious problems as well.

The worst transitions to independence were made by Belgian and Portuguese colonies. Here, the imperial masters had been particularly exploitative, and neither country took steps to prepare its colonies for independence. Guinea-Bissau gained freedom from Portugal in 1974 but only after a vicious guerrilla war. Angola fought a war of liberation against Portugal from 1961 to 1975. After achieving independence, Angola suffered years of civil war. Likewise, Mozambique fought Portugal from 1965 to 1975, only to descend into a long civil conflict.

Belgium pulled out of Rwanda in 1962, having artificially exacerbated differences between two tribes, the Hutu and Tutsi, who came to hate each other deeply. When the Belgians freed the Congo, postindependence violence was so pervasive from 1960 to 1964 that the United Nations had to intervene. The prime mover in the Congolese independence movement, the Marxist Patrice Lumumba, was assassinated by political rivals (almost certainly with U.S. knowledge, if not complicity) in late 1965.

South Africa and the Experience of Apartheid

As in Rhodesia/Zimbabwe, but for much longer, decolonization in South Africa was tainted by the clash between white and black citizens of the newly free country. The government that declared freedom from Britain was controlled by the white minority, largely descended from Dutch Boers. These Afrikaners practiced the policy of **apartheid** (extreme racial segregation). South Africa is one of the world's richest sources of gold and diamonds. Between the 1960s and the 1990s, the white government of South Africa turned the country into the wealthiest, most modern, and most industrialized on the continent.

However, South Africa became one of Africa's most repressive nations as well. By the 1980s, internal unrest, economic problems, and international revulsion were placing pressure on the South African government to abandon apartheid. The Zulu Confederation, the African National Congress (ANC), and other such groups opposed the white government. The ANC's leader, **Nelson Mandela**, gained the status of sympathetic dissident during his long imprisonment (1964–1990) by the white authorities. His wife, Winnie Mandela, continued the struggle on his behalf. Another moral figure in the antiapartheid movement was Bishop **Desmond Tutu**, a black clergyman in the Anglican Church and a Nobel Peace Prize recipient. In 1990, the government released Nelson Mandela. In 1994, free elections resulted in the ANC's victory. Mandela became the country's president.

Problems Facing Independent Africa

Unfortunately, many of Africa's original aspirations proved difficult if not impossible to attain. Few nations managed to achieve democratic governments, open societies, and economies that led to prosperity for all (or even many) citizens. Some of the problems that have interfered with African modernization include the following:

- *Dictatorship*: Despite beginning as democratic systems, many of Africa's governments degenerated into strongman regimes. Among the most notorious were Idi Amin of Uganda (1971–1979) and Mobutu Sese Seko of Zaire (1965–1997).
- *Corruption*: Dictatorial or not, many African regimes tended to function according to unlawful systems of patronage, nepotism, and graft.
- *Failure to modernize and diversify economies*: Rather than industrialize and diversify, many African regimes generated wealth by continuing to export the natural resources their former colonial masters took from them. This enabled foreign investors great control over African politics. It also kept profits in the hands of political rulers, rather than spreading wealth among the population at large.
- *The Cold War*: As with the rest of the developing world, many African nations became pawns in the global chess game between the United States and USSR.
- *Rapid population growth and food shortages*: The rate of African population growth has outstripped the rate of economic growth. Systems of food distribution are often inadequate, leading to food shortages and famine. The worst famines have been in Somalia and Ethiopia.
- *The HIV/AIDS pandemic*: From the 1980s onward, the HIV virus, which seems to have originated in Africa, has caused millions of deaths. Containing the virus has proven impossible, and African nations are too poor to afford large quantities of the medicines needed to treat it.

- *Lack of cultural or linguistic unity.* In Africa, the lines determining a nation's political borders often do not match where people of certain ethnicities or languages live. Most borders were drawn by European colonizers for their own benefit and convenience, leaving behind confusing varieties of ethnicities, languages, cultural practices, and religions in each country. This makes it difficult for a single state to govern all its people fairly.
- *Intertribal and interethnic conflict.* Frequently, the above problem becomes serious enough that it breaks out into violence. Since the colonial period, most of the wars in Africa have been fought within national borders, not between different countries.
- *Uncontrolled flow of small arms and light weapons.* Although this is a problem throughout the developing world, it is particularly dire in Africa. Small arms feature prominently in armed conflicts, postconflict situations, and everyday life. Thousands of children have been forcibly drafted into militias and paramilitaries.
- *Treatment of women:* In Africa's more developed countries and especially in the cities, women have attained a certain degree of economic and social equality: the right to an education, the right to work, the right to legal divorce and birth control, and so on. However, progress has been slow, and women are still dominated by men, especially in rural areas. In some regions, polygamy is still permitted. One infamous custom, clitoridectomy (female circumcision), is still practiced in some parts of Africa.

ASIA

Among the nations of the developing world, those of Asia have been the most successful in building stable governments and attaining economic prosperity. Regional organizations, notably the Association of Southeast Asian Nations (ASEAN, formed in 1967), have boosted economic, social, and cultural developments and cooperation among their members. Nonetheless, political repression, interethnic and interreligious strife, socioeconomic inequality, and periodic economic crises have caused problems as well. The Cold War also played a role in creating tensions.

The Philippines

In South and Southeast Asia, decolonization campaigns began immediately after World War II. Some were ended quickly, others dragged on. Almost all involved some degree of violence. The first colony in the region to be freed was the Philippines, which, during World War II, had been promised independence from the United States. Freedom was granted voluntarily in 1946. The United States hoped that this would provide an example to colonial powers such as France and Britain.

Indian and Pakistani Independence

India and Pakistan gained their independence next. In this case, Britain handed over power freely. In 1945, the British viceroy, Lord Louis Mountbatten, was ordered to prepare to transfer government to "responsible Indian hands" by 1948. Riots and disturbances, mainly consisting of clashes between Muslims and Hindus, sped up the British timetable.

Indian and Pakistani independence was granted on August 15, 1947. Although the British did not have to be expelled by force, independence still led to violence. Hindu-Muslim conflict cost at least a million lives. In January 1948, **Mohandas (Mahatma) Gandhi**, spiritual leader of the Indian freedom movement, was assassinated by a Hindu extremist who opposed his rhetoric of tolerance between the two faiths.

Despite their difficult beginnings, both nations survived. Pakistan became a modern Islamic republic and a major regional power. However, the original goal of its founder, **Muhammad Ali Jinnah**, has not been attained. Jinnah dreamed of a democratic, modernizing republic that could also remain true to Muslim traditions. Instead, Pakistan has been plagued by corruption, political repression, and military rule. It has also been caught up in a costly and dangerous diplomatic rivalry with its neighbor India. Both India and Pakistan developed nuclear-weapons capability during the 1990s, making their conflict even tenser.

Modern India

India has turned itself into the world's largest democracy. On the other hand, it has also suffered from sprawling inefficiency, an inability to balance population growth with economic growth, and interethnic and interfaith strife. The dominant political force in free India was the Congress Party, led by **Jawaharlal Nehru**, who served as India's prime minister from 1947 until his death in 1964. Unlike Gandhi, who had favored traditional Hindu values (although not religious bigotry) and economic simplicity, Nehru wanted to secularize India and turn it into a modern, educated industrial power.

Diplomatically, Nehru negotiated a difficult position: neighbor to a hostile China and an even more hostile Pakistan and not wishing to be a client of the Soviets, the British, or the United States, Nehru maintained a friendly, cooperative relationship with the USSR, without actually falling into the Soviet camp. As Sukarno had done in Indonesia (see below), Nehru preserved his country's status as a nonaligned nation.

From 1966 to 1975 and again from 1977 to 1984, Nehru's daughter, Indira Gandhi, was prime minister. She continued her father's policies of modernization and political **nonalignment**. Religious strife was her downfall. Her government's actions against the Sikh minority of Punjab provoked Sikh soldiers to assassinate her. From 1984 to 1991, her son, Rajiv Gandhi, served as prime minister, before being killed by Sri Lankan separatists. Since 1991, India's democratic government has continued to struggle with the same problems that Nehru and his descendants did—althogh the country has enjoyed a boom in high-tech industries like computers and film making.

After freeing India, Britain let go of its Southeast Asian colonies. Burma became independent in 1948, Malaysia in 1957, Singapore (which had been attached to Malaysia) in 1965. Hong Kong remained in British hands until 1997, when it was returned to mainland China.

Indonesia

Less willingly than the British, the Dutch and French were forced out of Southeast Asia. After World War II, the Netherlands retained control over the Dutch East Indies, or Indonesia. The charismatic leader of the Indonesian Nationalist Party, **Sukarno**, began to agitate for freedom, and a war of national liberation began in 1945. Afraid that continued combat would lead to a communist takeover of the region, the United States persuaded the Dutch to hand over freedom.

The new nation of Indonesia was born in 1949, with Sukarno as its leader. A huge archipelago, Indonesia is one of the world's largest and most populous nations. It is linguistically and ethnically diverse, although 80 percent of the population is Muslim. At first Sukarno governed democratically, but he became authoritarian over time. Like Nehru, he pursued a nonaligned foreign policy but was far more radical in calling for the Third World to defy the West. Eventually, he drew closer to the Indonesian Communist Party. In 1965, the army, allied with conservative Muslims, staged a coup against Sukarno. It turned into a popular uprising, in which as many as half a million people—mainly Communists—were killed. Sukarno was weakened by the coup, then forced out of office in 1967.

From 1967 to 1998, Indonesia was governed by a military strongman, Suharto. A dictatorial ruler with a record of frequent human-rights abuses, Suharto promoted economic growth, anticommunism, and alliance with the United States.

Vietnam, Laos, and Cambodia

The French attempted for almost a decade to hold on to their colony of Indochina (Vietnam, Laos, and Cambodia). In September 1945, the Vietnamese nationalist and communist **Ho Chi Minh** declared independence. Encouraged by the U.S. promise of freedom to the Philippines and proud of his movement's record of anti-Japanese resistance during World War II, Ho Chi Minh hoped that freedom would be granted without a struggle.

Instead, the French, with U.S. support, tried until 1954 to keep Indochina. Defeated by Vietnamese expertise in guerrilla warfare, the French withdrew. Laos, Cambodia, and Vietnam were given their independence. Vietnam was temporarily divided into a northern communist-dominated zone and a southern noncommunist zone.

Elections were to be held as soon as possible, but the French-educated, Catholic, U.S.-backed leader of South Vietnam, Ngo Dinh Diem, refused to allow elections, knowing that the Buddhist, anti-French peasant masses would vote against him. The North Vietnamese began to fight the south in 1959.

By the early 1960s, the United States was providing substantial military support for South Vietnam; it continued its military intervention for years. In 1968, the United States suffered a serious public-relations setback when the communists staged the Tet Offensive, catching the Americans and South Vietnamese off guard. America scaled back its war effort, withdrawing its troops in 1973. In April 1975, the communists captured the South Vietnamese capital and, with much violence, unified the country under their rule.

Militarism and Authoritarianism in Southeast Asia

Military or authoritarian government became the rule throughout much of Southeast Asia. The Communist **Khmer Rouge** movement in Cambodia took power and carried out a hideous reign of terror that claimed as many as 2 million victims. The U.S.-backed regime of Ferdinand Marcos, which governed the Philippines until the early 1980s, violated civil rights and was extravagantly corrupt. Myanmar (Burma) and Thailand came under military rule. As noted above, Indonesia was heavily authoritarian. Even prosperous and ultramodern Singapore, under prime minister Lee Kuan-yew, emphasized conformity and tradition over freedom and civil liberties.

Japan After World War II

Modernization came to the major nations of East Asia. Japan became the region's surprise powerhouse, just as West Germany, one of the defeated powers of World War II, became the economic dynamo of postwar Europe. At its peak during the 1980s, the Japanese economy was the world's third most productive, after the United States's and West Germany's. Per capita income was among the world's highest, and social services such as education and health care were excellent.

After World War II, Japan was occupied by the U.S. armed forces, which presided over democratic constitutional reform (1947) and the demilitarization of the country. The United States viewed Japan as a strategic anchor of its Cold War policy in Asia and invested in it heavily, both militarily and economically. Politically, Japan became a parliamentary democracy; although the emperor retained his symbolic role, the Diet (parliament) ran the government.

The Liberal Democratic Party came to dominate party politics, and while Japan's democratic system never ceased to function, the Liberal Democrats' influence over the Diet led some commentators to view Japan as slightly oligarchic. Much of Japan's postwar success depended on its population's dedicated work ethic and, through the 1980s, its willingness to place the needs of Japanese society above the desires of the individual.

The 1990s, however, brought not only an economic recession and revelations of deep-seated government corruption but also changes in social attitudes. Younger generations are less willing to conform, to work as selflessly as their parents and grandparents, or to accept traditional social roles. A desire for greater gender equality, in a society where women have generally been expected to play secondary and supporting roles, has also taken hold.

Taiwan, South Korea, and the "Little Tigers"

Like Japan, but to a lesser extent, Taiwan (the Republic of China) and South Korea developed prosperous and free societies. From the 1950s through the 1970s, neither Taiwan nor South Korea was truly democratic. Instead, they were anticommunist regimes that, while parliamentary, concentrated power in the hands of one dominant party. In the case of Taiwan, this was the Nationalist Party (Kuomintang) that had been defeated by Mao's Chinese Communist Party in 1949. Chiang Kai-shek remained in control of the Kuomintang—and thus Taiwan—until his death in 1975. By the end of the 1970s, Taiwan began to democratize.

South Korea remained authoritarian until 1987, when free elections were held. Despite their less than democratic nature, both Taiwan and South Korea became allies of the United States because of their staunch anticommunism. They also became economic success stories; along with Hong Kong, Singapore, and Thailand, they became known as the **"little tigers"** for their economic strength (as distinct from the great "tiger" of the Japanese economy).

Both Taiwan and South Korea were important to the United States's Cold War strategic posture. In 1950–1953, the United States spearheaded the United Nations coalition that kept South Korea safe from North Korean invasion. In the 1970s, even though the United States was forced to disclaim its formal recognition of Taiwan in order to establish ties with the People's Republic of China, the U.S.-Taiwanese relationship has remained strong, both politically and economically.

North Korea

Communism came to North Korea after World War II, when the country was divided by the Americans and Soviets. From the 1940s onward, North Korea has remained one of the most isolated and rigidly dictatorial societies on earth. Its longtime leader, **Kim Il Sung** (1948–1994), was an uncompromising Stalinist and ruthlessly oppressive. To the present day, North Korea retains its communist system, although economic collapse and its insistence on maintaining a huge military (which now includes a nuclear-missile capacity) have placed the population in danger of mass starvation.

The People's Republic of China

The People's Republic of China, established in 1949 by **Mao Tse-tung** and the Chinese Communist Party (CCP), has been the most populous communist nation on earth for more than five decades. Like the rest of East Asia, China has modernized, although not as consistently.

China was ruled by Mao from 1949 until his death in 1976. At first, Mao seemed to want to carry out pragmatic social and economic reform. His New Democracy of the early 1950s was greeted with some enthusiasm, as were his initial land reforms. His first Five-Year Plan (1953–1958), which imitated the USSR's five-year plans, led to industrial growth. Collectivization of agriculture began in 1955 but was (at first!) carried out more gradually than Stalin's collectivization of the late 1920s and early 1930s.

On the other hand, Mao's radical transformation of society, which included persecution of dissenters and so-called class enemies (members of the bourgeoisie or aristocracy), was harsh. Also, his aspirations became overly ambitious by the end of the 1950s, and he pressed too quickly for further modernization. In 1958, Mao began the **Great Leap Forward**, which included a rapid industrial buildup, even more grandiose than the Five-Year Plan's. In the agricultural sphere, it intensified collectivization and called for an unrealistic increase in food production. The trauma, stress, and confusion caused by the Great Leap Forward led to chaos and breakdown in industry. Even worse, agriculture collapsed altogether. The famines that resulted in 1959 and 1960 killed millions (the best estimate is 15 to 20 million). The Great Leap Forward was halted in 1960 but not before the damage was done. It caused splits within the CCP leadership, and opposition to Mao grew. (An interesting exercise is to compare Mao's method of rapid modernization to Stalin's.)

In 1966, Mao embarked on another program of radical modernization, the **Great Proletarian Cultural Revolution**, which lasted until 1976. This has been interpreted by historians as a policy used by Mao and his wife, Jiang Qing (the movement's primary architect), to strike at their political enemies, and also to instill absolute revolutionary purity within Chinese society and culture. Censorship was absolute, and indoctrination was crushingly heavy. The one acceptable source of all wisdom was *The Little Red Book*, a collection of Mao's sayings. Young communist activists, known as Red Guards, rampaged throughout the country denouncing and putting on trial any person—university professors, factory foremen, heads of collective farms, writers and journalists, and even politicians—whom they considered to be untrue to revolutionary communist ideals. Victims were demoted, harassed, often arrested and sent to labor camps for "reeducation," and sometimes executed. Even members of the CCP elite were not immune; among those arrested was Deng Xiaoping.

The Cultural Revolution ended with Mao's death in 1976. In 1978, **Deng Xiaoping**, having defeated Mao's widow and her allies (known afterward as the Gang of Four), came to power. Like Mao, Deng was a modernizer. However, while Mao had been inflexible and revolutionary, the pragmatic Deng was more concerned with China's well-being and growing strength than with absolute commitment to abstract Marxist ideals. Famously, he commented that whether a cat is black or white makes no difference, as long as it catches mice.

In contrast to Mao's anticapitalism, Deng allowed limited free-market reform and returned land to the farmers that Mao had communized. As a result, China experienced huge economic growth throughout the 1980s. Wages and standards of living improved. There was, however, a social and cultural effect as well. With greater wealth came the desire for greater freedom, a luxury Deng was not prepared to allow. By the end of the 1980s, China would have to deal with this growing problem. One of this era's most interesting comparisons is the success of Deng's reforms with the failure of Gorbachev's perestroika campaign.

LATIN AMERICA

Dictatorship and Economic Exploitation in Latin America

Latin America had freed itself from colonial domination in the 1800s, so national liberation and modernization here involved the struggle against dictatorship at home and the political and economic influence of the United States.

The Great Depression, despite its generally negative impact, compelled Latin American nations to diversify their economies somewhat. World War II also forced a number of the interwar period's dictators out of power. However, despite some temporary progress toward economic modernization and democratization during the late 1940s and early 1950s, many Latin American countries reverted to exploitative economies and dictatorial government from the late 1950s through the early 1980s. Moreover, in Latin America, "modernization" often led to a concentration of wealth in the hands of a narrow social stratum and weak social justice for the working classes and indigenous peoples.

Military governments and right-wing dictatorships appeared during these decades. By the mid-1970s, only Colombia, Venezuela, and Costa Rica could be considered democratic.

In 1943, military rule was established in Argentina. By 1946, the charismatic **Juan Perón** had come to dominate the military government by appealing to the poor. His wife, **Eva**, whose appeal among the lower-class *descamisados* ("shirtless ones") was great, helped him in this. During the 1950s, Perón became increasingly right-wing, even fascistic. He was overthrown by the army in 1955 and fled to Spain. Perón's popularity remained so high, however, that he was able to return in 1973 and become president until his death in 1974. A brutal military regime ruled from 1976 to 1983. This regime ruthlessly purged leftists, intellectuals, and dissidents, causing at least 30,000 to "disappear" over a decade and a half.

Brazil and Chile also had military regimes from the mid-1960s through the mid-1980s. In Chile, General **Augusto Pinochet** (backed by the U.S. Central Intelligence Agency) led a 1973 coup against the left-wing government of Salvador Allende—who, in 1970, had become one of the few Marxist politicians to come to power by means of democratic election. Pinochet remained in charge until the late 1980s. Like the military dictators of Argentina, Pinochet held the reins of power tightly, using force and violence to eliminate enemies and dissidents.

Mexico, although nominally democratic, was really an authoritarian oligarchy run by the **Institutional Revolutionary Party** (PRI). Its ability to keep the oil-based Mexican economy healthy during the 1950s and 1960s made the PRI's less than democratic nature acceptable to most Mexicans. By the end of the 1960s, however, economic stress, as well as the rising resentment of Indians, Mayans, and other minorities, who felt they were being treated as second-class citizens, stirred up discontent with the government.

The **1968 protests** shook Mexico City (as they did Paris, Prague, and many U.S. universities), showing how the PRI's democratic facade was wearing thin. By the 1980s, the Mexican government was starting to reform gradually but not completely.

Fidel Castro and the Cuban Revolution

Dictatorship from the left appeared in Cuba. In January 1959, the revolutionary movement led by **Fidel Castro** overthrew the right-wing dictator Fulgencio Batista. Within months, Castro had begun to nationalize industry and carry out land reform. His goals were to modernize, industrialize, increase literacy rates, and eliminate socioeconomic inequality. With his second-in-command, the Argentine radical Ernesto "Che" Guevara, he also wanted to combat what he saw as U.S. imperialism in Latin America. Accordingly, the Cuban revolutionaires declared themselves Marxists and turned to the Soviet Union for assistance.

Because of its proximity to the United States, Cuba became a Cold War hot spot from 1961 onward, as demonstrated by the Bay of Pigs incident (1961) and the **Cuban Missile Crisis** (1962). Domestically, the Castro regime's record is mixed. It is undeniable that Cuba has modernized under Castro, and the gap between rich and poor that had prevailed under Batista narrowed considerably. Educational levels have improved, and women (at least officially) are treated with greater equality than before. However, Castro's regime has been rigidly dictatorial and has violated human rights for more than four decades.

Latin America as Cold War Battlefield

Many problems plagued Latin America during the 1970s and early 1980s. Almost all of the military dictatorships found themselves heavily in debt, especially to the United States. Latin America had also become a great Cold War battlefield. Cuba, both on its own and on behalf of the USSR, consistently attempted to export Marxist revolution throughout Latin America. The Soviet Union did the same. For its part, the United States, fearing the spread of leftism directly to its south, made a practice of supporting any Latin American regime that opposed communism. Unfortunately, pro-U.S. regimes in Latin America tended to be right-wing and dictatorial.

One of the clearest examples of how Cold War politics were played out in Latin America during these years was the **Nicaraguan Revolution**. In 1979, the Marxist, Soviet-supported Sandinista movement overthrew the right-wing Somoza dictatorship that had ruled (with U.S. support) since 1937. In response, the U.S. government began to support a right-wing, counterrevolutionary guerrilla movement known as the Contras. In essence, the struggle between the Sandinista government and the Contra movement, both of whom were responsible for political abuses, was a proxy war between the Soviets and the Americans.

Democratization in Latin America

During the late 1980s and early 1990s, a wave of democratization swept Latin America. Much of it was tied to economic improvements, but just as much was due to the cooling down of the Cold War, which reduced the superpowers' anxiety about influence in the region. In addition, the Organization of American States (OAS), a regional organization of approximately forty countries, has promoted democratization, peace, and security in the region.

Argentina's dictatorship fell in 1983, and a free election peacefully handed power over in 1989. Brazil's dictatorship collapsed in 1985. Mexican elections in 1988 prompted the PRI to loosen its monopoly on power. The controversial Pinochet lost power in Chile in 1989.

One of the few exceptions to this trend was Cuba, where Castro's communist regime remained in power, despite the fall of communism in Eastern Europe and the USSR. Latin America's transition to democracy is still not complete. Corruption, backsliding toward authoritarian practice, the widespread economic dependence on illicit drug trafficking (especially in Colombia), and economic instability have troubled many of the region's new democracies. Nonetheless, the struggle to move toward democracy—or continue in that direction—continues.

Social Developments, Cultural Changes, and Intellectual Trends

CHAPTER 33

- The modern versus the postmodernist (contemporary) period
- Postindustrial (service and high-tech) economies
- Economic globalization (multinational corporations and international trade agreements)
- Socio-economic features of the developed world
- The developing (third) world and the north-south split
- Population growth and modern migration
- Social activism and nongovernmental organizations (NGOs)
- Women's liberation and feminism
- Multiculturalism versus Americanization
- Mass-media technology, the computer, and the information (digital) revolution
- Scientific advancements (quantum physics, genetics, rocketry, computers, robotics)

The twentieth and twenty-first centuries have witnessed an explosion of social, cultural, and intellectual changes. The pace of scientific and technological advancement is faster than ever before. The world's population has grown with breathtaking speed. The world's economies have become increasingly interconnected.

Different parts of the world experienced these transformations differently. As a general rule, the changes of the twentieth and twenty-first centuries can be said to have proceeded along four basic tracks:

- In Western Europe, the United States, and Canada—the West—and Australia and New Zealand, movement has been toward stable democratization, greater economic prosperity, thorough urbanization, commitment to social equality and individual liberties, and the creation of social welfare systems. Scientific and technological achievement has been tremendous. These nations have developed postindustrial economies that emphasize services, consumerism, and cutting-edge technology (especially biotech and computers).

- Prosperous nations in Asia—the so-called tigers, such as Japan and, to a lesser extent, Taiwan, South Korea, Indonesia, and Singapore—have made great strides toward economic and technological modernization. They have urbanized greatly and developed a variety of social services. Their economies are postindustrial and high-tech. In many respects, Japan has equaled or surpassed the West (even though its phenomenal economic growth slowed during the 1990s). However, these societies, although nominally democratic, have been relatively slow to embrace or even tolerate the diversity and individualism that have been the hallmarks of Western societies during the late 1800s and 1900s.
- The Soviet Union and Eastern Europe modernized economically, especially during the postwar era. They urbanized and developed social welfare services. Technological and scientific advancement was considerable. However, Soviet and East European economies remained industrial rather than postindustrial and, in terms of technological finesse (especially with regard to computers), were cruder than Western economies. Moreover, until the collapse of communism in this region from 1989 to 1991, political systems were dictatorial and repressive. Even after the collapse of communism, it has been difficult for this region to move toward democracy and economic prosperity.
- The developing nations of Asia, Africa, the Middle East, and Latin America are all, to one degree or another, striving to attain advanced economic systems, modern societies, and representative forms of government. Some have made progress, attaining a relatively high level of prosperity or functioning democracies, or both. Others are mired in backwardness, poverty, civil war, and dictatorship. Most are somewhere in between. Perhaps the most distinctive case is the People's Republic of China. Communist China has the geography, population, and military capacity of a major power, and its economic growth has been considerable from the 1980s onward. The government is still authoritarian, however, and social and economic progress remains uneven.

With regard to historical labels, it is common to speak of the **modern period** (ca. 1800–1945) as having come to an end, at least in the more developed West. The postwar era and the early twenty-first century are generally referred to by historians as the **contemporary** or **postmodern era**. The modern era was characterized by industrialization, the formation of the nation-state as the primary form of political organization, and the struggle for representative government and economic equality. The postmodern era is characterized by postindustrial and global forms of economic organization, multiculturalism and the blurring of national lines, and an extreme individualism that takes for granted the political and social equality won during the modern era.

One can argue convincingly that this description suits the Western world well. It is more difficult to fit the label "postmodern" to the less developed nations of Africa, Asia, Latin America, and the Middle East, many of which are still in the process of modernizing. This unevenness of social, political, and economic development is in and of itself a major characteristic of twentieth- and twenty-first-century world history.

ECONOMIC GLOBALIZATION

International Trade Before World War II

Systems of international trade had existed long before the twentieth century, and the scope and volume of that trade grew steadily between World War I and the **Great Depression** of the 1930s. The Depression sparked a wave of **protectionism**, as countries sought to shield their own industries and farms by imposing high tariffs on other nations' goods. The most notorious example of protectionism was the United States' **Smoot-Hawley Tariff Act** (1930). This act is widely considered to have spread the Depression to Europe, Latin America, and Asia by destroying the ability of these regions to export goods to the United States. World War II altered the patterns of international commerce in obvious ways.

Foundations of the Post-World War II Economic System

True globalization of the world economy began after World War II. Franklin Roosevelt, guided by the economic principles of John Maynard Keynes (and the convictions of Woodrow Wilson before him), believed that free trade was the key not only to economic prosperity but also to world peace. Nations whose economies interacted equitably, he felt, would be less likely to go to war.

In July 1944, Roosevelt met with Allied delegates at Bretton Woods, New Hampshire. It was here that the International Bank for Reconstruction and Development (the **World Bank**) and the **International Monetary Fund** (IMF), whose purpose was to rebuild Europe and lend assistance to countries in Asia, Africa, and Latin America, were created. In 1958, the first round of the **General Agreement on Tariffs and Trade** (GATT) was held, to establish the working rules governing imports, exports, and economic interaction among participating nations. The Soviet Union and the Eastern bloc refused to join this **Bretton Woods System**, and so their economies were cut off from much of the rest of the world's. Until the international economic crises of the 1970s, currency exchanges were fixed to the value of the U.S. dollar, the world's strongest. In turn, the U.S. dollar was based on the gold standard.

Varieties of Economic Development, 1940s–1970s

Over time, great prosperity came to the United States, Canada, Japan, and the nations of Western Europe. One way Western Europe staged its economic recovery was through **economic union** (the European Coal and Steel Community, the European Economic Community, the European Union), as described in Chapter 32. The reconstruction of war-torn Western Europe—particularly West Germany—was nothing short of incredible. The same was true of Japan.

The rest of the world developed unevenly. In Latin America and Africa, many governments relied on the export of small sets of natural resources or crops, just as they had done as colonies or economic dependents during the 1800s. The Middle East benefited from its dominance on oil production. The **Organization of Petroleum Exporting Countries** (OPEC), formed in 1960, consists mainly of Mideastern nations. OPEC has been one of the most successful and influential international economic coalitions in history.

The economies of the Soviet Union, its East European allies, and Communist China tended to remain largely but not completely isolated from the Western world.

Many nations in Asia, such as Japan, Taiwan, South Korea, Indonesia, and Singapore, were quick to adapt to global capitalism. As Western Europe had done, many Asian nations joined together in regional economic associations. Although the **Association of Southeast Asian Nations** (ASEAN), formed in 1967, was mainly a diplomatic group, it also tightened economic ties. The Asia-Pacific Economic Cooperation Group (1989) did the same.

A general economic crisis struck most of the world during the 1970s. OPEC's **oil embargo** severely affected the energy-dependent economies of the West. Recession and inflation plagued the United States and Western Europe. Although the USSR had its own oil reserves and was safe from OPEC's embargo, inefficiency, food shortages, the cost of the arms race, and governmental corruption sapped the economies of the Eastern bloc. In 1971, President Richard Nixon rocked the international community by taking the U.S. dollar off the gold standard.

Multinational Corporations

Nevertheless, Western economies recovered during the mid-to-late 1980s. Part of this recovery involved the growing strength of **multinational corporations**: huge conglomerates that, while technically "from" a single country, maintained factories, subsidiaries, and distribution networks all over the world, employing foreign workers and selling directly to foreign markets.

For years, the activities of these multinational corporations had been laying the groundwork for further globalization of the economy during the 1980s and 1990s. Critics say that multinational corporations have hurt indigenous populations by exploiting their labor, harming their environments, and preventing their own economies from producing homegrown industries and manufactured goods.

Economic Globalization During the 1990s

The 1990s brought about a high tide of **economic globalization**, at the same time as (and somewhat related to) the collapse of Soviet and East European communism and the democratization of much of the developing world, especially Latin America. The strength of multinational corporations increased. The explosion of computer technology facilitated the electronic transfer of money. Meetings of the **Group of Seven,** or **G-7** (the **Group of Eight**, or **G-8**, after 1998, when Russia joined), an informal association of the countries with the world's largest economies—the United States, Canada, Great Britain, Japan, Germany, France, and Italy—became more frequent and increasingly influential.

In 1995, the GATT regulations were upgraded and strengthened by the formation of the **World Trade Organization** (WTO), whose purpose is to regulate the economic interaction of the more than 100 nations that belong to it.

Regional economic unions became increasingly important. In 1994, the United States, Mexico, and Canada created a zone of free movement of money, goods, services, and labor by means of the **North American Free Trade Agreement** (NAFTA). Moves are afoot to enlarge this zone to include all of the Americas, through the auspices of the Organization of American States (OAS).

Asian nations have tightened their ties as well. By far the boldest experiment in economic integration, however, is Western Europe's. In 1991, the nations of the **European Union** (EU) agreed to the Maastricht Treaty, which provides for the creation of a single currency (the **euro**), the establishment of a European Central Bank, and common policymaking in the fields of immigration, environmental protection, and even foreign affairs and security issues. It took until the mid-1990s for EU nations to ratify the Maastricht Treaty, and friction between member states regarding the details of integration continues. Still, in 2002, many of the EU states abandoned their own currencies for the euro.

Costs and Benefits of Globalization

The costs and benefits of economic globalization are mixed. On one hand, it has generated great wealth, at least in a broad sense and in certain parts of the world. Proponents of globalization argue, with some justification, that free trade helps to preserve peace.

On the other hand, the fact that the economies of all (or most) nations influence each other so strongly means that negative trends in one region—financial crisis in Mexico in 1994 or Asia in 1997, for example, or Russia and Brazil in 1998—can adversely affect the entire world. In addition, it is questionable whether all nations will be willing to subject their individual economic policies to the dictates of the WTO or other international bodies. There have already been bitter disputes over this issue, especially between developing and developed countries.

Finally, globalization threatens to lead to a constant state of economic change and instability. Seeking profits, multinational corporations tend to move to wherever they can produce more cheaply. This means relocating to whatever city or country will provide them with the least expensive labor force, the most advantageous tax benefits or exemptions, and the most lenient environmental regulations. This can also mean the lowering of wages, the sudden unemployment or layoff of local labor forces, and great social stress. Agriculture has been greatly affected by globalization, as farmers in one country find themselves competing with cheap food being imported from other parts of the world. Some critics of globalization also point to its homogenizing effects on culture and fear that their own indigenous cultures are being crushed under the force of foreign (in particular, American) popular culture and values.

Whether or not economic globalization will continue remains to be seen. It most likely will. What also remains to be seen is whether the benefits will eventually outweigh the costs. This is much harder to predict and will remain a major issue into the twenty-first century.

SOCIAL TRENDS AND MOVEMENTS

Basic Features of Western Societies

Social change during the twentieth century was so rapid and thorough that it is difficult to generalize about it. By and large, Western nations and other developed states can be said to have evolved the following social features (albeit imperfectly and/or gradually in many cases):

- Elimination of legal distinctions between social classes.
- The replacement of aristocratic social elites by a professional, white-collar class that attains its elite status through earned wealth and/or educational status (often referred to as meritocracy or technocracy).
- Creation of a large, stable **middle class**.
- Access to at least a minimum standard of living and adequate level of material well-being, even among lower classes.
- **Urbanization**, as well as **suburbanization**.
- Establishment of a **social welfare system** that includes unemployment insurance, pensions, and health care (at least for the elderly, if not the population as a whole).
- Universal educational system.
- Equal political rights for all adult citizens, including females.
- Equal treatment of all citizens before the law.
- Equal rights for minorities (still an ongoing process, even in areas as advanced as the United States, Canada, Australia, New Zealand, Japan, and Europe).
- The participation of **nongovernmental organizations** (NGOs) in the political process. NGOs, representing the interests of various groups in society, pressure governments to implement policies and provide social services.

Standard-of-Living Disparity Between the West and Developing World

With varying degrees of success, countries in the developing regions of Africa, Asia, Latin America, and the Middle East attempted to bring about many of these same changes. Some managed to do so by the end of the century, others did not.

One of the most pressing issues affecting the globe is the vast standard-of-living disparity between the developed world and the **developing world**. Many political scientists and sociologists refer to this as the **north–south split**, because most of the world's advanced, postindustrial societies are located well above the equator.

TIP
In 1998, the United States alone consumed 25 percent of the world's energy, while its population makes up only 5 percent of the total world population.

The gap between the developed and developing worlds causes diplomatic friction, interferes with the smooth and equitable globalization of the world economy, and perpetuates tremendous socioeconomic inequality. An extremely small number of people in the developed nations possesses the majority of global wealth, uses up the bulk of the world's resources, eats a massive share of the world's food, and is responsible for most of the world's energy consumption and pollution. This trend has been in place during the entire twentieth century and showed no signs of reversing as the century ended.

Major Trends

Other important trends of the 1900s and/or early 2000s:

- *Population growth*: In 1900, the world population was 1.6 billion. At the century's end, that number had risen to 6 billion. Even in the developed world, where birthrates have tended to decline, population has increased. In the developing and less developed worlds, **population growth** has literally exploded. China and India each have populations of over 1 billion. The rate of growth in

Africa has averaged over 3 percent per year. Latin America went from 165 million in 1950 to 400 million in the mid-1980s. Cities such as Mexico City, Shanghai, and Buenos Aires are among the most densely populated in the world. Ironically, the true problems resulting from population growth—overconsumption of food and energy and overproduction of waste and pollution—have more to do with the developed world, where population growth is slower.

- *Migration*: Patterns of **modern migration** date to the last half of the 1800s, when millions of immigrants from Europe (and a smaller number from China) flooded to the United States, Canada, Argentina, and Chile. This trend continued through the early 1900s, until the United States instituted stricter immigration policies. The movement of peoples continued after World War II, however, and even intensified. During the late 1940s and 1950s, European refugees and displaced persons (largely from Eastern Europe, where Nazi genocide and then Soviet occupation led to massive population transfers) moved throughout the continent, mainly to Western Europe. All throughout the postwar period, economic opportunity, violence in the developing world (caused largely by brushfire conflicts related to the Cold War), and political repression have led millions of people to leave Asia, the Middle East, Latin America, and Africa for Western Europe and North America. Even as France and Britain dismantled their empires, many of their former colonial subjects migrated from Algeria, India, sub-Saharan Africa, the Caribbean, and elsewhere. Refugees have fled from Asia and Latin America to the United States and Canada, from Africa and the Middle East to Europe. Guest workers from the Middle East (especially Turkey) and elsewhere began to be admitted to Western Europe; by the 1980s, there were more than 15 million. Most recently, the collapse of communism in the former Soviet bloc, as well as ethnic conflict in the former Yugoslavia, has led to a rush of migration from Eastern to Western Europe. Migration has often provided a much-needed labor force and enriched the cultural diversity of the host nation. However, especially when economic times are tight, it has stirred up xenophobia, typically among right-wing extremists.

- *Rise of the consumer society*: In developed societies, inexpensive, mass-produced goods tend to be available to almost all people, even the lower classes. At the same time, fewer people in these societies earn their living by means of agricultural or even industrial production. Consumer societies therefore tend to be based on service, or postindustrial, economies.

- *Social activism*: Demonstrations, protests, and strikes have brought about social, political, and economic change ever since the French Revolution. During the twentieth century, however, **social activism** and the work of NGOs have become increasingly important. The most famous wave of activism came in the 1960s and early 1970s (especially the various **1968 protests** that broke out in Paris, Prague, Mexico City, and U.S. cities and universities). Social activism has toppled colonial regimes (for example, in India), helped to end wars (as in Vietnam), and achieved civil rights (including in South Africa and the American South). It has also been crucial to women's liberation and the environmental movement.

- *Environmentalism*: Ever since the Industrial Revolution, there has been a spirit of environmentalism, striving to prevent the natural world from overdevelopment or destruction. Conservation efforts date back to figures such as Henry Thoreau, Ralph Waldo Emerson, and John Muir. The modern **environmental (or green) movement**, however, is a product of the post-World War II era, when it became clear that pollution, species extinction, and uncontrolled industrialism posed a dire threat to the earth's ecological well-being. Such movements began during the 1960s, both in North America and Western Europe. A major boost came with the publication of Rachel Carson's *Silent Spring* (1962), which warned of the dangers connected with the insecticide DDT. The celebration of Earth Day in 1970 also popularized the environmental movement. NGOs working on behalf of the environment, such as Greenpeace and the World Wildlife Fund, have become globally influential. In some West European countries (particularly Germany), green parties play an important role in national politics. Contemporary environmental efforts, including the Kyoto Protocol are largely focused on the problem of **climate change** (see Chapter 34).

- *Terrorism*: The first major conflict of the twentieth century, World War I, was sparked by a terrorist. Ever since, it has become more common for political movements to achieve their goals by means of violence and assassination. Especially in the post-World War II era, **terrorist activity** has escalated. The first major terrorist act of the twenty-first century and the one that has had the greatest single impact on global affairs is the September 11, 2001 attack on the United States. Al-Qaeda terrorists linked to **Osama bin Laden** hijacked several aircraft and flew them into the World Trade Center and Pentagon, killing over 3,000 people.

> **TIP**
>
> Major terrorist groups have included the Palestinian Liberation Organization (PLO), the Irish Republican Army (IRA), the Red Brigades (a communist organization in Italy), a variety of anti-Israeli groups (including Hamas and Hizbollah), Chechen extremists, and Al-Qaeda.

- *Rise in extreme nationalism, ethnic hostility, and religious fundamentalism*: The most advanced age in human history has also been the most prone to hyper-patriotic **nationalism**, ethnic and religious violence, and **genocide**. The **Armenian genocide** and the **Holocaust** are instances from the first half of the century. The Arab-Israeli conflict, intertribal violence in Africa, and Hindu-Muslim tensions in South Asia have troubled the postwar era. Similar trends have been even more on the rise in the 1990s and early 2000s, as the end of the Cold War has removed many of the restraints keeping ethnic and religious tensions in check (see Chapter 34).

WOMEN AND THE SHIFT IN GENDER RELATIONS

One of the most important trends of the twentieth century—affecting slightly more than half of the world's entire population—is **women's liberation**. Progress here came mainly in the Western world, although other regions have also moved forward, if slowly and partially.

The Early Twentieth Century

Chapters 20 and 28 have already discussed the progress that women's movements in the West made during the late 1800s and World War I in agitating for **women's suffrage**, entering the workplace, and pushing for social, educational, and political equality.

Between 1917 and 1920, women got the vote in almost all Western nations, France and Italy being the most noteworthy exceptions. Except in the USSR (where rapid industrialization required as large a workforce as possible), the rate of female unemployment decreased in the 1920s, as men returned from World War I, and especially in the 1930s, when, during the mass unemployment of the Great Depression, it was considered "wrong" for women to have jobs if men were out of work.

The interwar dictatorships differed sharply in their treatment of women. In the USSR, Marxist ideology called for gender equality. The Soviets observed this ideal to a degree (but far from perfectly), and women made up a large part of the workforce. By contrast, Italian Fascism, German Nazism, and Japanese traditionalism were explicitly hostile to the notion of gender equality. In all three countries, women were expected to be principally mothers and homemakers.

Women and World War II

Famously, World War II brought women into the workplace in even greater numbers than World War I had. The image of "Rosie the Riveter" became a potent symbol of the role of women in U.S. wartime production. In the Soviet Union, women made up nearly 40 percent of the national workforce. Large numbers of American, Canadian, ANZAC, and British women served as war nurses and military personnel (although not combat troops). In the USSR, women served in the military and, in some limited but important cases, saw active duty in combat (mainly as pilots and snipers).

Although there was a temporary dip in female employment afterward, the war had served the purpose of permanently cementing women's place in the working world. Moreover, France and Italy gave women the vote in 1945.

Western Women and Feminism in the Postwar Era

During the postwar era, as Japan, Western Europe, the United States, and Canada moved on to ever-higher levels of economic advancement, women took an increasingly larger role in the workplace and public life. The same was true—and to an even larger degree—in Eastern Europe and the Soviet Union. However, during the late 1940s and 1950s, it was still generally considered that a woman's main roles were that of homemaker, childbearer, and caregiver to children. Even those women who worked suffered widespread gender discrimination: sexual harassment, unequal wages, lack of access to positions of leadership, and so on. The French philosopher Simone de Beauvoir analyzed women's place in modern society in *The Second Sex* (1949), which investigated the deep-seated cultural and biological reasons for male domination of women.

A great step toward equality was taken by women in the Western world during the 1960s and 1970s. This was the era of **feminism**, or women's liberation. Major figures here were Gloria Steinem and Betty Friedan, whose book *The Feminine Mystique* (1963) joined de Beauvoir's *The Second Sex* in providing the movement with an intellectual foundation.

The goal of the women's movement was not just to achieve legal equality but also to eliminate the cultural stereotype of women as the "weaker sex" and to remove social barriers blocking the way toward true equality. Achievements of the women's movement include better and more varied career opportunities, better pay, equal access to higher education, greater respect for women's athletics, a greater role in political life, and the right to birth control, legal abortion, and divorce.

Contemporary Gender Issues

Problems still remain, however. Informal discrimination and sexual harassment have not been eliminated. Access to the highest levels of business and political life is still not complete (a phenomenon commonly referred to as the "glass ceiling").

Moreover, women are still relegated to traditional and secondary roles in many non-Western societies. Although it is a stereotype to say that women are not treated equally in Asia, Africa, the Middle East, and Latin America, the fact remains that Islamic fundamentalism, conservative Catholicism, machismo, old-fashioned views of women as inferior (or wives as servants, even property) constrain women more commonly in these regions than in the West.

THOUGHT, CULTURE, AND SCIENCE

The hallmarks of twentieth-century thought and culture are rapid change and incredible diversity. Other major trends have included **multiculturalism**—the interaction and fusion of the world's various ethnic, artistic, and intellectual traditions—and the effect of **mass media technology** on culture and the arts. Scientific and technological advancement has proceeded at a breathtaking pace. The **information** (or **digital**) **revolution** caused by the computer has vastly altered life in the 1990s and beyond.

Pessimism and Uncertainty in Western Culture

After World War I, art and literature in the Western world tended to be dominated by the themes of uncertainty and anxiety that had already emerged in the late 1800s and early 1900s (see Chapter 20). The psychological theories of **Sigmund Freud**, as well as the philosophical implications of the theory of relativity and the new field of quantum physics, had dampened the overall optimism of the mid-to-late 1800s.

The demoralization caused by World War I increased the spirit of pessimism and relativism (the belief or attitude that there are no objective standards or truths). The best-selling nonfiction book in interwar Europe was the philosopher Oswald Spengler's *The Decline of the West*. The prose and poetry of T. S. Eliot and Franz Kafka dealt with dehumanization in an industrialized, bureaucratized era. By experimenting with stream-of-consciousness prose, authors such as Virginia Woolf, Marcel Proust, and James Joyce attempted to capture the workings of the human mind on the written page. Abstract painters, such as Pablo Picasso, distorted reality to demonstrate that things could be seen from a variety of perspectives. Surrealists, Salvador Dalí and others, placed realistic objects in unrealistic situations to confuse the viewer's sense of reality.

After World War II, the philosophical and literary school of **existentialism**, championed by the playwright Samuel Beckett and the philosophers Albert Camus and Jean-Paul Sartre, proposed that humanity was not guided by any deity, special destiny, or objective morality. Alone in the universe, the individual must learn to create a worthwhile, ethical existence for himself or herself without the benefit of religion or the hope of any life beyond the earthly one.

Mass Media

Mass media came to play an increasingly important role in cultural life. Radio, film, television, the inexpensive production of mass quantities of books, and computers have brought music, drama, literature, and information into the lives of a greater variety of people than ever before. In addition, in the hands of creative directors and filmmakers, cinema has been used to create genuinely great art.

On the other hand, critics of such **mass** (or **popular**) **culture** have argued that it tends to cheapen or dumb down culture by catering to the taste of the lowest common denominator. In addition, mass media have been used for political purposes, such as **propaganda** and indoctrination ("brainwashing"), especially in dictatorships. Even in free societies, critics say, mass media have become powerful tools in the hands of corporate entities, brainwashing people not for political purposes but to advertise goods and make a profit.

Another effect of mass media has been the westernization, even **Americanization**, of global popular culture. Before World War II, the lure of American jazz and Hollywood movies was immensely seductive. Afterward, when America dominated world markets and mass-media technology, Disney, McDonald's, and Coca-Cola, among others, became economic and cultural symbols recognizable not just in the United States but almost literally in every part of the globe. Some intellectuals, especially non-Western ones, have expressed concern about the corporatizing and Americanizing effects of mass culture; the Japanese novelist Yukio Mishima angrily condemned it as "coca-colonization." Others, however, have talked about the potential of mass media to draw people closer together. In the 1960s, Canadian sociologist Marshall McLuhan became famous for writing that modern communications would create a **"global village"**—a prediction that seems to have been at least partly realized, thanks to the Internet and World Wide Web.

Arts and Literature in the Non-Western World

The twentieth and twenty-first centuries have seen the literary and artistic traditions of the non-Western world achieve a status equal to—and in some cases surpassing—those of the West. In addition to maintaining their own indigenous traditions, non-Western authors and artists have adopted Western forms of writing, painting, and composing, often adapting, modifying, and adding native elements to them.

The Mexican painter Diego Rivera created powerful murals that vividly expressed the plight of the working poor, as well as that of Mayans and other indigenous peoples in his country. Chinese author Lu Xun (Lu Hsun) wrote hard-hitting stories about his nation's economic domination by outside powers, as well as the government's inability and unwillingness to care for the lower classes. The Indian poet Rabindranath Tagore, the first non-Westerner to win the Nobel Prize for literature, dazzled readers throughout the world with lyrical, mystical verses based on Hindu concepts.

Non-Western voices in the artistic world grew bolder and more eloquent after World War II. Common themes include the growing pains associated with decolonization, the difficulty of resisting Western (especially U.S.) cultural hegemony, the clash of Western and non-Western culture, and political opposition to one's own politically repressive regime. In *The Interpreters*, the Nobel laureate Wole Soyinka writes about corruption and dictatorship in his native Nigeria. A fellow Nigerian, Chinua Achebe, also takes on themes of decolonization and dictatorship, especially in *Things Fall Apart*. Ama Ata Aidoo describes the place of women in contemporary Ghana in *Changes: A Love Story*.

Cry, the Peacock is Anita Desai's famous treatment of women's lives in India. In Japan, Yukio Mishima, a traditional (but also gay) nationalist, bitterly opposed what he saw as the destruction of Japan's cultural values. His ritual, samurai-style suicide in 1970 elevated him to cult status.

In Latin America, authors such as Gabriel García Márquez and Isabel Allende pioneered magical realism: a richly textured style featuring detailed storytelling.

In the Islamic world, the novelist Naguib Mahfouz won the Nobel Prize for his *Cairo Trilogy*, a vibrant portrait of postwar Egypt. The Indian-born, English-speaking Muslim Salman Rushdie came to world attention in 1988 with *The Satanic Verses*, an irreverent treatment of Islamic orthodoxy. Both Mahfouz and Rushdie fell afoul of Muslim traditionalists. Mahfouz was stabbed by an Islamic extremist in 1984. Rushdie was declared a heretic by Iran's Ayatollah Khomeini, who openly called for Rushdie's assassination and forced him to go into hiding for years.

Science and Technology

Scientific and technological advancement during the twentieth and twenty-first centuries has been constant and spectacular. During the first half of the 1900s, the Western world fully industrialized, moving into a world where petroleum and electricity were the primary sources of energy.

Also in the Western world, great innovation has been made in all fields of science. Progress in certain areas has been most noteworthy. Physics was revolutionized at the beginning of the 1900s. First, **Albert Einstein** developed the **theory of relativity**, making the first major changes to the system of science and mathematics that had been synthesized by Isaac Newton in the late 1600s and early 1700s. Also in the early 1900s came the birth of **quantum physics**. Major figures here included Max Planck, Niels Bohr, Werner Heisenberg, and Enrico Fermi. The work of quantum physicists has completely altered our understanding of astronomy and subatomic particles. It also made atomic weaponry and nuclear energy possible.

Rocketry and space science emerged in the 1900s. Pioneers of rocket science included the American Robert Goddard and Russia's Konstantin Tsiolkovsky. The new science matured during World War II thanks largely to the efforts of German scientists. As discussed in Chapter 31, the nuclear arms race between the United

States and the Soviet Union spurred a parallel space race. The move toward a permanent presence in space was encouraged by the USSR's work in developing orbital laboratories and the United States' invention of the space shuttle. Rocket science has also made satellite communications possible.

Another field of special significance is **genetics**, which came into being in the late 1800s thanks to the work of an Austrian monk, Gregor Mendel. The field's great breakthrough came when James Watson and Francis Crick deciphered the **molecular structure of DNA** in 1953. Since then, scientists have gained an unprecedented wealth of knowledge about how living organisms work. Combined with innovations in computer technology, genetic science has allowed incredible medical advances.

Yet another significant advancement was the invention of the **computer**, during and shortly after World War II. Computers caused an information revolution that altered the way people communicate, transact business, entertain themselves, and work. A key innovation was the development of the **Internet**, originally created in the 1960s for U.S. defense research purposes. By the end of the 1990s, a World Wide Web had connected millions of users, and it continues to grow. Although a "digital divide" exists between those people who have better access to computer technology in the northern hemisphere and those who have poorer access south of the equator, the worldwide trend is toward greater access for all.

Apollo 15 Mission to the Moon, August 1971.
To this date, the United States is the only nation that has landed crewed spacecraft on the moon. The first moon landing came on July 20, 1969. The Apollo 15 mission, pictured here, was one of the several landings that followed. In recent years, trends in space exploration have included the deployment of crewless probes deep into the solar system (and beyond), long-term space station missions, space shuttle flights, and the use of remote-controlled technology to explore hostile environments, such as the surfaces of other planets.

CHAPTER 34

Integration or Fragmentation? Globalism in the Late Twentieth and Early Twenty-First Centuries

- Global integration vs. global fragmentation
- The end of the Cold War
- The September 11, 2001, attacks and the war on terror
- Asymmetrical warfare (terrorism, guerrilla conflict, and small arms versus WMDs and the revolution in military affairs)
- Nuclear proliferation and weapons of mass destruction (WMDs)

- Nationalist aggression and genocide
- Religious fundamentalism
- Environmentalism, climate change, and the Kyoto Protocol
- The United Nations
- Nongovernmental organizations (NGOs)
- Multiculturalism

Are the nations of the world growing closer together or further apart? Enduring symbols of the late 1900s and early 2000s would include the sight of McDonald's golden arches in cities such as Nairobi and Shanghai, as well as the all-pervasive presence of mass media and the Internet in every corner of the planet. One might argue that these are signs of **global integration**.

However, other images of the recent turn of the century would seem to indicate of **global fragmentation**. Ethnic cleansing in the former Yugoslavia. Genocidal butchery in Rwanda. The breakdown of peace talks between Israelis and Palestinians. The terrorist attacks of September 11, 2001, as well as the tensions caused by the resulting war on terror. All of these would appear to signal that world communities are growing apart, not together.

The fact of the matter is that, globally speaking, centripetal and centrifugal forces are both acting on the nations of the world, simultaneously pushing them together and pulling them apart. Which will prevail as the twenty-first century progresses remains to be seen.

DIPLOMACY AFTER THE COLD WAR

In 1992, U.S. President George Bush stated that the **end of the Cold War** had brought about a "new world order." The U.S.-Soviet arms race halted, as did the bipolar division of most of the world into two hostile camps. In this way, the nations of the world were free to emerge from underneath the nuclear umbrellas of the superpowers and associate with each other as they pleased. The risk of nuclear annihilation decreased dramatically, and as described in Chapter 31, the end of the Cold War coincided with a general rise in the level of democratization worldwide.

On the other hand, the end of the Cold War has left the world without a defining diplomatic framework. Instead of two superpowers, only one, the United States, remains. The fact that other countries are now free to join or clash as they wish has made international relations more unpredictable. New diplomatic alignments appear and disappear. Many old alliances have broken or weakened. Others have had to be redesigned. For instance, what purpose does NATO have in Europe now that the threat of Soviet invasion has been removed?

Furthermore, during the Cold War, any conflict anywhere carried with it the risk of superpower involvement and with it the possibility of nuclear war. In its way, then, the Cold War had something of a restraining effect, which contained certain ethnic and cultural pressures, especially within the superpowers' spheres of influence. With the restraining effect of the Cold War removed, many of those hostilities have emerged, breaking out of control in Yugoslavia, Rwanda, Indonesia, and elsewhere. In addition, the post-Cold War years have witnessed the gradual spread of nuclear-weapons capability.

Another point of tension in the post-Cold War era is the strained relationship between the United States and China, the largest remaining communist power on earth. China is not yet a superpower, but its economic growth has been rapid throughout the 1980s and 1990s, and the wealthy commercial center of Hong Kong returned to Chinese rule in 1997. China possesses the humanpower and geographical size eventually to achieve superpower status. Although the United States pursued a policy of engagement with China during the 1990s, trade disputes and diplomatic disagreements have been frequent. U.S. support for Taiwan, which China regards as a breakaway province, is another potential source of conflict. Although the United States does not officially recognize Taiwanese independence, it would probably help to defend Taiwan if China attempted a reunification by force.

As for Russia, America's briefly friendly relationship with it has cooled. During most of the 1990s, Russia was led by Boris Yeltsin, who was then succeeded by a former KGB operative, Vladimir Putin. Russia is still struggling to build democracy and regain its economic footing. Nationalist forces are building, and Russia wishes to retain its sphere of influence in parts of the former USSR (this desire has embroiled Russia in a war with Chechnya since 1995 and caused it to meddle, often unsuccessfully, in the political affairs of countries such as Ukraine and Georgia). On the other hand, its leaders do not want to seem overly aggressive or remain isolated from other parts of Europe. While Russia is, for the moment, too weak to renew its superpower hostility—or nuclear arms race—with the West, it is still an important force in Europe and Asia.

At the time, the end of the Cold War was thought to have brought about lasting global peace. It has not. It would be too much to say that the result has been global anarchy, the post-Cold War years have called for new and creative ways of thinking about diplomacy. As one U.S. government official said during the mid-1990s, "We have slain the dragon; but we now live in a jungle filled with a bewildering variety of poisonous snakes."

SECURITY CONCERNS

War After the Cold War

The end of the Cold War has by no means brought about an era of peace. One major war—the Iraqi invasion of Kuwait and the resulting Gulf War (1990–1991)—took place soon after. War raged in Yugoslavia during the 1990s. In 1999, NATO bombed Yugoslavia in an effort to stop Serb aggression against the Albanian population of the Serbian province of Kosovo. Russia has fought Chechnya.

Just as important, a large variety of brushfire wars, small armed conflicts, and civil disturbances have raged throughout the decade following the collapse of the Cold War, resulting in the deaths of hundreds of thousands. Many of these have been motivated by ethnic hostilities that the Cold War had helped to keep in check. Finally, the **Al-Qaeda attacks on September 11, 2001**, have resulted in a U.S.-led war on terror that spans the globe and looks likely to continue for some time.

Weapons of Mass Destruction

Other troublesome security issues involve **weapons of mass destruction**. From 1987 onward, the United States and Russia have made progress in restricting, even scaling back, the production and testing of nuclear weapons. (Recent tension between the two countries has slowed this process down.) Beyond that, there have been worries that, given the conditions of extreme economic and political breakdown in Russia, nuclear weapons or weapons-grade atomic material might be stolen or smuggled out of the former Soviet Union and end up in the hands of terrorists or rogue governments.

Even more worrisome is the issue of **nuclear proliferation**. Only five countries belong to the "nuclear club," the group of nations officially acknowledged to possess nuclear-weapons capability: the United States, Russia, China, France, and Great Britain. Most nations of the world have signed the Nuclear Non-Proliferation Treaty. Generally, the treaty's effectiveness and longevity have been remarkable.

Nonetheless, several countries, most notably Israel, developed nuclear arsenals during the 1970s and 1980s. In 1998, India and Pakistan, deadly enemies, each tested nuclear weapons, adding new peril to an already dangerous diplomatic situation. North Korea gained nuclear-weapons capability sometime after 2000, and Iran is actively seeking it. How long nuclear proliferation can be contained is one of the most pressing questions of the new century.

The same can be said for other weapons of mass destruction, such as biological weapons (various germs, viruses, and bacteria packaged in a delivery system) and chemical weapons (such as nerve gas and water-based toxins). These are relatively easy weapons to manufacture and deliver and extremely difficult to defend against. During the Cold War, both superpowers abided by international agreements banning the use of biological and chemical weapons. Whether or not all states will choose to honor such agreements, now that the Cold War is over, is an open question.

The Proliferation of Small Arms

At the other end of the weapons spectrum are small arms: pistols, rifles, submachine guns, and automatic rifles. During the Cold War, some 50 million people were killed, mainly in the developing world, because of small-scale conflicts of various types. This trend has continued since 1991. Certain parts of the world, such as Africa, Southeast Asia, and Latin America, are awash with small arms. A huge illegal trade in these weapons thrives. Societies in which large numbers of civilians, non-combatants, and members of paramilitary groups—as opposed to regular military forces—have access to heavy weaponry are inherently unstable.

The Revolution in Military Affairs and High-Tech Warfare

One of the most striking features of contemporary military life is the unprecedented disparity between the technological capabilities of the world's most advanced armed forces and those of the least advanced.

The gap between high-tech forces and the lowest level of military capability has always been important, as the West's imperial successes of the 1800s proved. After World War II, however, that gap widened considerably. Nuclear weapons, jet aircraft, third-generation tanks, helicopter gunships, nuclear submarines and aircraft carriers, and global airlift capacity—owned and used by the superpowers and the small group of other nations able to afford them—were a far cry from the assault rifles, grenade launchers, hand-to-hand weapons and other small arms available to most armies or paramilitary groups. On the other hand (as in the nineteenth-century era of imperialism), technological superiority in **asymmetrical wars**—conflicts that pit high-tech adversaries against low-tech enemies—was not always a guarantee of military success. That fact was made painfully clear to the superpowers in Vietnam and Afghanistan, where guerrilla warfare and other irregular forms of combat prevailed.

Computer technology has widened the military gap even further. During the 1990s and early 2000s, the United States and a tiny handful of other nations experienced what generals and strategists refer to as the "**revolution in military affairs**" (RMA). This involved the full integration of computer technology, satellite communications, and precision-guided ("smart") weapons into military operations. Whether such changes will guarantee future victories remains to be seen.

NATIONALIST EXTREMISM, ETHNIC TENSIONS, AND RELIGIOUS FUNDAMENTALISM

One of the forces that the Cold War tended to keep under control was nationalist and ethnic extremism. The collapse of the superpower rivalry has, in many cases, released national, ethnic, and religious pressures, allowing them to boil out of control.

Nationalist Extremism in the West

Even in Western Europe, with its democratic governments and tradition of respecting civil rights, there is a certain level of ethnic tension. Since 1975, the island of Cyprus has been divided between Turks and Greeks, with a United Nations force needed to keep the peace. In countries such as Britain, Germany, France, Switzerland, and Italy, the millions of Turks, Middle Easterners, Africans, Pakistanis, Indians, and Caribbean islanders who live and work there (many of them as **guest workers**) suffer varying degrees of prejudice and discrimination. Right-wing and neo-Nazi groups harass minorities and call for their deportation, especially in times of economic distress. Likewise, much the same applies to the United States, where **anti-immigration sentiment** sometimes rises up in opposition to America's "melting-pot" tradition.

East European Nationalism and the Breakup of Yugoslavia

In Eastern Europe, ethnic tensions are even higher than in the West. Each Eastern European state is home to substantial minority populations, many of which have long histories of conflict. Even the Eastern European states that have made the most progress toward democratization have found it difficult to ensure that the rights of national minorities—Romanians living in Hungary, for example, or Slovaks in the Czech Republic or Russians in the Baltic States—are protected. One group that is heavily discriminated against throughout Eastern Europe is the Roma, better known as Gypsies.

The most striking examples of ethnic hostilities in Eastern Europe are the various wars in the former Yugoslavia. With the collapse of communism in 1989 and 1990, Yugoslavia, an artificial nation created after World War I to unite the southern Slavs—Serbs, Croats, Bosnians, Slovenes, Montenegrins, and Macedonians—began to break apart. Complicating the matter was the fact that these groups practice three religions, Roman Catholicism (Croatians and Slovenes), Eastern Orthodoxy (Serbs, Montenegrins, Macedonians, the Serbian minority in Bosnia), and Islam (the majority of Bosnians). There is also a sizable Albanian minority in Serbia and Macedonia, most of whom are Muslims. All these peoples have a long history of conflict. However, from 1945 until 1980, the communist government of Josip Tito held these conflicts in check and encouraged multicultural coexistence. Even during the 1980s, the various people of Yugoslavia lived together reasonably amicably.

After 1989, **ethnic tensions** began to reemerge. Such tensions were due partly to the stress and strain of communist breakdown but also to the efforts of nationalist politicians (such as the Serbian leader Slobodan Milosevic), who deliberately whipped ethnic hostility out of control for their own purposes. Slovenia, Macedonia, and Croatia declared independence in 1991.

The first Yugoslav war resulted from Serbia's attempt to take territory from Croatia. When Bosnia declared independence in 1992, the Serbian minority there rose up in arms, with assistance from Milosevic and the Serbian government. Their goal was to create a "Greater Serbia."

From 1992 to 1995, while the Serbian-Croatian war came to an end, a second war raged in Bosnia. Serb forces took three-quarters of Bosnia. Even worse, Bosnian Serbs, with full support of Milosevic's Serbian government, carried out the policy of ethnic cleansing. This form of genocide involved the forced deportation of Bosnian Muslims from territories the Bosnian Serbs wanted for themselves. It also included mass executions and the systematic rape of large numbers of women. The Serbian campaign of ethnic cleansing was the worst military atrocity committed in Europe since the Nazi Holocaust. The failure of the United Nations and European community to deal effectively with the crisis was not only embarrassing but called into doubt the ability of international organizations to cope with international conflict in the post-Cold War era. The war in Bosnia was finally ended by the U.S.-sponsored Dayton Accords, in the fall of 1995, when the Serbs backed down under the pressure of U.S. airstrikes and a renewed Croatian offensive.

Another round of fighting came in 1998 and 1999, when Milosevic and the Serbs began another campaign of ethnic cleansing, this time against the Albanian minority living in the Serbian province of Kosovo. For three months in 1999, NATO, in its first-ever military action, bombed Serbia until Milosevic relented. Although, technically, a state of peace exists in the former Yugoslavia, ethnic resentment and bitterness boils just beneath the surface.

Ethnic Violence in Africa, Asia, and the Middle East

Other notorious examples of ethnic violence include the Hutu-Tutsi conflict in Rwanda. In 1994, these two tribes fought each other. In the process, the Hutu killed approximately 800,000 Tutsi men, women, and children. The long-standing effort of the people of East Timor, a Pacific island illegally annexed by Indonesia in 1975, to free themselves has led to great bloodshed. Indonesian suppression of the East Timorese has verged on the genocidal since the 1970s. In 1999, the reign of terror Indonesia visited upon the tiny island was so bloody that it prompted United Nations intervention. Along with a severe currency crisis, the disturbances and scandals connected with East Timorese independence also played a role in toppling Suharto, the dictator who had ruled Indonesia since 1967.

Perhaps the longest-lasting, and still problematic, ethnic clash is that of the Israelis and the Palestinians. The Oslo Accord of 1993, in which the PLO leader Yasser Arafat and the Israeli prime minister Yitzhak Rabin agreed to pursue peace, led to more than half a decade of relative calm in the Middle East. Negotiations came to a deadlock, however, and tensions began to mount once again. In 2001, those tensions broke out into open conflict, as the Palestinians began a second uprising, or intifada.

Religious Fundamentalism

Religious fundamentalism has experienced a revival during the late 1900s and early 2000s. In India, religious conflict among Hindus, Muslims, and Sikhs continues. Policy in Iran is still shaped largely by Islamic fundamentalism. In Afghanistan, Islamic fundamentalism led to the creation of a strictly theocratic government under the Taliban, which ruled from 1989 to 2002. Religious differences are at the heart of the Israeli-Arab conflict in the Middle East and largely at the heart of the ethnic tensions plaguing the former Yugoslavia. They played an overwhelming role in the September 11, 2001 bombings, and they have been heightened by the subsequent war on terror.

Ethnic and religious tensions and violence have to be counted among the fragmenting factors threatening to tear the world apart, rather than bring it together.

ENVIRONMENTAL ISSUES

Despite the existence of vibrant and active environmental movements since the 1960s, environmental problems still remain. In several ways, they have become more pressing during the 1990s and early 2000s.

Environmentalism in the Developed World

In the developed world—the United States, Canada, Western Europe, Japan, and others like them—strict environmental regulations have been put into place from the 1970s onward in an attempt to ensure clean air and clean water for all. Recycling has become common practice. Endangered species have received greater protections. Growing concern about the depletion of the ozone layer led to the elimination of chlorofluorocarbons (CFCs). The ongoing debate about the effect of carbon dioxide and other green-house gasses on planetary climate patterns—**global warming**—has raised awareness about this issue.

Consumption and Pollution in the Developed World

However, the developed world's economies continue to modernize. With that, the rate of consumption among the populations of these countries continues to escalate. This group—a small segment of the world population—eats more, generates more trash, burns more gasoline, uses more electricity, consumes more wood and paper products, and releases more additives and emissions into the air and water than the rest of the people in the world combined.

Modernization and Environmental Problems in the Developing World

Added to this issue is the modernization of the developing world. As large parts of Asia, Africa, Latin America, and the Middle East industrialize and

THE ENVIRONMENT

It is common to think of pollution and environmental crisis as modern problems. In fact, societies have affected—and been affected by—the environment from the Stone Age onward. Resource extraction and consumption, as well as pollution, have always been part of the human community. The downfall of civilizations like those of the Indus Valley and Easter Island has been linked directly to environmental disaster or, in the latter case, mismanagement. In countless ways, the industrial era has made humanity's footprint on the environment heavier than ever before: Societies consume more, rely more on machine production and fuel-driven transport, and possess engineering skills that involve the capacity to change the earth in ways unimaginable to preindustrial societies. Currently, climate change (global warming) serves as the clearest demonstration of how profoundly human action has affected the environment.

attempt to catch up with the developing world, their rates of energy use and resource consumption have been increasing. These countries also do not have the same clean-air, clean-water, and other regulations in place that nations in the developed world do.

The Failure of International Environmental Regulations

On the whole, international agreements to take greater care of the environment have met with limited success. A prime example of this is the Kyoto Summit (1997), where over 150 nations gathered to discuss environmental issues, especially the potential dangers of global warming. Although a **Kyoto Protocol** was hammered out, it is still contentious, and many countries, including the United States, have not ratified it. A particular point of conflict is the question of whether or not industrializing countries of the less developed world should be compelled to abide by the same clean-air regulations that nations of the developed world do.

Energy Sources

Another failure has been the inability or unwillingness to develop clean, sustainable sources of energy. Continued reliance on fossil fuels such as coal and especially petroleum has led not only to periodic shortages and economic difficulties but also to continued air pollution. Hydroelectric generation of electric power has its limits. Experiments with wind and solar power—potentially the cleanest sources of power possible—have not been supported by governments or corporations (at times, the latter, whose profits are dependent on oil-based technologies, have actively opposed such experiments).

The only alternative source of energy that has met with any success is nuclear power. This, however, carries with it serious risks, as nuclear accidents at Three Mile Island (1979) in Pennsylvania and Chernobyl (1986) in Ukraine—where 8,000 people were killed immediately and hundreds of thousands were made sick or born deformed afterward—have demonstrated.

Although a variety of environmental issues will confront the nations of the world in the twenty-first century, perhaps the most dangerous and the one that threatens all countries equally is global warming.

REGIONALISM, GLOBALIZATION, AND MULTICULTURALISM

Trends that would seem to encourage the integration rather than fragmentation of world communities include regionalism, economic globalization, and multicultural interaction. All are prominent features of contemporary life. However, they also have their limits.

The United Nations

Regional and international organizations and agencies serve to unite the efforts of countries around the world or in specific parts of the world. The **United Nations**, despite certain failures and flaws, has provided a forum for dispute resolution among the countries of the world since 1945. It oversees peacekeeping missions, monitors the observance of human rights and international treaties, and organizes humanitarian efforts, cultural preservation, and many other activities.

In terms of punitive measures, such as economic embargos, peacekeeping, and peacemaking, the United Nations' record is mixed. It has many successes to its credit, but events in Bosnia, Rwanda, Central Africa, and Sierra Leone have embarrassed it greatly. Its failure to dissuade the United States from invading Iraq in 2003 has called the United Nations' political effectiveness into some question.

Nongovernmental Organizations

A relatively recent trend has been the proliferation of **nongovernmental organizations** (NGOs). These nonprofit groups harness the effort of volunteers and activists locally, nationally, and around the world to work on various causes. Among the best-known NGOs are Greenpeace, the World Wildlife Fund, Amnesty International, Human Rights Watch, the National Organization for Women, Planned Parenthood, the National Rifle Association, and Medecins sans Frontieres (Doctors Without Borders).

Regional Organizations and Alliances

Regional organizations that have fostered international cooperation include the Organization for Security and Cooperation in Europe, the Association of Southeast Asian Nations, the Organization for African Unity, and the Organization of American States. Western Europe has made the greatest efforts to regionalize its economic, military, and political activities. In addition to the European Union and the OSCE mentioned above, many European nations belong to the NATO alliance and the Council of Europe.

Technology as an Integrating Force

Various cultural and technological factors seem to be bringing nations and regions closer together. Mass media technology has greatly increased people's awareness of other parts of the world. Enhanced means of communication—improved telephone networks, satellite transmissions, and above all the Internet and World Wide Web—have made it more possible than ever before for greater numbers of people to be continually in touch with other people in all parts of the globe. Cheaper and quicker modes of transport have enabled people to travel, work, study, or live abroad in vaster numbers than ever before. The celebration of art, literature, music, and traditions from all parts of the world—**multiculturalism**—has become extremely prominent during the 1990s and early 2000s. Cultural fusion and interaction have given multiculturalism even more of a boost.

Economic Globalization

The **globalization** of the world economy continues. The **European Union**, which, as of 2005, includes twenty-five members, has already removed barriers to the movement of people, goods, money, and services. In 2002, many of its members began to use a single currency, the euro. The North American Free Trade Agreement, in operation since 1994, is likely to serve as a model for similar agreements elsewhere. The **World Trade Organization**, formed in 1995, aims to bring the operations of the global economy under a single set of laws, rules, and practices.

However, economic globalization is not complete, nor is it self-evident that the trend is completely positive. Some of the flaws and potential dangers connected with globalization are discussed in Chapter 33. Not all nations belong to the WTO, and even member states quarrel with each other—and with the WTO's rulings. The great gap between the developed and developing worlds still remains—and, at least in some respects, it is widening.

Unit Six: Review Questions

SAMPLE ESSAY QUESTIONS (CCOT AND COMPARATIVE)

CCOT 1. Analyze the changes and continuities in the role played by non-governmental organizations (NGOs) between 1914 and the present.

CCOT 2. Analyze the changes and continuities in global economic exchange between 1914 and the present.

COMP 1. Compare and contrast the policy directions followed by the Chinese Communist leadership after the death of Mao and the Soviet government in the era of perestroika and glasnost.

COMP 2. Compare and contrast the political and social experiences of women between 1914 and the present in TWO of the following:

sub-Saharan Africa
India
the Middle East

MULTIPLE-CHOICE QUESTIONS

1. How did World War II change the patterns of international trade?

   (A) Most countries refused to trade with Japan or Germany after the war.
   (B) The World Trade Organization was created soon after the war's end.
   (C) The war diminished the European powers' control over world markets.
   (D) The USSR began trading extensively with Western Europe.
   (E) The United States stopped trading with countries in Asia.

2. What caused apartheid to end in South Africa during the 1990s?

   (A) White leaders came to realize how unjust it was.
   (B) Guerrilla violence committed by the African National Congress terrorized whites into ending it.
   (C) It was failing in its goal of fully segregating Africans from whites.
   (D) Pressure from the Vatican mobilized white opinion against it.
   (E) White leaders saw that it was harming its international reputation and trade ties.

3. During the 1960s and 1970s, the Sino-Soviet alliance

   (A) was strained by Soviet de-Stalinization, but remained intact.
   (B) came to an end, with the two nations agreeing to be friendly neutrals.
   (C) expanded by persuading India to join a Eurasian Treaty Organization.
   (D) broke apart, with great bitterness on both sides.
   (E) was untroubled and remained firmly in place.

4. After the Paris Peace Conference of 1919, Arab leaders

   (A) were frustrated by the limited autonomy granted them as mandate states.
   (B) were content with their newfound independence.
   (C) were overjoyed by the Balfour Declaration.
   (D) were grateful to Turkey's delegation for representing their interests.
   (E) were angered by the fact that Middle Eastern affairs were not discussed at the conference.

5. The image below most likely celebrates which Cold War–related event?

   (A) the first U.S. astronaut flight
   (B) the USSR's launch of the first human-made object into space
   (C) the testing of orbital missiles by the United States
   (D) the USSR's launch of an unmanned space probe toward Saturn
   (E) the European Space Agency's first space mission

6. During the 1990s, nationalist violence in the former Yugoslavia

   (A) was purposely stirred up by opportunistic politicians after communism's collapse.
   (B) grew no worse than it had already been under Tito's communist regime.
   (C) was unavoidable because of historically rooted and irrepressible hatred between ethnic groups.
   (D) resulted from covert intervention by radical Islamic fundamentalists.
   (E) was successfully averted by United Nations mediation.

7. Reza Shah Pahlavi of Iran is similar to Mustafa Kemal of Turkey in that both

   (A) democratized their countries.
   (B) introduced communism into their countries.
   (C) secularized their countries.
   (D) turned their countries into theocracies.
   (E) granted their countries liberal constitutions.

8. Which of the following is LEAST true of non-Western art and culture in the twentieth century?

   (A) The fusion of indigenous and Western forms and styles was common.
   (B) Non-Western authors won the Nobel Prize for literature.
   (C) Multicultural influences grew in importance.
   (D) Most non-Western intellectuals embraced the Americanization of global culture.
   (E) Many non-Western authors dealt with themes related to the legacy of colonialism.

9. Modern environmental movements

   (A) began only with the publication of Rachel Carson's *Silent Spring*.
   (B) have tended to avoid cooperation with non-governmental organizations (NGOs).
   (C) have not had an impact on national-level politics in any major country.
   (D) have stimulated greater public awareness of species extinction and climate change.
   (E) persuaded the U.S. government to ratify the Kyoto Protocol.

10. What effect did the liberation of Eastern Europe in 1989–1990 have on the USSR itself?

    (A) It stifled freedom movements within the USSR.
    (B) It drained badly needed finances from the Soviet economy.
    (C) It boosted Mikhail Gorbachev's prestige at home.
    (D) It provoked a territorial dispute between Poland and Soviet Ukraine.
    (E) It provided an example for non-Russians in the USSR who wanted freedom.

11. What is *satyagraha*?

    (A) a fusion of Marxism and Hindu theology
    (B) a policy of nonviolent resistance, mixed with Hindu theology
    (C) a fusion of Marxism and Muslim radicalism
    (D) an ethical justification for the use of violence to resist Western imperialism
    (E) a policy of nonviolent resistance, mixed with Islamic theology

12. Which of the following accurately describes World War II's impact on civilian populations?

   (A) Nearly half of the war's casualties were civilians.
   (B) Only Jewish civilians were killed in great numbers.
   (C) Combat rarely occurred near major population centers.
   (D) Most nations respected international conventions against the bombing of civilians.
   (E) Allied naval blockades caused the death of hundreds of thousands of Axis civilians.

13. Which of the following best describes the Communist takeover of Russia in 1917?

   (A) The Communists came to power after assassinating the royal family.
   (B) Defeat in World War I caused the masses to overthrow the tsar and vote the Communists into power.
   (C) Recognizing its weakness, the Provisional Government voluntarily handed power to the Communists.
   (D) Taking advantage of popular discontent with the Provisional Government, the Communists staged a successful insurrection.
   (E) The Communists used their majority in the Duma to take power by parliamentary means.

14. Which of the following describes developments in Mexico and Brazil during the 1930s?

   (A) The coffee trade generated great wealth for Mexico, and Brazil succeeded in developing its oil industry.
   (B) Mexico pursued populist reform and constitutional rule, and Brazil modernized its economy under an authoritarian regime.
   (C) Mexico sympathized with fascist regimes in Europe, and Brazil supported socialist governments there.
   (D) Mexico brutally suppressed peasants seeking land reform, and Brazil disbanded its secret police.
   (E) Mexico experienced political disorder and mass uprisings, and Brazil fought a border war against Peru.

15. Japanese war crimes between 1937 and 1945 did NOT include

   (A) the abuse of Chinese and Southeast Asian civilians.
   (B) the execution of U.S., British, and Australian prisoners of war.
   (C) the forced prostitution of Korean women.
   (D) the persecution of worshippers who practiced the Shinto faith.
   (E) the use of prisoners in chemical- and biological-weapons experiments.

16. Which of the following is NOT associated with the economic downturn experienced by the Western world during the 1970s?

   (A) the twentieth century's highest levels of unemployment
   (B) inflation
   (C) oil shortages
   (D) recession and slowdowns in production
   (E) the uncoupling of the U.S. dollar from the gold standard

17. Between the world wars, the League of Nations:

    (A) provided strong leadership and kept most of the world at peace.
    (B) proved effective at famine relief and dealing with refugees, but was otherwise weak.
    (C) benefited from U.S. leadership in stopping aggression in China and Spain.
    (D) had lost all its major European member states by the late 1930s.
    (E) was manipulated from within by Germany into granting several territorial concessions.

18. According to the map on page 359, which country did NOT become a member of the Commonwealth of Independent States?

    (A) Belarus
    (B) Moldova
    (C) Russia
    (D) Ukraine
    (E) Estonia

19. Which of the following has NOT been a factor interfering with modernization in Africa?

    (A) the HIV/AIDS epidemic
    (B) lack of cultural and linguistic unity in many Africans states
    (C) negative population growth
    (D) corruption on the part of political elites
    (E) interethnic conflict

20. What ethnic group is generally recognized to have suffered genocide during World War I?

    (A) the Palestinians
    (B) the Armenians
    (C) the Jews
    (D) the Roma (Gypsies)
    (E) Bosnian Muslims

Answers

1. **(C)** Germany and Japan received a great deal of economic assistance from other nations, allowing it to rebuild, and the United States stepped up its involvement with Asian markets after the war, so A and E are false. The postwar USSR was not completely cut off from the world economy, but tried to minimize trade with Western Europe—refusing, for example, to allow Eastern Europe to participate in the Marshall Plan. The World Trade Organization was not established until the 1990s. World War II did reduce Europe's global economic clout.

2. **(E)** Although some whites felt ethically uneasy about apartheid, and although clergy of many denominations denounced it (especially Desmond Tutu of the Anglican Church), moral pressures did not suffice to end it. Neither did ANC violence, which convinced many whites that more, not less, control over the black population was necessary. Answer C is also false. Only when South Africa was reduced to the status of international pariah—and had its wealth threatened by divestiture and sanctions—did the white leadership end apartheid.

3. **(D)** Soviet condescension, the USSR's unwillingness to share nuclear technology, and border disputes helped break the Sino-Soviet alliance. Especially as the USSR de-Stalinized, Mao perceived the Soviet brand of communism as ideologically impure. The split was not amicable, and China began competing with the USSR for influence over communist movements worldwide. India never entered into any kind of Soviet-Chinese alliance.

4. **(A)** The Arabs had rebelled against Ottoman rule, and would not have been represented by Turkey. Like most Middle Eastern Muslims, they were appalled by the Balfour Declaration, which pledged British support for a Jewish homeland in Palestine. On the whole, the

Arabs, who had expected to win full independence in exchange for supporting the Allies against Ottoman Turkey, were disappointed by the post–World War I settlement.

5. **(B)** The Cyrillic script indicates that a Russian mission is depicted, eliminating A, C, and E. Earth, not Saturn, is depicted, and the date of 1957 should recall the *Sputnik* launch—a major moment in both the "space race" and the Cold War arms race.

6. **(A)** Dictatorial as it was, Tito's regime succeeded in suppressing ethnic tensions in Yugoslavia. When violence broke out, the United Nations and most foreign powers acted slowly and weakly. Although some argued that ethnic hatred in the region was the "natural" state of affairs and therefore irresistible, the record shows that Serb politicians like Slobodan Milosevic deliberately stirred tensions up and exploited them to further their own agendas. Answer D is simply contrary to facts.

7. **(C)** Both of these rulers rapidly modernized their countries. Although Kemal was more ideologically flexible and inclined more toward constitutional governance, neither ruler was a communist or a liberal democrat. Both saw traditional Islam as an obstacle to progress and secularized their countries. Turkey succeeded at this more than Iran, where Islamic fundamentalists swept to power in 1979.

8. **(D)** The twentieth century, like the twenty-first, was an era of multicultural interchange. A number of non-Westerners gained global reputations and won awards like the Nobel Prize. National liberation and decolonization were major themes, as was a sense of unease about—or outright hostility toward—the worldwide influence of American mass culture.

9. **(D)** The United States has not ratified the Kyoto Protocol, and modern environmental awareness, stirred up by figures like John Muir, dates back to the 1800s and early 1900s.

NGOs have played a large (arguably the largest) role in promoting environmental issues, and "green" parties have had an impact on national politics in many countries, in several cases gaining seats in parliaments and legislatures.

10. **(E)** The Soviet regime under Gorbachev concluded fairly quickly that it would be better for the USSR's economy and international reputation to allow its East European bloc to go free. What the Soviets did not count on was how the East European example would encourage already-powerful nationalist feelings among non-Russian subject peoples in the USSR. Even at his peak, Gorbachev was always more popular in the West than at home, and "losing" the USSR's East European possessions did not boost his reputation domestically.

11. **(B)** Famously associated with the nonviolent resistance of Mohandas Gandhi, *satyagraha* played a huge role in Indian opposition to British rule by exposing Britain's failure to live up to its own liberal ideals. It blended Hinduism with principles that Gandhi absorbed from other idealists, such as Russian novelist Leo Tolstoy and the American philosophers Emerson and Thoreau. It remains an open question as to how effective nonviolent resistance can be in the face of an illiberal, oppressive authority.

12. **(A)** The unhappiest trend in modern warfare has been the steadily escalating level of civilian involvement. Roughly half of the 55 million to 60 million people who perished in World War II were noncombatants. Both sides bombed civilian populations, and combat often took place near or in cities and smaller settlements. Deaths by naval blockade were much more numerous in World War I, when the Allies succeeded in blocking shipments to Germany and Austria.

13. **(D)** Russia experienced two revolutions in 1917: the spontaneous February (March) Revolution that deposed the tsar, and the October

(November) Revolution that brought the Communists to power. In between, a Provisional Government attempted to govern the country, prepare for national elections, and continue Russia's World War I effort. Its failure to extract Russia from the war and to solve socioeconomic problems turned sentiment against it, leaving it vulnerable. Lenin and Trotsky led the Communists in a successful coup.

14. **(B)** Mexico under Lázaro Cárdenas came as close as it would to realizing the populist ideals of the 1910 revolution, and land reform on behalf of the peasants was a key priority. Its chief source of wealth was the oil industry, which Cárdenas nationalized. Brazil experienced authoritarian rule under Getúlio Vargas, who admired Europe's fascist regimes.

15. **(D)** Japan's leaders encouraged belief in Shinto, which they distorted to justify militarist aggression and a sense of racial superiority. All the other atrocities listed here took place and were prosecuted at the Tokyo Trials—the Japanese counterpart to the Nuremberg Trials held in Germany.

16. **(A)** The key clue here is the phrase "the twentieth century's highest levels." Unemployment in the 1970s did not surpass the levels reached during the Great Depression of the 1930s. All the other items are true of the 1970s.

17. **(B)** With no formal powers to enforce its rulings, and without America—whose idea the league was—as a member, the League of Nations proved impotent when it came to dealing with serious diplomatic or military crises. Although Germany and Italy left during the 1930s, most European nations still belonged to it on the eve of World War II. Germany either took territories by force during the 1930s or negotiated directly with countries such as France and Britain.

18. **(E)** Simple map-reading skills should suffice to answer this question. All three Baltic countries, highly motivated by nationalism and feeling no sense of unity with the Slavic states to the east, were eager to integrate with the West and wanted nothing to do with the Russian-dominated CIS.

19. **(C)** Many obstacles have stood in the way of African modernization since decolonization. Its population, however, has grown rather than shrunk—and to the point where *over*population has added to the other problems already listed.

20. **(B)** Although the Turkish government continues to deny it, the Ottoman Empire massacred somewhere between half a million and 2 million Armenians on the basis of race during World War I. Turkey maintains that these were "accidental" civilian deaths in uncontrolled military circumstances, but the record shows otherwise. In discussing how extermination of the Jews might be possible, Hitler alluded to how quickly the world public had forgotten the Armenians.

UNIT SEVEN

MODEL
ADVANCED PLACEMENT
WORLD HISTORY
EXAMINATIONS

Answer Sheet

MODEL TEST 1

Section I

1 Ⓐ Ⓑ Ⓒ Ⓓ Ⓔ   21 Ⓐ Ⓑ Ⓒ Ⓓ Ⓔ   41 Ⓐ Ⓑ Ⓒ Ⓓ Ⓔ   61 Ⓐ Ⓑ Ⓒ Ⓓ Ⓔ
2 Ⓐ Ⓑ Ⓒ Ⓓ Ⓔ   22 Ⓐ Ⓑ Ⓒ Ⓓ Ⓔ   42 Ⓐ Ⓑ Ⓒ Ⓓ Ⓔ   62 Ⓐ Ⓑ Ⓒ Ⓓ Ⓔ
3 Ⓐ Ⓑ Ⓒ Ⓓ Ⓔ   23 Ⓐ Ⓑ Ⓒ Ⓓ Ⓔ   43 Ⓐ Ⓑ Ⓒ Ⓓ Ⓔ   63 Ⓐ Ⓑ Ⓒ Ⓓ Ⓔ
4 Ⓐ Ⓑ Ⓒ Ⓓ Ⓔ   24 Ⓐ Ⓑ Ⓒ Ⓓ Ⓔ   44 Ⓐ Ⓑ Ⓒ Ⓓ Ⓔ   64 Ⓐ Ⓑ Ⓒ Ⓓ Ⓔ
5 Ⓐ Ⓑ Ⓒ Ⓓ Ⓔ   25 Ⓐ Ⓑ Ⓒ Ⓓ Ⓔ   45 Ⓐ Ⓑ Ⓒ Ⓓ Ⓔ   65 Ⓐ Ⓑ Ⓒ Ⓓ Ⓔ
6 Ⓐ Ⓑ Ⓒ Ⓓ Ⓔ   26 Ⓐ Ⓑ Ⓒ Ⓓ Ⓔ   46 Ⓐ Ⓑ Ⓒ Ⓓ Ⓔ   66 Ⓐ Ⓑ Ⓒ Ⓓ Ⓔ
7 Ⓐ Ⓑ Ⓒ Ⓓ Ⓔ   27 Ⓐ Ⓑ Ⓒ Ⓓ Ⓔ   47 Ⓐ Ⓑ Ⓒ Ⓓ Ⓔ   67 Ⓐ Ⓑ Ⓒ Ⓓ Ⓔ
8 Ⓐ Ⓑ Ⓒ Ⓓ Ⓔ   28 Ⓐ Ⓑ Ⓒ Ⓓ Ⓔ   48 Ⓐ Ⓑ Ⓒ Ⓓ Ⓔ   68 Ⓐ Ⓑ Ⓒ Ⓓ Ⓔ
9 Ⓐ Ⓑ Ⓒ Ⓓ Ⓔ   29 Ⓐ Ⓑ Ⓒ Ⓓ Ⓔ   49 Ⓐ Ⓑ Ⓒ Ⓓ Ⓔ   69 Ⓐ Ⓑ Ⓒ Ⓓ Ⓔ
10 Ⓐ Ⓑ Ⓒ Ⓓ Ⓔ   30 Ⓐ Ⓑ Ⓒ Ⓓ Ⓔ   50 Ⓐ Ⓑ Ⓒ Ⓓ Ⓔ   70 Ⓐ Ⓑ Ⓒ Ⓓ Ⓔ
11 Ⓐ Ⓑ Ⓒ Ⓓ Ⓔ   31 Ⓐ Ⓑ Ⓒ Ⓓ Ⓔ   51 Ⓐ Ⓑ Ⓒ Ⓓ Ⓔ
12 Ⓐ Ⓑ Ⓒ Ⓓ Ⓔ   32 Ⓐ Ⓑ Ⓒ Ⓓ Ⓔ   52 Ⓐ Ⓑ Ⓒ Ⓓ Ⓔ
13 Ⓐ Ⓑ Ⓒ Ⓓ Ⓔ   33 Ⓐ Ⓑ Ⓒ Ⓓ Ⓔ   53 Ⓐ Ⓑ Ⓒ Ⓓ Ⓔ
14 Ⓐ Ⓑ Ⓒ Ⓓ Ⓔ   34 Ⓐ Ⓑ Ⓒ Ⓓ Ⓔ   54 Ⓐ Ⓑ Ⓒ Ⓓ Ⓔ
15 Ⓐ Ⓑ Ⓒ Ⓓ Ⓔ   35 Ⓐ Ⓑ Ⓒ Ⓓ Ⓔ   55 Ⓐ Ⓑ Ⓒ Ⓓ Ⓔ
16 Ⓐ Ⓑ Ⓒ Ⓓ Ⓔ   36 Ⓐ Ⓑ Ⓒ Ⓓ Ⓔ   56 Ⓐ Ⓑ Ⓒ Ⓓ Ⓔ
17 Ⓐ Ⓑ Ⓒ Ⓓ Ⓔ   37 Ⓐ Ⓑ Ⓒ Ⓓ Ⓔ   57 Ⓐ Ⓑ Ⓒ Ⓓ Ⓔ
18 Ⓐ Ⓑ Ⓒ Ⓓ Ⓔ   38 Ⓐ Ⓑ Ⓒ Ⓓ Ⓔ   58 Ⓐ Ⓑ Ⓒ Ⓓ Ⓔ
19 Ⓐ Ⓑ Ⓒ Ⓓ Ⓔ   39 Ⓐ Ⓑ Ⓒ Ⓓ Ⓔ   59 Ⓐ Ⓑ Ⓒ Ⓓ Ⓔ
20 Ⓐ Ⓑ Ⓒ Ⓓ Ⓔ   40 Ⓐ Ⓑ Ⓒ Ⓓ Ⓔ   60 Ⓐ Ⓑ Ⓒ Ⓓ Ⓔ

Model Test 1

SECTION I: MULTIPLE-CHOICE QUESTIONS

TIME: 55 MINUTES FOR 70 QUESTIONS

> **Directions:** Each of the questions or incomplete statements below is followed by suggested answers or completions. Select the one that is best in each case and then fill in the corresponding oval on the answer sheet.

1. Which of the following accurately describes the Americas and West Africa before 1500?

   (A) Polytheism was the dominant belief system.
   (B) Sorghum and rye were the main food staples.
   (C) Large domesticated animals allowed for extensive agricultural production.
   (D) The most prevalent trade goods were bananas and salt.
   (E) Written languages were in wide use at the time.

2. Post-industrial modes of economic activity focus MAINLY on providing

   (A) manufactured goods.
   (B) services.
   (C) raw materials.
   (D) plastics.
   (E) biotechnical products.

3. Between 1450 and 1750, Russia

   (A) was at the forefront of the northern Renaissance.
   (B) remained Catholic despite Calvinism's growing appeal.
   (C) failed to keep up with its neighbors in adopting gunpowder weapons.
   (D) threw off Mongol rule and centralized under the Muscovite tsars.
   (E) abandoned the system of serfdom.

4. Which of the following did NOT contribute to worldwide population growth between 1700 and 1800?

(A) a decline in infant mortality rates
(B) the widespread introduction of state-supported systems of health care
(C) a decline in the number of deadly epidemics
(D) the introduction of American food crops to Europe and Africa
(E) the growth in the amount of land under cultivation

5. During and after the 1980s, the Latin American nations of Chile, Argentina, and Brazil made transitions to what kind of regime?

(A) democratic
(B) anarchist
(C) communist
(D) fascist
(E) theocratic

6. The Holy Inquisition was created to

(A) track down and punish heretics and religious nonconformists.
(B) canonize followers of Christ.
(C) build great cathedrals in capital cities of Europe.
(D) fight the Muslims in the Middle East.
(E) find the Holy Grail.

7. How did decolonization in British and French colonies differ from that in colonies once ruled by Belgium and Portugal?

(A) British and French officials better prepared their colonies for freedom and kept violence to a minimum.
(B) Belgian and Portuguese officials better prepared their colonies for freedom and kept violence to a minimum.
(C) British and French officials threatened violence, whereas Belgian and Portuguese officials did not.
(D) Belgian and Portuguese officials allowed native representation in transitional governments.
(E) Decolonization proceeded in about the same manner for all of these colonies.

8. For most of the 1800s, the Eastern Question

(A) caused European powers to unite against Islamic jihads launched from Egypt.
(B) forced European powers to manage Ottoman decline without upsetting the balance of power.
(C) confronted the European powers with the rise of Persia as a commercial rival.
(D) pitted the European powers against a militaristic Russia.
(E) divided the European powers over how to combat the East African slave trade.

9. Which invention did most to begin the Industrial Revolution?

   (A) the cotton gin
   (B) electricity
   (C) the internal combustion engine
   (D) the steam engine
   (E) the paddle wheel

10. How were trends in New Spain and Brazil similar during colonization?

   (A) Neither the Spanish nor the Portuguese used slaves.
   (B) Both European conquerors decimated Native American populations.
   (C) Both societies became ethnically homogeneous.
   (D) Copper mining dominated the economy in both colonies.
   (E) Both colonies gave equal rights to indigenous peoples and those of mixed ancestry.

11. What global pandemic struck the world just after World War I?

   (A) hepatitis C
   (B) cholera
   (C) the Spanish flu
   (D) the Ebola virus
   (E) the bubonic plague

12. How did pastoralism affect the development of early societies?

   (A) It caused wandering clans to become more sedentary.
   (B) It encouraged monotheistic forms of worship.
   (C) It did away with gendered divisions of labor.
   (D) It discouraged the domestication of plants.
   (E) It diversified the types of food available to a given social group.

13. What made Mali such a powerful state in the 1300s?

   (A) It mobilized large armies and armed them with gunpowder weapons.
   (B) It profited by cooperating with European slave traders.
   (C) It was a center of Christian worship, attracting pilgrims and wealthy patrons.
   (D) It was a center of Islamic instruction and possessed large deposits of gold.
   (E) It controlled the spice trade and was a significant center of Buddhist worship.

14. Which of the following did the MOST to encourage European exploration in the 1400s?

   (A) fear that Ming China might gain global supremacy by exploring first
   (B) scientific curiosity
   (C) the desire to seek out direct trade routes to China and the East Indies
   (D) the opportunity to gain new converts to Catholicism
   (E) the chance to search for gold, ivory, and slaves in Africa

15. The world's leading producer of cotton around 1700 was

   (A) the American South.
   (B) Flanders.
   (C) India.
   (D) China.
   (E) the Arabian peninsula.

16. The image below is best interpreted as an example of

   (A) U.S. military domination over the Middle East.
   (B) foreign takeover of U.S. corporations.
   (C) cultural autonomy on the part of the non-Western world.
   (D) the global influence of U.S. mass culture.
   (E) increased immigration of Middle Easterners to the United States.

17. Which of the following is a suitable comparison of political systems in China and Western Europe between 1000 and 1300?

   (A) China was unraveling politically, and in Western Europe the trend was toward unification.
   (B) Explorers from both regions were beginning to colonize parts of Africa.
   (C) Chinese leaders ruled a unified empire, whereas Western Europe was governed by many monarchies.
   (D) Both regions were undergoing a process of democratization.
   (E) Chinese law instituted civil rights, whereas Western law focused on protecting the feudal system.

18. Hindu-Muslim tension in the 1940s

   (A) persuaded a disheartened Nehru to abandon the independence movement.
   (B) persuaded many Hindus to collaborate with Japan during World War II.
   (C) led to the partition of India and Pakistan soon after independence.
   (D) was actively encouraged by leaders such as Gandhi and Jinnah.
   (E) was, in the end, resolved without violence.

19. During the 1800s, the Zulu

   (A) migrated to northwest Africa.
   (B) converted to Islam.
   (C) allied with British forces to conquer neighboring tribes.
   (D) were conquered and enslaved by the Boers.
   (E) united and militarized under a warlike chieftain.

20. As a result of the first Opium War, China

   (A) expelled European traders from Shanghai and Canton.
   (B) imposed steep tariffs on Western goods sold in China.
   (C) asserted the preeminence of Chinese law in foreign concessions.
   (D) ceded Hong Kong to Great Britain.
   (E) permitted Germany to annex Formosa (Taiwan).

21. How is the overall effect of World War I on European culture best described?

   (A) Poetry in the victorious nations reflected triumph and pride.
   (B) Artists quickly put the wartime experience behind them and ignored it.
   (C) Despair and uncertainty came to the forefront of intellectual life.
   (D) Abstract painting was equated with the war's brutality and rejected in
       favor of straightforward realism.
   (E) American jazz easily allowed Europeans to forget the trauma caused by
       the war.

22. Before the onset of the Neolithic era, Stone Age societies are NOT believed
    to have

   (A) domesticated the dog.
   (B) practiced monotheism.
   (C) expressed themselves by means of painting and music.
   (D) constructed dwellings out of wood and stone.
   (E) buried their dead.

23. Until the mid-1800s, Great Britain's colony in India was administered by

   (A) the British East India Company.
   (B) the House of Trade.
   (C) the Ministry of Overseas Colonies.
   (D) the Foreign Office.
   (E) the Bank of England.

24. What social trauma was experienced in common by China, the Middle East, and Europe during the fourteenth century C.E.?

(A) religious schisms dividing the official church
(B) peasant revolts caused by rising levels of taxation
(C) migration away from frontier zones caused by barbarian invasions
(D) the bubonic plague in pandemic form
(E) mass hysteria caused by fears of witchcraft

25. The poster shown below is most likely meant to communicate

(A) the Nazis' anti-Semitic ideology.
(B) the Nazis' attitudes toward women.
(C) the Nazis' preoccupation with racial purity.
(D) the Nazis' plans for economic recovery.
(E) the Nazis' opposition to communism.

26. Which of the following is NOT true of interwar Japan?

(A) Universal male suffrage was granted.
(B) *Zaibatsu* megacorporations persuaded the government to pass a generous package of worker-friendly labor laws.
(C) A state-sponsored form of Shintoism was used to justify militaristic and imperial policies.
(D) Japan became aggressive in a series of military campaigns in China and Manchuria.
(E) A number of high-level officials, including one prime minister, were assassinated.

27. Dutch colonization in the 1500s and 1600s

    (A) was carried out in partnership with Spanish allies.
    (B) was restricted to Southeast Asia.
    (C) resulted in the creation of the world's first stock-issuing corporation.
    (D) was carried out by Protestants driven out by religious intolerance in the Netherlands.
    (E) resulted in Dutch rule over Australia until the late 1800s.

28. How did the Russian revolutions of 1917 resemble the French Revolution?

    (A) Both involved a communist takeover.
    (B) The principal leaders of both came from the peasant class.
    (C) In both, the first stage was more liberal than later stages.
    (D) For both, the goal was the founding of a democratic republic.
    (E) Both respected the right of citizens to worship as they pleased.

29. The Bretton Woods System was created after World War II to

    (A) promote international environmental protection efforts.
    (B) promote international free trade.
    (C) protect Western militaries.
    (D) prevent a nuclear war.
    (E) engage the Soviet bloc in arms control talks.

30. Which of the following best characterizes Japan's relations with the outside world during the 1600s?

    (A) Japanese merchants persuaded the shoguns to allow free trade with Europe.
    (B) Christianity failed to gain any significant following among the Japanese.
    (C) Foreign traders and missionaries turned out to have little interest in Japan.
    (D) European presence was highly restricted, mainly to the port of Nagasaki.
    (E) The shoguns actively supported the missionary activity of European Christians.

31. What major factor changed the economic life of East Africa during the early 1500s?

    (A) the depletion of metal deposits
    (B) the arrival of European colonists
    (C) the abolition of the Arab slave trade
    (D) civil war
    (E) invasion by Berber warriors

32. Akbar the Great, Ashoka, and Gandhi are alike in that all three

    (A) considered Hinduism superior to other faiths.
    (B) wished to elevate Buddhism to the status of official religion.
    (C) advocated the expulsion of Muslims from India.
    (D) were devoted to the ideal of religious tolerance.
    (E) favored secularization over Hindu traditionalism.

33. Modernization in twentieth-century Latin America often led to

    (A) greater social equality.
    (B) the concentration of wealth in the hands of a small elite.
    (C) the elimination of racial prejudice.
    (D) the sharp reduction of illegal drug trafficking.
    (E) economic diversification.

34. Among the global effects of the Seven Years' War was

    (A) France's defeat of Bengal armies in India.
    (B) Prussia's naval triumph over Spanish fleets in the Caribbean.
    (C) Britain's acquisition of Canadian territory from France.
    (D) Prussia's victories over Austria on the battlefields of central Europe.
    (E) Russia's destruction of Chinese outposts along the Amur River basin.

35. During most of the nineteenth century, which two countries competed hardest for influence over Central Asia?

    (A) Japan and China
    (B) Germany and Russia
    (C) Britain and Russia
    (D) Japan and Britain
    (E) France and Russia

36. How did rugged terrain affect the formation of societies in the Andes Mountains?

    (A) People were forced to cooperate and work out an effective division of labor.
    (B) Very few buildings or roads were constructed.
    (C) The level of cultural sophistication remained quite low.
    (D) Tribal wars regularly broke out over scarce resources.
    (E) Individual clans remain isolated, retarding the development of large societies.

37. How did the discovery of agriculture affect Neolithic peoples?

    (A) The need to find new plots of arable land forced a nomadic lifestyle on early agriculturalists.
    (B) Earth-worshipping religions arose, causing many societies to become matriarchal.
    (C) With all members of society working in agriculture, specialization of labor became less necessary.
    (D) The effort involved with planting led newly sedentary societies to give up the domestication of animals.
    (E) Permanent settlement in one place gave rise to the concept of private property.

38. Which of the following best describes how West and Central African states reacted to the arrival of Europeans in the late 1400s and 1500s?

    (A) Most migrated to the east, displacing tribes native to the Indian Ocean coast.
    (B) Roughly half the population fell victim to European diseases such as smallpox and malaria.
    (C) They sent fleets across the Mediterranean to raid Spain's and Portugal's southern shores.
    (D) Some remained strong by taking slaves from their neighbors and exchanging them for guns.
    (E) Most managed to deny Europeans access to the region's networks of trade.

39. What made the Russo-Japanese War of 1904–1905 so significant?

    (A) Russia secured a foothold in Manchuria for the first time.
    (B) It allowed the Japanese to take control of the Trans-Siberian Railroad.
    (C) For the first time in the modern era, non-Westerners defeated Europeans in a full-scale conflict.
    (D) Machine guns and modern artillery made it the bloodiest war fought to that date.
    (E) Japan's defeat in the war transformed it from a militaristic nation to a more pacifistic one.

World Human Population Growth: 1 C.E.–1999	
Year	*Population*
1 C.E.	200 million
1650	500 million
1850	1 billion
1930	2 billion
1975	4 billion
1999	6 billion

40. According to the chart above, during which of the following intervals did world population grow at the fastest rate (people per year)?

    (A) 1 C.E.–1650
    (B) 1650–1850
    (C) 1850–1930
    (D) 1930–1975
    (E) 1975–1999

41. What did Jawaharlal Nehru's diplomatic policy have in common with Sukarno's?

    (A) Both fell firmly into the Soviet camp.
    (B) Both enjoyed cordial relations with their countries' former colonizers.
    (C) Both opted to remain unaligned in the Cold War superpower conflict.
    (D) Both considered Maoist China to be their most natural ally.
    (E) Both established closer ties with the United States than with the USSR.

42. How did slavery and indentured servitude differ in the New World before 1800?

    (A) There was no practical difference between these categories of labor.
    (B) Slavery was more common in New England; indenture was practiced more in Britain's southern colonies.
    (C) Indentured servants paid off debt with their labor; slaves were freed only if their masters wished.
    (D) Slaves were used only for agricultural labor; indentured servants performed household tasks.
    (E) Indentured servitude was principally a French practice, whereas slaves were used by all colonial powers.

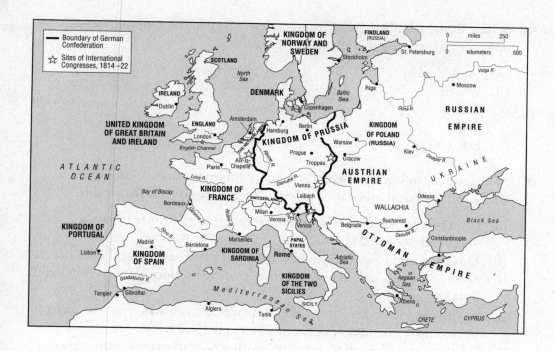

43. Which of the following is depicted by the map above?

    (A) the spread of French revolutionary ideology across Europe
    (B) the Napoleonic Empire at its peak
    (C) the resurgence of the Habsburg Empire under Franz Josef I
    (D) the map of Europe before the granting of Belgian independence
    (E) Europe as it was after the Franco-Prussian War

44. Many technological innovations stemmed from or were perfected during World War II, including

    (A) radio.
    (B) supersonic aircraft.
    (C) the tank.
    (D) the dry-cell battery.
    (E) radar.

45. Which crop dominated Southeast Asian agriculture in the 1400s?

    (A) rice
    (B) ginseng
    (C) soybeans
    (D) manioc
    (E) wheat

46. Where in the Middle East did women have the greatest range of educational opportunities during the 1920s and 1930s?

    (A) Saudi Arabia
    (B) Yemen
    (C) Turkey
    (D) Syria
    (E) Lebanon

47. Which of the following illustrates roughly simultaneous occurrences of a single technological innovation in two different regions of the world?

    (A) Chinese and Mesopotamian toolmakers creating bronze between 4000 and 3000 B.C.E.
    (B) European and Olmec engineers inventing the wheel around 2500 B.C.E.
    (C) Sumerian and Celtic scholars devising written scripts between 3500 and 3000 B.C.E.
    (D) Egyptians and Indus River valley agriculturalists discovering the secret of alcohol fermentation between 2500 and 1800 B.C.E.
    (E) Frankish and Flemish alchemists learning how to manufacture paper in the 1400s C.E.

48. During the 1700s, Ottoman janissaries and the aristocrats of continental Europe

    (A) led the way in abolishing feudalism.
    (B) frequently opposed reforms carried out by centralizing monarchs.
    (C) rejected gunpowder weaponry in favor of traditional forms of combat.
    (D) tended to be more religiously devout than the population at large.
    (E) invested heavily in joint-stock companies that funded overseas colonization.

49. How did the collapse of Han China resemble the Roman Empire's downfall?

    (A) Both were later absorbed by the Byzantine Empire.
    (B) Both weakened their military resolve by adopting Christianity.
    (C) The depletion of natural resources sapped both empires' economies.
    (D) Outside invaders contributed to the collapse of both empires.
    (E) Both collapsed because of lack of technological innovation.

50. Which statement below does NOT accurately reflect women's circumstances between 1000 and 1450?

    (A) Upper-class women in Europe tended to receive educations and manage household affairs in estates and castles.
    (B) At Japan's Heian court, aristocratic women could earn status by means of cultural and artistic accomplishment.
    (C) Certain societies in West Africa were matrilineal, rather than patrilineal.
    (D) In Islamic societies, women of the lower classes were, in practice, less restricted by religious law than those of the upper class.
    (E) The revival of Confucianism allowed Chinese women to gain greater rights and higher status.

51. Peasants living under the Tokugawa Shogunate

  (A) abandoned agricultural careers in large numbers to become traders.
  (B) benefited from a system of universal education.
  (C) readily adopted methods and scientific insights from Western agriculturalists.
  (D) gained the right to train with swords and serve in the armed forces.
  (E) found it extremely difficult to move from one social stratum to another.

52. Which of the following changes MOST distinguished the sixteenth century from the fifteenth in Europe and the Atlantic world?

  (A) The slave trade began.
  (B) The Renaissance spread to Russia and other regions to the east.
  (C) Absolutism reached its peak in Europe.
  (D) Systematic sugar production was introduced in the New World.
  (E) Triangular trade came abruptly to a halt.

53. How did European and Japanese feudal systems differ?

  (A) Japanese feudalism relied on serfdom, whereas the European system did not.
  (B) European knights had no code of conduct similar to the Japanese ethos of Bushido.
  (C) Gunpowder was restricted in Japan, and affected samurai less than it did knights in Europe.
  (D) Gunpowder weapons quickly ended the dominance of Japan's samurai, whereas European knights were not affected by such weapons.
  (E) Japanese feudalism was more repressive than European feudalism.

54. Which of the countries below was the last to grant suffrage to women?

  (A) United States
  (B) Canada
  (C) Great Britain
  (D) Italy
  (E) the USSR

55. A key difference between the Indian National Congress and the African National Congress was that

  (A) the former embraced communism, whereas the latter leaned toward anarchism.
  (B) the former committed itself to nonviolent resistance, whereas the latter turned more readily to violence.
  (C) the former collaborated with Britain's enemies during World War II, whereas the latter remained loyal.
  (D) the former's leaders spent long periods of time in prison, whereas the latter's did not.
  (E) the former was content to remain in the British Empire, but as a dominion, like Canada, whereas the latter wanted complete freedom.

56. The cartoon shown below depicts which nineteenth-century development?

(A) Western fears about the growing numbers of Japanese immigrants
(B) Chinese protests against the influx of Christian missionaries
(C) international outrage about the opium trade
(D) Burmese opposition to the French colonization of Indochina
(E) China's inability to prevent Western encroachments on its sovereignty

57. Which of the following accurately describes religious life in India during the 1300s?

(A) Islam had been forcibly introduced to much of India, especially in the north.
(B) Buddhism enjoyed a major revival and became the second-most popular faith after Hinduism.
(C) Islam became especially prominent in the southern and eastern parts of the country.
(D) Hinduism was nearly eradicated by seaborne invaders from East Africa.
(E) Hinduism remained unchallenged as India's dominant faith.

58. The movable-type printing press

(A) appeared first in China.
(B) helped spread Renaissance ideals to northern Europe.
(C) made it difficult for vernacular languages to gain literary importance.
(D) was outlawed by the Catholic Church.
(E) sparked a wave of Islamic expansion by mass-producing copies of the Qur'an.

59. Temples constructed in Cambodia and Thailand are most likely to reflect the influence of

    (A) Christianity and Hinduism.
    (B) Islam and Confucianism.
    (C) Taoism and Buddhism.
    (D) Hinduism and Buddhism.
    (E) Shinto and Buddhism.

60. In what way were Mesoamerican civilizations more sophisticated than those in North America before 1000 C.E.?

    (A) Mesoamerican peoples were more skilled at astronomy and architecture.
    (B) Mesoamerican societies developed monotheistic religions more quickly.
    (C) The Mesoamericans shunned human sacrifice, which North American tribes practiced extensively.
    (D) Mesoamerican city-states experimented with participatory forms of government similar to Athenian democracy.
    (E) Mesoamerican peoples had begun to domesticate the horse.

61. In what way were the student demonstrations on Tiananmen Square in May 1919 similar to those in May 1989?

    (A) The students called for the government to show more respect for the popular will.
    (B) The students called for an end to the communist regime.
    (C) The students called for violent overthrow of the government.
    (D) The students called for the radical transformation of culture and the arts.
    (E) The students called for capitalist reform of the economy.

62. The effect of the Upanishads on Hindu theology was to

    (A) provoke the schism that led to the birth of Buddhism.
    (B) reduce priestly authority in favor of individual responsibility for spiritual evolution.
    (C) nullify traditional justifications for the caste system.
    (D) elevate the status of the Vedic gods over that of deities such as Vishnu and Shiva.
    (E) cause the doctrines of karma and reincarnation to be declared heretical.

63. What marked the 1600s and 1700s as a period of scientific revolution in Europe?

    (A) the development of the theory of natural selection
    (B) the development of a workable and cost-effective steam engine
    (C) the development of navigational science and the invention of the compass
    (D) the development of the science of alchemy
    (E) the development of a unified system of physics, chemistry, and mathematics

64. One of the long-term effects of Mongol conquest was

(A) to eliminate Buddhism in China.
(B) to overthrow the fledgling Ottoman state.
(C) to bring Islam to parts of Hungary and Poland.
(D) to isolate Russia from Europe as the Renaissance got under way.
(E) to disrupt Silk Road commerce in Central Asia.

65. Why did the United States annex the Philippines after the Spanish-American War?

(A) purely for economic reasons
(B) for strategic purposes and because it thought American rule would benefit the natives
(C) to keep the Russians from gaining control of the islands
(D) because the Filipinos invited the Americans to occupy the bases there
(E) to encourage the spread of Christianity

66. Which of the following BEST encapsulates Confucian thought?

(A) Power is given to rulers by the gods; therefore, rulers may treat their people as they please.
(B) Husbands and wives should equally share the responsibility for family leadership.
(C) Harmony is attained when superiors treat those below them with kindness and inferiors respect those above them.
(D) Only members of the aristocracy are capable of cultivating the qualities of etiquette and grace.
(E) Society functions best when people are free to realize their individuality.

67. Which of the following sites was home to the greatest fusion of Arab, African, and Indian cultures in the nineteenth century?

(A) Alexandria
(B) Bombay (Mumbai)
(C) Djibouti
(D) Zanzibar
(E) Macau

68. Arab merchants

(A) contributed very little to the spread of Islam to Africa.
(B) lost control over Saharan caravan routes to Berber nomads in the ninth century C.E.
(C) refused for religious reasons to trade with Hindus from across the Indian Ocean.
(D) monopolized the growing trade in South African diamonds in the 1800s.
(E) dominated the East African slave trade until the late 1800s.

69. How did the adoption of parliamentary monarchies change the lives of ordinary Europeans in the 1700s?

(A) They were granted fewer civil liberties.
(B) They tended to enjoy more social mobility and greater freedom of religion.
(C) They successfully campaigned for the right to vote.
(D) Their average rate of literacy dropped.
(E) Social welfare systems protected them from poverty.

70. At the Berlin Conference (1884–1885)

(A) Socialist parties ratified *The Communist Manifesto*.
(B) The foreign ministers of Britain, Russia, and Germany resolved the Eastern Question.
(C) Germany, Austria, and Italy formed the Triple Alliance.
(D) An international gathering of suffragettes issued the charter *On the Equality of the Sexes*.
(E) European diplomats set boundary lines for African colonies and established rules for claiming new ones.

STOP

SECTION II: FREE-RESPONSE QUESTIONS

Part A: Document-Based Question

(SUGGESTED WRITING TIME—40 MINUTES)
PERCENT OF SECTION II SCORE—33⅓

Directions: The following question is based on the accompanying Documents 1–8. (The documents have been edited for the purpose of this exercise.) Write your answer on the lined pages of the Section II free-response booklet.

This question is designed to test your ability to work with and understand historical documents.

Write an essay that

- has a relevant thesis and supports that thesis with evidence from the documents.
- uses all of the documents.
- analyzes the documents by grouping them in as many appropriate ways as possible, and does not simply summarize the documents individually.
- takes into account the sources of the documents and analyzes the authors' points of view.
- identifies and explains the need for at least one additional type of document.

You may refer to relevant historical information not mentioned in the documents.

1. Using the documents, analyze the attitudes of Western and non-Western attitudes toward scientific and technological change from the 1500s onward. Identify an additional type of document and explain how it would help in assessing Western or non-Western actions and reactions.

DOCUMENT 1

Source: Charlotte Brontë, English novelist, upon viewing the Crystal Palace at London's Great Exhibition (1851).

> Yesterday I went for the second time to the Crystal Palace. . . . I must say I was more struck with it on this occasion than at my first visit. It is a wonderful place—vast, strange, new, and impossible to describe. . . . Whatever human industry has created you find there, from the great compartments filled with railway engines and boilers, with mill machinery in full work, with splendid carriages of all kinds, with harness of every description, to the glass-covered and velvet-spread stands loaded with the most gorgeous work of the goldsmith and silversmith. . . . It may be called a bazaar or a fair, but it is such a bazaar or fair as Eastern genii might have created. It seems as if only magic could have gathered this mass of wealth from all the ends of the earth.

DOCUMENT 2

Source: Victor Hugo, "This Will Kill That," *The Hunchback of Notre Dame* (1830).

Our readers must excuse us if we stop a moment to investigate the enigmatic words of the archdeacon: "This will kill that. The book will kill the edifice."

First of all, it was the view of a priest. It was the fear of an ecclesiastic before a new force, the printing press. It was the frightened yet dazzled man of the sanctuary confronting the illuminating Gutenberg press. . . . It signified that one great power was following upon the heels of another great power. It meant: The printing press will destroy the Church.

But besides this first thought, there was a second . . . but it no longer belongs to the priest alone, but to the scholar and to the artist as well. Here was a premonition that human thought had advanced, and, in changing, was about to change its mode of expression, that the important ideas of each new generation would be recorded in a new way, that the book of stone, [in which carvings and sculptures had provided the illiterate with a language of images and symbols], so solid and enduring, was about to be supplanted by the paper book, which would become more enduring still. In this respect, the vague formula of the archdeacon had a second meaning: That one art would dethrone another art. It meant: Printing will destroy architecture.

DOCUMENT 3

Source: Ito Hirobumi, young samurai from Japan, in letter to British official (1866).

Hitherto there have been a great number of stupid and ignorant persons in our provinces, who still adhered to the foolish old learning. They were unaware of the daily scientific progress of the Western nations, being like the frog at the bottom of a well. But lately they have learned. The eyes and ears of the stupid having thus been opened, the desirability of opening our country to foreign knowledge has become clear.

DOCUMENT 4

Source: Mohandas K. Gandhi, leader of Indian independence movement, *Gandhi: His Life and Message* (1954).

The incessant search for material comforts and their multiplication is such an evil, and I make bold to say that the Europeans themselves will have to remodel their outlook if they are not to perish under the weight of the comfort to which they are becoming slaves.

DOCUMENT 5

Source: Matteo Ricci, sixteenth-century Jesuit priest, showing a map of the world to the people of Canton during his visit to China (1578).

Of all the great nations, the Chinese have had the least commerce, indeed, one might say that they have had practically no contact whatever with outside nations, and consequently they are grossly ignorant of what the world in general is like. True, they had charts somewhat similar to this one, that were supposed to represent the whole world, but their universe was limited to their own fifteen provinces, and in the sea painted around it, they had placed a few islands to which they gave the names of different kingdoms they had heard of. . . . When they learned that China was only a part of the great east, they considered such an idea, so unlike their own, to be something utterly impossible. . . .

To them the heavens are round but the earth is flat and square, and they firmly believe that their empire is right in the middle of it. They do not like the idea of our geographies pushing their China into one corner of the Orient. They could not comprehend the demonstrations proving that the earth is a globe, made up of land and water, and that a globe of its nature has neither beginning nor end.

DOCUMENT 6

Source: Swiss author Henri Frédéric Amiel, on European industrialization, as seen at London's Great Exhibition (1851).

The useful will take the place of the beautiful, industry will take the place of art, political economy of religion, and arithmetic of poetry.

DOCUMENT 7

Source: Ali Akbar Davar, journalist and Iran's Minister of Public Works, editorial in *The Free Man* (1923).

Until we dedicate ourselves to an economic and technological revolution, nothing will move or change. We shall remain a nation of beggars, hungry and in ragged clothing, and we shall continue to suffer. We have six thousand years of history, but that will not translate into factories, railroads, hospitals, or schools. Schools alone without economic reforms will change nothing, as long as the environment outside the schools continues to reek of poverty. . . . When we have at least 5,000 kilometers of railways, 50 factories, 50 roads linking east and west, dams on the Karun River, and have eradicated locusts, we can then attend to the graduation of 1,000 students from institutions of higher learning.

DOCUMENT 8

Source: William Blake (1757–1827), English romantic poet, *Milton*.

> And did those feet in ancient time
> Walk upon England's mountains green?
> And was the Holy Lamb of God
> On England's pleasant pastures seen?
>
> And did the Countenance Divine
> Shine forth upon our clouded hills?
> And was Jerusalem builded here
> Among these dark Satanic Mills?
>
> Bring me my Bow of burning gold:
> Bring me my Arrows of desire:
> Bring me my Spear: O clouds unfold!
> Bring me my Chariot of fire.
>
> I will not cease from Mental Fight,
> Nor shall my Sword sleep in my hand
> Till we have built Jerusalem
> In England's green and pleasant Land.

Part B: Continuity and Change Over Time Question

(SUGGESTED PLANNING AND WRITING TIME—40 MINUTES)
PERCENT OF SECTION II SCORE—33⅓

Directions: You are to answer the following question. You should spend 5 minutes organizing or outlining your essay.

Write an essay that:

- has a relevant thesis and supports that thesis with appropriate historical evidence.
- addresses all parts of the question.
- uses world historical context to show continuities and changes over time.
- analyzes the process of continuity and change over time.

2. Analyze the economic–commercial changes and continuities associated with ONE of the following regions between 1200 B.C.E. and 1700 C.E.

the Indian Ocean
Central Asia
the Atlantic world

Part C: Comparative Essay

(SUGGESTED PLANNING AND WRITING TIME—40 MINUTES)
PERCENT OF SECTION II SCORE—33⅓

Directions: You are to answer the following question. You should spend 5 minutes organizing or outlining your essay.

Write an essay that

- has a relevant thesis and supports that thesis with appropriate historical evidence.
- addresses all parts of the question.
- makes direct, relevant comparisons.
- analyzes relevant reasons for similarities and differences.

3. For the period from 1945 to the present, compare the Southeast Asian experience of decolonization with that of sub-Saharan Africa.

STOP

END OF SECTION II

Answer Key
MODEL TEST 1

Section I

1. A	21. C	41. C	61. A
2. B	22. B	42. C	62. B
3. D	23. A	43. D	63. E
4. B	24. D	44. E	64. D
5. A	25. E	45. A	65. B
6. A	26. B	46. C	66. C
7. A	27. C	47. A	67. D
8. B	28. C	48. B	68. E
9. D	29. B	49. D	69. B
10. B	30. D	50. E	70. E
11. C	31. B	51. E	
12. E	32. D	52. D	
13. D	33. B	53. C	
14. C	34. C	54. D	
15. C	35. C	55. B	
16. D	36. A	56. E	
17. C	37. E	57. A	
18. C	38. D	58. B	
19. E	39. C	59. D	
20. D	40. E	60. A	

ANSWERS EXPLAINED

1. **(A)** Although the Maya had a sophisticated alphabet, written languages were not the norm in either region until quite recently, and neither was the use of animals in large-scale agricultural production. In neither place were sorghum and rye staple crops at the same time, or bananas and salt the most important commodities. Polytheistic forms of worship persisted in both places until and even after contact with the Europeans.

2. **(B)** Western nations have developed postindustrial economies that emphasize services, consumerism, and cutting-edge technology. In turn, a greater part of the workforce in these countries has been employed in the services, including the biotech and computer industries, and there is a smaller proportion of unionized, blue-collar factory workers.

3. **(D)** Eliminate answers B and E because Russia was Eastern Orthodox and kept serfdom in place until the mid-1800s. Thanks largely to Mongol rule, the Russians did not experience the Renaissance with the rest of Europe, but they did incorporate new weapons and fortifications in response to the spread of gunpowder. The main trend during this time frame was centralization under Moscow's leadership.

4. **(B)** Public health and state-run systems of medical care are modern inventions. All the other factors helped cause population growth during the 1700s.

5. **(A)** For decades, many regimes in Latin America were dictatorial, but the 1980s and 1990s witnessed a wave of democratization in such countries as Argentina, Brazil, Chile, and Nicaragua. One of the few exceptions to this trend was Cuba, which remained under the control of Fidel Castro.

6. **(A)** In 1231, the Holy Inquisition was established as a set of special courts with wide-ranging powers. Its goal was to hunt out and punish heresy and religious nonconformity.

7. **(A)** Methods for maintaining control over African colonies were particularly inhumane under the Belgians and Portuguese. In the process of extracting natural resources from the Congo, Belgian authorities maimed or murdered millions of Congolese people. Neither Belgium nor Portugal took steps to prepare their colonies for independence after World War II.

8. **(B)** By the 1800s, the Ottoman Empire was disintegrating, a fact that presented the European powers with the geopolitical challenge of managing its decline without upsetting their own balance of power or allowing a new power, possibly hostile to Europe, from taking the Ottomans' place.

9. **(D)** Powerful and cost-effective steam engines were developed near the end of the 1700s, when the English mining and textile industries, already having mechanized, badly needed a new and improved source of energy.

10. **(B)** Both the Spanish and Portuguese extracted natural resources from their colonies in the New World by exploiting slave labor from Africa. Although they quickly gave up enslaving Native Americans, the Europeans decimated large numbers of them because of the fact that they brought diseases and had the

advantage of more advanced military technology. Latin American societies were very hierarchical based on race.

11. **(C)** Spanish flu was a major pandemic in the twentieth century. It struck during the end of World War I and killed 20 million people (perhaps more) worldwide—twice as many people as died in the war.

12. **(E)** Pastoralism tended to cause nomadism, not permanent settlement, so A is false; on the other hand, herding did nothing to discourage early plant domestication, so D is false as well. Although the gender division of labor was more pronounced in agricultural societies, it was never absent, and there is no provable connection between certain modes of economic production and forms of worship.

13. **(D)** Between 1250 and 1460, Mali was the biggest and most powerful Islamic state in western sub-Saharan Africa. It had large deposits of gold and metal ore and, as a result, became a key center for trade in eastern and northern Africa. When European states began to coin money, the demand for gold there made Mali even richer.

14. **(C)** The Europeans' primary motivation for exploration was economic. During the Middle Ages, Europeans had become aware of the fabulous wealth of other parts of the world, particularly in the east. They planned to acquire this wealth by seeking out direct trade routes to China and the East Indies.

15. **(C)** Under Mughal rule, the economy thrived largely because of a boom in the Indian cotton trade. However, as the Europeans gradually gained the upper hand in India during the 1700s, they defeated the Mughal state and established their own control over cotton production.

16. **(D)** U.S. brands such as Coca-Cola and McDonald's (which are arguably no longer American, but multinational) enjoy worldwide recognition, as shown by this sign reading "McDonald's" in Arabic. Their omnipresence demonstrates the symbolic power and appeal of American mass culture.

17. **(C)** During this period in Europe, a large number of relatively centralized states had emerged and were led by monarchs. In China, centralization was achieved first by Mongol rule beginning in the 1200s. Later, after the mid-1300s, China underwent even greater centralization under the Ming dynasty.

18. **(C)** The Muslim League paralleled the Congress Party's independence efforts, but each had different aims. The Muslim League advocated a separate Muslim state called Pakistan. The failure of the Muslim League and Congress Party to resolve their differences peacefully led to great bloodshed after Indian independence occurred in 1947. India and Pakistan were partitioned, but they continued to fight over Kashmir, a province of India that is heavily Muslim.

19. **(E)** During the early 1800s, the Zulu were united and militarized under the chieftain Shaka Zulu. They went on to conquer and displace many neighboring tribes. Along with the Asante, they posed one of the greatest military threats to the British in Africa. They did not convert to Islam in any great numbers.

20. **(D)** The first Opium War, between China and Britain from 1839 to 1842, ended in a humiliating defeat for the Chinese, making answers A, B, and C impossible. The British took Hong Kong and asserted many other privileges in the Treaty of Nanking. Germany gained concessions in China only much later.

21. **(C)** World War I's cultural impact was so profound that B and E can easily be ignored. Not even the victors felt particularly triumphant, and the leading edge of art and literature did not retreat into the styles of the 1800s, meaning A and D are wrong as well.

22. **(B)** Although generalizing about Paleolithic humanity is difficult, we do know that early humans domesticated dogs, painted and created music, constructed dwellings out of wood and stone, and buried their dead. Concerning religious practices, early humans were polytheistic, meaning they worshipped more than one god.

23. **(A)** The British East India Company, a chartered joint-stock company created partly in imitation of the Dutch East India Company, administered British possessions in India politically and militarily as well as economically, until the Indian Mutiny of 1857. After the Mutiny was put down, the British crown stepped in to incorporate India directly into the British Empire.

24. **(D)** Although all these problems plagued all three regions at one time or another, the only one to strike all three during the time in question was the bubonic plague, which swept from China to the Middle East, and then to Europe. On average, it killed up to a third of any given population.

25. **(E)** The Nazis created propaganda dealing with all the topics listed. The snake representing the social evil to be crushed in this poster, however, bears the label "Marxismus"—a clear clue, even without reading German, that communism is the subject.

26. **(B)** Although Japan liberalized politically during the 1920s, it moved less in that direction where social and economic policy were concerned, especially because large corporations, the *zaibatsu*, had such a close relationship with the government that they could block trade-union efforts and labor legislation. Social tensions grew only worse with the depression, and violence and instability ended liberalization. By 1941, the Japanese military had gained control over the parliamentary government.

27. **(C)** The Dutch were enemies of Spain, not its allies, and they were for the most part religiously tolerant, so B and D are false. Although the British, not the Dutch, colonized Australia, and although Indonesia was the Netherlands' most important possession, the Dutch did colonize outside Southeast Asia. The Dutch established the Dutch East India Company, the first of its type, in the 1500s.

28. **(C)** Although the Russian revolution ended with a communist takeover, the French did not. In neither case did peasants play a leading role, and in both cases, the regimes interfered with the right to worship. The early French revolutionaries did not wish to found a democratic republic, although the Provisional Government that ruled Russia between the spring and fall of 1917

did. In both cases, a liberal attempt to overthrow despotism gave way to a more radical sort of revolution.

29. **(B)** In 1944, the United States and its allies met in Bretton Woods, New Hampshire, to create new economic institutions that would promote free trade and a stable monetary system. These new institutions included the World Bank and the International Monetary Fund.

30. **(D)** The key word here is *isolation*, which eliminates A and E. Foreigners wanted to trade with Japan, but although some interchange was allowed, it took place under highly restricted conditions, as in answer C. Despite this (and despite official disencouragement and occasional violence), a surprising number of Japanese embraced Christianity.

31. **(B)** During this period, the Portuguese were the most prevalent group of Europeans in the region. They conquered a chain of cities along the East African coast, turning them into colonies and garrisons. The Berbers lived far to the west, and the slave trade continued into the 1800s.

32. **(D)** All three of these Indian political figures, whatever their own faith, were famed for their religious tolerance.

33. **(B)** As in many non-Western parts of the world, modernization and industrialization were often carried out from above, by rulers and/or wealthy elites. In these cases, the wealth generated by modernization tended to stay in the hands of the elite, rather than being put to use for the good of the population at large.

34. **(C)** The only answers that are true of the Seven Years' War are C and D, and the latter has to do with the original European conflict, not its global ramifications. As for answer A, it was the British who defeated Bengal armies during this time.

35. **(C)** The so-called Great Game was an intense competition between Russia and Britain for influence over Central Asia. It involved espionage and diplomatic intrigue. Tensions over Central Asia never resulted in outright war, although this rivalry lasted until shortly before World War I.

36. **(A)** This cooperation and efficiency gave rise to a number of major South American cultures, both before and after 1000 C.E. They included the Nazca, the Moche, the Huari, the Tiahuanaco, and the Chimu.

37. **(E)** Agriculture discourages nomadism, but does nothing to discourage animal domestication. The shift away from hunter-gatherer and herding economies led to greater, not lesser, specialization of labor, and there is no evidence that agricultural societies had any special inclination toward matriarchal authority.

38. **(D)** All these answers accurately describe the impact the Europeans had on West and Central Africa during this period. The Portuguese continued to expand along Africa's western shore until 1488. Later, the Dutch, English, and French landed there, began trading, and built permanent outposts.

39. **(C)** The Russo-Japanese War of 1904–1905 was a great victory for Japan, which was better prepared for war and benefited from fighting close to home.

As a result, it annexed new territories and compelled Russia to agree to recognize its sphere of influence in southern Manchuria. The victory also encouraged a strong imperialistic streak, based on the slogan "Asia for the Asians," in Japan.

40. **(E)** Although world population grew by 2 billion both between 1930–1975 and 1975–1999, the second period is significantly shorter.

41. **(C)** Many governments of Third World countries, including those of Indonesia and India, did not want to remain aligned exclusively with either side during the Cold War. Instead, they thought it was in their best interests to remain neutral or at least switch sides every few years, depending on who was willing to grant them economic and military assistance.

42. **(C)** Many English settlers during the 1600s were indentured servants who agreed to work for their masters for a set number of years to pay for their passage across the Atlantic. On the other hand, slaves (who were used by every colonizing power) were forced to live in servitude. Both slaves and indentured servants could be used for agricultural or household labor.

43. **(D)** This map requires careful reading. Answers A and B would require more territory to be directly under French control. The Habsburg Empire did not experience "resurgence" under Franz Josef, and the fact that Germany is not united precludes answer E. Note that Belgium is not marked on the map—an easy way to arrive at answer D.

44. **(E)** Radar was made workable in time to help save Britain as it suffered German air attacks in 1940. All the other items listed were invented or perfected before or after World War II.

45. **(A)** Rice-paddy farming probably originated in the Vietnamese states around 500 B.C.E. By the 1400s, this method had spread to other parts of Asia, including China and Japan. However it was cultivated, it became Asia's mainstay crop.

46. **(C)** The modernization and secularization of Turkish life and politics under Colonel Mustafa Kemal, later named Ataturk, created greater opportunities for women as early as the 1920s. The other countries listed here were much slower to do so and still tend to be patriarchal.

47. **(A)** Diffusion—adapting a new technology or idea from a neighboring people—played a great role in how early societies learned to do things. Certain ideas, however, arose independently, as bronze metalworking appears to have done in these cases.

48. **(B)** Especially during the early modern period, monarchs who wished to centralize or modernize often met with opposition from aristocratic classes who wished to retain their privileges. European nobles and the Ottoman janissaries—who, as a military elite past its technological prime, had even greater reason to fear obsolescence—fell into this category. Opposition sometimes took the form of rebellion or assassination.

49. **(D)** Waves of Asiatic and Germanic barbarians attacked Roman lands from the east and the north for more than four centuries, finally wearing it down to a final collapse in 476 C.E. In Han China, outside invaders, bandits, and rebels on the frontiers prevented them from effectively guarding their borders. In 200 C.E., the Han dynasty collapsed.

50. **(E)** Neo-Confucianism, along with Chinese tradition, was used to justify the greater subordination of women. Upper-class women, whose families were most likely to follow Confucian dictates, were particularly subject to restrictions.

51. **(E)** The Tokugawa Shogunate was authoritarian and isolationist. It experienced considerable economic growth, but was very hierarchical.

52. **(D)** During the 1500s, Portuguese and Spanish colonies in Brazil and the Caribbean became major centers of sugar production. Massive profits from the sugar industry were built on the backs of African slaves. The Atlantic economy, with its triangular trade, boomed.

53. **(C)** The Tokugawa rulers maintained a monopoly on gunpowder technology and kept the number of guns in Japan to a minimum. European feudalism depended on serfdom, making A false, and gunpowder technology spread freely in Europe. European chivalry was similar in many respects to Japan's code of Bushido.

54. **(D)** After World War I, neither France nor Italy joined most of the rest of Europe and North America in giving women the vote. Both were traditionally patriarchal, and Italian fascism was decidedly anti-feminist.

55. **(B)** Both groups wanted full independence, and each had its leaders (Gandhi, Nehru, Mandela) jailed. Although there were pro-Japanese collaborationists in India, Congress did not endorse them. The ANC flirted with Marxism, but the Indian Congress did not. Gandhi and others put the Indian Congress firmly on the path of non-violent resistance.

56. **(E)** Facial expressions indicate that the outrage is Asian, not "Western" or "international," making A and C false. The caption on the pie reads *Chine*— French for "China"—making D unlikely. Choosing between B and E rests largely on remembering how much influence foreign powers gained over large portions of Chinese territory.

57. **(A)** By 1206, Muslim armies had captured Delhi, and most of northern India was in their hands. The major effect of the Muslim invasions and the establishment of the Delhi Sultanate was to introduce Islam into India.

58. **(B)** Johannes Gutenberg created the moving-type printing press, in which individual metal characters could be placed in a frame to form pages, used, taken out, rearranged, and used again to create a different page. It was instrumental in raising literacy rates, spreading information, increasing the impact of new ideas and scientific theories, and encouraging the expansion of libraries and universities.

59. **(D)** The Khmer adopted both Hinduism and Buddhism, and they built tens of thousands of temples reflecting the influence of both religions. The most famous example of Khmer architecture is Angkor Wat and Angkor Thom, former cities that consist of forty square miles of ornate palaces and pagodas. Thailand was mainly Buddhist.

60. **(A)** The Maya were accomplished astronomers and mathematicians. Their unusual calendar system was extremely intricate and accurate. They were also able architects, as shown by their pyramids and other buildings. Although North American peoples like the Hopewell and Mississippi civilizations built large mounds and at least one city, they were not as advanced. The horse was not native to the Americas at this time.

61. **(A)** On May 4, 1919, thousands of Chinese students gathered to protest against the military government that had derailed Sun Yat-sen's government. They desired political and social reform. In May 1989, student protesters chose to demonstrate at this time because it marked the seventieth anniversary of the May Fourth Movement, and they felt inspired by that event.

62. **(B)** The Upanishads revolutionized Indian religion by adding a new dimension to Vedic religion. They did not deny the doctrines of karma and reincarnation, but emphasized the ability of each person to further his or her spiritual evolution, rather than relying so much on priestly guidance. The Vedic deities were supplanted by gods like Vishnu and Shiva, not vice versa.

63. **(E)** The other innovations here are misdated. The Scientific Revolution ushered in a renewed interest in the ancient concept of the scientific method, as opposed to decision-making approaches based on superstition or narrow religious doctrines. Figures like Isaac Newton conceptualized the age's discoveries as a single system of thought.

64. **(D)** The Mongols facilitated Silk Road trade, making E false, and although some Mongols converted to Islam, they did not bring it to Eastern Europe. The rise of the Ottomans postdates the rise of the Mongols, and Mongol rulers in China, far from eliminating Buddhism, adopted it themselves. The Mongols ruled Russia for more than two centuries, cutting them off from Europe during the Renaissance.

65. **(B)** The United States wanted to keep the Philippines from falling into the hands of the Japanese, not the Russians. Most Filipinos were already Christian, thanks to centuries of Spanish colonization. Although possession of the Philippines made trade with China easier, the fact that it provided the United States with an excellent naval base was paramount. The Filipinos at first welcomed the Americans for liberating them from Spain, but did not ask to be occupied and fought a guerrilla war against U.S. troops for years.

66. **(C)** Answer A runs counter to the Chinese ideology of the Mandate of Heaven. Answers B and E fail to account for Confucianism's tendency toward hierarchy, while D neglects the fact that, in Confucian thought, people from any class can (and should) learn to behave gracefully and courteously.

67. **(D)** In the early 1800s, Zanzibar was the most important port in East Africa and controlled by Omani Arabs. Bombay (Mumbai) was its primary trading partner.

68. **(E)** Arab merchants did much to spread Islam to Africa; their religion did not bar them from trading with Hindus, and they retained control of Saharan trade routes much longer than B indicates. They had comparatively little to do with the emerging diamond trade in nineteenth-century South Africa.

69. **(B)** In parliamentary democracies in the 1700s, rulers became less powerful, because they governed in conjunction with some kind of lawmaking body. Although poverty and inequality existed in parliamentary monarchies during this era, society was more flexible, and social advancement more feasible, than in absolute monarchies.

70. **(E)** In 1884 and 1885, representatives of European nations, hosted by Otto von Bismarck, met in Berlin to set down rules for expanding further into Africa. They decided that no European state could make new claims there without demonstrating "effective occupation."

Answer Sheet
MODEL TEST 2

Section I

1 Ⓐ Ⓑ Ⓒ Ⓓ Ⓔ   21 Ⓐ Ⓑ Ⓒ Ⓓ Ⓔ   41 Ⓐ Ⓑ Ⓒ Ⓓ Ⓔ   61 Ⓐ Ⓑ Ⓒ Ⓓ Ⓔ
2 Ⓐ Ⓑ Ⓒ Ⓓ Ⓔ   22 Ⓐ Ⓑ Ⓒ Ⓓ Ⓔ   42 Ⓐ Ⓑ Ⓒ Ⓓ Ⓔ   62 Ⓐ Ⓑ Ⓒ Ⓓ Ⓔ
3 Ⓐ Ⓑ Ⓒ Ⓓ Ⓔ   23 Ⓐ Ⓑ Ⓒ Ⓓ Ⓔ   43 Ⓐ Ⓑ Ⓒ Ⓓ Ⓔ   63 Ⓐ Ⓑ Ⓒ Ⓓ Ⓔ
4 Ⓐ Ⓑ Ⓒ Ⓓ Ⓔ   24 Ⓐ Ⓑ Ⓒ Ⓓ Ⓔ   44 Ⓐ Ⓑ Ⓒ Ⓓ Ⓔ   64 Ⓐ Ⓑ Ⓒ Ⓓ Ⓔ
5 Ⓐ Ⓑ Ⓒ Ⓓ Ⓔ   25 Ⓐ Ⓑ Ⓒ Ⓓ Ⓔ   45 Ⓐ Ⓑ Ⓒ Ⓓ Ⓔ   65 Ⓐ Ⓑ Ⓒ Ⓓ Ⓔ
6 Ⓐ Ⓑ Ⓒ Ⓓ Ⓔ   26 Ⓐ Ⓑ Ⓒ Ⓓ Ⓔ   46 Ⓐ Ⓑ Ⓒ Ⓓ Ⓔ   66 Ⓐ Ⓑ Ⓒ Ⓓ Ⓔ
7 Ⓐ Ⓑ Ⓒ Ⓓ Ⓔ   27 Ⓐ Ⓑ Ⓒ Ⓓ Ⓔ   47 Ⓐ Ⓑ Ⓒ Ⓓ Ⓔ   67 Ⓐ Ⓑ Ⓒ Ⓓ Ⓔ
8 Ⓐ Ⓑ Ⓒ Ⓓ Ⓔ   28 Ⓐ Ⓑ Ⓒ Ⓓ Ⓔ   48 Ⓐ Ⓑ Ⓒ Ⓓ Ⓔ   68 Ⓐ Ⓑ Ⓒ Ⓓ Ⓔ
9 Ⓐ Ⓑ Ⓒ Ⓓ Ⓔ   29 Ⓐ Ⓑ Ⓒ Ⓓ Ⓔ   49 Ⓐ Ⓑ Ⓒ Ⓓ Ⓔ   69 Ⓐ Ⓑ Ⓒ Ⓓ Ⓔ
10 Ⓐ Ⓑ Ⓒ Ⓓ Ⓔ   30 Ⓐ Ⓑ Ⓒ Ⓓ Ⓔ   50 Ⓐ Ⓑ Ⓒ Ⓓ Ⓔ   70 Ⓐ Ⓑ Ⓒ Ⓓ Ⓔ
11 Ⓐ Ⓑ Ⓒ Ⓓ Ⓔ   31 Ⓐ Ⓑ Ⓒ Ⓓ Ⓔ   51 Ⓐ Ⓑ Ⓒ Ⓓ Ⓔ
12 Ⓐ Ⓑ Ⓒ Ⓓ Ⓔ   32 Ⓐ Ⓑ Ⓒ Ⓓ Ⓔ   52 Ⓐ Ⓑ Ⓒ Ⓓ Ⓔ
13 Ⓐ Ⓑ Ⓒ Ⓓ Ⓔ   33 Ⓐ Ⓑ Ⓒ Ⓓ Ⓔ   53 Ⓐ Ⓑ Ⓒ Ⓓ Ⓔ
14 Ⓐ Ⓑ Ⓒ Ⓓ Ⓔ   34 Ⓐ Ⓑ Ⓒ Ⓓ Ⓔ   54 Ⓐ Ⓑ Ⓒ Ⓓ Ⓔ
15 Ⓐ Ⓑ Ⓒ Ⓓ Ⓔ   35 Ⓐ Ⓑ Ⓒ Ⓓ Ⓔ   55 Ⓐ Ⓑ Ⓒ Ⓓ Ⓔ
16 Ⓐ Ⓑ Ⓒ Ⓓ Ⓔ   36 Ⓐ Ⓑ Ⓒ Ⓓ Ⓔ   56 Ⓐ Ⓑ Ⓒ Ⓓ Ⓔ
17 Ⓐ Ⓑ Ⓒ Ⓓ Ⓔ   37 Ⓐ Ⓑ Ⓒ Ⓓ Ⓔ   57 Ⓐ Ⓑ Ⓒ Ⓓ Ⓔ
18 Ⓐ Ⓑ Ⓒ Ⓓ Ⓔ   38 Ⓐ Ⓑ Ⓒ Ⓓ Ⓔ   58 Ⓐ Ⓑ Ⓒ Ⓓ Ⓔ
19 Ⓐ Ⓑ Ⓒ Ⓓ Ⓔ   39 Ⓐ Ⓑ Ⓒ Ⓓ Ⓔ   59 Ⓐ Ⓑ Ⓒ Ⓓ Ⓔ
20 Ⓐ Ⓑ Ⓒ Ⓓ Ⓔ   40 Ⓐ Ⓑ Ⓒ Ⓓ Ⓔ   60 Ⓐ Ⓑ Ⓒ Ⓓ Ⓔ

Model Test 2

SECTION I: MULTIPLE-CHOICE QUESTIONS

TIME: 55 MINUTES FOR 70 QUESTIONS

Directions: Each of the questions or incomplete statements below is followed by suggested answers or completions. Select the one that is best in each case and then fill in the corresponding oval on the answer sheet.

1. The Marshall Plan
   - (A) dedicated funds to the subversion of Soviet rule in Eastern Europe.
   - (B) ended the Cold War by reducing the number of Soviet and American nuclear warheads.
   - (C) granted the British control over Palestine after World War I.
   - (D) devised a new strategy to end the Vietnam War.
   - (E) injected billions of dollars into Western European economies to rebuild after World War II.

2. How did the German experience in colonizing Africa differ from that of the British and French?
   - (A) The Germans refrained from colonizing Africa.
   - (B) The British and French treated natives more brutally than the Germans did.
   - (C) German colonies were less desirable, lost money, and involved the Germans in brutal wars against the natives.
   - (D) The Germans colonized the northern coast of Africa, and the French and British took the eastern coast.
   - (E) German colonies were the most politically and economically successful in Africa.

3. The political and social effect of Neo-Confucianism in China was

 (A) to diminish public respect for China's emperor.
 (B) to reinforce the hierarchical organization of Chinese society.
 (C) to elevate the status of Chinese women.
 (D) to foster greater individualism among the Chinese.
 (E) to break down intergenerational relationships in Chinese families.

4. Which of the following is NOT true about the status of women in the twentieth century?

 (A) Fascist Italy, Nazi Germany, and militarist Japan actively encouraged the equal treatment of women.
 (B) During World War II, more women worked outside the home than during World War I.
 (C) At least in theory, Soviet ideology was committed to the ideal of gender equality.
 (D) Major goals of women's movements have been the achievement of legal equality and the elimination of culturally stereotyped gender roles.
 (E) Achievements of women's movements include equal access to higher education and a greater role in political life.

5. Which of the following trends is associated with Europe's Industrial Revolution?

 (A) outmigration from the cities to the countryside during the 1800s
 (B) a steep decline in population levels in the last quarter of the 1800s
 (C) a general increase in prosperity after the mid-1800s
 (D) the gradual shrinking of the middle class after the 1848 revolutions
 (E) an immediate improvement in the lives of the lower classes

6. In the early 1900s, what kinds of changes did the Young Turks wish to bring to the Ottoman Empire?

 (A) modernization and secularization
 (B) a return to Islamic fundamentalism
 (C) the revival of the janissary corps
 (D) a strengthening of the sultan's powers
 (E) closer diplomatic ties with the United States

7. The French colony of "Louisiana" consisted of

 (A) what is now the state of Louisiana.
 (B) what is now the province of Quebec.
 (C) the mid-Atlantic coast of North America.
 (D) the Great Lakes region and the Mississippi River valley.
 (E) the coast of the Gulf of Mexico from what is now Texas to Florida.

8. Existentialists would most likely agree that

   (A) a single God exists for the benefit of all humanity, and organized religion points the way to true morality.
   (B) every religion is valid, in that it helps people to reach true divinity.
   (C) the individual must learn to create his or her own ethical existence without the guidance of organized religion.
   (D) the universe is uncaring and amoral, and therefore all life is meaningless.
   (E) in the absence of a higher spiritual authority, might makes right, and everything is permissible.

9. Most historians consider that, during the Neolithic period, agriculture

   (A) was developed by all African and Eurasian cultures simultaneously.
   (B) was developed in many places independently, but also passed on or influenced by a process of cultural diffusion.
   (C) arose in one place, then was passed on to other cultures by means of cultural diffusion.
   (D) was brought to Eurasia by settlers migrating from the Americas.
   (E) did not develop at all, but emerged during the Stone Age.

10. The photograph below most likely illustrates an instance of

   (A) racial tensions breaking out into open conflict.
   (B) the tendency of Western imperial powers to train and deploy native troops.
   (C) intercultural commercial exchange involving the sale of military equipment.
   (D) forcible conversion of Africans to Catholicism.
   (E) technology transfer of gunpowder weaponry from West Africa to Europe.

11. What BEST explains the Russian conquest of Central Asia in the 1800s?

    (A) the regime's dedication to scientific and geographic research
    (B) the desire to convert the region's Muslims to Eastern Orthodoxy
    (C) fear that Germany might gain control of the Indian Ocean coast
    (D) the need to control the region's vast reserves of oil
    (E) anxiety about protecting a long and open southern frontier

12. What factor MOST encouraged the wave of democratization in Latin America in the 1990s?

    (A) a series of victories by Marxist guerrillas
    (B) new wealth generated by legalizing the narcotics trade
    (C) the end of the Cold War superpower conflict
    (D) the disbanding of the Organization of American States
    (E) the simultaneous death of several key dictators

13. Why did Europe's popes launch crusades during the medieval era?

    (A) to spread Christianity to Ireland
    (B) to fight Muslims, convert non-Catholics, and wipe out heresy
    (C) to enable England to conquer French lands
    (D) to grasp control of trade along the Silk Road
    (E) to conquer territory in sub-Saharan Africa

14. The travels of Ibn Battuta and Zheng He have what in common?

    (A) They demonstrate that the West did not have a monopoly on campaigns of exploration.
    (B) They were limited in their geographical scope.
    (C) They were motivated principally by the desire to gain religious converts.
    (D) Both compelled many of the places they visited to pay tribute to their home countries.
    (E) Both involved the projection of military force.

15. Why did the Spanish abolish the encomienda system in the mid-1500s?

    (A) Because Spain abolished slavery in all its colonial territories.
    (B) Because the system was allowing Native Americans to regain control of their former lands.
    (C) Because other countries agitated against its use.
    (D) There was no longer any use for it.
    (E) Because Catholic priests movingly protested against the system's abuses.

16. The Lend-Lease program

   (A) offered U.S. and British economic assistance to recently decolonized states in the 1950s and 1960s.
   (B) brought East European economies under tight Soviet control during the early years of the Cold War.
   (C) committed the United States to the economic support of Great Britain and the USSR during World War II.
   (D) created the foundations for greater economic union in Europe.
   (E) established a regional trade network in East and Southeast Asia.

17. By the 1750s, which European power had defeated the Mughals?

   (A) France
   (B) Great Britain
   (C) Holland
   (D) Spain
   (E) Italy

18. The Aryans and Magyars have which of the following in common?

   (A) They were among the most violent barbarians in history.
   (B) They contributed heavily to the ethnic mix of the places to which they migrated.
   (C) They both descended from the ancient Celts.
   (D) Their military campaigns accelerated Han China's downfall.
   (E) They are thought to be the first peoples to fight from horseback.

19. Which of the following does NOT belong to a list of common Enlightenment tenets?

   (A) Organized churches exploit superstitious beliefs to make themselves wealthy and powerful.
   (B) Rational thought can achieve a full understanding of the universe and its workings.
   (C) Logic and proper planning can alleviate most of society's problems.
   (D) Human beings should be guided as much by instinct and emotion as by the intellect.
   (E) Freedom from arbitrary rule is a political goal worth striving for.

20. Qing China's principal commodities for foreign trade were

   (A) cotton, silk, and gunpowder.
   (B) spices, porcelain, and cotton.
   (C) tea, gunpowder, and cloves.
   (D) gunpowder, silk, and glassware.
   (E) tea, silk, and porcelain.

21. The cartoon shown below most probably depicts

(A) Wilhelm II's dismissal of Otto von Bismarck.
(B) Wilhelm II's abandonment of the Anglo-German naval race.
(C) Wilhelm II's rejection of Otto von Bismarck's aggressive colonial policies.
(D) Wilhelm II's declaration of war against France.
(E) Wilhelm II's decision to disband the Reichstag.

22. Which of the following statements accurately describes tool use during the Stone Age?

(A) Stone Age people lived only in caves.
(B) Religious rituals were unknown during this era.
(C) Wheels and metal objects were in common use.
(D) The chief priority in tool design was ensuring a supply of food.
(E) Only stone was used to make tools.

23. Of the statements below, which is the BEST assessment of the Renaissance?

(A) It strengthened the Papacy by emphasizing Catholic orthodoxy.
(B) It boldly experimented with nonrealistic forms of artistic expression.
(C) It combined a revival of Greco-Latin learning with a conviction that worldly existence was worthwhile.
(D) Its primary emphasis was on painting and sculpture, and therefore there were few Renaissance writers or poets.
(E) Rigidly secular in its outlook, it ignored religious subject matter almost completely.

24. What European thinker's ideas were misappropriated during the 1800s to provide a "scientific" justification for imperialism?

(A) Cecil Rhodes
(B) Friedrich Nietzsche
(C) Ivan Pavlov
(D) Victor Hugo
(E) Charles Darwin

25. Which of the following is an accurate statement about slavery in the Americas?

(A) The Portuguese were the first to abolish it.
(B) Caribbean slaves worked mainly in cotton fields and silver mines.
(C) More slaves were brought to Latin America and the Caribbean than to the United States.
(D) The French enslaved entire native American tribes.
(E) The outlawing of slavery by European powers in the early 1800s ended slavery in the Americas.

26. Which of the following correctly describes the emergence of the first cities?

(A) No cities appeared before the Bronze Age.
(B) Urban populations were less diverse than rural populations.
(C) Cities allowed for the specialization of labor.
(D) The first cities are thought to have appeared in China.
(E) Only peoples who had developed a system of writing built cities

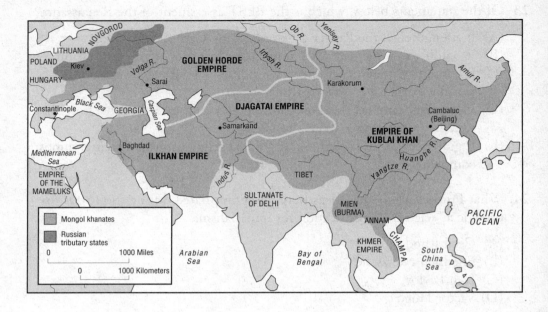

27. What is the central focus of the map above?

    (A) the Mongol Empire at its peak
    (B) the expansion of Muscovite Russia into Mongol territory
    (C) the breakdown of the Mongol Empire into smaller units
    (D) the decline and fall of the Delhi Sultanate
    (E) the rise of the Khmer Empire

28. Absolutism in seventeeth- and eighteenth-century Europe

    (A) was justified by political theories associated with the Enlightenment.
    (B) created systems in which there were no meaningful legal checks on the monarch's power.
    (C) generally involved the expansion of aristocratic power at the expense of the monarch's authority.
    (D) typically led to increased social mobility.
    (E) tended to encourage religious toleration.

29. What best describes the relationship between Islamic and medieval European culture?

    (A) Muslim orthodoxy in Spain prevented the emergence of the Renaissance there.
    (B) Muslim scholars and philosophers borrowed heavily from English and French thinkers and scientists.
    (C) Muslim science, as well as Muslim translations of ancient Greek writings, were indispensable to the cultural growth of Europe.
    (D) The Crusades brought European architectural and artistic forms to the Middle East, where they were eagerly absorbed into the local style.
    (E) There was little interaction between the two cultures, because of intense religious hostility.

30. Zimbabwe and Timbuktu were MOST alike in what respect?

(A) They were renowned centers of Islamic scholarship.
(B) They were key points in trade networks that extended beyond Africa's borders.
(C) They were great repositories of Swahili culture and learning.
(D) They were successful military powers that built powerful empires.
(E) They were largely cut off from all but their immediate surroundings.

31. Which of the following is NOT true of the Ottoman Turks' military campaigns between the late 1300s and late 1600s?

(A) They succeeded in capturing Constantinople and Vienna.
(B) They remained at or near the technological forefront with respect to weaponry.
(C) They attained naval mastery over the eastern Mediterranean.
(D) They conquered most of the Balkans and much of Hungary.
(E) They taxed non-Muslims who refused to convert after being conquered.

32. How have political developments changed in South Korea and Taiwan since the 1980s?

(A) Both countries have become more authoritarian.
(B) Taiwan has become more authoritarian than South Korea.
(C) Leaders in both countries would now prefer to unite with their communist counterparts.
(D) Both countries have democratized.
(E) Both countries have become allies of the People's Republic of China.

33. How did Great Britain gain control over the Suez Canal in the late nineteenth century?

(A) It colonized Egypt in the same way it had colonized India.
(B) It built the canal itself and established a zone of influence in the canal's vicinity.
(C) It seized the canal from Egypt in a short but bloody war.
(D) It bought up shares in the company that owned the canal, then used its economic interest as a pretext to install a pro-British regime in Egypt.
(E) It threatened to bombard the canal with gunships if the Egyptians did not hand over custody of it.

World's Major Consumers of Primary Energy (1998) Measured in quadrillions of British thermal units (Btu)	
United States	94.57 quadrillion Btu
China	33.93 quadrillion Btu
Russia	25.99 quadrillion Btu
Japan	21.21 quadrillion Btu
Germany	13.83 quadrillion Btu
India	12.51 quadrillion Btu
Canada	11.85 quadrillion Btu
France	10.00 quadrillion Btu
United Kingdom	9.75 quadrillion Btu
Brazil	8.08 quadrillion Btu

34. Based on the data presented in the above table, which of the following conclusions might one safely make?

    (A) Brazil has a smaller population than Canada does.
    (B) The top energy-consuming nations are to be found mainly in the developed world.
    (C) Russia is a more efficient consumer of energy than China is.
    (D) Japan has a larger population than India does.
    (E) Per capita, the people of France are less wasteful of energy than those in the United States.

35. How did the demise of the communist regimes in Eastern Europe tend to differ from the collapse of the USSR?

    (A) In most East European countries, revolutions were sparked by popular protest, whereas in the USSR, political elites largely caused the collapse.
    (B) In the USSR, popular uprisings instigated the ultimate collapse, whereas in Eastern Europe, political leaders decided to change the form of government.
    (C) The USSR collapsed purely for economic reasons, whereas in Eastern Europe, communist regimes collapsed mainly due to ethnic conflict.
    (D) East European regimes collapsed due to economic exhaustion, whereas the USSR's breakdown was caused by ethnic warfare.
    (E) The reasons for Soviet and East European collapse differed very little.

36. The image below represents

(A) an agrarian revolution on the brink of victory.
(B) the invasion of a less advanced nation by a more advanced one.
(C) the importation of a new technology into a traditional social order.
(D) a religious war at its most brutal.
(E) the inability of non-Western peoples to adapt to innovative technologies.

37. The millet system was

(A) a technique for improving agricultural production in Japan.
(B) the Ottoman Empire's method for grouping and governing peoples of various faiths.
(C) the Aztec government's system for gathering tribute from neighboring tribes.
(D) Tang China's method for keeping trade records.
(E) a Zulu form of tactical organization.

38. Which of the following is an incorrect description of agricultural societies?

    (A) Agriculture allowed humans to manipulate their environment like never before.
    (B) Women probably played a key role in promoting the transition from hunting and gathering to agricultural societies.
    (C) Agriculture promoted permanent settlements.
    (D) People began producing their own food nearly 12,000 years ago.
    (E) Agricultural societies were less organized than hunter-gatherer societies.

39. The ancient Athenians used the above structure for what purpose?

    (A) as a marketplace
    (B) as a government meeting place
    (C) as a temple
    (D) as a public bathhouse
    (E) as a museum

40. Russian domestic policy during the mid-to-late 1800s included which of the following?

    (A) the granting of a constitution
    (B) the improved treatment of Jews living in the Russian Empire
    (C) the emancipation of the serfs
    (D) the creation of a semiparliamentary legislative body
    (E) the abolition of the rights and privileges of the gentry class

41. Which of the following accurately describes patterns of trade in the Indian Ocean during the 1200s through the early 1400s?

    (A) ivory and gold from Africa; salt and cotton from India; porcelain and silk from China
    (B) gold and ivory from Africa; cotton from China; silk from India
    (C) spices from Africa; slaves from India; gold from China
    (D) ivory from India; porcelain and silk from China; tea from Africa
    (E) slaves and silk from China; gold and ivory from Africa; cotton from India

42. During the first century of Ming rule in China,

    (A) the religion of Daoism was born.
    (B) Beijing's Forbidden City became China's imperial capital.
    (C) Manchu armies broke through China's defenses in the north.
    (D) the government hosted Marco Polo during his visit from Venice.
    (E) China's fleet successfully invaded the Japanese home islands.

43. What best describes the Mississippian culture?

    (A) It erected large mounds for ritual purposes and built at least one large city.
    (B) It was the earliest civilization to appear in North America.
    (C) It was a highly warlike culture, attaining hegemony over most of North America.
    (D) It was one of the few monotheistic civilizations in the pre-Columbian Americas.
    (E) It is known for having built complex cliff dwellings in the walls of canyons.

44. Arabic numerals and the concept of zero are thought to have originated where?

    (A) the Middle East
    (B) West Africa
    (C) Mongolia
    (D) India
    (E) China

45. Which of the following applies to the Kongo kingdom?

    (A) Its rulers avoided outright colonization by ceding some of their powers to Portugal.
    (B) Superior military technology allowed Portugal to conquer it completely.
    (C) It avoided any economic entanglement in the Atlantic slave trade.
    (D) It fell under Berber rule for three centuries.
    (E) It was one of the most active participants in the Indian Ocean trade network.

46. Which of the following statements about European settlements in North America is NOT true?

   (A) The French, more than the English or Spanish, dominated the fur trade.
   (B) France's principal rival in the New World was England.
   (C) The Spanish once controlled the modern-day state of Louisiana.
   (D) The Russians settled along the Pacific coast.
   (E) The French drove the Acadians out of their Nova Scotia settlement to southern North America.

47. Nicolaus Copernicus is best known for which scientific accomplishment?

   (A) describing the chemical states of matter
   (B) elaborating the theory of elliptical orbits
   (C) devising the first workable microscope
   (D) mathematically proving the heliocentric theory
   (E) inventing the telescope

48. Why did the United States support Ferdinand Marcos's regime in the Philippines?

   (A) because Marcos was strongly committed to democratic principles
   (B) because Marcos was strongly anti-communist
   (C) because Marcos was trying to prevent takeover by a right-wing dictator
   (D) because Marcos faithfully observed international human rights standards
   (E) because of popular pressure from Filipino-American voters

49. Radicalism in the French Revolution manifested itself in which of the following ways?

   (A) the decision to allow Louis XVI to reign as a limited monarch
   (B) the peasant uprising in the Vendée
   (C) the Directory's willingness to allow aristocrats to return from exile
   (D) the extension of voting rights to women
   (E) the attempt to replace Catholicism with a deistic "cult of the supreme being"

50. Until the late 1980s, what did North Vietnam's regime have in common with South Korea's?

   (A) both were communist
   (B) both were ruled by peasant revolutionaries who had risen to power
   (C) both waged bitter campaigns against religious belief
   (D) both were less than completely democratic
   (E) both encouraged internationally successful electronics industries

51. In what key way did early Egyptian civilization resemble those in Mesopotamia?

   (A) They both buried their leaders in pyramids.
   (B) They both used cuneiform in preserving their important documents.
   (C) They both developed centralized societies ruled by a monarchy and a small caste of priests.
   (D) They both created law codes that protected the poor.
   (E) They both allowed women to act as priests.

52. What made the Silk Road unusual among premodern trade routes?

   (A) In an age when water transport was easier and cheaper, it allowed overland trade over great distances.
   (B) It was the only means by which the Mediterranean world could trade with East Asia.
   (C) It was the only major trade route the Mongols allowed to function after their campaigns of conquest.
   (D) Only along the Silk Road could large animals, such as oxen, elephants, and horses, be transported.
   (E) It allowed the influence of Hinduism and Buddhism to spread westward.

53. Which of the following statements about East Africa in the 1800s is inaccurate?

   (A) Swahili was the regime's dominant language for trade and interaction.
   (B) Ethiopia's leaders were Christian.
   (C) No major slave markets operated in East Africa.
   (D) At one point, more than 40 percent of the population was made up of slaves.
   (E) Arabs had gained a great deal of political influence.

54. When the Portuguese arrived in India and Southeast Asia, they

   (A) agreed with local powers not to allow Catholic priests to proselytize.
   (B) quickly conquered India and China, thanks to their naval superiority.
   (C) were unable to gain control over any parts of Southeast Asia, in great contrast to their colonial successes on the African coast.
   (D) established control over certain port cities and small islands, but not larger nations.
   (E) found that the difficulty of voyaging so far made trade with these regions unprofitable.

55. Which of the following events is NOT associated with religious fundamentalism in the post-1945 era?

(A) the Iranian revolution
(B) the growing popularity of evangelical denominations in South America
(C) the Rwandan genocide
(D) Sikh-Hindu conflicts in India
(E) the rise of the Taliban in Afghanistan

56. The Hittites are best remembered for

(A) persecuting early Christians.
(B) being among the first to use iron weapons.
(C) inventing the practice of coining money.
(D) devising the first alphabet.
(E) pioneering the use of the wheel.

57. Which of the following was NOT a major characteristic of Middle Eastern political life after World War II?

(A) widespread democratization
(B) independence of former colonies and mandates
(C) tensions between religious fundamentalism and Westernization
(D) the Arab-Israeli conflict
(E) the persistence of human rights abuses

58. To deter Germany's workers from embracing radical ideologies, Otto von Bismarck

(A) outlawed the sale of all books by Karl Marx.
(B) stirred up anti-Semitic resentment among German workers.
(C) imprisoned anyone who joined the Communist Party.
(D) granted universal male suffrage and gave workers many social benefits.
(E) gave women the vote.

59. The innovation most associated with the ancient Hebrews is

(A) monotheistic worship.
(B) metal coinage.
(C) the chariot.
(D) hieroglyphics.
(E) aqueducts.

60. Which of the following did the communist dictatorship of the USSR and the Nazi regime in Germany NOT have in common?

   (A) Both controlled society partly by means of a feared and powerful secret police force.
   (B) Both made use of propaganda to indoctrinate their populations and glorify the leaders.
   (C) Both subscribed to ideologies that viewed women primarily as homemakers and mothers.
   (D) Both promoted industrial buildup and the creation of large armed forces.
   (E) Both created an elaborate network of camps for purposes of concentration and forced labor.

61. Which of the following best describes the long-term results of the Latin American wars of independence?

   (A) Racial prejudice was for the most part eliminated.
   (B) The large states created by Simón Bolívar governed South America for almost two centuries.
   (C) Slavery was immediately abolished through South America and the Caribbean.
   (D) Peasant-led movements seized power in nearly all the states of Latin America.
   (E) Constitutional rule tended to weaken and fail a short time after Simón Bolívar's death.

62. What factor caused Southeast Asia to experience major political change between 1200 and 1400?

   (A) The Chinese and Mongols conquered parts of Southeast Asia at this time.
   (B) The countries of Southeast Asia adopted Confucianism.
   (C) The peoples of Southeast Asia began to adopt Christian ways.
   (D) Democracy became a leading force in political change.
   (E) Invading forces crossed the Indian Ocean from East Africa and raided coastal communities.

63. Which of the following best describes the effects of the eighteenth-century agricultural revolution in Europe?

   (A) Less organic food was grown.
   (B) There were fewer famines and better crop yields.
   (C) Serfdom was abolished.
   (D) Peasants revolted and took control of manors.
   (E) Poverty was eliminated.

64. Why did the European Economic Community form?

   (A) to prepare for economic mobilization in case of war
   (B) to coordinate economic production during World War II
   (C) to keep U.S. exports from flooding European markets
   (D) to encourage the free movement of goods, money, and labor within Europe
   (E) to increase the number of internal tariffs within Europe

65. Which country lost the Spanish-American War, and what happened to it?

   (A) the United States, which was forced to relinquish Cuba
   (B) the United States, which was forced to hand over the Philippines
   (C) Spain, which was stripped of its colonial possessions
   (D) Spain, which lost only Cuba to the United States
   (E) The war ended in stalemate.

66. How were the decolonization processes in Rhodesia and South Africa similar?

   (A) The African population in both countries was treated equitably.
   (B) The post-independence governments were led by whites who strictly controlled the black majorities.
   (C) In both cases, decolonization resulted in mass genocide.
   (D) French peacekeepers had to be brought in to maintain order.
   (E) Decolonization required the intervention of United Nations peacekeeping forces.

67. In what way did China's response to the growing presence of Western powers during the 1800s differ from Japan's?

   (A) Japan granted economic concessions to foreign powers, but China did not.
   (B) The Chinese modernized and industrialized, whereas the Japanese did not.
   (C) The Japanese modernized and industrialized, whereas the Chinese did not.
   (D) China defeated the Western powers in battle, whereas Japan tended to lose.
   (E) China and Japan interacted with Western powers in nearly identical fashion.

68. The Declaration of the Rights of Man and the Citizen

   (A) was adopted by the Constitutional Convention in Philadelphia.
   (B) guaranteed basic civil rights and liberties for male citizens in France.
   (C) enfranchised Hungarians living under Austrian Habsburg rule.
   (D) created a monarchy in Great Britain.
   (E) proclaimed the need for land reform in revolutionary Argentina.

69. Which of the following groups did the Nazi Party NOT target for persecution?

   (A) Roma (Gypsies)
   (B) Europeans of Mediterranean descent
   (C) homosexuals
   (D) Communists and other political dissidents
   (E) the mentally and physically disabled

70. Which of the following is NOT true of gunpowder?

   (A) Several African states boosted their regional power by acquiring firearms in the 1600s and 1700s.
   (B) Fearful of being made obsolete, Japan's samurai class carefully controlled access to and ownership of guns.
   (C) The Ottoman Empire and Mughal India both proved adept at using gunpowder weaponry in the 1500s and 1600s.
   (D) The appearance of gunpowder led immediately to Western domination of the world's other major civilizations.
   (E) It is generally considered to have been invented in China.

STOP

END OF SECTION I

SECTION II: FREE-RESPONSE QUESTIONS

Part A: Document-Based Question

TIME: 10 MINUTES TO READ DOCUMENTS; 40 MINUTES
TO COMPLETE ESSAY (RECOMMENDED, NOT OFFICIAL)

Directions: The following question is based on the accompanying Documents 1–7. (The documents have been edited for the purpose of this exercise.) Write your answer on the lined pages of the Section II free-response booklet.

This question is designed to test your ability to work with and understand historical documents.

Write an essay that

- has a relevant thesis and supports that thesis with evidence from the documents.
- uses all of the documents.
- analyzes the documents by grouping them in as many appropriate ways as possible, and does not simply summarize the documents individually.
- takes into account the sources of the documents and analyzes the authors' points of view.
- identifies and explains the need for at least one additional type of document.

You may refer to relevant historical information not mentioned in the documents.

1. Using the documents, compare and contrast European and non-European reactions to encounters with unfamiliar religious beliefs between roughly 1200 and 1900. Identify an additional type of document and explain how it would help in assessing such reactions.

DOCUMENT 1

Source: Thomas Coryate, English traveler in Turkey, on witnessing Sufi dervishes (1613).

> There is a College of Turkish Monks in Galata, that are called [Dervishes], . . . who every Tuesday and Friday do perform the strangest exercise of Devotion that ever I saw or heard of. . . .
>
> A little after I came into the room, the Dervishes repaired into the middle void space, sitting Cross-legged, bending their Bodies low toward the floor for Religion['s] sake, even almost flat upon their Faces . . . the whole company of them were about two and fifty. . . .

[A] certain Singing-man sitting apart in an upper room began to sing certain Hymns, but with the most unpleasant and harsh notes that ever I heard, exceedingly differing from our Christian Church singing, for the yelling and disorderly squeaking did even grate mine ears. . . . [T]hree Pipers sitting in the room with the Singer began to play upon certain long Pipes not unlike Tabors, which yielded a very ridiculous and foolish Music . . . whereupon some five and twenty of the two and fifty Dervishes suddenly rose up bare-legged and bare-footed, and casting aside their upper Garments, some of them having their breasts all uncovered, they began by little and little to turn about the Interpreter of the Law. Afterward they redoubled their force and turned with such incredible swiftness, that I could not choose but admire it.

DOCUMENT 2

Source: Council of the Aztec city of Huejotzingo, letter to the king of Spain (1560).

Catholic Royal Majesty!

When your servants the Spaniards reached us and your captain general Don Hernando Cortés arrived, not a single town surpassed us here in New Spain, in that first and earliest we threw ourselves toward you.

. . . we also say and declare before you that [when] your padres, the sons of St. Francis, entered the city of Huejotzingo, of our own free will we honored them and showed them esteem. When they [told us to] abandon the wicked belief in many gods, we did it. Very willingly we destroyed, demolished, and burned the temples. . . .

But now we are taken aback and very afraid, and we ask, have we done something wrong, have we somehow behaved badly, or have we committed some sin against almighty God?

DOCUMENT 3

Source: Jean Bodin, French philosopher (1530–1596), on Ottoman religious policy.

The King of the Turks, who rules over a great part of Europe, safeguards the rites of religion as well as any prince in this world. He constrains no one, but on the contrary permits everyone to live as his conscience dictates. What is more, even in his seraglio at Pera he permits the practice of four diverse religions, that of the Jews, the Christian according to the Roman rite, and according to the Greek rite, and that of Islam.

DOCUMENT 4

Source: Photograph of the Shrine of the Twenty-Six Martyrs, Nagasaki, Japan. Dedicated to twenty-six Japanese converts and Catholic priests crucified in 1597 at the orders of Japanese ruler Toyotomi Hideyoshi.

DOCUMENT 5

Source: Dante Alighieri, Florentine poet, *The Inferno,* Canto XXVIII, 28–36 (ca. 1307).

> I stood and stared at him from the stone shelf;
>   he noticed me and opening his own breast
>   with both hands cried: "See how I rip myself!
>
> See how Mahomet's mangled and split open!
>   Ahead of me walks Ali in his tears
>   his head cleft from the top-knot to the chin.
>
> All the other souls that bleed and mourn
>   along this ditch were sowers of scandal and schism:
>   as they tore others apart, so are they torn."

DOCUMENT 6

Source: The Regulations of the City of Avignon (1243).

> Likewise, we declare that Jews or whores shall not dare to touch with their hands either bread or fruit put out for sale, and that if they should do this they must buy what they have touched.

DOCUMENT 7

Source: Albert Schweitzer, German missionary, doctor, and humanitarian, letter to his sister (April 1913).

Medical knowledge made it possible for me to carry out my intention [of bringing Christ to Africa] in the best and most complete way, wherever the path of service might lead me. . . .

I'm really happy. I feel I've done the right thing in coming here, for the misery is greater than anyone can describe. . . . [T]here are all stages of leprosy. . . . I see a great deal of sleeping sickness. It is very painful for these poor souls. . . . And elephantiasis, that constantly increasing swelling of the limbs. It is dreadful; eventually the legs are so thick that the people can no longer drag them about.

Many heart cases; the people are suffocating. And then the joy when the digitalin works! Evenings I go to bed dead-tired, but in my heart I am profoundly happy that *I am serving at the outpost of the Kingdom of God!*

Part B: Continuity and Change Over Time Question

(SUGGESTED PLANNING AND WRITING TIME—40 MINUTES)
PERCENT OF SECTION II SCORE—33⅓

Directions: You are to answer the following question. You should spend 5 minutes organizing or outlining your essay.

Write an essay that:

- has a relevant thesis and supports that thesis with appropriate historical evidence.
- addresses all parts of the question.
- uses world historical context to show continuities and changes over time.
- analyzes the process of continuity and change over time.

2. Analyze continuities and changes in the political and social role of Confucianism in China between 1000 and 1900.

Part C: Comparative Essay

(SUGGESTED PLANNING AND WRITING TIME—40 MINUTES)
PERCENT OF SECTION II SCORE—33⅓

Directions: You are to answer the following question. You should spend 5 minutes organizing or outlining your essay.

Write an essay that

- has a relevant thesis and supports that thesis with appropriate historical evidence.
- addresses all parts of the question.
- makes direct, relevant comparisons.
- analyzes relevant reasons for similarities and differences.

3. Compare and contrast the aims and results of the Russian Revolution (1917) with ONE of the following:

the Mexican Revolution (1910)
the Iranian Revolution (1979)

STOP

END OF SECTION II

Answer Key
MODEL TEST 2

Section I

1. E	21. A	41. A	61. E
2. C	22. D	42. B	62. A
3. B	23. C	43. A	63. B
4. A	24. E	44. D	64. D
5. C	25. C	45. A	65. C
6. A	26. C	46. E	66. B
7. D	27. C	47. D	67. C
8. C	28. B	48. B	68. B
9. B	29. C	49. E	69. B
10. B	30. B	50. D	70. D
11. E	31. A	51. C	
12. C	32. D	52. A	
13. B	33. D	53. C	
14. A	34. B	54. D	
15. E	35. A	55. C	
16. C	36. C	56. B	
17. B	37. B	57. A	
18. B	38. E	58. D	
19. D	39. C	59. A	
20. E	40. C	60. C	

ANSWERS EXPLAINED

1. **(E)** Fearing a repetition of the interwar period, when economic desperation drove many regimes in Europe to political extremism, Secretary of State George Marshall proposed a large infusion of U.S. funds into the shattered economies of postwar Europe, to avoid having them become attracted to communism.

2. **(C)** Having come comparatively late to the empire-building competition, Germany was left with less desirable colonies in Africa. Inexperience in colonial administration and a harsh approach embroiled Germany in several bloody wars of suppression, especially against the Herero.

3. **(B)** A revival of Confucian beliefs during the Song dynasty reaffirmed China's cultural commitment to traditional patriarchal values and social and political hierarchy. It also led to a decline in the status of women.

4. **(A)** In the Western democracies, women made all the advances listed in this question. Marxist ideology committed the Soviet Union in principle (not always in reality) to gender equality. By contrast, the dictatorships in Germany, Italy, and Japan actively opposed the principle of gender equality.

5. **(C)** Even during its early stage, when conditions for the lower classes were at their hardest, the Industrial Revolution generated great wealth. Levels of overall prosperity in Europe rose. That prosperity slowly began to become more evenly distributed after the 1840s.

6. **(A)** The Young Turks were Westernizing modernizers who were impatient with the sultans' cautious, gradual approach to reform and dissatisfied with the influence of Islamic traditionalism in political life.

7. **(D)** The French colony of Louisiana encompassed much of the central portion of the present-day United States. It was resource-rich, and the Mississippi valley was economically and strategically crucial. Napoleon Bonaparte sold this territory to the United States in 1803, vastly expanding the size and potential power of the young country.

8. **(C)** Made famous after World War II by philosophers and authors such as Albert Camus, Jean-Paul Sartre, and Samuel Beckett, existentialism continued an intellectual trend begun earlier in the century by denying that there are any objective moral or religious truths to guide humanity. On their own, people must come to their own understanding of what is right, and then do it for its own sake.

9. **(B)** Agriculture arose partly as a result of independent innovation, partly as a result of cultural diffusion. Cultivation of crops is thought to have begun in the ancient Middle East around 8000 B.C.E., then spread to nearby areas, as well as Europe. It probably began independently in India (around 7000 B.C.E.) and China (perhaps 6000 B.C.E.).

10. **(B)** Answer E is easily discarded as contrary to facts. The absence of any signs of obvious violence or threat call A and D into question, and it does not appear that anything is being bought or sold, making C unlikely. These are Senegalese troops trained and armed by the French—much like Indian sepoys, Sikhs, and

Gurkha regiments were by the British—and sent to fight in Europe during World War I.

11. **(E)** Many factors motivated Russian imperialism in Central Asia. It desired for years to obtain warm-water ports on the Indian Ocean, and Central Asia's cotton fields were an economic inducement (oil in Persia and the Caucasus became relevant in the early 1900s). Also, as in the rest of Europe, nationalism spurred imperial tendencies. But of the items listed, the long, undefended frontier to Russia's south was a matter of great concern. When the Russians worried about the presence of another European power in the region, it was Britain, not Germany.

12. **(C)** Having been free from colonialism for more than a century and a half, Latin America had no need to decolonize in order to democratize in the 1990s. Greater prosperity eased the transition from dictatorship to democracy, as did regional cooperation assisted by the Organization of American States. The end of the Cold War not only provided examples of successful democratization elsewhere, but, by lessening superpower rivalry and interventionism there, helped to enable it in Latin America.

13. **(B)** Although the most famous crusades are those fought against the Middle East between 1096 and 1291, the popes launched crusades to combat heresy in Europe itself (especially in southern France) and to convert non-Catholic regions of Europe (such as Poland and eastern Europe) by force.

14. **(A)** Although they resemble each other in that they feature non-Westerners engaged in wide-ranging campaigns of exploration, the travels of Ibn Battuta and Zheng He are in fact quite different. They both traveled great distances, but Ibn Battuta's journey was a private venture, with no military purpose or results. Neither man was interested in religious conversion.

15. **(E)** By the mid-1500s, Spanish priests had converted many Native Americans to Christianity and were appalled by the conquistadors' treatment of native peoples, who were forced to labor under horrendous conditions. These priests petitioned authorities in Spain to end the encomienda system that allowed such abuses, with Bartolomé de las Casas's *The Tears of the Indians* proving particularly persuasive. Slaves from Africa replaced the Native Americans as the principal source of manual labor in Spanish America.

16. **(C)** Even before the United States became directly involved in World War II, it started to support Great Britain economically. After Germany invaded the USSR in the summer of 1941, the United States extended economic aid to the Soviets as well. U.S. assistance amounted to billions of dollars' worth of weapons and raw materials, and proved crucial in keeping the British and Soviet war efforts functioning during the dangerous months of late 1941 and 1942.

17. **(B)** Although their presence was restricted mainly to the coasts and the Ganges valley before the early-to-mid-1800s, the British, in 1757, handed the Mughals a decisive defeat at Plassey. This enabled the British to consolidate military power in India and gain great political influence over remaining Mughal rulers, most of whom the British controlled and used as pliable clients to govern on

their behalf. France's chances of building substantial colonies in India ended with Plassey, although they maintained an enclave at Pondicherry.

18. **(B)** After invading around 1500 B.C.E., Aryan tribes intermarried with local Dravidians, giving rise to many of India's diverse cultures. The Magyars, who invaded Europe from the east, are the ancestors of today's Hungarians. The latter are not at all related to the Celts, and the Magyars had no effect on China's development. Neither has a reputation for being any more violent than other nomadic warriors, and neither invented cavalry warfare.

19. **(D)** Largely a backlash against the Enlightenment, the Romantic movement, which began in the late 1700s and lasted well into the 1800s, stressed instinct and the emotions. All the other answers correctly reflect the ideals of the Enlightenment.

20. **(E)** The Chinese traded silk and porcelain for centuries. In the 1700s and 1800s, tea joined—and eventually surpassed—them as a commodity for export. In particular, the sale of tea to Great Britain caused such a trade imbalance that the British responded by shipping opium illegally and by force to China.

21. **(A)** All the possible answers mention Wilhelm II, ensuring that the cartoon is about Germany during the late 1800s or early 1900s. Although a boat is pictured, B cannot be true in light of Wilhelm's enthusiasm for naval affairs, and Wilhelm, despite autocratic tendencies, governed in conjunction with the Reichstag, making E false as well. Nothing about the cartoon hints at a declaration of war (as in D), and, although Bismarck was willing to fight wars if they were useful, he is known for cautious, not needlessly martial, diplomacy. Wilhelm dismissed Bismarck largely because of this cautious approach, and also because he wanted to pursue colonization more aggressively than Bismarck did.

22. **(D)** The need to provide food, then clothing and shelter, did the most to spur human invention during the Stone Age. By definition, C is false because metalworking was unknown during this era. Answer E is false, because tools were made of bone, fiber, and other materials; it is simply the fact that some of the most important tools (and the ones that survive the most easily for archaeologists to discover) were made of stone. Stone Age people built many kinds of dwellings and are known to have had religious beliefs.

23. **(C)** Combining the classical tradition of the Greco-Latin era with Christianity, the culture of the Renaissance was more secular in its outlook than the culture of the medieval period, but did not (and, practically speaking, could not) reject Christian belief altogether.

24. **(E)** Cecil Rhodes spoke out directly in favor of imperialism, so his ideas were not "misappropriated." The philosopher Nietzsche is best remembered for denying the existence of God and the worth of religious morality, and the novelist Hugo is known for his liberal views. Although the psychologist Pavlov's experiments with reflex have frequently been misapplied to social thought, they were not used to justify imperialism. A number of thinkers, especially Herbert Spencer, outlined the theory of "social Darwinism," according to which

supposedly better-adapted (in other words, scientifically advanced) peoples would naturally dominate weaker and more "backward" ones.

25. **(C)** The Atlantic slave trade began largely to meet Portugal's and Spain's desire for an exploitable labor force in the New World, and more slaves went to their colonies than to the United States. Although Britain and most other European nations outlawed slavery and the slave trade in 1814 and 1815, slavery itself did not end in the New World. The United States ended slavery after the U.S. Civil War, and Brazil and Cuba practiced slavery until the 1880s. The French tended to have friendly relations with Native American tribes, and Caribbean slaves worked in overwhelming numbers on sugarcane plantations.

26. **(C)** Urbanization led to labor specialization by creating food surpluses, which allowed some citizens to make a living in other ways besides food production. Cities were built long before the Bronze Age, and in some cases by civilizations that did not have a system of writing.

27. **(C)** After 1260, the Mongol Empire began to split apart into the khanates depicted on the map. The map thus represents the empire after, not at, the peak of its power.

28. **(B)** The tendency in absolutist regimes is toward greater centralization and increased monarchical power. Generally, there are no meaningful theoretical restrictions on the monarch's power (although informal factors or specific circumstances may limit the power of a particular monarch). Most Enlightenment philosophers disapproved of what they saw as absolutism's tyrannical nature. Religious toleration and social mobility were associated more with parliamentary monarchy.

29. **(C)** The European debt to Muslim and Jewish scholars (many of whom lived in Moorish Spain), especially concerning the recovery of knowledge about the ancient Greeks, was immense. The less advanced Europeans had less impact on Islamic culture at this time.

30. **(B)** The people of Mali were not descended from the Bantu, and Zimbabwe at its peak was not Muslim. Neither was part of the Swahili cultural group, and neither was close enough to West Africa to take direct part in the Atlantic slave trade. Both were vital trading centers.

31. **(A)** The Ottomans did everything listed except capture the Habsburg capital of Vienna. They besieged the city twice, in 1529 and 1683, but never took it. Failure to capture Vienna in 1683 led to a massive Christian counterattack that permanently ended the Ottomans as a serious threat to central and western Europe.

32. **(D)** During the Cold War, South Korea and Taiwan, although allies of the United States, were ruled by authoritarian governments. Political changes in the 1980s and 1990s brought greater democratization. Taiwan maintains an awkward relationship of undeclared independence from the People's Republic of China, which considers the island a renegade province. South Korea has remained divided from North Korea for more than half a century.

33. **(D)** The French, not the British, built the Suez Canal. It was America, in Panama, that employed the strategy of building a canal, then claiming military jurisdiction over the surrounding area. The British bought up a majority of the shares in the company that owned the canal. It then used its ownership as an excuse to intervene in a local political crisis and install a ruler, the khedive, who was pro-British and easily pliable.

34. **(B)** Without knowing the population of the countries listed on the chart, precise conclusions about population or per capita comparisons are impossible. What can be determined for certain from general knowledge is that most of the countries included on the chart are from the developed world.

35. **(A)** Mass movements, such as Polish trade union Solidarity and the dissident group led by Vaclav Havel in Czechoslovakia, played the decisive role in ending communist rule in Eastern Europe. Although popular discontent and breakaway tendencies on the part of non-Russian populations in the Soviet Union weakened the country, the final collapse came after the attempted coup against Gorbachev in August 1991, then the decision later that year by the leaders of Russia and other Soviet republics to form the Commonwealth of Independent States.

36. **(C)** Knowledge of the cultural advancement and inventiveness of India, the Middle East, and China—among others—is enough to eliminate E, and there are no clues pointing to religious war or agrarian uprising in the image, as in A and D (in fact, the heavy armament pictured here is a clue that these are *not* peasants). Only one side is depicted, so there is no evidence for B. The mix of armor and muskets makes C the likeliest answer. The image depicts Japanese samurai training with firearms and using rain-resistant gear.

37. **(B)** The Ottoman Empire organized its population into administrative groups based on religion. These were called millets, meaning "nations." For the most part, the Ottomans practiced religious tolerance, although non-Muslims had to pay special taxes and had certain rights restricted.

38. **(E)** Agricultural production required a great deal of organization and planning. It required manipulation of the environment, management of property, and, often, a high degree of social cooperation.

39. **(C)** The Athenian Parthenon, on the Acropolis ("high city"), served as the temple of Athena, the city's patron deity. It remains one of the best-known landmarks in Greece.

40. **(C)** During the reign of Alexander II (1855–1881), Russia experienced a brief period of relatively liberal rule, featuring the emancipation of serfdom. Tsarist Russia never had a true constitution, and only after the 1905 Revolution that nearly toppled Nicholas II from the throne was the Duma, Russia's semiparliamentary legislature, created. Anti-Semitic activity steadily worsened between the death of Alexander II and the Russian revolutions of 1917, and many gentry privileges remained in place until the 1917 revolutions.

41. **(A)** Africa contributed gold and ivory to the Indian Ocean trade network. India was a source of salt and cotton. China traded porcelain and silk, among

other goods. Southeast Asia took part as well, adding cinnamon and other spices; Japan was a source of silver.

42. **(B)** The events in A and D precede the rise of the Ming dynasty; that in C ended Ming rule, but not until the mid-1600s. Although Kublai Khan attempted it in the 1200s, China never successfully invaded Japan.

43. **(A)** Neither the first nor the most warlike civilization in North America, the Mississippian culture is best known for building large earth mounds. Cahokia, in what is now Illinois, was a sizable city. No Native American tribes are known to have practiced monotheism in the pre-Columbian era. The Anasazi and other peoples of the U.S. Southwest, not the Mississippians, are famed for cliff dwellings.

44. **(D)** Despite their name, Arabic numerals (and the concept zero) are thought to have been devised in Gupta India. They made their way to the Middle East, and it was from peoples there that Europeans learned about them.

45. **(A)** Like China in the 1800s, sixteenth-century Kongo gave up much of its national autonomy to foreign powers (in this case Portgual), but avoided being conquered outright. Its rulers converted to Catholicism and sold slaves to the Portuguese in exchange for guns and other manufactured goods. A West African state, Kongo did not participate directly in the Indian Ocean trade network. The Berbers did not conquer it.

46. **(E)** The Acadians, French-speaking colonists in Canada, were driven away from their homes by the British, who took over Quebec after the pivotal battle of Abraham Fields in 1759. The Acadians migrated south, many of them settling in the state of Louisiana, where their name evolved into the popular term "Cajuns." Don't confuse the larger Louisiana territory with the smaller state of Louisiana, which the Spanish did rule for a time.

47. **(D)** By proving mathematically that the earth and other planets revolve around the sun, Polish astronomer Nicolaus Copernicus set into motion an intellectual earthquake. During the late 1600s, his conclusions were confirmed by the observations of Tycho Brahe (who nonetheless did not believe in the heliocentric theory), Johannes Kepler, and Galileo. Because scientific orthodoxy and, more important, Catholic doctrine held that the sun revolved around the earth, home to humanity, God's favored creation, supporting the heliocentric theory was not only controversial, but was, until the 1700s, dangerous.

48. **(B)** During the Cold War, the United States pursued a strategy of containing Soviet expansion wherever it seemed to threaten U.S. interests. When choosing regimes to support, the United States tended to focus more on whether they were anti-communist rather than on whether they were democratic or observed human rights. Marcos was one of many authoritarian leaders who received U.S. backing during the Cold War.

49. **(E)** Answers A and C are examples of relative moderation, and women were not given the vote as in D. The Vendée uprising was a response to, not an example of, revolutionary radicalism. Not only did the Revolution separate church and state, but radical leaders attempted to displace or discourage

Catholicism by boosting alternatives such as the atheistic "cult of reason" or Robespierre's deistic "cult of the supreme being."

50. **(D)** Between 1945 and the free elections of 1987, South Korea's rulers, although not as dictatorial as Vietnam's Communists, were somewhat authoritarian. Answer E applies to South Korea, and C and A apply to Vietnam under the Communists. Answer B applies to neither, although the Vietnamese Communists worked to mobilize the country's peasants.

51. **(C)** Neither ancient Egypt nor the civilizations of Mesopotamia gave equal rights to the poor, and in both, males dominated the clergy. Only the Egyptians built pyramids; the Mesopotamians built ziggurats, which they used as temples, not tombs. Cuneiform was the Sumerians' system of writing; the Egyptians used hieroglyphics. Both had roughly the same system of social organization.

52. **(A)** Before industrial-era forms of transport such as railroads and highways made overland transport easy and cost-effective, most major trade routes grew up along rivers or coastlines. The Silk Road, which stretched for more than 5,000 miles between the Mediterranean and China, was remarkable in its ability to allow the transfer of goods, travelers, ideas, and new technologies over such great distances by land.

53. **(C)** Although the Atlantic slave trade was larger and remains more famous, the East African slave trade, largely run by Arab traders, played a signficant role in the life of the region and lasted until the 1800s.

54. **(D)** In the late 1400s and 1500s, countries such as China, Japan, and India were strong enough to resist Western colonial pressures. Portugal gained some footholds in South and Southeast Asia, but, like the other Europeans who followed them, could not conquer or intimidate the larger nations of Asia. Europe did not gain the ability to do that until the 1700s and 1800s.

55. **(C)** Religious fundamentalism has been a powerful force in the postwar world. Other political events affected by religious extremism have included Ireland's "troubles" (Catholic versus Protestant) and ethnic cleansing in the former Yugoslavia (Orthodox Serbs fighting Catholic Croats as well as Muslim Bosnians and Kosovars). The Rwandan genocide, however, was motivated more straightforwardly by racial tensions.

56. **(B)** Answer A applies to Rome (the Hittites preceded the birth of Christianity), C to the Lydians, and D to the Phoenicians. The wheel was invented before the rise of the Hittites.

57. **(A)** Middle Eastern regimes in the postwar era have tended to range from mild authoritarianism to severe dictatorship. Civil liberties and human rights have not been widely observed. One economic consequence has been a general failure to distribute wealth fairly, even in the region's oil-rich states.

58. **(D)** Although Bismarck governed Germany with an iron hand, he knew when to use positive inducements instead of outright repression. He put into effect labor laws and a social welfare system appealing enough to keep most workers from feeling that they did not have to join trade unions or socialist parties to

improve their lot. All German males could vote, but this was less significant, because the electoral system counted the vote of members of the upper classes for more than votes from the lower classes.

59. **(A)** The great contribution of the ancient Hebrews is monotheistic worship, the veneration of only one deity. This gave birth to the Judeo-Christian tradition, still a bedrock of Western culture.

60. **(C)** Despite the fact that fascism and communism are polar opposites on the ideological spectrum, many regimes based on them share similar features: dictatorship, rule by terror, propaganda, and state control over the economy. One noteworthy exception is their attitude toward women. Fascism tends to oppose gender equality, whereas communism embraces it. Furthermore, the superindustrialization campaigns of Soviet Russia required a large workforce, and female workers were needed just as much as male workers.

61. **(E)** Latin America's wars of independence did not achieve the utopian goals described in A and C. Leadership came from educated members of the privileged classes (like Simón Bolívar), not the peasantry, and the large states envisioned by Bolívar quickly splintered into smaller countries. The region had little experience with constitutional rule before independence, and Bolívar's constitutions were ignored or imperfectly observed.

62. **(A)** Mongol and Chinese conquest extended to Southeast Asia during the 1200s, changing political systems and patterns of economic activity. Compared with Hinduism and Buddhism, Confucianism and Christianity had little influence in the region. Democracy would not take root until the 1900s and 2000s—and even then, not in all places.

63. **(B)** By encouraging the use of better technology and more scientific methods of crop production, the agricultural revolution of eighteenth-century Europe increased yields, made crop failures rarer, and caused the rate of population growth to increase. It did not eliminate poverty or, by itself, cause political or social upheaval.

64. **(D)** Economic cooperation and the removal of obstacles to free trade were seen as ways to boost European prosperity and economic clout after World War II, which had badly damaged all European economies, even those of the victorious nations.

65. **(C)** Spain lost the Spanish-American War decisively, and its status as a colonial power steeply declined as a result. The United States took Puerto Rico, Cuba, the Philippines, and other colonial possessions from it—in effect, becoming an imperial power itself.

66. **(B)** Both in Rhodesia and South Africa, the population that won independence from Britain was governed not by blacks, but whites. In each case, racial tensions led to political turmoil: civil war in the case of Rhodesia (which became Zimbabwe after the overthrow of the white regime) and the prolongation of the apartheid system in South Africa until the 1990s.

67. **(C)** Until far too late, China's Qing regime remained oblivious to the need to modernize, if it wanted to stay free of foreign domination. Although it was not technically colonized, it lost territory to Western powers and was forced to grant them tremendous concessions. Upon the accession of the Emperor Meiji in 1868, Japan pursued a course of Westernization, focusing especially on industrial buildup and military modernization.

68. **(B)** The Declaration of the Rights of Man and the Citizen was a statement of the French Revolution's core beliefs, as well as the instrument that put them into political effect. It was a product of Enlightenment philosophy, political action, and influence from American revolutionaries.

69. **(B)** Although "Aryan" Germans were considered to be Europe's "purest" race, other peoples of Anglo-Saxon, Celtic, and Baltic descent were considered "acceptable," as were many Mediterranean peoples, such as the Spanish and Italians (the Germans' allies, after all). The groups listed in A, C, and E were considered "subhuman" and therefore "undesirable," and the regime cracked down on all political opponents, but especially Communists, whom Hitler despised.

70. **(D)** Although Europe came to use gunpowder weaponry more efficiently and more systematically than any other civilization, it took a number of years for this to happen. In the meantime, other cultures—the Ottomans and the Mughal Indians among them—used gunpowder weapons effectively as well. China invented gunpowder, and several West African states bartered slaves (generally taken from neighboring peoples) for Western guns.

Appendix: Map of Selected World Regions

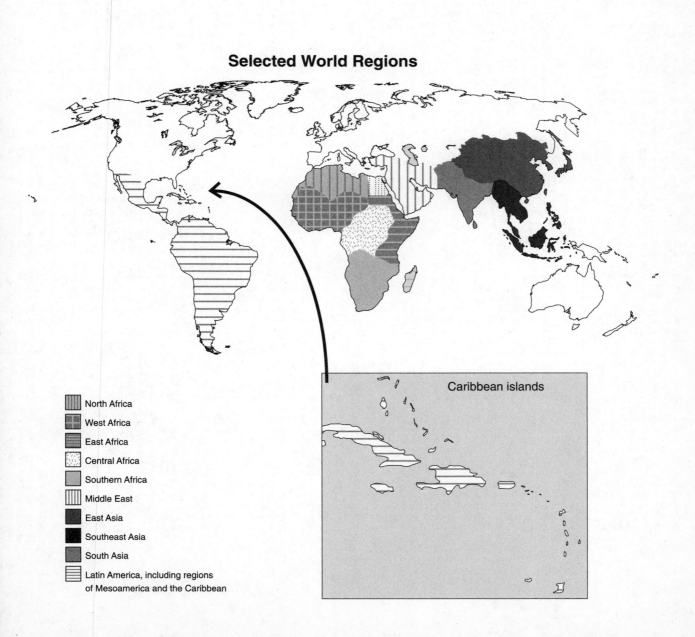

Selected World Regions

Caribbean islands

North Africa
West Africa
East Africa
Central Africa
Southern Africa
Middle East
East Asia
Southeast Asia
South Asia
Latin America, including regions
of Mesoamerica and the Caribbean

Index

THE FOLLOWING DOCUMENTATION APPLIES IF YOU PURCHASED
AP World History, 4th Edition with CD-ROM.
Please disregard this information if your edition does not contain the CD-ROM.

IMPORTANT NOTE
As of May 2011, ¼ point will no longer be deducted for each incorrect answer on the multiple-choice section of the exam. Because the CD-ROM does not currently reflect this recent scoring change, you will need to add in these deductions to determine your actual score.

SYSTEM REQUIREMENTS

The program will run on a PC with:
Windows® Intel® Pentium II 450 MHz
or faster, 128MB of RAM
1024 X 768 display resolution
Windows 2000, XP, Vista
CD-ROM Player

The program will run on a Macintosh® with:
PowerPC® G3 500 MHz
or faster, 128MB of RAM
1024 X 768 display resolution
Mac OS X v.10.1 through 10.4
CD-ROM Player

The software is not installed on your computer; it runs directly from the CD-ROM. Barron's CD-ROM includes an "autorun" feature that automatically launches the application when the CD is inserted into the CD-ROM drive. In the unlikely event that the autorun feature is disabled, follow the manual launching instructions below.

Windows®
1. Click on the Start button and choose "My Computer."
2. Double-click on the CD-ROM drive, which will be named **AP_WorldHistory**.
3. Double-click **AP_WorldHistory.exe** application to launch the program.

Macintosh®
1. Insert the CD-ROM.
2. Double-click the CD-ROM icon.
3. Double-click the **AP_WorldHistory** icon to start the program.